Learning SIMPLY ACCOUNTING
by Sage
Premium 2010

a modular approach

Harvey C. Freedman, CGA

Carol Smith, MBA, CMA

NELSON / EDUCATION

NELSON / EDUCATION

**Learning Simply Accounting
by Sage Premium 2010: A Modular Approach**

by Harvey C. Freedman and Carol Smith

**Vice President,
Editorial Director:**
Evelyn Veitch

**Editor-in-Chief,
Higher Education:**
Anne Williams

Senior Acquisitions Editor:
Craig Dyer

Executive Marketing Manager:
Dave Ward

Developmental Editor:
Toula Di Leo

Project Manager:
Becky Pembry-Spratley

Proofreader:
Gail Marsden

Senior Production Coordinator:
Ferial Suleman

Design Director:
Ken Phipps

Managing Designer:
Franca Amore

Cover Design:
Peter Papayanakis

Cover Image:
Comstock Images

Compositor:
Diane van Ingen

Printer:
RR Donnelley

Library and Archives Canada Cataloguing in Publication Data

Freedman, Harvey C.
    Learning Simply Accounting by Sage Premium 2010 : a modular approach / Harvey C. Freedman, Carol Smith.

Includes index.
ISBN 978-0-17-650409-0

    1. Simply Accounting (Computer file)—Textbooks.
2. Accounting—Computer programs—Textbooks.
I. Smith, Carol (Carol C.) II. Title.

HF5679.F747 2010
657.0285'536 C2010-903880-0

ISBN-13: 978-0-17-650409-0
ISBN-10: 0-17-650409-5

DEDICATION

This book is dedicated to all volunteers in your community who give their time and effort to help those in need. If you are a volunteer, may I offer my own thank you. We all appreciate the work you do to make your community a wonderful place to live.

ACKNOWLEDGMENTS

I would like to thank the individuals below who contributed to making this textbook a success. On behalf of the team, I hope that you find using this book a rewarding experience.

My wife **Marlene**, who reviewed the manuscript, my sons **Jeremy** and **Jason**, daughter-in-law **Julie-Ann**, grand-daughters **Jordan** and **Jessica,** for their support and encouragement while the book was in progress. I realize that I did not spend as much time with you as I would have liked.

Carol Smith, Professor at Humber College, my colleague, who was the technical reviewer for this textbook, reviewed the manuscript and offered numerous suggestions, ideas and helpful criticisms to make the textbook easy to understand.

Rosemary Imola, Professor at Mohawk College, who was the keystroke reviewer, for her assistance in checking the manuscript, and the slideshows, who offered numerous suggestions and helpful criticisms to make the textbook easy to understand.

Simply Accounting by Sage staff; **Melissa Lutman, Jim Collins, Alistair Ellis, Naz Gigaseri Hugo Croft-Levesque** and other members of Simply Education and Technical Support for their ongoing technical assistance.

Our students, who always come up with new ways of looking at the same information and whose suggestions help make the textbook material more effective.

Diane van Ingen, desktop technician, who contributed many suggestions and ideas to help make this textbook visually appealing.

Rebecca Pembry-Spratley, for creating the slideshows.

Alan Cohen, for his support and encouragement.

Toula Di Leo, Gordon Rollason, Susan Calvert and **Gail Marsden** of Nelson Education for their assistance on this project.

Harvey Freedman

> *Tell me and I forget.*
> *Show me and I remember.*
> *Let me do it and I understand.*
> *- Zen Proverb*

CREDITS

Becky Pembry-Spratley, Project Manager
Rosemary Imola, Keystroke Tester and Reviewer (Slideshows)
Diane van Ingen, Desktop Technician

Preface

This textbook is a comprehensive introduction to *Simply Accounting Premium 2010 version A* using the modular approach. It takes you step by step through **analyzing**, **recording** and **processing** transactions in all Simply modules. The text includes **converting from** a manual accounting system by setting up new Simply company data files. Month-End and Year-End processing, Project Costing, Account Reconciliation and Multi-currency features are also shown.

All Simply modules are covered in this text. They are:

1. COMPANY
2. RECEIVABLES
3. PAYABLES
4. EMPLOYEES & PAYROLL
5. INVENTORY & SERVICES
6. DIVISION*
7. BANKING

* The name of the DIVISION module can also be called Projects, Job Sites, Crops, Properties, etc., depending on the type of business you operate.

Software

The Simply Accounting Software 2010 Premium A **Student Version** software for use at home is available as a download from the Simply website. Do NOT load the software until you have read Appendix A, at the back of this textbook, for system requirements and instruction on loading the software as well as restrictions on its use.

Caution: Do not load the Simply software until you have read Appendix A at the back of this textbook.

Slideshows

The PowerPoint slideshows are located at www.simplyaccounting2010.nelson.com under **Student Resources**. They are designed to help you understand accounting concepts that relate to specific Simply Accounting features. You will be prompted to run these slideshows at relevant points throughout the book. For instructions on how to run the slideshows, click on **About the slideshows**.

Other Features

The textbook also includes numerous challenge exercises to provide additional experience in using the various Simply modules. A summary of the various assignments is given later in this Preface.

What's New in Simply 2010, Appendix C, at www.simplyaccounting2010.nelson.com under Student Resources will give you an overview of the new features of Simply. This information is useful for both new and experienced users of Simply Accounting.

A **Table of Contents** at the beginning of each chapter provides a detailed list of the topics in the chapter. A detailed index is also provided at the end of the textbook for your easy reference.

At the end of the textbook is a Glossary containing **Accounting and Simply Accounting Terminology** used in the chapters. Non-accounting words are used to help you understand the material. Review questions are also given at the end of each chapter.

The first three chapters, COMPANY (Photos Company), RECEIVABLES (Santos Luggage) and PAYABLES (Tyson's Toys) will guide you in entering transactions using the software as you would in many businesses.

Chapters 2 and 3 have been split into parts A and B. Part A contains basic transactions (e.g., sales, purchases, returns, receipts, payments) that occur on a regular basis, and part B contains more advanced topic transactions.

Each chapter and Challenge Exercise contains one or more transactions with the student name as a vendor or customer.

In Chapter 4 (Sarah's Kitchen Stores) you will set up a company's computer records by creating the data files, ledger accounts and other information.

In Chapter 5 (Sarah's Kitchen Stores) you will use **source documents** to record transactions in the COMPANY, RECEIVABLES and PAYABLES modules.

Chapter 6 (Shirts & Ties) is a comprehensive challenge exercise that requires you to set up a company from scratch and record transactions from source documents.

The later chapters cover the PAYROLL & EMPLOYEES (Creative Wallpaper), INVENTORY & SERVICES (Printers Company Ltd.), and DIVISION (HotTubs Company) modules, BANKING (Wedding Flowers Company) journal, and Foreign-currency (Saddles Company). These chapters reinforce learning by including transactions that require procedures learned in earlier chapters.

Challenge Exercises 08 C8-4 (Luggage–PI), C8-5 (Toys–PI) ,C8-6 (Shirts–PI and Bears-PI) require you to complete the Exercises using the Perpetual Inventory method.

As you complete each chapter, it would be a good idea to cross-reference your entries and reports with the solutions provided to the instructor.

Appendices

Various appendices provide you with additional information that would be useful to you both in your current course and when using Simply on the job.

Appendix A (in textbook) Installing Simply Premium 2010 Student Version B Software.

The following appendices are provided at www.simplyaccounting2010.nelson.com under Student Resources. References in the textbook that specify **Appendix —** refer to appendices on the website.

Appendix 2010-A   Basics of Accounting
Appendix 2010-C   What's New in Simply 2010
Appendix 2010-D   Printing a Tax (HST) Report
Appendix 2010-E   Budgets – General Ledger
Appendix 2010-F   Printing in Batches
Appendix 2010-G   Processing in Batches
Appendix 2010-H   New Business Guide
Appendix 2010-I   Checklists for Task Completion
Appendix 2010-K   Graphs Feature
Appendix 2010-M   Post-Dated Cheques
Appendix 2010-O   Security – Passwords
Appendix 2010-P   Payroll Garnishment
Appendix 2010-Q   Names Fields

Appendix 2010-R	Quick Reference Guide (*Print this guide for quick exercise references.*)
Appendix 2010-T	Reimbursement (Payroll)
Appendix 2010-U	Adding Notes/Footers to Statements
Appendix 2010-V	Mini-Guide Receivables—Payables (*in Excel*)
Appendix 2010-X	Removing an Account from a Wrong Section
Appendix 2010-Y	To Cancel a History Invoice
Appendix 2010-AA	Setting Up a New Company File using a Template
Appendix 2010-AC	Adding a Salesperson's Name to an Invoice
Appendix 2010-AD	Time and Billing Journals
Appendix 2010-AG	No Sales Taxes Event
Appendix 2010-AI	Transfer Funds – Transfer money between bank accounts

HST is explained in Chapter 2. GST and PST are explained in Chapter 15 to ensure that you understand the procedures for recording the HST, GST and PST collected from Sales and the HST, GST and PST paid on buying merchandise for resale and other goods and services.

Chapter Exercises and Challenge Exercises

Listed below is a summary of the company folders and the modules used for each chapter. The bottom chart indicates the challenge exercises provided at the end of each chapter and the modules reviewed in each exercise.

CHAPTER EXERCISES

Chapter	Folder Name	Company	G/L	A/R	A/P	Payroll	Inventory	Division	Banking
1	Photos	Photos Company	Yes						
2	Luggage	Santos Luggage	Yes	Yes					
3	Toys	Tyson's Toys	Yes		Yes				
4	Kitchen*	Sarah's Kitchens	Yes	Yes	Yes				
5	Kitchen*	Sarah's Kitchens	Yes	Yes	Yes				
6	Shirts*	Shirts & Ties	Yes	Yes	Yes				
7	Wallpaper	Creative Wallpaper	Yes	Yes	Yes	Yes			
8	Printers	Printers Company	Yes	Yes	Yes		Yes		
9	Kafa	Kafa Sweaters	Yes						
10	Kafa2	Kafa2 Sweaters	Yes						
11	HotTubs	HotTubs Company	Yes	Yes	Yes	Yes		Yes	
12	Wedding	Wedding Flowers	Yes	Yes	Yes				Yes
13	Corrections	Prizes	Yes	Yes	Yes	Yes	Yes		
14	Saddles	Saddles Company	Yes	Yes					

* Data files to be created by student.

CHALLENGE EXERCISES

Chapter	Folder Name	Company	G/L	A/R	A/P	Payroll	Inventory	Division	Banking
1	Driving	Driving School	Yes						
	Readings	Readings Company	Yes						
	Movers	Movers Company	Yes						
2A	Clocks	Clocks Company	Yes	Yes					
	Walkers	Walkers Company	Yes	Yes					
2B	Brides	Brides Dresses	Yes	Yes					
	Skis	Skis	Yes	Yes					
	Sitters	House Sitters	Yes	Yes					
3A	Wheelchair	Wheelchair Company	Yes		Yes				
	Radios	Radios Company	Yes		Yes				
3B	Network	Network Company	Yes		Yes				
	China	China Company	Yes	Yes	Yes				
	Dance	Dance Studio	Yes	Yes	Yes				
	Chairs	Chairs-Prov code	Yes	Yes	Yes				
4	Balloons*	Balloons Store	Yes	Yes	Yes				
	Kojokaro	Kojokaro Company	Yes	Yes	Yes				
	Skates*	Skates Stores	Yes	Yes	Yes				
	Uniforms	R. Park Uniforms	Yes		Yes	Yes			
7	Carpets	Carpets 4Home	Yes		Yes	Yes			
8	Stain	Stain Company	Yes	Yes	Yes		Yes		
	Hair	Charlie's Hair Styling	Yes	Yes	Yes		Yes		
	Vet	Vet Services	Yes	Yes	Yes		Yes		
	Luggage PI	Santos Luggage	Yes	Yes			Yes		
	Toys PI	Tyson's Toys	Yes		Yes		Yes		
	Shirts PI	Shirts & Ties	Yes	Yes	Yes		Yes		
	Bears	Bears Company	Yes	Yes	Yes		Yes		
10	Magazines	Rama Magazines	Yes		Yes				
	Gravel	City Gravel	Yes	Yes					
12	China	China Company	Yes	Yes	Yes				Yes
14	Saddles	Saddles Company	Yes		Yes				

* Data files to be created by student.

SLIDESHOWS

Chapter	Slideshow information	G/L	A/R	A/P	Payroll	Inventory	Division	Banking
1A	Simply Basics							
1B	General Ledger	Yes						
2A	Receivables Part A		Yes					
2B	Receivables Part B		Yes					
3A	Payables Part A			Yes				
3B	Payables Part B			Yes				
4	Setting up a New Company	Yes	Yes	Yes				
7A	Setting up the EMPLOYEES & PAYROLL Module				Yes			
7B	Processing PAYROLL Transactions				Yes			
8A	Setting up the INVENTORY & SERVICES Module					Yes		
8B	Journalizing Inventory- Related Transactions	Yes	Yes	Yes		Yes		
9	Month & Year-End Processing	Yes				Yes		
10	Year-End Closing	Yes				Yes		
11A	Setting up the DIVISION Module						Yes	
11B	Processing Transactions in the DIVISION Module			Yes	Yes		Yes	
12	BANKING Module							Yes
14	Multi-Currency	Yes	Yes	Yes				

Important tips in making the most of your Simply training

- When you see a number and a symbol similar to **7 ➤**, it means there is something on the line or paragraph in bold for you to type or a key or keys you must press.

- It is important that you follow the instructions in the order that they are given (don't jump around). Read each section before you do the work on the computer to get an idea of what will be done. This will help you avoid errors that could be prevented by knowing information presented a little further in the book. Ask your instructor if you are not sure. Asking your fellow students may help, but the final results are your responsibility, not your classmates.

- The instructor will have a Solutions Manual available for you to check your work. If you realize you have made an error after posting a transaction, don't panic; you can correct the error. Review Chapter 13, Correcting Transaction Errors After Posting, on ways to correct posted entries.

- Your transaction listing may not match the Solutions Manual exactly; e.g., you made a mistake, but the financial statements, Income Statement and Balance Sheet must be the same as the solution.

- Always back up your data after every work session either in the classroom or at home. This can save you hours of extra work. Look for the Backup icon to remind you to back up.

- Answer the **Before Moving On** questions at the end of each chapter before moving to the next chapter. This will help you understand the reasons behind the keystrokes and aid you in preparing for tests.

Perpetual Inventory

Many students have difficulty understanding Perpetual Inventory and how to use it in Simply Accounting; therefore, the authors have designed the textbook so that the following learning strategy can be used:

1. The students can first record entries for the first 3 modules, Chapter 1 – GENERAL JOURNAL (Photos), Chapters 2A and 2B – RECEIVABLES (Luggage) and Chapters 3A and 3B – PAYABLES (Toys) to get an understanding of how the basic modules work without Perpetual Inventory.

2. If the instructor deems it necessary to introduce Perpetual Inventory at this point, the students can then complete Chapter 8 – INVENTORY & SERVICES (Printers).

3. Two Challenge Case data files, <u>08 C8-4 Luggage-PI</u> and <u>08 C8-5 Toys-PI</u> are provided for additional work. Students can use their solutions from Chapters 2A and 3A for use with Perpetual Inventory.

4. A new case 08 C8-7 Bears, can be used to compare the inventory methods, Average costs (Avg) and First In First Out (FIFO) Inventory methods.

Your Feedback

Please send comments, suggestions or corrections to the author at:

freedmanh@rogers.com

Updates

You may access the Publisher's website especially set up, so that you may download files related to this text. The Publisher's website is:

http://www.simplyaccounting2010.nelson.com

Contents

Preface iv

Chapter 1
Getting Started and COMPANY Module
Photos Company. 1

   Simply Accounting 2010 Overview...4

   Getting Started...5

   Starting the Simply Program..8

       The Simply Accounting Start Window..................................9

       Network Procedures..10

       Range of Dates...12

     Home Window – Enhanced View 16

     Home Window – Classic View 17

       Menu Bar 17

       Toolbar 17

       Modules..17

     Tasks 18

     Accountant's Tasks..18

     Related Tasks 19

     Support & Services 19

     Reports 19

   Using Simply HELP 20

       Using Learning Centre Help 21

     Shortcuts (on left side)..22

   Revising company Information 22

   To Display Reports 23

       Displaying the Income Statement....................................23

       Displaying the Balance Sheet 25

   Processing transactions in the COMPANY Module...................26

     To Correct Errors 27

   Displaying the Journal Entry..31

   To Advance the Session Date 33

   Recording a Compound Entry and Adding a New Account 33

   Recurring Entries..38

   Owner Investment in Business..39

   Correcting an Entry – Cancel or Adjusting 40

   Displaying Corrected Entries with Reversals 42

       To Show Corrected Entries Only 43

   To Remove a Recurring Transaction Entry 44

   Using a Recurring Transaction 45

   Drill Down (Trace Back) 47

   To Display and Print the General Journal....................................48

   Display and Print the General Ledger Report 52

   Saying Your Work 55

   Why Back Up? 57

     Backup Procedures 57

     Using a Logbook or Diary...60

   Summary...61

     To View Corrections 62

   Before Moving On..63

     Challenge Exercise 01 C1-1, Driving School.................64

     Challenge Exercise 01 C1-2, Astrology Readings 65

     Challenge Exercise 01 C1-3, Movers............................66

   Relevant Appendices 67

Restoring a Data File from a Backup Date File.............. 69

Chapter 2A
RECEIVABLES Module--Basics

Santos Luggage. **73**

RECEIVABLES Module Overview 74
Company Profile – Santos Luggage 74
    Opening the RECEIVABLES Module 74
    To Display and Print the Customer Aged Report 77
The RECEIVABLES Journals 79
    The Sales Journals 80
    Customizing the Sales Journal Window 81
    Sales Invoice Styles 83
Entering Transactions in the RECEIVABLES Module 83
    Recording a Sales Quote 84
    Revising the Sales Quote Form 89
    Converting a Sales Quote into a Sales Order 91
Daily business Manager 93
    To View the Pending Sales Orders Report 95
Producing a Sales Invoice from a Sales Order 96
Journalizing Sales Returns 99
Receipts Journal 102
    Journalizing a Receipt with Cash Discount 102
    Journalizing a Partial Receipt with No Discount 108
    To Cancel an Invoice after Posting 111
The Customers Ledger 113
    Adding a New Customer Record 114
    Journalizing the Sale 122
Printing Reports When Needed 126
Relevant Appendices, Part A 126
Summary, Part A 127
Before Moving On, Part A 128
    Challenge Exercise 02 C2A-1, Clocks 129
    Challenge Exercise 02 C2A-2, Dog Walkers 130

Chapter 2B
RECEIVABLES Module—Beyond Basics

Santos Luggage. **131**

    Opening the RECEIVABLES Module, Part B 132
Using Simply's Special Features 134
    The Lookup Feature 134
    To Correct a Posted Invoice 135
    To Track Additional Transaction Details 135
Journalizing a Deposit 138
    To Record the Sales Order 139
Journalizing Cash/Cheque/Bank Card Sales 141
Journalizing a Credit Card Sale 143
Journalizing a Customer Account Write-off 145
    Record a Note in a Customer's File 145
Journalizing a Cash Sale with a Discount 149
Journalizing a Customer's NSF Cheque 152
Applying an Invoice to a Deposit 155
Journalizing Credit Card Receipts 157
Owner Investment in Business 159
    Recording a Receipt for a Non-Merchandise Item 160
Printing Customer Statements 162
Printing Period-End Reports 163
    To Print a Gross Margin Income Statement 164
    To Print the Sales Journal 165
    To Print the Receipts Journal 165

View/Print Graphs 165
To View Graphs 165
Summary, Part B 166
Before Moving On, Part B 166
Challenge Exercise 02 C2B-1, Brides 167
Challenge Exercise 02 C2B-2, Skis 168
Challenge Exercise 02 C2B-3, House Sitters 169
Mini-guide for Transactions in Chapter 2 170
Relevant Appendices, Part B 171

Chapter 3A
PAYABLES Module--Basics
Tyson's Toys. **173**

The PAYABLES Module Overview 174
Company Profile – Tyson's Toys 174
Session Date 176
Starting Simply for Payables 176
To Display the Vendor Aged Report 177
To Display and Print the Income Statement 178
Vendor Invoices Guidelines and Procedures.........................178
The PAYABLES Journals 178
The Purchase Orders Journal 180
Customizing the Purchase Orders Journal...........180
Toolbar Icons 181
Entering Purchase Orders..181
Pending Purchase Order Report 184
The Vendors Subledger 185
Purchase with No Purchase Order (PO) 189
To View a Vendor Account 192
Purchase of Services/Goods Not for Resale...192
Journalizing Purchases for Goods Not for Resale 192
Purchase of Services 194
Recording Arrival of Goods Ordered on a Purchase Order 199
Adjusting a Cheque 200
Journalizing Purchase Returns 202
To Review the Vendor Record 204
Viewing/Printing Special Reports 204
Outstanding Purchase Orders 204
The Payments Journal 205
Journalizing a Vendor Payment...205
Toolbar Icons 205
Payment with Merchandise Discount...208
Printing Reports When Needed..211
Summary, Part A 211
Before Moving On, Part A 212
Relevant Appendices, Part A...212
Challenge Exercise 03 C3A-1, Wheelchairs 213
Challenge Exercise 03 C3A-2, Radios 214

Chapter 3B
PAYABLES Module—Beyond Basics
Tyson's Toys. **215**

Opening the PAYABLES Module, Part B 216
Starting Simply for Payables 216
Cash Flow Projection Report...218
Credit Card Purchase..218
Payment with Non-Merchandise Discount...220
Purchase and Payment to a One-time Vendor 224

Journalizing Bank Reconciliation Items...227
    Entering Service Charges 227
Journalizing Partner's/Proprietor's Drawings...228
Recording a Purchase Order with a Prepayment to a Vendor 231
    Recording Lease Payments..232
Journalizing HST Remittance 234
    Calculating HST Remittance...235
    Viewing the Vendor Aged Report 237
Journalizing an Invoice with Reduced HST 238
    To Record Payment for Insurance...239
Printing Reports 241
Adjusting Ending Inventory – Periodic Method in Simply 241
    Periodic Inventory System 242
    Perpetual Inventory System 243
        To Enter the New Inventory Value..245
        The Comparative Income Statement..247
Other Period-End/Month-end Reports..247
        To View and Print the Purchase Journal 248
        To View and Print the Payments Journal 248
        To View and Print a Cheque Log...248
    To View Graphs 249
Summary, Part B...250
Before Moving On, Part B 250
Relevant appendices, Part B..251
    Challenge Exercise 03 C3B-1, Network 252
    Challenge Exercise 03 C3B-2, China 253
    Challenge Exercise 03 C3B-3, Dance Studio.................................255
    Challenge Exercise 03 C3B-4, Chairs 256
Mini-Guide for Chapter 3 257

Chapter 4
Setting Up a New Company
Sarah's Kitchen Stores **259**

Step 1: Creating Company Files..261
    Account Types 262
    Setting Up a New Company File from Scratch 264
Step 2: Setting User Preferences Defaults 271
    Changing Preferences Settings 274
Step 3: Changing System Defaults...276
Step 4: Changing Printer Settings 288
Step 5: Conversion Process with Accounts 290
    The Chart of Accounts...291
    Account Numbering System in Simply 291
    To Add an Account 292
    To Delete an Account 299
    Review and Check Account Coding Changes Made 299
    To Modify an Account 300
Step 6: Linking Modules/Accounts 302
    Linking the Modules 303
        COMPANY Module Links 303
        PAYABLES Module Links 304
        RECEIVABLES Module Links..305
Step 7: Entering Opening G/L Account Balances (History) 306
    Contra Account Balance..309
    Displaying the Trial Balance...311
Step 8: Setting Up Tax Classes, Codes, Rates & Customization 311
Step 9a: Setting Up Subledgers-Vendors 313
    Entering the Vendor Accounts 314
Step 9b: Setting Up Subledgers-Customers 318
    Entering Customers 318

Entering Customer Balances (History) 319
Step 10: To Add Credit Card Information 321
Step 11: Setting Modules to Ready 323
Setting the System to READY 324
Before Moving On 326
Challenge Exercise 04 C4-1, Balloons Store.......................327
Challenge Exercise 04 C4-2, Kojokaro 330
Challenge Exercise 04 C4-3, Skates Stores 331
Challenge Exercise 04 C4-4, R. Park Uniforms 334
Relevant Appendices 335

Chapter 5
Review of COMPANY, PAYABLES and RECEIVABLES Modules

Sarah's Kitchen Stores.. **337**
Sarah's Kitchen Stores Profile..338
Transactions 339

Chapter 6
Challenge COMPANY, RECEIVABLES, PAYABLES
Setup and Transactions

Shirts & Ties.. **349**
(Your Last Name) Shirts & Ties: Company Profile 350
Transactions 353

Chapter 7
EMPLOYEE & PAYROLL Module Setup and Processing

Creative Wallpaper... **363**
EMPLOYEES & PAYROLL Module 365
Difference between Manual Accounting and Simply Payroll 366
Creative Wallpaper: Company Profile...367
Making Payroll-Related Adjusting Entry 371
Step 1: Setting EMPLOYEES & PAYROLL Module Defaults 371
Step 2: Setting Up Linked Accounts 377
Payroll Conversion...380
Step 3: Entering Employee Payroll Information 381
Reviewing Related Payroll – G/L Balances 390
Step 4: Setting the PAYROLL Module to Ready........................390
Are you ready to make PAYROLL Ready? 390
Entering EMPLOYEE Transactions 391
Entering a New Employee...392
To Issue Paycheques 393
The PAYROLL Journal 398
To Review PAYROLL Entries After Posting........................403
Paying Receiver General Pay Withholdings................................406
Processing Vacation Pay 409
Making Payroll Corrections..411
Step 1: Reverse Original Entry...412
Step 2: Record the Correct Entry and Issue a New Cheque 414
Recording Payroll Accrued Wages 416
Processing T4 Slips (or Relevé 1) 417
Printing Month-End Employee-Related Reports 418
To Print the PAYROLL Journal 418
To Print the Balance Sheet as at Jan 31, 2014 419
To Display a Cheque Log for Jan 1 to Jan 31, 2014 419
To Print the Employee Detail Report 419
To Print the Employee YTD (Year-To-Date) Report............420
Payroll Entry with EHT (Employer Health Tax) 420
Converting During the Year 420

Garnishee and Reimbursement 421
Before Moving On 422
Relevant Appendices 422
Challenge Exercise 07 C7-1, Carpets 4Home 423

Chapter 8
INVENTORY & SERVICES Module Setup and Transactions Review: G/L, A/P, A/R

Printers Company **425**
INVENTORY & SERVICES Module Overview 426
Printers Company: Company Profile 427
INVENTORY Policies and Procedures 427
Conversion 431
The Inventory & Services Journals 432
Step 1: Setting the INVENTORY & SERVICES Module Defaults ... 433
Step 2: Setting the INVENTORY & SERVICES Linked Accounts 434
Step 3: Creating Inventory Item Ledgers 435
To Display Inventory Details 441
Step 4: Setting the INVENTORY & SERVICES Module to READY 443
Step 5: Journalizing Inventory-Related Sales 443
Preferred Pricing 444
Inventory-Related Sale on Credit 444
Determining Inventory Items or Order 448
Recording a New Item 448
Display the Pending Purchases Report 451
Journalizing Inventory Purchases 452
To Journalize a Cash on Delivery (COD) Sale 455
Journalizing an Inventory Sales Return 458
Step 1: Record the Sales Return 458
Step 2: Record the Cash Receipt from Computers and More 460
Journalizing an Inventory Purchase Return 460
Recording a Payment with Cash Discount 462
New Services Provided 463
To Create New Ledger Accounts 463
Class Options Tab 464
To Create New Service Items 464
Unit Tab 464
Pricing Tab 464
Linked Tab 464
Changing Selling Prices 466
Correcting Wrong Price after Posting 467
Making Inventory Adjustments 469
Correcting Inventory Errors 472
Build from Bill of Materials and/or Build from Item Assembly Journal ... 472
Quantities Tab 473
Pricing Tab 473
Linked Tab 473
Build Tab 473
Inventory Reports 476
Other Reports 476
Before Moving On 477
Relevant Appendix 477
Challenge Exercise 08 C8-1, Stain Company (Your Name) 478
Challenge Exercise 08 C8-2, Charlie's Hair Styling 480
Challenge Exercise 08 C8-3, Vet Services 481
Challenge Exercise 08 C8-4, Luggage-Pl 483
Challenge Exercise 08 C8-5, Toys-Pl 485
Challenge Exercise 08 C8-6, Shirts-Pl 487
Challenge Exercise 08 C8-7, Bears 489

Chapter 9
Month-End/Year-End Processing
Kafa Sweaters. **493**

Kafa Sweaters: Company Profile 494
    Reviewing Existing Accounting Data 494
    Trial Balance for Kafa Sweaters 494
Entering Month-End (Period-End) Adjustments 494
    Bank Reconciliation 496
    Prepaid Expense Adjustment: Office Supplies 497
    Prepaid Expense Adjustment: Prepaid Insurance 498
    Accrued Expenses 499
        Accrued Interest 501
        Accrued Wages Payable 502
    Amortization Adjustment 503
    Periodic Inventory: Month-End Adjustment 504
Backing Up the Data Files 505
Printing Month-End and Year-End Reports 505
Summary 506
Before Moving On. 506

Chapter 10
Year-End Closing
Kafa Sweaters. **507**

To Close the Books (Fiscal Year-End) 508
Kafa2 Sweaters: Company Profile 508
Starting a New Fiscal Year 512
Updating Inventory Accounts 515
Summary 516
Before Moving On 517
    Inventory Entry at the End of the First Month of the Fiscal Year 518
    Challenge Exercise 10 C10-1 (Chapters 9-10), Rama Magazines 519
    Challenge Exercise 10 C10-2 (Chapters 1-10), City Gravel 520

Chapter 11
DIVISION* Module Setup and Transactions
Hot Tubs Company Ltd.. .... **521**

The DIVISION Module 522
HotTubs Company: Profile 522
    Division Group Name 522
    Financial Reports and Other Information 523
Starting Simply Accounting 525
Setting up the DIVISION Module 525
    Step 1: To Display the DIVISION Module 525
    Step 2: To Set Up DIVISION Settings 525
    Step 3: To Set Up a DIVISION Name/Balance Forward 527
    Step 4: To Enter Other DIVISIONS 528
Processing Transactions in the DIVISION Module 528
Allocating a Purchase to a Division(s) 531
Allocating Cash Sales to a Division(s) 534
Allocating Payroll to a Division(s) 536
To Allocate Credit Sales to a Division(s) 539
Allocating Sales Returns to a Division(s) 540
    Correcting DIVISION Errors 541
    The Payroll Accrual 542
Adjusting INVENTORY and Cost of Sales 543
Printing Month-End DIVISION Reports 546
Before Moving On... 548

Chapter 12
BANKING Module – Reconciliation & Deposits
Wedding Flowers Company **549**
    Accounting and Simply Accounting Terminology 550
    Banking Codes 550
    BANKING Module 551
        The Reconciliation & Deposits Journal 551
    The Wedding Flowers Company 551
    Setting Up the Reconciliation & Deposits Journal 553
        To Set Up Linked Accounts 553
            Reconciliation & Deposits 553
    Reconciling Bank Accounts in Simply 555
        Steps to Complete a Bank Reconciliation in Simply 556
        Using the Reconciliation & Deposit Journal 556
    Printing Reconciliation & Deposits Reports 564
        Other Reconciliation & Deposits Features 566
    Summary 566
        Reconciliation Errors 566
    Before Moving On 568
    Relevant Appendix 568
        Challenge Exercise 12 C12-1, China 569

Chapter 13
Correcting Transaction Errors After Posting **571**
    Correcting General Journal Entries 573
    Correcting or Canceling Sales Orders or Quotes 576
    Correcting Sales Journal Entry for Merchandise 577
    Correcting Sales Receipt Entry 579
    Canceling or Correcting Purchase Orders or Quotes 581
    Correcting Purchase Journal Entries for Goods for Resale (Merchandise) 582
    Correcting Purchase Journal Entries for Non-Merchandise 584
    Correcting Vendor Payment 585
    Correcting Payments (Make Other Payments) 587
    Correcting Payroll Cheque Items 588
    Correcting Inventory Adjustments Journal Entries 589
    Correcting Build from Inventory Assembly Journal Entries 590

Chapter 14
Multi-Currency
Saddles Company **593**
    Foreign-Currency Overview 594
        To Print a Balance Sheet 605
    Challenge Exercise 14 C14-1, Saddles 607

Chapter 15
Taxes (GST, PST and HST)
Brittany Company **609**
    HST or GST Goods and Services Tax 610
    (PST) Provincial Sales Tax 610
    HST or GST Charged on Sales 610
    HST or GST Paid on Purchases 611
    Method of Recording HST or GST 611
        Registration 611
        HST or GST Paid to the Federal Government 612
        HST Example for Showing Remittances 612
    HST, What Account Do You Charge? 613

(PST) Provincial Sales Tax, (RST) Retail Sales Tax 614
    PST Paid to the Provincial Government...614
GST Sales Tax 615
PST, What Account Do You Charge?...615

Appendix A
Simply Accounting by Sale Premium 2010
Student Version B Software Installation Instructions .. 619

Glossary.. 631

Index 639

Work Logbook 643

Getting Started and COMPANY Module

Photos Company

Learning Objectives

After completing this chapter you will be able to:

- ☐ Use the General Journal to enter and post transactions using the Double-Entry method.
- ☐ Display General Journal entries.
- ☐ Advance the Session Date.
- ☐ Adjust a wrong Journal entry after posting.
- ☐ Set up, use and remove a recurring entry.
- ☐ Use the Additional Transaction Details feature.
- ☐ Display and print relevant reports.
- ☐ Save and back up the data file.
- ☐ Record backup information in a logbook.

Simply Accounting by Sage Premium 2010, which we will refer to as Simply Accounting, is sold in five different business releases: **First Step, Pro, Premium, Enterprise** and **Accountants Edition**.

FREE to you as a download program from the Simply server, is the **Simply Accounting by Sage Premium 2010**, **Student Version**, which we will refer to as the Student Version.

See Appendix A at the back of the textbook for computer system requirements, restrictions and installation instructions.

The Premium Educational Version (installed in your school lab) and the Student Version, that is available as a download, are the same program. *Note*: The 2010 version will work with Windows XP, Windows 2000, Windows Vista, and Windows 7, but will not work with previous Windows versions.

When you start Simply at school, you will see the following in the bottom left of the window:

Registered to: _____
Serial Number _____
Release A
Payroll Taxes Effective: Jul 1, 2009

Note: This window will only display for a few seconds.

If you are using the student version you will see:

Student version
xxx Days remaining
Release A
Payroll Taxes Effective Jul 1, 2009

For student version installation instructions, refer to Appendix A.

You will learn the features of the **Premium** version in this textbook. The Premium software is available as a 2-user networking software. Features such as multi-user mode and departmental accounting will be discussed, but you will not be given exercises using these features.

The first chapter, **Photos Company**, explains basic concepts to give you an idea of how Simply Accounting works using double-entry accounting. The exercises allow you to try out some of the basic techniques in recording transactions, using folders and windows, in the Simply General Ledger.

The contents of this chapter are as follows:

- Icon Reference.. 3
- Simply Accounting 2010 Overview.. 4
- Getting Started 5
    - Exercise 1-1a – Downloading the Master Data files using the Internet 6
    - Exercise 1-1b – Extracting the Master Data files 7
    - Exercise 1-1c – Unzipping the Master Data files using exe 7
- Starting the Simply Program... 8
    - Exercise 1-2 – Starting the Simply Program 8
- The Simply Accounting Start Window.. 9
    - Range of Dates.. 12
    - Home Window — Enhanced View 16
    - Home Window — Classic View 17
    - Menu Bar.. 17
    - The Toolbar 17
    - Modules 17
    - Accountant's Tasks 18
    - Related Tasks... 19
    - Reports... 19
    - Learning Centre 20
- Using Simply HELP.. 20
    - Exercise 1-3a – Using Help—Type a question for help 20
    - Exercise 1-3b – Using Help—Search... 21
    - Exercise 1-3c – Using Help—Database Search Tool 21
    - Exercise 1-3d – Using Help—Learning Centre 21
    - Exercise 1-4 – Changing Company Information 22
    - Exercise 1-5a – Displaying Reports Using Recently Viewed Reports Area.. 23
    - Exercise 1-5b – Display Balance Sheet Using the Report Menu................ 25
    - Exercise 1-5c – Display the Income Statement Using the Report Centre 25
- Processing Transactions in the COMPANY Module...................................... 26
    - To Correct Errors... 27
    - Exercise 1-6 – Entering Transactions in the General Journal...................... 27
    - Exercise 1-7 – Displaying a Journal Entry.. 32
    - Exercise 1-8 – To Advance the Session Date... 33
    - Exercise 1-9a – Recording a Compound Entry... 33
    - Exercise 1-9b – Adding a New General Ledger Account 34
    - Exercise 1-10 – Creating a Recurring Entry... 38
    - Exercise 1-11 – Journalizing Owner Investment in Business 39
    - Exercise 1-12 – Correcting an Entry 40
    - Exercise 1-13 – To Display Corrected Entries 42
    - Exercise 1-14 – Removing a Recurring Transaction Entry 44
    - Exercise 1-15 – Using a Recurring Transaction.. 45
    - Exercise 1-16 – Drill Down (Trace Back) 47
    - Exercise 1-17 – To Display and Print the General Journal 48
    - Exercise 1-18 – To Display/Print the General Ledger Report...................... 52
    - Exercise 1-19 – Printing the Financial Statements 53
    - Exercise 1-20 – Printing the Recurring Transactions Report...................... 53
    - Exercise 1-21a – Creating Custom Report Shortcuts 53
    - Exercise 1-21b – To Remove a Report Shortcut 54
    - Exercise 1-21c – To Add a Blank Space between Reports 55
    - Exercise 1-22 – Saving Your Work 55
- Why Back Up?.. 57
    - Exercise 1-23 – Backing Up Your Data.. 57
    - Exercise 1-24 – Maintaining a Logbook 60
- Summary 61

• Before Moving On…...63
    Challenge Exercise 01 C1-1, Driving School..64
    Challenge Exercise 01 C1-2, Astrology Readings.......................................65
    Challenge Exercise 01 C1-3, Movers...66
• Relevant Appendices 67
• **Chapter 1a**: Restoring a Data File from a Backup Data File.......................69
    Exercise 1a-1 – Restoring a Data File from a Backup 69

As you go through the text, you will come across the following icons that are accompanied by special notations. Study each one carefully.

 This icon alerts you to general information, usually relevant accounting or GAAP notation (Generally Accepted Accounting Principles). You will find the information box as a sidebar at the left of the main text.

 This icon signals caution, VERY IMPORTANT information or a reminder for you to do something that may affect processing results.

 Whenever you see this icon, run the slideshow relevant to the topic under study. It will help you to better understand concepts and procedures in the chapter.

 This icon indicates the availability of specific material for download from www.simplyaccounting2010.nelson.com under Student Resources. View the Appendix relevant to the topic under study. It will help you to better understand concepts and procedures.

 This icon will signal that you will purposely make an error which you will learn how to correct later.

 The Happy Face will alert you when you will correct an error that you purposely made earlier.

 This icon will remind you to back up your data.

 This icon will remind you to update your logbook. A logbook form is provided for you, at the back of this text, where you will log the page # and topic that you last completed.

 You will see these icons together to remind you to back up your data and update your logbook at the back of this text.

Simply Accounting 2010 Overview

Accrual Basis accounting
Generally Accepted Accounting Principles (GAAP) stipulates that revenue should be recognized and recorded when a service has been provided or a product has been delivered (for cash or on credit). Expenses should be recognized and recorded when a service has been provided or products have been delivered (for cash or on credit). This is the main premise of the **accrual** method.

Cash Basis accounting
Revenue is recognized and recorded when cash is received, and expenses are recognized and recorded when paid. This method is contrary to the accrual method and is not consistent with GAAP. The cash basis method can be used by farmers and fishermen, but is not accepted for income tax purposes.

The accrual method has been used in this book because it records revenues and expenses, when incurred, and provides appropriate reports that show profits or losses, at a specified accounting period, based on the time when actual business transactions occur and not when cash is received or paid. The accrual method is accepted for income tax purposes.

Simply Accounting is a simple, secure and integrated accounting software package designed to simplify bookkeeping functions using double entry accounting, i.e., Debit entries must equal Credit entries. You can view and/or print various financial statements and other reports whenever needed.

Subledgers, when in use, are linked to the GENERAL LEDGER (e.g., ACCOUNTS RECEIVABLE in Chapter 2A and 2B and ACCOUNTS PAYABLE in Chapter 3A and 3B). This means that when a transaction is processed in any of the subledgers, the General Ledger is automatically updated. The Accounts Payable and Accounts Receivable subledgers may be linked to the INVENTORY & SERVICES subledger (Chapter 8).

Simply provides a choice of either the **Cash** method or the **Accrual** method of accounting. This text uses the **Accrual** method (see side note box).

There are some powerful features of Simply that offer many advantages over using manual bookkeeping. For example:

1. Data entry errors may be easily corrected.

2. Controls are provided to prevent data entry errors, such as addition errors or duplicate invoice numbers, transposition of numbers, etc.

3. Posting transactions is automatically performed by clicking the Post [Post] icon or the [Post] icon depending on which module you are working in, and all ledgers are updated immediately.

4. Records are updated immediately.

5. Standard financial statements and reports may be printed at any time.

Company data files for you to work with are supplied on the textbook website: www.simplyaccounting2010.nelson.com. See Exercise 1-1a. Your instructor will explain which data files should be downloaded to your storage device and then extracted. If you have a damaged data file or if you want to repeat a chapter from the beginning you can extract the file again.

This text assumes that you are familiar with basic accounting. If you require help in this area, information on the *Basics of Accounting* can be found in Appendix A, at www.simplyaccounting2010.nelson.com under Student Resources.

As you work through each section of this textbook, you will learn how to use Simply in a business setting. The purpose of the procedures and various Simply features is explained in simple terms. A thorough **knowledge** of this software will make you a valuable employee.

Run **Slideshow 1A-SIMPLY BASICS** from the website: www.simplyaccounting2010.nelson.com under Student Resources.

It will give you a general overview of Simply Accounting Premium 2010 and the features that are available in all modules.

Getting Started

A basic understanding of Windows is required if you wish to use Simply Accounting effectively. You can find a glossary of accounting and Simply terminology at the end of each chapter.

If the Simply software has been installed using the Typical method (most common options) on the school computer/or network, the program is located in the path: **C:\ Program Files\Simply Accounting Premium 2010**.

It is assumed that:

1. You have access to the Simply Accounting software.

2. You will be storing your data files on a storage device. This text designates the storage device as drive **C:**. If your drive is other than C: replace **C:** with the appropriate drive letter when doing your exercises.

Throughout the text, you will see capitalized wording such as RECEIVABLES, PAYABLES, INVENTORY & SERVICES, EMPLOYEES & PAYROLL, PROJECTS (DIVISIONS) BANKING and COMPANY. These refer to the module being discussed.

When you see a number followed by an arrowhead such as 1➤, 2➤, etc., it means there is something on the line or the paragraph for you to do on the keyboard or with your mouse button. Icons will alert you to special notations.

Click   Means to click the left mouse button **once**.

Double-click   You must click the left mouse button **twice** quickly (without pausing).

Words you have to type or keys you have to press are shown in **BOLD**.

Throughout the text you will see shaded references similar to: See Exercise 7-8. These references are shaded to help you quickly find them in the textbook.

Read the instructions and explanation in the exercises before executing the keystrokes on your computer. If you read ahead and understand the instructions, you may avoid making errors.

VERY IMPORTANT:

Always back up your data at the end of EVERY work session, either in the classroom or at home. This can save you hours of redoing work (see side note). Answer the questions at the end of each chapter before moving on to the next chapter. This will help you understand the reasons for the various procedures. It will also aid you in preparing for tests.

A detailed index is provided at the end of the book for your easy reference.

A practical storage device to back up data is a USB storage device (see picture below) which is available in varying storage capacities. It plugs into a USB port and can be easily taken in and out. Ask your teacher where the USB port is located on your computer.

Most schools have an anti-virus program that protects the files in the school network. If your school does not, you should be aware that your files could be corrupted if there is a virus in the system. It is imperative, therefore, that you back up your data regularly.

If you do some of your work at home, you should invest in an anti-virus program with regular updates to ensure that your files will not be damaged, and that you do not take corrupted data to school, that can infect the network system.

Exercise 1-1a –Downloading the Master Data files using the Internet

---

The Master company data files you need to work through the exercises in this book are contained on the Nelson Education website. Each of the company data files are compressed using WinZip and are in self-extracting executable (exe) format. You need to download and unzip these files onto your storage device using the procedure below, which assumes that you are loading the data files to the C: drive. If you are loading the data files to a different storage device, use the procedure below, substituting the drive letter of the device for C.

> Backup files, created in Exercise 1-23, can be used to restore a data file (see Chapter 1a at the end of this chapter) if it becomes damaged or if you want to start an exercise again.

1 ➤ Using Windows Explorer, create a **Simply Exe** folder on the C: drive or other drive as requested by your instructor.

2 ➤ Start your web browser (Internet Explorer, Firefox, etc.).

3 ➤ In the locater bar, type **http://www.simplyaccounting2010.nelson.com/**. You will be taken to the Home page of the textbook.

4 ➤ On the menu, click **Student Resources**.

5 ➤ On the menu, click **Data Files**.

6 ➤ User Name: Type **freedman2010** as noted in the window.

7 ➤ Password As noted in the window, go to the page identified and type the password in the field. Click **OK**.

8 ➤ Scroll down to the Chapter Data Files area. Click the ▼ arrow.

9 ➤ This opens a new window with a list of the **exe** data files in chapter order.

> For an individual slide download, select the chapter from the <u>menu</u> below.
> select a file ▼

Chapter 1-2:

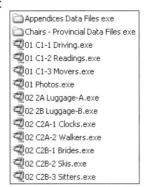

10 ➤ From the download list, double-click on the **01 Photos.exe** exe file you want to download. This will show you how to download the data file to your download location: C:**Simply Data 2010** folder, or location identified by your instructor.

11 ➤ You may see the following message bar.

> To help protect your security, Internet Explorer blocked this site from downloading files to your computer. Click here for options...

12 ➤ If you see this message, click on the bar, click on ⎣ Download File... ⎦ .

13 ➤ Repeat step 9.

14 ➤ Click **Save** in the File Download box, and save the file.

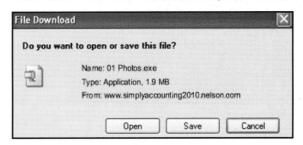

15 ➤ You may receive the following Security Warning. Ignore the warning. Click **Run**.

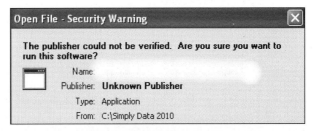

16 ➤ Click **Save** to save the file to the folder identified in step 1.

Exercise 1-1b – Extracting the Master Data files

If you use **Windows Explorer** or **My Computer**, you will notice that the 01 Photos folder contains a folder, with an extension of **SAJ** and a file with an extension of **SAI**. Inside the SAJ folder are 2 folders and additional files. The **mysql** folder contains the database and the **simply** folder contains the Simply files. Together these files contain information about the company, accounts, transactions, etc. When you open the data file, Exercise 1-2, step 10, you use only the **SAI** file in the window.

If you move your mouse over the SAI file, you will see information that this is a Simply Accounting Data File.

1 ➤ Go to the folder where your downloads are located. Double-click on the **01 Photos.exe** file and the following WinZip window will appear.

The WinZip Self-extractor, Unzip command will create the Photos data file in the Simply Data 2010 folder on your storage device. If you want to load the data files in a different drive/folder, change the field **C:\Simply Data 2010** to your specific location, or click **Browse** to locate the specific storage space.

---

2 ➤ Click **Unzip**.

The following window indicates that the data files have been successfully unzipped and are ready for you to use.

The data folder in your C:\ storage location should have the following name:

Folder	*Company Name*	*Module used (Main)*
01 Photos	Photos Company	COMPANY

3 ➤ Click **OK**, then **Close**.

To copy other company files (e.g., 01 C1-1 Driving, Chapter 1 Challenge Case; 02 2A Luggage-A, Chapter 2A; or other company files) to your storage space (e.g., C:\Simply Data 2010), repeat the above steps.

Refer to Appendix A, at the back of the text, for instructions on installing the Student version of the Simply program.

Using Windows Explorer, locate the Simply Data 2010 folder and the 01 Photos data file.

Starting the Simply Program

In a business setting, you may be required to enter a password before you can access a Simply data file. Passwords prevent unauthorized people from having access to your program and the company data. The exercises in this textbook do not require a password. Information on using a password can be found in Appendix O, *Security—Passwords* from www.simplyaccounting2010.nelson.com under Student Resources. See your instructor for more information.

Read the instructions and explanation in each exercise before attempting to record data using the Simply program. If you ignore the instructions and explanation, you may make errors that could easily have been avoided.

Remember...

Click   means to click the left button once.
Double-click   means to click the left button twice rapidly.

Exercise 1-2 – Starting the Simply Program

DO NOT open the Simply file from the Windows Explorer or My Computer window. Use the procedure shown in this Exercise.

You need to tell the Simply program where to locate the company data files that you will be using. You will start by using the Photos Company data folder.

Your instructor will advise you how to access Simply in the classroom. If you are using your home computer, follow this procedure:

1 ➤ Click the **Start** icon. .

2 ➤ Move the mouse to the **Programs** icon 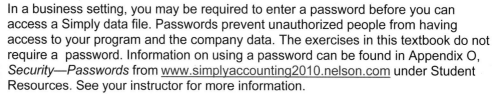, or to the   All Programs ▷ icon.

3 ➤ Move the mouse to   Simply Accounting Premium 2010 . (See side note box.)

The location of the Simply Accounting icon and/or name depends upon how your Windows program groups are set up for application software.

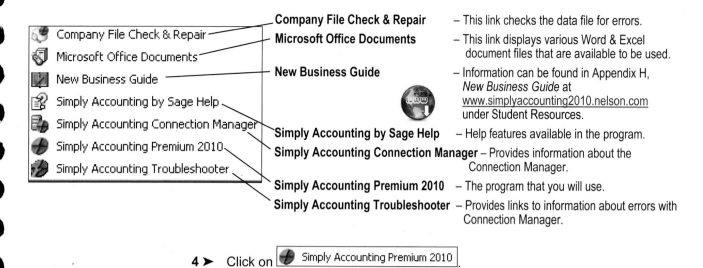

Company File Check & Repair – This link checks the data file for errors.

Microsoft Office Documents – This link displays various Word & Excel document files that are available to be used.

New Business Guide – Information can be found in Appendix H, *New Business Guide* at www.simplyaccounting2010.nelson.com under Student Resources.

Simply Accounting by Sage Help – Help features available in the program.

Simply Accounting Connection Manager – Provides information about the Connection Manager.

Simply Accounting Premium 2010 – The program that you will use.

Simply Accounting Troubleshooter – Provides links to information about errors with Connection Manager.

4 ➤   Click on   Simply Accounting Premium 2010

The Simply Accounting Start Window

ℹ️ If this is the first time the software is being used you will see screen Fig.1-1a. The next time the software is being used you will see a new item added to the list. Open the last company you worked on, Fig. 1-1b.

Fig. 1-1a: **Simply Accounting start window.** *(See side note box.)*

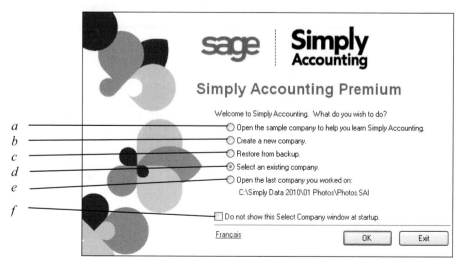

Fig. 1-1b: Simply Accounting start window, with Open last company.

a) **Open the sample company to help you learn Simply Accounting**. Used if you want to open the sample company (Universal Construction) that was installed in the computer. You may not have access to the sample companies.

b) **Create a new company**. Used when you need to create a new company. You will use this option in Chapter 4.

c) **Restore from backup**. Used when you want to open a backup file; (e.g., to replace a damaged data file). Instructions on using this feature (Restoring a Data File from a Backup Data File) is in Chapter 1a at the end of this chapter.

d) **Select an existing company**. Used when you want to open a company that is on your storage space. (See this exercise at step 5.)

e) **Open the last company you worked on**. This option may not be applicable in a classroom setting. If the student before you was working on a different company, this choice may not be appropriate.

f) **Do not show this Select Company window at startup**. Do NOT click this selection. This option is explained in Chapter 4.

5 ➤ Click **Select an existing company**.

6 ➤ Click **OK**. You will then see the Open Company window, Fig. 1-2.

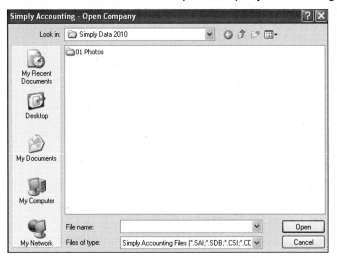

Fig. 1-2: Open Company window.

This window is the default data location. In a classroom network setting, this may not be correct. If your window does not resemble Fig. 1-2, follow the steps below (starting at step 7) to locate your drive folders.

Remember, if your data folders are located on another drive such as **D:**, **E:** or another letter, substitute your drive letter for **C:**.

Network Procedures

On a network, a window similar to Fig. 1-3 appears.

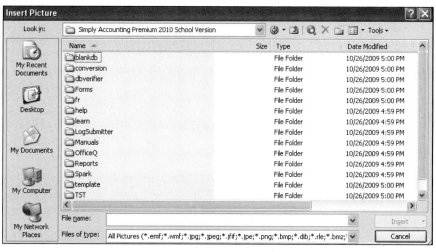

Fig. 1-3: Open Company window on a network.

7 ➤ Click the ▼ in the **Look in** box.

8 ➤ Locate and double-click the **Simply Data 2010** folder (Fig. 1-2).

9 ➤ Double-click the folder 01 Photos .

10 ➤ Click the file named Photos.SAI (*Note*: In Fig. 1-2, you may not see the **SAI extension** in the File name box; you should see the file name: Photos.)

11 ➤ Click **Open**. Wait for the program to load. A Session Date box appears.

If you are using the Simply Student Edition at home, see the note at the left.

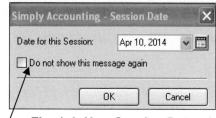

Fig. 1-4: New Session Date window.

If you are using the Student Version, the program can be used for a period of 14 months (425 days) from the date that you start using the program.

The number of days remaining will display on the left side when you start the program.

Simply uses the date format as defined by Windows. The author has used the long date format: **mm/dd/yyyy** (month, day, year) format. (Simply 2010 allows the date to be displayed using an abbreviated name, i.e., Apr 10, 2014 instead of 04/10/2014).

To change the date you have three choices.

Do NOT click this field. If you click this field and OK by mistake, you enter the Photos data file. The next time you open this company, the Session Date window will NOT display and you will have to change the session date inside the data file.

To correct the mistake, and have the session date displayed as above, each time you open the data file, from the top menu bar click, **Setup**, **User Preferences**, **View**, and click on the 3rd item at the bottom. ☑ Show Change Session Date at Startup , click **OK** to return to the Home window.

Experienced users may click this field, but as you are learning Simply, the authors suggest that you display the session date window.

1. You may type the date in the **Date for this Session** box.

2. You may click the ▼ arrow and select the appropriate date from a range of dates. See step 12.

3. You may click the Calendar button.

The most efficient way to enter a date is by using choice 3, the Simply Calendar. It is fast and it helps you avoid making date format errors.

You will click the ▼ arrow in the next step only to understand the concept of range of dates relevant to the Session Date.

12 ➤   Click the ▼ arrow. A drop-down list of dates appears.

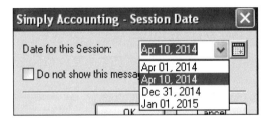

Range of Dates

The Photos Company is using a calendar fiscal year.

> Start of the fiscal year is: Jan 01, 2014
> End of the fiscal year is: Dec 31, 2014

Apr 01, 2014   This is the first day of the current month.

Apr 10, 2014   This is the last date that the Photos Company data file was used. This is known as the **session date**. In a business environment, the Session date is the current date when you are entering transactions. This date will change as you change the session date.

Dec 31, 2014   The end of Photos Company's fiscal year.

Jan 01, 2015   The start of Photos Company's next fiscal year. You must be careful NOT to select this. If you type or accept Jan 01, 2015, the start of Photos Company's next fiscal year, Simply will automatically perform year-end procedures, closing the Revenue and Expense accounts for the previous fiscal year to zero. In addition, the net profit or loss will be updated in the appropriate Equity account, e.g., Capital, Retained Earnings, etc.

You will now use the Calendar button 📅 to enter the session date. Although you can type the session date 04102014, Apr10, or select the appropriate date from the drop-down options, using the Calendar is by far the most efficient way.

13 ➤   Click the **Calendar** button 📅. The calendar for the current month appears. To move to future months click the ▶. To move back, click the ◀. Try going forward and backward now.

14 ▶ Move the Calendar to April. For this exercise, you need to enter **Apr 18, 2014** as your Session Date. Click **18**. Your window should resemble the next screen:

15 ➤ Click **OK**.

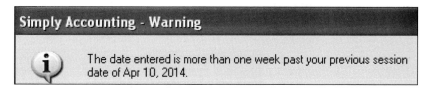

 The Warning window advises you if the date you entered is more than one week (7 days) ahead of the previous session date. However, it will not advise you if you have entered a new month or if you have entered the wrong date. If you have made an error in the date, the program will give you the opportunity to change it at this point by clicking Cancel.

16 ➤ If the date is correct, click **OK** to accept the new session date.

17 ➤ Depending on the configuration at your school, you may see the following online survey window. If you do not see the survey window, move to step 19.

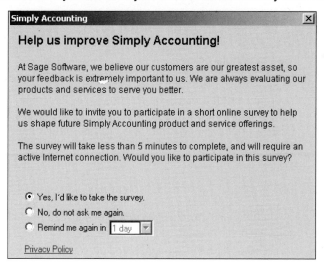

 Simply by Sage announces that you can only take the survey once. If you click the ☒ in the top corner, or click No, do not ask me again, this window will no longer appear in the future. If you click ▼ Remind me again in, you have a choice to select 1, 3, 7 or 10 days later.

18 ➤ You may select "Yes, I'd like to take the survey" or "No, do not ask me" again. Make your selection, then click **OK**.

If you were not connected to the Internet and had selected Yes, then clicked OK, you would have seen the following caution window.

> You must be connected to the Internet to respond to the survey. After connecting, please return to the survey window, select Yes, and click OK.

Students using the Student Edition will *not* see the following Welcome window.

The Welcome to the **Education Edition window shown next** will display each time you open a company data file at school. If you are using the student version, you will not see the Educational Version window shown next.

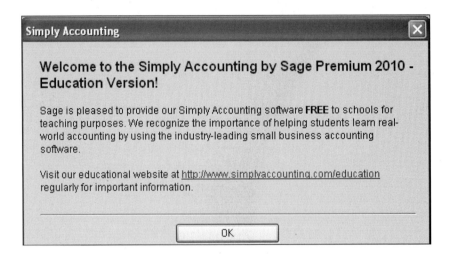

19 ➤   Click **OK**.

Students using the Student Edition will not see the Welcome window above step 19. Students using the Student Edition should jump to the information after step 19, starting with:

Your current data file...

(See side note box.)

Your current data file is for Photos Company. The Getting Started; Welcome to Simply Accounting window should look like Fig. 1-5a. The Simply **Home** window will be Fig. 1-5b. A brief explanation of the menus and icons is shown after step 24. You are welcome to experiment clicking on menu items or icons as you proceed with this overview.

Do not make any changes to any of the windows, as they may affect the data used in the practice exercises later in the chapter. To exit from this window or any window, click the $\boxed{X}$ in the top-right corner. If you click $\boxed{X}$ from the Home window Fig 1-5b Simply saves the work you completed and closes the file.

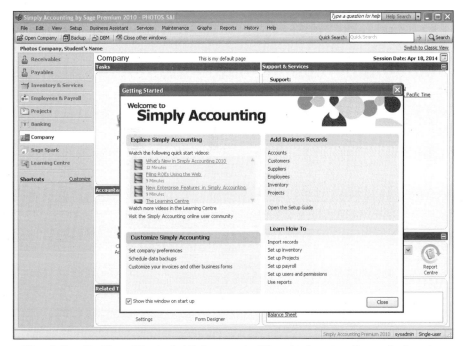

Fig. 1-5a: Getting Started; Welcome to Simply Accounting window.

The Welcome to Simply Accounting window is divided into 4 parts.

If you click on various choices, the Welcome to Simply Accounting window may disappear. You should see the [⬙ **Getting Started**] icon on the bottom taskbar. Click on the icon to return the Getting Started window to the foreground.

Explore Simply Accounting This section contains videos to learn about various parts of Simply. If you have used an older version of Simply (2009 or prior), you will want to review the 'What's New in Simply Accounting 2010' link, and the Learning Centre. Also see Appendix C—*What's New in Simply 2010* at www.simplyaccounting2010.nelson.com under Student Resources. The other selections will be discussed in various chapters.

Add Business Records This section contains links to add items identified. This text will show you how to add the records in each chapter: Accounts in Chapter 1, Customers in Chapter 2, etc. The link to Open the Setup Guide will be discussed in Chapter 4.

Customize Simply Accounting This section contains links that you will see in various chapters. Set Company Preferences will be discussed in Chapter 4, Schedule data backups will be discussed in Chapter 4 and Customize your invoices and other business forms will be discussed in Chapter 4.

Learn How to This section contains links to Help documents. You will be shown how to set up INVENTORY in Chapter 8, PROJECTS (can also be called DIVISIONS) in Chapter 11, PAYROLL in Chapter 7, Security (Users and permissions) in Appendix O, *Security – Passwords* at www.simplyaccounting2010.nelson.com under Student Resources.

20 ➤   To not see the Getting Started; Welcome to Simply Accounting window at startup and go directly to the Home window (Fig. 1-5b), click the ☑ **Show this window on startup** (this will remove the checkmark), then click [**Close**].

Note: For other companies the ☐ **Show this window on startup**, has been unchecked to not display on Startup. You will go directly to the Home page.
If you have clicked the button as indicated ☑ and you want to see the Welcome to Simply Accounting window, from the menu bar on the home window, click **Setup, Getting Started Guide**.

Home Window — *Enhanced View*

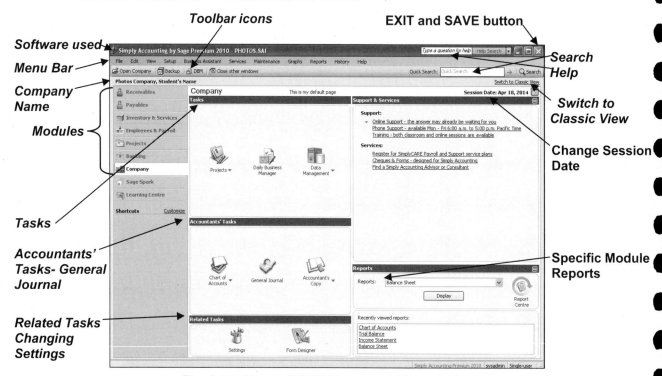

Fig. 1-5b: Simply HOME Enhanced View window.

Company Name: The internal data file company name `Photos Company, Student's Name` displays, above the module bars, near the top left side, as part of the Home window. You will be changing the "Student's Name" to your own name in Exercise 1-4. Your name will then display in the Home window and other journals.

Look at the top right side to see the location of the session date.
`Session Date: Apr 18, 2014` 📅 You will change the date using this feature in Exercise 1-8.

If you have seen previous versions of Simply (2007 and prior), you will notice a big change in the Home window.

21 ➤ On the right side, on the Support or Services line, click on the 🗕 at the end of the line. The section reduces to a single line and hides the information until you need it. This works with the 3 sections on the right.

22 ➤ To expand the section that is hidden, click on the ⊞.

You can still see and use the previous version Home page, now known as the Classic View.

23 ➤ To see the **Classic View** window, click `Switch to Classic View`.

Home Window — Classic View

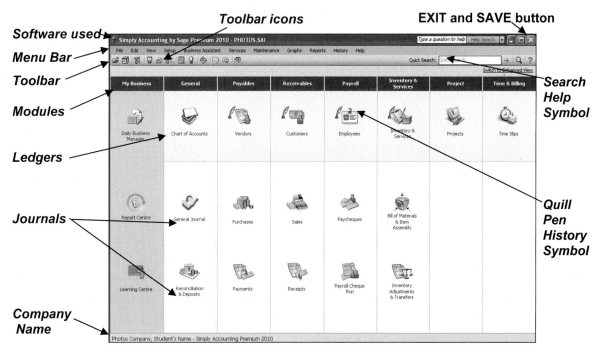

Fig. 1-5c: Simply HOME Classic View window.

24 ➤ To return to the **Enhanced View** window, click Switch to Enhanced View.

When you click the **X** button (Exit) in the top-right corner of the Home window, Simply **saves** all entries in memory to the data file in the storage location and closes the program.

Menu Bar

Each menu item contains a drop-down list of options related to the menu heading. You can display the menu list by clicking the menu item. Try clicking each menu item now.

Toolbar

Note that there is a row with 4 icons below the Menu Bar (this text calls them **Toolbar icons**). The icons are designed to allow easy access to changing to another company data file, backing up the current data file, opening the Daily Business Manager (shown in Chapter 2) and closing any open Simply journals or reports. When you move your mouse over a toolbar icon, an information box appears below it with a brief explanation. Position your mouse over each of the icons and read the explanation that appears.

Modules

A module is referred to, in Simply and this text, as a bar in the Home window. Each module will have different views for Tasks, Accountant's Tasks, and Related Tasks depending on the module selected. Click on each of the modules to see the differences. These will be explained in this and other chapters. The COMPANY module will be discussed in this chapter. Each module can be hidden or revealed as needed. You will see how this works in later chapters.

25 ➤ Click on the **RECEIVABLES** module and look at the Tasks area and the Customers icon.

History: This history symbol represents a module in which the history subledger information does not balance with the General Ledger. You can record Sales and Purchases to the RECEIVABLES and PAYABLES modules without having the previous balances recorded if the module has been set up. This feature would allow new users to start using the software and add previous balances when they have time.

Note: You cannot start a new fiscal year if the subsidiary ledgers do not agree with the General Ledger. This text does not record transactions until the module has been set up.

26 ➤   Click the **COMPANY** module.

Tasks

Projects: This feature can also be called Divisions, Territories or other appropriate name. This feature will allow revenues and expenses to be allocated and accumulated for projects, divisions, salesperson's territories, etc. (see Chapter 11).

Daily Business Manager: This feature allows the user to add notes for future reference and shows other Memo information, Recurring Invoices, Payments Due, Outstanding Purchase Orders, Sales Due and Sales Orders. You can also view various Business Performance ratios. You will be shown how to use this feature in Chapter 2A, Exercise 2A-7, or hide the option in Chapter 2A, Exercise 2A-11.

Data Management: You can right-click on any icon that shows the ▼ to see details of the features. This feature allows the user to Back up a data file, Restore a data file, Advanced Database Check, Consolidate Company (used when combining different businesses owned by an owner—this feature is not shown in this text) and Import and Export Records.

Accountant's Tasks

Chart of Accounts: The General Ledger (G/L) for a company. This ledger allows you to keep a complete G/L system from which you can produce financial statements. The G/L uses the following account grouping: Assets, Liabilities, Equities, Revenues and Expenses. This feature allows you to View, Add, Modify and Remove accounts. You can also add accounts from inside journals.

General Journal: This is the journal that you will use in this chapter.

You would normally use the Simply General Journal only to make entries, which cannot be made in subledgers and their associated journals. You use the Double Entry method to record these entries, which are usually banking transactions and those that relate to accrued adjustments. Transactions pertaining to sales and purchases are entered in the RECEIVABLES module (Chapters 2A, 2B) and PAYABLES module (Chapters 3A, 3B) respectively. You will learn how to record sales-related transactions in the RECEIVABLES module and purchases-related transactions in the PAYABLES module.

Some small companies, although not very many, use only the General Ledger and not any of the subledger modules. Photos Company is one of them.

Accountant's Copy: This feature allows the user to create a data file to be sent to the accountant for month or year-end entries. When the accountant sends you the updated data file, you can use the Import Entries from Accountant item. You can also Cancel the Accountant's copy.

Related Tasks

Settings

Settings This feature will allow you to change default settings in the software. This will be explained in more detail in Chapter 4.

Form Designer

Form Designer This feature will allow you to change default settings in various Simply forms.

Support & Services

Support & Services. Refer to the Installation instructions in Appendix A (at the back of the book) to see which support or services are not available for students.

Reports

Report Centre

Report Centre This feature allows the user to select a report from the Report Centre window, without having to click Reports from the menu bar, and selecting various types of reports. This feature also lets you see what the report will look like before you display it. You can also click the drop down arrow at Reports to see reports that are available in this module. Each module will have different reports available.

Recently viewed reports. This section will display the last 4 reports the user viewed. You can click any report in this section and it will display and can be printed.

Sage Spark

This section will display various services that are available to retail buyers of the software. The services displayed are not available to students.

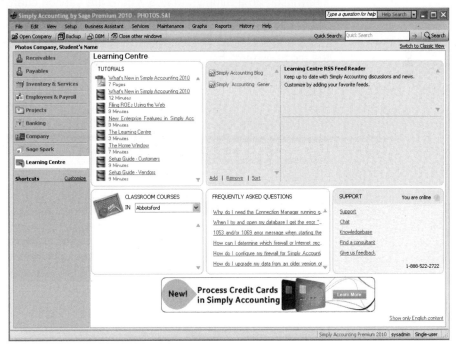

Fig. 1-5d: Learning Centre window.

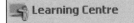

The Learning Centre window is divided into 6 parts (from left to right).

Note: This window may have a different configuration than the one displayed. (i.e., that is the Tutorials may be in the top row, and Classroom Courses may be in the 2ⁿᵈ row on the left. Other configurations are also possible.

This feature allows the user to use various tutorials.

Tutorials This section is similar to the Videos in the Getting Started window.

Learning Centre – middle section: This section contains links to a Simply Accounting Blog and General Forum.

Learning Centre RSS Feed Reader This section displays the results of the Blog or General Forum from the middle section.

Classroom Courses This section contains information about Simply courses in various locations for a fee.

Frequently Asked Questions This section contains links to most frequently asked questions to Simply forums.

Support This section contains links to various support options in the Retail version.

The lower portion of the window may be hidden. Click the **slider button** to display the following.

If your company accepts credit cards to pay for invoices, you can click to receive information on a Simply Service. There are service charges involved for this service.

The various tasks and journals are explained in the appropriate chapters, such as Sales and Receipts, where transaction information is recorded and posted. Each of the modules must be properly configured (set up).

Using Simply HELP

Simply provides four ways to find Help within the program.

$\mathbf{Q}$ Search , or using the ⬚ **Learning Centre** Frequently Asked Questions.

Exercise 1-3a – Using Help—Type a question for help

---

1 ➤ [Type a question for help Help Search ▼ ⊟ ⊡ ✕] This help field, at the top right of the window, enables the user to enter questions for assistance as if they were talking to the software. Click the Help Search ▼. Select either Simply Accounting Help (default) or On Line Community. Click in the field and type your question such as: **expense**, and press **Enter**. You will see the Simply Accounting Help window. You could click on a topic in the left pane and the right pane will display the response for that topic.

2 ➤ Click on ☒ in the top right corner to **Exit**, and return to Fig. 1-5b Home window.

Exercise 1-3b – Using Help—Search

---

1 ➤ In [Quick Search: Quick Search] type **expense**, and click the [→] (Quick Search) button, or press **Enter**. The Search button, searches all reports and customer, vendor and other modules for instances of the information recorded.

A report with a list of 11 accounts with the word Expense in the name will appear and the Advanced Search Results Summary report will display the information next.

> **Number of Matches: 11**
> Search <All Fields> Contains expense

2 ➤ As you move your mouse over the information, a magnifying glass appears. **Double-click** on any item in the window. Simply will drill down (this will be explained in more detail in Exercise 1-16) to the information and display it. In this situation, the General Ledger, where you can change account information, will appear.

3 ➤ Click X **twice** to return to the Home window. If you can see the

[☒ Close all other windows] icon on the tool bar, you can also click the icon and you will be returned to the Home window.

4 ➤ If you type [Quick Search: account] in the search field and click [→], or press **Enter**, you will see an Advanced Search Results report with 3 instances of the word 'account' in this file.

5 ➤ From the **Advanced Search Results** window click X in the top-right corner to return to the Home window.

Exercise 1-3c – Using Help—Database Search Tool

---

1 ➤ Click on [🔍 Search]. The Basic and Advanced tabs will display. Click the [▼] to see a list of records or transactions you can search for. This feature is not used in this text.

2 ➤ Click on the **Advanced** tab. This tab is similar to Exercise 1-17, between steps 3 and 4, Filter reports.

3 ➤ Click **Cancel**, to return to Fig. 1-5b Home window.

Exercise 1-3d – Using Help—Learning Centre

Using Learning Centre Help

1 ➤ Click the **Learning Centre** icon. Look in the **Frequently Asked Questions** list. You may have to scroll up or down to see more items.

2 ➤ Click on the **Company** icon to return to the Fig. 1-5b Home window.

The **F1** key for Help does not work in the Enhanced Home window.

Shortcuts (on left side)

You will be shown how to create a list of reports (Customize) that you may use often in Exercise 1-21a, Creating Custom Report Shortcuts. You can add or remove items in the list.

Revising Company Information

Simply allows you to make changes in the company information; e.g., the address needs to be changed if the company has moved, phone numbers may have changed, or the company may have installed additional phones. In the next exercise, you will change the company name information to include your name.

For a quick reference guide on various exercises throughout the textbook, refer to Appendix R—*Quick Reference Guide* at www.simplyaccounting2010.nelson.com under Student Rescores.

Exercise 1-4 – Changing Company Information

As you and your fellow students in class start printing reports, there could be confusion as to which printout belongs to whom, because you will all have the same heading, **Photos Company, Student's Name**. You will now change the company name to include your name, so you can easily identify your own printout.

You may use the same technique shown here to change any company information.

1 ➤ In the lower Related Tasks area, click on the **Settings** icon, in the left pane click on **Information**. The Company Information window will appear.

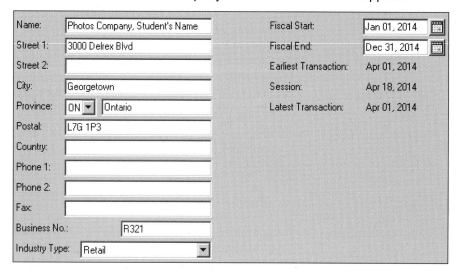

Fig. 1-6: A portion of the Company Information window.

2 ➤ In the Name box, highlight **Student's Name** and type your **last name** (surname) and **first name** (given), then click **OK**. The company name will be changed accordingly and now will appear at the top of the modules on the left side of the Home window.

Example: **Photos Company, Oliver Megan**

You should follow the name change procedure for each new company you work on. You need to do this only once for each company.

To Display Reports

Most new companies will start by setting up the various modules, e.g., COMPANY, RECEIVABLES, PAYABLES, EMPLOYEES & PAYROLL, etc. Some new companies, however, may start with only the COMPANY module and eventually add the other modules when they determine that they have enough transactions for these modules to warrant the effort to set them up.

As mentioned earlier, the COMPANY module allows you to enter transactions into a complete General Ledger system (double entry), and allows financial statements to be displayed and/or printed at any time. Note that the other modules are not active for the Photos Company (you can tell because the History symbol  is showing with the Tasks icons inside each of the other modules).

Financial Statements for a company are generated from previously entered data, and may be displayed or printed for a range of dates or a specific day.

To start this exercise you need to be at the Photos Company Home window.

Exercise 1-5a – Displaying Reports using Recently Viewed Reports Area

Displaying the Income Statement

You can display an Income Statement for any period of time:

- one day or a few days
- a week or a few weeks
- one month or a few months
- year-to-date

1 ➤ The Recently viewed reports area is displayed with 4 reports listed. In the **Reports** field, click ▼ , select **Income Statement**, click **Display**. The report will display. Only the top portion is shown.

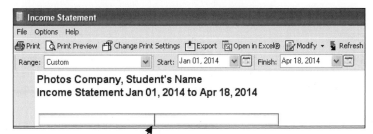

By clicking on the dividing line, you can move the columns to the left or right to change the way the columns display and/or print in statements.

2 ➤ To modify the Income Statement, click on the **Modify** icon.

Fig. 1-7: Modify Options menu.

3 ➤   Click on **Report Options**. You will see the following window.

Income Statement - Modify Report	
Template: <Last used report options> ▼	Save Template...

Report Options
Report Columns
Totals   Report Type: ☐ Comparative Income Statement
Print Settings
Font Settings   Range: Custom ▼   Start: Jan 01, 2014 ▼ 📅   Finish: Apr 18, 2014 ▼ 📅
Footer   ☐ Show Notes

The settings on the left side are the same as those in the Modify icon drop-down area.

Comparative Income statements will be discussed and shown in Chapter 3B.

You can customize the Income Statement Print settings and/or Font settings. The same customization information is for the Balance Sheet. There is no exercise for changing Print and Font settings.

Template drop-down : Click and two choices appear: <Default report options>
                                                                            <Last used report options>

> **<Default report options>** Options used by Simply without changes.
>
> **<Last used report options>** The options used the last time you requested the report and will be used to display the report this time.

Save Template button   You are able to save a report with any changed settings (date, terms, etc.) as a template and it can be retrieved later with the same settings.

☐ **Show Notes**   Do Not Change. You are able to add specific notes to viewed and printed statements. See Appendix U—*Adding Notes/Footers to Statements* for more information at www.simplyaccounting2010.nelson.com under Student Resources.

As noted previously at Exercise 1-2, you can change the date in reports using either the ▼ or the calendar feature.

4 ➤   **Range**   Click ▼ and a list of various reports dates appears. Click the ▼ again to use the **Custom** selection.

5 ➤   **Start**   Leave the date as **Jan 01, 2014**, the start of the fiscal year.

6 ➤   **Finish**   Using the calendar, change the date to **April 10, 2014** (because you have not entered data in April yet).

7 ➤   Click **OK** to display an Income Statement for the period Jan 01, 2014 to Apr 10, 2014 (see side note box). **DO NOT PRINT AT THIS TIME. You will print an Income Statement in Chapters 2A and 2B.**

To view the lower part of the statement, you can use the vertical scroll bar and/or the maximize button ☐. (See side note box.) Scroll back to the top of the Income Statement.

8 ➤   A management feature for the Financial Statements is now available. You will notice the symbol ⊟ to the left of the wording ⊟   **Revenue**, ⊟   **Cost of Goods Sold** and ⊟   **Store & Admin Expenses**.

ℹ️
You can view other parts of the report by scrolling down.

In the lower-left corner of the displayed statement is the wording:
Generated On: with the current date. When the statement is printed, the wording changes to:
Printed On: with the current date.

Note: This feature will hide the individual accounts and display the section total. The Revenue and Store & Admin Expense sections can be hidden for the Purchasing Manager. The Cost of Goods Sold & the Store & Admin Expense sections can be hidden for the Sales Manager and so on.

This feature will also work with the Balance Sheet.

9 ➤ To hide individual amounts, click on the ⊟ for the **Cost of Goods Sold** & the **Store & Admin Expense** sections. The Revenue section Sales accounts are still displayed. This report can be printed and distributed to managers in the Sales departments. Other reports can be distributed as needed.

To unhide statement details, repeat step 9.

As discussed previously, the individual amounts can be hidden. If you click on the ⊟ at Photo Equipment, two accounts are hidden and only the subtotal (Net Book Value) appears.

10 ➤ To display the previously hidden section, click on the ⊞ (**expand**) button. (See side note box.)

11 ➤ To close the Income Statement, click the ☒ **EXIT** button and return to the Home window. The Recently viewed reports area displays the Income Statement that you just viewed.

Displaying the Balance Sheet

Exercise 1-5b – Display Balance Sheet Using the Report Menu

You can display a Balance Sheet only at a certain date, not for a range of dates. To use another method of displaying reports, follow this procedure.

1 ➤ From the Menu bar, click **Reports**, move to **Financials**, move to **Balance Sheet**, then **click**.

You can customize the Balance Sheet Print settings and/or Font settings.

2 ➤ Template   Click the ▼ and select **Default Report Options** to match the text.

3 ➤ As at   Click the ▼ to see the range of dates that are available. Change to **Custom**.

The wording **Generated on**: with the current date will appear at the bottom of all displayed reports.

4 ➤ Date   Using the calendar, change the date to **Apr 10, 2014** (because you have not entered data in April yet). (See side note box.)

5 ➤ Click **OK** to display a Balance Sheet.

DO NOT PRINT AT THIS TIME; you will print a Balance Sheet in Chapters 2A and 2B.

6 ➤ To close the Balance Sheet, click the ☒ **EXIT** button and return to the Home window.

Exercise 1-5c – Display the Income Statement Using the Report Centre

---

1 ➤ Click the **Report Centre** icon.

2 ➤ In the COMPANY module, the default is Financials. Notice the 5 types of Income Statements that can be displayed.

3 ➤ Click on **Standard**. A sample of a similar Income Statement is displayed.

4 ➤ Click on | **Display** |, the Photos Income Statement is displayed. The dates will need to change depending on your situation.

5 ➤ **Start date**   Leave the date as **Jan 01, 2014**.

6 ➤ **Finish date**   Change to **Apr 10, 2014** (because you have not entered data in April yet). Press | Tab | or the **Refresh** ⟩ Refresh icon to update the information. The statement date is revised.

7 ➤ **Range**   Change to **This Calendar Year**. The Start date stays at Jan 01, 2014, and the Finish date changes to the session date Apr 18, 2014.

If you need to close the 01 Photos data file before completing the chapter, refer to Exercise 1-23 to complete the backup procedure.

DO NOT PRINT AT THIS TIME. You will print in Chapters 2A and 2B. (See side note box.)

8 ➤   Click ☒ to exit the Income Statement and return to the Report Centre. Other reports can be printed from the Report Centre. Click | Close | to return to the Home window.

Processing Transactions in the COMPANY Module

Run **Slideshow 1B-GENERAL LEDGER** from the website: www.simplyaccounting2010.nelson.com under Student Resources. It will give you a good idea of when and how to use the COMPANY module of Simply Accounting and a review of Generally Accepted Accounting Principles (GAAP) that you need to apply when processing transactions in Simply.

In Simply, it is only in the **GENERAL Journal** that you use double entry recording (enter both debit and credit items).

To record transactions, see Exercise 1-6 that follows these steps:

1. Enter the data into a **Journal**. Each entry must have equal debits and credits; otherwise, Simply will not allow you to post the entry.

2. View the entry to make sure it is correct. Simply will allow you to make corrections if necessary.

3. When the entry is correct, click the **Posting** icon ⟩ Post , and the entry is automatically posted to the appropriate accounts in the General Ledger.

To Correct Errors

Correct Errors

A: BEFORE Posting:
Click the field(s) that require changing and change the amounts or words.

B: Reverse Entry. To Correct Errors AFTER Posting –Cancelling the entry
If you make an error in the journal entry and realize after you have posted it, that it is completely in error and should be cancelled, use the **Reverse entry** feature. (See Exercise 2A-18.)

The Reverse entry reverses the original entry (debits and credits) which cancels the original entry.

C: Adjust a previously posted entry. To Correct Errors AFTER Posting – by
Adjusting the entry Exercise 1-12
If you make a minor error(s) in a journal entry and realize it after you have posted it, you can use an **Adjustment** entry to open the original entry and correct the error(s) and post the correction. This adjustment entry reverses the original entry (debits and credits) and records the correct entry. See Exercise 1-12 *Correcting an Entry*.

Correction Method A. In this exercise you will record, from a bank debit memo, the bank charges for printing new company cheques. Study the transaction:

Apr 18, 2014	**Received from the bank, new company cheques with a $31.00 bank debit memo, dated April 17, 2014 for the printing charge.**

The correct journal entry is:

Dr	Bank Charges Expense	31.00	
Cr	Cash in Bank		31.00

In order to show you how to correct errors before posting entries, you will deliberately make two errors (an account number at step 6 and an amount at step 11) and correct them before posting.

For this chapter only, HST is ignored. This will allow you to focus on understanding the basics of Simply Accounting at this early stage of your learning.

Exercise 1-6 – Entering Transactions in the General Journal

To start this exercise, you need to be at the Photos Company home window.

General Journal

1 ➤ Click the **General Journal** icon.

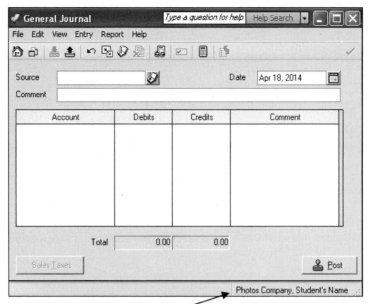

Fig. 1-8: General Journal window.

The name of the company is displayed on the bottom taskbar of the journals. This feature can be turned off and will be discussed in Chapter 4.

When you hold your mouse over each of the toolbar icons, a display below each indicates what they are used for. Try it now.

The ⌈Tab⌋ key is used to move to the next field in all journal screens.
If you want to move to a specific field, click the appropriate field or box.

Source: This field indicates where the information was taken from. It could be a bank debit or credit memo, an invoice number, a cheque number, return or adjustment numbers, a memo, etc.

2 ➤	**Source**	Type **Bank Debit memo** as the source, press the ⌈Tab⌋ key.

You move to the 🛡 icon. This icon will allow you to reverse and correct previously posted General Journal entries and will be shown to you in Exercise 1-12. Press ⌈Tab⌋ to move to the Date field.

3 ➤	**Date**	This is the date the transaction occurred. You may not always enter transactions on the day on which they occurred, depending on business volume. Although the printed cheques were received on the 18th, the bank charged (debited) our account on the 17th. The debit memo was issued on April 17; therefore, the transaction date is Apr 17, 2014. Using the calendar, change the date to **Apr 17, 2014**. ⌈Tab⌋ to move to the Comment field.

Comment: The comment line should include details of **who**, **what** and/or **why** you are making the entry. In this entry you need to record information about the printed cheques and any other important information. You may have to abbreviate the comments because the comments field allows only 65 characters.

4 ➤ Comment   Type **Bank charges printing new cheques SN** (where SN is your initials), press ⬚Tab to move to the Account field.

Account: If you know the account number, you would type it in this field.

To see a list of General Ledger accounts, press the ⬚Enter key or double-click the Account field.

You can also search for an account number or account name description. You will search by number.

To use this feature, type the account number (as you will do at step 6) and the lower portion of window will display the accounts near the number. You could also scroll down to find the account you need. It is easier to search by Number (see step 6).

To bypass the search field and use only the lower portion of the window, you would click the **Bypass Search Field** box in the top right and the setting will take effect the next time you use the **Select Account** feature.

5 ➤   Double-click the **Account** field or press ⬚Enter.

A portion of the General Ledger chart of accounts list is shown next.

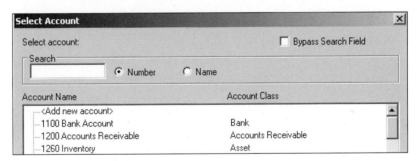

You may need to scroll down using the ⬚▼ scroll bar to the right of the Accounts box. You will notice that the first line indicates **<Add new account>**. The <Add new account> field can be used when you cannot find an appropriate account and decide that a new account in the ledger is needed. This option is explained in Exercise 1-9b and Chapter 4.

Study the following table that shows the account numbering system in Simply:

Account Number Starts with	Type of Account	Normal Balance	To Increase Account	To Decrease Account
1	Asset	Debit	+ Debit	- Credit
2	Liability	Credit	+ Credit	- Debit
3	Equity	Credit	+ Credit	- Debit
4	Revenue	Credit	+ Credit	- Debit
5	Expense	Debit	+ Debit	- Credit

You are going to choose the wrong account and then correct the account before posting.

From a Select Account window, in the lower portion, you could also scroll down to 5320 Business Salary Expense and double-click or click Select.

6 ➤ In the **Search** field type **5** (you will notice that the lower window moves to the 5 account numbers.) Type **2** and you move further into the 5 section account numbers. You should be at the line for Office Supplies Expense. If there were other numbers (e.g., 5325) you would continue entering numbers or scroll to the account needed. Press Enter or click **Select**.

5220 Office Supplies Expense is entered in the Account field and the cursor has moved to the Debits column (0.00) for the amount.

Oops, wrong account number. This is an error that needs to be corrected.

You will now correct the account number.

7 ➤ To delete the wrong account, click **5220 Office Supplies Expense** and press the Delete key.

8 ➤ Repeat steps 5 and 6 to locate and select (double-click) **5180 Bank Charges Expense** account. The account number has been corrected.

9 ➤ In the Debits column enter the amount **31** and press Tab. Simply puts in the missing 00 after the decimal point. If the amount was 50.25, you would need to enter 50, decimal point, 25 then Tab. The cursor moves to the Comment column.

10 ➤ **Comment**   Use this column when you want to record additional comments for each account. Type **Printing charge new cheques**. Press Tab to move to the Account field.

11 ➤ Double-click the Accounts field and select **1100 Bank Account**. The amount **31.00** automatically appears in the credit column. The software calculates the net amount of the Debit and Credit entries entered and displays the amount needed to make debits and credits equal. **Bank Account** is credited because when money is deducted from the account (by debit memo or cheque) Bank Account decreases.

You will enter the wrong amount in the current field to allow you to observe what happens when you try to post an entry with unequal debits and credits.

12 ➤ Change the **Bank Account** amount from 31.00 to **55.00,** Tab. This is an error which you will fix in step 15.

Notice that the totals at the bottom of the General Journal are not equal.

Total	31.00	55.00

13 ➤ Click the 🗄 Post button. Study the Error message box that appears:

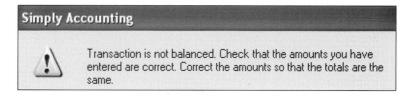

Simply Accounting

Transaction is not balanced. Check that the amounts you have entered are correct. Correct the amounts so that the totals are the same.

14 ➤ Click **OK** to return to the General Journal.

You will now enter the correct amount.

15 ➤ Highlight **55.00**, and type **31.00,** then press Tab. The Totals at the bottom of the Journal are now equal.

Do not post at this time.

Congratulations! You have entered a complete journal entry. Compare your window with Fig. 1-9.

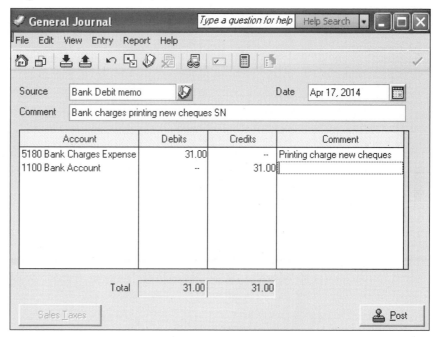

Account	Debits	Credits	Comment
5180 Bank Charges Expense	31.00	--	Printing charge new cheques
1100 Bank Account	--	31.00	
Total	31.00	31.00	

Fig. 1-9: General Journal Entry.

DO NOT POST YET. You need to verify your entry first.

The Sales Taxes button Sales Taxes is grayed out because HST is not used in this entry. This button will be discussed in Chapter 3B.

Displaying the Journal Entry

Before posting, it is best to check the accuracy of your journal entry. If there is an error, it may be easily corrected before posting.

There are two ways to correct an entry before posting:

1. Highlight the wrong entry item in the General Journal window and type the correct information.

2. If the entry has quite a few errors, it is best to start over. Click the **Undo** icon. A message box will appear verifying that you want to discard the entry. Click **Yes** to discard the entry, then retype the complete entry.

Exercise 1-7 – Displaying a Journal Entry

1 ➤   Click **Report** on the Menu Bar.

2 ➤   Click **Display General Journal Entry Ctrl + J** (Ctrl + J is a keyboard shortcut to display the entry). You can press Ctrl + J from Fig. 1-9 without having to complete steps 1 and 2. You will notice many other shortcuts in drop-down menus.

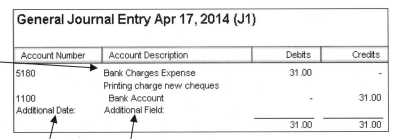

Notice the **Printing charge new cheques** comment which you entered in the **Comment** field in the journal entry.

General Journal Entry Apr 17, 2014 (J1)

Account Number	Account Description	Debits	Credits
5180	Bank Charges Expense	31.00	-
	Printing charge new cheques		
1100	Bank Account	-	31.00
Additional Date:	Additional Field:		
		31.00	31.00

Simply assigns a journal entry number, beginning with J1, to posted entries. This entry is displayed as J1. There are no previous Journal entries recorded in this data file.

The **Additional Date** and **Additional Field** information is displayed in all journal windows even if you don't enter information in these fields. The use of these fields will be explained in Exercise 1-11.

Review the entry to make sure it is correct. If it is not correct you need to close this window and correct the entry on the General Journal window before posting.

3 ➤   To exit, click the X box to return to the Journal window.

4 ➤   Click the **POST** button, the screen flickers and the following window appears.

This confirmation window is used to indicate that the entry was posted as Journal 1 (J1) to the General Ledger. Many students are not sure if they have posted the entry and record another entry. After you are comfortable knowing your entries are posted, you could click the "Do not show this message again" box.

If you click the "Do not show this message again" box by mistake, you can return the Transaction Confirmation window by clicking Setup, User Preferences. In the left hand window, click Transaction Confirmation, and click the right hand box, then OK.

5 ➤ Click **OK**, to accept the posting confirmation. The screen flickers, and returns to a blank journal window.

6 ➤ To exit to the Home window, click the **X**.

HST is ignored in this chapter and will be covered later in the text.

To Advance the Session Date

The current session date is April 18 and you need to record transactions dated for the week ending April 25. You do not need to exit the program to move or advance the date. You can advance the date from the Home window.

Exercise 1-8 – To Advance the Session Date

---

1 ➤ Click the calendar at **Session Date: Apr 18, 2014** 🖩 icon.

2 ➤ Using the calendar, change the date to **Apr 25, 2014** and click **OK**. You may see the following:

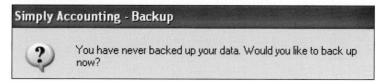

3 ➤ You do not need to back up at this time, so click **No**.

Recording a Compound Entry and Adding a New Account

So far, you entered a transaction where there is one Debit account and one Credit account. A compound entry uses three or more accounts.

The next transaction is a payment for a bank loan. Payments are normally recorded in the PAYABLES module. The PAYABLES module records all purchases and payments on credit, cash, cheque, credit card, or debit card. This transaction is entered in the General Journal because the bank debited the company bank account and a cheque is not being issued. You will be shown how to record payments by cheque in the PAYABLES module in Chapter 3.

Exercise 1-9a – Recording a Compound Entry

Study the following transaction:

> **Apr 21, 2014 Received debit memo, dated today, from the bank, indicating a $215.00 payment was made on the bank loan which includes Interest of $76.44. The loan was received on March 21.**

The correct compound entry is:

Dr	Bank Loan Payable	138.56	
Dr	Bank Loan Interest Expense	76.44	
Cr	Cash in Bank		215.00

A new general ledger account for Bank Loan Interest Expense will be created as part of Exercise 1-9b.

1 ➤   Click on the **General Journal** icon.

2 ➤   **Source**   Type **Bank Debit memo** as the source, and press Tab , Tab to move to the Date field.

3 ➤   **Date**   Using the calendar, change the date to **Apr 21, 2014**. Tab to move to the Comment field.

4 ➤   **Comment**   Type **Bank Loan Payment**, press Tab to move to the Account field.

5 ➤   **Account**   Type **2710**, Bank Loan Payable, Tab .

6 ➤   **Debits**   Type **138.56**, Tab .

7 ➤   **Comment**   **Principal repayment**, Tab .

Exercise 1-9b – Adding a New General Ledger Account

---

1 ➤   **Account**   Double-click the column or press Enter and click on <**Add new account**>, click Select.

Enter information shown in Fig 1-10a.

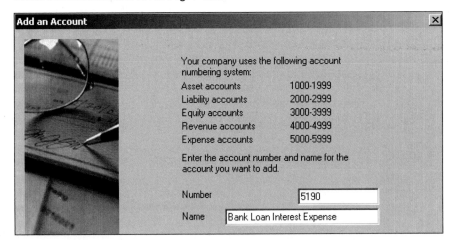

Fig 1-10a: Add an Account window.

Number   This is the number, the owner decided, to use for the new account that is to be added. You must make sure that it fits one of the numbering sequences as noted in the window.

Name   This is the name of the new account.

2 ➤ When the Add an Account window resembles Fig. 1-10a, click **Next >**.

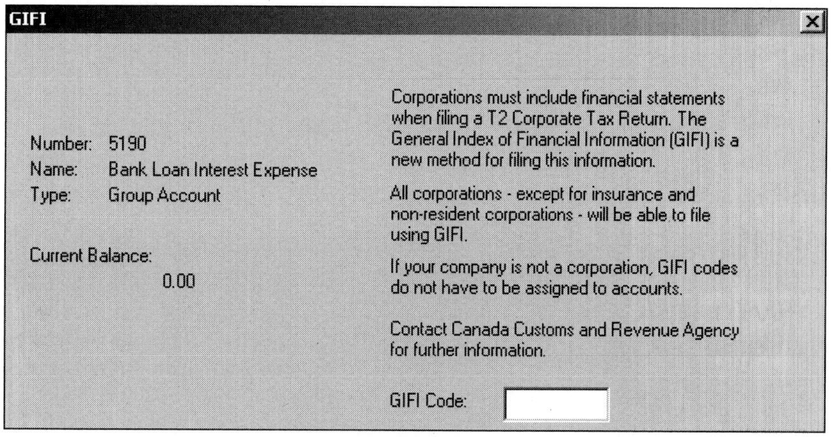

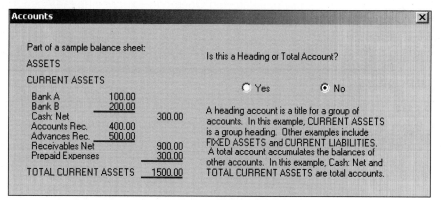

Fig. 1-10b: GIFI Code window.

Type   The default type of account code will be Group Account. It can be changed in step 5 or 6. Account Groups will be explained in more detail in Chapter 4.

Current   0.00. This is a new account for Photos Company. You cannot add a
Balance   balance to a new account in this company data file. The file is in Ready mode for the Company folder. You can create a balance for a company that is being created (History). This is discussed in Chapter 4.

If your business is a corporation, you would need to number the account number based on the GIFI codes as identified by Canada Revenue Agency (CRA). This section assumes that the business is not a corporation. If your business is a corporation, contact your accountant or Canada Revenue Agency for further information about the GIFI numbering sequences.

3 ➤ Photos Company is not a corporation; therefore, leave the GIFI field empty. Click **Next >**.

Fig. 1-10c: Accounts – Heading or Total window.

If the account to be added is a Heading or a Final Total of a section, you would click the 'Yes' button. Account 5190 is an account used to accumulate Bank Loan Interest Expense and is not a Heading or a Total account. Headings and Total accounts will be discussed in more detail in Chapter 4.

4 ➤ With a setting of **No**, click **Next>**.

If the account being added is to be added with another account to create a subtotal, similar to Bank A and Bank B shown next, then you would click Yes.

Account 5190 will not require a subtotal, similar to Prepaid Expenses.

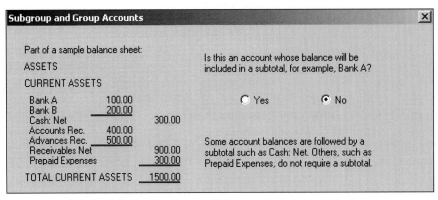

Fig. 1-10d: Subgroup and Group Accounts window.

5 ➤ With a setting of **No**, click **Next>**.

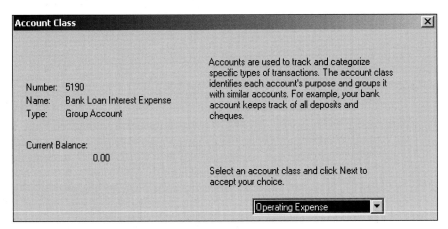

Fig. 1-10e: Account Class window.

Simply has selected Operating Expense as the Account Class. You will learn more about account classes in Chapter 4.

6 ➤ Click the ▼ and you will see various Account classes. Select the account class **Expense**, click **Next>**.

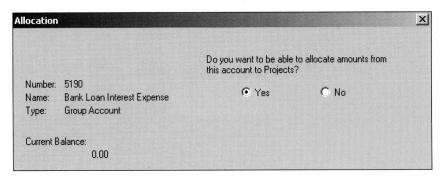

Fig. 1-10f: Allocation window.

7 ➤ If you need to allocate project revenue and expenses to this account, you would accept the Yes default selection. This business does not use the PROJECT module; therefore, change the setting to **No.** Click **Next>**.

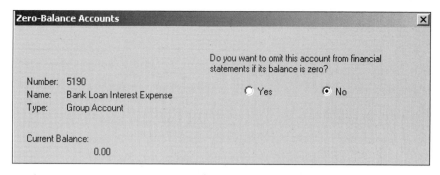

Fig. 1-10g: Zero-Balance Accounts window.

8 ➤ If you want accounts with zero balances to appear on financial statements, you would click No. If you do NOT want accounts with zero balances to appear on financial statements you would click Yes. With a setting of **No**, click **Next>**.

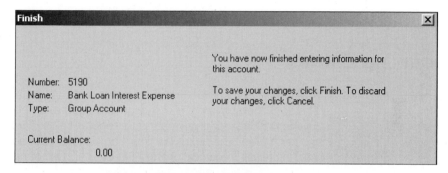

Fig. 1-10h: Finish window.

9 ➤ Click **Finish** to add the account to the General Ledger and the account column. Continue recording the entry as shown next.

10 ➤ **Account**   [Tab]

11 ➤ **Debits**   Type **76.44**, [Tab] to Account.

12 ➤ **Account**   Type **1100** (Bank Account), [Tab].

13 ➤ **Credits**   [Tab] to accept **215.00** and move to Comment.

14 ➤ **Comment**   Type **Bank Loan Payment**.

DO NOT Post the transaction until you complete the next exercise.

Your General Journal window should resemble the following:

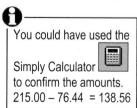

You could have used the

Simply Calculator
to confirm the amounts.
215.00 – 76.44 = 138.56

Source	Bank Debit memo				Date	Apr 21, 2014	
Comment	Bank Loan Payment						

Account	Debits	Credits	Comment
2710 Bank Loan Payable	138.56	--	Principal repayment
5190 Bank Loan Interest Exp	76.44	--	
1100 Bank Account	--	215.00	Bank Loan Payment

15 ➤ Don't forget to display the entry. Notice that this entry is J2 and is a compound entry.

General Journal Entry Apr 21, 2014 (J2)

Account Number	Account Description	Debits	Credits
2710	Bank Loan Payable	138.56	-
	Principal repayment		
5190	Bank Loan Interest Expense	76.44	-
1100	Bank Account	-	215.00
	Bank Loan Payment		
Additional Date:	Additional Field:		
		215.00	215.00

Note: In Simply 2010 the Additional Date and Additional Field will be shown in the journal entry display (as above) even when no information has been entered in the fields. See Exercise 1-11, step 7.

16 ➤ Click ☒ to return to the General Journal screen.

DO NOT POST YET! Continue with the next exercise.

Recurring Entries

A recurring entry refers to a transaction that may repeat many times during the year. The bank loan payment transaction is a good example. You know that you will be paying the bank loan payment on a regular basis. If you enter the above entry as a recurring entry, the next time your bank debits your account for the loan payment you can recall the entry, change the date and amounts, and it would be ready to Post. It saves time and helps you avoid errors.

Exercise 1-10 – Creating a Recurring Entry

1 ➤ To store this entry for future use, click the 3rd icon on the left side of the toolbar, **Store as recurring transaction** ⬇. The next window is where you will identify the name you wish to associate with this entry and the frequency you want Simply to remind you when it will reoccur.

2 ➤ Notice that in the Recurring Transaction box, the comment you entered in the General Journal is automatically entered. Change the recurring transaction name to **Bank Loan Payment Monthly** [Tab].

3 ➤ Frequency Click the ▾ to see the various choices available for how often you want this entry to appear. Leave Frequency as **Monthly**.

4 ➤ Click **OK**. The entry is now saved for future use. You will be using a different recurring entry in Exercise 1-15.

5 ➤ [Post] when correct.

6 ➤ You will see the J2 Transaction confirmation window. Click **OK**.

Owner Investment in Business

The owner's investment may be recorded in the General Journal as the funds were transferred, by the bank, from her personal account to the business to show the personal investment.

Exercise 1-11 – Journalizing Owner Investment in Business

> **Apr 24, 2014**   **Mrs. Chikowski called you to advise you that she decided to invest an additional $2,000.00 in the business, as she is going to purchase a new photo machine from another photo business. She is transferring $2,000.00 from her personal bank account to the company's bank account and asked you to record the investment.**

If you closed the General Journal prior to this exercise, click on the General Journal icon.

If you did not close the General Journal, you should be at a blank General Journal window.

　　1 ➤   **Record** the investment based on the following window.

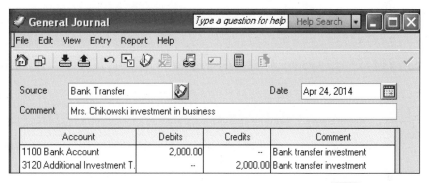

　　2 ➤   On the icon bar, click the **Enter Additional Information** [✓] icon and the Additional Information window appears.

This feature allows you to record additional information about the transaction, such as other dates and other information (e.g., voucher dates and voucher approvals, or entry recorded by person's name) that may be useful for the audit trail, or for future reference. This text does not use this feature in all entries.

　　3 ➤   **Additional Date**　　Select **Apr 24, 2014** the day the transaction was recorded. [Tab].

　　4 ➤   **Additional Field**　　Type **Mrs. Chikowski phone call message SN** (replace SN with your initials).

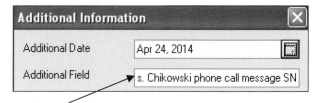

Note: the **s** refers to the word Mrs. that is partially hidden.

5 ➤ Click OK. Notice that the Additional Information window is gone and the General Journal window shown does not have any indication of the information just entered. This will be explained in the next 2 steps.

6 ➤ When your entry resembles the above investment window, click **Report, Display General Journal Entry**.

General Journal Entry Apr 24, 2014 (J3)

Account Number	Account Description	Debits	Credits
1100	Bank Account	2,000.00	-
	Bank transfer investment		
3120	Additional Investment T. Chiko...	-	2,000.00
	Bank transfer investment		
Additional Date: Ap...	Additional Field: Mrs. Chikowski ph...		
		2,000.00	2,000.00

7 ➤ Notice the additional information at the bottom. The additional information entered displays in the General Journal Entry window, and is retained by the system. Click X to close the entry. You will notice that the additional information is not shown in the General Journal.

8 ➤ When your entry is correct, click **Post,** and click **OK** to accept **J3**.

Correcting an Entry – Cancel or Adjusting

When you realize that an error has been made after you have posted a transaction, you can use the Reverse entry or Adjust the entry features in Simply. Simply 2010 makes this task very easy.

═══

Exercise 1-12 – Correcting an Entry

═══

Apr 25, 2014 Mrs. Chikowski advised you that she decided to increase the investment in the business to $3,000.00, when she was at the bank (April 24). She gave you the $3,000 bank transfer document.

In Exercise 1-11, you posted the following:

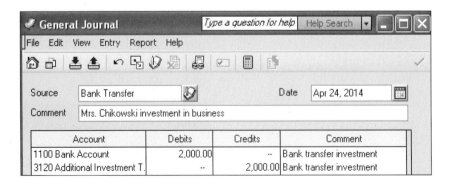

The investment was recorded for the wrong amount. Do not panic. You can reverse or correct an entry once it has been posted.

You have three ways to correct this:

1. You can manually reverse entry J3 by reversing the debits and credits. Then enter a new entry to record the entry correctly. You could make an error in the reversal and need to correct this error as well.

2. You can use the Reverse entry feature to allow Simply to reverse the debits and credits to cancel J3. Then you enter the correct entry if needed. Refer to Exercises 2A-17 and 2A-18 to see *To Correct a Receipt* or *to Cancel a Posted Invoice*.

> **ℹ**
> Refer to Chapter 13, Exercise 13-2, Correcting General Journal Entries.

3. You can use the Adjust a previously posted entry feature to adjust and correct J3. This will allow you to correctly record the entry. You do not need to reverse J3.

This exercise will use method 3 to adjust the J3 entry.

1 ➤ Click the **Adjust a previously posted entry** icon (it is to the right of the source field and also on the toolbar) and the following window appears.

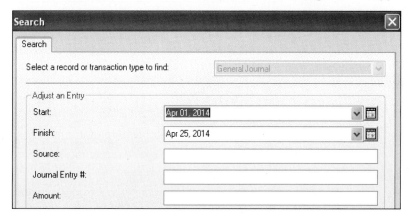

⚠ In business, you choose the dates of the entries you want to see displayed or sort by Source field description, Journal entry number or Amount.

You could leave the other fields blank and click OK to see what entries have been previously recorded.

2 ➤ Leave the other fields blank to see the entries recorded, click **OK**. Entries 1, 2 and 3 have been recorded previously and are displayed.

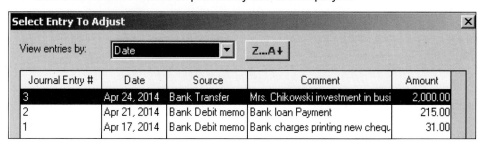

Journal Entry #	Date	Source	Comment	Amount
3	Apr 24, 2014	Bank Transfer	Mrs. Chikowski investment in busi	2,000.00
2	Apr 21, 2014	Bank Debit memo	Bank loan Payment	215.00
1	Apr 17, 2014	Bank Debit memo	Bank charges printing new chequ	31.00

3 ➤ You would click the entry that you need to reverse. **J3** should be highlighted in blue, click **Select**. Note that the previous entry with details appears and the header of the entry identifies the Source field.

> ✔ **General Journal - Adjusting Bank Transfer**

4 ➤ Change Debits and Credits to **3000.00**. You can change any fields (source, date, comments, account names and/or amounts). Do not change the date.

5 ➤ Display the Journal entry. Note that the entry number is **J5**. J4 is the reversal entry and J5 is the correct entry.

General Journal Entry Apr 24, 2014 (J5)			
Account Number	Account Description	Debits	Credits
1100	Bank Account	3,000.00	-
	Bank transfer investment		
3120	Additional Investment T. Chiko...	-	3,000.00
	Bank transfer investment		
Additional Date: Ap...	Additional Field: Mrs. Chikowski ph...		
		3,000.00	3,000.00

6 ➤ **Exit** the display window.

7 ➤ Click **Post**, click **OK** to accept confirmation number J5, click **X** and return to the Home window.

Displaying Corrected Entries with Reversals

When necessary, you can display entries that have been posted and subsequently corrected. The following exercise will show you how to display both the original incorrect entries and reversing entries. Later in the exercise, you will learn how to display the corrected entries only, without the incorrect entries.

This text uses displaying corrections as the default. However, your instructor may advise you to display only the correct entries without showing any of the entries you have reversed.

Exercise 1-13 – To Display Corrected Entries

1 ➤ At the Reports area, click ▼ and select **All Journal Entries,** click **Display**. The display shows J1, J2 and J5. We want to see what happened to the reversal and correction. Click the **Modify** button, select **Report Options**. Click the **Corrections** field.

Corrections: Make sure the field ☑ Corrections is checked.
Additional Information: Leave the field blank. We will concentrate on the correction and not the additional Information area.

2 ➤ Change the Start date and Finish date to **Apr 24, 2014**. This exercise will focus on the Investment correction entry. The Modify Report window should appear as shown next:

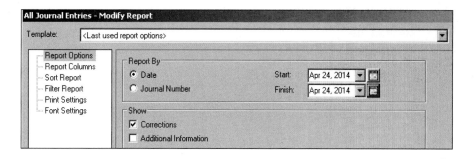

In a job situation, you would display and print all entries (with corrections) because this provides an audit trail (history) of entries that were recorded and changed. Notice that the Additional Information field is not checked.

3 ➤   Click **OK** and the following window will appear (see side note box):

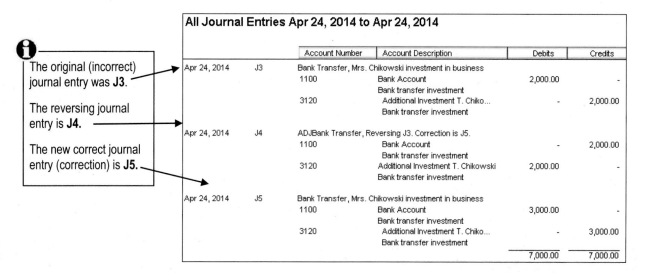

The original (incorrect) journal entry was J3.

The reversing journal entry is J4.

The new correct journal entry (correction) is J5.

J4 shows as the reversing entry and **J5** is the corrected Journal entry. The amount **7000.00** at the bottom of the entry is the total of the debits and credits displayed. This will be explained in more detail later.

4 ➤   In order to prepare for the next steps, click the [✏ Modify ▾] icon and select **Report Options**. The All Journal Entries- Modify Report window (seen at step 2) reappears.

To Show Corrected Entries Only

Notice that the [☑ Corrections] box is checked, which is now the default.

5 ➤   You do not want to show the original incorrect entry and the reversing entry in the report, therefore, click the [☑ Corrections] box to remove the check mark.

6 ➤   Click **OK**. Entry 3, with the error, and entry 4, the reversing entry, will not be displayed. Only the corrected entry J5 is displayed as shown next.

		Account Number	Account Description	Debits	Credits
Apr 24, 2014	J5		Bank Transfer, Mrs. Chikowski investment in business		
		1100	Bank Account	3,000.00	-
			Bank transfer investment		
		3120	Additional Investment T. Chiko...	-	3,000.00
			Bank transfer investment		
				3,000.00	3,000.00

Now, if you wish to display all entries, from a specific date only without corrections (e.g., Apr 17, 2014) follow the next step.

7 ➤ Click the **Modify** icon, select **Report Options**, and the **All Journal Entries** window reappears. Change the Start Date to **Apr 17, 2014** and make sure the ✓ has been removed from Corrections. Click **OK**.

All Journal Entries Apr 17, 2014 to Apr 24, 2014

		Account Number	Account Description	Debits	Credits
Apr 17, 2014	J1		Bank Debit memo, Bank charges printing new cheques SN		
		5180	Bank Charges Expense	31.00	-
			Printing charge new cheques		
		1100	Bank Account	-	31.00
Apr 21, 2014	J2		Bank Debit memo, Bank loan Payment		
		2710	Bank Loan Payable	138.56	-
			Principal repayment		
		5190	Bank Loan Interest Expense	76.44	-
		1100	Bank Account	-	215.00
			Bank loan payment		
Apr 24, 2014	J5		Bank Transfer, Mrs. Chikowski investment in business		
		1100	Bank Account	3,000.00	-
			Bank transfer investment		
		3120	Additional Investment T. Chiko...	-	3,000.00
			Bank transfer investment		
				3,246.00	3,246.00

Entry 3, with the error, and entry 4, the reversing entry, will not be displayed. Only the correct entries are displayed.

8 ➤ Exit the display window.

To Remove a Recurring Transaction Entry

Exercise 1-14 – Removing a Recurring Transaction Entry

You previously created a recurring transaction entry for Bank Loan Payment Monthly. This exercise will show you how to delete a recurring transaction entry, but you will not actually remove it.

1 ➤ Click the **General Journal** icon.

2 ➤ Click the 4th icon on the left ⬆ (Recall recurring transaction) and the following window appears.

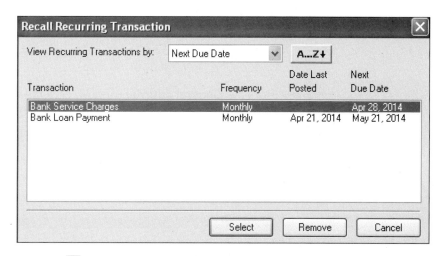

3 ➤ Click the ▾ and a drop-down list of report options is displayed. Leave the choice as **Next Due Date**. Click the `A...Z↓` and the report will be sorted automatically in descending or ascending order.

4 ➤ Return the display to ascending as shown in step 3.

5 ➤ Click the **Bank Loan Payment Monthly** listing, then click the `Remove` button and a warning message box appears.

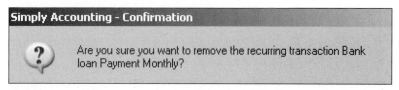

6 ➤ Click `No`, as you do not want to remove this item. This exercise is only to show you how you could remove a recurring entry. Click **Cancel** and you are returned to the General Journal window.

7 ➤ If the Home window is showing, you can click the 🗗 **Close All Other Windows** icon to close the General Journal window and any other Simply windows and return to the Home window. If you cannot see the 🗗 icon, click `X` to return to the Home window.

8 ➤ Advance the date to **Apr 30** and click `No` on the Simply Accounting – Backup window, if it appears, as you do not need to back up now.

Using a Recurring Transaction

Bank charges are levied each month and, as shown in Exercise 1-14, in the Recall Recurring Transaction window, an April 28 bank charges recurring transaction was set up for future use on April 28. You will also use a recurring entry in Chapter 3.

Exercise 1-15 – Using a Recurring Transaction

Apr 30, 2014	**You received a Bank Statement with a Debit memo dated April 29, 2014 from the bank advising that they have deducted $22.46 from your bank account for service charges.**

To use the Bank Charges recurring entry, complete the following steps:

1 ➤ Click on the **General Journal** icon.

2 ➤ From the **General Journal** window, click the **Recall Recurring Transaction** icon, 4th icon on the left, and the following window appears.

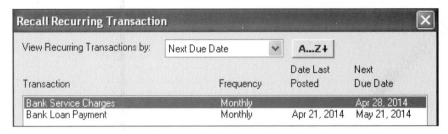

3 ➤ **Bank Service Charges**, should be highlighted in blue, click ⟨Select⟩ and the General Journal window appears with the recurring transaction information.

4 ➤ **Date**   Change the date to **Apr 29, 2014**. This is the date the money was removed from the bank account.

5 ➤ Change the **date** and the **amount** as shown in the journal below.

6 ➤ Click the **Enter Additional Information** ☑ icon.

This feature allows you to record additional information about the transaction, such as other dates and other information (e.g., voucher dates and voucher approvals, or entry recorded by person's name) that may be useful for the audit trail, or for future reference. This text does not use this feature in all entries.

7 ➤ **Additional Date**   Change the date to **Apr 29, 2014** the day the service charges were taken from the account.

8 ➤ **Additional Field**   Type **Recorded by SN** (replace SN with your initials).

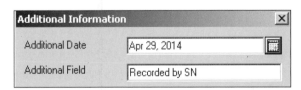

9 ➤ Click **OK**.

Source	Bank Debit Memo		Date	Apr 29, 2014
Comment	Bank Service Charges			

Account	Debits	Credits	Comment
5180 Bank Charges Expense	22.46	--	service charges
1100 Bank Account	--	22.46	

10 ➤ When your entry resembles the above window, click **Report, Display General Journal Entry**.

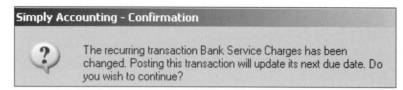

General Journal Entry Apr 29, 2014 (J6)

Account Number	Account Description	Debits	Credits
5180	Bank Charges Expense	22.46	-
	service charges		
1100	Bank Account	-	22.46
Additional Date: Ap...	Additional Field: Recorded by SN		
		22.46	22.46

11 ➤ Notice the additional information. Click X to close the entry.

12 ➤ When your entry is correct, click **Post**.

You will see the Confirmation message shown next:

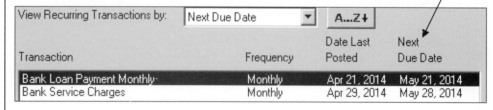

Simply Accounting - Confirmation

? The recurring transaction Bank Service Charges has been changed. Posting this transaction will update its next due date. Do you wish to continue?

13 ➤ Click **Yes**, J6 posting confirmation window appears. Click **OK**. The entry will be available for next month. (See the Next Due Date window in step 14.)

14 ➤ Click the 🔼 **Recall recurring transaction**. (See side note box and Next Due Date field.)

View Recurring Transactions by:	Next Due Date ▼	A...Z↓		
Transaction		Frequency	Date Last Posted	Next Due Date
Bank Loan Payment Monthly-		Monthly	Apr 21, 2014	May 21, 2014
Bank Service Charges		Monthly	Apr 29, 2014	May 28, 2014

15 ➤ Click **Cancel** and X to return to the Home window.

> ℹ️ You have recorded the bank charges for the period ending April 29. The recurring Due date (28th) is from the initial creation date. If the date or other information needs to change, the recurring entry could be resaved with the new information. Many businesses set up several recurring entries to help save time; you change only fields that need changing, and post.

Drill Down (Trace Back)

From an Income Statement, Balance Sheet or other reports, you can drill down (trace back) one level at a time to review a transaction in order to see the relevant information (including amounts) in the report.

This drill down feature works in all modules.

Exercise 1-16 – Drill Down (Trace Back)

Your manager has asked you to review the transactions you entered earlier, using the Income Statement. The following instructions will show you various techniques in tracing back transactions.

1 ➤   Display the **Balance Sheet** for Photos Company for **Apr 29, 2014** (see Exercise 1-5b).

2 ➤   As you move your cursor over the accounts, the cursor changes to a magnifying glass.

3 ➤   Move down to the **Equity section, Additional Investment – T. Chikowski** account and double-click.

The General Ledger Report for account 3120 displays for the same time period.

General Ledger Report Apr 01, 2014 to Apr 29, 2014 Sorted by: Transaction Number						
Date	Comment	Source #	JE#	Debits	Credits	Balance
3120 Additional Investment T. Chikowski						– Cr
Apr 24, 2014	Mrs. Chikowski investment in business	Bank Transfer	J5	–	3,000.00	3,000.00 Cr

This report is sorted by Transaction Number (default). As shown in Exercise 1-17 (Display and Print the General Journal), the report can be sorted by date. Using the Drill down feature, this report does not display the Adjusting entries (J3 and J4).

If you hide the error and reversing entry (J3 and J4) from the Journal Entries display as shown in Exercise 1-13, they will still display in the General Ledger report if the Show Corrections box is ✓.

4 ➤   Position the cursor on **J5**, or the amount, or the Source field information, and double-click. The General Journal entry that created the entry is displayed. (See side note box.) If you want to see the Journal entry window, double-click on J5 and you are taken to the journal window. Click ☒ to return to the step 3 window.

If you want to see the original and reversing entries, on the Modify icon, click on Report Options and click on ☑ Corrections . Click OK to see the original, reversing and correcting entry.

In the CUSTOMERS and VENDORS modules, Chapters 2A & 2B and 3A & 3B, when the journal entry is displayed, you will be able to see the aged report for that firm if you click the Customer or Vendor name.

5 ➤   Click the ☒ in the right corner of the open windows to return to the Balance Sheet.

6 ➤   Click ☒ to return to the Home window.

To Display and Print the General Journal

It is a good idea at this point to print a report of entries you have recorded from Session Date Apr 17 to Apr 29. The printed copy provides proof of what has been recorded in the company file.

Exercise 1-17 – To Display and Print the General Journal

The Reports area, will display only: All Journal entries. Use the following procedure to display and print only General Journal entries from the COMPANY module.

Although you might know that there are no transactions between April 1 to 17, you should use the beginning of the month for the Start Date to ensure that your system does not have entries posted before the entries you processed.

You should be at the Home window to start this exercise.

1 ➤ Click the **Report Centre** icon, in the left pane, click on **Accounts**, click on **General Journal Entries**. If you were sure of the setting to change, you could click on 'Modify this report' to change a setting. You will do this in step 2. Click **Display**.

When you choose the ✓ show **Additional Information,** the **Additional Date** and **Additional Field** will display in all entries regardless if you used the field or not.

In the future, if you do not want the **Additional Date** and **Additional Field** to appear in Journal windows or printouts, make sure the field is unchecked.

2 ➤ To change a setting, click on **Modify icon**, **Report Options**. The Start Date should be **Apr 01, 2014** (the first day of the month and the End Date should be **Apr 30, 2014** (current Session date).

3 ➤ Make sure the **Additional Information** boxes are ✓ to have this information shown in the report. (See side note box.)

There are a number of reports that can be customized to the user's requirements. See left panel shown next.

- Report Options
- Report Columns
- Sort Report
- Filter Report
- Print Settings
- Font Settings

There are no exercises in this text to use features other than Report Options. If you customize any of the reports, you must return to the original default choice; otherwise, future displays and/or reports will be different as compared to the text.

Report Options Shown previously.

Report Columns Customize column settings for this report. This feature will allow you to change the width of the columns and columns to be displayed/printed in reports. In the left pane, click on **Report Columns**, click on **Custom report column settings** button.

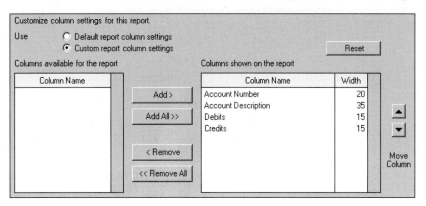

Sort Report — Custom sort order

Click **Sort Report**, and **Custom sort order**. This feature allows you to sort columns (fields) in reports.

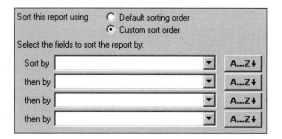

Click **Filter Report**, and click **Use your filter specification**.

This feature allows you to prepare reports in modules with various columns equal to the data requested; e.g., Customers with balances over $1,000.00.

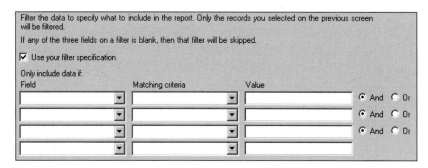

Print Settings — Custom page orientation and **Custom margins**

Click **Printer Settings,** click **Custom page orientation**.

This feature allows you to set Portrait or Landscape and to Customize the margins as the default print setting.

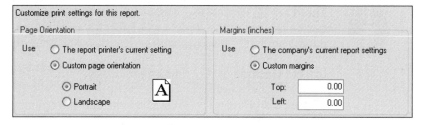

Font Settings — Custom font settings

4 ► Click **Font Settings**, click **Custom font settings**.

This feature allows you to change report fonts and colours, sizes, Bold, Italicize and Align information left, centre or right.

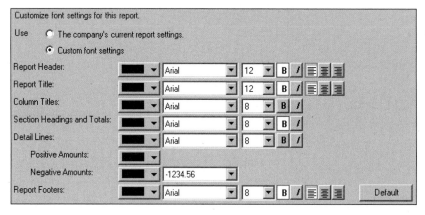

5 ➤ Click **OK** to display the Journal Entries.

 You may experiment with any of the customizations, but you must return to the default settings choice; otherwise, future displays and/or reports will be different as compared to the text.

General Journal Apr 01, 2014 to Apr 30, 2014

		Account Number	Account Description	Debits	Credits
Apr 17, 2014	J1	Bank Debit Memo, Bank charges printing new cheques SN			
		5180	Bank Charges Expense	31.00	-
			Printing charge new cheques		
		1100	Bank Account	-	31.00
Additional Date:		Additional Field:			
Apr 21, 2014	J2	Bank Debit memo, Bank Loan Payment			
		2710	Bank Loan Payable	138.56	-
			Principal repayment		
		5190	Bank Loan Interest Expense	76.44	-
		1100	Bank Account	-	215.00
			Bank Loan Payment		
Additional Date:		Additional Field:			
Apr 24, 2014	J3	Bank Transfer, Mrs. Chikowski investment in business			
		1100	Bank Account	2,000.00	-
			Bank transfer investment		
		3120	Additional Investment T. Chiko...	-	2,000.00
			Bank transfer investment		
Additional Date: Apr 24, 2014		Additional Field: Mrs. Chikowski phone call message SN			
Apr 24, 2014	J4	ADJBank Transfer, Reversing J3. Correction is J5.			
		1100	Bank Account	-	2,000.00
			Bank transfer investment		
		3120	Additional Investment T. Chikowski	2,000.00	-
			Bank transfer investment		
Additional Date: Apr 24, 2014		Additional Field: Mrs. Chikowski phone call message SN			
Apr 24, 2014	J5	Bank Transfer, Mrs. Chikowski investment in business			
		1100	Bank Account	3,000.00	-
			Bank transfer investment		
		3120	Additional Investment T. Chiko...	-	3,000.00
			Bank transfer investment		
Additional Date: Apr 24, 2014		Additional Field: Mrs. Chikowski phone call message SN			
Apr 29, 2014	J6	Bank Debit Memo, Bank Service Charges			
		5180	Bank Charges Expense	22.46	-
			service charges		
		1100	Bank Account	-	22.46
Additional Date: Apr 29, 2014		Additional Field: Recorded by SN			
				7,268.46	7,268.46

Fig. 1-11: General Journal Transactions (no hidden entries).

> The total amount, i.e., 7,268.46, is the sum of journal entries 1 to 6, and verifies the equality of debit and credits only. The total does not indicate the accuracy of the values recorded.

The total amount at the bottom (7,268.46) which is the sum of journal entries 1 through 6 does not have to equal your numbers if you have made more entries. (See side note box.)

To ensure you have processed your entries correctly, you must compare your entries to each entry in the solution set. (You cannot rely on the debit and credit column totals.)

You can use the [🔍 Print Preview] icon on the toolbar to view the report before printing to make sure it is what you want. If you see … on some lines, click **X** to return to the General Journal Display. You can click the top report header and move the columns to display the missing information. If you expand the columns, watch for the right column (dotted line) that indicates a page break.

6 ➤ To print this report, you can click Print in the Print Preview window, or return to the General Journal Display and click the 🖨 Print icon. Wait for the Print dialog box to disappear before moving on.

7 ➤ **Exit** to the Home window.

Display and Print the General Ledger Report

The General Ledger report displays the transactions posted to each General Ledger account.

The report could be printed by Transaction Number (the default) or by Date. The date feature would be useful if entries were recorded on a random date basis. The date report would place all entries with the same date together, regardless of the date when they were recorded. There is no exercise for the date feature. The report can also be printed with each account on a separate page (see step 3).

Exercise 1-18 – To Display/Print the General Ledger Report

To print all entries in the General Ledger:

> You can also view and print from the menu bar, click Reports, Financials, General Ledger.

1 ➤ In the Reports Area, click ▾, select **General Ledger**, click **Display**. (See side box.)

2 ➤ The report displays with the default of Apr 01, 2014 to Apr 30, 2014 and the default of printing with Transaction Number and Show transaction comment.

3 ➤ A feature in Simply is the ability to print each account on a separate page. This feature is demonstrated, but not completed, in order to save paper in a classroom setting.

From the General Ledger Report window, click the **File** menu, and click on the Separate Each Account on a New Page when Printed item. You are returned to the General Ledger Report window and can see the …… page separators.

4 ➤ Click the **File** menu and you will see a ✓ beside ✔ Separate Each Account on a New Page when Printed .

Click ✔ Separate Each Account on a New Page when Printed again to remove the ✓ check mark and you are returned to the General Ledger Report window with only 1 page separator lower in the report.

5 ➤ Click the 🖨 Print icon to print the report without printing on separate pages.

To display the report with journal line comments, instead of transaction comments, or if you wanted to print only 1 general ledger account, follow these steps.

6 ➤ Click on the **Modify** button, click on **Report Options**. To print only 1 account (e.g., 1100 Bank Account) in the middle pane, scroll up to **1100 Bank Account** and **click**. The other accounts turn white. If you also wanted to print account 3120 additional Investment T. Chikowski, **scroll down** to 3120 and press **CTRL** and click on **3120**. It turns blue like 1100. You could also change the lower setting to **Show line comment**.

7 ➤ Click **OK**. Only 2 accounts are displayed. Compare the Comments column in this report, with the Comments printed in the report in step 5. It is not possible to print the G/L report with both Comments in a report.

8 ➤ **Exit** from the display window.

If you wanted to see the report with the Corrections displayed, you would click the Modify button, select Show corrections, and OK. Many businesses will prefer to see the GL report without the corrections showing. Management may want to concentrate on the correct entries.

Exercise 1-19 – Printing Financial Statements

---

1 ➤ Refer to Exercise 1-5, and **print**:

- Income Statement for period Jan 01, 2014 to Apr 30, 2014.
  Net Income = $10,650.10.
- Balance Sheet as at Apr 30, 2014. Total Assets: $62,148.54.

Exercise 1-20 – Printing the Recurring Transactions Report

---

1 ➤ Click the **Report Centre** icon, in the left pane, click on **Recurring Transactions**. Select **General,** at the bottom under the right pane, click **Display**.

The report as shown next indicates the Module type.

Recurring Transactions

Type	Description	Frequency	Last Processed	Due Date
General	Bank Loan Payment Monthly	Monthly	Apr 21, 2014	May 21, 2014
General	Bank Service Charges	Monthly	Apr 29, 2014	May 28, 2014

2 ➤ Click **X** and **Close** to exit to the Home window.

Exercise 1-21a – Creating Custom Report Shortcuts

Look at the Recently viewed reports: area on the right side under Reports. This area displays the last 4 reports that are viewed in all modules. In future chapters, the section may no longer display the Income Statement and Balance Sheet links.

This exercise will create shortcuts (a maximum of 10 reports or reports and blank separators) under the Shortcuts area on the left side of the Home window for the Income Statement and Balance Sheet that are used often. Other reports can be added as you will see in this exercise.

1 ➤ From the Home window, in the Shortcuts area, click on **Customize**. The Customize Shortcuts window appears.

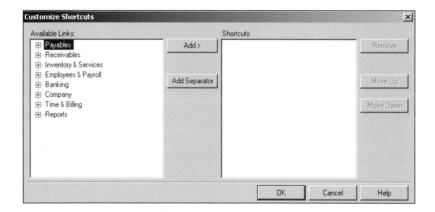

2 ➤ Click the ⊞ beside **Reports**, click the ⊞ at **Financials**, click the ⊞ at **Income Statement,** click on **Standard**.

3 ➤ Click **Add>**. The Standard item moves to the right side of the Shortcuts display window.

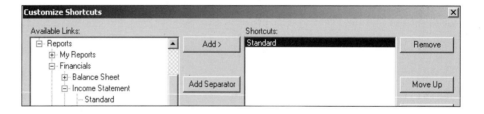

4 ➤ Click **OK**. In the Shortcuts pane you will see.

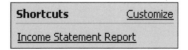

5 ➤ Repeat the procedure to add a Standard Balance Sheet Report, and a Gross Margin - Standard report (under Income Statement) to display the following:

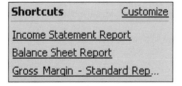

Exercise 1-21b – To Remove a Report Shortcut

---

1 ➤ In the Shortcuts area, click on **Customize**. The Customize Shortcuts window appears.

2 ➤ In the right side pane, click on **Gross Margin – Standard**.

3 ➤ Click the Remove button, and the item is removed.

Exercise 1-21c – To Add a Blank Space between Reports

This exercise will add a blank space between reports. Note you can have only 10 reports or a combination of reports and blank separator spaces equaling 10.

1 ➤ In the Shortcuts right pane window, click on the first **Standard** Item.

2 ➤ Click on the **Add Separator** button, and the window changes to:

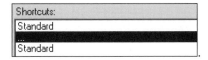

3 ➤ Click **OK** and the Shortcuts area changes to:

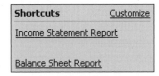

4 ➤ To remove the expander ..., click **Customize**, click on the blank line with **...** Click on the Remove button. Click **OK**.

The left side now displays.

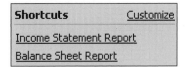

You can add reports from any of the modules shown in the left-hand pane.

Saving Your Work

If there is a power outage during your work session, you can lose what you have done before the power went out. To avoid this, you can save your work periodically during the work session.

The saving techniques in the next exercise may also be used for copying and backing up purposes. The main difference between the copy and backup functions is that when you copy the company file to another storage device, the copy has the same file size as the original; when you use the backup function in Simply, the file is compressed in a CAB file and your data file gets smaller (similar to a zip file).

Exercise 1-22 – Saving Your Work

To start this exercise, you need to be at the Photos Company Home window.

1 ➤ Click the **File** selection on the Main Menu. Study the different methods of saving:

Save As   Saves a copy of the current company data under a different file name on your hard drive, zip or other storage device. You have an option of changing the location and company name from the default file name of NEW.SAI.

DO NOT USE THIS FEATURE in your exercises in this book, because all future saves will be made to the new location and company name. If you leave the default settings, all future saves will be made to that same folder, but with a name **New**. When you open the file, the name on the top menu bar will be *New*.

If you use this feature outside of class, change the file name from *New* to a more descriptive name such as:

G:\Simply 2010 Backup\Backup_01_Photos_Sep_08_2010a_SN

G:\Simply 2010 Backup is the drive and folder where you will keep the backup copies of your work. Refer to **Exercise 1-23, step 3**.

Sept_08_2010a refers to the actual date that the student is working on the material and not the data file date and will help in identifying the saved file. If you were making a second backup on the same day, you would change 2010a to 2010b. Record in your logbook (see Exercise 1-24) the page you get to in the text.

Save a Copy

This feature is similar to the Save As choice. You can save the current company data under a different file name and location, and at the same time you will continue to work in the original storage location with the original company data file.

For the copy file, you should change the company name to a descriptive name such as:

    Backup_01_Photos_Sep_08_2010a_SN
    (The actual date you are making the backup.)

Be sure your storage device has enough space available. Use a USB storage device as discussed in the "Getting Started" section on page 1-5.

Backup

There are a number of options to backup. You can click this Backup option, or click on the [Backup] icon on the tool bar, or you can click ▼ on Data Management in the Tasks area and select Backup. In the next exercise you will back up using the Data Management option. Backing up will compress (make your data file smaller) for saving on your USB storage device.

Restore

Restore a data file from a previous saved file. You can also restore a data file by clicking ▼ on Data Management in the Tasks area and select Restore. See Restoring a Data File at the end of this chapter (Chapter 1a).

Exit

Save work and exit Simply. You can also Exit and Save by clicking on the X in the Home window on the top.

The computer stores the entries in the RAM memory of the computer. When you request a display of a Financial Statement, Ledger account or click X to exit, the program will add the entries in memory to the current balance of the accounts, and will update the files on your storage location.

This tool bar option is the same as **File, Backup** on the menu bar, or the Backup option in the Data Management icon. See the next exercise.

2 ➤   Click anywhere on the Home page to exit the menu list for File.

Why Back Up?

You have just spent a considerable amount of time recording entries and learning about the Simply Accounting software. What would you do if your hard drive crashed or you lost your storage device? It is always safe to have your backup stored in a different location from your original data.

If you need to restore your data files, see Restoring a Data File in Chapter 1a (at the end of this chapter).

Here are other recommendations:

- Use a USB storage device for storage of backups. Keep the protective tab for the computer end. This may reduce the possibility of damage from accidental spilling of pop, coffee, etc.

- Keep your storage device(s) at room temperature. Do not leave them in an automobile where they can be subjected to extreme hot or cold temperatures.

- Do not take your storage device out of the drive before you have completed the Exit or backup procedure. If you remove the device during the procedure you may lose some of the work you have just completed!

Backup Procedures

You will need to become familiar with the mechanics of backing up. There are a number of ways to back up your data.

As noted previously, Simply Accounting has provided a number of ways to back up your company's working data from your hard drive.

In the next exercise, you will use the Data Management option to back up. As noted it will condense (compress) your data and back up the information to a USB storage device that your computer supports.

You can back up many company folders to the USB device.

(See side note box.)

Exercise 1-23 – Backing Up Your Data

---

1 ➤   Click the ▼ at **Data management**, select **Backup** and a window similar to the following will appear.

This exercise assumes that you are using a USB storage device for storage of the backup files.

```
┌─────────────────────────────────────────────────────────┐
│ Simply Accounting - Backup                          [X] │
├─────────────────────────────────────────────────────────┤
│  Last backup:                                            │
│    Session Date:   --                                    │
│    System Date:    --                                    │
│                                                          │
│  File Name:    │Backup                              │    │
│                                                          │
│  Location:     │C:\SIMPLY DATA 2010\01 PHOTOS\Backup\│ ┌Browse...┐│
│                                                          │
│  Comment:      │Backup #0001 of company Photos.     │    │
│                                                          │
│  ☐ Compact data before backing up to save disk space    │
│  ☑ Verify backup file after back up completion           │
└─────────────────────────────────────────────────────────┘
```

Last backup:

Session Date:	The date is blank as you have not backed up previously. The window would indicate the Session date that was used on a previous backup.
System Date:	The date is blank as you have not backed up previously. The window would indicate the computer system date that was used on a previous backup.
2 ➤ File Name:	Change the File Name to: **Backup_01_Photos_Sep_08_2010a_SN**. This will identify the backup with a company name and date the backup was created. We are assuming an actual working date of Sep 08, 2010. The **01** refers to the chapter number of the data file and the 2010a refers to the first backup of the data file. If you were creating a second backup for the same day and chapter, you would use the next letter 2010b, then 2010c for the third backup if needed. This will allow you to have a backup for different saving points in the chapter in case you want to redo an Exercise that you have completed or your data file became corrupt. The **SN** (Student's Name) would be your initials as identification in case your instructor requires you to submit a backup file.
3 ➤ Location:	Change the location to: **E:\Simply 2010 Backup**. All backup files will be located in this folder.

Newer computers have DVD and CD-ROM drives and the drive letter available for the USB device may not be G. If your storage device's drive letter is different, substitute the appropriate drive letter for G. Use a backup file name that includes the company name and use the actual date the backup was created (in this example, September 08, 2010).

4 ➤ Comment	Do NOT change the Comment field. This identifies this backup as the first backup of the Company file named Photos. In future backups, Simply will update the backup by increasing the number accordingly; i.e., 0002, 0003, etc.

ℹ The location name may be truncated (reduced) (e.g., Simply~1\Photos\Backup) depending on your computer configuration.

ℹ Fragmented means that portions of this file or many data files are not together on the drive. Fragmentation can slow down the performance of the computer.

There is no exercise for this feature.

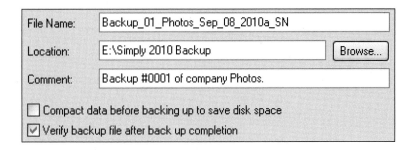

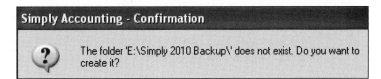 DO NOT CHANGE. You would ✓ this box if your drive and/or data file was fragmented and you wanted Simply to defrag the file before Backing up. This procedure is not necessary in the classroom. (See side note box.)

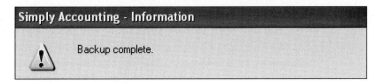 Leave this feature ✓. Verification of the backup file is important. If it was not verified, data corruption could occur during the backup and you would not know until you needed to use the backup. With the ✓, if data corruption occurred during the backup, the verification would display a warning message.

5 ➤ Click **OK** and the following Confirmation window appears:

Simply Accounting - Confirmation

? The folder 'E:\Simply 2010 Backup\' does not exist. Do you want to create it?

6 ➤ Click **Yes**. The backup may take a few minutes to complete.

7 ➤ When successful, a Backup complete window appears as shown next.

Simply Accounting - Information

⚠ Backup complete.

8 ➤ Click **OK** and you are returned to the Home window.

9 ➤ **Exit** Simply by clicking the **X** box in the top-right corner of the Home window.

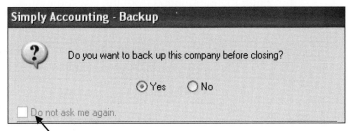

Simply Accounting - Backup

? Do you want to back up this company before closing?

⦿ Yes   ○ No

☐ Do not ask me again.

10 ➤ Change the selection to **No** as you have already backed up. It is also a reminder to back up if you forget.

☐ Do not ask me again. Do not select this. If you select this choice the Backup window will not display when you close Simply for this company. You can reset this choice and this will be discussed in Chapter 4.

11 ➤ Click **OK** to close the company.

When you click the EXIT ⊠ box in the top-right corner of the Home window, Simply saves all entries in memory to the data file in the storage device and closes the company and the program.

Go to the E: drive, or the drive letter of where you put your file, then double-click the **Simply 2010 Backup** folder. You should see the file:

Backup_01_Photos_Sep_08_2010a_SN1.CAB

This means a Photos backup CAB file was created with the creation date September 8, 2010. Simply added the **1** in 2010a_SN1 to indicate this is the first backup file in a series. There is no second backup (series) file for Photos.

You should back up your work on a USB drive or any storage device on a regular basis to reduce the chance of losing data.

From this point onward, back up whenever you see the icon at the left, before you leave the classroom or when you are moving to another exercise and you want to save the file at that point.

If there are any error messages during the Backup process, complete the Backup procedure again. If the same error messages or others appear, there may be some damage to the storage device. Write the error message(s) on paper and have your instructor look at the storage device and messages.

Using a Logbook or Diary

A logbook may be used to maintain a list of the work you have finished, and what backup drive you used on a specific date. This will be useful in determining where to start on your next work session. If you have a drive failure or you lose your backup drive, you can refer to your logbook to find out which drive and file name you used last.

Exercise 1-24 – Maintaining a Logbook

A logbook form is provided at the back of this book.

1 ➤ Enter the information from the backup that you completed in the previous exercise in the logbook. See the next example.

Date	Backup	Data Information Where you get to each class	Name of File in Storage Location
Sept 8	*1*	*Finished Ex. 1-13, page 1-44*	01_Photos_Sep_08-2010a
Sept 8	*2*	*Finished Ex. 1-23, page 1-60*	01_Photos_Sep_08-2010b
Sept 19	*1*	*Finished Ex. 2A-14, page 2A-102*	02_Luggage_Sep_18_2010a
Sept 26	*2*	*Chapter 2A finished, page 2A-126*	02_Luggage_Sep_25_2010b

It is recommended that you copy the backup file from the USB drive to your own computer as another form of backup away from the main computer. This will reduce the amount of work you have to redo if your storage location data is damaged or lost.

 Back up your data and update your logbook (located at the back of this textbook) now. **Remember, if it is important, back it up**.

Backing Up in an Office Environment

Most companies store their working data files on the hard drive of the computer and would back up daily to a hard drive of another computer, USB device, CD-ROM, DVD or other storage devices. The important thing is to ensure that the backup is not on the same storage device as the working data file and that the backup is kept at a different location. This way, if anything happens to one storage device, there is still a means to retrieve the company data.

 It is very important to record in a daily log the backup number and important information about the day or session. Information such as last cheque, last sales invoice, last purchase invoice recorded, etc., should also be recorded in the log. This way, if the working data file becomes damaged, you will have a record of what was entered on each of the backup disks.

Here is one backup procedure:

1. Use a set of 7 folders on an external storage device. Label each folder for every working day of the week: **Sunday, Monday**, **Tuesday**, **Wednesday**, **Thursday**, **Friday**, **Saturday**. It is assumed that many businesses record accounting information 7 days a week.

2. Prepare another set of 5 folders labelled **Week 1** to **Week 5**.

3. Prepare another set of 12 folders labelled for each month of the year: **January**, **February**, **March**, etc.

4. At the end of each day, back up your data into the appropriate backup folder; e.g., on Monday copy your data into the Monday backup folder, etc.

5. At the end of the week, copy the Saturday data file to a folder labelled Week 1, etc. to Week 5 (some months have 5 Saturdays).

6. At the end of each month, another backup should be made on the appropriate folder and dated.

The backup storage device should be stored off-site.

In a classroom situation, while you are learning to use the software, making a backup of your data at the end of every work session will be sufficient.

Do not take your storage device out of the drive before the light on your backup storage device goes off, because the backup procedure would not have been completed. If you remove the storage device, you may lose some of the work you have just completed.

Update your logbook regularly, identifying the page you last worked on, and which backup destination drive is being used on a specific date.

Summary

Some of the benefits of computerized bookkeeping, compared to manual bookkeeping, are:

1. Data entry errors may be easily corrected.

2. Controls are provided to prevent data entry errors, such as addition errors or duplicate invoice numbers, transposition of numbers, etc.

3. Posting transactions is automatically performed by clicking the Post icon, and all ledgers and journals are updated immediately.

4. Standard financial statements and reports may be printed any time.

When starting Simply, you are required to enter a date, which is the work session date. For each transaction you enter, you must enter the actual **Transaction** date, which could be either the same date as the Session date or earlier.

Simply is an integrated accounting system. The system contains **modules** that are similar to ledgers and subledgers in a manual system. The modules in Simply are:

-   RECEIVABLES subledger with Sales and Receipts journals.

-   PAYABLES   subledger with Purchases and Payments journals.

-   INVENTORY & SERVICES subledger with Build, Adjust and Transfer journals.

-   EMPLOYEES & PAYROLL subledger with Payroll Cheque and Pay Remittance journals. To automatically calculate payroll taxes, businesses must purchase a Payroll ID code to activate Automatic payroll calculations.

-   PROJECT module with Sales, Purchases, Paycheques and General Journal.

-   BANKING ledger with Receipt, Deposits, Transfer funds and Bank Reconciliation journals.

-   COMPANY ledger with General Journal.

-   In previous versions, module TIME SLIPS (formerly called TIME & BILLING) is now located in the RECEIVABLES AND EMPLOYEES & PAYROLL modules.

To save your work and exit from Simply, click the ⬚X⬚ in the top-right corner.

Budgets: Simply Accounting has a feature to record and display budget amounts. Information on Budget input and display can be found in Appendix E, *Budgets — General Ledger* at www.simplyaccounting2010.nelson.com under Student Resources. See your instructor for more information.

This chapter (Photos Company) uses only the GENERAL module and does not have a subledger section for each customer or vendor.

In Chapters 2A & 2B, using the Santos Luggage company files, sales are recorded in the RECEIVABLES subledger. Individual customer detail is available and includes items sold.

In Chapters 3A & 3B, Tyson's Toys, all purchases of merchandise for resale, services, e.g., rent paid, telephone bill, owner's withdrawals and goods for business use, are recorded in the PAYABLES subledger module. Individual Vendor transaction detail is available and includes details of items or services purchased.

The General journal would be used only for bank service charges, and adjustments that do not relate to specific customers or suppliers (vendors).

To View Corrections

To view corrections that need to be made to the text, please go to:

http://www.simplyaccounting2010.nelson.com

On the right side, click on Student Resources.

On the right side, click on Corrections.

Corrections to the text, if any, will be listed.

Before Moving On . . .

Read the following questions and make sure you know the answers to them; otherwise, read the corresponding part in the chapter before moving on:

1. What is the best way to open the Simply Accounting program and data files?

2. Describe Toolbar icons.

3. The firm's year-end (fiscal year) is on December 31, 2014. You received on January 22 a bank debit memo dated January 20, 2014, for service charges on the bank account:

    What would be your **Session date**? _____ Your **Transaction date**? _____

4. What important information does the **Source** field indicate?

5. What is the **Comment field** (box) used to record?

6. What is the **Comment column** used to record?

7. Describe two ways to display a list of accounts when entering a General Journal entry.

8. An Income Statement may be displayed/printed for only 1 day, a month at a time, or a time period which can be several months or parts of a month (e.g., January 1 to February 17). Explain why.

9. Why would you use the **Drill Down** feature in Simply?

10. Describe an effective backup routine in an office environment.

11. A logbook/diary, as discussed in this chapter, is used for what purpose?

12. How or where can you get help in Simply Accounting?

Challenge Exercise 01 C1-1, Driving School

(General Ledger Review)

1 ➤ Refer to Exercise 1-1 to unzip the **01 C1-1 Driving.exe** file.

2 ➤ Open the **01 C1-1 Driving** file.

The Driving school is a single-owner business, operated by Tanya Gauci. You should record the following transactions in the General Journal (double-entry accounting). You will learn how to record some of these entries more efficiently in the RECEIVABLES and PAYABLES module in Chapters 2A, 2B, 3A and 3B. The fiscal year is Jan 1 to Dec 31. Use appropriate additional Info and comment fields in 3 transactions.

Note: This assignment does not involve HST, similar to Photos Company.

This business uses the **Track Additional Transaction Details** feature where necessary.

3 ➤ **Record** and **Post** the following transactions in the General Journal for the month of January using the Double-Entry method.

Jan 2   Purchased $80.00 worth of office supplies from Kanwal Supplies and issued cheque #652. Note that these supplies are assumed to be used up by the end of the month.

Jan 2   Issued $80.00 invoice #324 to YOUR name (your name in the comment line) for 2 hours of lessons before your driving test.

Jan 3   Issued $600.00 cheque #653 to Uptown Mall for rent of a store in the mall.

Jan 4   Received cheque #113 from YOUR name (your name in the comment line) for invoice #324.

Jan 5   Issued $50.00 invoice #325 and received cheque #748 from Vito Campize for one-hour driving lesson ($40.00) and rule book test ($10.00) for his daughter Toula.

Jan 6   Issued $320.00 cheque #654 to Capilano Advertising for advertisements in flyers being delivered to homes in the area today.

Jan 8   A new client, Naomi Regalea, recommended by Marta Grez, took a 3-hour driving lesson. Received her $120.00 cheque #522 for invoice #326.

Jan 9   Issued $120.00 cheque #655 to Morton Medina (driving teacher) for wages.

Jan 11   Purchased 2 driving lesson DVDs at $75.00 each for use in the Beginners "In Class" course approved by the government. They will be used in the course starting tomorrow and once used they cannot be returned. Cheque #656 issued to Major Film Labs.

Jan 11   Beginners "In Class" course started today. Received cash $50.00 (2 clients) and cheques $200.00 (8 clients). Deposited $250.00 in the bank today.

Jan 12   Issued $110.00 cheque #657 to Amrit Devon (In Class teacher) for wages.

Jan 12   Record the $308.00 Bank Debit memo for a payment on the bank loan. This amount includes interest of $32.40.

4 ➤ **Print** the following:
   a) General Journal Entries for the period, Jan 02 to Jan 12, **with additional information**
   b) Income Statement for the period Jan 02 to Jan 12
   c) Balance Sheet as at Jan 12
   d) General Ledger for all accounts to Jan 12

Challenge Exercise 01 C1-2, Astrology Readings

(General Ledger Review)

1 ➤ Refer to Exercise 1-1 to unzip the **01 C1-2 Readings.exe** file.

2 ➤ Open the **01 C1-2 Readings** file.

The business is a sole proprietorship, owned by Harriet Patel. You should record the following transactions in the General Journal (double-entry accounting). You will learn how to record some of these entries more efficiently in the RECEIVABLES and PAYABLES module in Chapters 2A, 2B, 3A and 3B. The fiscal year is Jan 1 to Dec 31.

Note: This assignment does not involve HST, which is similar to Photos Company.

3 ➤ **Record** and **Post** the following transactions in the General Journal for the month of January using the Double-Entry method:

Jan 4   Paid $500.00 rent for the month to Eastwood Mall Inc. Cheque #131 issued to the attention of the manager, Mrs. Hilk.

Jan 4   Manager advised the rent has increased to $520.00 on new lease. Reverse and correct the previous entry to the correct amount. Cheque #132 issued.

Jan 4   Paid $50.00 to YourTown Newspaper for an advertisement in today's paper. Invoice #7622. Cheque #133 issued.

Jan 5   Issued invoice #231 for astrology reading (Your sign) to YOUR name (your name in the comment line). Received your cheque #788 in the amount of $130.00.

Jan 6   Issued invoice #232 for astrology reading for Sylvia Ciuciura (Leo). Received cash in the amount of $130.00.

Jan 7   Paid $20.00 for special computer paper, for astrology printouts, from Grand Supplies on invoice #8964. Cheque #134 issued. Charge to expense because it will be used by the end of the month.

Jan 9   Received $43.00 telephone bill for regular service from Metro Phones. Cheque #135 issued.

Jan 9   Issued invoice #233 for astrology reading for Ying Xiang (Scorpio). Received her cheque #465 in the amount of $120.00.

Jan 26   Received invoice #356. Issued $100.00 cheque #136 to Jeremy Design Studio, for graphic design work on new advertising brochure.

Jan 31   Issued invoice #234 for astrology reading for John Harwood (Scorpio). Received his cheque #611 in the amount of $125.00.

4 ➤ **Print** the following:

    a) General Journal Entries for Jan 1 to 31, **with corrections**
    b) Income Statement for Jan 1 to 31
    c) Balance Sheet as at Jan 31
    d) General Ledger at Jan 31

Challenge Exercise 01 C1-3, Movers

(General Ledger Review)

1 ➤ Refer to Exercise 1-1 to unzip the **01 C1-3 Movers.exe** file.

2 ➤ Open the **01 C1-3 Movers** file.

The business is a single-owner business, owned by Henry Kelly. You should record the following transactions in the General Journal (double-entry accounting). You will learn how to record some of these entries more efficiently in the RECEIVABLES and PAYABLES module in Chapters 2A, 2B, 3A and 3B. The fiscal year is Jan 1 to Dec 31.

Note: The store was closed from January 1 to January 3 and the transactions start at Jan 4.

Note: This assignment does not involve HST, which is similar to Photos Company.

3 ➤ **Record** and **Post** the following transactions in the General Journal for the month of January using the Double-Entry method.

Jan 4 Paid $700.00 rent for the month to Trudeau Realty; cheque #178 issued.

Jan 7 Purchased and received $500.00 of bubble wrap to be sold (use Purchases), from John Currie Wraps Ltd., invoice #28643. Terms Net 30.

Jan 11 Sold $140.00 of moving boxes and $65.00 of bubble wrap to YOUR name (your name in the comment line) on invoice #385. Received your cheque #232 in the amount of $205.00.

Jan 16 Received cheque #28426, for a $4,923.00 payment from a customer, Canadian Insurance Co., for invoice #360, dated December 14.

Jan 18 Paid $412.00 to Direct Advertising Co. for an advertisement in today's paper. Invoice #10-38962. Next cheque #179.

Jan 25 Sold $1,100.00 worth of boxes and $250.00 of bubble wrap to Gilmore Stores on invoice #386. Net 30 days.

Jan 26 Received $83.00 telephone bill #9901 from Metro Phones for regular service. Issued cheque #180.

Jan 30 Issued cheque #181 to Mrs. G. Sohi, $440.00, as an employee, for her work in the office.

Jan 30 Use the Recurring entry to record bank service charges for the month. This month's charges are the same amount as in the recurring entry.

Note: Remember, the store is closed January 31.

4 ➤ **Print** the following:

    a) General Journal Entries for the monthly activity with no corrections
    b) Income Statement for the monthly activity
    c) Balance Sheet as at Jan 30

Relevant Appendices

 The following appendices are available at www.simplyaccounting2010.nelson.com under Student Resources.

Appendix 2010 A	**Basics of Accounting**
Appendix 2010 C	**What's New in Simply 2010**
Appendix 2010 E	**Budgets – General Ledger**
Appendix 2010 H	**New Business Guide**
Appendix 2010 O	**Security – Passwords**
Appendix 2010 R	**Quick Reference Guide**
Appendix 2010 U	**Adding Notes/Footers to Statements**

Restoring a Data File from a Backup Data File

You would want to restore a data file when:

a) the data file is corrupt;

b) you have made one or more mistakes in recording transactions and want to start over again from a previous backup (before the mistake(s) were made), instead of correcting the mistakes.

The following procedure will allow you to restore a previous backup data file and continue recording transactions.

Check your logbook to ensure that you have chosen the correct backup data file stored on a storage device.

In this example, it is assumed that you are using a backup of the file named **Photos** (for Photos Company) in the G: drive. The file was created in Chapter 1, Exercise 1-23.

Use My Computer or Windows Explorer to look at the E: drive, and you will see a folder **Simply 2010 Backup** with a file ▨ Backup_01_Photos_Sep_08_2010a_SN1.CAB inside the folder. Depending on the configuration of your computer you may not see the .CAB.

Exercise 1a-1: Restoring a Data File from a Backup

---

1 ➤ Start Simply in the normal way and you will see a portion of the window similar to the following:

Simply Accounting Premium

Welcome to Simply Accounting. What do you wish to do?

○ Open the sample company to help you learn Simply Accounting.

○ Create a new company.

○ Restore from backup.

◉ Select an existing company.

○ Open the last company you worked on:
    C:\Simply Data 2010\01 Photos\Photos.SAI

2 ➤ Click **Restore from backup.**

3 ➤ Click **OK**.

Restore from Backup window

Make sure the storage device that you are using to restore files is in the E: drive (assumed USB drive).

4 ➤ Click **Next>**.

Select Backup File window- part 1

Simply assumes that the backup file is located on:

> C:\Simply Data 2010\01 Photos\Backup drive and folder.

5 ➤ Your backup file is not on the C: drive, therefore, click on the **Browse** button to locate the files.

6 ➤ Locate the **E:** drive, and double-click on the **Simply 2010 Backup** folder.

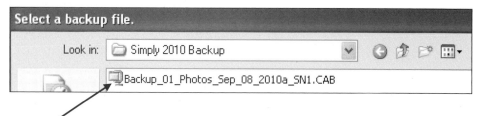

7 ➤ The icon in the lower field may be different on your computer. Double-click on **Backup_01_Photos_Sep_08_2010a_SN1.CAB**. Depending on the configuration of your computer you may not see the .CAB.

Select Backup File window – part 2

Scheduled Backup Files

There are no scheduled backups created in the textbook data files. See Chapter 4, Exercise 4-3 for a discussion on this topic.

8 ➤ Click **Next>**.

Confirm Backup file window

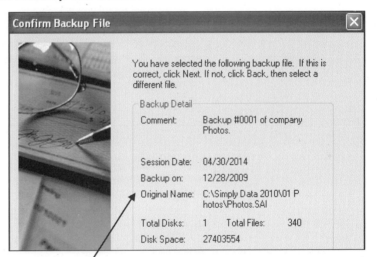

Session Date:	This is the session date of the data file. To make sure you are restoring the correct file, confirm the date with your log book.
Backup on:	12/28/2009. This is the actual date the backup was created by the author. Your date will be the actual date you backed up.
Original Name:	Depending on the configuration of your computer, this field is the path where the original file was created. It should read: C:\Simply Data 2010\01Photos\Photos.SAI.
Total Disks:	Each company data file contains a folder with an extension of SAJ. The MySQL data-base and company data files (accounts, transactions) are contained in the SAJ folder. A file with an extension of SAI is used by Simply to open the SAJ files.

9 ➤ This window contains information about the backup data file being restored. The information will be different depending on when and where you stored your backup. Click **Next>**.

New File Name window

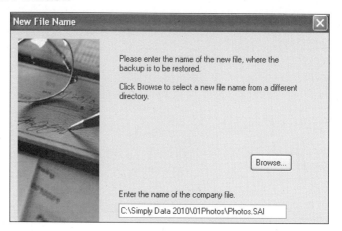

10 ➤ **Enter** the name of the folder and data file name you want to use. It is best to restore to the same folder and file name where you normally have your data. Using **Browse** to find the folder rather than typing in the name would be a faster and more accurate way.

11 ➤ Click **Next>**.

Confirmation window

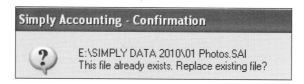

12 ➤ This window confirms your choice of folder and data file. Click **Yes** when the information is correct.

Finish Restoring from Backup window

13 ➤ Click **Finish** to complete the restoration process. The Session Date of your restored file will appear in the Session Date window.

14 ➤ If this is the correct session date you want to work with, click **OK**.

If you click OK, you will be at the Home window of the file you are going to use. It is best to print a Journal entry report to confirm the entries that you had previously posted and where you want to start from.

If you click Cancel you will return to step 1 of this procedure. You will need to find the backup storage device that contains the appropriate file that you want to restore. Refer to your logbook.

RECEIVABLES Module—*Basics*

Santos Luggage

Learning Objectives
After completing this chapter you will be able to:

☐ Process sales quotes, orders, invoices and sales returns.
☐ Add new customers and make changes to existing customers' data files.
☐ Process customers' receipts in full or partial payment of invoices with or without cash discounts and record cash and/or ATM (bank card) or credit card sales.
☐ Process deposits from customers for sales orders.
☐ Reverse and correct errors in invoices and cheques.
☐ Use Daily Business Manager and other Simply special features.
☐ Display and print various Receivable reports and journals.

Note: The Harmonized Sales Tax (abbreviated as HST) is being charged based on percentages available at time of preparation of this textbook.
See Exercise 2A-4 step 17.

Note: After finishing Chapter 2A and Chapter 8, you can complete selected transactions from Chapter 2A, using the Perpetual INVENTORY module. See Challenge Exercise 08 C8-4 Luggage-PI.

The contents of this chapter are as follows:

- RECEIVABLES Module Overview 74
- Company Profile – Santos Luggage 74
- Exercise 2A-1 – Opening the RECEIVABLES Module 74
  Exercise 2A-2 – Displaying/Printing Customer Aged Report 77
  Exercise 2A-3 – Deleting Columns (Customizing) & Resizing the Sales Journal 81
  Exercise 2A-4 – Recording a Sales Quote 84
  Exercise 2A-5 – Revising the Sales Quote Form 89
  Exercise 2A-6 – Converting a Sales Quote into a Sales Order 91
  Exercise 2A-7 – Using the Daily Business Manager (DBM) 93
  Exercise 2A-8 – Using the Notes Feature of the DBM 94
  Exercise 2A-9 – Using the Business Performance Feature of the DBM 95
  Exercise 2A-10 – To Display the DBM 95
  Exercise 2A-11 – To Hide the DBM 95
  Exercise 2A-12 – To View the Pending Sales Orders Report 95
  Exercise 2A-13 – To Produce a Sales Invoice from a Sales Order 97
  Exercise 2A-14 – Journalizing a Sales Return 99
  Exercise 2A-15 – To Record a Receipt with Discount 103
  Exercise 2A-16 – To Journalize a Partial Receipt without a Discount 108
  Exercise 2A-17 – To Correct a Receipt Error 110
  Exercise 2A-18 – To Cancel a Posted Invoice 111
  Exercise 2A-19 – Viewing a Customer Ledger 113
  Exercise 2A-20 – Creating a Regular Customer Ledger & Invoice in the Sales
              Invoice Window 115
- Printing Reports When Needed 126
- Relevant Appendices, Part A 126
- Summary, Part A 127
- Before Moving On…, Part A 128
  Challenge Exercise 02 C2A-1, Clocks 129
  Challenge Exercise 02 C2A-2, Dog Walkers 130

RECEIVABLES Module Overview

This chapter Parts A (Basics) and B (Beyond Basics), using **Santos Luggage**, will guide you through recording transactions that affect the amount of money owed to the company, involving Accounts Receivable subledgers and the General Ledger.

Below are two main types of transactions recorded in the RECEIVABLES module with the corresponding journals:

1. Sales of merchandise or services   - Sales Quotes
    (Sales Journal)   - Sales Orders
    - Sales Invoices on credit (on account)
    - Sales Invoices paid by Cash/Cheque
    - Sales Invoices paid by Credit Card (Part B)

2. Receipts from customers   - Partial payment
    (Receipts Journal)   - Full payment with or without cash discounts
    - Deposits against a future invoice (Part B)

Slideshow 2A – RECEIVABLES Part A will help you understand how the RECEIVABLES module works. It will also give you a review of the GAAPs applicable to accounts receivable transactions. Run it now from the website: www.simplyaccounting2010.nelson.com under Student Resources.

Company Profile – Santos Luggage

Santos Luggage has been selling luggage and accessories, for over 10 years, to various stores (wholesalers) and has an outlet store at the back of the warehouse to sell slightly damaged items and samples to retail customers. The business has an acceptable level of receivables outstanding based on selling to large stores with cash discounts for prompt payment.

Santos Luggage uses the Periodic Inventory method for calculating ending inventory. The Perpetual Inventory method will be demonstrated in Chapter 8. A perpetual inventory Challenge Exercise, 08 C8-4 using Santos Luggage part A, is available after completing Chapter 8.

Assume that you are a part-time bookkeeper and work at Santos Luggage on a variable time schedule. Some days you work an hour; some days you work for three hours, and other days you work the whole day.

The owner, Mrs. Santos, has decided at this time not to use the Track Additional Transaction Details feature of the software.

Opening the RECEIVABLES Module

In a job situation, it is most likely that you would work on an accounting system that has already been set up. Santos Luggage's RECEIVABLES module is ready to use. In this chapter, you will access the RECEIVABLES module of Santos Luggage and enter transactions related to sales and receipts of payment from customers.

Exercise 2A-1 – Opening the RECEIVABLES Module

> **ⓘ**
> Review Exercise 1-2 if you need help to open a data file.

1 ➤   Refer to Exercise 1-1c to unzip the **02 2A Luggage-A.exe** file.

2 ➤   Start **Simply Accounting**.

3 ➤   At the **Select Company** window, click **Select an existing company** button, **OK**.

4 ➤ At the Simply Accounting - **Open Company** window, in the **Look in**: box, locate your student location drive and folder, **Simply Data 2010**. **Double-click** on the **Simply Data 2010** folder.

5 ➤ Double-click the [02 2A Luggage-A] folder. You will see a [Luggage-A.SAJ] folder and a [Luggage-A.SAI] file in the window. The image at the left of Luggage may be different depending on the configuration of your computer and the SAI may be in lower case.

6 ➤ Click on [Luggage-A.SAI]. The lower **File name** box will change to: Luggage-A.SAI. (.SAI may not display or will be in lower case.)

7 ➤ Click **Open** to open the **Luggage-A.SAI** file.

8 ➤ The Session date will be **Feb 29, 2016**. This is the date when the file was last used. Click **OK**.

Study the Santos Luggage Home window: **EXIT and SAVE button**

Fig. 2A-1: Santos Luggage-A, Enhanced Home window.

Notice that on the right side, in the Customer's window, the name of the customer, telephone number and current balance are displayed. You can click on each of the column headings to sort the column in ascending or descending order. If you right click the column, you will see 2 check boxes for Telephone or Balance. Clicking the check mark will hide the column. You can bring back the hidden column by right clicking a column that is not hidden and clicking the column that is hidden and it will display.

> The History symbol appears for some icons in the **PAYABLES**, **INVENTORY & SERVICES** and **EMPLOYEES & PAYROLL** modules. This means that these modules have not been set up for use and cannot be used to record entries.

9 ➤ On the left, click on the following modules: **PAYABLES, INVENTORY & SERVICES, EMPLOYEES AND PAYROLL**, **PROJECTS, BANKING** and **COMPANY**.

10 ➤ Click the **RECEIVABLES** module on the left.

Notice that the History symbol does not appear for **RECEIVABLES, BANKING, and COMPANY** modules. This signifies that these modules are set up and ready for recording entries. (See side note box.)

11 ➤ Remember to change the company name to include your name; e.g., **Santos Luggage, Oliver Megan**.

12 ➤ Display the Trial Balance to make sure it agrees with the values shown in Fig. 2A-2. From the Menu bar, click **Reports**, **Financials**, **Trial Balance**, leave the date at Feb 29, 2016, then **OK**.

13 ➤ Study the Santos Luggage Trial Balance next. (First, see side note box.)

The majority of the transactions in this chapter will affect Balance Sheet accounts:
1020 Bank Chequing Account,
1030 Visa Credit Card Bank Account,
1200 Accounts Receivable,
2630 HST Charged on Sales, and Income Statement accounts
4100 to 4200 Sales accounts.
The above accounts are shaded in Fig. 2A-2. When you have confirmed that the Trial Balance is correct, exit to the Home window.

Santos Luggage, Student's Name
Trial Balance As At Feb 29, 2016

Account		Debits	Credits
1020	Bank Chequing Account	19,436.86	-
1030	Visa Credit Card Bank Account	0.00	-
1200	Accounts Receivable	12,656.00	-
1300	Inventory	23,680.00	-
1320	Prepaid Supplies	712.00	-
1420	Office/Warehouse Furniture/Equip...	25,163.00	
1425	Accum. Amort Office/Ware Furn/E...	-	4,100.00
2200	Accounts Payable	-	12,151.00
2630	HST Charged on Sales	-	1,120.00
2640	HST Paid On Purchases	525.00	-
3100	Capital, Maria Santos	-	63,683.68
3160	Additional Investment	-	0.00
3180	Drawings, Maria Santos	2,200.00	-
4100	Sales	-	40,125.00
4150	Sales-Discounts	320.00	-
4200	Sales-Returns & Allowances	355.00	-
5010	Beginning Inventory	21,000.00	-
5040	Purchases	28,000.00	-
5050	Purchase Returns	-	1,000.00
5080	Purchase Discounts	-	335.00
5090	Ending Inventory	-	23,680.00
5310	Wages Expense	8,000.00	-
5320	Advertising Expense	432.00	-
5330	Bank Charges & Interest	95.00	-
5340	Credit Card Charges	34.30	-
5350	Rent Expense	800.00	-
5370	Bad Debt Expense	0.00	-
5410	Office/Warehouse Supplies Expense	216.00	-
5450	Rent Expense Warehouse	2,000.00	-
5460	Utility Expense	263.89	-
5550	Telephone Expense	305.63	-
		146,194.68	146,194.68

Fig. 2A-2: Santos Luggage-A Trial Balance.

14 ➤ Click **X** to return to the Home window.

To Display and Print the Customer Aged Report

To find out the status of your company receivables, you can display and/or print the Customer Aged Report. Simply Accounting groups receivables calculated from the date of the invoice to the current Session Date, and provides a list of accounts that are **Current**, **31 to 60** days overdue, **61 to 90** days overdue, and **91+** days overdue.

Simply provides two options: **Summary** and **Detail**. Your choice depends on the purpose for which you need the reports. At this point, if you wish to acquaint yourself with the company customers, their purchasing pattern, their balances, and what accounts are overdue, you would then select **Detail**. You will display/print both report options in this exercise.

> When displaying this report, it is important the Session Date is correct; otherwise, the aging will not be accurate.

Exercise 2A-2 – Displaying/Printing Customer Aged Report

The default Detail report does not display Terms. In this exercise, you will display a **Detail** Customer Aged Report and modify it to display terms. Later you will display a **Summary** report. Observe the type of information each report provides, so you can determine which type you will need in the future.

1 ➤ On the left, click on **RECEIVABLES**, at the right in **Reports**, click ▼, select **Customer Aged Detail**, click **Display**. You will see the Customer Aged Detail window. Notice that the display shows a dotted line on the left side of 91+. This means the report will print on 2 pages. (See side note box.)

2 ➤ Click the **Modify** icon, click on **Report Options**. Click **Include Terms**. All customers should be in blue, meaning they have been selected. Click **OK**. The report will display with the right side showing 2 columns (dotted lines) and a portion will print on the second page.

3 ➤ To reduce the size of the columns, double-click on the divider line at **Source, Date, Transaction Type, Total, Current, 31-60, 61 to 90** and **91+**. You may have to move some of the divider line columns manually to the left, until the page divider line disappears, to save printed paper. See Fig. 2A-3. This will happen with a number of reports.

(See side box with revised column widths used in the 2A-3 report.)

4 ➤ At the top left, at **As at:**, click ▼ and you will see a number of choices. Select **Today**. The Date should be **Feb 29, 2016**. (See side note box.)

If you are able to change the printer to display/print in landscape mode, click File. Printer Setup, (on some computers you click Properties) and click the appropriate boxes on your system. You will have to ask your faculty member on which of the appropriate items to click to print in landscape mode. This text assumes you are printing in portrait mode (default).

You should now see the Customer Aged Detail report. Note the information it provides. (See side note box beside Fig. 2A-3.)

Side notes

Depending on the type of printer that is connected to the computer or network, you may see two dotted lines. One dotted line on the right side of 61 to 90 and another on the right of 91+. This means the report will print on 2 pages. This will be adjusted in step 3.

61 to 90	91+

Columns shown on the report	
Column Name	Width
Source	19
Date	14
Terms	15
Transaction Type	17
Total Balance Owing	14
Current	14
31 to 60	14
61 to 90	11
91+	11

Do **NOT** Print now. To print this report with an earlier date, change the **Date** accordingly. This is useful when the session date was advanced and you want to produce a report for a previous period. Do not change the Feb 29, 2016 date.

Customer Aged Detail As at Feb 29, 2016

Source	Date	Terms	Transaction Type	Total	Current	31 to 60	61 to 90	91+
Havarah Leather Goods								
2253	Feb 26, 2016	2%/10, Net 30	Invoice	2,373.00	2,373.00	-	-	-
Total outstanding:				2,373.00	2,373.00	-	-	-
Royes Luggage Inc.								
2212	Jan 31, 2016	2%/10, Net 30	Invoice	1,017.00	1,017.00	-	-	-
2256	Feb 27, 2016	2%/10, Net 30	Invoice	1,243.00	1,243.00	-	-	-
Total outstanding:				2,260.00	2,260.00	-	-	-
Sandler Travel Stores								
2197	Jan 26, 2016	2%/10, Net 30	Invoice	4,407.00	-	4,407.00	-	-
Total outstanding:				4,407.00	-	4,407.00	-	-
Spiller Luggage Stores								
2230	Feb 20, 2016	2%/10, Net 30	Invoice	3,616.00	3,616.00	-	-	-
Total outstanding:				3,616.00	3,616.00	-	-	-
Total unpaid invoices:				12,656.00	8,249.00	4,407.00	-	-
Total deposits/prepaid order:				-	-	-	-	-
Total outstanding:				12,656.00	8,249.00	4,407.00	-	-

Fig. 2A-3: Customer Aged Detail Report (reduced column sizes).

> ⓘ The arrow is pointing at **Total deposits/prepaid order:** this refers to all customers.
>
> If there are no deposits paid by customers, deposits/prepaid order will display blanks (-).

DO NOT PRINT NOW. You will print this report at the end of the chapter.

5 ➤ To save these column settings and have the same report style available for another time, click the **Modify** icon, click **Report Options**, at the top, click ⬚Save Template⬚ button. In the Save Template as: type, ⬚Receivable Aged Detail on 1 page⬚, click **Save** and **OK**. This template displays.

You will see Fig 2A-3, with a header change identifying your saved report.

⬚ **Customer Aged Detail As at Feb 29, 2016 - Receivable Aged Detail on 1 page** ⬚

You can repeat these steps for other module reports as well.

6 ➤ To exit your template, click ⬚X⬚, and you will see the Fig 2A-3 report.

7 ➤ To display the Summary report click the ⬚Modify⬚ icon, click **Report Options**, at Report Type, click **Summary** (the customers should be blue), the date should be **Feb 29, 2016,** click **OK**. (See side note box.)

> ⓘ Do **NOT** print now. To display/print this report with an earlier date, you would change the **As at: Date** accordingly. This would be useful if the Session Date was advanced and you want to produce a report for a previous period. For now, do not change the Feb 29, 2016 date.

The Customer Aged Summary report displays. This report does not need to have the column sizes reduced.

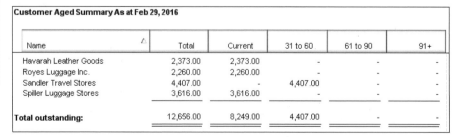

Customer Aged Summary As at Feb 29, 2016

Name	Total	Current	31 to 60	61 to 90	91+
Havarah Leather Goods	2,373.00	2,373.00	-	-	-
Royes Luggage Inc.	2,260.00	2,260.00	-	-	-
Sandler Travel Stores	4,407.00	-	4,407.00	-	-
Spiller Luggage Stores	3,616.00	3,616.00	-	-	-
Total outstanding:	12,656.00	8,249.00	4,407.00	-	-

Fig. 2A-4: Customer Aged Summary window.

You will notice that the **Detail** report shows the individual invoices owed by each customer, and that the **Summary** report shows only the total owed by each customer. You will print the Detail report at the end of the chapter.

8 ➤ **Exit** the Summary window, **exit** the Customer Aged Detail default window and return to the Home window.

9 ➤ To see your saved template report, at **Reports**, click ▼, select **Customer Aged Detail**, click **Display**. The Customer Aged Detail window will display with the right column displaying to print on 2 pages as shown before. Click the **Modify** icon, click **Report Options**. To the left of the **Save Template** button, click ▼, and select ⌐Receivable Aged Detail on 1 page⌐. Click **OK**.

10 ➤ Click **X** to **exit** your detail window and click **X** to **exit** to the Home window.

The RECEIVABLES Journals

The following types of transactions are entered in the three Sales journals:

Sales Quotes a form sent to a customer indicating the price of products or services as requested by the customer.

Sales Orders a confirmation of a commitment to purchase by a customer. A sales order can be issued without a previously issued sales quote. The product will be delivered at a later date, at which time a sales invoice will be issued.

Sales Invoices Pay Later a sale on account (credit), which may or may not be issued without a sales Quote and/or a Sales Order.

Sales Invoices Paid by a sale fully paid by cash, bank card, cheque or credit card.

Sales Invoices Adjustment an entry to record a return of goods or an adjustment to the sales price, also called a Credit Memo.

The following types of transactions are recorded in the **Receipts Journal**:

Receipts Payments (receipts) from customers on invoices, which may or may not be previously recorded.

Receipts can be:

1. Full payment of sales invoice on credit (Invoice-Pay Later) with or without cash discounts.

2. Partial payment of sales invoice on credit (Invoice-Pay Later) with or without partial cash discounts.

3. Deposits against a future sales invoice (Part B).

The Sales Journals

A customer may request a quote from a vendor (the selling company) to confirm/ guarantee sales prices. The vendor prepares a **sales quote,** which is recorded in the Sales Quote Journal. The sales quote is printed and sent to the customer. When you record the sales quote, neither the customer subledger nor any ledger account is updated with an accounting entry, as no sale has been made at this point. Although a sale is not made at this time, a record of the sales quote is useful for sales staff for follow-up purposes. Copies of printed quotes need to be kept because Simply does not provide a printed report of outstanding quotes.

When the customer confirms that the quote has been accepted, the quote can be converted into a **sales order**. At this point, the customer subledger and ledger accounts are still not updated with an accounting entry. The sales order is recorded in the company's **Sales Order Listing** and can be printed as a **Pending Sales Order** report. It is best to record the sales order to avoid the shipment getting missed in case there may be a delay in the delivery, or if the customer does not send a Purchase Order form. The Sales Order can also be displayed in the Daily Business Manager detail. See Exercise 2A-7.

When the goods/services are delivered, the sales order is converted into a **sales invoice**. At this time, an accounting entry is made and the sales transaction is posted to the corresponding ledger accounts and customer subledgers. (See side note box.)

Sales Quote ⟶ Sales Order ⟶ Sales Invoice

> ℹ️
> When a sales quote is converted into a sales order, the information on the **sales quote** is automatically entered into the **sales order** window. Likewise, sales order information is entered into the **sales invoice** window upon conversion.

In the Sales Journal, the following options are available for **Payment Method:**

Option	Payment Method	Linked with account
Pay Later	on credit	Accounts Receivable
Cash	when paid in cash	Bank account
Cheque	when paid by cheque	Bank account
Bank Debit Cd	when paid by ATM (debit card)	Bank Debit Card
Visa Credit	when paid by credit card	Bank Credit Card account

When you record entries in the Sales Journals, you enter only one part of the entry. The program knows you are in the RECEIVABLES module and will debit or credit the appropriate account (Receivable or other account shown above) and appropriate taxes, as required.

For example: If you had recorded a credit sale (invoice #239) transaction for a $70.00 Laptop Back Pak to J. Tang, the entry in the General Journal (double entry) would have looked similar to the following.

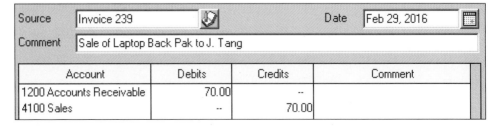

Source	Invoice 239			Date	Feb 29, 2016	
Comment	Sale of Laptop Back Pak to J. Tang					

Account	Debits	Credits	Comment
1200 Accounts Receivable	70.00	--	
4100 Sales	--	70.00	

To properly enter this type of transaction in the RECEIVABLE module, you need to enter the quantity, **credit** amount (base price) and account, which in this case is the 4100 Sales account, as shown next.

Quantity	Order	Back Order	Unit	Item Description	Base Price	Discount (%)	Price	Amount	Tax	Account
1			each	Laptop Back Pak	70.00		70.00	70.00	HS	4100 Sales

In the RECEIVABLE module, Simply will automatically debit the 1200 Accounts Receivable Account. *Note*: You cannot enter a credit sale transaction in the General Journal (or any transaction affecting 1200 Accounts Receivable (control account)), once you have activated (added customer history) and are using the RECEIVABLES module.

Exercise 2A-3 – Deleting Columns (Customizing) & Resizing the Sales Journal

1 ➤ Right click on the **Sales Invoice** icon. Notice the selections. Select **Create Invoice**. The Sales Invoice Journal will appear.

Study the basic format of the Sales Journal - Sales Invoice as shown next.

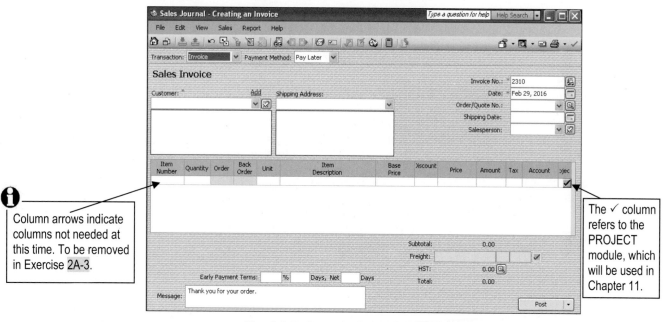

Column arrows indicate columns not needed at this time. To be removed in Exercise 2A-3.

The ✓ column refers to the PROJECT module, which will be used in Chapter 11.

Fig. 2A-5: Sample Sales Invoice window.

Customizing the Sales Journal Window

The **Item Number** column is not used when the company records sales or purchases of merchandise using the **periodic** inventory system. The other system, **perpetual** inventory, discussed in Chapter 8, requires detailed records of goods (merchandise) being sold or purchased and will use the **Item Number** column.

Santos Luggage in this chapter uses the **periodic** inventory system. You need to customize the Sales Journal window to include only columns for information you will enter in the Sales Journal.

Exercise 2A-3 will show you how to hide the **Item Number** and **PROJECTS** columns (see arrows in Fig. 2A-5) to customize the Sales Journal window for Santos Luggage. You may use the same procedure to hide any other column that you do not wish to appear on your sales journal. For example; a **service** company would not use **Ship Date**, **Order**, **Back Order**, and **Unit**. A service company would hide these columns to streamline invoices.

Follow the steps below to hide the **Item Number** and **PROJECTS** columns.

2 ➤ Click the **Customize Journal** icon and the Customize Journals window will appear, click on **Columns**. Form settings styles will be shown after step 8.

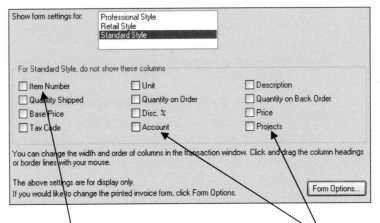

3 ➤ Click the **Item Number** box. A ✓ will appear and the **Account** name will fade.

4 ➤ You will also not need the **PROJECTS** field. Click the **PROJECTS** box and a ✓ will appear. (See side note box.)

5 ➤ On the left side of the window, click on the ➕ at **Sales Orders**, then **Columns**. (The author has completed steps 3 and 4 for you, as well as for the Retail and Professional styles.) You could also, in the left pane, select **Quotes**, then click **Columns**. The author has completed steps 2 and 3 to not display the Item Number and **PROJECTS** columns.

> ℹ️ Notice that the **Item** and **Allo** columns no longer display on the customized window.

6 ➤ Click **OK** when you are finished. The column area will now display as follows: (See step 7 to change the column widths.)

Quantity	Order	Back Order	Unit	Item Description	Base Price	Discount	Price	Amount	Tax	Account	

Fig. 2A-6a: Customized Sales Journal window (before sizing).

7 ➤ In order to show more information in the Description and Acct fields, type the information as shown in Fig. 2A-6b. Place your mouse over a column heading dividing line between 2 columns (e.g., Description), then use the windows icon to drag the column left or right to resize the columns to the approximate size as shown. This information will be deleted in step 8, but the column widths will remain the same size.

Quantity	Order	Back Order	Unit	Item Description	Base Price	Discount (%)	Price	Amount	Tax	Account
-100			each	Suitcase w/w regular size	23.00		23.00	-2,300...	HS	4200 Sales- Returns & Allowan...

Fig. 2A-6b: Customized Sales Journal window (after sizing).

8 ➤ When you have the columns to this approximate size, click the and you will see the following.

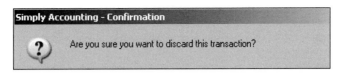

9 ➤ Select **Yes** to return to a blank invoice. The column sizes remain as you have set them up.

Sales Invoice Styles

1 ➤ From the menu bar, click **View, Invoice Style** and you will see that there are 3 invoice template styles available.

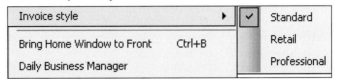

The headings that will appear on a Standard Invoice window are:

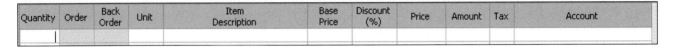

Quantity	Order	Back Order	Unit	Item Description	Base Price	Discount (%)	Price	Amount	Tax	Account

2 ➤ Click on **Retail**. You will see that the Order and Back Order columns are not displayed.

Unit	Item Description	Quantity	Base Price	Discount (%)	Price	Amount	Tax	Account

The **Retail** template could be used in a business that does not use Sales Quotes or Orders.

3 ➤ Click on **View, Invoice Style** and click on **Professional**. You will see that the Order and Back Order columns from the Standard template and Item, Quantity, Unit, Base Price, Disc % and Price columns are not displayed from the Retail template.

Item Description	Amount	Tax	Account

The **Professional** template could be used in a business that sells services (Accounting, real estate, legal, etc., and does not sell and list items or units).

In this text we will use the **Standard** style, and have modified the columns to not display Item and Allocation.

4 ➤ Click on **View, Invoice Style** and click on **Standard**.

5 ➤ **Exit** to the Home window.

Entering Transactions in the RECEIVABLES Module

A common question asked is, "When should transactions be entered?" The answer depends on the volume of transactions. Smaller volumes (10 to 20 transactions a week) may be entered weekly, anything more than 10 a day should probably be done on a daily basis.

Another factor is the type of transaction. In general, you would like your accounting records to be up to date, especially when it concerns customers; therefore, sales quotes, orders, invoices, receipts and adjustments (including sales returns and discounts) must be entered with the original date of the transaction in order to record cash discounts and full payment dates properly. If the invoice date is not recorded properly, the aging of invoices will not be accurate.

Recording a Sales Quote

One thing to remember about a Sales Quote is that a sales transaction has not taken place; therefore, a quote does not affect the company accounts. The quote is a record of an inquiry — with no commitment on the part of the customer to buy.

When a company sells items to a business that will resell the items to others, the buying company pays HST on these goods.

Exercise 2A-4 – Recording a Sales Quote

---

1 ➤ Change the Session date to **Mar 01, 2016**.

Sales Quotes ▼

There are 4 different ways to create a Quote. The same choices apply to Sales Orders, Sales Invoices or Receipts.

a) Right click on the Sales Quote icon, select Create Quote.
b) At the Sales Quote icon, click the ▼, notice the 3 choices, select Create Quote.
c) Click the Sales Quote icon to go directly to the Sales Quote window.
d) At the Sales Invoice icon, click the ▼, notice the 3 choices, select Create Invoice, at Transaction click the ▼, select Quote.

This text will use method c) to Create Sales Quotes, Sales Orders and Sales Invoices.

2 ➤ Click the **Sales Quotes** icon. The Sales Quote Journal will appear.

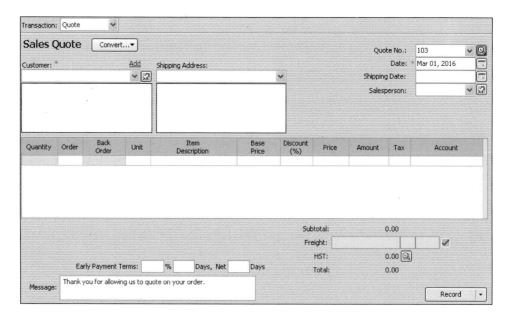

Study this transaction:

Mar 01, 2016 Luggage 4U has requested a quote for the following items that are to be picked up by their van on March 3. Their purchasing manager was very specific that the goods must be received by March 3 or the order will not be accepted. Their delivery van driver will pick up the quote before 2:30 p.m. today. Your manager has asked you to complete the Sales Quote, as the items requested are in stock and have been put aside for this customer:

5 Laptop Back Paks at $70.00 each
8 Suitcase w/w (with wheels) large size at $62.00 each
9 Suitcase w/w regular size at $56.00 each

Add HST at 13% on all items. Terms are 2/10, net 30.

To record the quote, complete the following steps:

Note: The Red * refers to required information in the window.

3 ➤ Customer

Click the ▼ arrow to display the list of customers to choose from. Notice that the customers are displayed in alphabetical order and require no customer numbers. You may have to move ▲ or ▼ to see more customers. Click to select **Luggage 4U**. (Also see side note.)

The address details for Luggage 4U are automatically shown in the Customer and Shipping Address fields.

> **ⓘ**
> You can also press the first letter of the company name. Simply will display the customer list with the names beginning with this letter.
>
> Click the yellow stick pin [📌] to enter sales information for the same customer on the next invoice. You do not have to choose the customer again until you need to enter information for a new customer.

4 ➤ Press the [Tab] key once to move to the yellow stick pin, (see side note box) and [Tab] again to move to the **Shipping Address** field. When you choose a customer in step 4, the Shipping Address field changes to:

| \<Mailing Address\> | ▼ |

If you click the ▼ the field can be changed to Ship-to Address. The shipping address could be inserted here if the goods are being ordered by a Head Office and the goods are to be shipped to one of the stores. This feature will be demonstrated in Exercise 2A-20. Leave the choice as Mailing Address.

5 ➤ Shipping Address

Pressing the [Tab] key moves the cursor to each line of the address. If there were no changes in this field you could use the mouse to click the next field, **Quote No.**

6 ➤ Quote No.

The number **103** is displayed, which is the number of the next quote in Santos Luggage company's records. [Tab] once to move to the Select Order or Quote button [🔍]. (This will be explained in Exercise 2A-6.) You will learn how to insert the automatic numbering in Chapter 4. [Tab] again to move to the Date field.

7 ➤ Date

This is the date the quote is given to the customer. The date should be **Mar 01, 2016**. This date is important because quotes, with sale items, may expire within a set number of days from the quote date. [Tab] [Tab] to move to the **Shipping Date** field.

HST refers to the **Harmonized Goods and Services Tax** applied by the federal government to goods and services sold.

HST rate of 13% is used in this text and reflected in the solutions. This rate, however, may have changed since publication date. When on the job, be sure to use the appropriate HST rates.

For additional information on HST, GST and PST, refer to Chapter 15, *Taxes*.

The codes **HS, and HI** are created by the company and may be different for each company. A company may make up any two-letter combination and wording for a tax code.

8 ➤	**Shipping Date**	This is the date agreed upon that the goods will be shipped to the customer. Use the calendar icon and change the date to **Mar 3, 2016**. [Tab] [Tab] to move to the **Salesperson** field.
9 ➤	**Salesperson**	You will not use this field in these exercises. See Appendix AC, *Adding a Salesperson's Name to an Invoice* at www.simplyaccounting2010.nelson.com under Student Resources, for information on the steps you would need to complete to have this field available. Not all companies would make use of this field. [Tab] [Tab] to move to the **Quantity** field.
10 ➤	**Quantity**	Although you stop at this field, this column will be used when goods are shipped to the customer, [Tab].
11 ➤	**Order**	Type **5,** [Tab].
	Back Order	The Back Order column is skipped on a Sales Quote or a Sales Order. It is used when a sales invoice is being produced and some of the goods ordered by the customer (part of the order) are not available. The goods will be shipped when stock arrives.
12 ➤	**Unit**	Type **each,** [Tab].
13 ➤	**Description**	Type **Laptop Back Paks,** [Tab].
14 ➤	**Base Price**	This field represents the price before any sale discounts are given to a customer. Type **70.00,** [Tab].
	Discount %	This field would be a sale discount percentage and does not represent a discount for paying an invoice within the discount terms. This field will be explained in Exercise 2B-33. [Tab].
15 ➤	**Price**	This field represents the price after any sale discounts from the Discount % column, [Tab].
16 ➤	**Amount**	This field represents the calculated amount from fields **Order** times **Price**. [Tab] to accept 350.00.
17 ➤	**Tax**	Press [Enter]. A list of Tax Codes and information is displayed (see below).

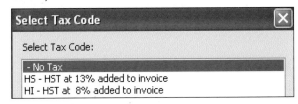

The Harmonized Sales Tax (abbreviated HST) is being charged based on percentages available at time of preparation of this textbook.

No tax   This includes items that are HST-exempt (No HST charged), HST Non-Taxable (No HST charged) and HST taxable (HST with a rate of 0%).

HS   Price of goods **plus** HST. The HST is not included in the selling price and must be added to the selling price of the items; e.g., Selling price of $200.00 plus 13% HST of the price ($26.00). Taxes total $26.00.

HI   This code applies on a sale where HST at a reduced rate of 8% is charged. (An example of this is when you buy or sell insurance. HST at 8% Sales Tax is charged.) The HI code will be used in Chapter 3.

---

18 ➤   Select **HS**. (You may also type hs) This means the selling price does not include HST.

19 ➤   **Account**   Press `Enter`. The G/L chart of accounts should be displayed. You may have to scroll using `▼` or `▲` to see more accounts. Simply is looking for an account to credit. Select account **4100 Sales** by double-clicking on it. You can also type **4** and the selection window changes to accounts beginning with 4. If needed, you could then type **2** and the account window would change to accounts beginning with 42. `Tab`.

20➤   Enter the next two items on the quote. The tax code and the sales account will be the same for all items (w/w means, *with wheels*).

   8   **Suitcase w/w large size at $62.00 each**
   9   **Suitcase w/w regular size in red colour at $56.00 each**

Note the **Description** field when you type "Suitcase w/w regular size **in red colour**." Simply will word wrap the required information to the next line(s) if the information does not fit on one line. You can use the ⊕ icon and drag left or right to resize the column as required. (See side note box.)

21➤   Remove the words: **in red colour**.

Comments box. This field displays a variety of messages you want customers to see on quotes, orders and invoices. Note the default for quotes. You will be shown how to enter other default comments in Chapter 4.

The **Terms** boxes should display **2.00%, 10 days, Net 30 days**, the terms previously agreed upon with the customer. If the terms are different from the default, click the appropriate box, and change as required.

   Freight   Santos Luggage does not charge for delivery; therefore, this field is not used.

22 ➤   **Shipped by**   On the **icon** bar, click 🖃 the **Track Shipments** icon.

23 ➤   Click the `▼` arrow to display a list of shippers. Select **Your Vehicle** (the customer's vehicle).

   Tracking Number   This will be blank because there is no need to track the shipment, since it is being picked up by the customer's vehicle. The software can track shipments; however, this text does not provide an exercise for tracking shipments on the Internet. Click **OK**.

   You will notice that the Shipping information does not display in the window. It prints on the printed Quote.

When you have completed entering the above information, the window display should look as follows:

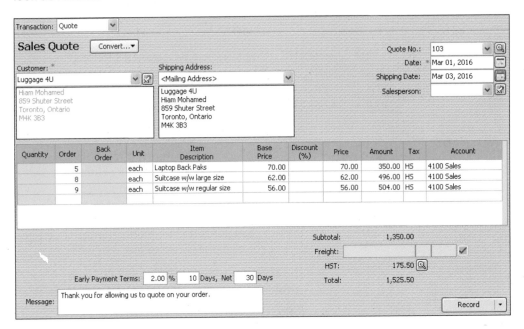

If your business uses pre-printed forms bearing the company name and/or logo and other relevant information, you would click the 🖨 from the Quote window. The information being printed on the Pre-printed form will look similar to Fig. 2A-7.

24 ➤   To display the Quote using the Custom Simply Form document, click on 🔲 . You should see the following error message.

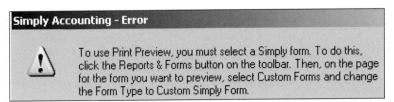

The settings for the Simply Custom Forms have not been selected.

25 ➤   Click **OK** to return to the Quote window.

Do not record; continue with Exercise 2A-5.

```
Santos Luggage-A, Student's Name
635 Semple Avenue
Toronto, Ontario M9L 1V5                              103

                                                     Mar 01, 2016

                                                     1 of 1


Luggage 4U                        Luggage 4U
Hiam Mohamed                      Hiam Mohamed
859 Shuter Street                 859 Shuter Street
Toronto, Ontario                  Toronto, Ontario
M4K 3B3                           M4K 3B3

    5       each      Laptop Back Paks         HS    70.00    350.00
    8       each      Suitcase w/w large size  HS    62.00    496.00
    9       each      Suitcase w/w regular size HS   56.00    504.00

                      Subtotal                               1,350.00

                      HS- HST at 13% added to invoice
                      HST                                      175.50


                      Terms: 2%/10, Net 30


Santos Luggage-A, Student's Name HST: #V8956325
Shipped by Your Vehicle.
Thank you for allowing us to quote on your order.           1,525.50
```

Fig. 2A-7: Sales Quote information printed on pre-printed forms (see side box).

Revising the Sales Quote Form

You can use Windows features such as Cut (selects text inside one column at a time), Copy and Paste from the Edit menu of the Sales Journal window (see side note box). You can cut, copy and paste text from one Simply window to another, or from a Simply window to another program (e.g., word processing). It will save time in typing information.

Using the Edit menu you can Insert or Remove a line in the Sales Quote, Sales Order or Sales Invoice.

In the following exercise you will use the Insert and Remove feature for the information in a row within a Quote.

Exercise 2A-5 – Revising the Sales Quote Form

The manager has asked you to move the regular size suitcase to the middle line of the invoice before you record the quote.

1 ➤ Click **8** in the Order field, then click **Edit, Insert Line**. You may see the following error message.

ℹ️ Pre-printed forms will normally have the company name and address printed on the form. The information shown in Fig. 2A-7 indicates the company name printed by Simply. If you are required to print the forms in the lab/classroom, the name printed by Simply will allow you to identify your printouts in class.

ℹ️ **Edit Notes...**
To Cut, Copy and Paste: Select (highlight) the text with the left mouse button. Choose **Edit** from the top menu of the window and then select either Cut (to remove) or Copy. The text is temporarily copied to the Windows clipboard, and can be retrieved using the Paste feature. Reposition the cursor, click **Edit**, then **Paste** to place the text at the new cursor location.

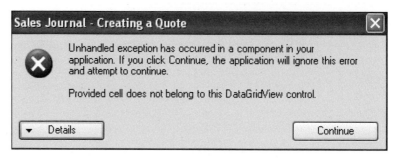

Ignore the message. Click **Continue**. A blank line appears as the second line of the invoice. The new line can be entered at the top, or between any items on the invoice. If you are not replacing any item, you could enter the item(s) you want as the second sales item.

2 ➤ **Retype** or cut and paste appropriate information, for the regular suitcases as the 2nd item.

3 ➤ Click **9** in the bottom item. Click the **Edit, Remove line** function, from the menu bar, to remove the bottom sales item. You will see the same error message. Click **Continue.** You could press the ⌐Delete⌐ key to remove the sales information from each of the columns for the regular size suitcase. (See side note box.)

The Quote information area should now resemble Fig. 2A-8.

Quantity	Order	Back Order	Unit	Description	Base Price	Disc. %	Price	Amount	Tax	Acct
	5		each	Laptop Back Paks	70.00		70.00	350.00	G	4100 Sales
	9		each	Suitcase w/w regular size	56.00		56.00	504.00	G	4100 Sales
	8		each	Suitcase w/w large size	62.00		62.00	496.00	G	4100 Sales

Fig. 2A-8: Revised Quote information area.

4 ➤ Make corrections to any fields, if necessary.

5 ➤ To display the Sales Journal entry created by this quote, click **Report**, then **Display Sales Journal Entry**.

The window should display:

Sales Journal Entry Mar 01, 2016 (J1)

Account Number	Account Description	Debits	Credits

There is no data to report.

See the Mini-guide at the end of Chapter 2B, before the Glossary. This form will help you identify when entries are recorded in the RECEIVABLES module of Simply and which journal they are recorded in. You can find the document at Appendix CD-V, *Mini-Guides Receivables—Payables* at www.simplyaccounting2010.nelson.com under Student Resources.

6 ➤ **Exit** from the Sales Journal Entry window.

7 ➤ Click the [🖊 Record] button. Notice that the confirmation window says Transaction recorded successfully, but it does not indicate a Journal entry #.

There is no entry made in the company records, because a sale has not taken place. At this point, the customer has requested a formal price quote and will decide whether to buy the goods at the quoted price. Santos Luggage must now wait for the customer to make a decision.

More Edit Notes...

To Move a Whole Column to a New Position:
Click and hold down the left mouse button positioned on a column heading. Drag the column to a new position, then release the mouse button.

Restoring the Original Column Width and Positions:
There is no selection to restore the window back after a column is moved. If you use the View menu, Restore feature it will return the window to the original default column size.

8 ➤ Click **OK** and **Exit** from the Sales Journal-Quote window to the Home window.

Converting a Sales Quote into a Sales Order

When you record a Sales Quote, it is recorded in the Sales Quote database and it will remain there until it is converted into a Sales Order or it is deleted. When converting a Sales Quote into a Sales Order, the details are automatically forwarded to the Sales Order, but may be revised.

Remember that a **Sales Order** does NOT affect the company books because no goods were shipped. The order, when recorded, goes to a Sales Order listing.

Exercise 2A-6 – Converting a Sales Quote into a Sales Order

The Purchasing Manager of Luggage 4U confirmed, by fax, to your Sales Manager the approval of Quote #103. To change the sales quote into a sales order, complete the following steps:

Sales Orders ▼

1 ➤ Advance the Session date to **Mar 02, 2016**.

2 ➤ At **Sales Orders**, click the ▼ to display the 3 choices. Click the **Create Order** item, or click the **Sales Order** icon. The Sales Journal – Creating an Order will appear.

3 ➤ **Order No.** Click the **Order No.** finder 🔍 icon.

The sales quote is recorded in the Sales Quote database of the program and cannot be printed as a report. You will be able to see a list of Quotes as shown in Exercise 2A-6. The Sales Quote does NOT get posted to the General Ledger.

(See side note box.)

You could also open the Sales Quote at 103 and click the ▼ | Convert...▼ | to convert the Sales Quote to a Sales Order.

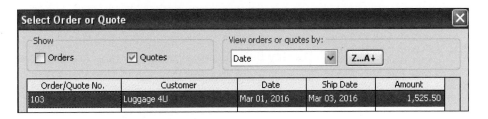

Order/Quote No.	Customer	Date	Ship Date	Amount
103	Luggage 4U	Mar 01, 2016	Mar 03, 2016	1,525.50

This window will display details about previously recorded customer quotes and orders for all customers. Quote **103** is the only outstanding quote at this time.

4 ➤ **View orders or quotes by**: Click the ▼ and you will see the different columns the report can be sorted by. Note the report can also be sorted in ascending or descending order.

5 ➤ Click **Select** or double-click **103** to accept the Quote.

The Sales Journal – Creating an Order window fills with the details from the Sales Quote.

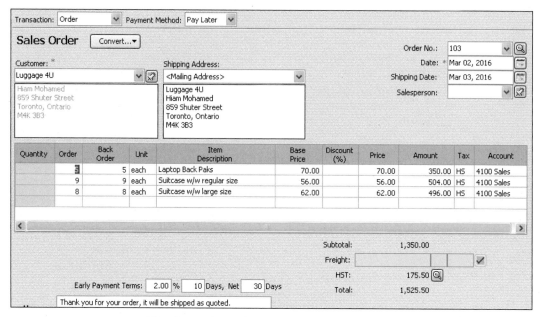

Fig. 2A-9: Sales Order window – filled in.

Back Order   The Back Order column shows **5**, **9 & 8** respectively, the quantity ordered. This means that 5, 9 and 8 of the specified items are backordered (not yet shipped since this is only a Sales Order form). The goods are due to be shipped to the customer on March 3, 2016. Do NOT change values in this column. Simply will keep track of the amounts.

All other details of the order are the same as entered in the quote. At this point, the quote could be revised. For example, the buyer might decide to increase or decrease the quantity. The price could also be changed if the final selling price was lower. Remember that a quote is a commitment by the seller to provide a product or service at the agreed upon price for the period of the quote (usually shown in **Ship Date**). If there is a price hike after the sales quote is issued and before the Ship Date, the buyer is protected from price increases. However, a price lower than the price quoted is to the advantage of the buyer, so it can be changed without consulting the buyer. For now, do not change any fields.

6 ➤ To display the Sales Journal entry created by this Sales Order, click **Report, Display Sales Journal Entry**. The window should display:

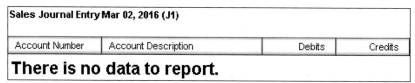

Account Number	Account Description	Debits	Credits

There is no data to report.

Similar to the Sales Journal Entry window for the sales quote, an entry to the company books has not been created, because a sale has not yet taken place.

To correct a Sales Order, refer to Chapter 13, Exercise 13-3.

7 ➤ **Exit** from this window by clicking the ☒ button.

8 ➤ Make corrections to the sales order, if necessary.

9 ➤ Click the 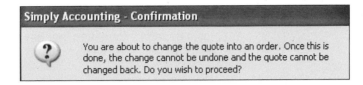 button. This records the sales order in the Pending Sales Order listing and does NOT post to the General ledger. Do not print the order.

Study the message that appears when you click the Record button:

> **Simply Accounting - Confirmation**
>
> (?) You are about to change the quote into an order. Once this is done, the change cannot be undone and the quote cannot be changed back. Do you wish to proceed?

10 ➤ Click **Yes** to proceed. The Confirmation window says the Transaction was recorded successfully, but it does not indicate a Journal Entry #, as a sale has not taken place. Click **OK**.

11 ➤ **Exit** from the Sales Order window.

Daily Business Manager

The Daily Business Manager (DBM) [DBM icon] is located **on the icon tool bar**. The Daily Business Manager is a business tool that can be displayed when you start Simply (the default setting), and/or when you advance the session date, or when you need to display the window. This window is very helpful for managing customer receivables in a business setting. You will see that outstanding Sales Orders are displayed in this window.

Exercise 2A-7 – Using the Daily Business Manager (DBM)

---

1 ➤ Change the Session date to **Mar 3, 2016**.

2 ➤ Click [DBM icon] the **Daily Business Manager** icon and the DBM will appear as shown next.

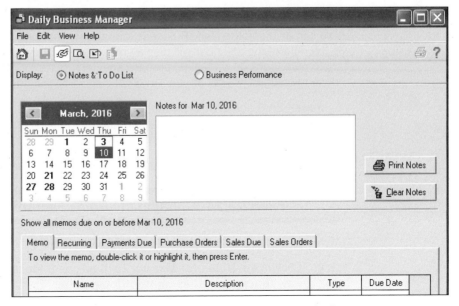

Fig. 2A-10: Daily Business Manager window.

The lower window will list reminders about tasks you need to do, for the next 7 days, relating to the various tabs shown (Memo, Recurring, Payments Due, etc.).

The **Reminder** date Mar 10, 2016 for all tabs is calculated from the **Session** date, Mar 03, 2016. *Note:* Sales Quotes will not display.

3 ➤ Click each of the tabs in the lower-half of the window.

> **Memo** Lists general information that has been placed in the customer file. This will be explained later in this chapter.

> **Recurring** Lists all recurring entries that are due within the next 7 days. Santos Luggage has not used recurring entries.

> **Payments Due** Shows all invoices that must be paid on or before Mar 10, 2016. This would include invoices for which discounts are available, if paid within the terms agreed upon (e.g., 2/10, net 30) when purchased. There are no items listed: Santos Luggage does not use the PAYABLES module.

> **Purchase Orders** Shows all purchase orders that are due to be shipped to your company on or before Mar 10, 2016. Santos Luggage does not use the PAYABLES module.

> **Sales Due** This tab lists overdue sales invoices and sales invoices that are due to be paid within the next 7 days.
>
> If you double-click on an invoice, you will be taken to the Receipts Journal. **Exit** from the Receipts Journal window to discard the receipt. (See side note box.)

> **Sales Orders** The display shows the Outstanding Order #103 for Luggage 4U. If you double-click any column, you will be taken to a filled-in Sales Invoice. It is assumed that you want to record a sale. **Exit** from the Sales Invoice window to discard the invoice.

> Sandler Travel Stores' invoice was due to be paid on Feb 25, 2016 and is now 6 days overdue. Someone from your company will have to contact this customer to follow up the outstanding invoice.

By studying the information in the various tabs, you may find items that may need to be followed up.

You can also use the Daily Business Manager to manage your daily tasks. The window to the right of the calendar will display messages that can be used to remind you to call customers, back up data files, prepare special reports for management, etc. However, those messages will not appear automatically. You will need to make notes for yourself.

Exercises 2A-8 and 2A-9 illustrate how you can use the Daily Business Manager to view outstanding invoices, orders, and memo notes to assist employees, and provide graphical analysis for management.

To use the **Notes** feature, follow the steps in the next exercise.

Exercise 2A-8 – Using the Notes Feature of the DBM

1 ➤ In the calendar on the left side of your screen, click **8** (Mar 08, 2016).

2 ➤ Click in the **Notes for Mar 08, 2016** box near the top. Type **Prepare draft newspaper advertisement for local paper.**

3 ➤ In the calendar on the left, click **March 10**. Type **Finalize newspaper advertisement for local paper**.

4 ➤ Click **March 8**. The previous message you typed is displayed.

Exercise 2A-9 – Using the Business Performance Feature of the DBM

---

1 ➤   **Display**   Click the ⦿ **Business Performance** item.

There are three Business Performance Measurements (ratios) shown in the top portion. A graphical representation of the measurements is shown in the lower portion. There are no entries made to this point; therefore, the graphs are a straight line.

2 ➤   Click the **Daily Business Manager Options** 🔍 icon. Click the **Business Performance** tab.

3 ➤   Management may like to see different measurements graphically. To set up a new measurement in the left window, click **Sales (Past 7 Days)**, click **Select >**, then **OK**. It is now moved to the right side pane. In Exercise 2B-25, you will return to this Business Performance window to see the graphical display.

4 ➤   To exit, click X to return to the Home window.

Exercise 2A-10 – To Display the DBM

---

1 ➤   In the menu bar, click **Setup, User preferences, View** in the left-side pane, and at Daily Business Manager, click **At Start Up**, to display the ✓. Notice the other choice is after Changing the Session Date, which would be appropriate in a business setting. Click **OK**. The module is displayed the next time you start up (open) the company file.

From this point on, it is assumed that the DBM will not display each time you open the company. See Exercise 2A-11. Your faculty member may ask you to display the DBM each time you open the file.

Exercise 2A-11 – To Hide the DBM

As noted in Exercise 2A-10, we do not want the DBM to appear each time we open the company file.

1 ➤   From the Home window, click **Setup**, **User Preferences**, **View**, at Daily Business Manager, click **At Start Up** to remove the ✓. Click **OK**. The DBM will be hidden next time you open the file.

To View the Pending Sales Orders Report

ℹ️ This report can also be viewed in **Detail** on two pages, before changing column widths. This report also lists the description and quantity of items that are backordered. The item column in the Detail report refers to **Perpetual** inventory data and will not contain any information for Santos Luggage.

You need to view and/or print the Pending Sales Orders Report regularly to ensure that no sales order is missed.

Exercise 2A-12 – To View the Pending Sales Orders Report

---

1 ➤   From the **Home** window, click **Report Centre**, the left pane should be **Receivables,** click **Pending Sales Orders Summary by Customer**, click the blue **Modify this report**. Change the **Date** to **Mar 10, 2016, OK**. This report will assist management in displaying all outstanding (pending) sales orders due within 1 week from the current Mar 03, 2016 session date. (See side note box.)

Orders with shipping dates due later than the date specified (Mar 10, 2016) will not display.

Pending Sales Orders Summary by Customer As at Mar 10, 2016			
Sales Order Number	Sales Order Date	Ship Date	Amount Original Order
Luggage 4U			
103	Mar 02, 2016	Mar 03, 2016	1,525.50
			1,525.50
			1,525.50

2 ➤ **Exit** to the Home window.

IMPORTANT: BACK UP your data after every work session and update your logbook.

Producing a Sales Invoice from a Sales Order

It is common practice to print multi-copy sales invoices and/or sales orders for distribution to the customer and various departments in the company as illustrated in Fig. 2A-11.

Santos Luggage
635 Semple Avenue
Toronto, Ontario M9L 1V5
Phone: (416)698-3333 ✦ Fax (416)698-3345

INVOICE
2310

Date: Mar 03, 2016

SOLD TO
Luggage 4U
Hiam Mohamed
859 Shuter Street
Toronto, Ontario M4K 3B3

SHIP TO
Luggage 4U
Hiam Mohamed
859 Shuter Street
Toronto, Ontario M4K 3B3

Re: Order No. 103

Business No.: V8956325

SHIP	ORDER	B/O	UNIT	DESCRIPTION	TAX	PRICE	AMOUNT
5	5			Laptop Back Paks	HS	70.00	$ 350.00
9	9			Suitcase w/w regular size	HS	56.00	504.00
8	8			Suitcase w/w large size	HS	62.00	496.00
				Subtotal			1,350.00
				HS- HST at 13% added to invoice			
				HST			175.50
				Terms: 2%/10, Net 30.			

Shipped by Your Vehicle.
Thank you for your order

TOTAL   **$ 1,525.50**

| Copy 1 Customer |
| Copy 2 Accounting |
| Copy 3 Sales |
| Copy 4 Packing Slip |

Fig. 2A-11: Sales Invoice Form and Distribution Schedule.

Exercise 2A-13 – To Produce a Sales Invoice from a Sales Order

Sales Invoices ▼

All goods ordered by Luggage 4U on Sales Order #103 are ready to be shipped. To record the sale, complete the following steps:

1 ➤ Right click the **Sales Invoices** icon, click **Create Invoice**. The Sales Journal-Sales Invoice window appears.

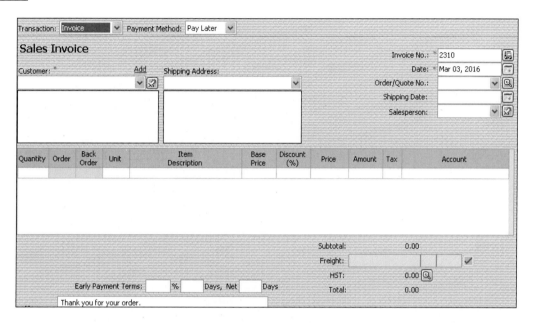

Transaction: Do NOT change the default from Invoice.

2 ➤ **Order/Quote No**. Click the **Finder** 🔍 icon.

As in Exercise 2A-6, this window will display details about previously recorded customer quotes and orders for all customers. Order 103 is the only outstanding order. Note: you may need to click the ☐ Orders field to see the Sales Order.

3 ➤ Click **Select** or double-click to accept Order #103. The Sales Invoice window fills with the details from Sales Order #103 recorded previously.

4 ➤ **Payment Method**   Click the ▼ arrow and 5 choices appear:

- *Pay Later*   for a sale on credit.
- *Cash*   used when cash is received as payment.
- *Cheque*   used when a cheque is received as payment.
- *Bank Debit Cd* used if a Bank Debit card is received as payment.
- *Visa Credit*   used if the Visa Credit Card is used as payment. This is the credit card that Santos Luggage accepts.

Because it is on account (on credit), select **Pay Later**, [Tab].

The full order is ready to ship. You can complete the invoice in one of two ways:

a. If you clicked in the **Quantity** column you would enter the quantity of each item shipped, `Tab` and continue entering the quantity shipped. Note that the Back Order column changes to blank because there are no goods backordered.

b. If you click the [icon] (Fill backordered quantities) icon Simply will fill in the Quantity columns for you. This would be used when all the items ordered are filled and there are no back orders.

5 ➤ Click the [icon] icon and the middle portion window will change to the following. The quantity field has been filled in and the Back Order field is blank, as the goods are being shipped.

Quantity	Order	Back Order	Unit	Item Description	Base Price	Discount (%)	Price	Amount	Tax	Account
5	5		each	Laptop Back Paks	70.00		70.00	350.00	HS	4100 Sales
9	9		each	Suitcase w/w regular size	56.00		56.00	504.00	HS	4100 Sales
8	8		each	Suitcase w/w large size	62.00		62.00	496.00	HS	4100 Sales

6 ➤ Display the Sales Journal entry created by this invoice.

Sales Journal Entry Mar 03, 2016 (J1)

Account Number	Account Description	Debits	Credits
1200	Accounts Receivable	1,525.50	-
2630	HST Charged on Sales	-	175.50
4100	Sales	-	1,350.00
Additional Date:	Additional Field:		
		1,525.50	1,525.50

ℹ️ **J1** (Journal Entry #1) indicates that this is the first Simply journal entry in the Santos Luggage Company records.

Notice the automatic debit to 1200 Accounts Receivable account made by Simply. Also notice the automatic credit to the HST CHARGED ON SALES calculated by Simply, based on the HST code or rate previously entered. The automatic linking to the debit and credit General Ledger accounts will be explained in Chapter 4.

7 ➤ **Exit** from the entry window.

In this text, you will not need to print Invoices or Packing Slips.

8 ➤ Click the ▾ on the right beside the Printer icon. You will see:

✔ Print Invoice	Ctrl+P
Print Packing Slip	Ctrl+Shift+P
Print Invoice and Packing Slip	Ctrl+Shift+K

The current default is to print an Invoice. This can be changed. You will see this in Chapter 4. Do NOT print the Invoice to save paper. Click in the invoice to exit this window.

In this text, we will not need to print Invoices or Packing Slips.

9 ➤ Click the **Post** button to post the invoice.

The next information box informs you that the complete sales order has been filled (no back order), and that the sales order will be removed from the Sales Order Listing.

> **Simply Accounting - Information**
>
> The sales order has been filled and removed from the system.

10 ➤ Click **OK**. The Posting Confirmation window displays that Journal entry J1 was posted successfully. Click **OK**.

11 ➤ **Exit** from the Sales Invoice window to the Home window.

Journalizing Sales Returns

Sometimes customers return goods that are damaged, goods that were delivered but not ordered, or goods delivered in excess of what was ordered. This type of transaction is referred to as a **Sales Return** and is recorded as a negative Sales Invoice.

	They are a CUSTOMER to you
Sale to your customer	Dr Accounts Receivable Cr HST on Sales Cr Sales
Sales Returns from your customer (Issue a Credit Note to the customer)	Dr Sales Returns/Allow Dr HST on Sales Cr Accounts Receivable

Sales Returns are journalized in the Sales Journal as a decrease to Sales (in the Sales section of the Income Statement). The **HST Charged on Sales** must also be reduced accordingly (in the Balance Sheet). Follow the steps in the next exercise.

Exercise 2A-14 – Journalizing a Sales Return

Mar 3, 2016	**Havarah Leather Goods returned 2 Laptop Back Paks, as they had ordered too many. Santos Luggage does not charge a Restocking Fee. The Back Paks were originally purchased on invoice #2253 at 70.00, plus HST. We sent Havarah Leather Goods our credit memo #124 dated today in the amount of $158.20, and referenced it to invoice #2253Rt.**

1 ➤ Right-click the **Sales Invoice** icon, select **Create Invoice**.

2 ➤ Sold To   Select **Havarah Leather Goods**, [Tab]. Click in the **Invoice** field.

3 ➤ Invoice   Many firms enter the invoice number with a return code (Rt) or other codes as shown below. This cross-references the return with the original sales invoice.

Type **2253Rt CM124**. When displaying the customer detail the invoice number will show first in the column. [Tab] [Tab] to Date.

Other invoice codes used to identify action taken are:

Ad	Adjustment	**Al**	Allowance Granted	**Co**	Correction
Dp	Deposit	**NS**	NSF	**Rt**	Returned goods
Rv	Reversal	**TS**	Transfer	**Wo**	Write-off

4 ➤ Date   **Mar 3, 2016** is the date the goods were received by our firm. [Tab]. You should not backdate the return to the original date of the sale (Feb 26, 2016). You want your records to reflect dates when transactions actually happened. Click in the **Quantity** field.

5 ➤ Quantity   Type **-2** (negative) (2 items returned), [Tab].

6 ➤ Unit   Type **each**, [Tab].

7 ➤ Description   Type **Laptop Back Paks Not needed**, [Tab].

8 ➤ Base Price   Type **70.00** (the original selling price). [Tab] [Tab] [Tab] to Amount as there is no % discount.

9 ➤ Amount   [Tab] to accept **-140.00**. The minus sign before the invoice amount will make this entry a **Debit** to the account selected and a **Credit** to Accounts Receivable.

10 ➤ Tax   [Tab]. The **HS** code is still valid for a sales return.

11 ➤ Acct   The default **4100 Sales** revenue account cannot be used because this is not a sale. It is a return of some or part of a sale. Many companies use a separate account to keep a record of returns.

Press [Enter]. The G/L accounts should be displayed.

Select account **4200 Sales - Returns & Allowances**. [Tab] to accept.

12 ➤ Early Payment Terms   Leave the 2.00%. Change the terms to **5 days** and **Net 25 days**. Goods were sold on the 26th, and returns were accepted on the 3rd. There are 5 days remaining in the discount period.

13 ➤ Message   Click in the **Message** field. The default comment code is not appropriate for a return. Change the comment by highlighting the current comment and typing **Return accepted, not needed**. [Tab]. You could leave the comment space blank, but it is best to enter a note for future reference.

14 ➤ Click the **Enter Additional information** 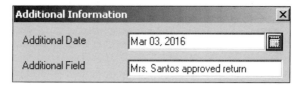 icon and type the information shown. (See side note box.)

> The Information about Mrs. Santos approving the return will not print on the customer return invoice.

Additional Information [×]

Additional Date	Mar 03, 2016
Additional Field	Mrs. Santos approved return

15 ➤ Click **OK**.

16 ➤ View the Sales Journal Entry as shown next.

Sales Journal Entry Mar 03, 2016 (J2)

Account Number	Account Description	Debits	Credits
2630	HST Charged on Sales	18.20	-
4200	Sales- Returns & Allowances	140.00	-
1200	Accounts Receivable	-	158.20
Additional Date: Ma...	Additional Field: Mrs. Santos appro...		
		158.20	158.20

17 ➤ **Exit** from viewing the Sales Journal entry.

The invoice window display should appear as follows:

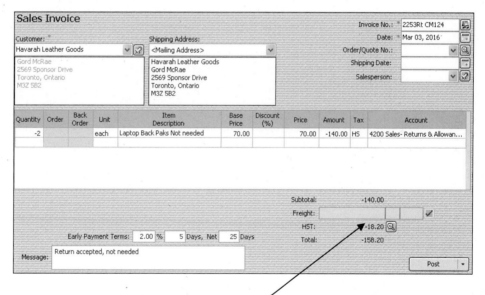

Notice that HST originally charged on this invoice has been reduced by the amount corresponding to the return. Negative **-18.20** is 13% of the $140.00 returned goods.

18 ➤ **Post** when correct, click **OK** for the J2 confirmation window and **Exit** to the Home window.

19 ➤ **Recently Viewed Reports Area** Display the Havarah Leather Goods Customer Aged Detail report at March 3, 2016, without terms. Click on **Customer Aged**, the report displays. Click the **Modify** icon, **Report Options**, select **Havarah Leather Goods, Detail** button should be selected. Leave the **Include Terms** ✓, click on **OK**. Notice the **2253Rt** reference, and the amount is shown with a minus.

Customer Aged Detail As at Mar 03, 2016					
Source	Date	Terms	Transaction Type	Total	Current
Havarah Leather Goods					
2253	Feb 26, 2016	2%/10, Net 30	Invoice	2,373.00	2,373.00
2253Rt CM124	Mar 03, 2016	2%/5, Net 25	Invoice	-158.20	-158.20
Total outstanding:				2,214.80	2,214.80
Total unpaid invoices:				2,214.80	2,214.80
Total deposits/prepaid order:				-	-
Total outstanding:				2,214.80	2,214.80

20 ➤ **Exit** the Aged Detail window and return to the Home window.

Remember to back up your data and update your logbook at the end of every work session.

The Receipts Journal

The Receipts Journal is used to record all types of payments from customers:

- Payment without discount
- Payment with discount(s)
- Deposits (see part B)

Most companies, that have a large volume of sales invoices, have a procedure to record receipts of payments. Upon receipt of the customer's cheque, it is usually stamped on the back with a notation "For Deposit Only" or "For Deposit to the Account of (company)." This prevents unauthorized persons from using the cheque for any other purpose. The date of receipt is also stamped on the back of the cheque, which is used in the journal entry as the date of the transaction.

The date of receipt may be backdated one or two days to accommodate a sales discount. This would apply when a customer's cheque was mailed on the tenth day from the invoice date. There may also be a delay in mail delivery or a cheque received on a Monday when the due date was on a Saturday or Sunday.

The receipts are usually deposited daily to update customer balances owing. A record of each receipt is detailed in the bank deposit book.

Journalizing a Receipt with Cash Discount

Cheques for payment of an invoice are usually accompanied by an advice, a detachable form that provides the details of the payment.

Fig. 2A-12 illustrates a cheque received for this transaction, accompanied by an advice. The date and security stamps on the back of the cheque are also shown. You will use the details shown on the cheque and the advice to journalize the payment.

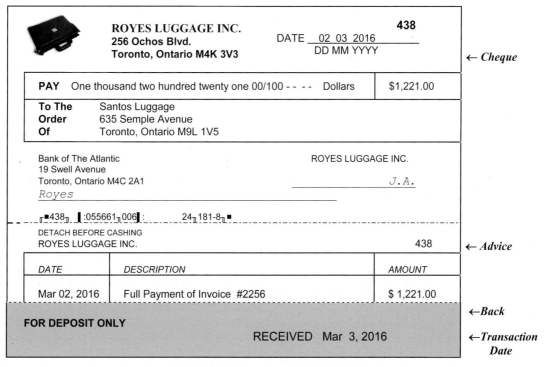

Fig. 2A-12: A Payment Cheque with Advice.

Exercise 2A-15 – To Record a Receipt with Discount

Study the following transaction:

> **Mar 03, 2016 Received from Royes Luggage Inc. cheque #438 for $1,221.00
> in full payment of invoice #2256.**

There are 3 different ways to create Receipts:

1 ➤ A) At the **Receipts** icon, click the ▼, notice the 3 choices. Select **Create Receipt**. In the **From** field, click ▼ and select the customer. The screen fills with the outstanding invoices. Click **X** to return to the Home window.

B) Click the **Receipts** icon, to go directly to the Receipts Journal window. In the **From** field click ▼ and select the customer. The screen fills with the outstanding invoices. Click **X** to return to the Home window.

C) In the **Customers** area, click the ▼ or **right click on the customer from whom we received the cheque**, select **Receive Payments**. The screen fills with the outstanding invoices. Click **X** to return to the Home window.

2 ➤ Using step 1, method **C**, click the ▼ at **Royes Luggage Inc.**, select **Receive Payments**. The Receipts Journal will display the name and address of the customer as shown:

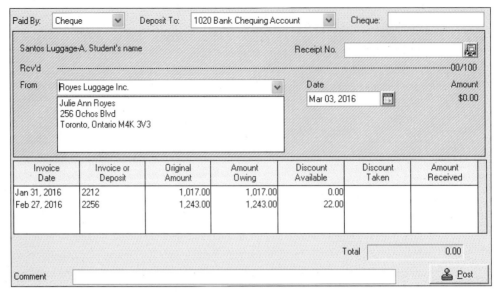

Fig. 2A-13: Receipts Journal window.

The menu bar items are the same as the Sales Journal, except for **Receipt**.

Receipt   Menu with choices for **Enter Deposits** and **Include Fully Paid Invoices/deposits** in the top detail section of the Receipts window. You can adjust a previously posted receipt or look up (view) a receipt.

The details of all outstanding invoices for a specific customer are listed in the lower section, including the original Invoice Date. Royes Luggage Inc. has two invoices that have not been paid in full. They are paying only invoice 2256 at this time.

The terms for this client are 2/10, net 30, (i.e., a discount of 2% if the invoice is paid within 10 days, or the full amount due in 30 days). The discount is calculated on the invoice amount **before** taxes (HST not included). HST is not affected by discounts taken.

Invoice #2256 amounts to $1,100.00 for various luggage goods, plus HST of 143.00 totaling $1,243.00. The 2% discount is calculated on the luggage sold at $1,100.00, which equals $22.00. To summarize:

Invoice #2256	
Luggage Sold	$1,100.00
HST	143.00
Total	$1,243.00
Discount	
.02 x $1,100.00 =	$22.00
Cheque received	
1,243.00 less 22.00 =	$1,221.00

3 ➤   **Paid By:**   Click the ▼ and 4 choices are available. Select **Cheque**, and Tab to the next field.

4 ➤ Deposit To: Click the [▼]. Simply Accounting allows the receipt to be deposited to one of many bank accounts. This would be useful if the business has Canadian, U.S. and other currency bank accounts; e.g., Euro, Mexican peso, etc. and accounts for depositing credit card receipts.

Santos Luggage uses two bank accounts:

1020 Bank Chequing Account is used for normal receipts from customers.

1030 Visa Credit Card Bank Account is used to deposit credit card receipts at a different bank.

5 ➤ Select **1020 Bank Chequing Account** and [Tab] to Cheque.

6 ➤ Cheque This field will show the cheque number received from the customer.

The cheque number will not appear in the Journal Entries All or Journal Entries Receipts entries. It will appear in the Reconciliation & Deposits Journal only.

Change the window to the following:

You will see an error message about the **Receipt No.** field in step 15. It will be corrected in step 16.

7 ➤ Receipt No. Leave blank. This field can also be used for a receipt number if the firm records cheques received with a sequence number.

8 ➤ Date The date should be Mar 03, 2016, the date the cheque was received. (This company is not using the additional information fields.) Change the date to **Mar 09, 2016**.

The **Discount Available** column should be **0.00** for both, indicating that the discount period has passed for both invoices. Simply will calculate the discount available within the days allowed by the terms of the invoice.

9 ➤ Change the date back to **Mar 03, 2016** and the correct discount of 22.00 shows in the **Discount Available** column. [Tab].

If the customer's cheque amount is less than the amount showing in the **Amount Owing** column and the discount amount shown is **0.00**, you should change the date back a few days (e.g., March 01) to see if the cheque reflects a discount taken by the customer.

Ask your manager what to do if a cheque is received a day or two late and misses the discount period. In most cases the manager will allow the discount.

10 ➤ Invoice Date The cursor jumps to this field. ***Note***: The payment is being made for invoice #2256 dated Feb 27, 2016. Use the ↓ key on the keyboard to move down to invoice 2256 dated Feb 27, 2016 that is being paid. You can also use your mouse to position the cursor on 2256. [Tab].

Invoice or Deposit	This field indicates the invoice number or deposit number issued.
Original Amount	This field indicates the original amount of each invoice.
Amount Owing	This field indicates the balance remaining on each invoice if partial payments have been received.
Discount Available	This field indicates the amount of any cash discounts available based on the terms agreed upon. This client's terms are 2/10, net 30. Most firms calculate the cash discount amount on the invoice price ($1,100.00) before taxes. The correct discount is $22.00.

> When a customer/ vendor takes a 2% discount for paying an invoice within terms of 2/10, net 30, HST regulations consider it a finance charge and not a reduction to the HST portion.

11 ➤ Discount Taken — The cursor jumps to this field. If the **Discount Available** field is blank, it indicates that no discount is available for this invoice. You can override the **Discount Taken** field by typing in an amount. [Tab] to accept the discount of 22.00. (See side note box.)

12 ➤ Amount Received — The field now shows 1,221.00, the amount of the outstanding invoice after the discount has been taken off, and is also the amount of the cheque received. [Tab] to accept the receipt of 1,221.00 against this outstanding invoice.

Total — This field (grayed out) shows the total of the Amount Received column. It should agree with the cheque received.

If the cursor was on the invoice 2212 line and you pressed the [Tab] key twice by mistake to move to the Amount Received column, the amount of 945.00 appears in the Amount Received field. Press the *Delete* key to remove the amount.

13 ➤ Display the Receipts Journal Entry. Click **Report**, then **Display Receipts Journal Entry**. The entry should appear as follows:

> The G/L account numbers did not need to be entered. All payments received will automatically be debited to the **Deposit To:** bank account identified in step 4, and credited to ACCOUNTS RECEIVABLE.
>
> All merchandise cash discounts will be debited to SALES DISCOUNTS.

Receipts Journal Entry Mar 03, 2016 (J3)

Account Number	Account Description	Debits	Credits
1020	Bank Chequing Account	1,221.00	-
4150	Sales -Discounts	22.00	-
1200	Accounts Receivable	-	1,243.00
Additional Date:	Additional Field:		
		1,243.00	1,243.00

14 ➤ When finished viewing, **exit** from the entry window. (See side note box.)

To change any of the amounts, click the incorrect field and enter the correct information. Remember to view the entry to make sure you have made the changes properly.

15 ➤ Click the [icon] (e-mail icon at the top-right corner of the window) and a message box appears. This is related to Step 7 earlier.

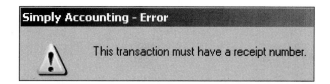

Simply requires a Receipt Number in the Receipt No. field to post the transaction.

 Most companies like Santos Luggage do not use receipt numbers, but record the **cheque number** in the **Receipt No.** field for easy verification (Audit trail). Using this method, they can see the cheque number in the journal entry as shown at step 24 and still be able to use the Reconciliation & Deposit Journal at a later time.

16 ➤ Click **OK** to return to the Receipts Journal.

17 ➤ **Complete your window** as shown next:

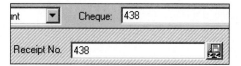

 This will now correct the error message seen at step 15.

All companies in this text use this method of recording cheque numbers in both fields.

18 ➤ Click the [email icon] (e-mail icon) again and the following message appears.

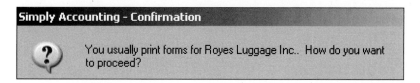

19 ➤ This is to advise you that you normally print forms for Royes Luggage Inc.

There is no Exercise to e-mail the receipt. Click **Cancel** to return to the Receipt Journal window.

20 ➤ **Post** when correct, click **OK** to accept the confirmation for J3. In future exercises, when the instruction is to Post, it also means to accept the confirmation.

21 ➤ **Exit** from the Receipts Journal.

22 ➤ **View** the Receipts Journal Entry. At **Reports,** click ▼, select **Receipts Journal Entries**, click **Display**. (See side note box.)

If there were other receipt entries and you wanted to display certain ones, click the **Modify** icon, **Report Options**, change the dates as required, or click Journal Number and change the information as required.

Receipts Journal Feb 29, 2016 to Mar 03, 2016				
	Account Number	Account Description	Debits	Credits
Mar 03, 2016 J3	438, Royes Luggage Inc.			
	1020	Bank Chequing Account	1,221.00	-
	4150	Sales -Discounts	22.00	-
	1200	Accounts Receivable	-	1,243.00
			1,243.00	1,243.00

The 438 cheque number is shown in the posted entry.

23 ➤ **Exit** from the Receipts Journal window.

24 ➤ View the Customer Aged Detail report only for Royes Luggage Inc. In the Customers area at **Royes Luggage Inc.**, click ▼ select **Display Customer Aged Detail Report**. The Detail report displays only Royes Luggage Inc.

Notice how the Payment and Discount appear, with a – minus sign, and the Discount wording in the Transaction Type column in Fig. 2A-14.

Customer Aged Detail As at Mar 03, 2016						
Source	Date	Transaction Type	Total	Current	31 to 60	61 to 90
Royes Luggage Inc.						
2212	Jan 31, 2016	Invoice	1,017.00	-	1,017.00	-
2256	Feb 27, 2016	Invoice	1,243.00	1,243.00	-	-
438	Mar 03, 2016	Discount	-22.00	-22.00	-	-
438	Mar 03, 2016	Payment	-1,221.00	-1,221.00	-	-
Total outstanding:			1,017.00	-	1,017.00	-

Fig. 2A-14: Customer Aged Detail.

> If you customize (filter) any report, the changes will affect all future reports and your report total may not agree with the General ledger control account; Accounts Receivable.

Cheque number **438** is shown on both the **Discount** and **Payment** lines. (See side note box.)

25 ➤ **Exit** from the Customer Aged Detail report. Notice that in the Customer Area on the Home page, the Balance for Royes Luggage Inc. now displays as 1,017.00.

Journalizing a Partial Receipt with No Discount

When a customer pays the full amount of an invoice within the discount period, the discount as per the terms of sale is allowed. However, if the customer pays only part of the invoice amount, discount on the partial payment is normally not allowed.

The procedure to journalize this transaction is similar to that in Exercise 2A-15. Enter the exact amount of the payment. Simply will deduct the partial payment from the invoice without discount and will show the remaining amount outstanding.

Exercise 2A-16 – To Journalize a Partial Receipt without a Discount

---

You are going to enter the wrong amount for the cheque and then correct the error after posting. You will later also make an error in an invoice and correct it after posting.

Study this transaction and complete the following steps.

Mar 03, 2016   **Received cheque #159, in the amount of $2,000.00, from Sandler Travel Stores as a partial payment on their outstanding invoice #2197 from January 26, 2016.**

---

1 ➤   Using the ▾ in the Customers area, click on **Receive Payments** for Sandler Travel Stores.

2 ➤   Cheque   Type **159** for the customer's cheque number, [Tab] to accept. The cursor moves to the From area.

3 ➤   Receipt No.   Type **159**, [Tab] [Tab].

4 ➤   Date   [Tab] [Tab] to accept Mar 03, 2016.

5 ➤   Invoice Date   At Jan 26, 2016, for Invoice **2197**, [Tab].

> A firm may allow a discount under special circumstances, even when the discount period has passed. If a customer asks for a discount or if you receive a payment showing an unauthorized discount, consult your manager.

Discount Available   There is no discount available, because it is more than 10 days since the invoice date of Jan 26, 2016.

6 ➤   Discount Taken   [Tab] to leave the field blank. (See side note box.)

To practise correcting an error after posting a transaction, you will deliberately make an error and then correct it later.

Amount Received   Type **2200.00** (This amount is not correct. You will correct it in the next exercise.) [Tab] to show a receipt of $2,200.00 against invoice #2197.

7 ➤   **View** the entry.

Receipts Journal Entry Mar 03, 2016 (J4)

Account Number	Account Description	Debits	Credits
1020	Bank Chequing Account	2,200.00	-
1200	Accounts Receivable	-	2,200.00
Additional Date:	Additional Field:		
		2,200.00	2,200.00

8 ➤   **Exit** to the Receipts Journal and **Post** J4 with the error.

You will be at a blank Receipt window.

9 ➤   From   Select **Sandler Travel Stores**. You will see that the **Amount Owing** column is reduced by the partial payment.

Invoice Date	Invoice or Deposit	Original Amount	Amount Owing
Jan 26, 2016	2197	4,407.00	2,207.00

You have just realized that you have made an error in the amount, as the Amount Owing should have been $2,407.00. Complete the next exercise to reverse and correct the error in posting.

Exercise 2A-17 – To Correct a Receipt Error

You will now correct the error that you deliberately made in the last exercise. You have two choices.

1. You can use the 🗒 **Adjust Receipt** icon as shown in this exercise. This would be useful if the amount or invoice(s) to be paid or customer would be changing.

2. You could use the 📑 **Reverse Receipt entry** icon to reverse and cancel the entry. This method would be useful if you posted the error to the wrong customer or you wanted to cancel the entry with the error and start the entry again. Refer to Chapter 13, To Reverse a Cash Receipt.

To correct a Sales Receipt, refer to Chapter 13, Exercise 13-5.

1 ➤ **Receipt No.**   Click the 🖼 **Lookup a Receipt** icon.

2 ➤ Click **OK**. The **Select a Receipt** window appears.

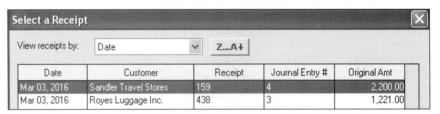

Date	Customer	Receipt	Journal Entry #	Original Amt
Mar 03, 2016	Sandler Travel Stores	159	4	2,200.00
Mar 03, 2016	Royes Luggage Inc.	438	3	1,221.00

3 ➤ Select **Sandler Travel Stores**.

4 ➤ The **Receipts Journal - Receipt Lookup** window appears and the **Paid By:**, **Deposit To:**, **Cheque:**, **Receipt No.**, **From** and **Date** fields are grayed out.

5 ➤ Click the 🗒 **Adjust Receipt** icon. The top header changes to **Receipts Journal - Adjusting Receipt 159** and only the lower portion of the **From** field is grayed out. The customer cannot be changed, because we are reversing an entry to their account.

6 ➤ Click the **Amount Received** column and change the amount to **2000.00**, `Tab`.

If you display the entry, it will display as J6. **Exit** the entry.

7 ➤ **Post** when correct.

8 ➤ **Exit** from the Receipts Journal.

9 ➤ **Display** the Customer Aged Detail report for **Sandler Travel Stores**.

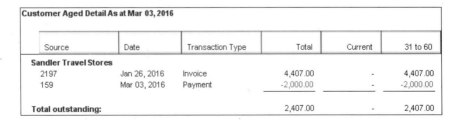

Customer Aged Detail As at Mar 03, 2016					
Source	Date	Transaction Type	Total	Current	31 to 60
Sandler Travel Stores					
2197	Jan 26, 2016	Invoice	4,407.00	-	4,407.00
159	Mar 03, 2016	Payment	-2,000.00	-	-2,000.00
Total outstanding:			2,407.00	-	2,407.00

Note that only the correct posting of -2,000.00 displays.

10 ➤ **Exit** from the Customer Aged Detail.

11 ➤ Display the **Receipts Journal Entries** as shown in Exercise 2A-15.

The default display is to NOT show corrections (e.g., J4 and J5). To see the Corrections, click **Modify, Report Options**, click **Corrections** to have a ✓, click **OK**. You will notice that J5 is the reversing entry for J4 (the error) and J6 is the correct entry.

12 ➤ **Exit** from the Receipts Journal window and return to the Home window.

Remember to back up your data and update your logbook at the end of your work session.

To Cancel an Invoice After Posting

There may be situations where you need to cancel an invoice. You posted a sale to the wrong customer, or a customer decides they don't want/need the product just purchased. This would be different from a sales return. The customer did not take the merchandise out of the store, so it is technically not a sales return.

1 ➤ Advance the date to **Mar 04, 2016**.

2 ➤ **Record** and **Post** the following transaction.

Mar 04, 2016   **A clerk from Havarah Leather Goods is being sent to pick up 2 Laptop Back Paks.** **Record and Post the sale (invoice #2311) in the regular way at $70.00 each, plus HST. Terms 2/10,n30. Invoice total $158.20.**

Exercise 2A-18 – To Cancel a Posted Invoice

---

1 ➤ In this exercise, you will cancel the invoice, based on the information below.

To correct a Sales Invoice, refer to Chapter 13, Exercise 13-4.

Mar 04, 2016   **As the Havarah Leather Goods clerk is preparing to leave the store, he receives a cell-phone message that he is to change the order to 3 extra large Laptop Back Paks. Your store does not carry this particular item and your supplier does not stock this item. The clerk confirms with his boss that the order for 2 Laptop Back Paks is to be cancelled. They will go elsewhere.**

2 ➤ Click the **Lookup an Invoice** icon and the Invoice Lookup window appears.

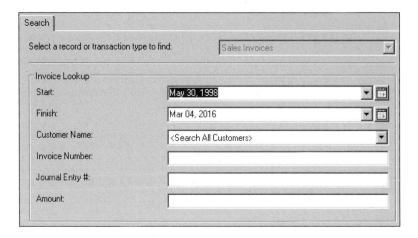

A range of dates and/or customers, invoice numbers or Journal entry numbers may be selected at this point. In this exercise you will view all posted invoices.

3 ➤ Click **OK**. The *Select An Invoice* window is displayed listing the invoices you have entered in this chapter. *Note*: Only a partial window is shown.

Date	Customer	Invoice #	Journal Entry #	Original Amt
Mar 04, 2016	Havarah Leather Goods	2311	7	158.20
Mar 03, 2016	Havarah Leather Goods	2253Rt CM124	2	-158.20
Mar 03, 2016	Luggage 4U	2310	1	1,525.50

4 ➤ **Select** invoice **2311**. The invoice details are inserted into the Sales Journal-Invoice Lookup window for *review only*.

> The icon ![icon] remains the same, but the wording in each Journal window will change.
>
> If you reverse a receipt the same icon is named "Reverse Receipt".

5 ➤ You want to cancel invoice 2311; therefore, click the ![icon] **Reverse Invoice** entry icon. (See side note box.)

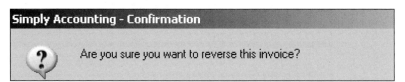

Simply Accounting – Confirmation

Are you sure you want to reverse this invoice?

6 ➤ Click **Yes**.

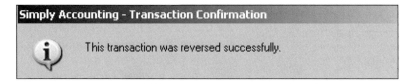

Simply Accounting – Transaction Confirmation

This transaction was reversed successfully.

7 ➤ Click **OK**. The window returns to a blank invoice. The reversing entry has been posted; therefore, the original entry has been reversed.

8 ➤ **Exit** the invoice and return to the Home window.

9 ➤ Display the **Sales Journal Entries** for Mar 04, 2016 (change the Start date) with Corrections ✓. Click **Modify**, **Report Options**, click **Corrections**, change the **Start Date** to **Mar 04, 2016**, **OK**.

Sales Journal Mar 04, 2016 to Mar 04, 2016					
		Account Number	Account Description	Debits	Credits
Mar 04, 2016	J7	2311, Havarah Leather Goods			
		1200	Accounts Receivable	158.20	-
		2630	HST Charged on Sales	-	18.20
		4100	Sales	-	140.00
Mar 04, 2016	J8	ADJ2311, Reversing J7. Correction is J8.			
		2630	HST Charged on Sales	18.20	-
		4100	Sales	140.00	-
		1200	Accounts Receivable	-	158.20
				316.40	316.40

Journal entry 8 has cancelled Sales journal entry 7. The above information will not display in the Customer Aged Detail report as there was no sale.

This procedure can also be used to cancel Sales Quotes, Sales Orders, Receipts, Purchase Quotes, Purchase Orders, Purchase Invoices, and Payments.

10 ➤ Exit the Sales Journal window and **X** to return to the Home window.

The Customers Ledger

When you set up a customer account in the RECEIVABLES module, you are creating a ledger for that customer. When you enter sales or payment transactions referring to the particular customer in the RECEIVABLES module, the corresponding customer's ledger will be updated.

Exercise 2A-19 – Viewing a Customer Ledger

In this exercise, you will familiarize yourself with the Customers window and view a customer ledger. You would need to view a customer's ledger when you receive an inquiry about the customer's account.

1 ➤ Advance Session date to **Mar 05, 2016**.

2 ➤ In the **Tasks** area, at **Customers** icon, click ▼ to see the 4 choices. Select **View Customers**. As discussed in previous Exercises, you can also click the Customers icon to go directly to the Customers window. Study Fig. 2A-15.

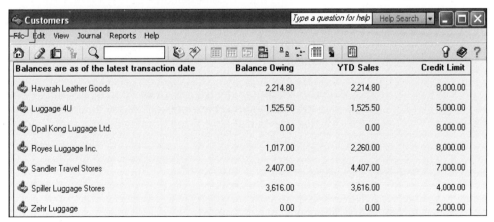

Balances are as of the latest transaction date	Balance Owing	YTD Sales	Credit Limit
Havarah Leather Goods	2,214.80	2,214.80	8,000.00
Luggage 4U	1,525.50	1,525.50	5,000.00
Opal Kong Luggage Ltd.	0.00	0.00	8,000.00
Royes Luggage Inc.	1,017.00	2,260.00	8,000.00
Sandler Travel Stores	2,407.00	4,407.00	7,000.00
Spiller Luggage Stores	3,616.00	3,616.00	4,000.00
Zehr Luggage	0.00	0.00	2,000.00

Fig. 2A-15: Customers Summary Information.

This window shows summary information about the customer, including the credit limit the customer is allowed.

The find customer

feature. Click the magnifying glass on the left, and the **Find Customer Search** window appears. You would use this if you want to find a specific customer in a long list of similar names (e.g., Smith, Singh, etc.).

The FIND icon is a quick way to locate an item from a long list. Simply provides this facility in various fields in most windows. Use it. It can save you time!

You will see that the Customers window has the following menu bar choices: (Also see side note box.)

File	Menu with choices for opening a customer, creating a new customer or removing a current customer (only if balance is nil and prior invoices have been cleared).
Edit	Menu item allows you to search for a customer record.
View	Menu choice for displaying customer information (changing the size of the icons for the display). **Icon** displays 2 customers on a line, **Small icon** displays 3 customers on a line, or **Name** displays customer detail information as shown in Fig. 2A-15. If you maximize the window, depending on the monitor, resolution and icon you are using, you may see 2, 3 or 4 customer names on a line, and Restore Window to default setting.
Journal	Menu choice of either the **Sales** or **Receipts** Journal for data entry. (Icons are also provided on the toolbar for this.)
Reports	A drop-down menu listing reports available for display.
Help	The Simply Help menu.

3 ➤ Return to the **Home** window.

Adding a New Customer Record

Simply allows you to create two basic types of customers and add new customers in two different ways:

1. **Regular Customer** – You create individual ledgers for customers who buy from the company more than once during the accounting period. The ledger would include the customer's name, address and other details of the company. You can enter a new customer:

   a) using the Customers icon.
   b) using the Sales Invoice Journal.

   In Exercise 2A-20, you will create a ledger for a new regular customer using method b.

2. **One-time Customer** – There are two options available when you need to record a sale to a customer who is not likely to buy again. These options are available when you use the Sales Invoice icon, and select Create Invoice. When you enter a name of a customer that is not in the Customers List you have two choices.

   a) **<One-time customer>** (see Exercise 2B-27) with customer information *not retained* in the customer list.

      Simply allows you to record the details of the individual sale including the customer's name and address (in the lower box), but Simply will not create a ledger for the customer. You can view the record of the sale (Journal entry) at a later time, as it will be in the list of transactions.

When you record a sale using this option, Simply will allow you to enter a cash sale only (cash, cheque, bank card or credit card). Payment from the customer for the sales amount is journalized at the same time as the sale.

b) Type the customer's name and use the **Continue** button (see Exercise 2B-28) with customer information *retained* for the new customer in the Journal Entry report but not in the customer list. Simply will not create a ledger for the customer.

Exercise 2A-20 – Creating a Regular Customer Ledger & Invoice in the Sales Invoice Window

---

Study this transaction:

Mar 05, 2016 **You have made a sale to a new customer. The details are: A-Your Name Luggage Rack; Contact: Your Name; 256 Trillium Way, Oakville, Ontario, L6J 2H8; telephone 905-699-8000, extension 2563; fax number 905-699-8010; credit limit $3,000.00**

The goods ordered and shipped on this first order are:

6 Carry on bags – small @ $21.00 each, plus HST
3 Suitcase w/w large   @ $62.00 each, plus HST
4 Power adapters   @ $10.50 each, plus HST

The goods **are to be picked up by their own delivery truck and delivered** to the Hamilton store, operated by Jackie Welland, as follows: **939 Fennel Avenue West, Hamilton, Ontario, L9N 3T1.**

Note: You will be recording the Hamilton Store information in the Customer Ledger Address tab.

Your Name Luggage Rack is a good example of a regular customer, as they are likely to buy from you again. Since there is no existing ledger for this new customer, you need to create a Customer Ledger, and then record the sale.

1 ➤ Click the **Sales Invoices** icon, at **Customer**: type, **A-Your Name Luggage Rack**, Tab . The following window will display.

This is where you would identify the customer type by clicking the appropriate button:

⊙ Continue   You would select this when you type the name of the one-time customer in the **Customer** field. It allows you to continue recording the sale without adding the customer to the customers list. Remember, however, that if you select this option, you can enter only a cash or credit card sale.

○ Quick Add   This feature will add the customer to the Customers Ledger but will omit details about the customer (address, phone number, terms, credit limit, etc.), **⌷ Tab** . The cursor will move to the **Shipping Address** field. Type the customer address and complete the invoice. You can use this feature with a quote or order. You will need to go back to the customer account and add the details later.

○ Full Add   This feature will add the customer to the Customers Ledger and will open the Receivables Ledger window to record details about the customer. When the details have been entered, you are returned to the previous window. You can then produce the invoice. ***Note:*** The address information will be automatically entered from the Customer Ledger information. You can use this feature with a quote or order.

Cancel   To cancel the current operation. Simply will then allow you to enter a different customer name.

2 ➤   Select **Full Add, OK**. The Receivables Ledger window will open with the name of the customer displayed. The Receivables Ledger window opens.

Address tab

3 ➤   Enter the information for A-Your Name Luggage Rack, as shown next:

In this window, you can add a new customer's details on various tabs. You can also click the ✏ Edit icon to amend details on the tabs for a customer.

Customer:	A-Your Name Luggage Rack		

Address | Ship-to Address | Options | Taxes | Statistics | Memo | Import/Export | Additional Info

Contact:	Your Name	Phone 1:	(905) 699-8000 2563
Street 1:	256 Trillium Way	Phone 2:	
Street 2:		Fax:	(905) 699-8010
City:	Oakville	E-mail:	
Province:	Ontario	Web Site:	
Postal Code:	L6J 2H8	Salesperson:	
Country:		Customer Since:	Mar 05, 2016

Customer	Type **A-Your Name Luggage Rack**, `Tab`. The A- is used to place your name at the beginning of the customer list regardless of the first letter of your name.
Contact	Your name as the contact person for this company.
Postal Code	When you type **L6J2H8** or l6j2h8 and press `Tab`, the postal code will format automatically.

Enter the phone/fax numbers without dashes. Simply will automatically format them with a dash and brackets as you press `Tab`.

Phone	Type **9056998000** (without dashes) and `Tab`.
	To add the extension number **2563** to the phone number, click at the end of the phone number, press the space bar and type the extension number (up to 10 numbers), `Tab` `Tab`. If you type the number and extension as 90569980002563 and then press `Tab`, the number and extension will not format.
Fax	Type **9056998010** (without dashes) and press `Tab`.
E-mail:	Leave blank. This text does not show sending E-mail.
Web Site:	Leave blank. This text does not show accessing a customer's web site.
Salesperson:	As discussed earlier, this field is not used in this chapter. See Appendix AC, *Adding a Salesperson's Name to an Invoice* at www.simplyaccounting2010.nelson.com under Student Resources'.
Customer Since:	This feature lets clerks see, at a glance, when the customer started buying goods from Santos Luggage.
	Note: Santos Luggage has not updated previous customers. It is assumed that they have been customers for many years.

Ship-to Address

4 ➤ Click the **Ship-to Address** tab. This window information would be used when you are sending the invoice to the mailing address of a company (usually the Head Office) and always send the goods to a different store location.

The address information is grayed out as it is assumed that this is the default mailing address and shipping address for all invoices.

5 ➤ Click the **Add New** button, Type the Address Name information as shown next. Each customer can have up to 100 different shipping addresses. You can also add shipping addresses from the invoice. Shown later in this Exercise, Journalizing the Sale, step 1.

6 ➤ Click **OK**. You are returned to the Receivables ledger.

7 ➤ Enter the information shown next. Ignore Phone and other information.

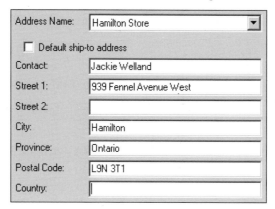

Options

8 ➤ Click the **Options** tab, and **complete** the information as shown.

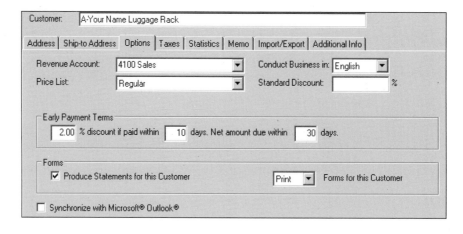

> The **Price List** field would be used with the **Perpetual Inventory** module for special pricing for customers who buy a lot of goods or services. Simply 2010 supports 1,000 different price lists. This is discussed in Chapter 8.

Revenue Account

This will make **4100 SALES** the default account which will display in the Sales Quotes, Orders or Invoice window for this particular customer. Note this default will be for the first line of each invoice only.

Price List

(See side note box.)

Conduct Business in

This field indicates the ability to have screen displays and printouts in French for the customer. Santos Luggage has not had requests to conduct business in French.

Standard Discount

This field would indicate the discount that would apply to each item the customer buys. This is not to be confused with a cash discount for paying early (within term time limits). This discount is for good customers who buy a lot of goods and deserve a reduction to the selling price. If an amount is entered here, it will appear in the Discount % column for the customer. Santos Luggage will not be using this field, in part A. See Exercise 2B-31 after step 7, 2nd information area for a discussion on the Quantity or Trade Discount.

Early Payment Terms

When customers are given time to pay for the goods or services they purchase, it is called purchasing goods on credit. The time is normally 30 days.

Some customers are allowed special terms of 2/10, net 30. This means that if the customer pays the balance owing within 10 days they can deduct 2% of the cost of the goods bought as a cash discount; otherwise, the balance is to be paid within 30 days. These terms with discount are what are referred to as **Early Payment Terms. 2/10 net 30** is the default.

A-Your Name Luggage Rack is a new customer, and as a general practice, your company allows payment terms of 2/10 net 30 days to new customers to provide an incentive to pay early.

Do NOT change from the default.

Produce Statements for this Customer

Do NOT change. A ✓ in the box will allow you to print a summary statement to be sent to a customer. You will learn how to produce a customer statement in Exercise 2B-37.

Forms for this Customer

There are two choices: **E-mail** and **Print**. Leave the choice as **Print**.

Synchronize with Microsoft® Outlook®

When this box is ✓, the customer's e-mail address will be placed in the Microsoft® Outlook® Mailing address list. Do NOT change. There is no exercise for this feature.

Taxes

9 ➤ Click the **Taxes** tab and complete the information as shown.

Indicate which taxes this customer is exempt from by entering Yes for Tax Exempt.

Tax	Tax Exempt	Tax ID
HST	No	

Choose the tax code that includes the taxes that you normally charge this customer:

HS - HST at 13% added to invoice

Tax Exempt   HST, do not change. This customer is not exempt from HST.

Tax ID   This field would be used if the customer was exempt from the HST. An identification number would be given to the customer by the provincial and/or federal government.

In the lower box, click the ▼ and a list of Tax codes appears.

Select **HS - HST at 13% added to Invoice.** The HS code will appear on the first line of the sales invoice.

Statistics

10 ➤   Click the **Statistics** tab and enter the information as shown.

Credit Limit:	3,000.00

This is the customer's credit limit.

Many companies give each customer a maximum credit balance. When the customer's balance is larger than its preset limit, a warning message box will appear when you try to post a new sale to the customer's account. Although a customer may have exceeded its limit, sales to that customer can still be processed in Simply, but you would first consult your manager on how to properly handle this situation. Management may require a payment from the customer to reduce the Accounts Receivable before any additional sales could be made, or your manager may approve the extended credit limit based on financial records of the customer.

You should check the sale and payment history of customers on a regular basis to ensure that each customer is making payments within the agreed terms.

Memo

The open space allows you to make notes about the customer. Click in the open box and the status bar informs you that you have up to 255 characters to make your note.

11 ➤   Click the **Memo** tab and enter the information as shown.

Customer:	A-Your Name Luggage Rack

Address | Ship-to Address | Options | Taxes | Statistics | Memo | Import/Export | Additional Info

Memo: Follow up payment for new customer in 10 days to see if they took advantage of the 2% discount.

Goods can also be shipped to the Fennel Avenue West address.

To-Do Date: Mar 17, 2016   📅   🗐 Clear Memo
☑ Display this memo in the Daily Business Manager

You will see this message in Exercise 2B-25, step 2.

To-Do Date: This is the date (10 days from the date of the sale, plus two days for late mail delivery) that you want to be reminded to deal with the information in the box.

Display this memo in the Daily Business Manager   Click the box to enter a ✓ in this field. This ✓ will allow the above messages to appear in the Daily Business Manager display.

Import/Export

12 ➤   Click the **Import/Export** tab.

| Address | Ship-to Address | Options | Taxes | Statistics | Memo | Import/Export | Additional Info |

☐ This customer has Simply Accounting and can import invoices and quotes

☐ This customer uses my item numbers on orders

Match the customer's item number to my item number or an account number for importing orders:

Customer's Item No.	My Item No.	My Account	

This customer has...   Leave this box blank. You would ✓ this box if you know the customer uses *Simply Accounting,* and can import your quotes and invoice information. The text does not have an exercise for importing or exporting information to another company. This feature is not used often.

This customer uses my item numbers...   You would click in the box to insert a ✓ only if your company uses the perpetual inventory method in recording sales and you know the customer uses the item numbers of your goods when ordering from your company.

Additional Info

13 ➤   Click the **Additional Info** tab. The fields in this window allow you to add additional information that will display when the customer is selected in a transaction. Complete the information as shown.

		Display this information when the customer is selected in a transaction
Field1 :	Remind new customer of 2% discount in 10 days	☑
Field2 :	when buying goods	☑

See the Appendix Q, *Names Fields* at www.simplyaccounting2010.nelson.com under Student Resources for more information.

14 ➤   Click [💾 Save and Close]. The customer account is created and you are returned to a Sales Invoice window.

15 ➤   The Sales Invoice window, with the name and address you entered, with the **HS** tax code and the **4100** default **Sales** account indicated is displayed. [Tab].

16 ➤   The Additional Info note window for fields 1 and 2 will appear in front or behind
        the Sales Invoice window. If the Info window is partially hidden, click on the box,
        and then click **Close**. You can also click Close later.

Journalizing the Sale

Now that you have completed the new customer file, follow these steps to journalize the
sale to this customer:

Transaction	Do not change the default **Invoice**.
Payment Method	Do not change the default **Pay Later**.

1 ➤   **Customer**   The goods are being shipped to the Hamilton store. Click the
                          ▼ and select **Hamilton Store**. The address field changes.
                          [Tab] .

Invoice   The next invoice number is **2312**.

Date   **Mar 05, 2016** This is the date the goods are shipped to the
                       Customer.

Order/Quote   This field will be blank, as no previous sales quotes
No.   or orders were received from this customer.

Shipping Date   This date field can be left blank as the goods were not
                       ordered on a Sales Quote or Sales Order, and the goods are
                       being shipped the same day as the invoice date.

A-Your Name Luggage Rack ordered the following items:

6 Carry on bags - small   @ $21.00 each, plus HST
3 Suitcase w/w large   @ $62.00 each, plus HST
4 Power adapters   @ $10.50 each, plus HST

**The goods are to be picked up by their own delivery truck and delivered to the
Hamilton store.**

2 ➤   **Quantity**   Type **6**, [Tab] . (These are the units being sold and shipped.)

Order   This column is skipped. The goods are ordered and shipped.

Back Order   This column is skipped. There are no goods backordered on
                       this invoice.

3 ➤   **Unit**   Type **each**, [Tab] .

4 ➤   **Description**   Type **Carry on bags - small**, [Tab] .

5 ➤   **Base Price**   Type **21.00**, [Tab] [Tab] [Tab] to Amount.

6 ➤   **Amount**   This field represents the calculated amount from fields
                          Quantity times **Price**. [Tab] to accept **126.00**.

7 ➤ **Tax**   The default code **HS** is entered as you set this up earlier. This is correct. [Tab] to accept.

HST is not included in the selling price of each item. (See Exercise 2A-4, for a discussion of the tax codes.)

8 ➤ **Acct**   4100 is shown as the default General Ledger account number as you set this up earlier. If you want to change the account number, press [Enter]. The G/L chart of accounts available should be displayed. You may have to move [▲] or [▼] to see more accounts. Select or type account **4100** Sales and [Tab] to accept 4100.

9 ➤ Enter the remaining sales information from step 1.

The default tax code HS and G/L account **4100** is used only for the first item. You will have to type or select the tax code and account number for each of the additional items.

Subtotal   This field is the subtotal of the goods being sold without taxes.

Early Payment   Should show **2.00%, 10 days, Net 30 days**, the terms you set
Terms   up earlier. If the terms are different, you can click on these fields and enter the correct terms.

Message   This field would display a variety of messages you want the customers to see on quotes, orders and invoices. The default for all invoices is shown. You will learn how to enter this type of information in Chapter 4.

Freight   Your company does not charge for delivery and, therefore, does not use this field.

10 ➤ **Track**   Click the [icon] **Track Shipments** icon. Click [▼] and a
Shipments   drop-down list of shipping companies is displayed. Select **Your Vehicle**, [Tab]. The shipped information will not display in the Invoice window, but will print on the invoice.

11 ➤ **Tracking**   This will be blank because there is no need to track the
Number   shipment if it is being picked up by the customer's vehicle. Click **OK**.

12 ➤ When you have completed recording the above information, the window display should look like Fig 2A-16.

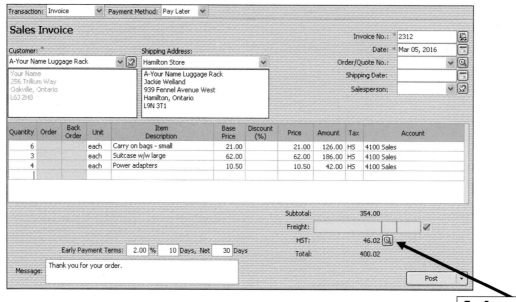

Fig. 2A-16: A-Your Name Luggage Rack Invoice.

Tax Summary icon

ℹ

When an invoice is created to record cash register summary tapes, there may be a few cents difference in the HST amounts. As stated in the **Tax Summary** window, the amount field can be changed. If in doubt, use the Simply calculator and make the changes, if necessary.

13 ➤ To see information about the taxes, click the **Tax Summary** icon 🔍 and the summary displays as shown next. This would be a summary of the HST fields to the left. (See side note box.)

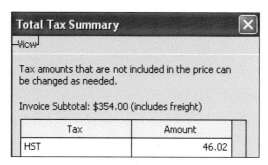

14 ➤ Click **OK**.

15 ➤ Display the Sales Journal entry created by this invoice. The window should display as follows:

Sales Journal Entry Mar 05, 2016 (J9)

Account Number	Account Description	Debits	Credits
1200	Accounts Receivable	400.02	-
2630	HST Charged on Sales	-	46.02
4100	Sales	-	354.00
Additional Date:	Additional Field:		
		400.02	400.02

Recording this invoice allows the preparation of a journal entry, given that a sale has taken place. Notice the automatic debit to the Accounts Receivable account made by Simply. Notice that the automatic credit to the HST Charged on Sales, calculated by Simply, is based on the HST code or rate entered.

16 ➤ **Exit** from this window by clicking the **X** button.

17 ➤ Make corrections to any fields that have errors in them. Click the **Post** icon. The entry will be posted to the customer's account in the RECEIVABLES module and will also be posted to the General Ledger.

18 ➤ **Exit** to the Home window.

19 ➤ If the Additional Info window is displayed **close** it now.

Additional Transactions

1 ➤ Advance the Session date to **Mar 07, 2016**.

Process the following transactions:

Mar 06, 2016	**Sold to Zehr Luggage (PST Exempt) Terms 2/10, net 30, 10 Suitcases w/w large size at $62.00 each, 4 Suitcases w/w regular size @ $56.00, plus HST on all items. Invoice 2313, $953.72.**

Mar 06, 2016	**You made a sale to a new customer, Hanlan's Luggage Store, contact: Liam Hanlan, 2318 Avondale Drive, Oakville, Ontario, L6H 5A1; telephone 905-399-5000, Revenue Account 4100, Terms No %, 0 days, Net amount 0 days, HST code. Credit limit $3,000.00, and they paid by business cheque #739. You will record this as a sale and then record the receipt separately. You will see how to combine this into one transaction in Chapter 2B.** **The goods ordered and shipped on this first order are: 6 Carry on bags – small @ $21.00 each, $126.00 plus HST**

When a business has a lot of customers and they cannot see all of them in the Customers area, you can scroll down the listing and/or expand the area. In the Reports area, click the ▬ minimize icon. The Reports area is minimized. *Note*: This will only work for the current session. To expand the Reports area, click the ⊞ expand icon.

Mar 07, 2016	**Zehr Luggage returned 3 Suitcases w/w large as the zippers do not work properly. The suitcases will need to be returned to the manufacturer. Record the Sales Return. You do not need to record a return to the manufacturer. Purchases Returns will be shown in Chapter 3A, Toys.** **Issued Credit Memo #125, with reference to original sales invoice. Terms amended to 9 days, net 29 days.** **–3 Suitcases w/w large @ $62.00, plus HST (net return –$210.18).**

Remember to back up your data and update your logbook at the end of your work session.

Printing Reports When Needed

The following reports may be printed for management's information and for filing for the audit trail.

- Journal Entries may be printed in one of two ways (see Exercise 1-17).

  a) **Journal Entries All** will print all journal entries from all modules (with or without corrections). All transactions, in the time-period requested, are numbered in this journal in sequential order (even if entered in a subledger; i.e., RECEIVABLES or PAYABLES module).

  b) **Journal Entries General** will print journal entries entered in the COMPANY module only.

  1 ➤ To save time and paper, **print** only the following:

a) Journal entries, All (with corrections)	Mar 01 to Mar 07
b) Income Statement for period	Jan 01 to Mar 07
c) Balance Sheet at	Mar 07
d) Customer Aged Detail report at	Mar 07
e) General Ledger	Mar 01 to Mar 07

Your instructor may request printouts of the Sales and/or Cash Receipts Journals. See Exercise 2B-38.

Refer to the back of the text for a complete list of Accounting and Simply Accounting Terminology for the Receivables chapter.

Relevant Appendices, Part A

The following appendices are available at www.simplyaccounting2010.nelson.com under Student Resources.

Appendix 2010 Q   **Names Fields**

Appendix 2010 V   **Mini-Guide Receivables—Payables**

Appendix 2010 AC   **Adding a Salesperson's Name to an Invoice**

Note: After finishing Chapter 2A and Chapter 8, you can complete selected transactions from Chapter 2A, using the PERPETUAL INVENTORY module. See Challenge Exercise 08 C8-4 Luggage-PI.

Summary, Part A

Here is a summary of the transactions entered in this chapter:

Transaction:	Journal/Ledger:	Remarks:
Sales Quotes	*Sales Quotes*	Creates a quote that may be printed and sent to a customer. Simply records it in the Sales Quote database, but does not post to the General Ledger.
Sales Order	*Sales Orders*	Creates a sales order record when an order is received from a customer. May be created by converting an existing sales quote. Simply records in the Sales Order Listing, but does not post to the General Ledger.
Sale on Account	*Sales Invoices*	Records SALES amounts only. User selects the appropriate HST code. Simply automatically debits Accounts Receivable and credits the appropriate tax accounts.
Sales Adjustment	*Sales Invoices*	Use Adjustment icon.
Receipt	*Receipts*	Select the invoice(s) paid.
Receipt with Discount	*Receipts*	Apply the receipt against the original invoice less the discount amount calculated on the sales amount before taxes.
Return on Account/ Credit Memo	*Sales*	Enter the memo as a minus amount with HST.
New Customer	*Customers*	Remember to select an appropriate Revenue account and appropriate tax code for each customer.
Cancel an Invoice	*Sales*	Use the **Reverse Invoice** icon to reverse the original invoice. Can also be seen in Chapter 13.
Revise a Cash Receipt	*Receipts*	Use **Lookup** to find the original receipt and adjust the amounts as required. Can also be seen in Chapter 13.

Before Moving On..., Part A

Read the following questions and make sure you know the answers to them; otherwise, review the corresponding section in the chapter before moving on.

1. What types of transactions are journalized in the RECEIVABLES module?

2. What is the main difference in journalizing transactions between the RECEIVABLES module and the COMPANY module?

3. What occurs when you post journal transactions in the RECEIVABLES module?

4. Why would a business need to use more than one bank account?

5. Explain the concept of aging in customer accounts.

6. Name at least two uses of the Customer Aged Detail report.

7. What is the difference between a sales quote and a sales order?

8. The default Revenue account is used for what purpose?

9. What is a cheque payment advice?

Challenge Exercise 02 C2A-1 Clocks

RECEIVABLES and COMPANY Modules

Clocks is a business that sells various type of clocks (e.g., table, desk, grandfather, etc.) and is open 7 days a week.

You do *NOT* need to print Sales invoices or receipts. Terms are varied for different customers. HST is 13%.

1 ➤ Refer to Exercise 1-1 to unzip the **02 C2A-1 Clocks.exe** file.

2 ➤ Open the **02 C2A-1 Clocks** file, and enter the following Accounts Receivable transactions for May:

May 1	Sold 10 model #256 desk clocks at $30.00 each, plus HST, to Carney's Clocks. Invoice #212 issued with terms 2/10, net 30.
May 1	Issued Sales Quote #136 to **Your Name** (Your actual name must appear). Terms net 5 days. Other information: 623 Autumn Breeze Way, Mississauga, Ontario, L5B 9P2. Phone and fax numbers may be left blank. Credit limit $2,500.00 for a grandfather clock at $2,000.00, plus HST. Free delivery and setup of the clock. Your Name will return from a business trip on Friday, May 4 and will advise about the quote on the clock. Ship date Tuesday, May 8.
May 4	**Your Name** accepted quote #136 and ordered the grandfather clock. The order was increased to include 2 travel alarm clocks at $35.00 each, plus HST.
May 5	Issued invoice #213 for sale of one antique style desk clock model #128 for $140.00, plus HST, to Carlton Shippers. Cheque #258 received.
May 8	The grandfather and travel alarm clocks on Order #136 were delivered to **Your Name** and the grandfather clock was installed. Invoice #214 was left at the home.
May 9	Issued sales order #137 to wholesale customer, Sandy's Clock Town, for 10 desk clocks model #899 at $62.50 each, plus HST. The clocks are scheduled to be shipped May 14. Terms are net 2/10, net 30 days.
May 10	Your Name returned one of the travel alarm clocks as it does not work. Your Name does not want a replacement. Credit his account.
May 11	Received cheque #847 from Carney's Clocks to pay for outstanding invoice #212.
May 13	Received cheque #148, as payment from Your Name re invoice #214.
May 14	Issued invoice #215 to Sandy's Clock Town for 9 desk clocks from their order. One clock is back ordered and will be shipped on May 23. If you see a confirmation window, click **NO**.

3 ➤ When you have recorded the above entries, **print** the following reports:
   a. Customer Aged Detail Report as at May 14
   b. Journal Entries All, for May 1 to 14
   c. Sales Journal for May 1 to 14
   d. Cash Receipts Journal for May 1 to 14
   e. Income Statement for Jan 1 to May 14
   f. Pending Sales Order report with an As at date of May 14.

Challenge Exercise 02 C2A-2, Dog Walkers

RECEIVABLES and COMPANY Modules

Dog Walkers is a business that looks after pets during the day, evening or when the owners are away for a period of time. The business takes the dogs for walks and play in parks.

You do *NOT* need to print Sales invoices or receipts.

Note: All invoices are left at the residence or business at the end of each week (5 day walking) or at the end of the walking period if the period is less than a week. Terms are varied for different customers. HST is 13%.

1 ➤ Refer to Exercise 1-1 to unzip the **02 C2A-2 Walkers.exe** file.

2 ➤ Open the **02 C2A-2 Walkers** file, and enter the following Accounts Receivable transactions for May.

May 1   Issued Sales Quote #362 to Ms. Sadia Kalirai for 3 walking services at $20.00 plus HST per day for her dog "Ranger", while they are out of town starting on Friday, May 4. Terms net 3 days.

May 2   Left invoice #782 for 4-day walking services for Ms. Rachel Tran's dog, Duffer, at $20.00 plus HST per day with terms of net 3 days.

May 2   Ms. Sadia Kalirai accepted quote #362 for Ranger.

May 5   Received cheque #829 from Ms. Rachel Tran for invoice #782.

May 6   Issued and left invoice #783, on order #362, for $67.80 (3 day service at $20.00 per day plus HST) at Ms. Sadia Kalirai's home.

May 7   Issued sales order #363 to a new business client, Your Name Transport (Your Name must appear), to take their 2 security dogs for walks in the park during the day when they are not able to. The first Sales order is for a minimum of 10 days for the month. Use May 31 as the Ship Date. The dogs are to go on longer walks and play sessions and the charge will be $40.00 plus HST per visit. Other information: 889 Ancaster Avenue, Stoney Creek, Ontario, L8E 6Z9, phone and fax numbers may be left blank. Terms are 2% 10 days net 20 days. (Special terms arranged for business clients.) Credit limit $500.00.

May 8   Received $41.00 Bank Debit memo re service charges on the Bank account.

May 8   Received cheque #529 from Ms. Kalirai for invoice #783.

May 11   Issued invoice #784 against sales order #363 to Your Name Transport for 3 days walking for the dogs.

May 21   Received cheque #8961 from Your Name Transport for invoice #784.

May 21   Issued invoice #785 to Manpreet Foss for 2 day walking services at $20.00 per day, plus HST. Mr. Foss left cheque #603 on the kitchen table for us.

3 ➤ When you have recorded the above entries, **print** the following:
   a. Customer Aged Detail Report as at May 21
   b. Journal Entries All, for May 1 to 21
   c. Journal Entries-General, for May 1 to 21
   d. Sales Journal for May 1 to 21
   e. Pending Sales Order report at May 31
   f. Income Statement for Jan 1 to May 21

Chapter 2B

RECEIVABLES Module—*Beyond Basics*

Santos Luggage

Learning Objectives

After completing this chapter you will be able to:

☐ Revise (increase or decrease) invoices for quantity or prices.
☐ Track Additional Information in transactions.
☐ Use the Daily Business Manager and other Simply special features.
☐ Journalize Deposits with a Sales Order.
☐ Journalize Cash/Cheque/Bank Card sales.
☐ Journalize Credit Card Sales.
☐ Journalize a Customer Account Write-Off and/or NSF Cheques.
☐ Apply Deposits to Invoices.
☐ Journalize a Cash Sale with a Discount and/or Credit Card Receipts.
☐ Journalize Owner Investment.
☐ Journalize non-merchandise receipt.
☐ Process deposits from customers for sales orders.
☐ Use Display and print various Receivable reports and journals.

This chapter is a continuation of Chapter 2A. You should download the 02 Luggage 2B data file for use with this chapter.

The contents of this chapter are as follows:

- Exercises:
  - Exercise 2B-21 – Opening the 02 2B Luggage-B data file 132
  - Exercise 2B-22 – To Set Up a Default Revenue Account for a Customer.. 133
  - Exercise 2B-23a – To Process a Transaction with an Increase in Quantity 134
  - Exercise 2B-23b – To Correct a Posted Invoice (Lookup Feature) 135
  - Exercise 2B-24 – Using the Additional Transaction Details 135
  - Exercise 2B-25 – Using the Daily Business Manager (DBM) 137
  - Exercise 2B-26 – Journalizing a Deposit with a Sales Order 138
  - Exercise 2B-27 – Journalizing a Retail Sale (by cheque) 141
  - Exercise 2B-28 – Journalizing a Credit Card Sale 143
  - Exercise 2B-29 – Record a Note in a Customer's File 145
  - Exercise 2B-30a – Journalizing a Partial Write-off 146
  - Exercise 2B-30b – Journalizing the Receipt.. 147
  - Exercise 2B-31 – Journalizing a Cash Sale with a Discount (Senior) 149
  - Exercise 2B-32 – Journalizing an NSF Customer Cheque....................... 153
  - Exercise 2B-33 – Applying an Invoice to a Deposit.................................. 156
  - Exercise 2B-34 – Journalizing a Credit Card Receipt 157
  - Exercise 2B-35 – Journalizing Owner Investment in Business 159
  - Exercise 2B-36 – Journalizing a Non-Merchandise Cheque..................... 160
  - Exercise 2B-37 – Printing Customer Statements 162
  - Exercise 2B-38 – To Print Period-End Reports 164
    - To Print a Gross Margin Income Statement 164
    - To Print the Sales Journal 165
    - To Print the Receipts Journal 165
  - Exercise 2B-39 – Viewing/Printing Graphs... 165

- Summary, Part B 166

- Before Moving On…Part B 166

     Challenge Exercise 02 C2B-1, Brides.. 167
     Challenge Exercise 02 C2B-2, Skis 168
     Challenge Exercise 02 C2B-3, House Sitters 169

- Mini Guide for Transactions in Chapter 2 170
- Relevant Appendices, Part B.. 171

Opening the RECEIVABLES Module, Part B

In this chapter (2B), you will access the RECEIVABLES module of Santos Luggage and enter transactions related to sales, receipts of payment from customers, and other Receivable transactions, starting from March 8.

The 02 2B Luggage-B exe file contains the ending balances of the General Ledger accounts and Customers files from Chapter 2A of this text (see Trial Balance shown on next page). These balances will be the starting point of the B file and journal entries will start at J1.

Exercise 2B-21 – Opening the 02 2B Luggage-B data file

ℹ

Review Exercise 1-2 if you need help to open a data file.

1 ➤ Refer to Exercise 1-1 to unzip the **02 2B Luggage-B.exe** file.

2 ➤ Start **Simply Accounting**.

3 ➤ At the Select Company window, click **Select an existing company** button, and **OK**.

4 ➤ At the Simply Accounting - **Open Company window**, in the **Look in**: box, locate your student location drive and the **02 2B Luggage-B** folder.
📁 02 2B Luggage-B

5 ➤ **Double-click** the 📁 02 2B Luggage-B folder and the 📄 Luggage-B.SAI will appear in the box. (The image at the left of Luggage may be different depending on the configuration of your computer and the SAI may be in lower case.)

6 ➤ Click the 📄 Luggage-B.SAI icon. The **File name** box will change to Luggage-B.SAI (.SAI may not display).

7 ➤ Click **Open** to open the **Luggage-B.SAI** file.

8 ➤ The Session date will be Mar 07, 2016. Click **OK**.

Santos Luggage, Student's Name
Trial Balance As At Mar 07, 2016

		Debits	Credits
1020	Bank Chequing Account	22,800.24	-
1030	Visa Credit Card Bank Account	0.00	-
1200	Accounts Receivable	11,923.86	-
1300	Inventory	23,680.00	-
1320	Prepaid Supplies	712.00	-
1420	Office/Warehouse Furniture/Equip...	25,163.00	
1425	Accum. Amort Office/Ware Furn/E...	-	4,100.00
2200	Accounts Payable	-	12,151.00
2630	HST Charged on Sales	-	1,425.24
2640	HST Paid On Purchases	525.00	-
3100	Capital, Maria Santos	-	63,683.68
3160	Additional Investment	-	0.00
3180	Drawings, Maria Santos	2,200.00	-
4100	Sales	-	42,799.00
4150	Sales-Discounts	342.00	-
4200	Sales-Returns & Allowances	681.00	-
5010	Beginning Inventory	21,000.00	-
5040	Purchases	28,000.00	-
5050	Purchase Returns	-	1,000.00
5080	Purchase Discounts	-	335.00
5090	Ending Inventory	-	23,680.00
5310	Wages Expense	8,000.00	-
5320	Advertising Expense	432.00	-
5330	Bank Charges & Interest	95.00	-
5340	Credit Card Charges	34.30	-
5350	Rent Expense	800.00	-
5370	Bad Debt Expense	0.00	-
5410	Office/Warehouse Supplies Expense	216.00	-
5450	Rent Expense Warehouse	2,000.00	-
5460	Utility Expense	263.89	-
5550	Telephone Expense	305.63	-
		149,173.92	149,173.92

Exercise 2B-22 – To Set Up a Default Revenue Account for a Customer

In Exercise 2A-4, step 19 you had to locate and select the Revenue account for Luggage 4U. In Exercise 2A-20, step 8 you set up a default revenue account for A-Your Name Luggage Rack. (All customers except Luggage 4U have a default Revenue account.)

1 ➤ Return to the Customer's Receivable Ledger window of Luggage 4U and add

the default **Revenue Account 4100,** [Tab]. All regular customers will then have a default revenue account. This will help avoid errors and will make inputting information faster.

2 ➤ Click **Save and Close** to return to Home window.

Slideshow 2B – RECEIVABLES Part B demonstrates the use of Simply's special features and more transaction processing techniques. Run it now.

Using Simply's Special Features

Simply has some special features that maximize efficiency in your everyday tasks and optimize the use of a computerized accounting software. You learned earlier how to use the Daily Business Manager. Below are special features relevant to tasks involving sales and customers.

The Lookup Feature

The **Invoice Lookup** feature shown in the next exercise can be used when management wants to view previously posted invoices in order to verify details. This is especially useful if the paper copy of the invoice(s) cannot be located, or to locate a previously posted invoice that you wish to correct.

Exercise 2B-23a – To Process a Transaction with an Increase in Quantity

In this exercise you will record a transaction while the customer, Mr. Tran, is still in the store and the order is being prepared. After the invoice is **Posted**, the customer decided to increase the quantity for the carry on bags. You could prepare a new invoice for the additional items, but the customer wants all the items on one invoice.

You will be shown how to correct the posted invoice in the exercise that follows.

1 ➤ Advance the Session date to **Mar 08, 2016**.

2 ➤ **Record** and **Post** the following transaction.

 On future invoices, if **Shipped by** details are not provided, do not enter any information. Also assume **Mailing address** and **Ship to** address are the same if not specified.

Mar 08, 2016   Sold 15 Carry on bags – small at $21.00 each and 3 Power adapters at $10.50 each, plus HST, to a new customer, Tran's Luggage Warehouse, contact person is Huong Tran, 875 Burke Avenue, Markham, Ontario L2S 2Y9. Phone number 905-768-3620, the default Revenue account is 4100, price list is Regular, terms are 2/10, net 30, tax code is HS, credit limit is $1,500.00. Invoice #2315 for $391.55 including $45.05 HST.

To Correct a Posted Invoice

You will now correct the invoice that you just posted.

Exercise 2B-23b – To Correct a Posted Invoice (Lookup Feature)

It is assumed that you are still in the Sales Journal-Invoice window.

1 ➤ Invoice   Click the 🖳 **Invoice Lookup** icon and the Invoice Lookup window appears.

2 ➤ Click **OK**, and the Select Invoice Window appears.

3 ➤ With **Invoice 2315** highlighted, click **Select**. The Sales Journal-Invoice Lookup window appears with the original 2315 invoice. (See side note box.)

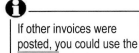

If other invoices were posted, you could use the **Look up previous** or **Look up next** icons to move forward or backward in the list of invoices.

4 ➤ Click the 🗑 **Adjust Invoice** icon. (The icon is identical to the Adjust Receipt icon used previously.) The 🖳 **Sales Journal - Adjusting Invoice 2315** banner appears at the top.

5 ➤ Change the 15 Carry on bags - small to **18**, Tab . The Invoice total changes to $462.74, which includes $53.24 HST. Mr. Tran is pleased that you could make the change for him.

6 ➤ **Post** this transaction and **Exit** to the Home window.

7 ➤ Advance the date to **Mar 10, 2016**.

To Track Additional Transaction Details

This feature is the same as the feature you used in Chapter 1, Exercise 1-11. You will be able to add additional information about transactions when required.

Exercise 2B-24 – Using the Additional Transaction Details

Mrs. Santos has decided to have the **Additional Date and Information** fields available and used when appropriate. You have been asked to use this feature.

> **Mar 08 2016**   Received cheque #1256 dated Mar 07, 2016 in the amount of **$2175.60 (after a net $39.20 discount after the return) from Havarah Leather Goods on invoice 2253. Use additional transaction detail information as noted in this exercise.**

1 ➤ Click the **Receipts** icon. **Record** this transaction using the **Mar 08, 2016** date as the transaction date (the actual date the cheque was deposited — this will match up to the bank statement). Don't forget to input cheque #1256 into the cheque number and receipt fields.

The cheque was mailed by the customer on the 10th day of the discount period and should be given the discount. In steps 3 and 5, at the Discount Taken field, you will type the Discount taken amount to override the blank amount shown.

Invoice Date	Invoice or Deposit	Original Amount	Amount Owing	Discount Available	Discount Taken	Amount Received
Feb 26, 2016	2253	2,373.00	2,373.00	0.00		
	2253Rt CM124	-158.20	-158.20	-2.80		

Note the Invoice Date column. Simply 2010 does not display the date of the return or other credits.

Change the date to Mar 07, 2016 and the **Discount Available** field changes to 42.00 with the return discount -2.80 as a negative. Goods were returned, therefore, no discount is allowed on the returned goods. (See side note box.)

Invoice Date	Invoice or Deposit	Original Amount	Amount Owing	Discount Available	Discount Taken	Amount Received
Feb 26, 2016	2253	2,373.00	2,373.00	42.00		
	2253Rt CM124	-158.20	-158.20	-2.80		

Change the date back to Mar 08, 2016. You will note that the **Discount Available** field is back to 0.00, `Tab`.

2 ➤ **Invoice/Deposit** At invoice 2253, `Tab`.

3 ➤ **Discount Taken** Type **42.00** to allow the discount, `Tab`. Management will usually allow a 2 or 3 day grace period as there could be mail delivery problems or holidays affecting the delivery. (See side note box.)

If it is longer than 3 days, you need to speak to a manager to approve the discount.

4 ➤ **Amount Received** `Tab` to accept 2,331.00. The cursor moves to the 2253Rt CM124 Discount Taken line.

Original Purchase	$ 2,100.00	Discount available	$ 42.00
Less Return	$ (140.00)	Return Discount lost	$ (2.80)
Net Sale	$ 1,960.00 x 2% = $39.20	Net Discount	$ 39.20

5 ➤ **Discount Taken** At **-2.80**, `Tab` to allow the negative discount on the return.

6 ➤ **Amount Received** `Tab` to accept -155.40. The lower portion should resemble the following.

Invoice Date	Invoice or Deposit	Original Amount	Amount Owing	Discount Available	Discount Taken	Amount Received
Feb 26, 2016	2253	2,373.00	2,373.00	0.00	42.00	2,331.00
	2253Rt CM124	-158.20	-158.20	-2.80	-2.80	-155.40
					Total	2,175.60

7 ➤ Click the **Additional Information** icon and record the information to show that a cheque dated on the 7th was received and deposited on the 8th. Click **OK**.

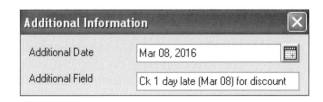

The journal entry window should look like the following:

Receipts Journal Entry Mar 08, 2016 (J4)			
Account Number	Account Description	Debits	Credits
1020	Bank Chequing Account	2,175.60	-
4150	Sales -Discounts	39.20	-
1200	Accounts Receivable	-	2,214.80
Additional Date: Ma...	Additional Field: Ck 1 day late (Mar...		
		2,214.80	2,214.80

8 ➤   **Exit** the journal window, **Post** this transaction and **Exit** to the Home window.

9 ➤   **Record** and **post** the following two transactions:

Mar 09, 2016   **Sold to Havarah Leather Goods, 10 Briefcases narrow at $70.00 each, 3 Briefcases large at $105.00 each, 3 Carry on bags - small at $21.00 each, 15 Suitcases w/w large at $62.00 each, plus HST. Terms are 2/10, net 30. HST in the amount of $261.04 is added to the goods purchased to give a final invoice total of $2,269.04.**

Mar 10, 2016   **Sold to Royes Luggage Inc., 10 Laptop Back Paks at $70.00 each, 10 Locks one size at $3.50 each, and 14 Suitcases w/w small at $49.00, each plus HST. Terms are 2/10, net 30. HST in the amount of $184.73 is added to the goods sold to give a final invoice total of $1,605.73.**

---

10 ➤   When finished processing the transactions, **Exit** from the Sales Journal and return to the Home window.

Exercise 2B-25 – Using the Daily Business Manager (DBM)

---

1 ➤   Advance the Session date to **Mar 17, 2016**.

2 ➤   In Exercise 2A-20 at step 11 you identified Mar 17 as the date to display the memo note in the Daily Business Manager. To see the note in the Related Tasks Area, click the **Daily Business Manager** icon on the tool bar. Click the **Notes & To Do List** bullet, then select **Mar 17**. If the Memo tab information is not displayed in the lower window, click the **Memo** tab. The clerk would advise management about the memo note for further action.

3 ➤   **Display**   In Exercise 2A-9, you were shown how to display the Business Performance window. Select **Business Performance**. You can now see that the straight line (in Exercise 2A-9) has changed with the entries you have recorded.

4 ➤   **Display**   Click **Sales (Past 7 Days)** to see another change. This information can be very helpful for management when planning staff work schedules.

5 ➤   Return to the Home window.

Journalizing a Deposit

Assume a special order of **clothes and laptop suitcases** for March 29 (a future date) of $6,000.00, plus HST of 780.00 for a total of $6,780.00. The customer pays a deposit of $3,500.00 to ensure that the goods are delivered on time. This is similar to paying a fraction of the total price to lay away a special dress or suit. The seller will take the dress/suit off the rack or special order the goods, but would want assurances that you will come back. The deposit is usually applied toward the final price.

When you record a deposit of $3,500.00 before a sale is completed, it is entered as a **credit** in the customer RECEIVABLES Ledger. Since there is no sale, it is, in essence, a negative receivable and the money is owed to the customer until the corresponding service is rendered or goods are delivered.

Exercise 2B-26 will show you how to record a deposit as you record a Sales order.

Remember: A deposit cannot be recorded on a Sales Quote.

A deposit transaction is not a sale but rather a deposit on a future sale.
Simply would record the following entry as an example:

Dr BANK ACCOUNT	**$3,500.00**	
Cr ACCOUNTS RECEIVABLE		**$3,500.00**

This, in effect, gives the customer a **credit** balance of $3,500.00.

When the goods or services are delivered, the sale is recorded with a **debit** invoice ($6,780.00) in the customer RECEIVABLES Ledger.

When the remaining outstanding balance ($3,280.00) on the invoice is received, the $3,280.00 receipt and the $3,500.00 prepayment are applied to the total invoice of $6,780.00, to clear the invoice from the outstanding list. (The invoice would then be fully paid.)

Exercise 2B-26 – Journalizing a Deposit with a Sales Order

You will now journalize the $3,500.00 deposit as you record the Sales Order.

Study the transaction:

Mar 15, 2016 Opal Kong Luggage Ltd. has placed a special order for 30 Clothes and Laptop suitcases w/w with embossed Price Company logos (approved by the CEO of the Price Company). The cost will be $200.00 each, plus HST. Total order including HST is $6,780.00. Estimated shipping date is Mar 29, 2016. We have received Opal Kong Luggage Ltd.'s cheque #433 for a $3,500.00 deposit (or prepayment) on this special order.
Due to the company's logo on the goods, the goods are not returnable unless defective.

To Record the Sales Order

1 ➤   Create an Order using the **Sales Order** icon.

2 ➤   **Transaction**   Do not change, from Order.

3 ➤   **Customer**   Select **Opal Kong Luggage Ltd.**, ⎡Tab⎤ .

Before you continue, look at the Date and Shipping Date fields. There is no field between them.

4 ➤   **Payment**   Select **Cheque**. You will now see the

      Method   fields ⎡Deposit Ref. No.: *　　　　　⎤ between the Date and Shipping Date fields. You will also see
⎡Deposit Applied:　　　　　　⎤ field in the lower section. You will use these fields in steps 8 and 11 of this exercise. ⎡Tab⎤ .

      Deposit To   Do not **change**.

5 ➤   **Cheque No.**   Type **433**. ⎡Tab⎤ .

6 ➤   **Order No.**   You have to type order number **104.** Simply creates the Quote numbers, but cannot create the Order numbers.

7 ➤   **Date**   Select **Mar 15, 2016** the day the cheque is received. ⎡Tab⎤
      ⎡Tab⎤ ⎡Tab⎤ to Order.

      Deposit   **Dp SO#104** refers to Deposit Special Order #104. Some
      Ref No.   companies will use the number of the cheque received and others may use a deposit reference number, which is different than the cheque number received. ⎡Tab⎤ .

8 ➤   Complete the rest of the information as follows:

| Transaction: | Order ▼ | Payment Method: | Cheque ▼ | Deposit To: | 1020 Bank Chequing Account ▼ | Cheque No.: | 433 |

Sales Order   Convert...▼

Order No.:	104
Date: *	Mar 15, 2016

Customer: *
Opal Kong Luggage Ltd. ▼

Opal Kong
33 Evans Avenue
Streetsville, Ontario
L5N 1V5

Shipping Address:
<Mailing Address> ▼

Opal Kong Luggage Ltd.
Opal Kong
33 Evans Avenue
Streetsville, Ontario
L5N 1V5

Deposit Ref. No.: * Dp SO#104
Shipping Date: Mar 29, 2016
Salesperson:

Quantity	Order	Back Order	Unit	Item Description	Base Price	Discount (%)	Price	Amount	Tax	Account
	30	30	each	Clothes and Laptop suitcase w/w with embossed company logos for the Price Company	200.00		200.00	6,000.00	HS	4100 Sales

Subtotal:	6,000.00
Deposit Applied:	
Freight:	
HST:	780.00
Early Payment Terms: 2.00 % 10 Days, Net 30 Days	
Total:	6,780.00

Message: Thank you for your order, it will be shipped as quoted.

Record ▼

9 ➤ Display the Sales Journal entry.

Sales Journal Entry Mar 15, 2016 (J7)

Account Number	Account Description	Debits	Credits

There is no data to report.

10 ➤ J7 reports no data because no goods have been sold. **Exit** to the Sales Order window.

11 ➤ Enter the information in the lower part of the window as shown.

Deposit Applied: 3,500.00   The amount will be applied to the client record.

Notice that the Sales Order Total (6,780.00) has not changed. The order is still for the full amount.

12 ➤ Display the Sales Journal entry; it should look like the following. The entry records the money received on the Sales Order.

Sales Journal Entry Mar 15, 2016 (J7)

Account Number	Account Description	Debits	Credits
1020	Bank Chequing Account	3,500.00	-
1200	Accounts Receivable	-	3,500.00
Additional Date:	Additional Field:		
		3,500.00	3,500.00

13 ➤ Exit from the entry and **Record** the transaction.

14 ➤ Exit to the Home window.

15 ➤ Display the **Customer Aged Detail Report** for Opal Kong for **Mar 17, 2016** (see Exercise 2A-2: Displaying/Printing Customer Aged Report).

Customer Aged Detail As at Mar 17, 2016				
Source	Date	Transaction Type	Total	Current
Opal Kong Luggage Ltd.				
Dp SO#104	Mar 15, 2016	Prepaid Order	-3,500.00	-3,500.00
Total outstanding:			-3,500.00	-3,500.00
Total unpaid invoices:			-	-
Total deposits/prepaid order:			-3,500.00	-3,500.00

The Opal Kong report shows a deposit (Prepaid Order) of **-3,500.00** in two places.

16 ➤   **Exit** from the Aged Detail Report and return to the Home window.

Journalizing Cash/Cheque/Bank Card Sales

This type of sale can be recorded in the Sales Journal as a One-time customer, because you do not expect to have repeat sales with the customer. This option is appropriate because there is no need to keep detailed computer records for a One-time customer. However, the sales record is useful for the audit trail or for inquiries of goods sold, etc.

When you use this option, Simply automatically allows you to enter only a sale paid by cash, cheque, credit or bank debit card. This means that nothing (name or amounts) will be posted to the ACCOUNTS RECEIVABLE account in the G/L. The One-time Customer transaction will appear in the journal and ledger printouts similar to:

Mar 15, 2016	J8	456, 2318, <One-time customer>

The sales invoice will, however, record the name/address of the customer in the lower box and can be viewed at a later time.

The next exercise shows you how to enter the name of the customer in the lower **Sold to** field to enter a cash sales transaction with a One-time customer, which allows you to have the One-time customer wording (instead of name) as shown above to appear in journal entries.

Exercise 2B-27 – Journalizing a Retail Sale (by cheque)

Mar 15, 2016   **Mrs. Arlene Hirsch has purchased from the outlet store, at the back of the warehouse, 2 Suitcases w/w large at $80.00, 2 Carry on bags - small at $28.00, and 2 Locks at $4.50 each, plus HST. (The Outlet store selling prices, although seconds and samples, are higher than goods sold to chain stores but lower than regular retail prices.) Cheque #456 for $254.25 was accepted, as Mrs. Hirsch is a friend of one of our staff.**

1 ➤   Create an invoice using the **Sales Invoices** icon.

> **Transaction**   Do not change the default Invoice.

2 ➤   **Payment Method** Select **Cheque,** [Tab] .

3 ➤ Deposit to   DO NOT CHANGE, [Tab] to accept 1020 Bank Account.

4 ➤ Cheque   Type **456**. [Tab].

5 ➤ Customer   Click the ▼ and select **<One-time customer>**. [Tab] [Tab].

For audit trail information and verification purposes you should type in the name of the customer (as shown) and address information. The manager, however, decided you do not need the cash customer's address. Mrs. Hirsch is a friend of one of the employees. Enter the information as shown next.

6 ➤ Ship-to-Address Type **Outlet Store**. This, in effect, indicates that the customer has picked up the goods from the Outlet Store. [Tab] , and click the Invoice field.

7 ➤ Invoice   [Tab] to accept 2318. [Tab] to Date.

8 ➤ Date   Select **March 15, 2016**. [Tab] and click the Quantity field.

9 ➤ Enter the information shown in Fig 2B-17.

Tax	Mrs. Hirsch is purchasing this for personal use. Mrs Hirsch still pays the HST on this retail sale. Select **HS**.

The Sales Invoice window should appear as follows: (See side note box.)

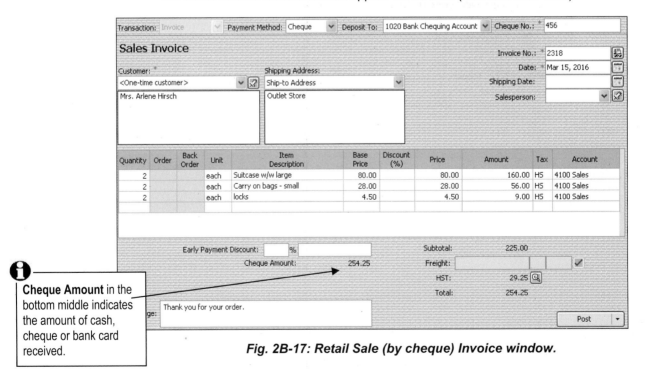

Cheque Amount in the bottom middle indicates the amount of cash, cheque or bank card received.

Fig. 2B-17: Retail Sale (by cheque) Invoice window.

The Early Payment Discount field would be used for a customer who received terms of 2/10, net 30 days who buys today and pays today. Mrs. Hirsch does not receive this discount.

10 ➤　**Display** the Sales Journal Entry. The window should appear as follows:

Sales Journal Entry Mar 15, 2016 (J8)			
Account Number	Account Description	Debits	Credits
1020	Bank Chequing Account	254.25	-
2630	HST Charged on Sales	-	29.25
4100	Sales	-	225.00
Additional Date:	Additional Field:		
		254.25	254.25

11 ➤　**Exit** from the display window.

12 ➤　**Post** when correct and **Exit** to the Home window.

Journalizing a Credit Card Sale

Credit Card sales are, in essence, **cash** sales. However, journalizing them is a bit different from a sale where the customer pays cash or uses an ATM (debit) card. When a customer pays with a credit card, the vendor's credit card company charges the vendor a fee for the privilege of accepting the credit card. This is called a **discount charge**. The credit card discount rate varies depending on the dollar volume of sales processed by the vendor.

When journalizing this type of sale, the sale amount is reduced by the amount of the credit card company's discount fee, and the discount fee is entered as a separate item.

Depending on the arrangement with the credit card company, your bank may credit your account for this type of sale, or you may be required to deposit credit card receipts at your bank.

Exercise 2B-28 – Journalizing a Credit Card Sale

Santos Luggage has arranged to have credit card receipts credited automatically to their bank account.

The credit card discount fee for Santos Luggage is 3.5% of the sales amount (including taxes) and is entered in a separate account; e.g., 5340 Credit Card Charges.

Mar 17, 2016 **Another sale from the Outlet store. Mr. Jerry Tyson, of Tyson's Toys, used his business credit card to purchase 1 Briefcase wide for $135.00, plus HST. The invoice total was $152.55, including taxes.**

1 ➤　Create an invoice using the **Sales Invoice** icon.

　　Transaction　　Do not change Invoice.

2 ➤　**Payment**　　Select **Visa Credit**. Santos Luggage accepts the Visa Credit
　　Method　　Card. `Tab`.

3 ➤　**Customer**　　**Mr. Jerry Tyson**, `Tab`, click **Continue**, click **OK**. This is
　　　　　　similar to selecting <One-time Customer>, but as noted
　　　　　　previously, the customer's name will appear in the printouts,
　　　　　　similar to `Visa Credit, 2319, Mr. Jerry Tyson`. This is the author's

recommended way to record this type of transaction, as the customer's name will display and print in the journals and G/L. To ensure privacy, do not type credit card numbers on screen. They should be recorded on paper only. Type

Outlet Store as shown. [Tab].

Invoice	Accept **2319**.
Date	Accept **Mar 17, 2016**.

4 ➤ Enter the information shown next:

Quantity	Order	Back Order	Unit	Item Description	Base Price	Discount (%)	Price	Amount	Tax	Account
1			each	Briefcase wide	135.00		135.00	135.00	HS	4100 Sales

Tax	Mr. Tyson is purchasing this for personal use. He pays 13% HST.
Discount	There is no discount on this sale.

The screen display should display the following:

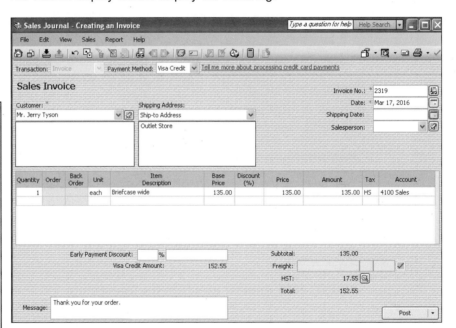

Because you selected **Visa Credit** in the **Paid By** box on the sales invoice when you journalized the transaction, Simply automatically deducted the $5.34 discount fee (invoice total of $152.55 * 3.5%) and posted it to **5340 Credit Card Charges**. The remainder $147.21 is debited to **1030 Visa Credit Card Bank Account**.

The **Total** and **Visa Credit Amount** of $152.55 on the sales invoice remain the same.

Fig. 2B-18: Sales Journal – Sales Invoice for credit card sale (see side note box).

5 ➤ Display the Sales Journal entry.

Sales Journal Entry Mar 17, 2016 (J9)

Account Number	Account Description	Debits	Credits
1030	Visa Credit Card Bank Account	147.21	-
5340	Credit Card Charges	5.34	-
2630	HST Charged on Sales	-	17.55
4100	Sales	-	135.00
Additional Date:	Additional Field:		
		152.55	152.55

6 ➤ **Exit** from the display window.

7 ➤ **Post** when correct and **Exit** to the Home window. You may see the Simply Accounting *Sign UP for Sage Payment Solutions* information. This feature requires the user to pay a user fee for this service. This feature will not be discussed in this text. Click **Do Not Show Me again**, to exit to the Home window.

8 ➤ Advance the Session date to **Mar 18, 2016**.

Journalizing a Customer Account Write-off

A write-off may be either a reduction by the full amount or by a partial amount from a specific invoice or the balance in the customer ledger. When all attempts to collect the amount from the customer have failed due to bankruptcy, business closing, etc., the account balance of the customer would be written off.

If there is a dispute over the goods or services supplied, a partial or full write-off on the specific invoice may be made. In the next exercise, a portion of an invoice will be written off after you received notification from the customer's lawyer that the company declared bankruptcy and the cheque received, a partial payment of an invoice, will be the final amount paid.

Mar 18, 2016 **Received cheque #3431 for $904.00 and a letter from Spiller Luggage Stores' lawyer advising our company that Spiller Luggage had a severe uninsured fire at their store, and they have declared bankruptcy. The cheque received is the final amount to be received.**

Maria Santos, the owner, reviewed the letter and advised you to write off the $2,520.00 difference to the following accounts: BAD DEBT EXPENSE $2,400.00
HST ON SALES $ 312.00

Mrs. Santos advised you to record a notation in the client memo file that $2,712.00 has been written off.

ℹ️ The user could confirm the invoice/balance outstanding and related details (.e.g., invoice #, date) by viewing the Customer Aged record for Spiller Luggage Stores, before writing off the account.

To record the write-off properly, you should do it in three steps:

1. Update the customer memo notes if required.
2. Record the write-off.
3. Record the receipt.

Mrs. Santos has asked you to first enter a note in the customer's file, then record the write-off and record the receipt.

Exercise 2B-29 – Record a Note in a Customer's File

Record a Note in a Customer's File

Refer to Exercise 2A-20, which specifically describes the memo tab in the customer's Receivables Ledger file.

1 ➤ Click the ▼ at **Spiller Luggage Stores** in the Customers area, click **View Customer Record**.

2 ➤ Click the **Memo** tab, and enter the following information.

> Mar 18, 2016 Received $904.00 cheque ($800.00 plus $104.00 HST) from customer's lawyer regarding business bankruptcy. Wrote off the account balance of $2712.00 per memo from Mrs. Santos.

To-Do Date   Leave blank. No need to have this information reported later.

3 ➤ Click Save and Close, return to the Home window.

Exercise 2B-30a – Journalizing a Partial Write-off

Follow this procedure to write off the $2,712.00 difference for invoice #2230 using a negative invoice.

1 ➤ In the Customers area, click the ▼ at **Spiller Luggage Stores**, click **Create Invoice**.

Transaction	Do not change from **Invoice**.
Payment Method	Do not change from **Pay Later**. (You must use **Pay Later** to match the write-off to the previous sale.)

2 ➤ Invoice   Type **2230Wo**, Tab Tab . Simply does not allow the entry of an invoice number twice, so adding **Wo** (code for **write-off**) to the original invoice number allows you to reference the write-off to the original sales invoice.

3 ➤ Date   Tab to accept Mar 18, 2016 (18th is the date the decision was made to write off the amount). Tab . Click on **Description**.

4 ➤ Description   Type **Write-off partial invoice balance.** Tab . Click on **Amount**.

5 ➤ Amount   Type **-2400.00**. The minus sign before the amount will make this entry a Debit to the account selected. Tab to accept.

6 ➤ Tax   Tab to select code **HS**.

7 ➤ Acct   Press Enter . Select account **5370** for Bad Debts Expense, Tab . (See side note box.)

8 ➤ Message   Type **Write-off approved by Mrs. Santos.** Tab .

9 ➤ Terms   Remove **2, 10, 30**. There is no discount on a write-off.

ℹ️ Alternatively, some companies estimate hard-to-collect accounts and set up an **Allowance for Doubtful Accounts** or **Allowance for Bad Debts**. The allowance is adjusted at year-end (or more frequently) to **Bad Debts Expense**. Actual Accounts Receivable write-offs reduce **Allowance for Doubtful Accounts**.

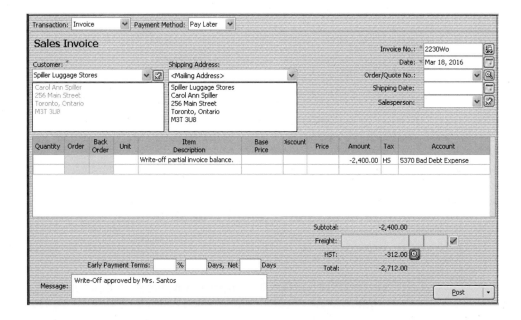

10 ➤ Display the Sales Journal Entry.

Sales Journal Entry Mar 15, 2016 (J10)

Account Number	Account Description	Debits	Credits
2630	HST Charged on Sales	312.00	-
5370	Bad Debt Expense	2,400.00	-
1200	Accounts Receivable	-	2,712.00
Additional Date:	Additional Field:		
		2,712.00	2,712.00

11 ➤ **Exit** from the display window.

12 ➤ **Post** after verifying accuracy and **Exit** to the Home window.

Exercise 2B-30b – Journalizing the Receipt

1 ➤ In the Customers area, click the 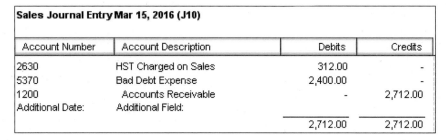 at **Spiller Luggage Stores**, click **Receive Payments**.

2 ➤ **Cheque**   Type **3431**, ⬚Tab .

     From   Spiller Luggage Stores is filled in.

3 ➤ **Receipt No.**   Click in the No. field, type **3431**, ⬚Tab ⬚Tab .

4 ➤ **Date**   ⬚Tab ⬚Tab to accept **Mar 18, 2016**.

5 ➤ **Invoice Date**   ⬚Tab to accept Feb 20, 2016.

6 ➤ **Discount Taken** ⬚Tab there is no discount.

7 ➤ **Amount Received**   ⬚Tab to accept the original 2230 invoice $3,616.00.

8 ➤ **Discount Taken** ⬚Tab there is no discount.

If your invoice 2230Wo line has a **-48.00 Disc. Available** amount showing, it means that you did not remove the 2% terms in the previous exercise. Use the [**Delete**] or [**Backspace**] key to remove **-48.00**.

9 ➤ Amount Received [Tab] to accept the write-off of **-2,712.00**. The lower portion to the Receipts window will look similar to the following:

Invoice Date	Invoice or Deposit	Original Amount	Amount Owing	Discount Available	Discount Taken	Amount Received
Feb 20, 2016	2230	3,616.00	3,616.00	0.00		3,616.00
	2230Wo	-2,712.00	-2,712.00	0.00		-2,712.00
					Total	904.00

The **Total** box 904.00 at bottom will indicate the amount of the cheque received, which is the net amount of invoice 2230 ($3,616.00), less the write-off allowed (-2,712.00).

10 ➤ Display the Receipts Journal entry.

Receipts Journal Entry Mar 18, 2016 (J11)

Account Number	Account Description	Debits	Credits
1020	Bank Chequing Account	904.00	-
1200	Accounts Receivable	-	904.00
Additional Date:	Additional Field:		
		904.00	904.00

11 ➤ Exit from the display window.

12 ➤ Post when correct and **Exit** to the Home window.

13 ➤ Display the Customer Aged Detail Report, using the [▼] in the Customers area for Spiller Luggage Stores at March 18.

The screen should look as follows:

Customer Aged Detail As at Mar 18, 2016

Source	Date	Transaction Type	Total	Current
Spiller Luggage Stores				
2230	Feb 20, 2016	Invoice	3,616.00	3,616.00
3431	Mar 18, 2016	Payment	-3,616.00	-3,616.00
2230Wo	Mar 18, 2016	Invoice	-2,712.00	-2,712.00
3431	Mar 18, 2016	Payment	2,712.00	2,712.00
Total outstanding:			-	-

The lower portion of the report has hyphens (-) to indicate no dollar values.

Notice that cheque **3431** has been applied to both the **invoice 2230** and **invoice 2230Wo**. For future reference, the negative invoice 2230Wo is shown to be applied to original invoice 2230.

14 ➤ The following procedure works with the RECEIVABLES AND PAYABLES modules and assumes that you want to display details of the original invoice(s). Double-click on any item on the invoice **2230Wo** line. The original invoice that created the $ values is displayed with a **PAID** image. This will assist you in verifying if payment was received on an invoice.

15 ➤ **Exit** the Invoice Lookup, and **Exit** the Aged Detail report.

Journalizing a Cash Sale with a Discount

You learned earlier how to journalize a payment for a sale on credit with a discount. In this exercise, you will learn how to journalize a cash sale with a discount; e.g., a senior's discount. This procedure would also apply if the business was giving a discount to a firm for buying a lot of merchandise or services (trade discount).

Exercise 2B-31 – Journalizing a Cash Sale with a Discount (Senior)

Santos Luggage has had a number of inquiries from senior citizens who want to buy various luggage articles, and would appreciate a senior's discount, similar to what other businesses allow. Mrs. Santos has decided that it would be appropriate to offer a 10% discount to senior citizens (this is not the same as a cash discount for paying early on credit sales). Mrs. Santos has decided that she did not need to track this type of discount and does not need a new ledger account for senior's discount. See the information after step 10 for alternate ways to track this type of discount by setting up a new General Ledger account; e.g., SENIOR'S DISCOUNT.

These sales will be recorded in the Sales Journal by typing the customer's name and using the **Continue** button because the business wants a record of the customer's name in the entry, similar to other entries made from the Outlet Centre. See Exercise 2B-28 **Customer** area.

Mar 18, 2016   Mr. Ronald Peddle, a senior citizen, provided you with a senior's card and purchased 2 Suitcases w/w large at $80.00 each, before a 10% senior's discount. HST would be added to the price after the discount as follows:

Suitcases w/w large, 2 @ $80.00	$160.00	
Senior's discount less 10%	$ (16.00)	
Net Sales amount before taxes		$144.00
HST 13% on $144.00		$ 18.72
Amount to be paid		$162.72

Mr. Peddle paid the bill in full with his cheque #749.

You will record the sale with the regular selling price and also show the discount. *Note*: The cash discount on goods is not a discount for paying within the invoice terms. However, only the $72.00 net amount for each suitcase (total $144.00) is posted to the Sales account. Follow these steps:

1 ➤ Create an invoice using the **Sales Invoices** icon.

   Transaction   Do not change from Invoice.

2 ➤ **Paid By**   Select **Cheque**, [Tab] to Deposit To.

3 ➤ **Deposit To**   Do not change the default 1020 Bank Chequing Account, [Tab] to Cheque.

4 ➤ Cheque No. Type **749**, [Tab] .

5 ➤ Customer area Type **Mr. Ronald Peddle**, [Tab] , click **Continue**, then click **OK**, then [Tab] [Tab] to move to the address area and type **2569 Plaster Lane**, [Tab] , type **Mississauga, ON**, [Tab] , type **L5N 3K7**, [Tab] . Click the **Ship to** field.

6 ➤ Shipping Address If you click the [▼] there will not be an address listed. A cash sale customer would not require a Ship-to-Address. [Tab] to move to the lower box. Type **Outlet Store**, [Tab] . Click on **Quantity**.

7 ➤ Quantity Complete the information as shown next.

Quantity	Order	Back Order	Unit	Item Description	Base Price	Discount (%)	Price	Amount	Tax	Account
2			each	Suitcase w/w large size with senior's discount	80.00	10.00	72.00	144.00	HS	4100 Sales

Other Information:

Discount (%) This column is used to record reductions in the price of the goods being sold. The price reduction can be for senior's discount, quantity or trade discounts.

Tax **HS** Retail Sale 13% HST will be removed from 10% of the original Sales price.

Early Payment Discount:		%	
	Cheque Amount		162.72

 Do not type an amount in the Early Payment Discount field. This field is linked to the Sales Discount account for paying within 2% 10 days discount terms and is not applicable to Senior's Discounts.

 Some firms would also use the Disc % column to give discounts to businesses that buy a lot of goods or services. This is usually called **Quantity** or **Trade discount**. If so, then the original sales price is shown, with the appropriate discount for the customer in the Discount column. The Price column would show the reduced price for each item on the invoice.

Quantity	Order	Back Order	Unit	Item Description	Base Price	Discount (%)	Price	Amount	Tax	Account
5			each	Suitcase w/w large	80.00	15.00	68.00	340.00	HS	4100 Sales

The Sales Invoice window for the senior's discount should look like the following:

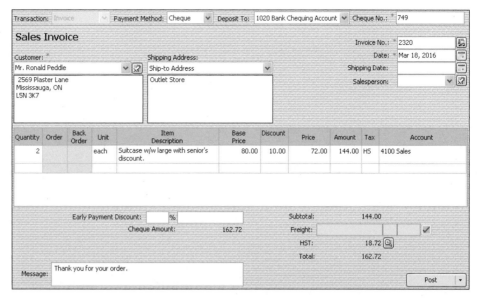

Fig. 2B-20: Sales Invoice window – Senior's Discount.

8 ➤ **Display** the Sales Journal Entry. It should resemble the following:

Sales Journal Entry Mar 18, 2016 (J12)

Account Number	Account Description	Debits	Credits
1020	Bank Chequing Account	162.72	-
2630	HST Charged on Sales	-	18.72
4100	Sales	-	144.00
Additional Date:	Additional Field:		
		162.72	162.72

9 ➤ **Exit** from the display window and **post** the entry when correct.

10 ➤ **Exit** to the Home window. (See the Information note box that follows.)

Some firms want to keep track of the dollar value of discounts given to seniors and would create a new G/L account **Senior's Discount**. If so, the invoice window would be similar to that shown below.

Quantity	Order	Back Order	Unit	Item Description	Base Price	Discount (%)	Price	Amount	Tax	Account
2			each	Suitcase w/w large	80.00		80.00	160.00	HS	4100 Sales
2			each	Senior's Discount	-8.00		-8.00	-16.00	HS	4170 Senior's Dis…

The journal entry would be similar to:

Sales Journal Entry Mar 18, 2016 (J12)

Account Number	Account Description	Debits	Credits
1020	Bank Chequing Account	162.72	-
4170	Senior's Discount	16.00	-
2630	HST Charged on Sales	-	18.72
4100	Sales	-	160.00
Additional Date:	Additional Field:		
		178.72	178.72

Additional Transactions

1 ➤ Record and **Post** the following transaction information.

The Additional Info note box for **A-Your Name Luggage Rack** (normally appears in the top left corner of the window) appears to remind you to discuss the 2% discount in 10 days with the customer. **Close** the Additional Info box.

Mar 18, 2016 **Sold to the Oakville branch of A-Your Name Luggage Rack the following: 4 Suitcases w/w large @ $62.00 each, plus HST Total Invoice including HST of $32.24, is $280.24. Credit terms 2%/10 n30.**

Mar 18, 2016 **Havarah Leather Goods returned 2 briefcases narrow ($70.00 plus HST each on invoice #2316). The locks are damaged. Total return is $158.20 including HST of $18.20 Credit terms 2/1 net 21.**

Mar 18, 2016 **Judy Morrison, a part-time staff member, purchased 1 suitcase w/w large at 80.00 less a 20% staff discount, plus HST. Cheque #225 received.**

Additional Transactions

1 ➤ Advance the Session date to **Mar 21, 2016**.

2 ➤ Record and Post the following transaction information.

Mar 21, 2016 **Receipt from Havarah Leather Goods from sale on March 09, less the return. Note cheque 786 dated March 19. Allow the discount.**

Mar 21, 2016 **Sale at Outlet Store to Henry Taylor of 2 suitcases w/w large at $70.00 plus HST. Cheque 683 received.**

Journalizing a Customer's NSF Cheque

When a customer's cheque is returned by the bank as **NSF** (**N**ot **S**ufficient **F**unds), it means the customer did not have enough money in their account to cover the cheque that they had sent to you for payment. In a real sense they still owe you money for the invoice that you now show as paid in your records.

To correct this situation, enter in the Sales Journal an increase (Debit) to **Accounts Receivable** in the amount of the NSF cheque plus bank charges, if any, and a decrease (Credit) to **Bank Account** (or Cash) for the same amount as the debit. To keep track of the fact that the entry is due to an NSF cheque, you can use the same invoice number as the original invoice with the code NS or NSF; e.g., Invoice #12345NSF.

DO NOT use the Reverse Entry icon. You do not want to reverse the original sale. The sale has taken place, only the payment is not valid.

Exercise 2B-32 – Journalizing an NSF Customer Cheque

1 ➤ Advance the Session date to **Mar 25, 2016**.

Study this transaction:

Mar 23, 2016	**You were notified by a bank debit memo, from your bank, that Mrs. Arlene Hirsch's cheque #456 in the amount of $254.25 was returned NSF (Not Sufficient Funds). The bank charged an additional service fee of $15.00 for the NSF transaction.**
	You called Mrs. Hirsch and she explained that she has changed banks, as she moved recently and inadvertently used the wrong cheque. She promised that she will send you a replacement cheque to cover the above. Her new home is at *993 Ashdown Crescent, Toronto M3H 2K8*, new phone number *905-585-6366*.

To locate the details of the entry made in the accounting records, when the cheque was originally received, use the Reports, Journal Entries, All to display the entries. Locate the entry with the amount of the original cheque $254.25. You can then drill down to locate the original entry and invoice number. Verify the information before recording the NSF cheque.

Some banks charge an NSF service fee for processing the returned cheques. If your company is charged a fee, the amount will be added to the amount the customer owes your firm (original account receivable $254.25 plus the service fee, e.g., $15.00). (See following information note for an entry if a service fee was not charged.) You will charge Mrs. Hirsch the bank service fee that was charged by the bank for this transaction.

If the bank did not charge a fee to process an NSF cheque, the entry would be similar
to: 1200 Accounts Receivable   254.25
       1020 Bank Chequing Account   254.25

When you recorded the cheque on Mar 15, 2016 from Mrs. Hirsch, you journalized the entry as an **Invoice Paid by Cheque** for a **One-time customer** in the Sales Journal, and made the following entry:

Sales Journal Entry Mar 15, 2016 (J8)

Account Number	Account Description	Debits	Credits
1020	Bank Chequing Account	254.25	-
2630	HST Charged on Sales	-	29.25
4100	Sales	-	225.00
Additional Date:	Additional Field:		
		254.25	254.25

The bank, by the debit memo, has reduced our bank account balance by $269.25 (the amount of the $254.25 NSF cheque plus $15.00 service fee); therefore, Mrs. Hirsch now owes the company the same amount. We need to set up Mrs. Hirsch as a customer and show this amount as being outstanding until her replacement cheque is recorded.

When you record the NSF cheque, you will record the following entry:

1200	Accounts Receivable	269.25*	
1020	Bank Chequing Account		269.25
	(* 254.25 +15.00)		

2 ➤ Using the **Sales Invoices** journal icon, create an Invoice as follows.

3 ➤ **Customer**   Type **Mrs. Arlene Hirsch** [Tab].

4 ➤ Select **Full Add** and set up **Mrs. Hirsch** as a customer with the **address information** provided; customer since **Mar 15, 2016.** Leave Revenue Account field blank, terms will be **0%** discount, and **Net amount due within 4 days**. Use **No** Tax code. Credit Limit **0.00**.

There is no sale when you record an NSF cheque. The sale took place on March 15, and you are now recording the fact that the customer owes you the money originally received.

She will have a **0.00** credit limit, and the memo note could be:

> Replacement cheque for NSF cheque required from customer
> NSF cheque #456 received in Outlet Store. Friend of employee (put in your name).

To-Do date   Select **Mar 29, 2016,** as a reminder to verify that the cheque was received.

Display this Memo   Click this field to place a ✓ in the box.

Click the Save and Close button when done.

5 ➤ **Invoice**   Type **2318NS Cheque 456** and `Tab` `Tab`. Remember that Simply prevents the entry of an invoice number twice, so adding NS (for Not Sufficient Funds) to the invoice number will allow you to enter the original invoice number twice. This will also indicate to you, later, that this entry is a re-entry of a previous sale due to an NSF cheque. The 456 represents the cheque number that was received NSF. 456 is recorded for tracing purposes, if required.

6 ➤ **Date**   Select **Mar 23, 2016,** `Tab`. Click on **Item Description**.

7 ➤ **Item Description**   Type **NSF cheque #456,** `Tab`. Click on **Amount**.

8 ➤ **Amount**   Type **269.25,** `Tab` `Tab` to Acct. This will leave a blank Tax field. This is the same as double-clicking and selecting - No Tax.

9 ➤ **Acct**   Press `Enter`. Select **1020 Bank Chequing Account**. This results in a credit to the Bank Account.

10 ➤ **Remove** the Message box information, `Tab`. The lower section should look like the following:

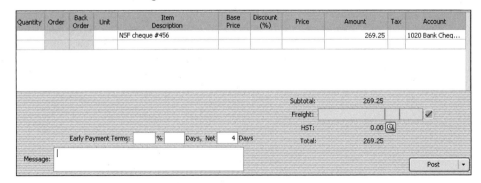

Fig. 2B-19: NSF Sales Invoice.

11 ➤ Display the Sales Journal Entry. The window should appear as follows:

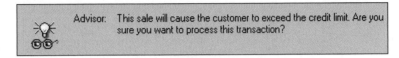

Sales Journal Entry Mar 23, 2016 (J18)			
Account Number	Account Description	Debits	Credits
1200	Accounts Receivable	269.25	-
1020	Bank Chequing Account	-	269.25
Additional Date:	Additional Field:		
		269.25	269.25

> An alternate method to record a returned cheque is to reverse the payment transaction (see Chapter 13, *Correcting Transaction Errors after Posting*).
>
> The invoice method shown in this exercise is preferred by many businesses because it allows you to send an invoice to the customer advising them that they owe you the money.

Notice that there is no amount posted to the Sales account. The sale was recorded on March 15, 2016. The credit to the Bank Account shows that the payment from Mrs. Hirsch was NSF. This entry reverses the bank deposit entry of March 15, and debits (increases) the customer's Accounts Receivable account.

12 ➤ **Exit** the Sales Journal Entry window and **Post** the entry.

You should receive the following warning message. (The credit limit was set to 0.00.) (See side note box.) If not, proceed to step 14.

> Advisor: This sale will cause the customer to exceed the credit limit. Are you sure you want to process this transaction?

13 ➤ Click **Yes**. You entered a 0.00 credit limit for this customer.

14 ➤ **Exit** from the Sales Journal. Return to the Home window.

Another Transaction

1 ➤ **Journalize** and **post** the following transaction: Return to the Home window.

> **Mar 24, 2016** **Cheque #186 from Sandler Travel Stores in the amount of $2,407.00 for Jan 26, 2016 invoice #2197 received and deposited to the bank.**

1 ➤ **Record** and **Post** the following transaction information.

> **Mar 24, 2016** **Bank by debit memo, returned Henry Taylor cheque #683 as NSF. The bank charged a $15.00 service fee. Mrs. Santos, sent a letter to Mr. Taylor requesting a replacement cheque for the NSF cheque, plus the bank service fee.**

1 ➤ Advance the Session date to **Mar 29, 2016**.

Applying an Invoice to a Deposit

On March 15, 2016 Opal Kong Luggage Ltd. placed a $6,780.00 sales order with a deposit of $3,500.00. The customer ledger shows a **-3,500.00** balance.

When the goods are shipped, you would convert the sales order into a sales invoice for $6,780.00.

The $6,780.00 sales invoice less the deposit of $3,500.00 you recorded earlier, will leave a receivable balance owing of $3,280.00.

Exercise 2B-33 – Applying an Invoice to a Deposit

Here is the full transaction description:

> **Mar 25, 2016** **The special order of 30 Clothes and Laptop suitcase with embossed company logos for Opal Kong Luggage Ltd. was received this morning from your supplier. The cases were checked and then sent to Opal Kong. The $6,780.00 price is per sales order #104.**

1 ➤   Change Sales Order #104 to an invoice #2324 (see Caution information below). **Record** and **Post** the invoice as the order has been filled. The Sales Invoice window lower portion should display as shown next.

Simply may have changed the **Paid By** field to **Cheque** (last used selection when the Sales Order was created). Change it to **Pay Later**.

Quantity	Order	Back Order	Unit	Item Description	Base Price	Discount (%)	Price	Amount	Tax	Account
30	30		each	Clothes and Laptop suitcase w/w with embossed company logos for the Price Company	200.00		200.00	6,000.00	HS	4100 Sales

	Subtotal: 6,000.00
Deposit Applied: 3,500.00	Freight: ✔
	HST: 780.00 🔍
Early Payment Terms: 2.00 % 10 Days, Net 30 Days	Total: 6,780.00
Message: Thank you for your order.	Amount Owing: 3,280.00 [Post ▼]

The Deposit Paid wording has changed to **Deposit Applied**.

The **Total** field shows the invoice amount as the correct $6,780.00. See Step 2 Journal entry.

The **Amount Owing** field now shows the balance owing (after reduction of the deposit). You will also see it reduced in Step 4, when you display the Aged Detail report. However, the printed invoice does not show the reduced balance.

2 ➤   Display the Sales Journal entry; it will look similar to the following:

Sales Journal Entry Mar 25, 2016 (J21)

Account Number	Account Description	Debits	Credits
1200	Accounts Receivable	6,780.00	-
2630	HST Charged on Sales	-	780.00
4100	Sales	-	6,000.00
Additional Date:	Additional Field:		
		6,780.00	6,780.00

3 ➤   **Exit** the entry, **Post** the sale. The information box Sales Order has been filled and removed from the system displays. Click **OK**.

4 ➤ **Exit** to the Home window. Display a Customer Aged Detail report at March 25, for Opal Kong Luggage Ltd., and note how Simply displays the deposit and sale. The report should display as follows:

Customer Aged Detail As at Mar 25, 2016

Source	Date	Transaction Type	Total	Current
Opal Kong Luggage Ltd.				
Dp SO104	Mar 15, 2016	Prepaid Order	-3,500.00	-3,500.00
2324	Mar 25, 2016	Applied	3,500.00	3,500.00
2324	Mar 25, 2016	Invoice	6,780.00	6,780.00
2324	Mar 25, 2016	Payment	-3,500.00	-3,500.00
Total unpaid invoices:			3,280.00	3,280.00
Total deposits/prepaid order:			-	-

Dp SO#104 and **Prepaid Order**	This is the deposit received when Opal placed her order on the 15th.
Applied	The **Prepaid** amount is transferred from the Sales Order record to the invoice, when you changed the sales order into a sales invoice, shown at line 4 (in the Aging report) as a payment.
Invoice	This is the regular **$6,780.00** Invoice recorded previously.
Payment	This is from the **Applied** amount discussed above.

You will note that the amount **Unpaid by Opal** in this transaction is **3,280.00** ($6,780.00 sale less the $3,500.00 deposit).

5 ➤ **Exit** from the display and return to the Home window.

Journalizing Credit Card Receipts

A credit card received as a payment on any ACCOUNTS RECEIVABLE amount owing may be recorded directly to a specific credit card account which may be linked to one of the bank accounts. In your company's Chart of Accounts, 1030 Visa Credit Card Bank Account is linked to the Visa Credit Card. If you record a payment using a credit card from Visa, it updates the 1030 Visa Credit Card Bank Account.

Exercise 2B-34 – Journalizing a Credit Card Receipt

Study the following transaction:

> **Mar 29, 2016 Mrs. Hirsch came in to pay her account. She decided to pay her account (NSF cheque) using her Visa card. Process her payment using the credit card.**

1 ➤ Using Mrs. Arlene Hirsch from the Customers Area, use **Receive Payments**.

2 ➤ **Paid By**   Select **Visa Credit**, [Tab] to From.

   From   Mrs. Arlene Hirsch is selected.

3 ➤ **Receipt No.** This is a credit card receipt which does not have a cheque or invoice number. You do NOT want to record the Authorization code from the credit card company on this document because of privacy concerns. Click the field, type **Visa**. `Tab` `Tab` to Date.

4 ➤ **Date** `Tab` to accept. `Tab` to Invoice Date.

5 ➤ **Invoice Date** `Tab` `Tab` to Amount Received.

Discount Taken There is no discount on this invoice (NSF cheque).

6 ➤ **Amount Received** `Tab` to accept 269.25.

7 ➤ **Comment** Type **Paid by Visa Credit Card**.

The Receipt window should look like the following:

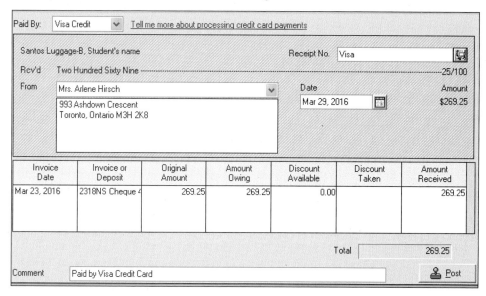

8 ➤ **Display** the Receipts Journal entry. It should resemble the following:

Receipts Journal Entry Mar 29, 2016 (J22)

Account Number	Account Description	Debits	Credits
1030	Visa Credit Card Bank Account	259.83	-
5340	Credit Card Charges	9.42	-
1200	Accounts Receivable	-	269.25
Additional Date:	Additional Field:		
		269.25	269.25

9 ➤ **Exit** from the display window and **Post** the entry when correct.

10 ➤ **Exit** to the Home window.

11 ➤ Advance Session date to **Mar 31, 2016**.

Owner Investment in Business

The owner's investment may be recorded by either of the following methods:

1. Recording a General Journal entry to show the personal investment where funds have been transferred by the bank.

2. Setting up a customer ledger with the owner's name and recording a sales invoice (using the Capital account or Additional Investment by Owner account) paid by cheque whenever the owner invests more money into the business.

Method #1 is the preferred method.

Exercise 2B-35 – Journalizing Owner Investment in Business

> **Mar 31, 2016 Mrs. Santos has decided to invest an additional $6,000.00 into the business, as she is going to purchase a large number of suitcases from a company that is going out of business. She, therefore, transferred $6,000.00 from her personal bank account to the company's bank account. She brought the bank transfer form as a source document for the business.**

The General Journal method will be used to record the investment.

1 ➤ Click on the **COMPANY** module and click on the **General Journal** icon. **Record** and **Post** the investment based on the following window.

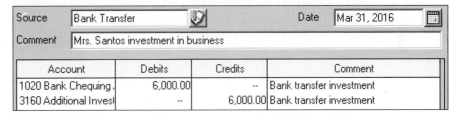

2 ➤ **View** the General Journal entry. The window should appear as follows:

General Journal Entry Mar 31, 2016 (J23)			
Account Number	Account Description	Debits	Credits
1020	Bank Chequing Account	6,000.00	-
	Bank transfer investment		
3160	Additional Investment	-	6,000.00
	Bank transfer investment		
Additional Date:	Additional Field:		
		6,000.00	6,000.00

3 ➤ **Exit** from viewing the General Journal entry.

4 ➤ **Post** when correct and **Exit** to the Home page.

Additional Transactions

Process the following two transactions:

Mar 31, 2016　**Mrs. Santos visited the Royes Luggage Inc. store yesterday evening, and discussed the problems (conditions of goods received) with their manager. Mrs. Santos and the manager agreed that there is a problem with the goods. Mrs. Santos will give a Sales price allowance for the goods on invoice #2212, in the amount of $100.00 plus HST. Mrs. Santos received Royes Luggage Inc.'s cheque #496 in the amount of $904.00 as payment for this invoice less the allowance. There are no discount terms on this allowance as it is more than 10 days from the purchase date.**

　　　　　　　　　1. Record the allowance.
　　　　　　　　　2. Record the cheque received.

Mar 31, 2016　**Sold to Luggage 4U, to be picked up today, 5 Suitcases w/w large @$62.00 plus HST, and 4 Power Adapters @ $10.50 each plus HST. Issued invoice #2325 for $397.76 including 45.76 HST, terms 2/10 net 30 days.**

Recording a Receipt for a Non-Merchandise Item

There will be situations when the business receives a cheque(s) for goods that are not being resold (e.g., sale of your old equipment, rebate cheque, etc.).

This next exercise shows you how to enter the rebate information as a cash transaction (refer to Exercise 2B-27), as an invoice is normally created for the cheque received. The name of the firm issuing the cheque will appear in journal entries.

Exercise 2B-36 – Journalizing a Non-Merchandise Cheque

Mar 31, 2016　**Mrs. Santos handed you a $10.20 mail-in-rebate cheque #2897561 that she forgot was in her briefcase. The rebate cheque is for a case of computer paper the business purchased last month from the Office Supply Store.**

　　　　　　　　　You would not create a customer ledger for the Office Supply Store as they are a vendor in the PAYABLE module.

---

1 ➤　Create an invoice using the **Sales Invoice**s icon.

　　　　Transaction　　　Do NOT change the default Invoice.

2 ➤　**Payment Method** Select **Cheque**, [Tab].

3 ➤ Deposit to   Do NOT change, [Tab] to accept 1020 Bank Chequing
                    Account.

4 ➤ Cheque   Type **2897561** [Tab].

5 ➤ Customer   Enter the information shown next.

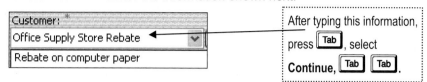

6 ➤ Enter the information shown next.

Quantity	Order	Back Order	Unit	Description	Base Price	Disc. %	Price	Amount	Tax	Acct
				Rebate on computer paper				10.20		1320 Prepaid Supplies

Tax   You will not be able to recover tax (HST) on a rebate. Leave
                the field blank.

Account   Select **1320 Prepaid Supplies**, as this is the account that
                was charged when the computer paper was purchased.

7 ➤ Comments   **Remove** the comments. They are not needed for a rebate.
                    The complete Invoice window is shown next.

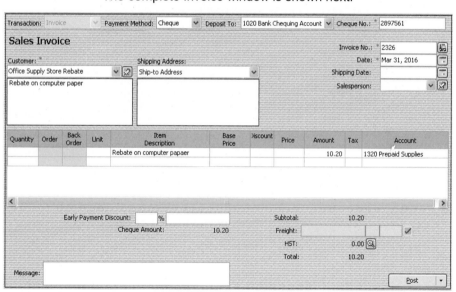

8 ➤ **View** the Sales Journal Entry. The window should appear as follows:

Sales Journal Entry Mar 31, 2016 (J25)

Account Number	Account Description	Debits	Credits
1020	Bank Chequing Account	10.20	-
1320	Prepaid Supplies	-	10.20
Additional Date:	Additional Field:		
		10.20	10.20

9 ➤ **Exit** from the display window.

10 ➤ **Post** when correct and **Exit** to the Home window.

The following would appear in the Reports, Journal Entries - All display.

2897561, 2326, Office Supply Store Rebate

Printing Customer Statements

Many businesses send their customers a statement, which is a record of the transactions recorded in their account. This will give customers a chance to check their own records and investigate any invoices that do not agree. It is also a very effective reminder to customers of any overdue amounts. Statements may be printed or e-mailed for all customers or for individual customers at any time during the month.

If a firm prints statements for mailing, they can use the built in Simply Custom forms or they can purchase pre-printed forms from a printing company, which can include the company logo and will have shaded column headings for Simply to print the information that is shown in Fig. 2B-20. A brochure of various forms available is included in the software manufacturer's package. You can order the forms through Simply, or you would take the brochure to a commercial printer to have forms customized for your company. You can also e-mail a version of the statement to the customer if you have their e-mail address.

Remember that statements may be printed at any time (whenever there is a customer account inquiry, to collect an overdue account, etc.), not only at the end of the month. To reduce paper use, your instructor may request you to print only one statement (on plain paper) for an individual customer to allow you to see what will print on preprinted forms.

Exercise 2B-37 – Printing Customer Statements

For practice, you will print one customer statement on blank paper. Be sure your printer is ready.

1 ➤ From the Home window, in the **Customers** area, at **Royes Luggage Inc.**, click on ▼ and click on **View Customer Record**.

2 ➤ Click the **Options** tab.

3 ➤ Make sure the **Produce Statements for this Customer** box is (✓). Statements for customers may be printed only if this box is (✓).

4 ➤ **Exit** from the Receivables Ledger window.

There are two options for printing statements:

1. In the Tasks area click on the ▼ at **Customer's** icon, click on **View Customers**. From the menu bar, click **Reports, Customer Statements** and you will see the Customer Statements window displayed. Select **Royes Luggage Inc.** the customer who will receive the statement. With a setting of **Print**, click **OK** and the statement prints.

   Return to the Home window to see another way to print this statement.

2. From the Home window, click **Reports, Receivables, Customer Statements** and you are at the Customer Statements window.

5 ➤ Using either method, make sure the ⊙ Print button, in the top-right corner, is selected. Select **Royes Luggage Inc.**, then **OK**. The statement should print.

Your printout on plain paper should resemble Fig. 2B-20. This information will be printed on the pre-printed form, or similar information can be e-mailed to your customer.

```
Santos Luggage-B, Student's Name
635 Semple Avenue
Toronto, Ontario M9L 1V5

                                                    Mar 31, 2016

Royes Luggage Inc.                          Royes Luggage Inc.
Julie Ann Royes
256 Ochos Blvd.
Toronto, Ontario M4K 3V3            Mar 31, 2016


Jan 31, 2016    2212      Invoice    1,017.00
Mar 31, 2016    496       Payment   -1,017.00  _____
                                                0.00   2212              0.00


Feb 27, 2016    2256      Invoice    1,243.00
Mar 03, 2016    438       Discount     -22.00
Mar 03, 2016    438       Payment   -1,221.00  _____
                                                0.00   2256              0.00

Mar 10, 2016    2317      Invoice             1,605.73  2317         1,605.73
Mar 31, 2016    2212AI    Invoice    -113.00
Mar 31, 2016    496       Payment     113.00   _____
                                                0.00   2212AI            0.00



        Current       31-60     Over 60
        1,605.73       0.00       0.00           1,605.73            1,605.73
```

Fig. 2B-20: *Customer Statement information printed on pre-printed forms.*

Notice how Simply displays information for sales (Invoices) and receipts (Payment and Discount). Information for invoice #2212 is shown in two places (2212AI) as the report lists invoices by date order.

 Be sure to back up your data and update your logbook at the end of every work session.

Printing Period-End Reports

The following reports may be printed for management's information and for filing for the audit trail.

- Journal Entries may be printed in one of two ways (see Exercise 1-17).

  a) **Journal Entries All** will print all journal entries from all modules (with or without corrections). All transactions, in the time-period requested, are numbered in this journal in sequential order (even if entered in a subledger; i.e., RECEIVABLES or PAYABLES module).

  b) **General Journal Entries** will print journal entries entered in the COMPANY module only.

- The General Ledger — complete general ledger listing of transactions for the month.

- The Receivable Sales Journal for the month.

- The Receivable Receipts Journal for the month.

- The Balance Sheet as at March 31.

- The Income Statement for the year to March 31.

- The Customer Aged Detail report.
- The Aged Overdue Receivables Detail.

The HST Report — all transactions in the month with HST are shown in this report (see Appendix D, *Printing a Tax Report* at www.simplyaccounting2010.nelson.com under Student Resources for more information).

1 ➤ To save time and paper, **print** only the following:

    a) All Journal entries, with corrections Mar 07 to Mar 31
    b) General Journal entries   Mar 07 to Mar 31
    c) Income Statement for period   Jan 01 to Mar 31
    d) Income Statement for period   Mar 07 to Mar 31 for Sales Manager. Hide details of Cost of Goods Sold and Office/Warehouse Expenses.
    e) Balance Sheet at   Mar 31
    f) Customer Aged Detail report at   Mar 31
    g) General Ledger   Mar 07 to Mar 31

Your instructor may request printouts of the Sales and/or Cash Receipts Journals.

2 ➤ Compare the amount in the ACCOUNTS RECEIVABLE account on the Balance Sheet with the Customer Aged Detail total balance. They should be the same!

3 ➤ Compare your printouts with the RECEIVABLE data files for Santos Luggage provided on the Solutions Disk with your instructor.

As you were going through the lessons earlier, you learned how to print some of the reports above. Instructions for reports that you have not printed earlier follow.

Exercise 2B-38 – To Print Period-End Reports

To Print a Gross Margin Income Statement

The **Gross Margin Income Statement** can also be called the **Gross Profit Income Statement** and is an income statement that breaks down Expenses into two categories; **Cost of Goods Sold** (takes into account items that refer to goods purchased for resale) and **Expenses** (referred to as purchases of goods/services not for resale).

1 ➤ Click **Report Centre,** click **Financials,** click the **+** at Income Statement, select **Gross Margin – Standard,** click **Modify this Report.**

2 ➤ The Start and Finish dates should be **Jan. 01, 2016** and **March 31, 2016.** You can change the dates to display the report for different dates. Click **OK** to display the Income Statement.

3 ➤ Click the **Print** icon to print the report. Note the change in wording for various lines; Net Sales and Total Revenue to: TOTAL REVENUE and TOTAL OPERATING REVENUE. A GROSS MARGIN line has been added and the information below the Total Expenses line. Refer to your accounting textbook for discussion of these changes as this text does not explain the various changes.

4 ➤ **Exit** from the display window.

To Print the Sales Journal

1 ➤ Click **Report Centre**, move to **Receivables, Sales Journal Entries.** Click **Modify this Report.** The **Start date** should be **Mar 07, 2016** (the day the file was started). If required, click Modify, Report Options, to add or remove the ✓ at Corrections. Click **OK** to display the sales journal entries.

2 ➤ Click the **Print** icon to print the report.

3 ➤ **Exit** from the display window.

To Print the Receipts Journal

1 ➤ Click **Report Centre**, move to **Receivables, Receipt Journal Entries.** Click **Modify this Report**. The **Start date** should be **Mar 07, 2016** (the day the file was started). If required, click Modify, Report Options, to add or remove the ✓ at Corrections. Click **OK** to display the Receipt Journal entries.

2 ➤ Click the **Print** icon to print the report.

3 ➤ **Exit** from the display window.

View/Print Graphs

Simply also has a Graph feature that allows you to view and/or print your data in graph format.

Additional information on using the graph feature (pie and bar charts) can be found in Appendix K, *Graphs Feature* at www.simplyaccounting2010.nelson.com under Student Resources

---

Exercise 2B-39 – Viewing/Printing Graphs

To View Graphs

1 ➤ From the Home page, click **Graphs** from the menu bar.

2 ➤ Click Receivables **by Customer**, **Select All**, **OK**. A pie chart will display.

The Generated on date will correspond to the date you display the graph.

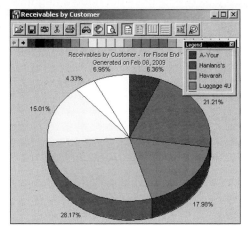

3 ➤ At this point, you may print the graph by clicking the **Print** button. The Legend will not print with the graph.

4 ➤ **Exit** from the graph display.

Summary, Part B

Here is a summary of the transactions entered in Chapter 2B.

Transaction:	Journal/Ledger	Remarks:
Deposit	*Receipts*	Enter a deposit when you receive a partial payment with the Sales Order.
Cash Sale	*Sales*	Select **Transaction Invoice** and **Paid by: Cash/Cheque** with Payments; **One-time Customer,** or type the **customer's name** in the Sold to field and click **Continue**, for an automatic cash/cheque sale.
Credit Card Sale	*Sales*	Select **Transaction Invoice**, and choose the Credit Card Company in the **Paid by** drop-down box.
Write-off	*Sales*	Enter write-off as a minus amount with HST.
NSF cheque	*Sales*	Enter a revised invoice or new invoice for the original cheque (plus bank charges) with **no** taxes. Select the **Cash in Bank** account *(not* Sales).
Post-dated cheques	*Receipts*	The post-dated entry (debit Bank, credit Accounts Receivable) will not appear in reports until the date the cheque is deposited. More information is found in Appendix M, *Post-Dated Cheques* at www.simplyaccounting2010.nelson.com under Student Resources.
Revise an Invoice		Use **Lookup** to find the original invoice and adjust with the corrected amounts. Can also be seen in Chapter 13.

Review **Slideshows 2A** and **2B**.

Before Moving On..., Part B

Read the following questions and make sure you know the answers to them; otherwise, review the corresponding section in the chapter before moving on.

1. What is a deposit? In what circumstances would a business require a deposit? Where do you record the deposit?

2. Which of the following business events does not need a negative amount to record the transaction?
    a) A retail sale invoice for a pair of sunglasses was issued for $172.89 ($153.00 plus taxes) and should have been issued for the correct amount of $152.55 ($135.00 plus taxes).
    b) Write off a customer balance due to the bankruptcy of the customer.
    c) Record a sale with HST to a customer.
    d) Return of an unopened DVD movie by a customer.
    e) None of the other choices.

3. How would you record a senior's discount?

4. Give the journal entry (or entries) for a $210.00 NSF cheque for which the bank has added bank charges of $15.00 (no HST) to your company bank statement. Indicate the Simply module in which the entry is made.

5. What is a customer account write-off? In what circumstances would a business write off a customer account?

6. A customer wants to pay an outstanding invoice $339.00 (which includes $39.00 of HST) with a credit card. Which Journal would you use to record it and what entry is made in the accounting records assuming the bank charges 3% for processing credit cards?

7. Your manager would like you to prepare a Gross Margin Income Statement. What is it?

8. How do you record a Quantity discount for a good customer?

Challenge Exercise 02 C2B-1, Brides

RECEIVABLES and COMPANY Modules

1 ➤ Refer to Exercise 1-1 to unzip the **02 C2B-1 Brides.exe** file.

2 ➤ Open the **02 C2B-1 Brides** file and enter Receivable transactions for May for a company that sells bridal gowns, other dresses, and accessories. HST is 13%. Brides Company does not print Sales invoices or receipts.

Note: All sales are personally picked up; therefore, leave 'Shipped by' field blank.

May 3   Issued Sales Order #30 to Marlene's Bridal Fashions for 4 pink bridesmaid dresses. Each dress will sell for $410.00, plus HST. Accept default terms 2/10, net 30. Total order $1,853.20. Delivery date will be May 27.

May 3   Received cheque #689 for $3,330.00 (net of $60.00 discount) as payment in full from Bev's Bridal Shop re outstanding invoice #381.

May 5   Retail sale to credit card customer Navneet Banwait of 1 bridal gown for $1,200.00 and 4 accessories at $30.00 each (all items plus HST). Credit card authorization #D1962 for $1,491.60.

May 6   Sold 3 bridal gowns to Brenda's Dresses at $800.00 each, plus HST. Terms 2/10, net 30 days. Invoice total $2,712.00.

May 9   Sold 3 bridal gowns at $800.00 each and 10 accessories at $25.00 each, plus HST, to new customer, **Your Actual Name Dresses**, contact **Your Actual Name**, 967 Spadina Street, Markville, Ontario, L3X 2Z9. Phone and fax number are 905-826-3820. Credit limit will be $5,000.00 with terms of 2/10, net 30 days, Invoice total $2,994.50.

May 14   **Your Actual Name Dresses** returned 10 accessories, as the customers did not like the style. Return accepted, and credit note referring to invoice #784 sent to customer.

May 19   Sold a dress at $250.00, plus HST, to Mrs. Petra Kurek, a senior citizen, for an engagement party. Mrs. Kurek qualifies for the 10% senior's discount. Use any of the methods discussed in the chapter. Cheque #556 received.

May 19   **Your Actual Name Dresses** cheque #613 as payment in full was received.

May 24   The bank advised that Mrs. Kurek's cheque #556 for $254.25 was returned 'Account Closed.' Mrs. Kurek was contacted and she will be sending a certified cheque to cover the error.

May 24   A new customer, Saira Heggie (any address information is acceptable), ordered a $900.00, plus HST cream wedding dress to be delivered by June 12. Sales Order #31 was issued and a $300.00 cheque #134 was received as a deposit. Leave discount terms blank.

May 25   The pink bridesmaid dresses ordered on sales order #30 arrived and were picked up by Marlene's Bridal Fashions. Invoice amount per the May 3 order.

May 31   The owner, Mrs. Mehta, gave you a bank transfer for $4,000.00 which is for her additional investment in the business.

> If an Additional Investment account does not exist in the Chart of Accounts, use the Capital Account for the investment.

3 ➤ When you have recorded the above entries, print the following:

   a.   Customer Aged Detail Report as at May 31
   b.   Journal Entries All, for the monthly activity
   c.   Journal Entries-General, for the monthly activity
   d.   Sales Journal for May
   e.   Cash Receipts Journal for May
   f.   Income Statement for May 1 to May 31
   g.   Pending Sales Order as at June 12

Challenge Exercise 02 C2B-2, Skis

RECEIVABLES and COMPANY Modules

1 ➤ Refer to Exercise 1-1 to unzip the **02 C2B-2 Skis.exe** file.

2 ➤ Open the **02 C2B-2 Skis** file and enter Receivable and General Ledger transactions for March for a company that sells skis and related sporting equipment. HST is 13%.

Note: All sales are personally picked up; therefore leave 'Shipped by' field blank.

Mar 2   Retail sale of 1 pair of Blanchard skis and bindings $550.00 plus HST to Miss Devon Cutronia. Received her Universal credit card for payment.

Mar 3   Issued Sales Order #212 to Jordan's Sports Equipment for 10 Jock SnowBoards at $500.00 each plus HST. Snowboards shipping date will be March 31, terms 2/10, net 30 days. (Note special price for long-time customer.)

Mar 5   Owner Hong Duaog invested an additional $5,000 in the business. Received a bank receipt showing the money was put in the bank account today.

Mar 5   Sold to Mr. Lopez a package containing 1 pair of used skis, bindings, and poles for $300.00 plus HST. Mr. Lopez produced a senior card from a competitor and the manager allowed a 10% senior's discount. Cheque #326 received.

Mar 6   As a new customer, **Your actual Last (Family) name Skiing Lodge** (add any address, ID S39-454) ordered and received 3 Jock SnowBoards at $510.00 and 3 ski goggles (glasses) at $60.00 each. All items plus HST. Credit limit $7,000 and terms 2/10, net 30.

Mar 9   **Your actual Last (Family) name Skiing Lodge** returned 1 Jock SnowBoard ($510.00 plus HST) because it has a tiny crack in the middle. The board has not been used and the manager approved a credit to the account.

Mar 16   Sold one set of ski poles to Mr. Obi for $56.00 plus HST. Received his cheque #985 in full payment. This customer is moving at the end of April to Edmonton.

Mar 16   Received cheque #638 from **Your actual Last (Family) name Skiing Lodge** as payment on the goods ordered on the 6th and the return on the 9th.

Mar 23   Bank advised that Mr. Obi's cheque #985 was returned NSF. Sent registered letter to Mr. Obi. The mailing address was on the cheque.

Mar 26   Received a $13.10 bank debit memo for bank service charges to Mar. 23.

Mar 31   Only 8 snowboards ordered by Jordan's Sports Equipment on the 3rd arrived. The other 2 Jock SnowBoards are to be delivered within 5 days. Called Jordan's and they agreed to receive the 8 boards we received. Issued next sales invoice for this order, and the company picked up the boards.

3 ➤ When you have recorded the above entries, print the following:

a. Customer Aged Detail report as at Mar 31
b. Journal Entries All, for the monthly activity
c. Journal Entries-General, for the monthly activity
d. Income Statement for the year-to-date activity, for the Sales Manager. Hide appropriate information.
e. Sales Journal
f. Pending Sales Order as at March 31

Challenge Exercise 02 C2B-3, House Sitters

RECEIVABLES and COMPANY Modules

House Sitters is a business that looks after your house or apartment while you are away. The business waters plants, looks after pets, makes sure the furnace, water heater and air conditioning are working, and brings in the mail and newspapers, etc.

House Sitters Company does *NOT* print Sales invoices or receipts.

Note: All invoices are left at the residence or business on the day the client returns. Terms are varied for different customers. HST is 13%.

1 ➤ Refer to Exercise 1-1 to unzip the **02 C2B-3 Sitters.exe** file.

2 ➤ For this review assignment open the **02 C2B-3 Sitters** file, and enter the following Accounts Receivable transactions for May.

May 1   Completed 4-day sitting for Hagos Aulakh at $30.00 plus HST per day. Invoice #177, in the amount of $135.60 with terms of net 5 days.

May 3   Received $101.70, cheque #752, as payment from Winston Chun re outstanding invoice #170.

May 6   Left $101.70 invoice #178, at Mr. & Mrs. Thomas Royes' home for service for three days at $30.00 plus HST per day. Terms net 5 days.

May 6   Received $135.60, cheque #829 from Mr. Hagos Aulakh for invoice #177.

May 9   Received $101.70, cheque #256 from Mr. & Mrs. Thomas Royes as payment for invoice #178.

May 10   Completed 2-day sitting for Mrs. Manpreet Foss at $30.00 plus HST per day. Invoice #179, in the amount of $67.80 with terms of net 3 days left in the house.

May 12   Mrs. Foss came to the office and paid invoice #179 in full with $67.80 cash.

May 18   A new business client, ***Your Actual Name Ceramics***, requested us to check her store 3 times a day at $30.00 plus HST per visit. She will be out of town May 19 and 20 for a family function. Other information: 889 Ancaster Avenue, Stoney Creek, Ontario A0A 3C3, phone and fax numbers may be left blank. Terms are 2%, 10 days, net 30. (Special terms arranged for business clients.) Credit limit $200.00.

May 20   Left invoice #180 for $203.40 in the office at the back of ***Your Actual Name Ceramics*** store.

May 28   Received ***Your Actual Name Ceramics*** cheque #158 in the amount of $199.80 as payment in full for invoice #180 with $3.60 discount taken.

May 31   Completed 2-day sitting for Hagos Aulakh at $30.00 plus HST per day. Invoice #181 issued for $67.80 with terms net 5 days.

3 ➤ When you have recorded the above entries, **print** the following:
   a.   Customer Aged Detail Report as at May 31
   b.   Journal Entries All, for May 1 to 31
   c.   Sales Journal for May 1 to 31
   d.   Cash Receipts Journal for May 1 to 31
   e.   Income Statement for Jan 1 to May 31

Mini-guide for Transactions in Chapter 2

Mini-guide for transactions in Simply Accounting Premium 2010*
Not all types of transactions listed here.

***Study Suggestion - Add additional transactions from your chapters.**

Receivable Events	Entry	Module	Journal	Comments	You fill in the Text Ref
Customer asks for price quote	No entry	RECEIVABLE	Sales, Orders & Quotes	No sale, customer asking for prices	
Customer confirms quote & places order for later delivery	No entry	RECEIVABLE	Sales, Orders & Quotes	No sale, price confirmed for future delivery	
Sale of Merchandise	A/Rec	RECEIVABLE	Sales, Orders & Quotes	may be preceded by sales quote	
	Sales			may be preceded by sales order	
	HST collected on Sales			may be a sale without prior quote or order	
Sales Rtn of Merchandise	Sales Rtns & Allowances	RECEIVABLE	Sales, Orders & Quotes	Add "Rt" to invoice number	
	HST collected on Sales			If credit memo listed, then add "CMxxx"	
	A/Rec				
Receipt (no discount)	Cash	RECEIVABLE	Receipts	-can be partial or full receipt	
	A/Rec			-can be after a return	
Receipt, with discount	Cash	RECEIVABLE	Receipts	-full receipt	
	Sales Discount			-can be after a return	
	A/Rec				

 * Note: Refer to the Appendix V, *Mini-Guide Receivables—Payables* at www.simplyaccounting2010.nelson.com under Student Resources.

Relevant Appendices, Part B

The following appendices are available at www.simplyaccounting2010.nelson.com under Student Resources.

Appendix 2010 D	**Printing a Tax (HST) Report**
Appendix 2010 F	**Printing in Batches**
Appendix 2010 G	**Processing in Batches**
Appendix 2010 K	**Graphs Feature**
Appendix 2010 M	**Post-Dated Cheques**
Appendix 2010 U	**Adding Notes/Footer to Statements**
Appendix 2010 V	**Mini-Guide Receivables—Payables**

Chapter 3A

PAYABLES Module—*Basics*

Tyson's Toys

Learning Objectives
After completing this chapter you will be able to:

☐ Record purchase orders, invoices and returns.
☐ Add new vendors and make changes to existing vendors.
☐ Record payments to vendors in full or partial payment of invoices with or without cash discounts.
☐ Record payments to other suppliers.
☐ Display and print various payable reports (vendor balances outstanding, etc.) and journals.

Note: After finishing Chapter 3A and Chapter 8, you can complete selected transactions from Chapter 3A, using the Perpetual INVENTORY & SERVICES module. See Challenge Exercise 08 C8-5 Toys-PI.

The contents of this chapter are as follows:

- The PAYABLES Module Overview 174
- Company Profile – Tyson's Toys 174
- Starting Simply for Payables 176
- Exercises:
    - Exercise 3A-1 – Opening the PAYABLES Module 176
    - Exercise 3A-2 – Displaying the Detail Vendor Aged Report 177
    - Exercise 3A-3 – To Display/Print Income Statement & Balance Sheet 178
    - Exercise 3A-4 – Customizing the Purchase Orders Journal 180
    - Exercise 3A-5 – Entering a Purchase Order 182
    - Exercise 3A-6 – Revising a Purchase Order 184
    - Exercise 3A-7 – To View/Print Outstanding Purchase Orders 184
    - Exercise 3A-8 – To Enter a New Vendor 185
    - Exercise 3A-9 – Recording a Purchase with NO Purchase Order (PO)...... 190
    - Exercise 3A-10 – To Display a Vendor Account 192
    - Exercise 3A-11 – Recording Purchase of Goods Not for Resale 193
    - Exercise 3A-12 – Recording Purchase of Services – Cheque Issued 195
    - Exercise 3A-13 – Recording Purchase of Services – Pay Later 197
    - Exercise 3A-14 – Recording a Purchase Invoice from a PO....................... 199
    - Exercise 3A-15 – Adjusting a Posted Cheque 200
    - Exercise 3A-16 – Recording Purchase Returns.. 202
    - Exercise 3A-17 – To View/Print a Pending Purchase Orders Report 204
    - Exercise 3A-18 – Recording a Vendor Payment.. 205
    - Exercise 3A-19 – Recording a Payment with Merchandise Discount 208
    - Exercise 3A-20 – Printing Period-End Reports 211
- Summary, Part A.. 211
- Before Moving On…, Part A 212
- Relevant Appendices, Part A 212
    - Challenge Exercise 03 C3A-1, Wheelchairs 213
    - Challenge Exercise 03 C3A-2, Radios 214

The PAYABLES Module Overview

The PAYABLES module consists of the Vendors Ledger, the Purchase Quotes (Tyson's Toys does not use the Purchase Quotes Journal), Purchase Orders, Purchase Invoices and the Payments Journals. The Vendors Ledger is the same as the Accounts Payable (A/P) subledger in a manual accounting system.

Purchase Quotes and Purchase Orders are recorded (not posted) in the database. Purchase Invoices and Payments Journal transactions are posted to the individual vendor ledger accounts and to the linked accounts in the General Ledger.

The following transactions are normally recorded in the **Purchase** journals:

- Purchase quotes, purchase orders, and/or purchase invoices on credit from vendors (suppliers).

- Prepayments with a purchase order.

- Purchases on company credit card.

The following are recorded in the **Payments** journal:

- Payments to vendors (suppliers):
    - partial payment of an invoice.
    - full payment of an invoice with discount.
    - full payment, no discount.
    - cash purchase paid with a cheque, credit card or ATM card.

- Payments for expenses: all other payments such as rent, electricity, water bills, owner drawings, tax payments (HST) to the government, etc.

At any time, reports (e.g., Aged Vendor reports, etc.) can be produced that show the balances that are payable to vendors. Remember, the total of all payable balances to vendors must match the balance of the ACCOUNTS PAYABLE account in the General Ledger.

In working with the PAYABLES module, you must be very careful in determining the difference between purchases of **goods for resale** (also referred to as merchandise) and purchases of **services or goods not for resale**.

Slideshow 3A – PAYABLES Part A is designed to help you understand how the PAYABLES module works and the GAAP related to it. Notice the similarities (and differences) between the RECEIVABLES and PAYABLES modules. Run the slideshow now.

Company Profile – Tyson's Toys

Jerry Tyson and his wife, Helen, owners of Tyson's Toys, sell wooden toys for children from a store in the local mall. Helen works in the store and also travels to toy conventions in search of new toys to sell in their store and to promote their business.

Only the COMPANY and PAYABLES modules, for the month of April, are used in the following exercises in this chapter Parts A and B.

Jerry normally waits until the last day of the invoice terms to pay for goods purchased on credit. Helen has been trying to get him to pay the outstanding invoices so that he can take advantage of the 2% discount. However, he has been focusing on selling the toys rather than good money management. With your help he can manage the business more effectively.

In Part A, Tyson's Toys uses the data folder **03 3A Toys-A**. Cost of ending inventory is calculated monthly using the **Periodic** method.

The business does not use the Track Additional Details feature to record information.

Study Tyson's Trial Balance.

Tyson's Toys-A, Student's Name
Trial Balance As At Mar 31, 2016

		Debits	Credits
1010	Bank Account	11,425.00	-
1020	Bank Account US funds	580.60	-
1200	Accounts Receivable	12,899.90	-
1310	Toys and Parts Inventory	6,907.29	-
1330	Prepaid Office Supplies, etc.	625.00	-
1340	Prepaid Insurance	0.00	-
1510	Store Equipment	25,138.45	-
1515	Accum. Amort. Store Equipment	-	11,393.00
1520	Office Furniture/Equipment	2,812.60	-
1525	Accum. Amort. Office/Furniture/Equi	-	1,605.00
2200	Accounts Payable	-	10,666.96
2210	Visa Credit Card Payable	-	0.00
2550	HST Charged On Sales	-	1,738.25
2560	HST Paid On Purchases	650.14	-
2610	Bank Loan Payable	-	14,310.86
3100	Capital Jerry Tyson	-	11,924.65
3120	Drawings Jerry Tyson	3,500.00	-
3200	Capital Helen Tyson	-	11,924.65
3210	Drawings Helen Tyson	3,500.00	-
4100	Sales	-	34,191.08
4150	Sales - Discount	212.30	-
4200	Sales - Returns & Allowances	604.00	-
5010	Beginning Inventory	5,421.49	-
5040	Purchases	18,408.80	-
5050	Purchases Returns	-	300.00
5080	Purchase Discounts	-	289.93
5090	Ending Inventory	-	6,907.29
5310	Rent Expense	6,000.00	-
5340	Advertising Expense	516.00	-
5345	Bank Loan Interest	301.00	-
5350	Bank Charges	135.00	-
5355	Credit Card Charges	0.00	-
5360	Insurance Expense	303.00	-
5370	Auto Lease Expense	1,200.00	-
5440	Office/Store Supplies Expense	750.00	-
5450	Telephone Expense	912.00	-
5460	Utility Expense	1,250.00	-
5470	Bad Debts Expense	0.00	-
5480	Delivery Expense	1,200.00	-
		105,251.67	105,251.67

Fig. 3A-1: Trial Balance, Tyson's Toys-A.

Session Date

In Chapter 2 (A and B) you entered transactions for Santos Luggage at various times and advanced the Session Date as needed. Tyson's Toys has adopted a policy of entering its Accounts Payable transactions on a daily basis, unless you, the clerk, are not available.

Advance the Session Date as noted in the instructions for each exercise.

Starting Simply for Payables

Exercise 3A-1 – Opening the PAYABLES Module

---

1 ➤ Refer to Exercise 1-1 to unzip the **03 3A Toys-A.exe** file.

2 ➤ Start **Simply Accounting**.

3 ➤ At the Select Company window, click **Select an existing company** button and **OK**.

4 ➤ At the **Simply Accounting - Open Company** window, in the **Look in** box, locate your student location drive, and the Toys folder 📁03 3A Toys-A.

5 ➤ Double-click the 📁03 3A Toys-A folder and the 📟 Toys-A.SAI will appear in the box below. (The image at the left of Toys may be different depending on the configuration of your computer and the SDB may be in lower case sdb.)

ⓘ

Review Exercise 1-2 if you need help to open a data file.

6 ➤ Click the 📟 Toys-A.SAI icon. The **File name** box will change to Toys-A.SAI.

7 ➤ Click **Open** to open the Toys-A file.

8 ➤ The **Session Date** window will be **Mar 31, 2016**. Click **OK**.

Study the Toys Home window. The other modules are hidden.

The Vendor ledger does not have the **History** (quill pen) symbol. This indicates that this ledger with journals is ready to use.

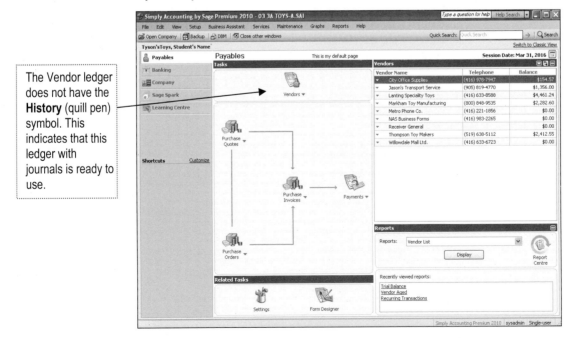

Fig. 3A-2: Toys-A Home window.

9 ➤ Remember to revise your company information to add *your name* to the company information in order to have your name printed on your printouts. Refer to Exercise 1-4 if you need help. **This is the last reminder. It is assumed you will add your name to each of the company records from here on.**

To Display the Vendor Aged Report

As in the RECEIVABLES module, you can find out the status of the company payables by displaying and/or printing the Vendor Aged Report. Similarly, Simply groups payables calculated from the date of the invoice to the current Session Date. It provides a list of accounts that are **Current**, **31 to 60** days overdue, **61 to 90** days overdue, and **91+** days overdue.

Also, as in the RECEIVABLES module, Simply provides two options: **Summary** and **Detail**. Your choice depends on the purpose for which you need the reports. At this point, if you wish to acquaint yourself with the balances owing to vendors, and which vendor invoices are overdue, you would select **Detail**. In the next exercise you will display the Detail Vendor Aged report.

When printing this report, it is important that the **Session Date** is correct; otherwise, the aging will not be accurate.

Exercise 3A-2 – Displaying the Detail Vendor Aged Report

1 ➤ From the menu bar click **Reports**, **Payables**, **Vendor Aged**, **Detail** should be selected. If necessary, **Select All** to highlight all Vendors in blue, click **OK**.

Compare the window display to Fig. 3A-3. Notice that the screen shows columns that are based on the age of the invoices. As in the RECEIVABLES module, the aging schedule can be changed. This is covered in Chapter 4. Notice that the Detail Report has the session date (As at date) on which the aging of invoices is based.

◄ As at date

Vendor Aged Detail As at Mar 31, 2016

Source	Date	Terms	Transaction Type	Total	Current	31 to 60	61 to 90	91+
City Office Supplies								
1235	Mar 02, 2016	2%/10, Net 30	Invoice	154.57	154.57	-	-	-
Total outstanding:				154.57	154.57	-	-	-
Jason's Transport Service								
6691	Mar 01, 2016	Net 30	Invoice	1,356.00	1,356.00	-	-	-
Total outstanding:				1,356.00	1,356.00	-	-	-
Lanting Speciality Toys								
6198	Feb 22, 2016	2%/10, Net 30	Invoice	1,057.68	-	1,057.68	-	-
6211	Feb 25, 2016	2%/10, Net 30	Invoice	3,403.56	-	3,403.56	-	-
Total outstanding:				4,461.24	-	4,461.24	-	-
Markham Toy Manufacturing								
1622	Mar 22, 2016	2%/10, Net 30	Invoice	1,154.86	1,154.86	-	-	-
1638	Mar 30, 2016	2%/10, Net 30	Invoice	1,127.74	1,127.74	-	-	-
Total outstanding:				2,282.60	2,282.60	-	-	-
Thompson Toy Makers								
886	Mar 15, 2016	2%/10, Net 30	Invoice	2,412.55	2,412.55	-	-	-
Total outstanding:				2,412.55	2,412.55	-	-	-
Total unpaid invoices:				10,666.96	6,205.72	4,461.24	-	-
Total prepayments/prepaid order:				-	-	-	-	-
Total outstanding:				10,666.96	6,205.72	4,461.24	-	-

Fig. 3A-3: Tyson's Vendor Aged Detail window.

As in the RECEIVABLES module, the aged report will show the total for each vendor when there are two or more invoices listed.

2 ➤ **Exit** from the display window.

To Display and Print the Income Statement

As part of your task in getting acquainted with the company, you would display and/or print the Income Statement.

Exercise 3A-3 – To Display/Print Income Statement & Balance Sheet

---

1 ➤ Display and **print** the **Year-to-date Income Statement** with start and end dates of **Jan 01, 2016** and **Mar 31, 2016**. Keep this printout because you will be using it to compare with the Income Statement printed at Exercise 3B-33. Do Not Hide any amounts.

2 ➤ Display and **print** the **Balance Sheet at Mar 31, 2016**. Keep this printout because you will be using it to calculate the HST amounts in Exercise 3B-30. Do Not Hide any amounts.

Vendor Invoices Guidelines and Procedures

Tyson's Toys follow common accounting procedures in processing transactions in the PAYABLES module.

When journalizing vendor invoices in the Purchases Journal, you must know to which G/L account the purchase should be charged. The following guidelines are used by Tyson's Toys:

- Toys and parts purchased, to be sold to customers (stores and retail), are charged to **PURCHASES**.

- Other payables (rent, advertising, utilities: water, gas, electricity, etc.) are charged to the appropriate expense account.

- Any goods or services paid for in advance (e.g., office supplies, insurance, etc.) are charged to a **PREPAID ASSET** account.

When a purchase invoice is received, the invoice is usually stamped on the back with the date of receipt and an approval stamp (see Fig. 3A-11).

The purchase invoice is then sent to a department manager or other supervisor who is authorized to approve payment and will assign a G/L account number to the amount(s) purchased. It is then signed or initialed, dated, and sent to the accounting department for recording and issuing of the cheque. The owner, Jerry Tyson, would then review the relevant documents and sign the cheque(s) for payment.

The PAYABLES Journals

The PAYABLES Module has four journals: **Purchase Quotes, Purchase Orders, Purchase Invoices** and **Payments Journals**. The following options are available in the Purchase Journals when entering transactions:

Purchase Quotes   used to record a form received from a vendor indicating the price of products or services that they will sell the product or service to you. Tyson's Toys does not use this Journal.

Purchase Orders (PO) used to record a confirmation of a commitment to purchase. You would normally send a copy of the purchase order to a vendor. You may record a purchase order although there is no purchase quote recorded earlier.

The following options are available in the Home page in the Purchase Journal – Purchase Invoices when entering transactions:

Create Invoice used to enter a purchase on account (credit). A purchase quote and/or a purchase order may or may not have been issued earlier. When a purchase invoice is posted, an accounting entry is recorded affecting both General Ledger and Payables subsidiary ledger accounts.

Find Invoice look up a posted invoice.

Adjust Invoice using a negative invoice, this is used to record a return of goods or an adjustment to the purchase price, also called a **Debit Memo**. Similar to the Create Invoice option above, when an Adjustment invoice is posted, an accounting entry is recorded affecting both General Ledger and Payables subsidiary ledger accounts.

When entering the Purchase Journal – Purchase Invoice window, the following option is available.

Payment Method You can record a purchase with Pay Later, Cash, Cheque,
(Chapter 3, Part B) or Visa Credit.

The following options are available in the Payments Journal icon, when entering transactions:

Pay Purchase Invoices used to record payments to vendors for invoices previously recorded using the Purchase Invoice-Pay Later option.

Pay Credit Card Bill used to record payments where a credit card is used for invoices previously recorded. Tyson's Toys does not use this feature.

Make Other Payment used to record payments for invoices or debit/credit memos that have not been recorded previously; e.g., rent, drawings, purchases paid by cash, cheque, credit card or bank card.

Pay Remittances used to record payments for payroll deductions (e.g., CPP,
(Chapter 7) EI, and Income Tax).

When entering the Payments Journal window, you can record a payment with the following options.

Type Pay Purchase Invoices, Pay Credit Card Bill, Make Other Payment (Pay Expenses from home window) and Pay Remittance.

By You can record a payment by: Cash, Cheque or Visa Credit.

The Purchase Orders Journal

This journal is intended to look like a future invoice, and is used to record purchase quotes. Purchase orders and purchase invoices windows are similar. Similar windows were seen in sales quotes, sales orders and sales invoices in the RECEIVABLES module.

Similar to the Sales Journal, when you record entries in the Purchases Journal, you enter only one part of the entry. The program knows you are in the PAYABLES module and will automatically debit or credit the Accounts Payable account and appropriate taxes.

Customizing the Purchase Orders Journal

As with the Sales Journals, you may also customize the Purchase Journals. Tyson's Toys uses the **Periodic Inventory** method, and does not need the **Item** and **Allo** columns. In this exercise, you will customize the Purchase Orders journal by removing the Item and Allo columns. You were shown how to do this in Exercise 2A-3.

Exercise 3A-4 – Customizing the Purchase Orders Journal

---

1 ➤ Advance the Session date to **Apr 01, 2016**.

2 ➤ As in the RECEIVABLE module, you can click the ▼ to see the choices available. Click the **Purchase Orders** icon and the Purchase Order window displays.

3 ➤ Click the **Customize** 🖳 icon, click on **Columns**. Make sure a ✓ appears in the **Item Number** (the Account field is grayed out) and **Division** fields to not display these columns.

4 ➤ Click **OK** when you are finished.

5 ➤ Type the following into the columns shown. Resize the columns as shown in Exercise 2A-3.

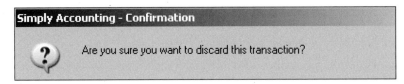

Quantity	Order	Back Order	Unit	Item Description	Price	Tax	HST	Amount	Account
				Cheques Special order					1330 Prepaid Office Supplies etc.

Fig. 3A-4: Customized Purchases Journal window (after sizing).

6 ➤ When you have the columns to this approximate size, click the 🔄 and you will see the following.

> **Simply Accounting - Confirmation**
>
> ❓ Are you sure you want to discard this transaction?

7 ➤ Select **Yes** to return to the Purchase Order window.

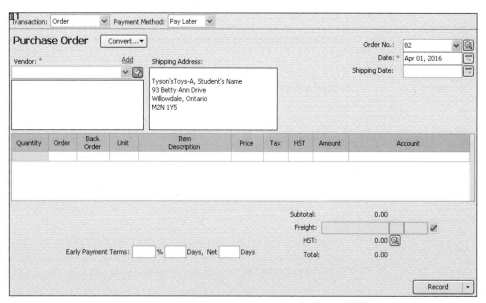

Fig. 3A-5: The Purchase Order Journal window.

Toolbar Icons

The toolbar icons are similar to the icons seen in the RECEIVABLES module Fig. 2A-5, Sample Sales Invoice window.

Entering Purchase Orders

When a purchase quote is converted into a purchase order, the information on the purchase quote is automatically entered into the Purchase Order window. Likewise, purchase order information is entered into the Purchase Invoice window upon conversion.

A purchase order is a commitment by a purchaser to buy goods, merchandise or services, etc., at the agreed-upon price, terms and date. The goods are to be delivered, or services provided, within the stated time period.

In the PAYABLES module you can:

1. enter a Purchase Quote;

2. convert it into a Purchase Order (PO); then

3. convert the PO into a purchase invoice.

(See side note box.)

Purchase Quote ⟶ **Purchase Order** ⟶ **Purchase Invoice**
                               Purchase Order ⟶ **Purchase Invoice**
                                                           Purchase Invoice

---

Similar to the RECEIVABLES module, the purchase quote and the purchase order do not affect the subledgers; they are simply recorded in a Purchase Quote or Purchase Order Listing.

Tyson's Toys records purchase orders; it does not record purchase quotes. Although there are no serious consequences if you do not record purchase quotes, it is important to record purchase orders in order to make sure that all ordered goods or services are provided by the vendor(s). Remember, PURCHASES are goods for resale; if you do not receive your shipments from your vendors, you might not have anything to sell!

Exercise 3A-5 – Entering a Purchase Order

> **Apr 01, 2016**   Jerry Tyson issued purchase order #82 to Markham Toy Manufacturing for 35 Trucks small for $14.32 each, plus HST. The trucks will be delivered on Apr 5. Credit terms are 2/10, net 30.

Some firms may use a numbering sequence for purchase orders that reflects the date; e.g., 100401 (for PO#100 for Apr 1). Mr. Tyson has decided to use a numerical sequence. The next PO is **#82**.

When entering a purchase transaction, from a Purchase invoice, in the Purchases Journal, Simply will automatically **credit** the Vendor account and ACCOUNTS PAYABLE in the G/L with the total invoice amount (including taxes).

1 ➤	**Transaction**	Click the ▼ arrow and note that the choices are similar to the Receivables Journal, select **Order**. [Tab].
2 ➤	**Payment Method**	Click the ▼ arrow and note the four choices available. If you use the Cash, Cheque or Visa Credit option, the software assumes you are making a prepayment (a payment in advance to a vendor) on the Purchase Order. (See side box.) Leave the choice as **Pay Later**. [Tab] to Vendor.
3 ➤	**Vendor**	Select **Markham Toy Manufacturing**.

ⓘ
*Simply records money **paid** on a future order in the PAYABLES module (Chapter 3B) as a **Prepayment**. In the RECEIVABLES module (Chapter 2B), Simply records money **received** on a future order as a **Deposit**.*

Note that the address for Tyson's Toys is recorded in the **Shipping Address** box. If the goods are to be shipped to a different address, you will need to type the information in the box, as no field is available to list different Addresses as is available in the RECEIVABLES module.

Notice that the **Tax** and **Account** fields have already been filled in, based on the Vendor Options tab, Expense account identified. You can change the tax and account fields when necessary.

	Order No.	82 will be the next Purchase Order number. Do Not Change.
	Date	Accept **Apr 01, 2016**, [Tab] [Tab] to Order.
	Quantity	This field is skipped because we have not received the goods that were ordered.
4 ➤	**Shipping Date**	Click the **calendar** and choose **Apr 05**, [Tab] [Tab].
5 ➤	**Order**	Type **35**, [Tab].
6 ➤	**Back Order**	These are items that have not been received from a purchase order. [Tab] to accept 35.
7 ➤	**Unit**	Type **each**, [Tab].
8 ➤	**Description**	Type **Trucks small**, [Tab].
9 ➤	**Price**	Type **14.32**, [Tab].

10 ➤	**Tax**	Press Enter or double-click. You will see tax codes like those used in Santos Luggage, Chapter 2A and 2B. Select **HS**. Tab .
11 ➤	**HST**	The HST amount should be 65.16 which is 13% of 501.20 (35 pieces x 14.32 = 501.20) in the Amount column, Tab .
12 ➤	**Amount**	This column should be 501.20 (35 pieces times the cost 14.32) with a total amount of 566.36 including HST, Tab to accept.
13 ➤	**Acct**	The default account, **5040 Purchases**, is displayed (see side note box). You will be shown how to set a default account in Exercise 3A-8. If 5040 is not correct, you would press Enter , or double-click to see a list of General Ledger account numbers. Tab to accept **5040**.
14 ➤	**Terms**	Verify that the terms **2**% **10** Days Net **30** Days are recorded correctly. Correct if necessary.

ⓘ
A default account is the account that is used most often with each vendor.

This is a purchase of **goods for resale** and should be charged to the PURCHASES account.

The purchase order is now complete and is displayed in Fig. 3A-6.

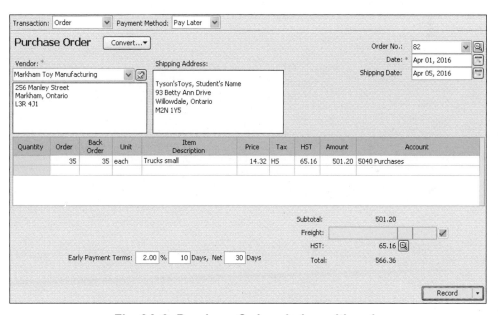

Fig. 3A-6: Purchase Order window with order.

15 ➤ Display the **Purchases Journal Entry**. It should be as shown in Fig 3A-7:

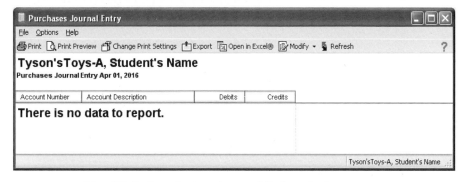

Fig. 3A-7: Purchases Journal Entry window.

There is no journal entry created with a PO, because the goods have not been purchased. When the goods arrive, the PO is converted into a purchase invoice and a journal entry is then created and posted.

16 ➤ **Exit** from the Purchases Journal Entry window.

The Reports and Forms Options have been set at Pre-printed. You do not need to print the Purchase Order.

17 ➤ After verifying that the PO is correct, click the **Record** button.

18 ➤ Click **OK** to exit the Transaction Confirmation window. **Exit** the Purchase Order window to return to the Home window.

Exercise 3A-6 – Revising a Purchase Order

Apr 01, 2016 **Jerry Tyson reviewed purchase order #82 to Markham Toy Manufacturing and decided to increase the order to 40 Trucks small for $14.32 each, plus HST. The other information did not change.**

1 ➤ Click **Purchase Orders** icon, click 🔍 **Find Order** icon. The Select Order or Quote window appears with **Quote 82** highlighted. Click **Select** and the window changes to the PO with 35 items backordered.

2 ➤ Click the 🗔 **Adjust Purchase Order** icon.
     The header changes to: **Adjusting Order 82**.

> 🛈
> To correct or cancel a Purchase Quote, Purchase Order or Purchase Invoice after recording, you would repeat this procedure which is also appropriate for a Quote or Invoice. You may refer to Chapter 13, *Corrections*.

3 ➤ **Order**   Change the quantity to **40**, ⌨ Tab , and the Subtotal amount changes to 572.80 and the total changes to 647.26. Mr. Tyson is pleased with the change.

4 ➤ After verifying that the PO is correct, click the **Record** button.

5 ➤ Click **OK** to exit the Transaction Confirmation window, and **exit** to the Home window. (See side note box.)

Pending Purchase Order Report

It is good practice to view/print the Pending Purchase Order report to ensure that all goods you have ordered are either received or have been scheduled for shipping by the vendor(s).

Exercise 3A-7 – To View/Print Outstanding Purchase Orders

---

1 ➤ To display the Pending PO report, click **Report Centre,** from the Payables tab, select **Pending Purchase Orders Summary by Vendor,** click **Display**. The report will display that there is no data to report. Simply defaults to the last time the report was used Apr 01, 2016. Click the **Modify** button, **Report Options** and change the Date to: **Apr 08, 2016** (a week in the future; all items should be in blue (if not, click Select All), click **OK**.

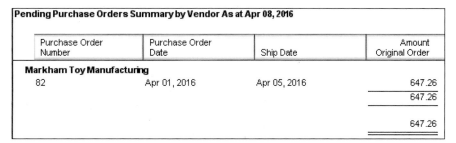

Fig. 3A-8: Purchase Order Summary window.

This report displays the outstanding Purchase Orders and the dates the goods are expected to be shipped.

2 ➤ **Exit** from the Pending Purchase Order window and return to the Home window.

The Vendors Subledger

Before you can enter transactions for a vendor, you need to create a Vendors Subledger account for that vendor. The procedure is very similar to creating a customer subledger in the RECEIVABLES module.

Exercise 3A-8 – To Enter a New Vendor
---

1 ➤ Advance the Session date to **Apr 05, 2016**.

Study this transaction:

Apr 05, 2016	**Mr. Tyson issued PO #83 to a new vendor A-Your Name Toy Parts, contact Your Name, 956 West Credit Avenue, Mississauga, Ontario, L6X 3K9. Phone number 905-820-3865 extension 2056, Fax 905-820-3866. Ordered 100 Truck wheels (to be sold as parts) at 99 cents plus HST per wheel, terms 2/10, net 30. Total Purchase Order is $111.87 and the wheels are to be shipped on Apr 15.**

Before you can enter a transaction for Your Name Toy Parts, you need to enter a new Vendor account in the Vendors (Accounts Payable) subledger.

2 ➤ From the Home window click on **Purchase Orders** ▼ and select **Create Order**.

3 ➤ **Transaction**   Do not change from **Order,** `Tab` `Tab` `Tab`.

4 ➤ **Purchased From**   Type **A-Your Name Toy Parts,** `Tab`. Type **A-** in front of your name. (See side note box—there is no Continue button.)

Notice that in the PAYABLES module, there is no **Continue** button.

You can enter a one-time vendor while entering a Purchase Invoice transaction. As in the RECEIVABLES module, the purchase from a one-time vendor must be paid at the same time as the date of purchase in cash, cheque, credit card or ATM card.

If you select **<one-time vendor>** the window changes to a Purchase Invoice.

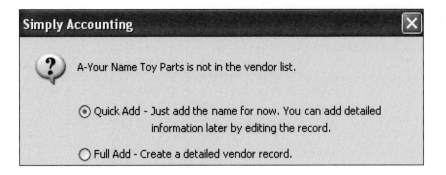

5 ➤ Similar to the RECEIVABLES module, you can create a new vendor in the Payables ledger as you enter transactions. Click **Full Add**.

Address

6 ➤ **Enter** the appropriate information as shown in Fig. 3A-9.

 Enter the phone/fax numbers without dashes. Simply will automatically format them with a dash and brackets as you press ⌨Tab. Refer to Exercise 2A-20 to record the extension number.

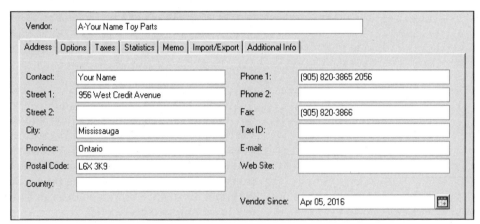

Fig. 3A-9: Payables Ledger window – Address tab.

Tax ID	This field would be used for subcontractor tax numbers required by Canada Revenue Agency for T5018 forms. Tyson's Toys does not use subcontractors for selling toys.
E-mail	Not used in this case.
Web Site	Not used in this case.
Vendor Since	As noted in Receivables, this field lets the user know how long they have been using that particular vendor. It is assumed that previous vendors have been used for a long time.

Options

7 ➤ Click the **Options** tab, and enter information as shown:

Vendor:	A-Your Name Toy Parts					

Address | Options | Taxes | Statistics | Memo | Import/Export | Additional Info

Expense Account: 5040 Purchases ▾

Conduct Business in: English ▾

Early Payment Terms

2.00 % discount if paid in 10 days. Net due in 30 days. ☑ Calculate Discounts before Tax

Forms

☐ Include this Vendor When Printing T5018 Slips   Print ▾ Purchase Orders for this Vendor

☐ Print Contact on Cheques   ☐ E-mail Confirmation of Purchase Invoices and Quotes

☐ Synchronize with Microsoft® Outlook®

☐ Inactive Vendor   Balance Owing   0.00
☐ Payroll Authority

Expense Account	**5040 Purchases**. This becomes the default for this vendor and will show in all purchase orders or invoices for this vendor. It can be changed if necessary.
Conduct Business in	There is the ability to have screen displays and printouts in French for the customer. Tyson's Toys has not had any requests to conduct business in French. Do Not Change.
Early Payment Terms	Type as shown. This is the discount for paying within the terms time period.
Calculate Discounts before Tax	Checking this box instructs Simply to calculate discounts, on the price before tax, when the company pays within the early payment terms. Click the box. A ✓ will appear, Tab .
Include this Vendor when Printing T5018 Slips	DO NOT CHANGE. This box would be ✓ to include this vendor when printing the T5018 slips. Leave blank as Tyson's Toys does not use subcontractors and does not need T5018 forms.
Print Contact on Cheques	DO NOT CHANGE. You would click this box to print the contents of the "Contact" field on the cheques printed for this vendor. Mr. Tyson does not want to print the contact name on cheques produced by the program; therefore, you may leave the box blank.
Purchase orders for this Vendor	DO NOT CHANGE. You have a choice of sending a purchase order by e-mail or printing and mailing the purchase order. Leave choice as **Print**.
E-mail Confirmation of Purchase Invoices and Quotes	DO NOT CHANGE. This box would be ✓ if the vendor was able to e-mail you their quotes and/or invoices. Leave blank, as this text does not have an exercise to receive e-mail.
Synchronize with Microsoft® Outlook®	DO NOT CHANGE. As discussed in Chapter 2A, when this box is ✓, the vendor's e-mail address will be placed in the Microsoft® Outlook® Mailing address list. There is no exercise for this feature.

Payroll Authority	DO NOT CHANGE. This field is checked if the "vendor" is to send payroll related remittances (used in Chapter 7).

Taxes

8 ➤ Click the **Taxes** tab. This tab will indicate the appropriate taxes that are applied to purchases from this vendor.

9 ➤ Enter the information as shown. Select Tax code **HS**.

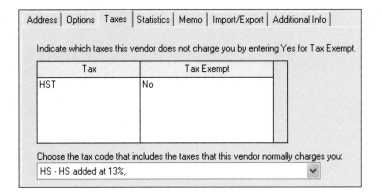

Statistics

10 ➤ Click the **Statistics** tab. DO NOT CHANGE. This tab will show the value of purchases and payments with each vendor.

Memo

11 ➤ Click the **Memo** tab. DO NOT CHANGE. This tab will allow you to keep information about the vendor and have the information shown in the Daily Business Manager.

Import/Export

12 ➤ Click the **Import/Export** tab. DO NOT CHANGE. This tab is similar to the Import/Export tab in RECEIVABLES. It refers to importing quotes and invoices from your vendors with your firm's item numbers.

Additional Info

13 ➤ Click the **Additional Info** tab. DO NOT CHANGE. This tab could show additional information about the vendor. Refer to the Appendix Q, *Names Fields* at www.simplyaccounting2010.nelson.com under Student Resources for more information.

14 ➤ Click Save and Close button to save this vendor in the Payables Ledger and return to a Purchase Order window.

15 ➤ You can now enter purchase order **#83** information for A-Your Name Toy Parts.

100 Truck wheels at 99 cents plus HST per wheel, terms 2/10, net 30. Total Purchase Order is $111.87 and the wheels are to be shipped on Apr 15.

16 ➤ **Record** the Purchase order when correct. **Exit** to the Home window.

You can also create a new vendor as follows:

a)   From the Home window, click the **Vendors** ▼ arrow, select **View Vendors**. The Vendors window (Fig. 3A-10) displays icons and information for all vendor accounts.

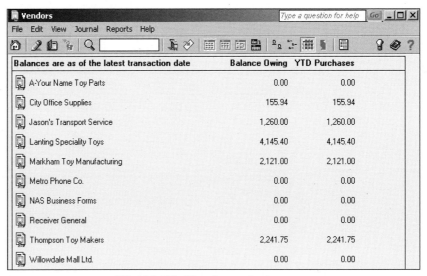

Fig. 3A-10: Vendors window.

The new toolbar icons at the top of the Vendors window mean the following:

Purchases: Displays a blank Purchases Journal for entry of purchase invoices. If a vendor icon is highlighted and this icon is clicked, the vendor address details are automatically inserted in the blank Purchases Journal.

Payments: Displays a blank Payments Journal for entry of a payment to a vendor. If a vendor icon is highlighted and this icon is clicked, the vendor address details are automatically inserted in the blank Payments Journal.

b)   From the **Vendors** window, click the **Create** icon [icon] , and the Payables Ledger window appears similar to Fig. 3A-9, with a red asterisk beside Vendor* and a red *Required Field to the right.

c)   **Enter** the appropriate vendor information.

d)   **Exit** the Vendors window and return to the Home window.

Purchase with No Purchase Order (PO)

Simply will also allow you to enter a purchase in the Purchases Journal without a Purchase Quote or a Purchase Order.

Study the sample Vendor Invoice:

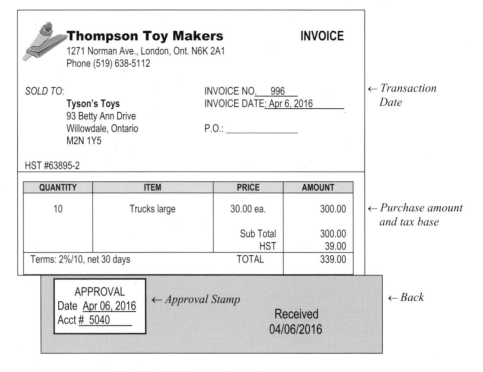

Fig. 3A-11: Vendor Invoice.

Exercise 3A-9 – Recording a Purchase with NO Purchase Order (PO)

Remember that a **purchase** refers to buying goods for resale. Buying services and goods that are not for resale are recorded as **expenses or prepayments**.

1 ➤ Advance the Session date to **Apr 06, 2016**.

The vendor invoice in Fig. 3A-11 is a credit purchase of toy trucks for sale and should be charged to the Purchases account in the G/L.

There are three ways to create a Purchase invoice.

a) Click the ▼ at Purchase Invoices icon, view the choices, select Create Invoice, at Purchased From: select your vendor. The window fills with the vendor name and address.

b) Click on Purchase Invoices icon to open the Purchase Invoice Journal, at Purchased From: select your vendor. The window fills with the vendor name and address.

c) In the Vendor section, at top right, scroll to the vendor, click the ▼ select Create Invoice. The window fills with the vendor name and address.

We will use method c) for this transaction.

2 ➤   In the Vendors section, move to **Thomson Toy Makers**, click the ▼ select **Create Invoice**. The window fills with the vendor name and address, Tax code and Account number.

3 ➤ **Transaction** [Tab] to accept Invoice.

4 ➤ **Payment** Note that the choices are similar to the Receivables Journal.
Method Accept **Pay Later**, [Tab].

5 ➤ **Vendor** [Tab] to accept **Thompson Toy Makers**, [Tab].

6 ➤ **Invoice Received** It is assumed that all invoices have been received, [Tab].

7 ➤ **Invoice** Type **996**, the invoice number, [Tab] [Tab].

8 ➤ **Date** [Tab] [Tab] to accept Apr 06, 2016 (the date of the purchase).

9 ➤ **Order/** [Tab] [Tab] (a previous purchase order was not issued).
Quote No.

10 ➤ **Quantity** Type **10**, [Tab].

Order Not used if PO not issued.

Back Order Not used if PO not issued.

11 ➤ **Unit** Type **each**, [Tab].

12 ➤ **Description** Type **Trucks large**, [Tab].

13 ➤ **Price** Type **30.00**, [Tab].

14 ➤ **Tax** [Tab] to accept HS.

15 ➤ **HST** The HST amount. We have purchased $300.00 of toy trucks to resell to customers, 13% HST on the $300.00 is calculated.
[Tab] to accept 39.00. (See side note box.)

16 ➤ **Amount** [Tab] to accept 300.00. The 300.00 is the calculated amount of Quantity multiplied by Price.

17 ➤ **Acct** [Tab] to accept the default account 5040 Purchases.

18 ➤ **Terms** Verify that the terms 2%/10, net 30 days are recorded correctly. Correct the terms if the record is incorrect.

19 ➤ Click **Report**, **Display Purchases Journal Entry**. The display window should appear as follows:

Purchases Journal Entry Apr 06, 2016 (J1)

Account Number	Account Description	Debits	Credits
2560	HST Paid On Purchases	39.00	-
5040	Purchases	300.00	-
2200	Accounts Payable	-	339.00
Additional Date:	Additional Field:		
		339.00	339.00

Notice the automatic credit to Accounts Payable. Check to ensure that the details on your screen are the same.

Side note box:

When Tyson's Toys buys goods, the HST the business pays is recorded separately from the HST collected on Sales. Other companies may put the HST collected and HST paid in the same account.

At the end of a period (e.g., month, quarter) the business subtracts the HST PAID ON PURCHASES from the HST COLLECTED FROM SALES. (Calculation of HST amount shown in Exercise 3B-30.) If the HST collected (e.g., $800.00) is more than the HST paid (e.g., $300.00) the difference ($500.00) is sent to the government (shown in Exercise 3B-31 for remittance entry preparation and posting). If the HST collected (such as $700.00) is less than the HST paid (e.g., $900.00) the difference ($200.00) is requested from the government.

HST PAID ON PURCHASES is a Contra Liability account on the Balance Sheet, and has a debit balance.

20 ➤ **Exit** from the Journal Entry window. Changes can be made to the invoice, if required, by clicking on the field to be changed, and entering the revised details. Make sure you display the entry again, after changes, to ensure that it is correct.

(See side note box below.)

21 ➤ **Post** when correct and **Exit** to the Home window.

To View a Vendor Account

ℹ️ To correct or cancel a recorded purchase quote, purchase order or posted purchase invoice, refer to Chapter 13. A procedure similar to Exercises 2A-18 and/or 3A-6 could also be followed.

Sometimes you may need to view a vendor account; e.g., you want to take advantage of a discount so you need to check the date of the invoice, or you want to know how much you owe a particular vendor. At any time, you can display or print the details in a vendor account.

As in the RECEIVABLES module, you can display a **Vendor Aged** report.

Exercise 3A-10 – To Display a Vendor Account

To display the Vendor Report for Thompson Toy Makers you have two choices:

a)   If the Vendor Aged is listed in the *Recently Viewed Reports* area, click on it. This will display all vendors.

b)   If the Vendor Aged is not listed in the *Recently Viewed Reports* area, use step 1 to display only Thompson Toy Makers.

1 ➤ Click **Report Centre**, from the Payables tab select, **Vendor Aged Detail**, click **Modify this report**, click on **Thompson Toy Makers** (it remains blue). The date should be Apr 06, 2016, click **OK**. The report could be displayed with Include Terms.

Notice that all invoices are in the Current (0 to 30 days) column.

2 ➤ **Exit** from the display window and return to the Home window.

Purchase of Services/Goods Not for Resale

Inevitably you need to purchase goods not for resale, such as shipping supplies. Although these items may be related to your sales, the items themselves are not for resale. Therefore, they should be recorded differently.

Other examples of items not for resale are office supplies, printed cheques for paying bills, customer bags, utilities (Electricity, Water), etc.

Journalizing Purchases for Goods Not For Resale

When a firm purchases goods or services that will be used by the business and not sold to customers, the HST, that is part of the invoice price, becomes part of the HST recoverable.; e.g., supplies used in the office and store, telephone, electricity, etc.

HST is calculated on the invoice amount of goods or services. Remember, HST paid on purchases is recoverable from the federal government. For example:

Value of supplies purchased	300.00
HST paid and recoverable	39.00
Total cost of goods and taxes	**339.00**
HST to be recovered	39.00
True cost of amount paid for supplies	300.00

Simply allows you to record the cost price, HST to match the information from the purchase invoice, and the software does the rest.

Exercise 3A-11 – Recording Purchase of Goods Not for Resale

Apr 06, 2016 **Mr. Tyson ordered and received 1 box of 1,000 cheques, form style, number #10188 from NAS Business Forms. The special printing of cheques, on invoice #4556 dated today, is in the amount of $300.00, plus HST $39.00. Terms are 2/10, net 30. A purchase order number was not issued for this purchase.** *Note*: **Charge 1330 Prepaid Office Supplies because the cheques have not been used. The cost will be charged to an expense (adjustment) as they get used.**

NAS **Business Forms**

8599 Hamel Avenue   **INVOICE 4556**
Toronto, Ont. M8W 3X9
Phone 416-983-2265 ❖ Fax 416-983-2266

SOLD TO:

Tyson's Toys   P.O. _____
93 Betty Ann Drive   Date: _Apr 06, 2016_____
Willowdale, Ont. M2N 1Y5

#	UNIT CODE	QTY.	DESCRIPTION	AMOUNT
1	10188	1000	Cheques Special Order	$ 300.00
			HST	39.00
Terms: 2/10, net 30			TOTAL	$ 339.00

Fig. 3A-12: Purchase of non-merchandise.

1 ➤ **Record** the entry as shown in Fig. 3A-13.

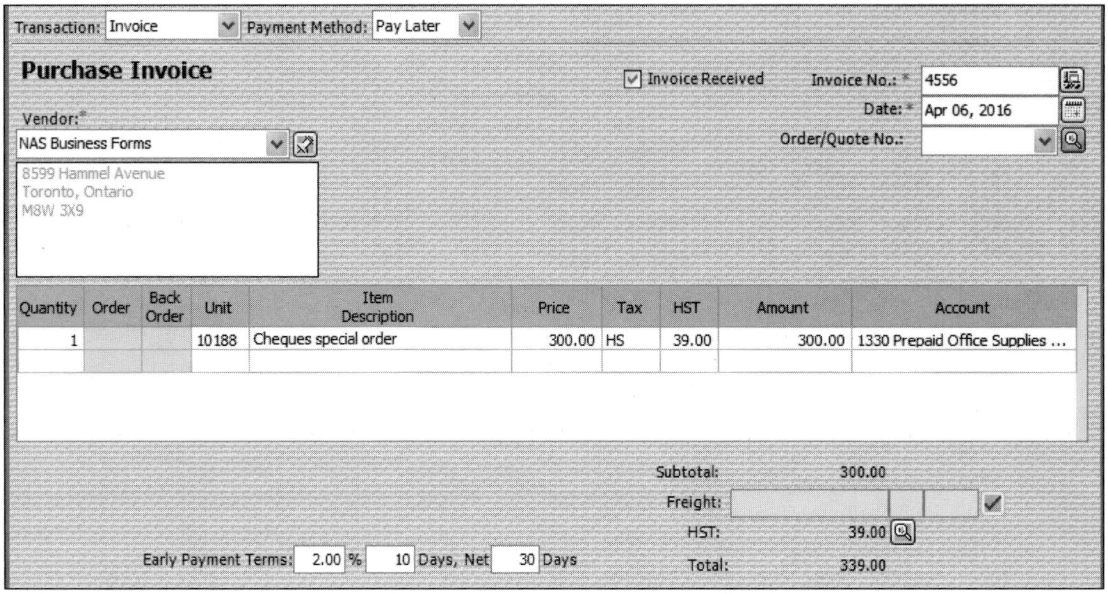

Transaction: Invoice	Payment Method: Pay Later

Purchase Invoice

☑ Invoice Received   Invoice No.: * 4556
Date: * Apr 06, 2016

Vendor: *
NAS Business Forms

8599 Hammel Avenue
Toronto, Ontario
M8W 3X9

Order/Quote No.:

Quantity	Order	Back Order	Unit	Item Description	Price	Tax	HST	Amount	Account
1			10188	Cheques special order	300.00	HS	39.00	300.00	1330 Prepaid Office Supplies ...

Subtotal: 300.00
Freight:
HST: 39.00
Early Payment Terms: 2.00 % 10 Days, Net 30 Days
Total: 339.00

Fig. 3A-13: Purchases Journal window.

2 ➤ View the Purchases Journal Entry. Simply calculates the cost of the cheques correctly.

Purchases Journal Entry Apr 06, 2016 (J2)

Account Number	Account Description	Debits	Credits
1330	Prepaid Office Supplies etc.	300.00	-
2560	HST Paid On Purchases	39.00	-
2200	Accounts Payable	-	339.00
Additional Date:	Additional Field:		
		339.00	339.00

> If you make an error in a recorded purchase quote or order, or in a posted invoice, you can use the icon to adjust (Exercise 3A-6) or cancel the quote, order or invoice. You can also Reverse the entry. Refer to Exercise 2A-18 which would be similar, but use the appropriate Purchases Quotes, Orders or Invoices Journal instead. See also Chapter 13 to make corrections.

3 ➤ When your entry is complete, **Post** the transaction and return to the Home window. (See side note box.)

Purchase of Services

Non-merchandise transactions such as rent, utility (electricity or water) expenses, accountant's fees, drawings, HST payments, etc., should be entered in the Purchases Journal, if it will be paid later just as any other purchase, or in the Payments Journal, if it is paid when you get the bill/invoice. A vendor subledger should be created for each non-merchandise supplier.

Exercise 3A-12 – Recording Purchase of Services – Cheque Issued

---

This exercise illustrates the steps to record a cheque issued for a service.

1 ➤ Advance the Session date to **Apr 07, 2016**.

Apr 07, 2016   **Mr. Tyson called you on his cell phone. He will pick up a cheque payable to Willowdale Mall Ltd. for $2,000.00 plus 13% HST cheque for the monthly mall rent at 93 Betty Ann Drive.**

> ℹ️ The term, Pay Expenses, is not exactly correct. You use this choice to pay expenses that are being paid without being recorded as a payable (rent cheques, office supplies that are purchased and not being used during this accounting period, Owner's Drawings, which is not a business expense and/or other miscellaneous expenses that are being paid by cheque).

2 ➤   From the Home window at the **Payments** icon, click the ▼ arrow and there are 6 choices.

Pay Purchase Invoices ──→	Pays Invoices previously posted
Pay Credit Card Bills ──→	Pays Credit Card bills previously posted
Pay Expenses ──→	Pays other bills not previously posted
Pay Remittances ──→	Pays Government amounts previously posted – HST (see Exercise 3B-31) and Income Tax, CPP, EI (see Chapter 7).
Find Payment ──→	Find payments previously posted.
Adjust Payment ──→	Adjust a payment previously posted. (See Exercise 3A-15.)

3 ➤   Select **Pay Expenses**. (See info note box.)

4 ➤   The choice at top left is Make Other Payment. Click the ▼ to see the choices available. Select **Make Other Payment**. `Tab`.

5 ➤ **By**   Click the ▼ to see the choices available. Select **Cheque**, `Tab`.

6 ➤ **From**   If the company used more than 1 bank account you would click the ▼ arrow and select a bank account. Tyson's Toys uses only 1 bank account. `Tab`.

7 ➤ **To the Order of**   Select **Willowdale Mall Ltd.** `Tab`.

     Cheque No.   The next cheque number is 2511. Cheque #2511 was set up as part of the company defaults. You will learn how to do this in Chapter 4.

8 ➤ **Date**   Click this field. You could select a different date. `Tab` `Tab` to accept the date (see side box) and move to Acct. The Payments Journal window shows the cheque date as Apr 07, 2016, but the printed cheque will display the date as follows: 0 7 0 4 2 0 1 6 based on the CPA cheque guidelines. D D M M Y Y Y Y (See side note box.)

> ℹ️ *Note*: Effective Jan 1, 2007, the Canadian Payments Association (CPA) has issued guidelines for cheque dates. Simply Accounting has adopted the same DDMMYYYY standard that Canadian cheque printers have adopted.

9 ➤ **Acct**   `Tab` to accept this field because this is the default expense account. If you need to change this column, you would double-click on **5310** and change it to the appropriate account number. DO NOT CHANGE.

10 ➤ **Description**   Type **Mall rent for April** `Tab`.

11 ➤ **Amount**   Type **2000.00**. `Tab`.

12 ➤ Tax [Tab] to accept code HS.

13 ➤ HST [Tab] to accept HST calculated amount.

14 ➤ Invoice Ref Type **Lease 04-2016** [Tab]. This field will contain appropriate invoice numbers, memo codes, or other descriptive notations that help describe why the payment is being made. This information will display in the Vendor Aged Report. You cannot use the same Invoice Reference twice; therefore, **04-2016** would indicate the month and year of the lease payment.

15 ➤ Comment Type **Mall rent for Apr at 93 Betty Ann Drive**. This field can be used to record an additional comment on the cheque at the bottom of the detail section. See the Make Other Payment window next. See next information note (under cheque) re printed journal.

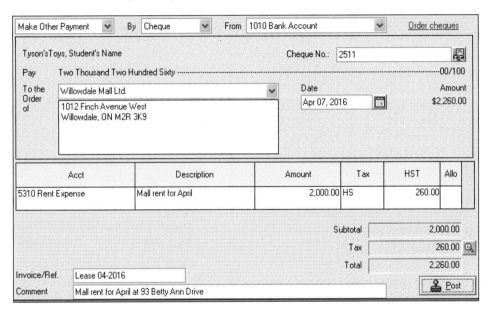

In the printed Journal, the comment field will display to the right of the vendor name; e.g., 2511, Willowdale Mall Ltd.: Mall rent for Apr at 93 Betty Ann Drive .

16 ➤ Display the **Payments Journal Entry**. The window should appear as follows:

Payments Journal Entry Apr 07, 2016 (J3)

Account Number	Account Description	Debits	Credits
2560	HST Paid On Purchases	260.00	-
5310	Rent Expense	2,000.00	-
1010	Bank Account	-	2,260.00
Additional Date:	Additional Field:		
		2,260.00	2,260.00

Notice that Simply has automatically credited the BANK account.

17 ➤ Exit the display and **Post** when correct.

18 ➤ Exit to the Home window.

A bill with amounts this large should be accrued as an adjustment at the end of each month. You have advised the accountant and they will begin recording monthly accruals starting at the end of this month. (Adjustments like this will be discussed in Chapter 9.)

Exercise 3A-13 – Recording Purchase of Services – Pay Later

This exercise illustrates the steps necessary to record an invoice to be paid later. To record this transaction, the procedure is similar to Exercise 3A-9, but we will use the Purchase Invoices icon. (See side note box.)

> **Apr 07, 2016** The March telephone bill was received today. The bill, with no invoice number but dated Mar 31, was from **Metro Phone Company**. This bill was not accrued in the month of March. The amounts of the bill were: Phone service rental and long distance charges **$352.00**, HST **$45.76**. Phone bill is due for payment on Apr 24, 2016. Total amount **$397.76**.

1 ➤   From the Home window click the **Purchase Invoices** icon.

Use an appropriate code for other bills or memos that do not have an invoice number (e.g., for electricity bill use **Hydro0410**, for water bill use **Water0410**, etc.).

2 ➤ Vendor   Click the ▼ arrow and select **Metro Phone Co.**, .

3 ➤ Invoice   Type **PHMar31**, Tab Tab. This coding indicates that the invoice is from the phone company (PH), and that the date the information was sent by the phone company was March 31. (See side note box.)

Date: If you use a Mar 31, 2016 date and try to post the entry, you will get the following message:

> **Simply Accounting - Confirmation**
>
> ❓ The date for this transaction precedes the session date and will affect prior period reports. Are you sure you want to continue?

This means that the entry will go back to March 2016 data and change the account postings. The reports dated Mar 31, 2016 have already been printed and sent to the various managers and owners, and would now be incorrect. It is better to date this type of entry as being received on Apr 01, 2016.

The advanced date (Apr 1) would not have a significant effect on the financial results of April.

This approach is reasonable as long as the amount is not significant. A significant transaction amount (large dollar value) would have to be recorded in March; otherwise, the reports may be misleading. Some companies may want to backdate this type of entry. If so, revised reports would be required for all managers and necessary staff. Be sure to provide an explanation to the managers and staff why the previous report was revised.

4 ➤ Date   Select **Apr 01, 2016**, Tab to move to Quantity.

5 ➤ Quantity   Type **1**, Tab Tab to Description.

6 ➤ Description   Type **Phone bill to Mar 31**, Tab.

7 ➤ Price   Type **352.00**, the invoice amount before taxes, [Tab].

8 ➤ Tax   [Tab] to accept HS code.

9 ➤ HST   [Tab] to accept 45.76.

10 ➤ Amount   [Tab] to accept 352.00.

11 ➤ Acct   The default account **5450 Telephone Expense** is displayed.

If you need to select a different account number press [Enter] or double-click. Remember, Simply will debit the account chosen, [Tab]. The cursor moves to the next line of the purchase invoice. No more entries are required.

The total at the bottom should equal the total phone billing of **$397.76**.

12 ➤ Terms   Leave % blank, leave **Days** blank, type **23** in **Net _Days** box (payment due by Apr 24).

The Purchase Invoice window should appear as follows:

Transaction: Invoice	Payment Method: Pay Later							

Purchase Invoice   ☑ Invoice Received   Invoice No.: * PHMar31

Vendor: *   Date: * Apr 01, 2016
Metro Phone Co.   Order/Quote No.:

678 Boxlane Road
Willowdale, Ontario
M2N 9B7

Quantity	Order	Back Order	Unit	Item Description	Price	Tax	HST	Amount	Account
1				Phone bill to Mar 31	352.00	HS	45.76	352.00	5450 Telephone Expense

Subtotal: 352.00
Freight: ☑
Early Payment Terms: ___ % ___ Days, Net 23 Days   HST: 45.76
Total: 397.76

> **ⓘ**
> This transaction has been posted to Apr 2016. This does not follow the Matching Principle. However, if a March date is used, all of the reports for March will be changed. In cases like this, most companies would prefer to date this transaction as Apr 1, 2016 so that reports for Mar 2016 are not changed.
>
> Monthly accruals should be recorded by the accountant.

13 ➤ Display the Purchases Journal Entry as follows:

Purchases Journal Entry Apr 01, 2016 (J4)

Account Number	Account Description	Debits	Credits
2560	HST Paid On Purchases	45.76	-
5450	Telephone Expense	352.00	-
2200	Accounts Payable	-	397.76
Additional Date:	Additional Field:		
		397.76	397.76

Simply has automatically credited Accounts Payable. Check the accuracy of the details.

14 ➤ **Exit** the Journal window, **Post** when correct and **Exit** from the Purchases Journal window. (See side note box at step 13.)

Recording Arrival of Goods Ordered on a Purchase Order

When goods on a purchase order arrive, an invoice usually accompanies them. This is now a purchase transaction; therefore, it should be recorded (and posted).

Exercise 3A-14 – Recording a Purchase Invoice from a PO

> **Apr 07, 2016** **The items ordered from Markham Toy Manufacturing on purchase order #82 arrived today in good condition with Invoice #1693 dated Apr 06, 2016. Record the transaction with a purchase date of Apr 06, 2016 because the 2% discount period starts on the 6th. Mr. Tyson was aware the trucks would arrive late.**

Enter the appropriate information into the fields as required.

1 ➤ From the Home window click the **Purchase Invoices** icon.

2 ➤ **Order/Quote No**. Click 🔍 **Look up an Order/Quote**. Select **82**, Tab.

The screen should flicker and the information from the Purchase Order is displayed in the window.

3 ➤ **Invoice**　　　Type **1693**, Tab Tab.

4 ➤ **Date**　　　　Type or select **Apr 06, 2016**, Tab.

5 ➤ **Quantity**　　Type **40**, Tab or use the ▨. The Backorder column is now blank because it shows the correct amount of items that have not been shipped as Nil. The complete order has been received.

The Purchases Journal window should appear as follows:

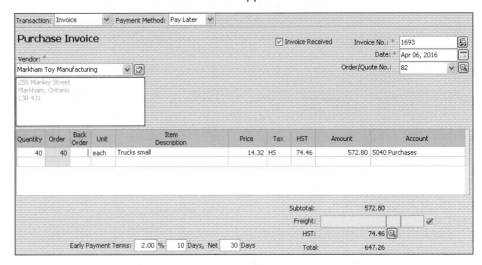

6 ➤ **View** the Purchases Journal entry. The display window should appear as follows:

Purchases Journal Entry Apr 06, 2016 (J5)			
Account Number	Account Description	Debits	Credits
2560	HST Paid On Purchases	74.46	-
5040	Purchases	572.80	-
2200	Accounts Payable	-	647.26
Additional Date:	Additional Field:		
		647.26	647.26

7 ➤ **Exit** from the Journal entry window and **Post** when correct.

A message box appears.

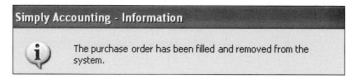

Simply Accounting - Information

> The purchase order has been filled and removed from the system.

8 ➤ Click **OK**. Click **OK** again, to accept the confirmation window. The window flickers and returns to a blank Purchases Journal.

9 ➤ **Exit** to the Home window.

Back up your data and update your logbook (located at the back of this textbook) now. **Remember, if it is important, back it up**.

Adjusting a Cheque

There may be situations where a cheque was printed with the wrong amount, or to the wrong vendor. This exercise will show you how to adjust the Payment to the correct amounts. You could have cancelled the cheque (using the Reverse Cheque icon) and then issued a new cheque. In this exercise we will adjust the cheque and change the cheque number. You cannot reprint a cheque using the same cheque number.

Exercise 3A-15 – Adjusting a Posted Cheque

This exercise illustrates the steps to adjust a cheque.

Apr 07, 2016 **Mr. Tyson arrived, and realized that he did not tell you the rent increased to $2,100.00 plus 13% HST as of April 1. Cancel cheque #2511 and issue a corrected cheque #2512 payable to Willowdale Mall Ltd. for the monthly mall rent at 93 Betty Ann Drive.**

1 ➤ From the Home window click the ▼ at the **Payments** icon.

2 ➤ Select **Adjust Payment**, and the Search window opens. Click **OK**.

3 ➤ Select **cheque 2511**, and a payment window with this header appears.

Payments Journal - Adjusting Other Payment 2511

4 ➤ **Cheque No.**   Change the cheque number to **2512** (the next cheque) [Tab].

If there was an error in the vendor name, you could click the [▼] arrow and select the correct vendor.

5 ➤ **Amount**   Type **2100.00,** [Tab].

HST   The amount changes to 273.00 (2,100.00 x 13%).

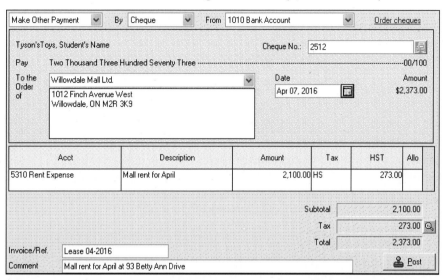

6 ➤ **View** the Payments Journal entry. The display window should appear as follows:

Payments Journal Entry Apr 07, 2016 (J7)

Account Number	Account Description	Debits	Credits
2560	HST Paid On Purchases	273.00	-
5310	Rent Expense	2,100.00	-
1010	Bank Account	-	2,373.00
Additional Date:	Additional Field:		
		2,373.00	2,373.00

7 ➤ **Exit** from the Journal entry window and **Post** when correct.

8 ➤ **Exit** to the Home window.

9 ➤ Click **Report Centre**, **Banking**, **Cheque Log**, **Modify this report**, The Start Date should be **March 31** and a Finish Date of **April 7**, click **OK**.

Cheque Log for 1010 Bank Account from Mar 31, 2016 to Apr 07, 2016

Cheque No.	Che... Type	Payee	Amount	Cheque Date	Times Prin...	Entered... system	JE#	JE Date
2511	Payment	Willowdale Mall Ltd.	2,260.00	Apr 07, 2016	0	Reversed	J3	Apr 07, 2016
2512	Payment	Willowdale Mall Ltd.	2,373.00	Apr 07, 2016	0	Yes	J7	Apr 07, 2016

Notice that each cheque is shown as not being printed.

Good Audit Trail information, cheque 2511 is shown as Reversed, for the managers, accountants and owners.

10 ➤ **Exit** to the Home window.

Journalizing Purchase Returns

There are times when you may return merchandise for the same reasons that your customers would return goods you have shipped (they were damaged, defective, or not as ordered). This type of transaction should be recorded in the Purchase Returns account. You may send a return invoice (DEBIT MEMO) to the vendor along with the returned goods because you are **debiting** your ACCOUNTS PAYABLE account. The vendor would then credit the ACCOUNTS RECEIVABLE account in their books that corresponds to your company. They may send you a credit invoice (CREDIT MEMO) to verify the transaction.

Study this summary:

Transactions	*Recorded in YOUR books*	*Transactions*	*Recorded in THEIR books*
	They are a VENDOR to you		**You are a CUSTOMER to them**
Purchases from your vendor	Dr Purchases Cr Accounts Payable	Sale to you	Dr Accounts Receivable Cr Sales
Purchase Returns to your vendor (Receive their Credit Note)	Dr Accounts Payable Cr Purchase Returns/Allow	Sales Return from you (Issue Credit Note to the customer)	Dr Sales Returns/Allow Cr Accounts Receivable
	They are a CUSTOMER to you		**You are a VENDOR to them**
Sale to your customer	Dr Accounts Receivable Cr Sales	Purchase from you	Dr Purchases Cr Accounts Payable
Sales Returns from your customer (Issue a Credit Note to the customer)	Dr Sales Returns/Allow Cr Accounts Receivable	Purchase Return from you (Receive your Credit Note)	Dr Accounts Payable Cr Purchase Returns/Allow

Exercise 3A-16 – Recording Purchase Returns

> **Apr 07, 2016**   Returned 13 Trucks small, received this morning from Markham Toy Manufacturing due to paint peeling from the driver's side of truck. The cost of each returned item is $14.32, plus HST from invoice #1693. Markham Toy Manufacturing faxed us their credit memo #CM265 today in the amount of $-210.36.

Record the entry as follows:

1 ➤ From the Home window, click the **Purchase Invoices** icon.

2 ➤ **Purchased From**   Select **Markham Toy Manufacturing** vendors, `Tab`.

3 ➤ Invoice

Many firms would enter the old invoice number 1693 with an Rt code; i.e., **1693Rt**. Some firms, in addition, may also enter the credit memo number. Type **1693Rt CM265**. This coding method shows both the original invoice and the credit note. `Tab` `Tab` to Date.

4 ➤ Date

Apr 07, 2016 is the date goods are returned. `Tab`.

5 ➤ Quantity

Type **-13** (minus), `Tab`. The minus sign represents the return of the trucks.

6 ➤ Unit

Type **each**, `Tab`.

7 ➤ Description

Type **Trucks small - returned paint peeling**, `Tab`.

8 ➤ Price

Type **14.32**, `Tab`.

9 ➤ Tax

`Tab` to accept HS.

10 ➤ HST

`Tab` to accept -24.20. The HST PAID ON PURCHASES account will be credited (reduced).

11 ➤ Amount

`Tab` to accept -186.16 (negative).

12 ➤ Account

You cannot use account 5040 because we are **returning** goods, not buying. Mr. Tyson wants to keep track of the goods returned in a separate account.

Select **5050 Purchase Returns**, `Tab`. This account will be credited because of the minus amount. The cursor moves to the next line of the purchase invoice. No more entries are required. (See side note box.)

> A credit memo received is entered as a **negative** purchase invoice which reduces NET PURCHASES in the Income Statement.

13 ➤ Terms

Change to **2%, 9 days, net 29 days** to match the original terms on invoice #1693. *Note*: Some firms would not change terms.

The lower portion of the window should appear similar to the following:

Quantity	Order	Back Order	Unit	Item Description	Price	Tax	HST	Amount	Account
-13			each	Trucks small - returned paint peeling	14.32	HS	-24.20	-186.16	5050 Purchase Returns

Subtotal:		-186.16
Freight:		✔
HST:		-24.20

Early Payment Terms: 2.00 % 9 Days, Net 29 Days   Total: -210.36

14 ➤ Display the Purchases Journal Entry as follows:

> Entering a *negative* amount in the **Quantity** column results in a **debit** to **Accounts Payable**, and **credits** to **HST Paid on Purchases** and **Purchase Returns**.

Purchases Journal Entry Apr 07, 2016 (J8)

Account Number	Account Description	Debits	Credits
2200	Accounts Payable	210.36	-
2560	HST Paid On Purchases	-	24.20
5050	Purchase Returns	-	186.16
Additional Date:	Additional Field:		
		210.36	210.36

(See side note box.)

15 ➤ **Post** when correct. **Exit** from the Purchases Journal window and return to the
     Home window.

Save your work on a regular basis and update your logbook.

To Review the Vendor Record

To view the return memo (negative purchase invoice) just recorded and posted,
display the Vendor Aged detail as follows:

1 ➤ In the Vendors area, click ▼ at **Markham Toy Manufacturing, Display Vendor
     Aged Detail Report**, click **Modify, Report Options, Include Terms** and **OK** to
     display the detail for Markham Toy Manufacturing.

Notice that the return memo is displayed in the "Current" column because of the date
used to enter the transaction.

Vendor Aged Detail As at Apr 07, 2016

Source	Date	Terms	Transaction Type	Total	Current	31 to 60
Markham Toy Manufacturing						
1622	Mar 22, 2016	2%/10, Net 30	Invoice	1,154.86	1,154.86	-
1638	Mar 30, 2016	2%/10, Net 30	Invoice	1,127.74	1,127.74	-
1693	Apr 06, 2016	2%/10, Net 30	Invoice	647.26	647.26	-
1693Rt CM265	Apr 07, 2016	2%/9, Net 29	Invoice	-210.36	-210.36	-
Total outstanding:				2,719.50	2,719.50	-
Total unpaid invoices:				2,719.50	2,719.50	-
Total prepayments/prepaid order:				-	-	-
Total outstanding:				2,719.50	2,719.50	-

2 ➤ **Exit** from the display window.

Viewing/Printing Special Reports

Exercise 3A-17 – To View/Print a Pending Purchase Orders Report

Outstanding Purchase Orders

This report displays the outstanding Purchase Orders and the dates the goods are
expected to be shipped. It is good to print this report periodically to ensure that no
purchase orders are missed. The information in this report is also used for budgeting,
particularly forecasting future receipts to ensure that cash is available for payment of
bills.

1 ➤ To display this report, click **Report Centre, Payables, Pending Purchase
     Orders Detail by Vendor, Modify this report**, change the date to: **Apr 15,
     2016** (just over 1 week in the future), **OK**. The Pending PO (A-Your Name
     Toys Parts) is displayed and includes a description of the items being
     purchased and Backordered quantity 100.00 (100 wheels have been ordered).
     Note that this report is different than the Summary report in Exercise 3A-7.

2 ➤ **Exit** from the Pending Purchase Orders window and return to Home window.

Another Transaction

1 ➤ **Record** and **Post** the following transaction: Return to the Home window.

> **Apr 07, 2016** **Per special arrangements, Mr. Tyson sent back 30 trailer cars at $10.00 each plus HST, to Lanting Speciality Toys, that were originally purchased on invoice #6198 dated Feb 22, 2016. Total return including HST is -339.00 (negative). There are no terms on this return.**

The Payments Journal

Payments to vendors for invoices that were previously recorded are entered in the **Payments** Journal. The Payments Journal is also used to record payments for prepayments and cash purchases where invoices are paid at time of purchase (invoices that have not been previously recorded and require a cheque). For cash purchases, you would record the invoice and the cheque at the same time.

Journalizing a Vendor Payment

When entering a vendor payment, Simply will automatically record a debit to ACCOUNTS PAYABLE and a credit to CASH IN BANK for the amount of the payment.

Simply can print cheques with an advice; however, Simply prints only the details of the cheque and advice. The cheques have to be formatted and printed with the bank codes according to bank specifications, ideally on preprinted cheques.

You can also select an option to display a reminder window to print cheques before posting. This has not been done for Tyson's Toys but will be covered in Chapter 4.

Exercise 3A-18 – Recording a Vendor Payment

---

1 ➤ Click the **Payments** icon from the Home window to open the Payments Journal.

Toolbar Icons

The new icon in the Payments Journal is:

 Enter vendor Prepayments Allows you to record payments in advance of receiving goods and/or services. Used with or without a purchase order (see Exercise 3B-28).

 The **Include Fully paid invoices prepayment** icon means that any invoice recorded as a Purchase Invoice (not paid using the Pay Expense selection) that was previously fully paid and not cleared (from the data file) will be displayed in the **Original Amt.** column. This feature allows a review of the invoice and payment activity for this vendor. (If you check the box while entering payments, the journal will be reset and amounts will have to be re-entered.)

Process the following transaction:

Apr 07, 2016 Mr. Tyson made arrangements to pay Lanting Speciality Toys for Invoice #6198 and the return of goods from that invoice. Cheque #2513 issued (see below).

As the information in Fig. 3A-14 indicates, cheque 2513 is paying only Invoice #6198 less the #6198 return. Invoice #6211 is not being paid at this time.

Enter the payment as follows:

2 ➤ To the Order of   Select **Lanting Speciality Toys**. Notice the program shows all unpaid invoices for this vendor (supplier). [Tab].

Cheque No.   2513, is the next available cheque number for Tyson's Toys. If the cheque number is different, you would type the correct number.

3 ➤ Date   Click the date field. [Tab] [Tab] to accept Apr 07, 2016.

4 ➤ Due Date   The cursor is on Mar 23, 2016 for invoice 6198. [Tab].

The Due Date column, displays the net 30 days due date, not the discount period date.

Invoice #	Invoice Date	Discount Date*	30 Days Due Date*
6198	Feb 22, 2016	Mar 03, 2016	Mar 23, 2016
6211	Feb 25, 2016	Mar 06, 2016	Mar 26, 2016
6198Rt	Apr 07, 2016	- none- **	Mar 23, 2016***

* February 2016 is a leap year.

**The 6198Rt (return) does not have a discount date, as the discount period for the original purchase has passed.

***Simply does not display the Due Date for negative invoices (returns and Allowances), therefore, the Mar 23, 2016 date is not shown.

Discount Available   The cursor does not stop in this field, as it is an information column that shows if a discount is available (this invoice is more than 10 days from the purchase date and, therefore, over the discount period).

5 ➤ Discount Taken   As discussed above, there is no discount on this invoice, [Tab] to leave blank.

6 ➤ Payment Amount   The amount **1,057.68**, which is the amount of invoice 6198, appears in this field and is highlighted.

[Tab] to accept 1,057.68.

> **ℹ**
>
> If the Disc. Available column has a **-6.00** discount showing, it was because you forgot to remove the terms from the return you recorded in the previous entry. Press **Delete** to remove the -6.00.

7 ➤ Discount Taken

The cursor drops to the next invoice and the Discount Taken column. The current payment is for invoice 6198 and the return 6198Rt associated with the same invoice. Use the down arrow key ↓ to move to the **Discount Taken** field on the line for **6198Rt**. ⌷Tab⌷ . (See side note box.)

If you pressed ⌷Tab⌷ by mistake before moving down, and 3,403.56 appears in the Payment Amount column, press the *Delete* key to remove 3,403.56 from the column.

8 ➤ Payment Amount

The amount of **-339.00** is highlighted, ⌷Tab⌷ . The total of the cheque to be issued is $718.68 If other invoices were listed and required payment, you would use the ↑ or ↓ key to move to the invoices that were being paid, and repeat the above procedure.

9 ➤ Comment

This field (maximum 39 characters) could be used to record an additional comment which will appear at the bottom of the detail section on the cheque. (See Fig. 3A-14.)

Type **Payment as discussed with Mr. Lanting**, ⌷Tab⌷ .

The lower portion window should display as follows:

> **ℹ**
>
> The Due Date field does not display the date of the debit note (return or allowance). See Chapter 2, Exercise 2B-24, step 6.

Due Date	Invoice or Prepayment	Original Amount	Amount Owing	Discount Available	Discount Taken	Payment Amount
Mar 23, 2016	6198	1,057.68	1,057.68	0.00		1,057.68
Mar 26, 2016	6211	3,403.56	3,403.56	0.00		
	6198Rt	-339.00	-339.00	0.00		-339.00

Total　718.68

Comment　Payment as discussed with Mr. Lanting　　　　　　🖊 Post

Fig. 3A-14 Lower portion of Payments Journal.

10 ➤ Display the Payments Journal Entry.

Payments Journal Entry Apr 07, 2016 (J10)

Account Number	Account Description	Debits	Credits
2200	Accounts Payable	718.68	-
1010	Bank Account	-	718.68
Additional Date:	Additional Field:		
		718.68	718.68

Notice that Simply has automatically debited Accounts Payable and credited the Bank Account.

11 ➤ Exit from the display window.

Do NOT print a cheque at this time. Pre-printed cheques can be printed on 81/2 x 11 paper with one or two advice stubs. If the cheque has two stubs, one advice stub may be sent to the vendor and the second advice stub would be attached to the invoice with other documentation required to approve the payment. If only one advice stub is used, it will be sent to the vendor with the cheque.

12 ➤ **Post** when correct.

> Advisor: There are older outstanding invoices for this vendor. Are you sure you want to process this transaction?

To correct or cancel a vendor payment refer to Chapter 2, Exercise 2A-17, To Correct a Receipt Error, which would be similar, or see Chapter 13, for the PAYABLES correction.

The message box informs you that there are older invoices that should have been paid first. Mr. and Mrs. Tyson have made arrangements to pay invoice #6211 by Apr 16. In a business setting, the clerk would advise a supervisor that an older invoice has not been paid, and the supervisor would take appropriate action.

13 ➤ We want to pay this invoice less the return; therefore, click **Yes**.

14 ➤ **Exit** to the Home window. (See side note box.)

To Review the Vendor Record

15 ➤ Display the **Vendor Aged Detail** report, without terms, for Lanting Speciality Toys.

Vendor Aged Detail As at Apr 07, 2016

Source	Date	Transaction Type	Total	Current	31 to 60	61 to 90
Lanting Speciality Toys						
6198	Feb 22, 2016	Invoice	1,057.68	-	1,057.68	-
2513	Apr 07, 2016	Payment	-1,057.68	-	-1,057.68	-
6211	Feb 25, 2016	Invoice	3,403.56	-	3,403.56	-
6198Rt	Apr 07, 2016	Invoice	-339.00	-339.00	-	-
2513	Apr 07, 2016	Payment	339.00	339.00	-	-
Total outstanding:			3,403.56	-	3,403.56	-

16 ➤ **Exit** from the display window to the Home page.

17 ➤ Advance the Session date to **Apr 15, 2016**.

Payment with Merchandise Discount

Many firms take a cash discount on the price of the goods before HST. Most firms will not allow a discount on the HST. You would set a default for the Simply program to specify how to calculate discounts (to include or not include HST). Tyson's Toys has set Simply to allow cash discounts before taxes. You saw this step when you set up a new vendor in Exercise 3A-8.

Exercise 3A-19 – Recording a Payment with Merchandise Discount
---

> **Apr 15, 2016 Issued cheque #2514 to Thompson Toy Makers for $2,745.55 in payment of Invoices #886 and #996. Tyson's Toys took a cash discount on Invoice #996. Mr. Tyson wants the cheque to arrive before the end of the discount period.**

Tyson's Toys calculates the cash discount on the $300.00 merchandise purchased on invoice #996, before taxes; therefore, the discount available on this invoice is $6.00 which is 2% of $300.00.

1 ➤ Click the **Payments** icon from the Home window to display the Payments Journal.

2 ➤ **To the Order of**   Select **Thompson Toy Makers,** `Tab` .

Cheque No.   **2514** (the next cheque number).

Date   **Apr 15, 2016**.

The lower portion of the journal is displayed in Fig. 3A-15 and the Discount Available column shows 6.00.

Due Date	Invoice or Prepayment	Original Amount	Amount Owing	Discount Available	Discount Taken	Payment Amount
Apr 14, 2016	886	2,412.55	2,412.55	0.00		
May 06, 2016	996	339.00	339.00	6.00		

Fig. 3A-15: Payments Journal window showing discount.

> **If you advance the date more than 10 days from the date of the invoice, the automatic discount calculation will report zero discount available.**

3 ➤ Date   Change the date to **Apr 16, 2016**. The discount remains at 6.00.

4 ➤   Change the date to **Apr 17, 2016**. The Discount Available field now shows 0.00. (See side note box.)

5 ➤   Change the date back to **Apr 15, 2016, [Tab]**. The Discount Available field now shows 6.00.

6 ➤ Due Date   The cursor should be at Apr 14, 2016 in this field, [Tab].

7 ➤ Discount Taken There is no discount because it is more than 10 days from the invoice date for invoice #886. [Tab].

8 ➤ Payment Amount   [Tab] to accept 2,412.55.

The cursor should be in the **Disc. Taken** field.

9 ➤   Double-click **6.00** in the **Disc. Available** field. The screen drills down to the original invoice. You can see the original purchase amount of $300.00 and can verify the discount of 2%. Simply does the calculation automatically.

10 ➤   **Exit** from the Purchases Journal - Invoice Lookup window, [Tab].

11 ➤   **Discount Taken** [Tab] to accept 6.00.

12 ➤   **Payment Amt.** [Tab] to accept $333.00.

The amount of the cheque should be $2,745.55. The lower portion of the Payments Journal window should resemble Fig 3A-16:

Due Date	Invoice or Prepayment	Original Amount	Amount Owing	Discount Available	Discount Taken	Payment Amount
Apr 14, 2016	886	2,412.55	2,412.55	0.00		2,412.55
May 06, 2016	996	339.00	339.00	6.00	6.00	333.00
					Total	2,745.55

Fig. 3A-16: Payments Journal window.

13 ➤   Click **Report**, click **Display Payments Journal Entry**. The display window should appear as follows:

Payments Journal Entry Apr 15, 2016 (J11)		Debits	Credits
Account Number	Account Description	Debits	Credits
2200	Accounts Payable	2,751.55	-
1010	Bank Account	-	2,745.55
5080	Purchase Discounts	-	6.00
Additional Date:	Additional Field:		
		2,751.55	2,751.55

Notice the Debit to Accounts Payable and the Credit to Purchase Discounts.

14 ➤ Exit from the display window. If the cheque were printed on pre-printed forms, with Easy-Align, it would resemble Fig. 3A-17. You do NOT need to print the cheque.

Tyson's Toys, Student's Name
93 Betty Ann Drive
Willowdale, Ontario M2N 1Y5

CHEQUE NO.   2514

DATE 1 5 0 4 2 0 1 6
           D D M M Y Y Y Y

Two Thousand, Seven Hundred Forty Five and 55/100

$**2,745.55

Thompson Toy Makers
1271 Norman Avenue
London, Ontario N6K 2A1

Tyson's Toys, Student's Name

Thompson Toy Makers   Apr 15, 2016   2514

Discount   Amount Paid
886 . . . . 2,412.55
996. . . . .   6.00 . . . . 333.00

Total 2,745.55

**Fig. 3A-17: Information printed on Easy-Align pre-printed cheque form
(note Discount).**

15 ➤ Post when correct, and **Exit** the Payments Journal.

16 ➤ Display the **Vendors Aged Detail** Report (no terms) for this vendor at Apr 15, 2016.

The report should look like the following (note the Discount):

Vendor Aged Detail As at Apr 15, 2016						
Source	Date	Transaction Type	Total	Current	31 to 60	61 to 90
Thompson Toy Makers						
886	Mar 15, 2016	Invoice	2,412.55	-	2,412.55	-
2514	Apr 15, 2016	Payment	-2,412.55	-	-2,412.55	-
996	Apr 06, 2016	Invoice	339.00	339.00	-	-
2514	Apr 15, 2016	Discount	-6.00	-6.00	-	-
2514	Apr 15, 2016	Payment	-333.00	-333.00	-	-
Total outstanding:			-	-	-	-

To display details of a recorded invoice, you could double-click on any item on the invoice **996** line. The invoice that created the $ values is displayed with a **PAID** image. This will assist you in not paying an invoice twice. To see the cheque that paid the invoice, you would double-click on the Payment line. The Cheque Lookup window will appear.

17 ➤ Exit from the Vendor Aged Detail display window.

Printing Reports when needed

It is normal to print some of the following reports during the month and file them for your audit trail:

- The Journal Entries - All of the transactions entered to date.
- The Vendor Aged Detail report, as at an appropriate date Apr 15, 2016.
- The Purchases Journal for the current period Apr 1 to Apr 15.
- The Payments Journal for the current period Apr 1 to Apr 15.
- The Cheque Log for the current period Apr 1 to Apr 15.

Exercise 3A-20 – Printing Period-End Reports

Make sure the printer is ready. You should be at the Tyson's Toys Home window to start this exercise.

1 ➤ **Print the All Journal Entries** report - as shown in previous chapters.

2 ➤ **Print the Vendor Aged Detail** at Apr 15, 2016. To ensure that everything is correct, you should compare the Balance Sheet Accounts Payable amount with the total of the Vendor Aged Detail report. They should be the same!

3 ➤ If required by your instructor, at Apr 15, refer to Exercise 3B-36 to View and/or Print the Purchases Journal, Payments Journal and/or Cheque Log.

Summary, Part A

Here is a summary of tasks and transactions in Chapter 3A:

Transaction	Journal	Remarks
Purchase Quote	Purchase Quotes	Enter amounts as positive including HST where applicable. Does not update the General Ledger. Can be changed to a Purchase Order.
Purchase Order	Purchase Orders	Similar to Purchase Quote. Enter amounts as positive. A purchase order can be entered without a purchase quote being recorded. Does not update the General Ledger.
Purchase	Purchase Invoices	A purchase can be entered by changing a Purchase Order to an invoice, or can be recorded without recording a purchase order. Enter amounts as positive. HST amounts are entered in appropriate fields. Updates the General Ledger.
Purchase Return	Purchase Invoices	Enter amount as a minus amount. HST is recorded as a negative amount. Updates the General Ledger.
Payment to Recorded invoice	Payments	Select the invoice(s) to be paid. Updates the General Ledger.
Payment with Discount	Payments	Applies a payment against the original invoice and the calculated discount.
New Vendor (Supplier)	Vendors Ledger	At the Taxes tab, change the Tax Exempt status for HST where necessary and select the appropriate tax code. Select an appropriate default expense account.

Before Moving On..., Part A

Read the following questions and make sure you know the answers to them; otherwise, read the corresponding part in the chapter before moving on:

1. Name the types of transactions that are recorded in the PAYABLES module.

2. Describe the procedure for approving vendor invoices from the time they are received until they are paid. What is the significance of this procedure?

3. What types of entries are **not** recorded in the PAYABLES module? (Ignore Sales entries.)

4. When journalizing non-merchandise purchases with HST, how is the **HST** recorded?

5. Give the journal entry for a merchandise purchase return of $300.00 plus HST of $39.00.

6. Describe briefly the steps in recording an invoice payment in full, net of a cash discount. [Assume that a) merchandise for resale was purchased, and b) discounts are calculated on pre-tax amounts.]

7. What happens when you post journal transactions in the PAYABLES module?

8. When journalizing non-merchandise purchases with HST, on what amount is **HST** based?

Relevant Appendices, Part A

The following appendices are available at www.simplyaccounting2010.nelson.com under Student Resources.

| Appendix 2010 V | **Mini-Guide*** |
| Appendix 2010 Q | **Names Fields** |

Refer to Mini-guide at the end of Chapter 3B for transactions.

Note: After finishing Chapter 3A and Chapter 8, you can complete selected transactions from Chapter 3A, using the Perpetual INVENTORY module. See Challenge Exercise 08 C8-5 Toys-PI.

Challenge Exercise 03 C3A-1, Wheelchairs

PAYABLES and COMPANY Modules

Wheelchairs is a business that sells various kinds of wheelchairs to wholesale and retail customers.

Note: The business is open 7 days a week. HST is 13%.

1 ➤ Refer to Exercise 1-1 to unzip the **03 C3A-1 Wheelchairs.exe** file.

2 ➤ Open the **C3A-1 Wheelchairs** file, and enter the following Accounts Payable transactions.

Mar 1 Issued Purchase order #81 to Your Name Chairs (Your name must appear) for 8 new model #CP-3 wheelchairs at $1,500 each, plus HST. Ship date is Mar 4. Other information: 156 Octavia Street, Belleville, Ontario, K8P 1H3, phone and fax numbers may be left blank. Terms are 2% 10 days, net 30 days, calculate discounts before tax.

Mar 1 Issued $2,250.00 plus HST cheque to Gordon Mall Management for lease rent for March.

Mar 4 Received 7 wheelchairs from Your Name Chairs from PO#81. Invoice #4568 received. The other chair is backordered and should be delivered by Mar 25th.

Mar 5 Returned 1 wheelchair from PO#81, as there is a crack in the metal frame. Credit note CN-56 received by fax.

Mar 6 Purchased and received from The Paper Place, 2 boxes of invoices with a new logo, that will be used during the year. Invoice #2256 received for $300 plus HST, Terms 2/10, net 30.

Mar 7 We discovered that ¼ of the invoices (value $75.00) received on invoice #2256 were printed without logos. The Paper Place manager agreed to an allowance (2256Al) of $75.00 plus HST which can be used to reduce the cost of the current order.

Mar 13 Received Belleville Hydro bill #1565-3 for $112.00 plus HST. Service bill dated Mar 12, and payment date is Mar 27.

Mar 14 Issued next cheque to Your Name Chairs for amount owing, less the return.

Mar 17 Purchased from Avery Parts, 3 boxes of various repair parts for wheelchairs at $100.00 per box. Invoice #8897 in the amount of $300.00 plus HST. Terms 2/10, net 30.

Mar 20 Received a bank debit memo, dated today, regarding the loan payment of $400.00, which includes $67.00 of interest.

3 ➤ When you have recorded the above entries, **print** the following:
   a. Vendor Aged Detail Report as at Mar 20
   b. Journal Entries All, for Mar 1 to 20
   c. Journal Entries-General, for Mar 1 to 20
   d. Purchase Journal for Mar 1 to 20
   e. Income Statement for Jan 1 to Mar 20
   f. Pending Purchase Order report with an as at date of Mar 20

Challenge Exercise 03 C3A-2, Radios

PAYABLES and COMPANY Modules

Radios is a business that sells various kinds of radios to wholesale and retail customers.

Note: The business is open 7 days a week. HST is 13%.

1 ➤   Refer to Exercise 1-1 to unzip the **03 C3A-2 Radios.exe** file.

2 ➤   Open the **03 C3A-2 Radios** file, and enter the following Accounts Payable transactions.

Aug 1   Issued $2,000 plus HST cheque to Royal Mall Management for lease rent for August.

Aug 1   Purchased from Town Printing Co, 4,000 advertising flyers at $.35 (35 cents each) plus HST on invoice #9974 Terms 2/10, net 30. The flyers are being distributed today to homes and businesses in the local area.

Aug 4   Received 20 radios model #26583 from Radio Manufacturing Ltd., at $40.00 each plus HST on Invoice #2583 with terms 2/10, net 30.

Aug 4   Ordered on Purchase Order #135, 15 boom box radios at $83.00 plus HST, from new vendor Your Name Radio Wholesale. (Your name must appear). Ship date is Aug 06. Other information: 688 Coleman Street, Belleville, Ontario, K8P 7P3, phone and fax numbers may be left blank. Terms are 2% 10 days, net 30 days, calculate discounts before tax.

Aug 6   Complete order received from Your Name Radio Wholesale on invoice #3865 dated today.

Aug 7   Returned 1 boom box from the Your Name Radio Wholesale order of Aug 6, as one of the speakers is broken. Credit note CN-86 received.

Aug 14   Issued next cheque to Radio Manufacturing Ltd. for invoice #2583.

Aug 15   Purchased from Oksana Radio Sales 2 specialty wide band radios at $150.00 each plus HST on invoice #3489. Terms 2/10, net 30.

Aug 15   Issued next cheque to Your Name Radio Wholesale for amount owing, less the return.

Aug 20   Issued next cheque to Gananoque Telephone for telephone service $160.00 and yellow pages advertising $40.00, plus HST. Service bill dated August 19.

Aug 20   The owner does not want the cheque mailed to Gananoque Telephone as there is an error in the advertising amount. Reverse the cheque. We have requested a revised invoice.

3 ➤ When you have recorded the above entries, **print** the following:
   a.   Vendor Aged Detail Report as at Aug 20
   b.   Journal Entries All, for Aug 1 to 20, **with Corrections**
   c.   Purchases Journal for Aug 1 to 20
   d.   Income Statement for Jan 1 to Aug 20

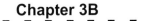

Chapter 3B

PAYABLES Module—*Beyond Basics*

Tyson's Toys

Learning Objectives

After completing Chapter 3B you will be able to:

☐ Continue to record purchase orders, invoices and returns.
☐ Continue to add new vendors and make changes to existing vendors.
☐ Record payments to vendors in full or partial payment of invoices with or without cash discounts.
☐ Record payments to other suppliers (one-time vendor, owner for drawings, etc.).
☐ Record tax payments for HST to the federal government.
☐ Record prepayments to vendors.
☐ Display and print various payable reports (vendor balances outstanding, etc.) and journals.

This chapter is a continuation of Chapter 3A. You should download the 03 3B Toys-B data file for use with this chapter.

The contents of this chapter are as follows:

- Opening the PAYABLES Module, Part B 216
- Starting Simply for Payables 216
- Exercises:
  - Exercise 3B-21 – To Open the 03 3B Toys-B data file 216
  - Exercise 3B-22 – To View/Print a Cash Flow Report 218
  - Exercise 3B-23 – Recording a Credit Card Purchase 219
  - Exercise 3B-24 – Recording a Payment with Non-Merchandise Discount .. 221
  - Exercise 3B-25 – Recording a Purchase from a One-time Vendor 225
  - Exercise 3B-26 – Recording Bank Reconciliation Entries 227
  - Exercise 3B-27 – Recording Owner's Drawings 228
  - Exercise 3B-28 – Recording a Purchase Order and Prepayment Cheque . 231
  - Exercise 3B-29 – Recording a Lease Payment 232
  - Exercise 3B-30 – Calculating the HST Remittance 235
  - Exercise 3B-31 – Recording the HST Remittance 236
  - Exercise 3B-32 – Recording an Invoice with reduced HST 238
  - Exercise 3B-33 – Printing Reports 241
  - Exercise 3B-34 – Adjusting Inventory.. 244
  - Exercise 3B-35 – Printing Statements.. 246
  - Exercise 3B-36 – Printing Period-End Reports 247
    - To View and Print the Purchases Journal 248
    - To View and Print the Payments Journal 248
    - To View and Print a Cheque Log 248
    - To View Graphs 249

- Summary, Part B.. 250
- Before Moving On…, Part B 250

* Relevant Appendices, Part B...251

    Challenge Exercise 03 C3B-1, Network 252
    Challenge Exercise 03 C3B-2, China 253
    Challenge Exercise 03 C3B-3, Dance Studio 255
    Challenge Exercise 03 C3B-4, Chairs 256

* Mini-Guide for Chapter 3 257

Opening the PAYABLES Module, Part B

In this Chapter (3B), you will access the PAYABLES module of Tyson's Toys and enter transactions related to purchases, payments to vendors, one time payments and other payable transactions starting from April 16.

The 03 3B Toys-B.exe file contains the ending balances of the General Ledger accounts and Vendor files from Chapter 3A of this text (see Trial Balance on following page). These balances will be the starting point of the B file and journal entries will start at J1.

View **Slideshow 3B – PAYABLES Part B** to prepare for more transaction processing in the PAYABLES module. Pay particular attention to the Accounting principles related to the various tasks.

Starting Simply for Payables

Exercise 3B-21 – To Open the 03 3B Toys-B data file

Review Exercise 1-2 if you need help to open a data file.

1 ➤ Refer to Exercise 1-1 to unzip the **03 3B Toys-B.exe** file. (See side note box.)

2 ➤ Start **Simply Accounting**.

3 ➤ At the Select Company window, click **Select an existing company** button and **OK**.

4 ➤ At the **Simply Accounting - Open Company** window, in the **Look in** box, locate your student location drive, and the Toys folder 📁03 3B Toys-B.

5 ➤ Double-click the 📁03 3B Toys-B folder and the 📄Toys-B.SAI file will appear in the box below. (The image at the left of Toys may be different depending on the configuration of your computer and the SAI.)

6 ➤ Click the 📄Toys-B.SAI icon. The **File name** box will change to Toys-B.SAI.

7 ➤ Click **Open** to open the Toys-B.SAI file.

8 ➤ **Date**   Accept **Apr 15, 2016**.

9 ➤ Display the Trial Balance.

The following is the Tyson's Toys Trial Balance at the end of Chapter 3A.

Study Tyson's Trial Balance.

Tyson's Toys-B, Student's Name
Trial Balance As At Apr 15, 2016

		Debits	Credits
1010	Bank Account	5,587.77	-
1020	Bank Account US funds	580.60	-
1200	Accounts Receivable	12,899.00	-
1310	Toys and parts Inventory	6,907.29	
1330	Prepaid Office Supplies, etc.	925.00	-
1340	Prepaid Insurance	0.00	-
1510	Store Equipment	25,138.45	-
1515	Accum. Amort. Store Equipment	-	11,393.00
1520	Office Furniture/Equipment	2,812.60	-
1525	Accum. Amort. Office/Furniture/Equi	-	1,605.00
2200	Accounts Payable	-	8,370.39
2210	Visa Credit Card Payable	-	0.00
2550	HST Charged On Sales	-	1,738.25
2560	HST Paid On Purchases	1,058.16	-
2610	Bank Loan Payable	-	14,310.86
3100	Capital Jerry Tyson	-	11,924.65
3120	Drawings Jerry Tyson	3,500.00	-
3200	Capital Helen Tyson	-	11,924.65
3210	Drawings Helen Tyson	3,500.00	-
4100	Sales	-	34,191.08
4150	Sales - Discount	212.30	-
4200	Sales - Returns & Allowances	604.00	-
5010	Beginning Inventory	5,421.49	-
5040	Purchases	19,281.60	-
5050	Purchases Returns	-	786.16
5080	Purchase Discounts	-	295.83
5090	Ending Inventory	-	6,907.29
5310	Rent Expense	8,100.00	-
5340	Advertising Expense	516.00	-
5345	Bank Loan Interest	301.00	-
5350	Bank Charges	135.00	-
5355	Credit Card Charges	0.00	-
5360	Insurance Expense	303.00	-
5370	Auto Lease Expense	1,200.00	-
5440	Office/Store Supplies Expense	750.00	-
5450	Telephone Expense	1,264.00	-
5460	Utility Expense	1,250.00	-
5470	Bad Debts Expense	0.00	-
5480	Delivery Expense	1,200.00	-
		103,447.26	103,447.26

Fig. 3B-18: Trial Balance, Tyson's Toys-B.

Cash Flow Projection Report

The Cash Flow Projection report shows how the bank account is expected to change by anticipated payments to outstanding vendor accounts, and expected customer payments (receipts) to be received within the number of days specified, as well as, recurring entries and other payments that will affect the bank balance. (See Bank Account projection in step 1 and side note box beside step 1.)

Exercise 3B-22 – To View/Print a Cash Flow Report

> **Apr 15, 2016 Mr. Tyson is concerned about the amount of money he will have in the bank and the amount he owes his suppliers. He has asked you to print a Cash Flow report.**

The Cash Flow **Summary** report shows a summary of amounts that will affect the bank account balance. This chapter shows only Accounts Payable transactions and does not show any receipts from Accounts Receivable.

1 ➤ To display the Cash Flow report, click **Report Centre, Financials, Cash Flow Projection Summary, Display**. This report does not indicate when the account will be in a negative position.

1010 Bank Account. Cash flow projection from Apr 15, 2016 to May 15, 2016	
Description	Balance
Balance as of Apr 15, 2016	5,587.77
Total receipts	0.00
Total payments	-8,344.65
Total recurring general journal transactions	-884.20
Total recurring other payment transactions	0.00
Ending balance	-3,641.08
Net change in cash balance:	-9,228.86
Lowest balance in the account:	-3,641.09
Highest balance in the account:	5,587.77

An overdraft occurs when you have issued cheques for more money than you have in your bank account.

2 ➤ Click **Modify, Report Options**, select **Detail**, **1010 Bank Account** is selected, click **OK**. The report shows the balance per day (Total for the day) and that the bank account will go into a negative position, (overdraft), on Apr 16 if current ACCOUNTS PAYABLE vendors are paid on time. Mr. and Mrs. Tyson are drafting a payment plan with the bank and all vendors. (See side note box.)

3 ➤ **Print** the Report.

4 ➤ **Exit** from the Cash Flow Projection window, return to the Home window.

Credit Card Purchase

Similar to credit card sales in the RECEIVABLES module, credit card purchases are considered cash purchases.

In Chapter 2B, the credit card company charges the vendor (Mrs. Santos) a fee for each transaction for allowing a customer to use a credit card. In the case of the customer who uses a credit card to pay for a purchase, the customer does not pay a fee for every transaction. The credit card company usually collects an annual fee from the credit card holder. Study how the credit card purchase transaction is recorded in the next exercise.

Exercise 3B-23 – Recording a Credit Card Purchase

Apr 15, 2016	Mrs. Tyson purchased a second new briefcase (wide) for **$135.00**, plus 13% HST, for a total price of **$152.55** from Santos Luggage. She is going to Vancouver for a toy conference and her old briefcase does not look good and needs some repairs. Mrs. Tyson used her business credit card to pay for the purchase. Received invoice 2401.

Follow these steps to record the transaction:

1 ➤ From the Home window, click the **Purchase Invoices** icon.

      Transaction   DO NOT CHANGE.

2 ➤ Payment method   Select **Visa Credit**, `Tab`.

3 ➤ Vendor   Type **Santos Luggage** `Tab`, **Continue** should be selected. Click **OK**, then `Tab` `Tab`. The Tysons do not plan to buy other goods from Santos.

4 ➤   Type **635 Semple Avenue** `Tab`, **Toronto, ON** `Tab`, **M9L 1V5**. `Tab`.

5 ➤ Invoice No.   For a credit card transaction, some vendors will issue a regular invoice and other vendors will issue a cash register receipt. Type **2401**, because Santos Luggage issued invoice 2401, `Tab` `Tab`.

6 ➤ Date   `Tab` to accept **Apr 15, 2016**, `Tab` to Quantity.

7 ➤ Quantity   Type **1**, `Tab`.

8 ➤ Unit   Type **each**, `Tab`.

9 ➤ Item Description   Type **Briefcase wide**, `Tab`.

10 ➤ Price   Type **135.00**, `Tab`.

11 ➤ Tax   Select **HS**, `Tab`. (This is a retail purchase.)

12 ➤ HST   `Tab` to accept 17.55.

13 ➤ Amount   `Tab` to accept 135.00.

14 ➤ Account   Select **5440 Office/Store Supplies Expense**. (See side note box.)

> 🛈 Some firms may have specific expense accounts to charge this type of item. This item would not be charged to an asset account due to the low dollar value (the amount is not material). Your teacher will explain in more detail.

The lower portion of the window appears as follows:

Quantity	Order	Back Order	Unit	Item Description	Price	Tax	HST	Amount	Account
1			each	Briefcase wide	135.00	HS	17.55	135.00	5440 Office/Store Supplies E…

The following is shown at the bottom of the Invoice window:

Early Payment Discount:	%	
Visa Credit Amount:		152.55

There is no Early Payment Discount on this purchase. The Early Payment Discount referred to here is for a regular customer who has 2/10 terms, who pays when the purchase is made. The discount does not apply to a Visa purchase.

15➤   **Display** the entry as follows.

Purchases Journal Entry Apr 15, 2016 (J1)

Account Number	Account Description	Debits	Credits
2560	HST Paid On Purchases	17.55	-
5440	Office/Store Supplies Expense	135.00	-
2210	Visa Credit Card Payable	-	152.55
Additional Date:	Additional Field:		
		152.55	152.55

ℹ️ Because you selected **Visa Credit** in the **Paid By** field, Simply automatically entered a credit to 2210 VISA CREDIT CARD PAYABLE, instead of a credit to ACCOUNTS PAYABLE.

(See side note box.)

16 ➤   **Post** when correct, and **Exit** to the Home window.

Payment with Non-Merchandise Discount

At this point, it is important to differentiate between **Purchase Discount** and **Cash Discount**.

A **Purchase Discount** account is used **ONLY** to show **reductions** (for paying within the discount period) to the cost of merchandise to be resold. When you are able to take a cash discount on goods or services that are **not for resale** (non-merchandise items, e.g., office supplies) and, therefore, not charged to the PURCHASES account, you should not record the discount to the Purchase Discount account.

Simply will allow an automatic discount entry to only 1 account. The Purchase Discount account has been set up as the default discount account.

Before you can record a payment with a discount on goods that are not for resale, (e.g., Office Supplies, Advertising Expense, etc.), you need to record a negative invoice. This invoice is charged to the same account, e.g., office supplies, which is a reduction to the original account where the cost was charged.

There are two steps to record a payment that involves a non-merchandise discount:

1. Record a negative purchase invoice for the discount. There are two ways to calculate the discount:

   i) You can use the lookup feature to view the details of the original invoice, and manually calculate the discount.

   ii) You can use the Payment cheque icon to view the items that are owing for each vendor, and let Simply calculate the discount for you. ***Do not post the transaction. This method is used to calculate the discount only.***

2. Record the payment including the discount using method part (i) above.

Exercise 3B-24 – Recording a Payment with Non-Merchandise Discount

Apr 15, 2016   **Paid $333.00 with your cheque #2515 to NAS Business Forms in payment of their invoice 4556 taking a cash discount because you are paying within the credit terms. The amount of the discount is $6.00 (2% of the $300.00 printing costs).**

The discount of $6.00 is a reduction of the cost of the printed cheques and is not charged to the Purchase Discounts account.

Note that this purchase of non-merchandise items was originally entered, in Chapter 3A Exercise 3A-11 Journal entry 2, as shown:

Purchases Journal Entry Apr 06, 2016 (J2)

Account Number	Account Description	Debits	Credits
1330	Prepaid Office Supplies etc.	300.00	-
2560	HST Paid On Purchases	39.00	-
2200	Accounts Payable	-	339.00
Additional Date:	Additional Field:		
		339.00	339.00

To record the payment with a cash discount:

Step One: Record the Discount

1 ➤ Click **Purchase Invoices** icon.

2 ➤ Payment method   Select **Pay Later** to match original invoice.

3 ➤ Vendor From   Select **NAS Business Forms**, [Tab].

4 ➤ Invoice No.   Type **4556Di**, [Tab] [Tab]. (See side note box.)

5 ➤ Date   [Tab] to accept **Apr 15, 2016**, [Tab] to Quantity.

6 ➤ Quantity   Type **1**, [Tab] [Tab] to Item Description.

7 ➤ Item Description   Type **Discount on invoice 4556**, [Tab].

8 ➤ Price   Type **-6.00**(negative amount to reduce the cost of supplies), [Tab].

9 ➤ Tax   **Delete** the default HS tax code, as there are no taxes on a discount. [Tab] [Tab] to Acct.

10 ➤ Account   The default account 1330 Prepaid Office Supplies, etc., appears in this field. The cheques were originally charged (posted) to this account; therefore, [Tab] to accept. This will reduce the cost of the supplies.

Di is added to the end of the invoice number to distinguish the discount as relating to a cash discount for non-merchandise items, and not a purchase discount for goods purchased for resale.

11 ➤ **Terms**   Remove **2% 10 Days, Net 30 Days**. There are no terms when claiming a discount, [Tab].

Your Purchases Journal display should be as follows:

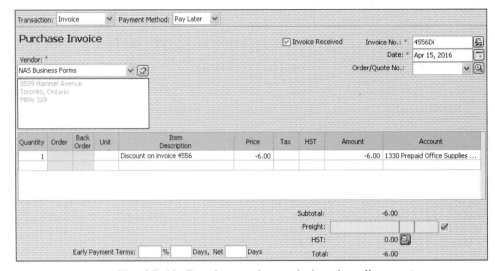

Fig. 3B-19: Purchases Journal showing discount.

12 ➤ **Display** the Journal entry, it should appear as follows:

Account Number	Account Description	Debits	Credits
Purchases Journal Entry Apr 15, 2016 (J2)			
2200	Accounts Payable	6.00	-
1330	Prepaid Office Supplies etc.	-	6.00
Additional Date:	Additional Field:		
		6.00	6.00

Notice the **credit** to PREPAID OFFICE SUPPLIES, etc., and the **debit** to ACCOUNTS PAYABLE.

13 ➤ **Exit** from the Journal Entry window.

14 ➤ **Post** when correct, and **Exit** to the Home window.

Step Two: Journalize the Payment

15 ➤ Click the **Payments** icon.

16 ➤ **Pay to the order of**   Select **NAS Business Forms,** [Tab].

      Cheque No.   2515 is the next cheque number.

      Date   Apr 15, 2016 is the correct date.

17 ➤ **Due Date**   **Click** May 06, 2016. We want to pay invoice 4556 and 4556Di; therefore, press [Tab].

18 ➤ **Discount Taken**   Automatic calculation shows 6.00. Accepting the discount amount in this column means you want the discount to be charged to the Purchase Discount account. We have recorded a 6.00 non-merchandise discount on the next line. Press the *Delete* key to remove the 6.00, Tab .

19 ➤ **Payment Amount**   Tab to accept $339.00, the amount of the original invoice.

20 ➤ **Discount Taken**   The cursor moves to the Discount Taken field for invoice **4556Di**, Tab .

21 ➤ **Payment Amount**   Tab to accept -6.00. This will charge the discount on non-merchandise to the account specified in step 10. The cheque amount total at the bottom is the correct amount (333.00) for this payment

The lower portion of the Payments Journal should resemble Fig. 3B-20.

Due Date	Invoice or Prepayment	Original Amount	Amount Owing	Discount Available	Discount Taken	Payment Amount
May 06, 2016	4556	339.00	339.00	6.00		339.00
	4556Di	-6.00	-6.00	0.00		-6.00
					Total	333.00

Fig. 3B-20: Payment with Prepaid Office Supplies discount.

22 ➤ **Display** the Journal entry, it should appear as follows.

The discount on this payment was charged to PREPAID OFFICE SUPPLIES in step 10.

Payments Journal Entry Apr 15, 2016 (J3)

Account Number	Account Description	Debits	Credits
2200	Accounts Payable	333.00	-
1010	Bank Account	-	333.00
Additional Date:	Additional Field:		
		333.00	333.00

23 ➤ **Exit** from the Payments Journal Entry window.

24 ➤ **Post** when correct and **Exit** to the Home window.

25 ➤ **Display** the Vendor Aged Detail report for NAS Business Forms at Apr 15, 2016 and it should appear as follows. Do *not* click Include Terms. The report should appear similar to Fig. 3B-21.

Vendor Aged Detail As at Apr 15, 2016					
Source	Date	Transaction Type	Total	Current	31 to 60
NAS Business Forms					
4556	Apr 06, 2016	Invoice	339.00	339.00	-
2515	Apr 15, 2016	Payment	-339.00	-339.00	-
4556Di	Apr 15, 2016	Invoice	-6.00	-6.00	-
2515	Apr 15, 2016	Payment	6.00	6.00	-
Total outstanding:			-	-	-

Fig. 3B-21: Vendor Aged Detail.

26 ➤   **Exit** from the Vendor Aged Detail window.

27 ➤   Advance the date to **Apr 16, 2016**.

More Transactions

1 ➤   **Record** and **Post** the following transactions: (See side note box.)

> If you make an error in a cheque amount and realize it after you have posted the payment, refer to Exercise 2A-17 or Chapter 13. A cheque reversal in PAYABLES is similar to a reversal in RECEIVABLES.

Apr 16, 2016	**Received invoice #646 dated today, in the amount of $384.93 for 15 Cars medium at $22.71 each plus HST, from Thompson Toy Makers. A PO was not issued. Terms 2/10, net 30.**

Apr 16, 2016	**The complete Purchase Order #83 of truck wheels from A-Your Name Toy Parts arrived in good condition with invoice # 65839 for $111.87 dated today.**

2 ➤   Advance the date to **Apr 18, 2016**.

Apr 18, 2016	**Cheque issued to pay Lanting Speciality Toys $3,403.56 on invoice #6211.**

Apr 18, 2016	**After receiving numerous telephone calls from Jason's Transport Service, Mr. Tyson paid their invoice #6691 with the next cheque.**

Apr 18, 2016	**Cheque issued to pay City Office Supplies for invoice #1235 in full.**

Purchase and Payment to a One-time Vendor

Similar to the RECEIVABLES options, Simply allows you to enter a purchase and payment to a vendor with whom you may not deal with again (One-time vendor). For example, you may hire a company to deliver advertising flyers, or you may purchase curtains for the office from a store, etc.

You can enter this type of purchase/payment by either using the:

1. **Cheque** option in the **Purchase Invoices** Journal, or
2. **Make Other Payment** option in the **Payments** Journal.
3. Click the ▼ in **Payments**, select **Pay Expenses,** the Make Other Payment option is shown.

The Payments Journal option 2 will be used in this exercise.

Simply will record the transaction to the appropriate General Ledger account, but this type of entry will not be displayed in the Vendor Aged Detail report because no vendor was set up. The journal entry may be viewed in the Payments Journal or the Journal Entries-All report.

Exercise 3B-25 – Recording a Purchase from a One-time Vendor

1 ➤ Advance date to **Apr 19, 2016**.

Apr 19, 2016	Issued cheque to Alan Cohen & Associates, 2340 Eglinton Avenue East, Toronto ON M6E 2L6 for work done on setting up our website. The invoice #589 dated today, was for $412.00 plus HST $53.56 for a total invoice of $465.56. Mr. Tyson is not sure if he will deal with this firm again.

---

2 ➤ Click the **Payments** icon.

3 ➤ At `Pay Purchase Invoices ▼`, select **Make Other Payment,** `Tab`.

4 ➤ **Cheque**   Select **Cheque,** `Tab` `Tab`.

5 ➤ **To the**   Type **Alan Cohen & Associates,** `Tab`, click **Continue,**
     Order of   then `Tab`.

6 ➤ In the box, type the address as indicated above. This information would appear on the cheque if it were printed. Also, the payee name is recorded in the Payments Journal for audit trail purposes. `Tab`.

     Cheque No.   The next cheque is 2519.

     Date   Apr 19, 2016.

7 ➤ **Account**   Select **5340 Advertising Expense.**

8 ➤ **Item**   Type **Setup Website,** `Tab`.
     Description

9 ➤ **Amount**   Type **412.00,** `Tab`.

10 ➤ **Tax**   Type **HS,** `Tab`.

11 ➤ **HST**   `Tab` to accept **53.56**.

12 ➤ **Invoice/Ref.**   Type **589,** `Tab`.

13 ➤   Comment   Type: **Alan Cohen & Associates created our website, Tab**.
(See side note box.)

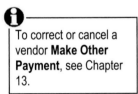

The **Comment** field replaces the **Vendor name** in the Journal entry display and printout. If you use the comment field, always use the vendor name as part of the comment.

14 ➤   The Payments Journal window should resemble the following:

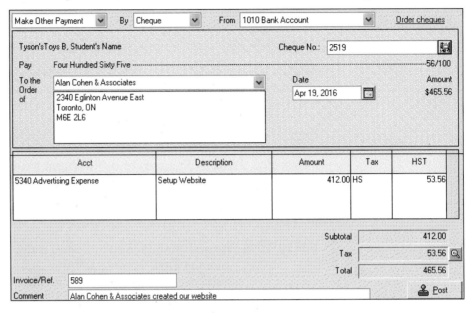

15 ➤   View the Payments Journal Entry. The display window should appear as follows:

To correct or cancel a vendor **Make Other Payment**, see Chapter 13.

Payments Journal Entry Apr 19, 2016 (J9)			
Account Number	Account Description	Debits	Credits
2560	HST Paid On Purchases	53.56	-
5340	Advertising Expense	412.00	-
1010	Bank Account	-	465.56
Additional Date:	Additional Field:		
		465.56	465.56

16 ➤   Exit the Payments Journal Entry window.

17 ➤   Post after verifying accuracy.

A warning message box appears.

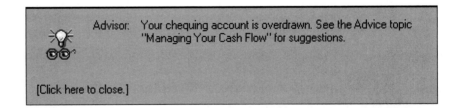

18 ➤   Mr. & Mrs. Tyson have previously made arrangements to issue cheques when they do not have enough money in their bank account. (This can be called a line of credit or overdraft protection.) You will see this message window when you post cheques later in this chapter. Accept the message by **clicking inside the box** to continue.

19 ➤   Exit the Payments Journal.

Journalizing Bank Reconciliation Items

Bank charges and various items recorded on the bank statement (e.g., any special charges, etc.) but not recorded in the company accounting records would need to be entered in your Simply files. This type of entry would be entered in the General Ledger and would not affect the Vendors Ledger because it does not concern any vendor and a cheque is not issued.

Exercise 3B-26 – Recording Bank Reconciliation Entries

Study the next memo:

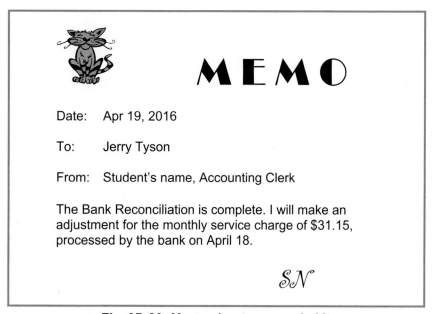

MEMO

Date: Apr 19, 2016

To: Jerry Tyson

From: Student's name, Accounting Clerk

The Bank Reconciliation is complete. I will make an adjustment for the monthly service charge of $31.15, processed by the bank on April 18.

SN

Fig. 3B-22: Memo about unrecorded item.

Entering Service Charges

Tyson's Toys has set up a General Journal recurring entry for regular monthly service charges.

1 ➤ Click on the **COMPANY** module, click the **General Journal** icon. (See side note box.)

2 ➤ Click the **Recall Recurring Transaction** icon [icon] and the Recall Recurring Transaction window will appear as follows:

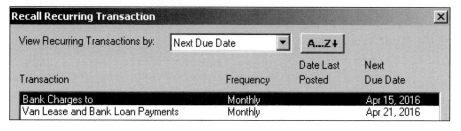

3 ➤ Select **Bank Charges to**, and the General Journal window will fill in with the recurring information.

Change the fields to resemble the following window. (See side note box.)

The entry date (Apr 18) is the date the bank took the bank charges from your account.

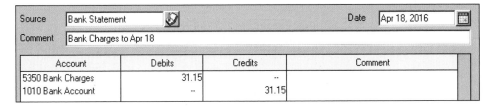

4 ➤   **Post** after verifying accuracy. A Confirmation box will appear.

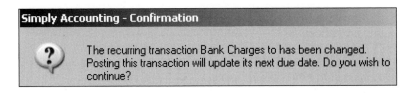

5 ➤   Click **Yes**. Click the **Recall Recurring Transaction** icon. The recurring entry has been posted and will be updated to the next scheduled due date of May 15, 2016. (See side note box.)

Recurring due dates update from the original date and do not correspond to the date last used/posted.

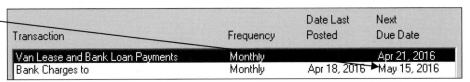

6 ➤   Click **Cancel** and **Exit** to the Home window.

Journalizing Partner's/Proprietor's Drawings

Although proprietorship withdrawals are not considered a normal vendor transaction, it is entered in **the PAYABLES module because this module is used to keep track of all payments made by the business.** Sole proprietorships or partnerships use an account called DRAWINGS or WITHDRAWALS when an owner withdraws money for personal use.

Jerry and Helen Tyson will be withdrawing money on a regular basis; therefore, vendor accounts should be set up. At any time Jerry or Helen can check their vendor account to see what amounts they have withdrawn during the year.

Exercise 3B-27 – Recording Owner's Drawings

1 ➤   Advance the Session date to **Apr 20, 2016**.

Study the following memo:

MEMO

Date: Apr 20, 2016

To: Accounting

From: Jerry Tyson

Please issue a cheque to me as a personal draw in the amount of $900.00.

Jerry

Fig. 3B-23: Memo requesting personal draw.

Apr 20, 2016   **Issued next cheque to the owner, Jerry Tyson, for $900.00 as a drawing.**

To Record the Withdrawal

> Other payments that would use the **Make Other Payment** option are: Rent, HST payments to Receiver General, Insurance, purchases paid by cash, cheque and credit card.

2 ➤ From the Home window, click on **PAYABLES** module, click the **Payments** icon to display the Payments Journal. (See side note box.)

3 ➤ At `Pay Purchase Invoices ▼`, select **Make Other Payment**, `Tab`.

4 ➤ **To the Order of**   Type **Jerry Tyson**, `Tab`.

5 ➤ Select **Full Add**. The **Address** tab (Home address), is **556 Betty Ann Drive, Willowdale, Ontario, M2N 1Y7**. Click **Options** tab, **Expense Account**, select **3120 Drawings Jerry Tyson**, click **Taxes** tab, change **Tax Exempt** to **Yes** for **HST**, select **-No tax** (there are no taxes on owner's withdrawals).

Click **Save** and **Close** when complete and you are returned to the Payments Journal, `Tab`.

Date   Apr 20, 2016.

6 ➤ **Description**   Type **Draw Apr 20, 2016**, `Tab`.

7 ➤ **Amount**   Type **900.00**, `Tab`.

Tax   Leave blank; there is no tax when an owner withdraws money from the business.

8 ➤ Invoice/Ref   Jerry or Helen would normally give you a memo to request a cheque indicating the reason for issuing the cheque. This is important for the audit trail. They will be giving you a number of memos during the year, and you will need to identify which memo was your authority to issue for each cheque. Type **Memo Apr 20** or Draw # 1, April (draw Apr, 1st draw of month), Tab .

Leave the **Comment** field blank for this and the other cheques that follow.

The Payments Journal should look like Fig. 3B-24.

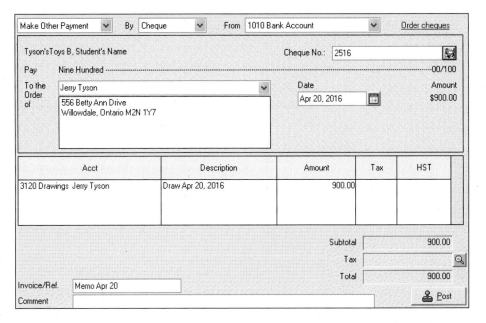

Fig. 3B-24: Jerry Tyson's Draw entry window.

9 ➤ Display the journal entry and it should appear as follows:

Payments Journal Entry Apr 20, 2016 (J11)

Account Number	Account Description	Debits	Credits
3120	Drawings Jerry Tyson	900.00	-
1010	Bank Account	-	900.00
Additional Date:	Additional Field:		
		900.00	900.00

10 ➤ Exit from the Payments Journal Entry window.

11 ➤ Post when correct.

12 ➤ Exit from the Payments Journal.

This entry could be displayed in the **Vendor Aged Detail**. You do not need to view the Aged report at this time.

Recording a Purchase Order with a Prepayment to a Vendor

It is common business practice to give a prepayment to a vendor against future invoices to show the commitment to purchase items (special orders) or use their services.

In the Simply PAYABLES module, this type of transaction is called a **Prepayment**. In RECEIVABLES it is called a **Deposit**.

> Although we will use the Purchase Order paid by Cheque option, the cheque will not be issued in Simply. A manual cheque will need to be issued.

Exercise 3B-28 – Recording a Purchase Order and Prepayment Cheque

---

Apr 20, 2016	**A local service club has ordered 16 Orderly Vanline trucks. The trucks need to be received on Apr 29, 2016, as 10 of the trucks will be used as prizes in a children's contest, sponsored by the service club. Issue a Purchase Order (#84) to Thompson Toy Makers for these trucks at $25.66 each plus HST, Total $463.93. Terms 2/10, Net 30. Thompson requires a $200.00 prepayment, as this is a special order of trucks.**

To issue the Purchase Order and a prepayment cheque to Thompson:

1 ➤ Click the **Purchase Orders** icon from the home window.

      Transaction   **Order, do NOT change.**

2 ➤ **Payment Method**   Select **Cheque,** a new field displays above Shipping Date

          Prepay Ref. No. `2521`   2521 is the next cheque # or reference # for the prepayment.

3 ➤ **Vendor**   **Select Thompson Toy Makers.**

4 ➤ **Shipping Date**   Select **Apr 28, 2016.**

5 ➤ **Order**   Type **16,** [Tab] [Tab].

6 ➤ **Unit**   Type **each,** [Tab].

7 ➤ **Description**   Type **Orderly Vanline Trucks,** [Tab].

8 ➤ **Price**   Type **25.66,** [Tab].

9 ➤ **Tax**   [Tab] to accept **HS**.

10 ➤   Prepayment Applied: _____ Type **200.00,** [Tab].
The Prepayment will be applied to the final invoice.

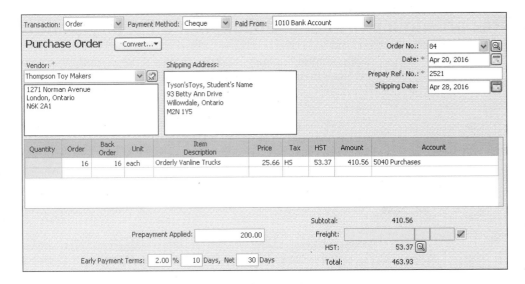

11 ➤ The Purchases Journal–Purchase Order Entry should appear as follows:

Purchases Journal Entry Apr 20, 2016 (J12)

Account Number	Account Description	Debits	Credits
2200	Accounts Payable	200.00	-
1010	Bank Account	-	200.00
Additional Date:	Additional Field:		
		200.00	200.00

12 ➤ **Exit** the Purchases Journal–Purchase Order Entry window.

13 ➤ **Record** when correct and **Exit** to the Home window.

14 ➤ Display the Vendor Aged Detail Report for **Thompson Toy Manufacturers** at Apr 20. The lower portion is shown next. The Prepayment (Prepaid order) is identified separately.

2521	Apr 20, 2016	Prepaid Order	-200.00	-200.00
Total unpaid invoices:			384.93	384.93
Total prepayments/prepaid order:			-200.00	-200.00
Total outstanding:			184.93	184.93

15 ➤ Advance the Session date to **Apr 21, 2016**.

Recording Lease Payments

Because Tyson's Toys pays the lease of their van on a monthly basis, they have set up a recurring transaction entry for this transaction.

Exercise 3B-29 – Recording a Lease Payment

Apr 21, 2016   Received Bank Debit memo dated Apr 21, 2016 in the amount of $852.00 for the van lease payment ($400.00 plus $52.00 HST) and $400.00 payment on the bank loan ($304.59 to reduce the loan and $95.41 interest).

You will use the **Recall Recurring Transaction** option, which has been set up for this transaction earlier.

1 ➤ Click on the **COMPANY** module. Click on the **General Journal** icon.

2 ➤ Click the **Recall recurring transaction** icon and the Recall Recurring Transaction window will appear as follows:

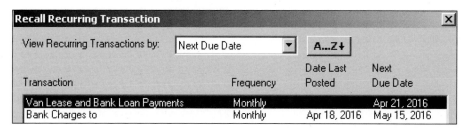

3 ➤ Select **Van Lease** and **Bank Loan Payments**, and the General Journal window is filled in.

4 ➤ Make necessary changes as shown in Fig. 3B-25.

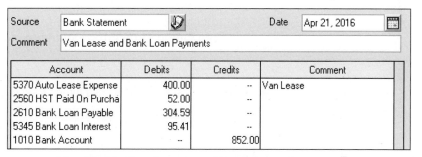

Fig. 3B-25: Van Lease and Bank Loan Payment entry.

5 ➤ In order to update the HST taxes properly, for the HST report when using the General Journal, click the Sales Taxes button.

6 ➤ **Enter** the information as shown next. This will update the HST report, which can be seen in the Appendix D, *Printing a Tax (HST) Report* at www.simplyaccounting2010.nelson.com under Student Resources.

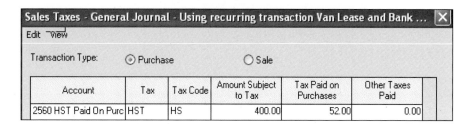

7 ➤ Click **OK**. You will notice a blue ✓ in the ✓ Sales Taxes button. This means that the Sales Taxes will be updated for the HST report.

8 ➤ **Post** when correct, click **Yes** to update the recurring entry.

9 ➤ **Exit** the General Journal to the Home page.

More Transactions

1 ➤   Advance the date to **Apr 29, 2016**.

2 ➤   **Record** and **Post** the three transactions below.

Apr 26, 2016	**Paid $109.89 to A-Your Name Toy Parts for invoice 65839.**

Apr 27, 2016	**Received 3 boxes of various coloured paper at $56.00 each, plus HST and 3 binders ½ inch at $4.00 each plus HST, from City Office Supplies. Invoice #2640 dated Apr 27, 2016 with terms of 2/10 n30. Total invoice $203.40.**

Apr 28, 2016	**Received 14 of the trucks ordered on PO #84, from Thompson Toy Makers. The other 2 trucks will be delivered on May 4, 2016. Invoice #1007 dated Apr 27, 2016 was received. Total invoice $405.94. You will need to change Payment Method from Cheque to Pay later. See caution and information boxes.**

Simply remembers the last setting you used for the **Paid By** field.
You may have to click the **Paid By** ▼ and change it to **Pay Later**.

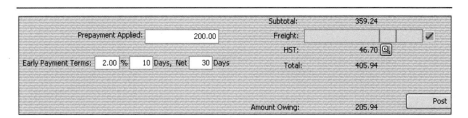

Notice that the Prepayment made on Apr 21, has been applied to the invoice total of 405.94 which leaves an amount owing of 205.94.

Journalizing HST Remittance

The federal government (Canada Revenue Agency) requires that **HST CHARGED ON SALES** be paid to the government (**Receiver General**) on a regular basis.

Companies are allowed to subtract from the payment any **HST PAID ON PURCHASES** (this includes all goods and services). This is why many companies keep track of HST Paid on Purchases separately from HST Charged on Sales Invoices.

The balance of the HST PAID ON PURCHASES account is a **debit** (meaning **receivable**) and HST CHARGED ON SALES is a **credit** (meaning **payable**). However, both accounts are located in the Liabilities section of the Balance Sheet.

In a job situation, the task of reconciling HST PAID ON PURCHASES and HST CHARGED ON SALES and journalizing HST remittance may be part of your routine responsibilities. You may or may not receive a memo from your supervisor when it is time to do it. It depends on the procedure that has been set up at your company.

Exercise 3B-30 – Calculating the HST Remittance

Study the following memo:

MEMO

Date: Apr 29, 2016
To: Accounting Clerk
From: Helen Tyson

Please pay the Receiver General the net March 31 HST balance.

Helen

Fig. 3B-26: HST Remittance memo.

Apr 29, 2016	**Paid the Receiver General the net HST payable outstanding at the end of March 2016.**

First, you must find out the General Ledger account balances for HST CHARGED ON SALES and HST PAID ON PURCHASES at the end of March. In a normal business environment you would display the Balance Sheet or the Trial Balance at the end of March.

Chapter 3 was split into parts A and B. As part B starts at Apr 15, 2016 you cannot display a Mar 31, 2016 Balance Sheet in Part B. In Exercise 3A-3 you were asked to print a Balance Sheet at Mar 31 and retain it for use in this Exercise. If you cannot locate the Mar 31, 2016 Balance Sheet, refer to the Mar 31, 2016 Trial Balance in Fig 3A-1 for the HST amounts.

In a business environment, you could also print a HST report as shown in Appendix D, *Printing a Tax (HST) Report* at www.simplyaccounting2010.nelson.com under Student Resources. The Tyson's Toys 3A data file was started at Mar 31; therefore, there are no transactions recorded for March. There will be a message that there is no data to report.

Calculating HST Remittance

1 ➤   Refer to the Balance Sheet printed in Exercise 3A-3.

2 ➤ Circle the amounts for **HST CHARGED ON SALES** and **HST PAID ON PURCHASES**. The net HST amount owing should be $680.09.

HST Charged on Sales	1,738.25
HST Paid on Purchases	- 650.14
Net HST amount owing	1,088.11

OR:

Refer to the Trial Balance (Fig. 3A-1) at the end of Mar 31, 2016, and write on a piece of paper the balances for HST CHARGED ON SALES and HST PAID ON PURCHASES, and calculate the difference. It should amount to **$1,088.11**.

There may be situations when the HST paid on purchases/services is higher than the HST collected on sales.

HST on Sales	$1,730.00
HST on Purchases/Services	$1,750.14
HST overpaid (refund requested)	$ 20.14

In this situation, the business would submit the HST return and claim a refund.

In a business environment you could also print the Balance Sheet or Trial Balance noted above as proof of the amounts used. Print the Income Statement for the dates specified on the HST Tax Form. The Sales and Purchase information will be used to fill in the tax form. This would be attached to the documentation for the cheque request and would be part of the audit trail information.

The Receiver General has been set up as a vendor for regular HST payments. Using a vendor will retain information in the PAYABLES module about payments made. This record can be used by Revenue Canada auditors to verify that a payment has been made.

Exercise 3B-31 – Recording the HST Remittance

To record the amount payable to the Receiver General, you would use the same procedure as in the payment to Mr. Tyson in Exercise 3B-27.

1 ➤ Click the **Payments** icon.

2 ➤ Select **Make Other Payment**, `Tab`.

By Cheque	DO NOT CHANGE.
From 1010 Bank Account	DO NOT CHANGE.

3 ➤ To the Order of Select **Receiver General** and `Tab`.

4 ➤ Acct The default account **2550 HST Charged on Sales** appears. HST Charged on Sales is a 2 series Liability account number. The program treats all 2 series numbers as **Liability** accounts, which have normal **credit** balances. We need to **debit** the HST CHARGED ON SALES account and transfer the amount to the ACCOUNTS PAYABLE account. `Tab`.

5 ➤ Description Type **Payment for Mar HST on Sales**, `Tab`.

6 ➤ **Amount**   Type **1738.25**, [Tab]. (A positive number will debit the account used.)

7 ➤ **Tax**   [Tab] not used when paying the Receiver General.

8 ➤ **Acct**   Select **2560 HST Paid on Purchases**.

9 ➤ **Description**   Type **Payment for Mar HST on Purchases**, [Tab].

10 ➤ **Amount**   Type negative **-650.14** (a negative amount will credit the account used), [Tab].

11 ➤ **Invoice/Ref**   We need to create a visual record of what is taking place. Some companies would use codes similar to: HST@Mar 31 (Net HST at the end of March), Mar HST (March HST being paid) or HST1QTR (HST 1st Quarter of year).

Type **Mar HST**, [Tab]. The window should resemble Fig. 3B-27:

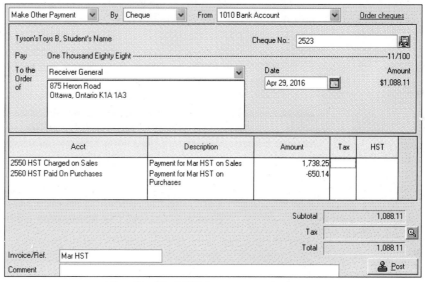

Fig. 3B-27: HST Payment window.

12 ➤ **Display** the Journal Entry and the window should appear as follows:

Payments Journal Entry Apr 29, 2016 (J17)

Account Number	Account Description	Debits	Credits
2550	HST Charged on Sales	1,738.25	-
1010	Bank Account	-	1,088.11
2560	HST Paid On Purchases	-	650.14
Additional Date:	Additional Field:		
		1,738.25	1,738.25

13 ➤ **Exit** from the Payments Journal Entry window. You could store this transaction as a recurring entry for future periods.

14 ➤ **Post** when correct and **Exit** from the Payments Journal.

Viewing the Vendor Aged Report

1 ➤ The above entry can be displayed using the Vendor Aged Detail report. Your screen display for the Receiver General, should be similar to:

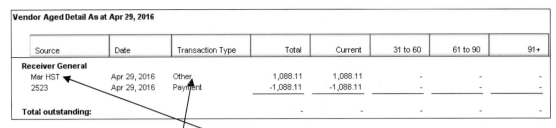

Source	Date	Transaction Type	Total	Current	31 to 60	61 to 90	91+
Receiver General							
Mar HST	Apr 29, 2016	Other	1,088.11	1,088.11	-	-	-
2523	Apr 29, 2016	Payment	-1,088.11	-1,088.11	-	-	-
Total outstanding:			-	-	-	-	-

Notice the Source **Mar HST** information.

Also notice **Other** in the Transaction Type column. Future payments should have similar good audit trail information.

2 ➤ **Exit** the Vendor Aged Detail Report.

Journalizing an Invoice with Reduced HST

Current federal HST legislation exempts insurance from HST at a rate of 5%; therefore, at present there is HST on insurance at a rate of 8% (using the HI tax code). However, this legislation may change, so watch for HST changes in the future.

Insurance is normally paid in advance, and the cost is charged to PREPAID EXPENSES and then charged to INSURANCE EXPENSE every accounting period over the life of the insurance policy.

Exercise 3B-32 – Recording an Invoice with reduced HST

Study this transaction and the invoice below:

Apr 29, 2016	**Received the following invoice #4799 from Meadows Insurance Brokers Inc. HST is applicable on insurance invoices at 8%.**

Meadows **I**nsurance **B**rokers Inc.

197 Larange Avenue, Suite 125   **INVOICE**
Toronto, Ontario M8Z 4R9   **4799**
Phone/Fax (416) 233-5886

SOLD TO:
   Tyson's Toys
   93 Betty Ann Drive   Date: Apr 28, 2016
   Willowdale, Ont M2N 1Y5

COVERAGE	

Renewal Policy #3224321
To insure building at 93 Betty Ann Drive, Willowdale, Ontario

Coverage for the period Apr 01, 2016 through Mar 31, 2017	$1,200.00
HST	96.00
Terms: upon receipt TOTAL	$1,296.00

Fig. 3B-28: Insurance Invoice.

Because the company will be buying additional insurance during the year, you will set up **Meadows Insurance Brokers Inc.** as a vendor, using the Full Add option.

The invoice will be allocated to prepaid expense based on the following:

- $1,296.00 divided by 12 months equals $108.00 per month.

- April expense (#5360 Insurance Expense) account will be $108.00, and as the remaining $1,188 prepaid amount expires (gets used), it will be charged to INSURANCE EXPENSE.

You could set up a recurring adjusting General Journal entry for the insurance expense portion for future use.

To Record Payment for Insurance

1 ➤ Click the **Payments** icon.

2 ➤ Select **Make Other Payment**.

3 ➤ To the   Type **Meadows Insurance Brokers Inc.**, `Tab`.
Order of

4 ➤ Click `Full Add`. Use Invoice information to complete the data fields.

5 ➤ Click the **Options** tab. Expense Account field, select **1340 Prepaid Insurance**.

6 ➤ Click the **Taxes** tab. **Tax Exempt** field for HST, Do NOT change from No.

7 ➤ Tax code.   Select **HI** (HST at 8%). Click `Save and Close` when complete. `Tab`.

Cheque No.   2524, the next cheque number.

Date   Apr 29, 2016, the date the cheque is being issued.

Acct   Account 1340 Prepaid Insurance is shown since you created this in step 5.

8 ➤ Description   Type **Insurance - Building Prepaid**, `Tab`.

9 ➤ Amount   Type **1,100.00**, `Tab`.

10 ➤ Tax   `Tab` to accept HI.

11 ➤ HST   `Tab` to accept 88.00.

12 ➤ Acct   Select **5360 Insurance Expense**.

13 ➤ Description   Type **Insurance - Building Expense**, `Tab`.

14 ➤ Amount   Type **100.00**, `Tab`.

15 ➤ Tax   `Tab` to accept HI.

16 ➤ HST   `Tab` to accept 8.00.

17 ➤ Invoice/Ref   Type **4799**, `Tab`.

The $1,188 charged to **Prepaid Expenses** is for the 11 months from May 1, 2016 to Mar 31, 2017. As the insurance expires in future months, this amount will be reduced and allocated to **Insurance Expense**.

The lower portion of the Payments window should appear as follows:

Acct	Description	Amount	Tax	HST
1340 Prepaid Insurance	Insurance - Building Prepaid	1,100.00	HI	88.00
5360 Insurance Expense	Insurance - Building Expense	100.00	HI	8.00

Subtotal	1,200.00
Tax	96.00
Total	1,296.00

Invoice/Ref. 4799

Comment

      Post

18 ➤ Display the Payments Journal Entry. It should look like the following:

Payments Journal Entry Apr 29, 2016 (J18)

Account Number	Account Description	Debits	Credits
1340	Prepaid Insurance	1,188.00	-
5360	Insurance Expense	108.00	-
1010	Bank Account	-	1,296.00
Additional Date:	Additional Field:		
		1,296.00	1,296.00

19 ➤ **Exit** from the Payments Journal Entry window.

20 ➤ **Post** after verifying accuracy, and **Exit** to the Home window.

More Transactions

Record and **Post** the following transactions:

Apr 29, 2016	Returned 3 binders ½ inch at $4.00 each plus taxes, to City Office Supplies. Original Invoice #2640. Binders too small.

Apr 29, 2016	Purchased various parts, odd size wheels, doors, etc., which will be sold as parts (record as 1 lot of various parts) from A-Your Name Toy Parts. PO was not issued. Received their invoice #9765 dated today, for $182.10 (including $20.95 for HST), terms net 30 for this invoice.

1 ➤ Advance the date to **Apr 30, 2016**.

Apr 30, 2016	Paterson's Wood Working, 698 Beech Avenue, Suite 6, Toronto, Ontario, M4E 9A3, delivered and installed 2 new Store Equipment (display) cabinets. They were ordered by Mrs. Tyson to display new and current toys. A PO was not issued. The cabinets cost $900.00 each, plus HST. Received $2,034.00 invoice #2696 dated today, with terms net 10 days.

Printing Reports

As you have seen in previous chapters, an Income Statement may be viewed or printed at any time. However, for the Income Statement to be accurate, the ending inventory needs to be updated to the correct value of goods on hand that have not been sold.

An Income Statement shows the current financial position re SALES, COST OF GOODS SOLD and EXPENSES. This chapter deals with PURCHASES; therefore, there will be no change to the Revenue (Sales) section of the Income Statement. (See side note box.)

Exercise 3B-33 – Printing Reports

---

1 ➤ Print the following and compare them to the same report you printed at the beginning of this chapter, Mar 31, 2016, at Exercise 3A-3.

    a. Income Statement for period **Jan 01, 2016** to **Apr 30, 2016**.

    b. Balance Sheet at **Apr 30, 2016**.

2 ➤ Print a Trial Balance. Click **Reports, Financials, Trial Balance**, Date: **Apr 30, 2016**. Click **OK**, then **Print** Report.

You should notice that in both Income Statements, ENDING INVENTORY accounts (#5090) have the same negative -$6,907.29. You should also notice that both Balance Sheets have a Current Asset TOYS AND PARTS INVENTORY account (#1310) in a value of $6,907.29.

In business, it is extremely unlikely that inventory values would not change from one month to the next, especially with sales and purchases being made during the month. The ending inventory value $6,907.29 needs to be updated to reflect the actual cost value of goods on hand.

Adjusting Ending Inventory – Periodic Method in Simply

There are three inventory values (one on the Balance Sheet and two on the Income Statement) needed to complete financial statements. They include:

Balance Sheet:

- Asset Inventory on the Balance Sheet (what is "owned" on that date).

Income Statement:

Cost of Goods Sold (COGS) Calculation.

- COGS Beginning Inventory
- COGS Ending Inventory

How inventory accounting is recorded will depend on:

1. Which system is used (perpetual or periodic), and
2. If the company uses manual bookkeeping or computerized bookkeeping (e.g., Simply Accounting).

Review the comparison between Periodic Inventory System and Perpetual Inventory System. Remember that in this chapter we are using a **Periodic** Inventory system in a **computerized** bookkeeping environment.

Periodic Inventory System

For companies that are still using manual bookkeeping, there are no inventory entries until closing entries at fiscal year-end. Interim financial statements are prepared with inventory information supplied by management, but inventory amounts are not recorded in the accounting records.

For companies that use computerized bookkeeping (e.g., Simply Accounting), inventory values must be recorded in the Simply system for all reports. This means inventory entries (to adjust inventory values) are required every time financial statements are produced.

Review the following comparison between **manual** and **computerized** environments assuming a company uses the calendar year as its fiscal year.

Manual Bookkeeping

For the entire fiscal year, the value for inventory in the G/L INVENTORY (Asset) account as of January 1 will not change. For financial statement reporting throughout the year, it is reported as the value of **COGS Beginning Inventory** on the **Income Statement**.

In order to properly reflect the amount of inventory still "owned" versus "sold" each month, a physical count is conducted at month-end and reported:

1. On the **Balance Sheet** as the **asset** INVENTORY value to accurately report what is "owned", <u>and</u>
2. On the **Income Statement** as the **COGS Ending Inventory** value. The ending inventory as part of the COGS calculation (which includes the COGS **Beginning Inventory** value and **Net Purchases**), will ensure accurate reporting of what has been "sold" to date.

There are NO entries made in the company files for either of 1 or 2 above.

After the physical inventory count at fiscal year-end has been approved and reported, the asset INVENTORY value in the General Ledger will be updated to the new count and closing entries are posted. As in the year just finished, this value will be in the General Ledger INVENTORY Asset account for the entire next fiscal year.

During the **next** fiscal year, it will be "used" for Income Statement reporting as the "COGS Beginning Inventory."

Computerized Bookkeeping

In contrast, computers cannot "borrow" information from G/L accounts to complete the financial statements. The information must be recorded in the system. Therefore, we need to use three inventory accounts to parallel the one account we use in manual systems. These accounts are:

Financial Statement	Type of Account	Account Name
Balance Sheet	Asset	Inventory
Income Statement	COGS	Beginning Inventory (See side box.)
Income Statement	COGS	Ending Inventory

The **INVENTORY** value as of January 1 is reported in the **COGS Beginning Inventory** account. This balance does NOT CHANGE during the year.

The asset **INVENTORY** value and the **COGS Ending Inventory** value are the actual physical count, usually on a monthly basis. At the end of each month, you update these two accounts by removing last month's values and replacing them with the current month's values. This will be shown to you in Exercise 3B-34. Again, this is done to ensure accurate reporting of what is "owned" on the Balance Sheet and what has been "sold" on the Income Statement.

> **i**
> BEGINNING
> INVENTORY is also
> referred to as OPENING
> INVENTORY.

Perpetual Inventory System

See the 'Comparison of Periodic and Perpetual Inventory Methods' chart at the beginning of Chapter 8, for a visual display of entries required in both the Perpetual and Periodic inventory methods. You will also be able to record the transactions in 3A using the 08 C8-5 Toys-PI data file using the Perpetual Inventory method (after you have completed Chapter 8).

In Chapter 8, you will have a chance to work with the **Perpetual** Inventory system. In contrast to a **Periodic** Inventory system, a Perpetual Inventory system's features include:

1. Updating Asset INVENTORY and COGS balances as inventory is bought and sold.
2. Using inventory adjustment entry to update the accounts to match the actual inventory on hand; e.g., adjust inventory value based on the physical count and/or record decrease due to lost/damaged items, etc.

As you have seen, when you record purchase of goods for resale (or purchase of goods to make goods for resale), the INVENTORY accounts, as mentioned above, do not change. They are adjusted only at period-end or when you want to produce accurate financial statements.

Study this information:

> The **Mar 31, 2016** and **Apr 30, 2016 inventory balances** are as follows:
>
> | Section | Name of Account | Debit | Credit |
> |---|---|---|---|
> | ASSET | 1310 Toys and parts Inventory | $6,907.29 | |
> | COGS* | 5010 Beginning Inventory | $5,421.49 | |
> | COGS* | 5090 Ending Inventory | | $6,907.29 |
>
> *Cost of Goods Sold

Just as inventory values are adjusted and closed in a manual accounting system, inventory amounts need to be adjusted in Simply. Management decides the time period for the financial statements, (e.g., monthly, quarterly, etc.), and by an actual count or estimate, a reasonable dollar value ENDING INVENTORY must be determined.

You are provided with the new INVENTORY value by the following memo:

MEMO

Date:　　Apr 30, 2016

To:　　　Accounting Clerk

From:　　Jerry Tyson

Would you please print a year-to-date Income Statement for me.

The ending inventory on Apr 30, 2016 rounded to nearest dollar is $8,297.00 based on an inventory count taken.

Jerry

Fig. 3B-29: ENDING INVENTORY memo.

There are two methods to adjust the inventory:

Method 1 requires two steps. 1 Remove the previous inventory $6,907.29 2 Set up the new inventory value $8,297.00	**This method is recommended by the authors**. You can see the old value removed and the new value entered.

Method 2 requires only one step: Adjust the inventory for the $1,389.71 difference between the two inventory amounts.	This method can cause problems because you may deduct from the inventory when you should have added to inventory, or vice versa.

Method 1 will be explained in this chapter. Method 2 will be explained in Chapter 9.

Exercise 3B-34 – Adjusting Inventory

To Remove Previous INVENTORY Value

To remove the old ENDING INVENTORY, the General Journal is used, because the entry does not affect Receivables or Payables.

1 ➤ Click the **COMPANY** module, and click the **General** icon.

2 ➤ **Source**   Type **Memo Apr-JT** (Memo Apr- Jerry Tyson), <kbd>Tab</kbd> to Comment.

3 ➤ **Comment**   Type **Remove March ending inventory**, <kbd>Tab</kbd>.

4 ➤ **Account**   Select **5090** (Ending Inventory in Cost of Goods Sold), <kbd>Tab</kbd>.

5 ➤ **Debits**   Type **6,907.29**. <kbd>Tab</kbd><kbd>Tab</kbd> to accept 6,907.29 and bypass the **Comment** column field.

The 5 series accounts normally have a **debit** balance, but closing inventory (a contra account) has a **credit** balance. It reduces the cost of goods available for sale to what was actually sold. We need to debit #5090 to reduce the account. Enter as a Debit (positive) amount.

6 ➤ **Account**   Select **1310** Toys and parts Inventory (Asset), <kbd>Tab</kbd>.

7 ➤ **Credits**   The cursor is in the **Credits** column to balance the entry.

<kbd>Tab</kbd> to accept 6,907.29 and bypass the **Comment** column. The 1 series accounts normally have a **debit** balance. We need to credit the account to reduce the ASSET account amount to nil.

8 ➤ **Display** the General Journal Entry. The screen should resemble the following:

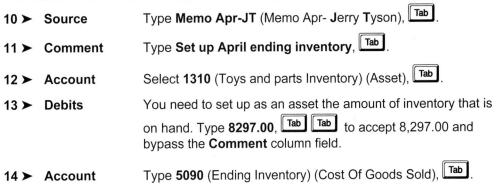

General Journal Entry Apr 30, 2016 (J22)

Account Number	Account Description	Debits	Credits
5090	Ending Inventory	6,907.29	-
1310	Toys and parts Inventory	-	6,907.29
Additional Date:	Additional Field:		
		6,907.29	6,907.29

9 ➤ **Exit** the General Journal entry and **Post** when correct.

This inventory entry and the next, which happen monthly, are excellent examples of entries that could be set up as recurring entries.

This procedure has reduced both accounts to nil. You need to record the new inventory value of $8,297.00 (estimated) by reversing the above procedure.

To Enter the New INVENTORY Value

10 ➤ **Source**   Type **Memo Apr-JT** (Memo Apr- Jerry Tyson), <kbd>Tab</kbd>.

11 ➤ **Comment**   Type **Set up April ending inventory**, <kbd>Tab</kbd>.

12 ➤ **Account**   Select **1310** (Toys and parts Inventory) (Asset), <kbd>Tab</kbd>.

13 ➤ **Debits**   You need to set up as an asset the amount of inventory that is on hand. Type **8297.00**, <kbd>Tab</kbd><kbd>Tab</kbd> to accept 8,297.00 and bypass the **Comment** column field.

14 ➤ **Account**   Type **5090** (Ending Inventory) (Cost Of Goods Sold), <kbd>Tab</kbd>.

15 ➤ Credits   The cursor is in the **Credits** column. `Tab` `Tab` to accept. The 5 series accounts normally have a **debit** balance, but ENDING INVENTORY needs a **credit** balance. It reduces the cost of goods available for sale to what was actually sold.

16 ➤ Display the General Journal entry:

General Journal Entry Apr 30, 2016 (J23)

Account Number	Account Description	Debits	Credits
1310	Toys and parts Inventory	8,297.00	-
5090	Ending Inventory	-	8,297.00
Additional Date:	Additional Field:		
		8,297.00	8,297.00

17 ➤ **Exit** the General Journal entry and **Post** when correct.

18 ➤ **Exit** to the Home window.

Apr 30, 2016 trial balance would contain the following values:

Section	Name of account	Debit	Credit
ASSET	1310 Toys and parts Inventory	$ 8,297.00	
COGS*	5010 Beginning Inventory	$ 5,421.49	
COGS*	5090 Ending Inventory		$ 8,297.00

*Cost of Goods Sold
Notice that account #5010 Beginning Inventory (Jan 1, 2016) did NOT change.

To see the effect each of the above transactions had on each of the INVENTORY accounts, drill down to each of the accounts. You will see that each account shows the opening balance; the first adjustment reduces the account to nil, and the second adjustment updates the account with the new balance.

The asset inventory general ledger account has been updated as follows:

General Ledger Report Apr 15, 2016 to Apr 30, 2016
Sorted by: Transaction Number

Date	Comment	Source #	JE#	Debits	Credits	Balance
1310	**Toys and parts Inventory**					6,907.29 Dr
Apr 30, 2016	Remove March Ending Inventory	Memo Apr-JT	J22	-	6,907.29	- Dr
Apr 30, 2016	Set up April ending inventory	Memo Apr-JT	J23	8,297.00	-	8,297.00 Dr
				8,297.00	6,907.29	

Exercise 3B-35 – Printing Statements

1 ➤ Print an **Income Statement** with starting date of **Jan 01, 2016** and finish date **Apr 30, 2016**. The statement should now show the new ending inventory. Exit to the Home page.

When you start a new fiscal year the inventory entries are slightly different. See Chapters 9 and 10 for discussion on this topic.

Mr. Tyson wants to see the Income Statement activity from Apr 16 as well as the year-to-date activity.

The Comparative Income Statement

To print a Comparative Income Statement follow these steps:

1 ➤ Click **Report Centre**, **Financials**, click the **+** at **Income Statement**, select **Comparative 2 Period**, click **Modify this report**. A new Options window appears.

2 ➤ To see what changes occurred in the period Apr 16 to April 30, as well as the year-to-date information, change the **First Period Start** date to **Apr 16, 2016**, `Tab`, change the Report On item as shown, then click **OK**.

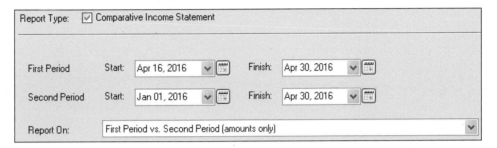

The Comparative Income Statement is displayed. The first column of amounts is the activity that occurred from the entries you recorded from April 16 to the 30th. The other column is the year-to-date values in the accounts.

3 ➤ **Exit** to the Home window.

The BEGINNING INVENTORY account value in the first group of columns is 0.00. This is because there was no change in the account for the period requested, namely April 16 to the 30th. Beginning Inventory will not change throughout the fiscal year.

The ENDING INVENTORY account value in the first group of columns is -1,389.71. This is because there was a credit increase from 6,907.29 to 8,297.00 to this account for the period requested, namely April 16 to the 30th.

Other Period-End/Month-End Reports

At the end of the month it is normal to print the following additional reports for the month and file them for your audit trail:

- The All Journal Entries for the transactions entered Apr 15 to April 30.
- The Balance Sheet as at Apr 30, 2016.
- The General Ledger for Apr 15 to Apr 30.
- The Vendor Aged Detail report, as at Apr 30, 2016.
- The Purchases Journal for Apr 15 to 30 - includes cash purchases.
- The Payments Journal for Apr 15 to 30.
- The Cheque Log for the month of Apr 15 to Apr 30.

Exercise 3B-36 – Printing Period-End Reports

Make sure the printer is ready. You should be at the Tyson's Toys Home window to start this exercise.

1 ➤ **Print the All Journal Entries** as shown in previous chapters.

2 ➤ **Print** the **General Ledger for Apr 16-30** as shown in previous chapters.

3 ➤ **Print** the **Vendor Aged Detail** at **Apr 30, 2016**. To ensure that everything is correct, you should compare the Balance Sheet Accounts Payable amount with the total of the Vendor Aged Detail report. They should be the same!

> When you see the magnifying glass with the + sign in any of the reports, it means you can drill down (if you click the Journal entry number) to see the original invoice that made the entry.
>
> If you drill down from the account number or name, you will see the ledger account and all entries that make up the account. Try drilling down for one or two entries.

To View and Print the Purchases Journal

To print the **Purchases Journal** for Apr 2016:

1 ➤ Click **Report Centre**, **Payables**, **Purchases Journal Entries**, **Modify this report**.

    By Date   DO NOT CHANGE.

2 ➤ **Start**   Select **Apr 15, 2016**, ⌨Tab .

3 ➤ **Finish**   ⌨Tab to accept Apr 30, 2016.

4 ➤ Click **Corrections** or **Additional Information** if required. Click **OK** to display the Purchases Journal.

5 ➤ **Print** the report.

6 ➤ **Exit** from the display window. (See side note box.)

To View and Print the Payments Journal

To print the **Payments Journal** for Apr 2016:

1 ➤ Click **Report Centre, Payables, Payments Journal Entries, Modify this report**.

    By Date   DO NOT CHANGE.

2 ➤ **Start**   Select **Apr 15, 2016**, ⌨Tab .

3 ➤ **Finish**   ⌨Tab to accept Apr 30, 2016.

> ☑ Invoice Payments
> ☑ Credit Card Payments
> ☑ Other Payments
> ☐ Remittance Payments
> ☑ Corrections

Click the boxes shown, even though you have not made a credit card payment or corrections. The Remittance Payments option will be discussed in Chapter 7 (Payroll).

4 ➤ Click **OK** to display the Payments Journal.

5 ➤ **Print** the report.

6 ➤ **Exit** from the display window.

To View and Print a Cheque Log

1 ➤ Click **Report Centre, Banking, Cheque Log, Modify this report**, select the options as shown next:

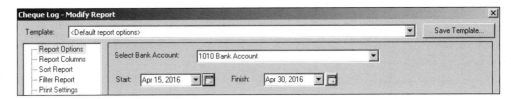

2 ➤ Click **OK** and the cheque log will display.

3 ➤ You may **Print** this report, and return to the Home window.

Cheque Log for 1010 Bank Account from Apr 15, 2016 to Apr 30, 2016

Cheque No.	Che... Type	Payee	Amount	Cheque Date	Times Prin...	Entered... system	JE#	JE Date
2515	Payment	NAS Business Forms	333.00	Apr 15, 2016	0	Yes	J3	Apr 15, 2016
2516	Payment	Lanting Speciality Toys	3,403.56	Apr 18, 2016	0	Yes	J6	Apr 18, 2016
2517	Payment	Jason's Transport Service	1,356.00	Apr 18, 2016	0	Yes	J7	Apr 18, 2016
2518	Payment	City Office Supplies	154.57	Apr 18, 2016	0	Yes	J8	Apr 18, 2016
2519	Payment	Alan Cohen & Associates	465.56	Apr 19, 2016	0	Yes	J9	Apr 19, 2016
2520	Payment	Jerry Tyson	900.00	Apr 20, 2016	0	Yes	J11	Apr 20, 2016
2522	Payment	A-Your Name Toy Parts	109.89	Apr 21, 2016	0	Yes	J14	Apr 21, 2016
2523	Payment	Receiver General	680.09	Apr 29, 2016	0	Yes	J17	Apr 29, 2016
2524	Payment	Meadows Insurance Broke...	1,296.00	Apr 29, 2016	0	Yes	J18	Apr 29, 2016

The cheque log (from Part 3A) is shown below:

Cheque Log for 1010 Bank Account from Mar 31, 2016 to Apr 15, 2016

Cheque No.	Che... Type	Payee	Amount	Cheque Date	Times Prin...	Entered... system	JE#	JE Date
2511	Payment	Willowdale Mall Ltd.	2,260.00	Apr 07, 2016	0	Reversed	J3	Apr 07, 2016
2512	Payment	Willowdale Mall Ltd.	2,373.00	Apr 07, 2016	0	Yes	J7	Apr 07, 2016
2513	Payment	Lanting Speciality Toys	718.68	Apr 07, 2016	0	Yes	J10	Apr 07, 2016
2514	Payment	Thompson Toy Makers	2,745.55	Apr 15, 2016	2	Yes	J11	Apr 15, 2016

This report displays the cheque numbers, amounts and dates the entries were recorded. As noted early in the chapter, in order to conserve paper you would not print cheques, unless your instructor requires you to do so.

In the 3A report above, cheque 2511 was recorded and reversed. Cheque 2512 was printed. In a job situation, the **Times prin** (Times Printed) column would indicate a **1** (for cheques printed) and perhaps **2** if there was a printer jam and the cheque had to be reprinted. The report would ensure that management knew the number of times cheques were printed in order to prevent fraud (the same cheque printed more than once). The manager would want to see all damaged cheques and make sure that they were voided and unusable.

4 ➤ Compare your printed reports to the reports for Tyson's Toys in the data files from your instructor.

To View Graphs

You may find information on using the graph feature (pie and bar charts) for PAYABLES comparisons in Appendix K, *Graphs Feature* at www.simplyaccounting2010.nelson.com under Student Resources.

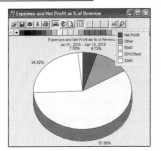

Summary, Part B

Here is a summary of tasks and transactions in Chapter 3, Part B.

Transaction	Journal/Ledger	Remarks
Prepayment	Purchase Orders	Record a Vendor prepayment with a Purchase Order.
New Vendor (Supplier)	Vendors Ledger	At the Taxes tab, change the Tax Exempt status for HST, GST or PST where necessary and select the appropriate tax code. Select an appropriate default expense account.
Drawings	Payments	Create owner's Vendor record. Use Make other Payment option to record a memo and a cheque together.
HST Remittance	Payments	Create Receiver General as a Vendor. Use Make other Payment option to record a memo and a cheque together. Determine balance of HST Charged On Sales and HST Paid on Purchase accounts to be paid. Enter a negative amount to HST paid on Purchases account.
Inventory Adjustment	General	Remove and set up inventory values as required.

Review **Slideshows 3A** and **3B** now. They will help you better understand the next chapter on **Setting Up a Company**.

Before Moving On..., Part B

Read the following questions and make sure you know the answers to them; otherwise, read the corresponding part in the chapter before moving on.

1. When journalizing non-merchandise purchases with HST, how is **HST** recorded?

2. Give the journal entry for a purchase return of $300.00 plus HST of $39.00:

   a) for merchandise for resale.

   b) for merchandise not for resale, plus $39.00 HST (non-purchase items - office supplies).

3. Describe briefly the steps in recording a payment of an invoice when taking a cash discount, using as the base the cost before taxes:

   a) for merchandise for resale.

   b) for merchandise not for resale (Office Supplies).

4. Give the journal entry for a prepayment of $100.00 to a vendor.   How is it entered in Simply?

5. Describe briefly how the HST remittance is calculated.

6. What happens when you post journal transactions in the PAYABLES module?

7. When journalizing non-merchandise purchases with HST, on what amount is **HST** based?

8. The month-end inventory adjustment consists of two entries. What is the Journal entry for the reversal of the old inventory?

9. What would a manager look for when reviewing the cheque log?

10. What is the difference in the periodic inventory method of accounting between the Simply process and the manual books process? Which method requires more inventory accounts?

Relevant Appendices, Part B

 The following appendices are available at www.simplyaccounting2010.nelson.com under Student Resources.

Appendix 2010 D   **Printing a Tax (HST) Report**

Appendix 2010 K   **Graphs Feature**

Challenge Exercise 03 C3B-1, Network

(PAYABLES and GENERAL Ledger)

1 ➤ Refer to Exercise 1-1 to unzip the **03 C3B-1 Network.exe** file.

2 ➤ Open the **03 C3B-1 Network** file and enter **PAYABLES transactions for Mar** for a company that sells various computer parts. Apply HST of 13% when needed. Network Company does *not* print cheques.

The business is open every day. You worked on March 5, 12, 19, 26, and March 31.

3 ➤ Record and **Post** the following transactions:

Mar 2   Ordered on PO# 651, 28 Ethernet cable-ready network cards for $75.00 each, plus HST, from PC Cards Company. Shipping date to be Mar 12. Terms 2/10, net 30 days. PO total $2,373.00.

Mar 3   A $300.00 cheque is issued to Umax Cables as a prepayment for a special order of 80 RJ45 cables at $21.50 each, plus HST. Total cost $1,720.00, plus HST. Issue next PO. These cables are required by Mar 28. Terms are 2/10, net 30.

Mar 9   Purchased from new vendor, Your Last Name (surname) Supplies, various store supplies for $145.00, plus HST. Goods arrived and were placed in the storage cabinet. Invoice #8261, terms 2/10, net 30, calculate discounts before tax. The default Expense Account field in the Vendor Setup, Options tab window, can be an Asset or other account type. Select an appropriate account for this field.

Mar 10   Next cheque issued to J.D. Long for 2 Network Hubs at $81.00 each, plus HST, invoice #10005 received.

Mar 12   Received 28 Ethernet cable-ready network cards from PC Cards Company ordered on PO# 651. Invoice #6638 was received totaling $2,373.00. Terms 2/10, net 30 days.

Mar 15   Issued cheque to the Receiver General for the HST owing at the end of February. Note that the Trial Balance HST amounts at February month-end are correct.

Mar 16   Returned 1 Ethernet cable-ready network card to PC Cards Company because it is damaged. Our technician could not get it to work. PC Cards accepted the return with a credit note 6638RT.

Mar 19   Issued cheque to Your Last Name (surname) Supplies, for invoice #8261.

Mar 22   Issued cheque to PC Cards Company as payment in full for invoice #6638, after return.

Mar 28   80 RJ45 cables arrived with invoice #8964 from Umax Cables Company (P.O. #652). Each cable cost $21.50, plus HST. Terms on the order are 2%10, net 30.

Mar 30   Bank statement as of March 29 arrived with debit note that the bank charge for the period ending March 29 is $19.35. No HST.

Mar 31   The manager advised you that the ending inventory value was $84,286.00. Adjust the inventory to allow you to prepare accurate financial statements.

4 ➤ When you have recorded the above entries, **print** the following:

a) Vendor Aged Detail report as at Mar 31.
b) All Journal Entries for the monthly activity with ✓ Show Corrections
c) Journal Entries-General for the monthly activity with ✓ Show Corrections
d) Purchases Journal for Mar.
e) Payments Journal for Mar.
f) Income Statement for the year to date.
g) Cheque log for the month.

Challenge Exercise 03 C3B-2, China

(GENERAL, PAYABLES and RECEIVABLES)

1 ➤ Refer to Exercise 1-1 to unzip the **03 C3B-2 China.exe** file.

This exercise is a review of the 3 modules (GENERAL, PAYABLES and RECEIVABLES).

2 ➤ Open the the **03 C3B-2 China** file.

The China Company sells various kinds and sizes of china for everyday use and for special occasions. 13% HST are applied to sales. Terms for non-retail sale customers are 2/10, net 30. Vendor invoices normally have terms of 2/10, net 30, except where additional information is given.

All sales invoices and cheques are issued in numerical order. China Company does not print invoices or cheques. The company does not use the **Shipped** field in Purchase Invoices. Cash discounts when appropriate are calculated on the cost price before HST. You normally work on March 5, 12, 19, 26 and March 31. You advance the session date when you open the data file.

3 ➤ Record and **Post** the following transactions:

Ignore phone and fax numbers for new customers and vendors.

Mar 1   Issued Purchase order #106 to BNS Printing Ltd. for new invoices with a revised logo. Delivery date is Mar 5. Cost of the new invoices will be $100.00, plus HST, with terms 2/10, net 30.

Mar 1   Advertisement in today's issue of Yourtown Newspaper, a new vendor, 5569 Ace Avenue, Yourtown, Ontario L5N 1X6, contact Eugene Korobok. Invoice #1099 received for $200.00, plus HST. Terms Net 15 days. Use an appropriate account for the default Expense field.

Mar 2   Purchased 30 dinner plates at $25.00 each, plus HST, from Specialty Manufacturer. All plates were received in good condition. Invoice #361 dated today with terms of 2/10, net 30.

Mar 3   Sold on invoice #5270, one specialty item, a British luncheon service set, to a new customer, **Your Actual Name**, 85 Lake Avenue, Rockton, Ontario L6N1B9. The service set selling price is $1,000.00, plus HST. **Your Actual Name** will pay the net amount in 15 days. Credit limit $2,000.00.

Mar 5   The new invoices from BNS Printing ordered on PO#106 are received in good condition with invoice #875 dated today.

Mar 5   We returned 4 plates from the Mar 2 order from Specialty Manufacturer Ltd., because the pattern is not centered properly. Original cost of the plates was $25.00 each, plus HST.

Mar 6   Sold 1 dozen soup bowls at $15.00 per bowl, plus HST, to Plates and More. Normal terms.

Mar 6   Issued cheque to pay Receiver General the HST owing at the end of February.

Mar 7   Plates and More returned 5 of the soup bowls because they arrived damaged. We have called the shipping company to determine what happened. Plates and More purchased replacement bowls from another store and have requested a reduction to their account. We accepted the returned bowls by issuing a credit note with the original Invoice number as a reference.

Mar 8   Issued an $800.00 cheque to Mary Opal, owner, based on a memo received. The money is for personal expenses.

Mar 12   Issued cheque to Specialty Manufacturer Ltd. to pay only for dinner plates purchased, after returns, on invoice #361.

Mar 15   Issued cheque to pay BNS Printing Ltd. for invoice #875.

Mar 16   Received $116.55 cheque #789 from Plates and More re: invoice #5271.

Mar 16   Issued cheque to Yourtown Newspaper for outstanding invoice #1099.

Mar 19   Received cheque #788 from Your Actual Name for invoice #5270.

Mar 19   The bank manager called and requires an Income Statement as of business today. The manager advised you by memo to adjust the ending inventory as counted by staff to $12,380.00.

4 ➤ **Print** the following reports:

    a)   Year-to-date Income statement.
    b)   Journal Entries - All for the transactions above.
    c)   Journal Entries General, Mar 1 – Mar 19.
    d)   Bank Reconciliation Transaction Detail report Mar 01 to Mar 19.
    e)   Accounts Receivable - Aged Detail for all customers.
    f)   Accounts Payable - Aged Detail for all vendors.
    g)   Cash Flow Projection (detail) for the next 30 days.

Challenge Exercise 03 C3B-3, Dance Studio

(GENERAL, PAYABLES and RECEIVABLES)

1 ➤   Refer to Exercise 1-1 to unzip the **03 C3B-3 Dance.exe** file.

2 ➤   Open the **03 C3B-3 Dance** file and enter transactions for Mar.

The Dance Studio instructs students in various types of dance classes (Tap, Scottish, Irish, Ballet, etc.). Dance lessons are taxable at 13% HST.

Terms for customers are net 5 days with a few customers being given 2/10, net 30. Vendor invoices normally have terms of 2/10, net 30, except where additional information is given. Discounts for paying vendor invoices early are charged to Cleaning and Repairs Expense. All sales invoices and cheques are issued in numerical order. Dance Studio Company does not print invoices or cheques. Ignore Shipped by field. HST is 13%.

You work on a weekly basis, Mar 5, 12, 19, 26 and Mar 31, therefore, advance the date as needed. Ignore phone and fax numbers for new customers and vendors.

3 ➤   Enter the following transactions:

Mar 1   Purchased 10 boxes of special wax (Cleaning & Repairs Expense) at $32.00 each, plus HST for the new dance practice studio floor from new vendor Speciality Services (any address information). These will be used in the next two weeks. Invoice #748 received with terms 2/10, net 15 days, calculate discounts before tax.

Mar 2   Issued cheque #897 to pay for invoice #1962 owing to Quinton Cleaning Services.

Mar 5   Sold on invoice #426, dance lessons for the week $40.00 plus HST, to **Your Actual Name**. You paid with a Universal credit card.

Mar 5   Returned 1 box of the special wax to Speciality Services, as the wax was too oily. Credit note #748RT received.

Mar 8   The owner, Rajwinder Opuku, issued a memo requesting an $800.00 cheque to cover personal expenses. Cheque #898 is issued.

Mar 14   Purchased 1 box of sales invoices from NAJ Printing Ltd. Invoice #875, $100.00, plus HST. Terms, net 20 days.

Mar 15   Paid Speciality Services with cheque #899, for invoice #748 after taking off the return.

Mar 19   Sold on invoice #427 dance lessons, for the week $40.00, plus HST to **Your Actual Name**. You paid with your cheque #158.

Mar 26   The bank advised by $428.00 debit memo dated today that the bank interest on the loan was $28.00 and the loan payment was $400.00.

Mar 29   Sold on invoice #428 dance lessons for the week $55.00, plus HST, to Ying Zhu. Ying paid cash for the invoice.

Mar 30   Received invoice #456 in the amount of $80.00, plus HST, for cleaning of classroom from Quinton Cleaning Services. Terms 2/10, net 20.

Mar 30   Received insurance bill #A4589 for $175.00, plus HI (8% portion of HST) from Metro Insurance (any address information) for the month of March. Bill to be paid in 5 days.

4 ➤   Advance the date to **Mar 31** and **print** the following:

   a)   Income Statement for Jan 1 to Mar 31.
   b)   Journal Entries-All, for Mar 1 to Mar 31.
   c)   Journal Entries-General, for Mar 1 to Mar 31.
   d)   Accounts Receivable - Aged Detail for all customers, for Mar 1 to Mar 31.
   e)   Accounts Payable - Aged Detail for all vendors, for Mar 1 to Mar 31.

Challenge Exercise 03 C3B-4, Chairs

This exercise is a review of 3 modules – COMPANY, PAYABLES & RECEIVABLES

1 ➤ Refer to Exercise 1-1 to unzip the Chairs exe file and Chairs document file that is appropriate for your province or territory located at www.simplyaccounting2010.nelson.com under Student Resources: **Chapter Data files\Chairs-Provincial Data Files**.

Chairs-Alberta.exe	Chairs-Nova Scotia.exe
Chairs-British Columbia.exe	Chairs-Ontario.exe
Chairs-Manitoba.exe	Chairs-Prince Edward Island.exe
Chairs-New Brunswick.exe	Chairs-Quebec.exe
Chairs-Newfoundland.exe	Chairs-Saskatchewan.exe
Chairs-North West Territories.exe	Chairs-Yukon.exe

2 ➤ Open the appropriate **Chairs** file.

3 ➤ **Print** the appropriate **Chairs Adobe PDF file** for your province or territory.

If you do not have Adobe Reader on your computer, click the Adobe Reader button/link on the website at www.simplyaccounting2010.nelson.com under Student Resources, or go directly to: http://get.adobe.com/reader/.

Each data file has the HST, GST or PST rates appropriate for that province or territory.

A list of HST, GST and PST rates are shown below and can also be found in Chapter 15, *Taxes*.

The HST rate of 13% is used in this text and reflected in the solutions. This rate, however, may have changed since the publication date. When on the job be sure to use the appropriate HST, GST or PST rates.

4 ➤ **Record** the transactions listed in the PDF document.

5 ➤ **Print** the reports required in step 3 of the PDF document.

HST, GST and PST rates by Province & Territory (at July 1, 2010)	HST	GST	PST	Total
Prince Edward Island	-	5.0	10.0	15.0
New Brunswick	13.0	-	-	13.0
Newfoundland & Labrador	13.0	-	-	13.0
Nova Scotia	13.0	-	-	13.0
Ontario	13.0		-	13.0
Quebec	-	5.0	7.5	12.5
British Columbia	12.0	-	-	12.0
Manitoba	-	5.0	7.0	12.0
Saskatchewan	-	5.0	5.0	10.0
Alberta	-	5.0	-	5.0
North West Territories	-	5.0	-	5.0
Yukon	-	5.0	-	5.0

Mini-Guide for Chapter 3

Mini-guide for transactions in Simply Accounting 2010*
Not all types of transactions listed here.

***Study Suggestion – Add additional transactions from your chapters.**

Purchase Events	Entry	Module	Journal	Comments	You fill in the Text Ref
You ask vendor for price quote	No entry	PAYABLE	Purchases, Orders & Quotes	No Purchase, you are asking for prices	
You confirm quote & place order for later delivery	No entry	PAYABLE	Purchases, Orders & Quotes	No Purchase, price confirmed for future delivery	
Purchase of merchandise	Purchases	PAYABLE	Purchases, Orders & Quotes	may be preceded by purchase quote	
	HST on Purchases			may be preceded by purchase order	
	Accounts Payable			may be a purchase without prior quote or order	
Purchase Rtn of Merchandise	Accounts Payable	PAYABLE	Purchases, Orders & Quotes	Add "Rt" to invoice number	
	Purchase Rtns & Allowances			If credit memo listed, then add "CMxxx"	
	HST on Purchases				
Payment (no discount)	Accounts Payable	PAYABLE	Payment	-can be partial or full payment	
	Cash			-can be after a return	
Payment, with discount	Accounts Payable	PAYABLE	Payment	-full payment	
	Purchase Discount			-can be after a return	
	Cash				

* Note: Refer to the Appendix V, *Mini-Guide Receivables—Payables* at www.simplyaccounting2010.nelson.com under Student Resources.

Chapter 4

Setting Up a New Company

Sarah's Kitchen Stores

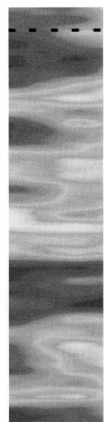

Learning Objectives

After completing this chapter you will be able to:

☐ Set up a company from scratch.
☐ Add account names with specific account types for displaying reports.
☐ Modify and delete accounts as required.
☐ Set up links from modules to the General Ledger.
☐ Record opening balances for General Ledger accounts.
☐ Set up Tax Classes, Codes and Rates.
☐ Set up Receivable and Payable accounts and balances.
☐ Turn the modules to Ready mode.
☐ Display and Print reports.

In this chapter you will create (SET UP) a company's data file from scratch. You will convert a manual set of accounting records to a computerized accounting system.

> If you are setting up a recent new company or one that has been in business for some time, refer to Appendix H, *New Business Guide* at www.simplyaccounting2010.nelson.com under Student Resources, for a Checklist of forms or registration items the company should be aware of.

Before you can use Simply Accounting software to process company transactions, you need to create the data file, enter defaults and various settings, add accounts, customers, vendors and balances and set the module to READY. It is important to prepare the system carefully, to avoid problems when you start processing transactions.

This chapter explains the typical procedure in setting up a company in Simply. Since every company is different, some of these requirements may vary. To help you learn the setup procedures, we will guide you in setting up the COMPANY, PAYABLES and RECEIVABLES modules for **Sarah's Kitchen Stores**, a business that buys and sells kitchen cabinets and accessories.

The contents of this chapter are as follows:

- Step 1: Creating Company Files 261
  - Account Number Structure.. 261
  - Account Types 262
  - Exercise 4-1 – Setting Up a New Company File from Scratch 264
- Step 2: Setting User Preferences Defaults 271
  - Exercise 4-2a – To Set User Preferences–View Defaults 271
  - Exercise 4-2b – To Set User Preferences–Options Defaults 274

- Step 3: Changing System Defaults 276
    - Exercise 4-3 – Changing System Defaults 276
- Step 4: Changing Printer Settings 288
    - Exercise 4-4 Changing Printer Settings 288
- Step 5: Conversion Process with Accounts 290
    - Exercise 4-5 – Setting Up (Adding) the Chart of Accounts 292
    - Exercise 4-6 – Deleting an Account 299
    - Exercise 4-7 – To Modify an Account 300
    - Exercise 4-8 – Change Next Cheque Number & Settings 301
- Step 6: Linking Modules/Accounts 302
    - Exercise 4-9 – Linking the Modules 303
        - COMPANY Module Links 303
        - PAYABLES Module Links 304
        - RECEIVABLES Module Links 305
- Step 7: Entering Opening G/L Account Balances (History) 306
    - Exercise 4-10 – Entering Opening G/L Balances (History) 309
- Step 8: Setting Up Tax Classes, Codes, Rates & Customization 311
    - Exercise 4-11 – Setting Up Tax Classes, Codes, Rates & Customization 311
- Step 9a: Setting Up Vendor Subledgers 313
    - Exercise 4-12 – Setting Up Subledgers–Vendors 314
- Step 9b: Setting Up Subledgers 318
    - Exercise 4-13 – Setting Up Subledgers–Customers 318
- Step 10: To Add Credit Card Information 321
    - Exercise 4-14 – To Add Credit Card Information 321
- Step 11: Setting Modules to Ready 323
    - Exercise 4-15 – To Set the System to READY 324
    - Exercise 4-16 – Verify Information in SAI Data File 325

- Before Moving On. 326
    - Challenge Exercise 04 C4-1, Balloons Store 327
    - Challenge Exercise 04 C4-2, Kojokaro 330
    - Challenge Exercise 04 C4-3, Skates Stores 331
    - Challenge Exercise 04 C4-4, R. Park Uniforms 334

- Relevant Appendices 335

Run **Slideshow 4 – Setting Up a New Company**. You will get a good idea of what is involved in setting up a new company from scratch and how to link the various modules.

Step 1: Creating Company Files

Creating Simply Files

A company data file must be created in Simply for Sarah's Kitchen Stores that is the same as the existing company's manual system. This is known as the **CONVERSION** process. Simply provides a selection of sample companies, with General Ledger Chart of Accounts already set up (called templates). One of these company templates may be copied to a new Simply company folder to save the time required to enter the G/L accounts.

Normally, these sample companies are located in a folder called **SAMDATA**. You would select a company that has a chart of accounts most similar to that of your own company. A template chart of accounts for the Retail Company contains 167 accounts.

Using the template, you would have to delete accounts you do not need, such as 1920 Goodwill, 1930 Incorporation Costs and others. You would then modify account names to match your own Chart of Accounts, such as 1060 Chequing Bank Account to 1060 Nova Scotia Bank Account and others. You would add accounts that are not on the list, such as 5010 Beginning Inventory, and 5340 Ending Inventory and others.

The text will show you how to set up a company from scratch. This structure will start with one account 3600 Current Earnings, which will allow for the transfer of the Net Income or Loss from the Income Statement to the Balance Sheet Equity section.

To start a company from a template is covered in Appendix AA, *Setting Up a New Company File using a Template* at www.simplyaccounting2010.nelson.com under Student Resources.

As you are going through this chapter, remember to save at regular intervals.

Account Number Structure

It is important that you understand how the Simply account numbering structure works to make sure that the program processes transactions properly.

Simply uses an Account Number Range shown next to identify the type of account and how to process each accordingly.

Study the next example regarding the position of account numbering in Simply:

Account Type	Account # Range	Normal Balance	Amount Entered
Assets	1000 – 1999	Debit	positive
Liabilities	2000 – 2999	Credit	positive
Equity	3000 – 3999	Credit	positive
Revenue	4000 – 4999	Credit	positive
Expense *	5000 – 5999	Debit	positive

* Includes **Cost of Goods Sold** and **Expenses**.

Simply will allow account numbers up to 8 digits. This text uses 4 digits in account numbers; therefore you cannot use an account number outside of this structure, i.e., a number lower than 1000 or higher than 5999.

Account Types

If you use a template to create your company file, print the chart of accounts before you make changes to the structure.

View the structure of the Current Assets section shown below. The complete financial statements with account codes (HASGT) are shown in Fig. 4-37b. The displayed or printed Chart of Accounts shows only the account code.

Look carefully at the type of account and where it is located in the statement structure; i.e., column 1, the first dollar value on the left (coded as **A** 'Subgroup **A**ccount' [values that accumulate]), or column 2, the second dollar value column which is on the right (coded as **S** '**S**ubgroup Total,' **G** '**G**roup Account' or **T** '**G**roup **T**otal').

Acct #	Description	Type	Code	Column 1 Amount	Column 2 Amount
1000	Current Assets	Group Heading	H		
1005	Petty Cash	Subgroup Account	A	100.00	
1010	Bank Account Chequing	Subgroup Account	A	17,106.00	
1011	Bank Account Credit Card	Subgroup Account	A	0.00	
1080	**Cash Total (subtotal)**	**Subgroup Total**	**S**		17,206.00
1200	Accounts Receivable	Subgroup Account	A	12,173.90	
1210	Allowance for Bad Debts	Subgroup Account	A	-550.00	
1219	**Net Accounts Receivable**	**Subgroup Total**	**S**		11,623.90
1240	Store/Office Supplies/Prepaid	Group Account	G		400.00
1260	Inventory of Goods	Group Account	G		102,500.00
1299	**Total Current Assets**	**Group Total**	**T**		131,729.90

It is very important that you understand the use of the Simply type of accounts:

Group **H**eadings   Group Headings start each section. They provide descriptions of section account types, are **not postable** and have no balances.

Acct #	Description	Type	Code	Amount	Amount
1000	Current Assets	Group Heading	H		

Other Examples:

1400	Capital Assets	
2000	Current Liabilities	
2300	Long Term Liabilities	

Subgroup **A**ccount   **Postable** accounts. Subgroup **A**ccounts are used when you need to add accounts together to get a subtotal. **A** accounts can have opening balances and are updated whenever debits and credits from journal entries are posted to them.

They are not in Debit or Credit columns. They are printed in the left column of the appropriate group on the financial statement.

Subgroup Total   **S**ubgroup Total accounts are used when you want to subtotal
(Accumulates   **A** accounts. **S** type of accounts are **not postable** and create a
A accounts)   subtotal of **A** accounts above the **S**. **S** accounts are printed in the right column of the appropriate group on the financial statement. This makes your financial statement easier to understand.

Study the example below regarding the position of the **A**, **S** accounts.

Example:

Acct #	Description	Type	Code	Amount	Amount
1005	Petty Cash	Subgroup Account	A	100.00	
1010	Bank Account Chequing	Subgroup Account	A	17,106.00	
1011	Bank Account Credit Card	Subgroup Account	A	0.00	
1080	**Cash Total (subtotal)**	**Subgroup Total**	**S**		17,206.00

The **A** type of accounts **are postable** and their balances are printed in the left column of the appropriate group on the financial statement. **A** type of accounts require an **S** type of account to subtotal the amounts.

The **S** account **1080 Total Cash**, is the subtotal of the **A** type of accounts (#'s 1005, 1010 and 1011) and it is printed in the right column of the appropriate group on the financial statement.

Another example:

Acct #	Description	Type	Code	Amount	Amount
1200	Accounts Receivable	Subgroup Account	A	12,173.90	
1210	Allowance for Bad Debts	Subgroup Account	A	-550.00	
1219	**Net Accounts Receivable**	**Subgroup Total**	**S**		11,623.90

Group Account   **Postable** accounts. **Group** accounts are used when there are no **A** accounts to be subtotaled. These accounts are in the right column and can have an opening balance and are updated with debits and credits from journal entries posted to them.

Study the example below regarding the position of the **G** accounts.

Acct #	Description	Type	Code	Amount	Amount
1240	Store/Office Supplies/Prepaid	Group Account	G		400.00
1260	Inventory of Goods	Group Account	G		102,500.00

Notice that the amounts for the **G** accounts 1240 and 1260 are placed at the right column, whereas amounts for the **A** accounts were placed in the left column.

Group **T**otal   Used to end each section. They are **not postable**, and will subtotal all the **G** and **S** accounts in the section above it. They are descriptions only of the section above.

Acct #	Description	Type	Code	Amount	Amount
1299	Total Current Assets	Group Total	T		131,729.90

Other examples of **T**otals are:

1499	Net Capital Assets	
2299	Total Current Liabilities	
2399	Total Long Term Liabilities	

Important things to remember:

1) Each section must begin with an **H** (Heading) and end with a **T** (Total account). You cannot have 2 Hs or 2 Ts together.

2) **A** (Subgroup accounts) and **G** (Group accounts) are the only postable account types.

3) **A** (Subgroup accounts) must be followed by an **S** (Subgroup Total) account. **Always**.

4) The Group Total **T** account adds all **G** (Group accounts) and **S** (Subgroup Total accounts) between the **H** (Heading; e.g., 1000 Current Assets) and the **T** (Total account; e.g., 1299 Total Current Assets).

Current Earnings **X**   **Not Postable**. The **X** account is like the manual accounting INCOME SUMMARY account. It is used only to move dollar values from the Income Statement to the Balance Sheet.

Simply assigns the number 3600 **Current Earnings** to the **X** account. **This cannot be changed**. It automatically adds the **Net Revenue Earned** and subtracts the **Cost of Goods Sold** and **Expenses**. The difference, the **Net Profit or Loss**, is carried forward to the Balance Sheet in the Equity Section.

Setting Up a New Company File from Scratch

You will now set up the company file for Sarah's Kitchen Stores using the Scratch method.

Exercise 4-1 – Setting Up a New Company File from Scratch

This exercise will demonstrate the creation of a new company data file from scratch. If you want to use a template, refer to Appendix AA, *Setting Up a New Company File using a Template,* at www.simplyaccounting2010.nelson.com under Student Resources, in case you need to use one in the future.

1 ➤ Start **Simply Accounting** the normal way.

Fig. 4-1: What do you wish to do window.

Note: You may not see | ○ Open the last company you worked on: | at the bottom.

2 ➤ Click the **Create a new company** button, then **OK**.

New Company Setup

✓	Introduction	Welcome to the New Company Setup Wizard. This wizard will help you set up your company quickly and easily.
✓	Name & Address	
✓	Dates	
✓	List of Accounts	
➧	File Name	
➧	Finish	

Fig. 4-2a: New Company Setup Wizard using School Edition.

This window informs you that the wizard will help in setting up the new company, and that changes may be made to any options chosen. If you click the Help button, you will see a checklist of steps to complete when setting up a new company using the scratch method.

 If you are using the **Student** version that came with the text, you will see Fig. 4-2b. As noted in Appendix A, Installation Instructions, the links shown (Customer Support and Accounting expert) are not available for Students. The links require an upgrade to the retail version.

Fig. 4-2b: New Company Setup Wizard using Student Edition.

3 ➤ Click **Next >**.

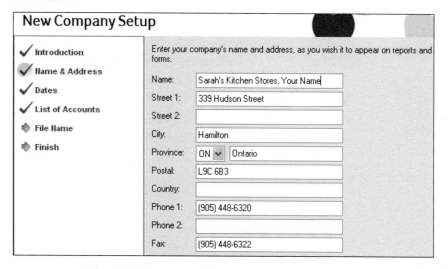

Fig. 4-3: Company Name and information.

4 ➤ **Type the information** from Fig. 4-3 into the fields in your window. Remember to type your actual name, in place of Your Name, to identify your printouts. When complete click **Next >**.

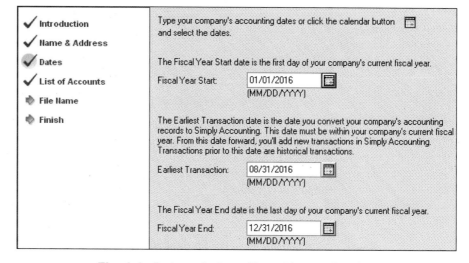

If your computer has been set up to display dates as DD/MM/YYYY, then the dates would appear as follows:
Start   01/01/2016
Earliest   31/08/2016
Year End 31/12/2016

Fig. 4-4: Dates window. (See side note box.)

5 ➤ Sarah's Kitchen Stores, a single-owner business, has a calendar fiscal year ending Dec 31 of each year. Enter the dates shown in Fig. 4-4. You will see the setting for changing the dates display to show the month name in Exercise 4-3, step 25. The default setting for dates when starting a company is **Short Dates** (01/01/2016).

Fiscal Year Start   **01/01/2016**   (Jan 1, **Start date** of the fiscal year.)

Earliest Transaction **08/31/2016**   (Aug 31, this is the last date the accounting records were completed manually, or were completed on another computer system, or the day the records were converted to Simply. This may also be called a **conversion date**. The records are being created in Simply as of this date.)

Fiscal Year End   **12/31/2016**   (Dec 31, **End date** of the fiscal year.)

6 ➤ When complete click **Next >**.

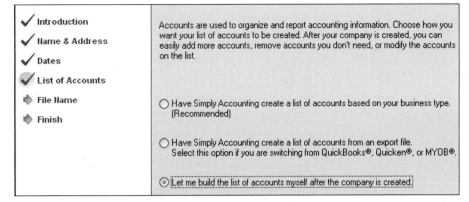

Fig. 4-5: Setup Method.

> ⦿ Have Simply Accounting create a list of accounts based on your business type. (Recommended)

With this option, Simply will create a company with approximately 167 General Ledger accounts that would be used by similar businesses. Using a template may save time in setting up a company; however, if you have a small company, using a template may take more time because you have to modify, delete and/or add new accounts and change the default settings using **Setup, Simply Settings, Settings** window. Refer to Appendix AA, *Setting Up a New Company File Using a Template* at www.simplyaccounting2010.nelson.com under Student Resources.

> ○ Have Simply Accounting create a list of accounts from an export file. Select this option if you are switching from QuickBooks®, Quicken®, or MYOB®.

Using this option, Simply will create a list of General Ledger accounts ***from a Quickbooks®, Quicken®, MYOB® export file*** ® (other accounting software programs). This means that Simply will convert the data from the export file to a Simply data file structure.

> ⦿ Let me build the list of accounts myself after the company is created.

Using this method, Simply will create a company with only 1 General Ledger account (i.e., **3600 Current Earnings**) in the chart of accounts. You would create (add) accounts into each section as needed. In the authors' view, this is the best way for students to create a company as you will build each section containing the H A S G T accounts.

This is the method you will be using in this chapter.

7 ➤ Click method **c) Let me build the list of accounts myself after the company is created,** then **Next >**.

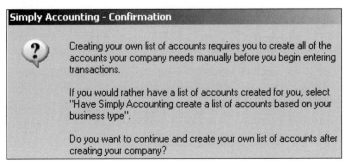

Fig. 4-6: Warning Message.

8 ➤ This window informs you that you have chosen to create your own list of accounts method. Click **Yes**.

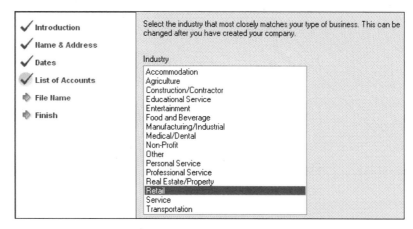

Fig. 4-7: Type of Business window (Choose a Template).

This window lists a number of different types of businesses.

9 ➤ Select the **Retail** Industry (type of business). Click **Next >**.

Fig. 4-8: Enter the name of company file window.

10 ➤ **Type the information** from Fig. 4-8 into the fields in your window (see caution box).

Remove your name here. Do NOT type your name here as part of the company file name. If you type your name here, it will become part of the company data file name; e.g.,

Sarah's Kitchen Stores Oliver Megan.SAI

Change the **C:** to your drive letter. Delete any other information that may remain in the boxes. Maximum 52 characters including spaces.

11 ➤ When Fig. 4-8 is complete, click **Next >**.

C:\Simply Data 2010\
Sarah's Kitchen Stores
means that Simply will
create on the **C:** drive,
inside the Simply Data
2010 folder, a folder
named **Sarah's Kitchen
Stores.SAJ**, and will
create the **Sarah's
Kitchen Stores.SAI** file
in the Kitchen folder.

.SAI may also be lower
case, as in **.sai.**

12 ➤ Simply informs you that the folder and file do not exist in the location you
have specified. Verify the location and when correct, click **Yes** and Simply
will create the folder and file. (See side note box.)

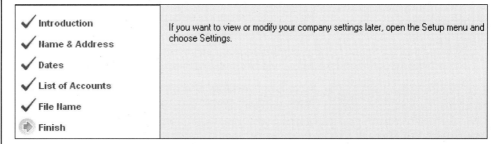

13 ➤ The above display informs you that in order to view or modify settings after
continuing, you need to change settings. Click **Finish** to have Simply set up
the files for the company.

After you click Finish, a message box will appear to advise you, ***Creating
new database***, similar to the following.

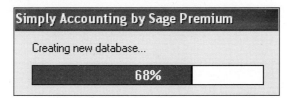

 The creating database procedure can take up to *3 minutes or more*, depending on
the type of computer system you are using – it might look as if the computer has
stalled at the 10% or other point. Closing the Simply program or shutting the
computer off can cause a major problem to the data file and you will have to redo the
setup procedure again. Moreover, it is possible that the file cannot be deleted from
your storage space. **Wait until the system has set up the data file before
proceeding.**

When Simply has created the data files, the program will display the next window.

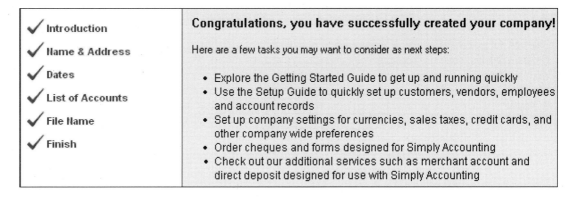

Fig. 4-9: Successfully created the company data file.

This window lists some of the tasks that may be needed to finish setting up the company data file.

    a.   Explore the Getting Started Guide to view tutorials that are available.

    b.   Modify the company settings to those needed by the company (Exercise 4-2a, 4-2b, 4-3 and 4-4).

    c.   Use the Setup Guide to add and link General Ledger accounts with open balances (Exercise 4-5 to 4-10 inclusive).

    d.   Add list of vendors and record unpaid invoices (Exercise 4-12). Note the text adds vendors first.

    e.   Add list of customers and record unpaid invoices (Exercise 4-13).

    f.   If required, add inventory items and services, with quantities. Sarah's Kitchen Stores does not require the INVENTORY module at this time.

    g.   Get customized cheques, quotes, orders and invoices from a printer.

14 ➤   Click **Close**, then **OK**, then **Close** the Getting Started window.

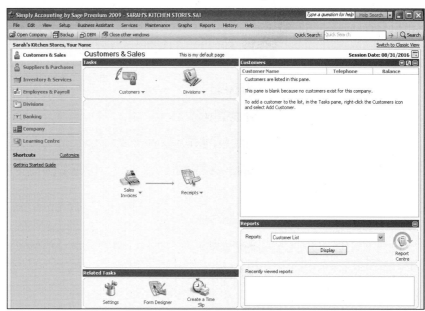

> The menu bar may be on two lines. You can resize the window by placing your mouse over the right edge of the outside border of the Simply window; when it changes to ↔, drag the edge to the right to widen the window so the menu bar can be on one line.

Fig. 4-10: Sarah's Kitchen Stores Home window (see side note box).

The Customers & Sales window does not display Sales Quotes or Sales Orders.

The Suppliers & Purchases window does not display Purchase Quotes or Purchase Orders. (See side note box.)

> Note that Purchases and Sales do not indicate Orders & Quotes. You will make these selections in Exercise 4-3, step 10.

The following modules display the History symbol, (quill pen): CUSTOMERS & SALES, SUPPLIERS & PURCHASES, INVENTORY & SERVICES, EMPLOYEES & PAYROLL, AND COMPANY.

15 ➤   You can view the Chart of Accounts created for a scratch company, using two methods:

    a) Click the **Report Centre**, **Accounts**, **Chart of Accounts**, click **Display**.

    b) Click the **COMPANY** module, click the **Chart of Accounts** icon.

    Use method a) to view the **Chart of Accounts**.

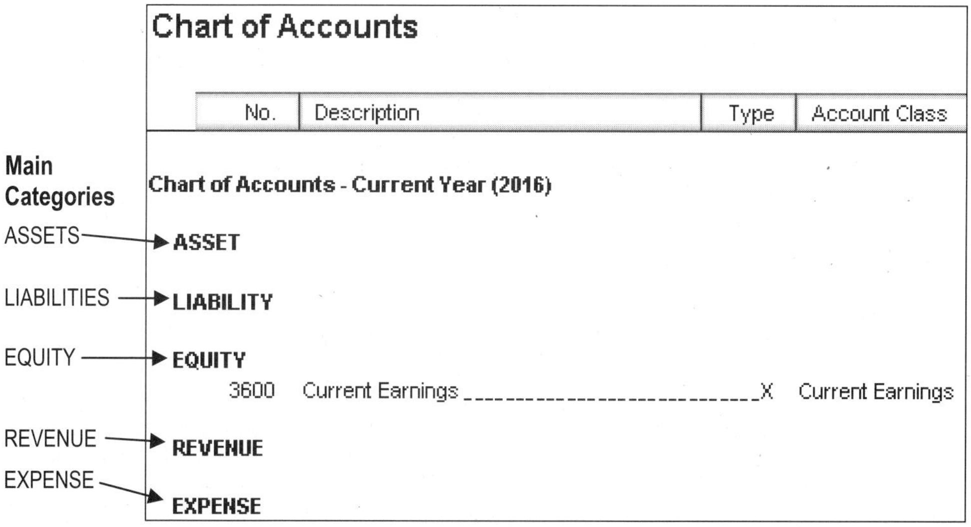

Chart of Accounts

	No.	Description		Type	Account Class

Main Categories

Chart of Accounts - Current Year (2016)

ASSETS ————▶ **ASSET**

LIABILITIES ————▶ **LIABILITY**

EQUITY ————▶ **EQUITY**
              3600   Current Earnings _____X   Current Earnings

REVENUE ————▶ **REVENUE**

EXPENSE ————▶ **EXPENSE**

Fig. 4-11: Chart of Accounts from scratch.

The Chart of Accounts structure is created with the five main financial statement categories and the X account **3600 Current Earnings**. You will be adding accounts to this structure to create Sarah's Kitchen Stores Chart of Accounts before linking accounts. Remember, if you use the template, you would have to remove (delete) the accounts you don't need, change (modify) the names of accounts to those that your firm would use, and add other accounts that are not listed. If you decide to use a template, you should print the default Chart of Accounts to determine which accounts to keep, delete, modify or add. (See side note box.)

Congratulations! You have successfully set up the scratch company files in your data location!

At the end of this chapter, after setting up the company, you will be shown how to turn the COMPANY, PAYABLES, and RECEIVABLES modules to READY.

You will also set up the linked accounts to the General Ledger that will be used by the PAYABLES and RECEIVABLES modules. This will be explained in Exercise 4-9.

16 ➤ Click **X** and **Close** to return to the Home window.

> ℹ️ If you had used the template option (see Appendix AA, *Creating a New Company using a Template* at www.simplyaccounting2010.nelson.com under Student Resources) Simply would have created a set of standard default General Ledger accounts (167 or more) for the company and created the linked accounts.

Step 2: Setting User Preferences Defaults

A **default** is a pre-selected option that is automatically set until you choose a different option. Each of the next windows will allow you to either accept the defaults or select new options to set as defaults for various windows and reports.

Exercise 4-2a – To Set User Preferences–View Defaults

We are going to hide the modules that we will not use in this chapter. The procedure can be reversed later to reveal the modules as you need them.

1 ➤ To hide modules, click **Setup**, **User Preferences**.

2 ➤ In the left pane click on the **View** item.

User Preferences				
Options **View** Colour Scheme Transaction Confirmation	**Pages** Customers & Sales ☑ Vendors & Purchases ☑ Inventory & Services ☐ Employees & Payroll ☐ Division ☐ Banking ☑	**Icon Windows** Customers ☑ Vendors ☑ Inventory & Services ☐ Employees ☐ Division ☐ Accounts ☑	**Features** Time & Billing ☐	

Home Window Toolbar
- ⦿ Icons and Text
- ○ Icons only

Daily Business Manager	Checklists
☐ At Startup	☐ At Startup
☐ After Changing Session Date	☐ After Changing Session Date

☑ Show Company Name in Status Bars
☑ Automatic Advice
☑ Show Change Session Date at Startup
☑ Show Paid stamp on fully paid sales invoices during lookup
☑ Show Paid stamp on fully paid purchase invoices during lookup

Fig 4-12 User Preferences View window (after changes).

Window (Fig. 4-12) will allow you to choose the modules you plan to use for your company. Unclick a Pages item (e.g., Division ✓ and the corresponding Icon Windows ✓ is unchecked as well).

Customers & Sales	Allows you to keep track of your Accounts Receivable.
Vendors & Purchases	Allows you to keep track of your Accounts Payable.
Inventory & Services	Allows you to maintain individual records using the perpetual inventory method. (Shown in Chapter 8.)
Employees & Payroll	Allows you to record employee paycheques with payroll deductions and prepare government reports (T-4s). (Shown in Chapter 7.)
Division	This option allows you to maintain records of cost centres (projects, jobs, departments, etc.) for sale of goods and/or sale of services you provide to others. (Shown in Chapter 11.)
Banking	Allows you to Receive Payments (Receipts from Chapter 2), make Deposits, Pay various bills (Payments Chapter 3), Transfer funds between Company bank accounts and Reconcile accounts (Chapter 12).
Time and Billing 	Used with Customers & Sales, Employees & Payroll. Allows you to maintain time for employees and using the information to bill the customer. Shown in Appendix AD, *Time & Billing Module* at www.simplyaccounting2010.nelson.com under Student Resources.
3 ➤ **Pages**	Remove the ✓ at **Inventory & Services, Employees & Payroll** and **Division**. This will hide the modules in the Home window.
4 ➤ **Features**	Remove the ✓ at **Time & Billing**.

Home Window Toolbar

Leave the selection as . If you select icons only the home window icons will display without wording.

Daily Business Manager

The default setting is to display the Daily Business Manager ✓ **After Changing the Session Date**.

5 ➤ Click ✓ **After Changing the Session Date** to NOT display the Daily Business Manager. The ✓ has been removed.

> Daily Business Manager
> ☐ At Startup
> ☐ After Changing Session Date

Checklists

You can find information on Checklists in Appendix I, *Checklists for Task Completion* at www.simplyaccounting2010.nelson.com under Student Resources.

The default setting is to display the **Checklists After Changing the Session Date**.

6 ➤ To change the Checklists to not display, click on ✓ **After Changing Session Date**. The ✓ has been removed.

> Checklists
> ☐ At Startup
> ☐ After Changing Session Date

Checklists will not display unless you repeat the procedure.

Lower section

> ☑ Show Company Name in Status Bars
> ☑ Automatic Advice
> ☑ Show Change Session Date at Startup
> ☑ Show Paid stamp on fully paid sales invoices during lookup
> ☑ Show Paid stamp on fully paid purchase invoices during lookup

> ☑ Show Company Name in Status Bars Do NOT change. The default is to have the company name displayed at the bottom of each journal.

> ☑ Automatic Advice Do NOT change. This will provide advice on the Help menu if requested.

7 ➤  ☑ Show Change Session Date at Startup Click this field. This will provide the change session date window when you open a company data file.

> ☑ Show Paid stamp on fully paid sales invoices during lookup
> ☑ Show Paid stamp on fully paid purchase invoices during lookup Do NOT change. This will display the Paid stamp on fully paid invoices during lookup.

Colour scheme

8 ➤ In the left pane, click on the **Colour scheme** item. You will see the current colours used in journal windows. Simply allows the user to change the background colour of the Journals.

Many businesses use different background colours for quotes, orders and invoices. It is easier to see and know that you are in the correct window by the colour of the window.

The network system at your school may not allow you to change the background colour settings. You can change the colour background (appearance) of any window (from the default) by clicking the ▼ to see the various choices available from the list. Many of the default windows already have different colour backgrounds. There is no exercise for changing the settings. (See side note box.)

Transaction Confirmation

9 ➤ In the left pane, click on the **Transaction Confirmation**.

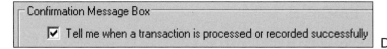

Do NOT change.

This choice will provide a window advising you the entry was posted or recorded. You may uncheck this box if you do not want the advice window.

Exercise 4-2b – To Set User Preferences–Options Defaults

1 ➤ In the left pane, click **Options** to move to the Options window.

Changing Preferences Settings

Use the following procedure to customize the options for your data file. If a row or rows of information is not discussed, leave the default unchanged.

Terminology

Fig. 4-13: Terminology window.

2 ➤ Click **Use Accounting Terms** button. This will allow you to display familiar accounting terms.

Microsoft Excel Language

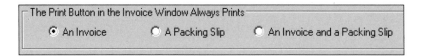

Do NOT change from English.

Print Button

3 ➤ Leave the choice as **An Invoice**.

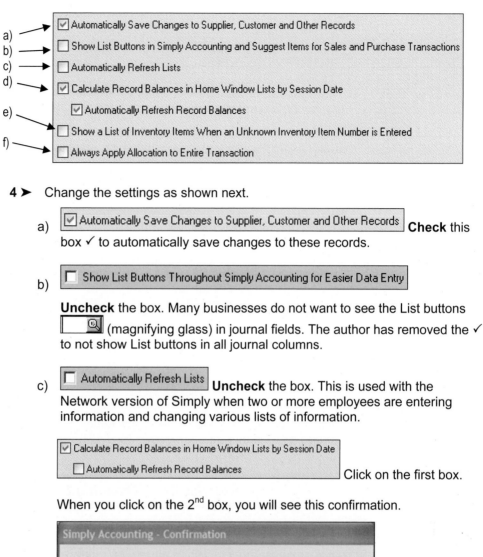

4 ➤ Change the settings as shown next.

a) 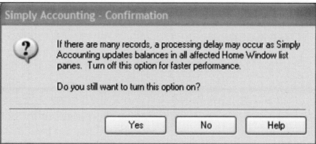 **Check** this box ✓ to automatically save changes to these records.

b) ☐ Show List Buttons Throughout Simply Accounting for Easier Data Entry

Uncheck the box. Many businesses do not want to see the List buttons ☐ 🔍 (magnifying glass) in journal fields. The author has removed the ✓ to not show List buttons in all journal columns.

c) ☐ Automatically Refresh Lists **Uncheck** the box. This is used with the Network version of Simply when two or more employees are entering information and changing various lists of information.

☑ Calculate Record Balances in Home Window Lists by Session Date
☐ Automatically Refresh Record Balances   Click on the first box.

When you click on the 2nd box, you will see this confirmation.

> **Simply Accounting - Confirmation**
>
> ❓ If there are many records, a processing delay may occur as Simply Accounting updates balances in all affected Home Window list panes. Turn off this option for faster performance.
>
> Do you still want to turn this option on?
>
> [Yes]   [No]   [Help]

Click **Yes**. A second checkmark appears.

d) ☐ Show a List of Inventory Items When an Unknown Inventory Item Number is Entered
Uncheck the box. This choice would be checked when you are using Perpetual Inventory. Discussed in Chapter 8.

e) ☐ Always Apply Allocation to Entire Transaction   Do NOT change. This choice is used with the DIVISION module. This selection will be removed from this window when you click OK in step 5.

5 ➤ Click **OK** to return to the Home window.

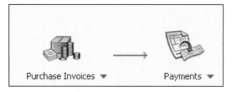

Fig. 4-14: Sarah's Kitchen Stores Payable display before Update Exercise 4-3.

The program, based on your choices earlier, has amended the scratch company data file and displays the RECEIVABLES, PAYABLES, BANKING and COMPANY modules, and the LEARNING CENTRE Module.

Since you did not use a template, you will need to add accounts and link appropriate accounts for the COMPANY, PAYABLES, and RECEIVABLES modules.
This window does not display the EMPLOYEES, INVENTORY, DIVISION or TIME and BILLING modules, because you removed the ✓ in Exercise 4-2a, step 3.
See View item information Fig. 4-12, User Preferences View window.

Step 3: Changing System Defaults

In this section, you will be confirming and/or changing some of the system settings defaults. If you need to change any settings in the future (e.g., comments to appear on sales quotes, orders or invoices), this section is where you would come to make the change.

In this section, you will be looking at new settings that were not shown before in Exercise 4-1 and/or 4-2.

Exercise 4-3 – Changing System Defaults

1 ➤ **Related Tasks**   From the Home window, area, click on **Settings**.

Information

2 ➤ In the left pane, click the ⊞ at Company. Click on **Information**.

3 ➤ **Business No.**   Type **R4675 2567**. ⬚Tab⬚. Some companies have one registration number for both HST and Employee payroll. This number is issued by Canada Revenue Agency (CRA) [formerly called Canada Customs and Revenue Agency (CCRA)] and needs to be printed on Sales invoices and T4 slips.

Industry Type

Fig. 4-15: Business Number window.

4 ➤ Click the ▼ to view the choices available. *Note*: These are the same choices available in Fig. 4-7. Select **Other**.

System

5 ➤ In the left pane, click on **System**. You will see the following confirmation.

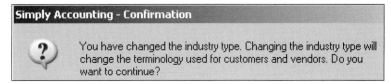

Simply Accounting - Confirmation

You have changed the industry type. Changing the industry type will change the terminology used for customers and vendors. Do you want to continue?

6 ➤ Click **No** to return to the Retail setting. You do not want to change the Industry type settings. In the left pane, click on **System**.

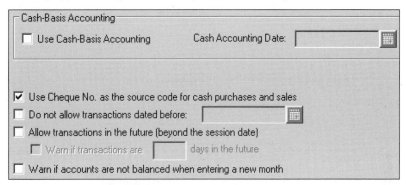

Fig. 4-16: Settings window – System.

Cash-Basis Accounting	Recognizes revenue when cash is received, and recognizes expenses when cash is paid. The cash basis of accounting is used by farmers and fishermen and is *NOT* covered in this text. Sarah's Kitchen Stores uses **Accrual Based** accounting. Do NOT click the box.

☑ Use Cheque No. as the source code for cash purchases and fees DO NOT CHANGE this field. It should be ✓. When using the Reconciliation and Deposits journal, it is useful to know the cheque number for a cash purchase or sale. Checking this option results in Simply using the cheque number as the source code rather than the invoice number.

☐ Do not allow transactions dated before: DO NOT CHECK THIS BOX. This feature will allow you to post transactions in previous months (e.g., May, July, or previous years). If you check this box ✓, the date field and box will be available to change. Sarah's Kitchen Stores does not plan on using this feature.

7 ➤ ☐ Allow transactions in the future (beyond the session date) Remove the ✓ from this box. This feature would allow you to record transactions in the future (e.g., post-dated cheques). At this time Sarah's Kitchen Stores does not want to allow future postings. Information on *Post-Dated Cheques* can be found in Appendix M at www.simplyaccounting2010.nelson.com under Student Resources.

☐ Warn if accounts are not balanced when entering a new month DO NOT CHANGE. This feature will allow the user to buy and install the software and immediately start to record transactions before putting in the previous month's General Ledger balances and CUSTOMERS and PAYABLES invoice details called **History**. If you record transactions in a new month, a warning message will appear to advise you that the subledger(s) do not balance with the General Ledger. Do not change the settings.

Backup

8 ➤ In the left pane, click on **Backup**.

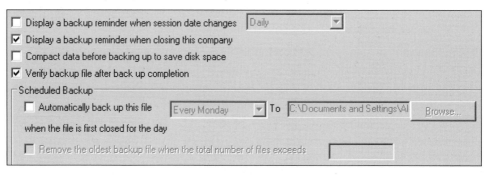

Fig. 4-17: Backup window.

This feature assumes you are backing up as shown in Exercise 1-23.

9 ➤ Change the settings as shown in Fig. 4-17.

If you are using a different backup procedure (e.g., creating backups outside of Simply), then these settings would not be required.

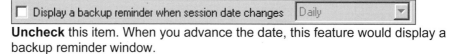

Uncheck this item. When you advance the date, this feature would display a backup reminder window.

In a business setting, this item could be used, but in a classroom environment it is not required.

☑ Display a backup reminder when closing this company   DO NOT CHANGE. When closing the company (exiting), you will be reminded to back up before exiting. Discuss a backup procedure with your instructor.

The authors recommend that daily backups be completed, and a copy of the data on USB storage device, CD or other media be taken off-site to ensure safety of the material. There are many cases where a business has suffered losses due to fire, etc., and has recovered because the accounting records were backed up and stored away from the business location. See Exercise 1-23.

☐ Compact data before backing up to save disk space   DO NOT CHANGE. In a classroom environment there is no need to Compact Data when exiting. In a business environment when the file contains hundreds of entries, there would be a need to compact the data file.

☑ Verify backup file after back up completion   DO NOT CHANGE. When using any backup procedure, it is recommended that you maintain a setting to verify the backup data.

Scheduled Backup ☐ Automatically back up this file **Uncheck** this item. In a classroom environment, there is no need to schedule backups. In a business environment, it is recommended that you schedule backups daily.

Features

10 ➤ In the left pane, click on **Features**.

Sarah has decided that she will not use Purchase Quotes for vendors/suppliers. She will use only Purchase Orders to confirm orders placed with vendors. She will use customer Quotes and Orders and will not use Packing Slips.

Fig. 4-18: Orders, Quotes and Packing Slips.

11 ➤ **Change** the selections as shown in Fig. 4-18.

Language

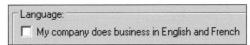

DO NOT CHANGE. Sarah's Kitchen Stores does not have any customers using French.

Credit Cards, Sales Taxes

The following items in the left pane will be left for a later exercise as they need account number information to proceed. **Sales Taxes** (Exercise 4-11) **Credit Cards** (Exercise 4-14).

Currency

12 ➤ In the left hand pane, click on **Currency**.

You will notice that the Home Currency is Canadian Dollars. You will also notice that the window has a column for Foreign Currency, but you cannot enter information unless you click the ☐ Allow Transactions in a Foreign Currency.

Click the **Allow Transactions in a Foreign Currency** box, a ✓ appears and the Enter your home currency changes to Enter your home currency and the account used to track exchange differences. The Track Exchange and Rounding Differences in: field is not grayed out.

13 ➤ Double-click on the **Foreign Currency** column, to see a list of foreign currencies available in Simply. You could select a foreign currency or click cancel.

14 ➤ Click **Cancel** in the Select Foreign Currency list window. Sarah's Kitchen Stores does not plan to sell to the U.S. or any other country at the current time. See Chapter 14 for information on Foreign Currency.

15 ➤ Click the box again to remove the ✓ in ☐ Allow Transactions in a Foreign Currency.

Forms

16 ➤ In the left pane, click on **Forms**.

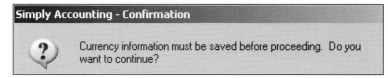

Simply needs to save currency information, even though you changed the setting to the original default setting.

17 ➤ Click **Yes**.

	Next Form Number	Verify Number Sequence	Confirm Printing/E-mail	Print Company Address on	Print in Batches	Check for Duplicates
Invoices:	922	☑	☐	☑	☐	☑
Sales Quotes:	1	☑	☐	☑	☐	--
Sales Order Confirmations:	--	--	☐	☑	☐	--
Receipts:		☐	☐	☑	☐	☐
Statements:	--	--	--	☑	--	--
Customer Deposits:		☐	--	--	--	--
Purchase Orders:	1	☑	☐	☑	☐	--
Cheques:	--	☑	☐	☑	☐	--
Deposit Slips:	--	☐	☐	--	--	--

Fig. 4-19: Settings – Forms tab (see side note box).

> **ⓘ**
> There is no box for Cheque Number. The next cheque number will be entered when you set up bank accounts (see Exercise 4-8, step 6).

The number entered in these fields is the next number that will print on the appropriate form. Simply has the capability to print any number from 1 to 200,000,000 on all forms.

18 ➤ `Invoices:`   This number is the invoice number that will print on the next sales invoice to be issued by Sarah's Kitchen Stores. Type **922**, `Tab`.

19 ➤ `Sales Quotes:`   This number is the next number that will print on sales quotes to be given to customers. Leave at **1**, `Tab`. Sarah's will start to use this feature.

20 ➤ `Receipts:`   Delete **1** from this field. A blank field in the receipts journal will allow you to record the cheque number received from your customer, `Tab`.

21 ➤ `Customer Deposits:`   Delete **1** from this field. If your company issued numbered printed receipts for deposits, you can assign that number to customer deposits in the Receipts Journal. Sarah's Kitchen Stores does not issue receipts for deposits at this time.

22 ➤ `Purchase Orders:`   **This number is the next number that will print on purchase** orders given to vendors. Leave at **1** (Sarah's Kitchen Stores will start using purchase orders in the near future), `Tab`.

Verify Number Sequence   **Uncheck** Deposit slips and DO NOT CHANGE the rest. This will make sure the numbers of forms identified increase by 1 each time you use the next form.

| **Confirm Printing/ E-mail** | DO NOT CHANGE. In business, you check the boxes to confirm that you want to print or e-mail a client. For classroom use, leave the boxes unchecked. |
| **Print Company Address on** | DO NOT CHANGE. When this option is ✓, the company name and address (as set up in the Company Information window) will print on forms. Note: This field is ✓ for classroom/lab use to identify students' work. In a business setting the name and address would be on the pre-printed document. |

Print in Batches

DO NOT CHANGE. You can enter many invoices during a day and then print them at one time. For classroom use, leave the boxes unchecked so you can print individual forms, as required. You will find information in Appendix F, *Printing in Batches* at www.simplyaccounting2010.nelson.com under Student Resources.

23 ➤ Check for Duplicates

Click the **Invoice** box ✓. This will verify that duplicate numbers are not used on invoices.

(See side note box.)

> If you click on the bottom computer link, "Order cheques and forms" you would be taken to a Simply Accounting Business Services window with more information about buying customized forms.

E-mail

24 ➤ Click the **E-mail** item.

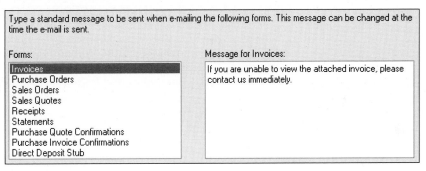

Type a standard message to be sent when e-mailing the following forms. This message can be changed at the time the e-mail is sent.

Forms:
Invoices
Purchase Orders
Sales Orders
Sales Quotes
Receipts
Statements
Purchase Quote Confirmations
Purchase Invoice Confirmations
Direct Deposit Stub

Message for Invoices:
If you are unable to view the attached invoice, please contact us immediately.

Fig. 4-20: Settings – E-mail.

DO NOT CHANGE. This text does not have an exercise to send or receive e-mail, Sarah's Kitchen Stores will not be e-mailing documents to customers or vendors. Click each of the forms and notice the wording in the message box. This wording can be changed when the form is being e-mailed.

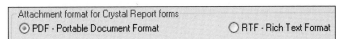

Attachment format for Crystal Report forms
⦿ PDF - Portable Document Format   ◯ RTF - Rich Text Format

DO NOT CHANGE. You can send e-mail documents to your customers and vendors in either of the two formats shown. This text does not have an exercise to send the different forms.

Dates

25 ➤ Click the **Date Format** item.

| On the screen, use: | ◯ Short Dates | ⦿ Long Dates |
| In reports, use: | ◯ Short Dates | ⦿ Long Dates |

Select the choices as shown. The dates will display and print in words (e.g., Aug) instead of 08.

Shippers

26 ➤ Click the **Shippers** item.

Sarah's Kitchen Stores is not going to record Shipper information at this time. You can return here at a later date and add information as required.

Logo

27 ➤ Click the **Logo** item.

Sarah's Kitchen Stores is not going to use a logo on forms. There is no exercise to use this feature.

Names

28 ➤ Click the **Names** item.

DO NOT CHANGE. Refer to Appendix Q, *Names Fields* at www.simplyaccounting2010.nelson.com under Student Resources.

General Accounts

29 ➤ Click the **+** at General (Accounts), the list is expanded.

Budget

30 ➤ Click the **Budget** item.

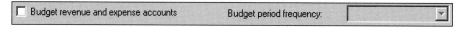

Budget	You would record budgeted amounts for reporting and
revenue	control purposes. You can select the frequency of the
and expense	budget period from a drop-down list. If this option is
accounts	checked, each Revenue and Expense account can be

You can find information on using the *Budget Feature* in Appendix E at www.simplyaccounting2010.nelson.com under Student Resources.

Budget revenue and expense accounts — You would record budgeted amounts for reporting and control purposes. You can select the frequency of the budget period from a drop-down list. If this option is checked, each Revenue and Expense account can be modified to include budgeted amounts by budget period. (See side note box.)

The Income Statement can then be displayed with a comparison of actual to budget for the period.

At this time, Sarah's Kitchen Stores is not planning to set up a budget. DO NOT CHANGE. **Leave** the box **unchecked**. This default can be changed at a later date, if desired.

Numbering

31 ➤ Click **Numbering**. DO NOT CHANGE.

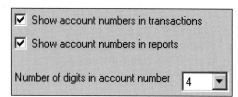

Fig. 4-21: Numbering.

Show account numbers in reports — DO NOT CHANGE. If you select this option, account numbers (e.g., 5330 for Telephone Expense) will not appear in the General Ledger printouts.

32 ➤	**Number of digits in account number**	Click the 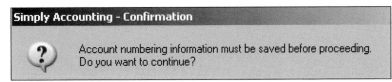. You can extend the account number up to 8 digits. **Change** to 8 digits. **Change** back to 4 digits. This text will use only 4 digits in all account numbers. DO NOT CHANGE.

Departments

33 ➤ Click **Departments**.

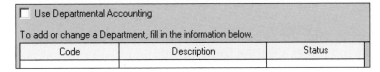

34 ➤ This confirmation is aware that you clicked the 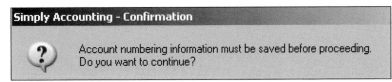, and assumes that you changed a setting. Click **Yes** to continue.

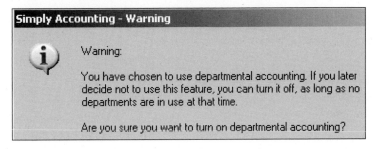

Fig. 4-22: Departmental Accounting.

35 ➤ Click **Use Departmental Accounting**, the following warning appears.

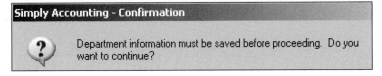

36 ➤ Select **Cancel**. Sarah's Kitchen Stores has decided not to use Departmental Accounting at this time.

Names

37 ➤ Click the **Names** item, and the following warning message appears.

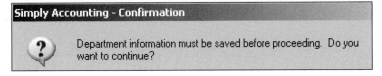

This message appears because you changed a setting in Departments and changed it back to the default. Click **Yes** to continue without creating Departments. Simply does not realize there is no change.

A list of 5 Field Names appears. DO NOT CHANGE. See Appendix Q, *Names Fields* at www.simplyaccounting2010.nelson.com under Student Resources for discussion on this topic.

Linked Accounts

38 ➤ Click the **Linked Accounts** item.

You will return here after entering the General Ledger accounts.

Payables

39 ➤   In the left pane, click on + at **Payables**, the list is expanded.

Address

40 ➤   Click the **Address** item.

> Enter default address information for new suppliers.
>
> City: | Hamilton
> Province: | Ontario
> Country: |

41 ➤   Change the information as shown. This default information will appear when you add new suppliers (vendors).

Options

42 ➤   Click the **Options** item.

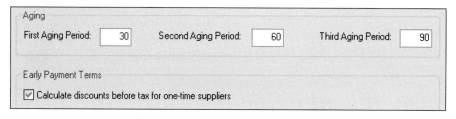

Fig. 4-23: Settings – Payables Options.

Aging	DO NOT CHANGE. Aging is a process of sorting Accounts Payable transactions in the Vendor Aged reports using predefined categories; e.g., 30, 60, or 90 days based on the current session date. Aging enables you to easily see which invoices are due within the time periods.
	Some companies use 10, 30, and/or 60 days as the aging periods. If you wish to change the aging period, you would click on the appropriate box, and type in the new setting. The second number must be larger than the first, and the third larger than the second.
43 ➤ Early Payment Terms	Click the **Calculate discounts before tax for one-time suppliers** field. A ✓ appears. This will allow cash discounts for early payments to be taken from One-time Suppliers (when appropriate) on the value of goods purchased before HST was added to the invoice value. The name Suppliers will change to Vendors after step 45.

Duty

44 ➤   Click **Duty**.

> ☐ Track duty on imported items
>
> Import Duty Account: [▼]

DO NOT CHANGE. Sarah's Kitchen Stores does not plan on importing merchandise at this time.

Names

Ignore Additional Information Titles at this time. See Appendix Q, *Names Fields* at www.simplyaccounting2010.nelson.com under Student Resources, for discussion on this topic.

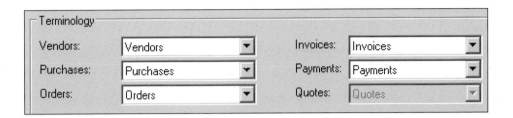

45 ➤ Click **Names**. Click each of the ▼ to see the various choices. Change the settings as shown.

Linked Accounts

You will return here after entering the General Ledger accounts.

Receivables

46 ➤ You may need to scroll down in the left hand pane to see Receivables. Click the **+** at **Receivables**. The list is expanded.

Address

47 ➤ Click the **Address** item.

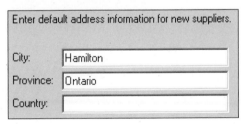

48 ➤ Change the information as shown. This default information will appear when you add new customers.

Options

49 ➤ Click the **Options** item.

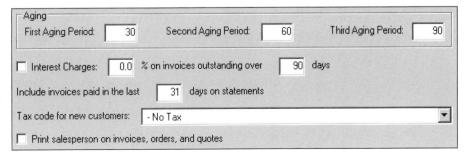

Fig. 4-24: Settings – Receivables Options.

Aging	DO NOT CHANGE (see Payables Aging).
Interest Charges	DO NOT CHANGE. Interest on overdue invoices can be calculated by checking this box. If desired, you may enter an interest rate and the number of days the invoice is overdue before interest applies. The interest charges will appear on the customer statement. When this is used, Simply shows only the amount on the statement. It does not automatically post it as an interest charge to the account. Leave the default blank.
Include invoices paid in the last 31 days on statements	DO NOT CHANGE. You can print details of paid invoices with receipts on customer statements for the selected number of days with this option. If you have cleared paid invoices from the system, no paid invoices will be printed.
Tax code for new customers	You are unable to change this field as you have not set up individual tax codes. You will set up Sales Tax codes in Exercise 4-11.

☐ Print salesperson on invoices, orders, and quotes Refer to Appendix AC, *Adding a Salesperson's Name to an Invoice* at www.simplyaccounting2010.nelson.com under Student Resources.

Discount

50 ➤ Click on **Discount**.

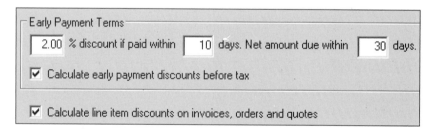

51 ➤ **Early Payment Terms**	Add the following in each box: **2**%, **10** days, net **30** days. This will allow these terms to be applied to all future invoices. However, the default can be changed in individual invoices, if desired.
52 ➤ **Calculate early payment discounts before tax**	Click **this field**. A ✓ appears. This will allow cash discounts for early payment to be taken on the value of goods purchased before HST is added to the invoice value.
53 ➤ **Calculate line item discounts on invoices, orders & quotes**	This field should have a ✓. If there is no ✓, click this field. A ✓ appears. This will allow a Disct (Discount) % to appear in Sales Invoices. See Fig. 2A-5 in Chapter 2A.

Comments

54 ➤ Click the **Comments** item.

Fig. 4-25: Settings – Comment tab.

55 ➤ **Type** the comments as shown in Fig. 4-25. They will appear on the appropriate form when recording quotes, orders and invoices.

Names

56 ➤ Click the **Names** item. DO NOT CHANGE. Click each of the ▼ to see the various choices.

> Ignore Additional Information Titles at this time. See Appendix Q, *Names Fields* at www.simplyaccounting2010.nelson.com under Student Resources, for discussion on this topic.

Linked Accounts

You will return here after entering the General Ledger accounts.

57 ➤ Click **OK** to accept the setting changes and return to the revised Home window, shown next.

Study the Home window in Fig. 4-26. Modules CUSTOMERS & SALES, and VENDORS & PURCHASES are changed to RECEIVABLES and PAYABLES. The following modules are hidden: INVENTORY & SERVICES, EMPLOYEES & PAYROLL and DIVISIONS. The middle Tasks diagram displays the Sales Quotes icon.

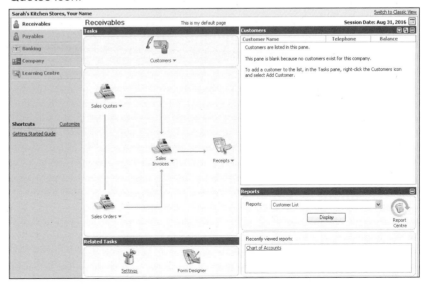

Fig. 4-26: Revised Kitchen Home window after changes.

58 ➤ Click the PAYABLES module. Notice the icon **Purchase Quotes** is not displayed as a result of the setting made in step 11, Fig. 4-18 to not use Quotes.

Step 4: Changing Printer Settings

The Network system at your school may not allow you to change the printer settings. Check with your teacher. If you click Printer Settings by mistake, the Simply program may exit and you may have to restart the Setup procedure again.

If you are NOT able to change the Printer Settings, go to Step 5: Conversion Process with Accounts.

Exercise 4-4 – Changing Printer Settings

Report & Form Options

1 ➤ If you are able to change printer settings, on the menu bar, click **Setup**, **Reports & Forms**. The Report & Form Options window is displayed.

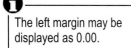

The left margin may be displayed as 0.00.

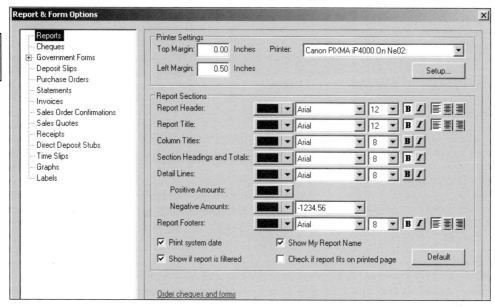

Fig. 4-27: Printer Settings window before changes. (See side note box.)

Reports

The left pane lists the various reports and forms that are available to change. The right pane lists the various selections that can be changed within the various reports and forms.

Printer Settings

This section allows you to select Top and Left Margin settings and a printer.

        Left Margin   The left margin should be **0.50** (reports will indent one-half inch from the left edge of the paper).

2 ➤ Printer   Click on the ⏷ arrow to view the printers available. In most cases do not change the default printer. If a different printer is to be used, your instructor will advise you. On some networks the printer font and size may not be changed. DO NOT CHANGE the default.

Reports Sections

This section allows you to customize the colour of various headings and titles, change the font and font size, and see the various printer settings available for each report identified. Sarah's Kitchen Stores prints with default settings, except those noted below. Sarah may change settings in the future. Cheques and invoices are not printed.

If you are able to, you will change settings for Reports and Purchase Orders. If not, it would still be worthwhile going through the steps below (without setting the defaults) in order to see the available options in each step. (See side note box.)

> **ℹ** You are not able to change printer settings for cheques as bank accounts have not been set up at this time. Refer to Exercise 4-8.

3 ➤	**Report Headers**	**Colour** ▣▼. Click on the ▼ arrow. You will see a Colour chart window. Click **Cancel** to leave the settings.
		Change *only* the Report Header and Report Title font and size in steps 4 and 5. Do not change other items.
4 ➤	**Arial**	Click on the ▼ arrow beside Arial to display the fonts that are available for the printer selected. Choose **Arial**.
5 ➤	**12**	Click on the ▼ arrow beside 12 to see the various font sizes available. You must select a size that will print the reports clearly on the paper for your printer. This may require some test prints. Choose size **10**.
6 ➤		Repeat steps 4 and 5 for Report Title.

 Settings for Bold and Italics

 Settings for left, centre and right justified.

Print system Date	DO NOT CHANGE. The current date (the computer system date) will appear at the bottom of each printed report, e.g., Printed On: Aug 31, 2010.
	This will enable you to know the date the report was printed.
Show if report is filtered	DO NOT CHANGE. If reports are filtered, a note, "This report has been filtered" will appear at the bottom-right corner of each printout.
Show My Report Name	DO NOT CHANGE. The template report name can be saved (e.g., Mrs. Kafa report) in the My Reports section of Simply. When selecting a report from **Report Centre, My Reports**, you can select the appropriately named report. When you display the report, you will see the report name in the title section of the report as follows.

> Balance Sheet As at Aug 31, 2016 - Mrs. Kafa report

7 ➤	**Check if report fits on printed page**	If this choice is not ✓, click on this choice. When printing, a message box will inform you if the printout will print over the right margin.

Purchase Orders

> 8 ➤ In the left pane click the **Purchase Orders** item.

> 9 ➤ In the right pane the selection should be ⊙ Pre-printed. If not, click on Pre-printed.

10 ➤   Form Type   Click ▾ and you will see 2 choices.

8½ × 11 in. (long source or item no.)   ▼
8½ × 7 in. (long source or item no.)

Selection **8½ x 11 in**. (**long source or item no**.) will allow more space to record information in invoice no. and other boxes. The report will print on a regular size paper. If you are using the Student version, select **8½ x 11 in**. (long source or item no.)

Selection **8½ x 7 in**. (**long source or item no**.) will allow more space to record information in invoice no. and other boxes, but will print on a smaller size page.

☐ Warn when there are less than	0 forms remaining. There are	0 forms on hand.

This option would be ✓ if Simply was checking on the remaining blank forms available. There is no exercise for this feature.

In the E-mail Form section at the bottom, you will see the Form box grayed out. This is where the e-mail Purchase Order form is located on the hard drive.

11 ➤   Click **OK** to return to the Home window.

Step 5: Conversion Process with Accounts

The next step is to enter accounting data such as accounts and account balances from the manual records of the company. This is required not only for Sarah's Kitchen Stores, but also for any company converting to Simply.

Conversion, in this chapter, means changing from one accounting system to another. There are two types of conversion:

1.   Changing from a manual system to a computerized system.
2.   Changing from one computerized system to another computerized system.

When a company buys the Simply software program it has two choices:

a)   After setting up the Chart of Accounts, the company can record transactions immediately without entering previous history balances in the General Ledger, and Customer and/or Vendor subledgers. They would add previous history during the next month(s), but before a year-end.

b)   The company can set up the Chart of Accounts, then record their previous history balances at a specific time, normally from the end of a month. This is done when all accounting records from the original accounting system have been updated, and the Trial Balance and financial statements have been prepared.

Regardless of the method the company chooses, the new computerized Chart of Accounts should accurately reflect the company's Chart of Accounts. Then the Trial Balance amounts, and customers' and vendors' balances are entered in the computer records.

It is possible to have more than one conversion date. A company may decide to use a computerized GENERAL LEDGER on one date; e.g., January 1, and could start to use the computerized RECEIVABLE subledger on another date, e.g., March 1. In either case, the accounts and balances for the manual system and computer system must be the same on the dates when information is converted.

At this time, both the manual and computer records should agree. This specific time is called the **Conversion Date**. Simply refers to it as the **Earliest Transaction Date**. When all information and dollar values have been entered in Simply and they agree with the old records, you will change the system from a HISTORY mode to a READY mode. After this date, the company would stop using the manual records and start to enter transactions using the computer system. (See side note box.)

Sarah's Kitchen Stores has decided to use method **b)**. They will take the time to set up the completed company records, namely, COMPANY, ACCOUNTS PAYABLE and ACCOUNTS RECEIVABLE modules before recording new transactions.

The Chart of Accounts

Part of the conversion process is to ensure that the General Ledger accounts are the same for the manual system and the computerized system. The G/L accounts for Sarah's Kitchen Stores need to be set up.

Using the COMPANY module of Simply you can add, change or delete the G/L accounts. Before making any changes, it is important to understand how Simply sets up the chart of accounts.

The following is a summary of the information provided at the beginning of the chapter: Step 1 Account Number Structure.

Account Numbering System in Simply

The account numbering system for this company and all companies in this text starts with 1000 and ends with 5999. Each section of a classified statement must always:

- start with an **H** account (Group Heading), and
- end with a **T** (Group Total) account.

Postable accounts that require a subtotal are shown in the first dollar value column on the left as an **A** (subgroup Account).

The account that adds the **A** type of accounts is the **Subgroup Total** account and is shown in the second dollar column.

Postable accounts that do not require a subtotal are shown in the second dollar value column on the right as a **G** (group account).

Leave spaces between account numbers for adding accounts in the future without having to make new account groups to accommodate the new accounts. For example, if you start **Cash In Bank** at 1050, and the next account Is Accounts Receivables, assign Accounts Receivable number 1060 so that if you need to insert other bank accounts in the future, you can assign them numbers close to the first bank account.

You will now start setting up Sarah's Kitchen Stores, Chart of Accounts. You will be starting with the scratch Chart of Accounts, which Simply sets up when you select the option to start the Chart of Accounts from scratch (shown next). You will add accounts under each account category. Refer to Fig. 4-33 (Chart of Accounts) to see the accounts and structure that you will be setting up.

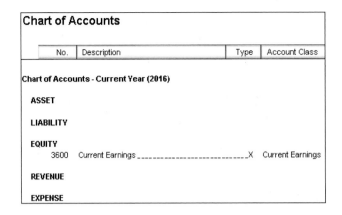

Exercise 4-5 – Setting Up (Adding) the Chart of Accounts

To Add an Account

For illustrative purposes, you will add 3 accounts:

> **1000 Current Assets**
> **1005 Petty Cash**
> **1010 Bank Account Chequing**

There are 3 ways to enter new accounts:

A. From the Home window, click on the **COMPANY** module, click the ▾ at Chart of Accounts to view the 4 choices. The blue quill pen icon (History) means this module is still in History mode. Select **Add Account** to display Fig. 4-28a.

B. From the Home window, click the Company module, then the **Chart of Accounts** icon to open the Accounts window, click the **Create** 🗐 icon. The General Ledger window (Fig. 4-28a) will be displayed. This method will be shown for information purposes for Ex 4-5.

C. Click **Setup**, **Setup Guide**, click on **Accounts** to open new window, Fig 4-28b.

1 ➤ You will use method **B** to display the General Ledger window, as you will be using the Accounts window in step 18.

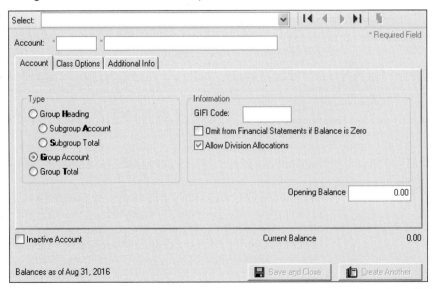

Fig. 4-28a: New Account window. *Note the red * referencing Required Field.*

2 ➤ Account   Notice that there are 3 tabs. Type **1000** a number within the Asset section. Notice that three new tabs appear: Reconciliation & Deposits, Related Historical Accounts and Notes. The Reconciliation & Deposits tab is covered in Chapter 12.

The Related Historical Accounts tab information is created by Simply when you move into a new fiscal year. The information for this tab is only available when you have recorded transactions in Premium in a previous fiscal year.

Notes .A feature to add Notes to display and print on Financial Statements. See Appendix U, *Add Notes/Footer to Statements* at www.simplyaccounting2010.nelson.com under Student Resources, for more information.

Tab to move to the next field which is the Account Name field. Type **Current Assets**, Tab .

3 ➤ Type   Click ○ Group Heading . Current Assets is the heading (H) for the Current Assets section on the Balance Sheet.

You will see that some of the options (under GIFI Code) are now hidden. They will be seen and explained in step 13.

Information

GIFI Code: DO NOT CHANGE. This field is used for electronic filing of Corporate Tax Returns. Sarah's Kitchen Stores is not a corporation.

4 ➤ Click on Class Options tabs.

> There are no Class Options for accounts which are used as a Group Heading, Subgroup Total, or Group Total.

5 ➤ Click on the Additional Info tab. You can add up to 5 additional lines of description about this account (e.g., the manager or assistant manager responsible for the account). See Appendix Q, *Names Fields* at www.simplyaccounting2010.nelson.com under Student Resources for information about these fields.

6 ➤ Click on the Reconciliation & Deposits tab.

> Account Reconciliation cannot be performed on Group Heading, Subgroup Total, Group Total, and most linked accounts.

The Options are available only for **postable** type accounts (**A** and **G**).

7 ➤ Click on the Related Historical Accounts tab.

> There are no Related Historical Accounts for accounts which are used as a Group Heading, Subgroup Total, or Group Total.

8 ➤ Click on the Notes tab. As mentioned in step 2, you can add notes to display and print on Financial statements.

9 ➤ Click once again on Account tab. Click **Save and Close**, **X** to return to the Home window.

10 ➤ From the menu bar, click **Setup**, **Setup Guide**, **Accounts** to display the Accounts window (Fig 4-28b).

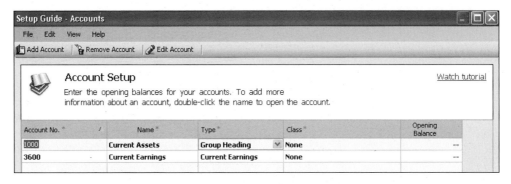

Fig. 4-28b: New Account Setup window. Note the red * Required Fields.

Account 1000 is there from the previous steps.

11 ➤ Account   Below account 3600 Type **1005**, [Tab].

12 ➤ Name   Type **Petty Cash**, [Tab].

13 ➤ Type   Click the [▼]. Select **Subgroup Account** because this
                     account will require a subtotal. [Tab].

Remember: If you use a **Subgroup Account (A)**, then you must also use a
Subgroup Total (S) after the last A in a group.

14 ➤ Class   Click the [▼]. A list of account classes displays. They can be
                     used for sorting and filtering reports in later versions of the
                     Simply program. Enter the classes as indicated. (See side
                     note box.)

                     Not all classes are discussed below. (See side note box.)

The author has used a minimum number of account class options in the setup of accounts to allow you to understand the basic setup of the account classes without spending too much time on it.

Account classes can be changed at a later time if the business needs to break down the accounts into specific groupings.

Asset:	All Items owned by a company.
Cash:	Amount of cash on hand.
Bank:	A bank account (chequing or savings).
Credit Card Receivable:	Amount owed by credit card company to you for sales made to customers.
Accounts Receivable:	Amount that is owed to you for goods and services sold on credit.
Other Receivable:	Amount that is owed to you that is not a normal sale of goods and services (e.g., sale of old office equipment).
Inventory:	Goods on hand for sale to customers.
Current Asset:	Assets that will be replaced/or used up within a year (e.g., Prepaid Items, Investments, etc.).
Capital Asset:	An asset that will be used for a long period of time (e.g., Building, Computer Equipment, etc.).
Other Asset:	An asset that does not fit into any of the other categories.

15 ➤   Sarah has decided to keep a minimum number of classes of accounts as
            shown with the names of the accounts (see Fig. 4-33). Simply requires
            certain types with specific accounts such as the Accounts Receivable ledger
            account to be an Accounts Receivable Option type. Select **Cash**. [Tab].

	Opening Balance	DO NOT CHANGE. Sarah's Kitchen Stores has decided to add all the accounts and the account structure (**H A S G T**) before adding the account balances in Exercise 4-10. See side box.

You may also add each account's balance as you create the account. Accounts and Class Options are entered in this exercise, and Account Balances will be entered in Exercise 4-10. When you become more comfortable with account types and contra balances, you may try to add the account balances as you create the accounts.

16 ➤ Name   Double-click on **Petty Cash** to display the General Ledger window.

Information Section

	GIFI Code	DO NOT CHANGE.
	Omit from Financial Statements if Balance is Zero	DO NOT CHANGE. If you click this box and the account has a zero balance, it will not show when viewing or printing the financial statements. Sarah's Kitchen Stores has decided to show all accounts when viewing or printing statements.
	Allow Division Allocation	DO NOT CHANGE. Sarah's Kitchen Stores will not use the DIVISION module. The DIVISION or PROJECT module will be discussed in Chapter 11. Leave blank.

Class Options Tab

17 ➤ Next Deposit No. [＿＿＿＿] Sarah Kitchen Stores will not keep track of receipts by deposit numbers. Remove **1**, Tab.

To see information about the different types of classes, you would click on the **Help** menu, **Contents**, **Search**, and in the top field, type **classes**. You will see a list of categories below classes. Click on any one that you would like information about. **Exit** the Help window. Click Save and Close.

18 ➤ Create account **1010 Bank Account Chequing**, with **Subgroup Account** type and with a **Class Option of Bank**. Double-click on **Name**, and click the **Class Options** tab.

19 ➤ Institution: Click on ▼ and you will see a list of banks that allow electronic transfer of funds using Simply. Select **Other**.

DO NOT CHANGE the Branch, Transit Number, and Account Number fields.

20 ➤ Next Deposit No. [＿＿＿＿] Sarah Kitchen Stores will not keep track of receipts by deposit numbers. Remove **1**, Tab.

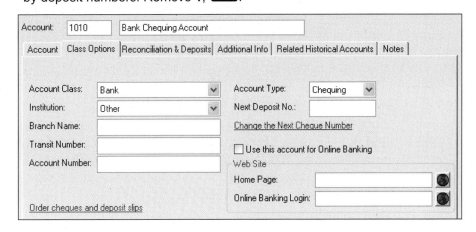

Fig. 4-29: Bank Class Options window.

If you choose the Account Class Option: Cash, you will be able to link the Principal Bank Account in Exercise 4-9 (Figures 4-35 and 4-36), but you will not be able to record the Next Cheque No. as shown in Exercise 4-8, step 6.

When you attempt to record a Payments Journal entry, you will see the following warning message.

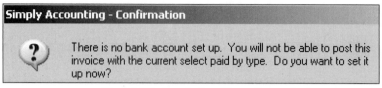

Fig. 4-30: Bank Confirmation window.

If you choose an Account Class Option other than Cash or Bank (e.g., Asset, Current Asset), the Principal Bank Account in Exercise 4-9 (Figures 4-35 and 4-36) will not display the Bank account for linking.

21 ➤ Click **Save and Close** to add the account.

22 ➤ After reviewing the possible warning messages below, turn to the next page to create the remaining accounts from the lists (2 pages).

Note: If you attempt to add an account number that has already been set up, you may see the following error message. If you see this message, click OK to continue.

You should see a message similar to the following:

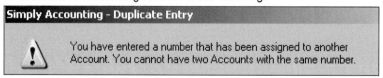

Click **OK**. Remember that the account number has already been entered/created.

Note: Simply may not allow you to enter more accounts after entering the first screen or later. If this happens, click Close. You will see an error message about accounts are not in logical order or the accounts are not balanced. Click **Continue** to be returned to the Setup Guide. Click **Accounts** and continue entering accounts.

Some users prefer **HEADING** and **TOTAL** names in all capital letters, while others capitalize only the first letter (**Heading** and **Total**). Sarah's Kitchen Stores uses the latter format.

* When you create account 1080 Cash Total, select type Subgroup Total account **S**.

To **delete** an account set up in error, see Exercise **4-6**. To **modify** an account, see Exercise **4-7**.

Acct #	Account Name	Type of Account	Code	Class
1011	Bank Account Credit Card Receivable	Subgroup Account	A	Credit Card Receivables (no other changes)
1080	Cash Total	Subgroup Total	S*	(See side note box.)
1200	Accounts Receivable	Subgroup Account	A	Accounts Receivable
1210	Allowance for Bad Debts	Subgroup Account	A	Allowance for Bad Debts
1219	Net Accounts Receivable	Subgroup Total	S	
1240	Store/Office Supplies/Prepaid	Group Account	G	Current Asset
1260	Inventory of Goods	Group Account	G	Inventory
1299	Total Current Assets	Group Total	T	
1400	Capital Assets	Group Heading	H	
1410	Display Equipment	Subgroup Account	A	Capital Asset
1415	Accumulated Amortization Display Eq	Subgroup Account	A	Accum. Amort. & Depreciation
1419	Display Equipment: Net Value	Subgroup Total	S	
1420	Office Furniture/Equipment	Subgroup Account	A	Capital Asset
1425	Accumulated Amort. Office Fur/Eq	Subgroup Account	A	Accum. Amort. & Depreciation
1429	Office Furniture/Equipment: Net Val	Subgroup Total	S	
1499	Net Capital Assets	Group Total	T	

The **Liabilities** section heading is automatically put in by the program. Create the Liability accounts as shown next:

2000	Current Liabilities	Group Heading	H	
2010	Accounts Payable	Group Account	G	Accounts Payable
2030	Visa Credit Card Payable	Subgroup Account	G	Credit Card Payable*

> * DO NOT CHANGE other fields in the Class Options tab for this account.

2210	HST Charged on Sales	Subgroup Account	A	Sales Tax Payable
2220	HST Paid on Purchases	Subgroup Account	A	Sales Tax Payable
2230	Net HST Owing/Receivable	Subgroup Total	S	
2299	Total Current Liabilities	Group Total	T	
2300	Long Term Liabilities	Group Heading	H	
2310	Bank Loan Payable	Group Account	G	Long Term Debt
2399	Total Long Term Liabilities	Group Total	T	

The **Equity** section heading is automatically put in by the program. Create the Equity accounts as shown next:

3000	Owner's Equity	Group Heading	H	
3020	Capital Beginning Sarah Kafa	Subgroup Account	A	Retained Earnings
3030	Capital Additional Investments	Subgroup Account	A	Equity
3040	Drawings Sarah Kafa	Subgroup Account	A	Equity
3050	Net Capital before Current Earnings	Subgroup Total	S	
3699	Total Owner's Equity	Group Total	T	

Notice that the full details of the Statement of Owner's Equity have been built into the equity section of the Balance Sheet (including the Current Earnings account #3600).

The **Revenue** section heading is automatically put in by the program. Create the Revenue accounts below:

4000	Sales Revenue	Group Heading	H	
4010	Sales Kitchen Cabinets	Subgroup Account	A	Revenue
4020	Sales Kitchen Sinks	Subgroup Account	A	Revenue
4030	Sales Kitchen Accessories	Subgroup Account	A	Revenue
4099	Sales Total	Subgroup Total	S	Revenue
4210	Sales Returns	Subgroup Account	A	Revenue
4220	Sales Discounts	Subgroup Account	A	Revenue
4229	Sales Deductions Total	Subgroup Total	S	Revenue
4399	Sales Net	Group Total	T	

The **Expense** section heading is put in by the program. Create the Cost of Goods Sold and Expense accounts next.

5000	Cost of Goods Sold	Group Heading	H	
5020	CGS Beginning Inventory	Subgroup Account	A	Cost of Goods Sold
5030	Purchases	Subgroup Account	A	Cost of Goods Sold
5040	Purchase Returns	Subgroup Account	A	Cost of Goods Sold
5050	Purchase Discounts	Subgroup Account	A	Cost of Goods Sold
5060	Goods Available for Sale	Subgroup Total	S	
5090	CGS Ending Inventory	Group Account	G	Cost of Goods Sold
5099	Total Cost of Goods Sold	Group Total	T	

5300	Store Expenses	Group Heading	H	
5310	Rent Expense	Group Account	G	Expense
5320	Store Salaries Expense	Group Account	G	Expense
5330	Telephone Expense	Group Account	G	Expense
5340	Advertising Expense	Group Account	G	Expense
5350	Amortization Expense-All	Group Account	G	Expense
5360	Delivery Costs to Customers	Group Account	G	Expense
5370	Bad Debts Expense	Group Account	G	Expense
5380	Utilities (Hydro/Water) Expense	Group Account	G	Expense
5399	Total Store Expenses	Group Total	T	
5500	Other Expenses	Group Heading	H	
5510	Bank Charges Expense	Group Account	G	Expense
5520	Credit Card Charges	Group Account	G	Expense
5530	Bank Interest on Loan	Group Account	G	Expense
5599	Total Other Expenses	Group Total	T	

You will not be able to view the Income Statement or Balance Sheet until all sections are set up.

If you place an account in a wrong section, refer to Appendix X, *Removing an Account from a Wrong Section* at www.simplyaccounting20 10.nelson.com under Student Resources to correct the account.

You should be aware that there are many different ways to number and structure accounts. Some companies would subtotal accounts 5510 and 5520 to show bank costs before Interest on loans. (See side note box.)

23 ➤ When you have entered all the accounts click on the **Validate** button. If everything is okay, you will see Fig. 4-31. If your accounts are not in logical order, Exercise 4-6 will provide some insight as to what needs to be done to resolve these issues.

To Delete an Account

To delete an account, complete the following steps:

Exercise 4-6 – Deleting an Account

This exercise is used to show you the steps involved in removing an account.

1 ➤ Click on account **5530 Bank Interest on Loan**, to highlight the account in blue.

2 ➤ Click 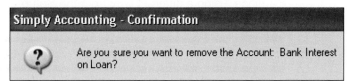 icon, and the following message box will request confirmation that you want to remove the account.

Simply Accounting - Confirmation

(?) Are you sure you want to remove the Account: Bank Interest on Loan?

3 ➤ Click **No**. If you wanted to remove the account, you would click **Yes** and the account would be removed.

Review and Check Account Coding Changes Made

There are three ways to verify that the account structure you added is correct.

a) Use the Validate button.

b) Display an Income Statement or Balance Sheet to indicate the structure is correct.

c) From the Home page, click on the Chart of Accounts icon, and click the validity of accounts icon.

4 ➤ Click the **Validate** button. If there are no errors you will see the message box Fig. 4-31.

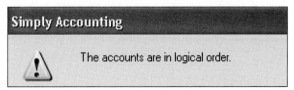

Simply Accounting

⚠ The accounts are in logical order.

Fig. 4-31: Accounts in order.

5 ➤ Click **OK**. Click **Close** to return to the Home window.

6 ➤ **Display** an Income Statement or Balance Sheet. If there are any errors in your account coding (accounts not in logical order) the message box Fig. 4-32 will advise you where the account coding error has occurred. If there are a number of coding errors, you may see a similar message box a number of times.

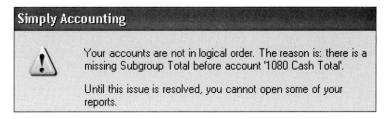

Simply Accounting

⚠ Your accounts are not in logical order. The reason is: there is a missing Subgroup Total before account '1080 Cash Total'.

Until this issue is resolved, you cannot open some of your reports.

Fig. 4-32: Example of an Account Coding Error window.

It may be helpful to display or print the Chart of Accounts and check your structure near the account number given. You would then change the account coded in error and try again.

You may need to do this a number of times due to an incorrect **H A S G T** structure.

7 ➤   You may need to repeat steps 4, 5 and 6 until such time as your **H A S G T** account structure is validated as "logical."

To Modify an Account

Sarah has decided that she wants to change the name of account 3600 Current Earnings, using a different way from the Setup guide.

Exercise 4-7 – To Modify an Account

---

1 ➤   From the Account Setup window, locate and double-click the **3600 Current Earnings** Account No. or Name column.

The General Ledger window similar to Fig. 4-28a will appear.

2 ➤   **Account**   Change the name to: **Net Income from Income Statement,** ⌨ Tab .

As explained earlier, this account will transfer the balance of the Net Income from the Income Statement to the Owner's Equity section of the Balance Sheet.

The Account with no Type coding cannot be changed. If you clicked the Class Options tab, you will see the grayed out Account Class as Current Earnings. (See side note box.)

> ❶
> Other types of accounts could be changed; however, the Current Earning **X** account cannot be changed.

3 ➤   **GIFI Code**   Remove **3620**. A single-owner non-incorporated business does not use GIFI codes.

4 ➤   Click the ▶ or ◀ to save the changes. On the last account to be modified use the **Save and Close** button.

All the accounts have been added. Refer to Fig. 4-33.

5 ➤   **Exit** to the Home window.

Sarah's Kitchen Stores - Student Name
Chart of Accounts

ASSETS

1000 Current Assets...............................H
  1005 Petty Cash ....A Cash
  1010 Bank Account Chequing ....A Bank
  1011 Bank Account Credit Card Receivable ....A Credit Card Receivable
  1080 Cash Total...................................S
  1200 Accounts Receivable ....A Accounts Receivable
  1210 Allowance for Bad Debts ....A Allowance for Bad Debts
  1219 Net Accounts Receivable............................S
  1240 Store/Office Supplies/Prepaid ....G Current Asset
  1260 Inventory of Goods ....G Inventory
1299 Total Current Assets......................T

1400 Capital Assets.............................H
  1410 Display Equipment.....................A Capital Asset
  1415 Accumulated Amortization Display Eq........A Accum. Amort & Depre
  1419 Display Equipment: Net Value...................S
  1420 Office Furniture/Equipment.......................A Capital Asset
  1425 Accumulated Amort. Office Fur/Eq ....A Accum. Amort & Depre
  1429 Office Furniture/Equipment Net Val............S
1499 Net Capital Assets........................T

LIABILITIES

2000 Current Liabilities............................H
  2010 Accounts Payable .... G Accounts Payable
  2030 Visa Credit Card Payable .... G Credit Card Payable
  2210 HST Charged on Sales............................A Sales Tax Payable
  2220 HST Paid on Purchases ....A Sales Tax Payable
  2230 Net HST Owing/Receivable......................S
2299 Total Current Liabilities ....T

2300 Long Term Liabilities ....H
  2310 Bank Loan Payable.................................. G Long Term Debt
2399 Total Long Term Liabilities ....T

EQUITY

3000 Owner's Equity ....H
  3020 Capital Beginning Sarah Kafa ....A Retained Earnings
  3030 Capital Additional Investments....................A Equity
  3040 Drawings Sarah Kafa................................A Equity
  3050 Net Capital before Current Earnings ....S
  3600 Net Income from Income Statement...........X Current Earnings
3699 Total Owner's Equity ....T

REVENUE

4000 Sales Revenue ....H
  4010 Sales Kitchen Cabinets .... A Revenue
  4020 Sales Kitchen Sinks................................ A Revenue
  4030 Sales Kitchen Accessories....................... A Revenue
  4099 Sales Total....................................... S
  4210 Sales Returns.................................... A Revenue
  4220 Sales Discounts.................................. A Revenue
  4229 Sales Deductions Total .... S
4399 Sales Net..T

EXPENSE

5000 Cost of Goods Sold .... H
  5020 CGS Beginning Inventory...................... A Cost of Goods Sold
  5030 Purchases....................................... A Cost of Goods Sold
  5040 Purchase Returns............................... A Cost of Goods Sold
  5050 Purchase Discounts .... A Cost of Goods Sold
  5060 Goods Available for Sale....................... S
  5090 CGS Ending Inventory........................... G Cost of Goods Sold
5099 Total Cost of Goods Sold ....T

5300 Store Expenses...............................H
  5310 Rent Expense.................................G Expense
  5320 Store Salaries Expense...........................G Expense
  5330 Telephone Expense ....G Expense
  5340 Advertising Expense.............................G Expense
  5350 Amortization Expense - All ....G Expense
  5360 Delivery Cost to Customers ....G Expense
  5370 Bad Debts Expense..............................G Expense
  5380 Utilities (Hydro/Water) Expense.................G Expense
5399 Total Store Expenses ....T

5500 Other Expenses ....H
  5510 Bank Charges Expense...........................G Expense
  5520 Credit Card Charges ....G Expense
  5530 Bank Interest on Loan ....G Expense
5599 Total Other Expenses........................T

| H = Group Heading |
| A = Subgroup Account |
| S = Subgroup Total |
| G = Group Account |
| T = Group Total |

Fig. 4-33: Sarah's Kitchen Stores Chart of Accounts before linking accounts.

Exercise 4-8 – Change Next Cheque Number & Settings

You were not able to change the Payment Cheque Information in Exercise 4-3, because the bank accounts were not set up at that time. The bank accounts are now set up and you can update the next cheque number.

1 ➤ Click **Setup, Reports & Forms,** in the left pane click **Cheques**, in the right pane click `1010 Bank Account Chequing`. The window contains the default settings for Payment Cheque, Payroll Cheque and Cheque Settings.

Payment Cheque Setting

2 ➤ In the right pane ensure the selection is  .

3 ➤ At Form Type select the following to conform to the Canadian Payments Association guidelines for cheques. Information on the guidelines can be seen at Exercise 3A-12, step 8.

Form Type:	8½ × 11 in. - Easy Align	▼

Payroll Cheque Setting

4 ➤ In the right pane ensure the selection is Pre-printed .

5 ➤ At Form Type there are two Easy-Align form types available to conform to the Canadian Payments Association guidelines for cheques.

a) 8½ × 11 in. (two stub) - Easy Align

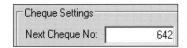

b) 8½ × 11 in. (long single stub with YTD) - Easy Align ▼

Select **b**, with 1 stub.

Cheque Setting

┌─ Cheque Settings ──────────────┐
│ Next Cheque No: 642   │
└────────────────────────────────┘

6 ➤ Type **642** for the next cheque number.

7 ➤ Click **OK** to return to the Home window.

 8 ➤ Now that your structure is correct, *This is a good time to do a **backup***. Use a folder name for your backup similar to **Sarah's Kitchen Stores_with_accts**.

The next step is to link the accounts before entering the $ values to the accounts from the Trial Balance.

Step 6: Linking Modules/Accounts

The Simply program allows you to copy information (Debits and Credits) from the RECEIVABLES and/or the PAYABLES modules to the General Ledger. This process called **Linking** permits the modules to talk to each other to ensure information is up to date across the modules.

Remember that earlier in the RECEIVABLES and PAYABLES modules you entered only one side of an entry; e.g., when you entered a SALES amount for a sales transaction on credit, Simply automatically debited ACCOUNTS RECEIVABLE and credited HST ON SALES. This is because these accounts have been linked from the RECEIVABLES module (see linked windows in this exercise). The person setting up the linked accounts determines which account data needs to be copied to General Ledger linked accounts.

One thing to remember: you can change the account structure and links **before** setting the module to **Ready**.

If you have to change the account structure and the links after setting the module to READY, you need to be very careful as you adjust the links. If you had posted transactions to a Sales Discount account and then had to change the account number, you will also need to change the links.

You can change the links between General Ledger accounts at any time.

When a General Ledger account is linked, it is impossible to delete the account without deactivating the link of the accounts. A General Ledger account cannot be deleted if it contains posted transactions.

If you had used a template to create a company, Simply would have created a set of linked accounts for you.

When using a template, there are two ways to set up or change the links:

1. Remove the links before changing the accounts.
2. Change the accounts while using the default links.

The author believes it is easier to use method 1. Remove the links, then change the default chart of accounts to the company's needs. Then you would return and link the appropriate accounts.

Changes or deletions to the linked accounts are made by using the **Setup** options from the menu bar. A link to a General Ledger account can be removed (deactivated) or changed. A deactivated linked account cannot be deleted if the Ledger account contains posted transactions.

You now need to set up your own linked accounts because you have not used a template. This will allow you to better understand the process of linking accounts.

Linking the Modules

The next step in the setup process is to make the modules "talk" to each other. Before transactions can be entered in the appropriate subledger modules, links to General Ledger accounts must be specified. This procedure is also called **Integration**.

Exercise 4-9 – Linking the Modules

COMPANY Module Links

1 ➤ From the Home window Related Tasks area, click **Settings**, click on **General** (**Accounts**), in the right pane select **Linked Accounts**, and a window similar to the following is displayed.

When you start a new fiscal year, the balances from your income and expense accounts are moved to the Retained Earnings account.

Retained Earnings: 3020 Capital Beginning Sarah Kafa

Current Earnings: 3600 Net Income from Income Statement

☐ Record opening balances in my Retained Earnings account

Fig. 4-34: COMPANY Linked Accounts window.

2 ➤ Retained Earnings: In a single-owner business, the proper account name is Capital (account 3020). Simply will not allow you to change the program heading **Retained Earnings**. Account 3020 accumulates the profits of the firm from prior years. It is automatically updated by the program when a new accounting year is started.

When you start a new fiscal year, the program closes the prior year's accounting records and transfers the balance in the Net Income from the Income Statement or Current Earnings (account 3600) to the identified Retained Earnings account.

Select **3020 Capital Beginning Sarah Kafa**, Tab .

You cannot change the program heading **Retained Earnings**.

Do not click Record opening balances in my Retained Earnings account, as it will update the account automatically. You want to record your own balance.

Current Earnings: The program transfers the year-to-date Net Income or Loss from the Income Statement, and adds the value to the Equity section of the Balance Sheet.

3 ➤ When your window resembles Fig. 4-34, move to the PAYABLES module as shown next.

PAYABLES Module Links

1 ➤ In the left pane click **Payables,** in the right pane select **Linked Accounts**, to display the Payables Linked Accounts window.

When you process invoices or payments, these accounts are used as needed.

Principal Bank Account: 1010 Bank Account Chequing

Accounts Payable: 2010 Accounts Payable

Freight Expense:

Early Payment Purchase Discount: 5050 Purchase Discounts

Prepayments and Prepaid Orders: 2010 Accounts Payable

Fig. 4-35: Payables Linked Accounts window.

2 ➤ Select the accounts shown above.

Principal Bank Account   **1010 Bank Account Chequing**. This will allow the program to credit the bank account in the General Ledger when you record a cheque being issued in the PAYABLES module.

Accounts Payable	**2010 Accounts Payable**. This will allow the program to credit ACCOUNTS PAYABLE in the General Ledger when you purchase goods or services on credit. It will also debit ACCOUNTS PAYABLE when you return goods and issue cheques.
Freight Expense	Leave this field blank. This account is used for freight costs that cannot be included in purchases. Sarah's Kitchen Stores does not use this account.
Purchase Discount	**5050 Purchase Discounts**. This is the account Simply will credit when a purchase discount is taken on a purchase merchandise for resale invoice.
Prepayments and Prepaid Orders	**2010 Accounts Payable**. This is the account Simply will debit when a prepayment is made on a purchase order.

3 ➤ In the left pane, click **Receivables**. In the right pane select **Linked Accounts**, to display the Receivables Linked Accounts window.

RECEIVABLES Module Links

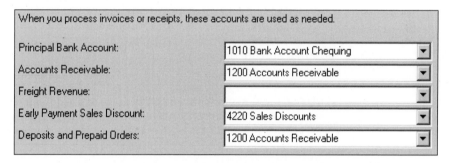

Fig. 4-36: RECEIVABLES Linked Accounts window.

4 ➤ Select the accounts shown above.

Principal Bank Account	**1010 Bank Account Chequing**. Receipts from customers entered in the Receipts journal will be debited to this account in the General Ledger.
Accounts Receivable	**1200 Accounts Receivable**. This account will be automatically debited and credited when entering sales transactions for customers.
Freight Revenue	Leave this field blank. This account is used for **freight** revenue that is not part of sales. Sarah's Kitchen Stores does not use this account.
Sales Discount	**4220 Sales Discount,** for paying early (within discount terms), is taken off a sales invoice.
Deposits and Prepaid Orders	**1200 Accounts Receivable**. This account will be automatically credited when a deposit is received on a Sales Order.

5 ➤ Click **OK** and you are returned to the Home window.

Step 7: Entering Opening G/L Account Balances (History)

Important: Back up your data before proceeding.

You have now set up the chart of accounts, but the ledger accounts do not have the current manual record dollar balances. We need to enter the August 31, 2016 Trial Balance so that the starting point in the computerized system is the ending point of the manual records.

As you have learned before, Simply structures G/L accounts into five categories (or groups):

1. Assets
2. Liabilities
3. Equity
4. Revenue
5. Expense

Simply also breaks up the previous categories into subgroups (class options) as seen in Exercise 4-5, step 14. How does Simply know whether an amount entered is a debit or a credit? The answer is based on the **normal balance** of the account.

If the account has a normal **debit balance** (e.g., asset – OFFICE SUPPLIES), then a **positive** amount entered is a **debit** and a negative amount, for a contra account, is entered for a **credit**.

Similarly, if the account has a normal **credit balance** (e.g., SALES) then a **positive** value entered is a **credit** and a **negative** amount, for a contra account, is entered for a **debit**.

VERY IMPORTANT:

To enter a **contra balance** (a decrease) to an Asset, Liability, Equity or Revenue account (normal debit balance) you must enter the amounts with a **negative**. For example, DRAWINGS is an Equity section contra account. **Equity** normally has a credit balance. When you enter the Drawings amount with a **negative** sign it will cause Simply to **debit** it.

To enter a **Sales Return** or a **Purchase Return**, you would enter the amount with a **negative** sign. As SALES RETURNS is a contra (decrease) balance to SALES (with a normal credit balance), entering a negative amount will cause Simply to **debit** it. On the other hand, PURCHASE RETURNS is a contra (decrease) balance to PURCHASES (with a normal debit balance), so entering a negative amount will cause Simply to **credit** it.

Here are the rules for entering debits or credits to accounts:

#	*Category/ Group*	*Normal Balance*	*Normal Balance to be entered*	*Contra Balance to be entered*
1	Asset	Debit	Positive	Negative (Credit)
2	Liability	Credit	Positive	Negative (Debit)
3	Equity	Credit	Positive	Negative (Debit)
4	Revenue	Credit	Positive	Negative (Debit)
5	Cost of Goods and/or Expenses	Debit	Positive	Negative (Credit)

Sarah's Kitchen Stores, Your Name
Trial Balance As At Aug 31, 2016

		Debits	Credits
1005	Petty Cash	100.00	-
1010	Bank Account Chequing	17,106.00	-
1011	Bank Account Credit Card Receivable	0.00	-
1200	Accounts Receivable	12,848.10	-
1210	Allowance for Bad Debts	-	550.00
1240	Store/Office Supplies/Prepaid	400.00	-
1260	Inventory of Goods	102,500.00	-
1410	Display Equipment	30,700.00	-
1415	Accumulated Amortization Display Eq	-	11,000.00
1420	Office Furniture/Equipment	8,125.00	-
1425	Accumulated Amort. Office Fur/Eq	-	3,450.00
2010	Accounts Payable	-	12,134.25
2030	Visa Credit Card Payable	-	0.00
2210	HST Charged on Sales	-	3,517.50
2220	HST Paid on Purchases	1,410.00	-
2310	Bank Loan Payable	-	51,256.00
3020	Capital Beginning Sarah Kafa	-	83,496.35
3030	Capital Additional Investments	-	0.00
3040	Drawings Sarah Kafa	16,900.00	-
4010	Sales Kitchen Cabinets	-	338,165.00
4020	Sales Kitchen Sinks	-	22,560.00
4030	Sales Kitchen Accessories	-	53,289.00
4210	Sales Returns	6,200.00	-
4220	Sales Discounts	5,731.00	-
5020	CGS Beginning Inventory	91,500.00	-
5030	Purchases	308,986.00	-
5040	Purchase Returns	-	12,600.00
5050	Purchase Discounts	-	7,212.00
5090	CGS Ending Inventory	-	102,500.00
5310	Rent Expense	16,800.00	-
5320	Store Salaries Expense	46,980.00	-
5330	Telephone Expense	3,216.00	-
5340	Advertising Expense	7,468.00	-
5350	Amortization Expense-All	0.00	-
5360	Delivery Costs to Customers	9,645.00	-
5370	Bad Debts Expense	0.00	-
5380	Utilities (Hydro/Water) Expense	1,796.00	-
5510	Bank Charges Expense	743.00	-
5520	Credit Card Charges	9,842.00	-
5530	Bank Interest on Loan	2,734.00	-
		701,730.10	701,730.10

Fig. 4-37a: Sarah's Kitchen Stores Trial Balance.

Note: This information will be recorded in Exercise 4-10.

Sarah's Kitchen Stores, Student's Name
BALANCE SHEET As at Aug 31, 2016

ASSETS		Column 1 Subgroup	Column 2 Group Subtotal Total
Current Assets	H		
Petty Cash	A	100.00	
Bank Account Chequing	A	17,106.00	
Bank Account Credit Card Receivable	A	0.00	
Cash Total	S		17,206.00
Accounts Receivable	A	12,848.10	
Allowance for Bad Debts	A	-550.00	
Net Accounts Receivable	S		12,298.10
Store/Office Supplies/Prepaid	G		400.00
Inventory of Goods	G		102,500.00
Total Current Assets	T		132,404.10
Capital Assets	H		
Display Equipment	A	30,700.00	
Accumulated Amortization Display..	A	-11,000.00	
Display Equipment: Net Value	S		19,700.00
Office Furniture/Equipment	A	8,125.00	
Accumulated Amortization – Office F..	A	-3,450.00	
Office Furniture/Equipment: Net Val	S		4,675.00
Net Capital Assets	T		24,375.00
TOTAL ASSETS			156,779.10
LIABILITIES			
Current Liabilities	H		
Accounts Payable	G		12,134.25
Visa Credit Card Payable	G		0.00
HST Charged on Sales	A	3,517.50	
HST Paid on Purchases/Services	A	-1,410.00	
Net HST Owing/Receivable	S		2,107.50
Total Current Liabilities	T		14,241.75
Long Term Liabilities	H		
Bank Loan Payable	G		51,256.00
Total Long Term Liabilities	T		51,256.00
TOTAL LIABILITIES			65,497.75
EQUITY			
Owner's Equity	H		
Capital Beginning Sarah Kafa	A	83,496.35	
Capital Additional Investments	A	0.00	
Drawings Sarah Kafa	A	-16,900.00	
Net Capital before Current Earning	S		66,596.35
Net Income from Income Statement	X		24,685.00
Total Owner's Equity	T		91,281.35
TOTAL EQUITY			91,281.35
LIABILITIES AND EQUITY			156,779.10

Sarah's Kitchen Stores, Student's Name
INCOME STATEMENT Jan 01, 2016 to Aug 31, 2016

REVENUE		Column 1 Subgroup	Column 2 Group Subtotal Total
Sales Revenue	H		
Sales Kitchen Cabinets	A	338,165.00	
Sales Kitchen Sinks	A	22,560.00	
Sales Kitchen Accessories	A	53,289.00	
Sales Total	S		414,014.00
Sales Returns	A	-6,200.00	
Sales Discounts	A	-5,731.00	
Sales Deductions Total	S		-11,931.00
Sales Net	T		402,083.00
TOTAL REVENUE			402,083.00
EXPENSE			
Cost of Goods Sold	H		
CGS Beginning Inventory	A	91,500.00	
Purchases	A	308,986.00	
Purchase Returns	A	-12,600.00	
Purchase Discounts	A	-7,212.00	
Goods Available for Sale	S		380,674.00
CGS Ending Inventory	G		-102,500.00
Total Cost of Goods Sold	T		278,174.00
Store Expenses	H		
Rent Expense	G		16,800.00
Store Salaries Expense	G		46,980.00
Telephone Expense	G		3,216.00
Advertising Expense	G		7,468.00
Amortization Expense-All	G		0.00
Delivery Costs to Customers	G		9,645.00
Bad Debts Expense	G		0.00
Utilities (Hydro/Water) Expense	G		1,796.00
Total Store Expenses	T		85,905.00
Other Expenses	H		
Bank Charges Expense	G		743.00
Credit Card Charges	G		9,842.00
Bank Interest on Loan	G		2,734.00
Total Other Expenses	T		13,319.00
TOTAL EXPENSE			377,398.00
NET INCOME			24,685.00

Fig. 4-37b: Balance Sheet and Income Statement after changes (with codes).

Account names with boxes around them, | ASSETS | | TOTAL REVENUE | and others, are automatically put in by the computer program. You cannot delete or change them.

Note: This information will be recorded in Exercise 4-10.

Exercise 4-10 – Entering Opening G/L Balances (History)

One **VERY IMPORTANT thing to remember:** You may change the balances you have entered for G/L accounts up until you set the modules to **Ready** (ready to record transactions). Once the modules are **Ready**, balances can be changed only by making journal entries. Setting modules to **Ready** is covered in Exercise 4-15.

1 ➤ From the menu bar, click **Setup, Setup Guide, Accounts**.

Group Heading (H) type of accounts, (a non-postable account), do not have amounts associated with it.

Subgroup Accounts (S) and **Group Accounts (G)** accounts have amounts posted to them.

Subgroup Total (S) and **Group Totals (T)** and the **Current Earnings (X)** account balances are non-postable accounts, but have amounts that are calculated by Simply based on the balances you enter for the corresponding postable accounts.

---

2 ➤ Click on the **Opening Balance** field for **1005 Petty Cash** (from Fig. 4-37a).

3 ➤ **Opening Balance** Type **100** [Tab]. Simply puts in .00 to input 100.00.

If you make a mistake in entering the dollar amount or you forgot to press the negative (minus) key for an opposite balance, you can return to the field and correct the amount. The new amounts will replace the incorrect values you entered before.

4 ➤ Move down the **Opening Balance column**, where the 0.00 fields are, and **continue entering balances** from the Trial Balance (Fig. 4-37a), subject to the Contra Account Balance notes in the next section. If the account does *not* have a 0.00 displayed, it is a non-postable account like an H (Group Heading), S (Subgroup Total), or T (Group Total).

5 ➤ See steps 6 and 7 for entering a contra account balance.

Contra Account Balance

As you have learned earlier, **Contra** means **opposite**. For example, a **contra asset account** (e.g., ACCUMULATED AMORTIZATION of an asset account such as a truck or computers) is placed in the Asset section, but since it **decreases** the value of the asset, it is entered with a **negative** sign, causing Simply to **credit** this account, instead of the normal debit entry for Assets.

Other examples of Contra accounts are:

Section	*Contra Account Name*
Asset	Allowance for Bad Debts
	Accumulated Amortization Display Eq
	Accumulated Amortization Office Fur/Eq
Liability	HST Paid on Purchases
Equity	Owner's Withdrawals (**Drawings** in a sole proprietorship)
	Dividends Declared (used in a corporation)

| **Revenue** | Sales Returns & Allowances |
| | Sales Discounts |

Cost of Goods Sold	Purchase Returns & Allowances
	Purchase Discounts
	Ending Inventory

6 ➤ Click on the **0.00** field, for the **Allowance for Bad Debts** account.

7 ➤ Opening Balance   Type **-550 (negative)**, ⬛Tab . The -550.00 shows up in the Accounts window in the Debit column with a negative -550.00. If you display a Trial Balance, you will see the amount in the Credit column.

Continue entering the **other accounts**.

Only **postable** accounts [Subgroup (**A**) and Group (**G**)] have balances.

Subgroup totals and Group Totals are calculated automatically. The **X** account balance is calculated automatically based on the total of revenues less expenses (net income).

If you do not enter all the account balances during one session and you need to quit, or if you have an error in the amounts you entered, you will receive a message window similar to the following:

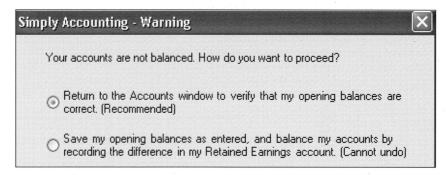

8 ➤ Select the first choice and check the amounts entered. *Note*: Verify that you have recorded the Contra accounts with negative amounts. If the amounts appear correct, see step 9.

9 ➤ Select the 2nd choice: Save my opening balances as entered.

This window will allocate the amount difference to the 3020 Capital Beginning Sarah Kafa (Retained Earning account). The 'Cannot undo' means that you can't undo the balance at this time. You can amend amounts that are in error.

10 ➤ Print a Trial Balance and check that the amounts agree with the amounts in Fig 4-37a.

11 ➤ Return to the Setup Guide and correct the Opening Balance amounts.

You can take your time to locate the error(s). When the account with the error is found (e.g., Sales discount entered as a positive amount and should have been a negative amount), return to the Setup Guide and update the accounts that have the errors.

12 ➤ When all corrected account balances have been entered, Click Close and you are returned to the Setup Guide window, without the error message from step 7. **Exit** to the Home window.

Displaying the Trial Balance

13 ➤ Display the **Trial Balance**. Check that the amounts agree with the Trial Balance in Fig. 4-37a and make corrections if necessary.

14 ➤ It would be a good idea to print the Trial Balance, Income Statement and Balance Sheet. Compare them to Fig. 4-37a and Fig. 4-37b. This would be done in an office setting to prove that the starting computer General Ledger accounts agree with the manual General Ledger.

15 ➤ Back up your data before moving on. Identify the backup with a name similar to Sarah's Kitchen Stores_B4_Ready. You are returned to the Home window when the backup is complete. Make a note in your logbook similar to **Starting balances**, **not ready**. If you make a major mistake and want to start back at this point, it will be easy with a backup data file.

Step 8: Setting Up Tax Classes, Codes, Rates & Customization

In this section, you will enter the appropriate taxes (HST) with the corresponding linked accounts. You will also set up abbreviated tax codes for each tax class.

Exercise 4-11 – Setting Up Tax Classes, Codes, Rates & Customization

Taxes

1 ➤ Click **Setup**, **Settings,** in the left pane click ⊞ at **Company**, click ⊞ at **Sales Taxes**, click **Taxes** and enter the information shown in the Fig. 4-38.

To add a tax, enter the tax name on a new line in the Tax column.

Tax	Tax ID Included on Forms	Exempt from this tax?	Is this Tax taxable?	Acct. to track tax paid on purchases	Acct. to track tax charged on sales	Report on taxes
HST	R4675 2567	No	No	2220 HST Paid on Purchase	2210 HST Charged on Sales	Yes

Fig. 4-38: Sales Tax Information window.

> Using the Report on Taxes feature (Yes) will use a lot of memory space on the drive. Some firms would use the procedure shown in Exercise 3B-30 to determine the amount of HST to pay.
>
> **Report on taxes:**
> This field will accumulate the HST to be included in an HST Report. You will find information on the *Printing a Tax (HST) Report* in Appendix D at www.simplyaccounting20 10.nelson.com under Student Resources.
>
>

Tax   HST.

Tax ID Included on Forms   R4675 2567 (the Business registration number), [Tab].

Exempt from this tax?   No. The business must **collect** HST on Sales and **pay** HST on Purchases.

Is this Tax taxable?   No. In the province of Ontario, you do not pay tax on HST.

Acct. to track tax paid on purchases   Double-click in the field and scroll down and select **2220 HST Paid on Purchases.**

Acct. to track tax charged on sales   Double-click in the field and scroll down and select **2210 HST Charged on Sales**.

Report on taxes   Press the **spacebar**, or click on the field to change it to **Yes** for HST. (See side note box.)

Tax Codes

2 ➤ In the left pane, click on **Tax Codes** and enter the information shown.

To add a tax code, enter in a code and description.

To see tax code details, double-click on a tax code or description.

Code	Description	Use In
	No Tax	All journals
HS	Harmonized Tax at 13%	All journals
HI	Harmonized Tax at 8% (insurance)	All journals

Code   An abbreviation for the tax code.

Description   A description of the tax being collected.

Use In   Select All Journals.

3 ➤ Code   Double-click the **HS** field and the Tax Code Details window appears. **Type** the information as shown. The tax code HS is shown first, as it is the one that will be used in the majority of transactions.

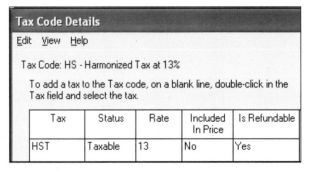

Tax Code Details

Edit   View   Help

Tax Code: HS - Harmonized Tax at 13%

To add a tax to the Tax code, on a blank line, double-click in the Tax field and select the tax.

Tax	Status	Rate	Included In Price	Is Refundable
HST	Taxable	13	No	Yes

> When entering the tax rate (e.g., **13.0**, the **.0** does not show). If the rate does not have a decimal point, the .0 does not display even if you type it in.
>
> The **Is Refundable** column (for HST) is set to **Yes** because the HST **collected** is deducted from the HST **paid** and the difference can be recovered (receive a refund) from the federal government.

(See side note box.)

4 ➤ Click **OK** to accept the information, codes and rates.

5 ➤ Repeat **steps 3** and **4** to enter the information for the HI code as follows:

Code **HI** Set up HST (for insurance) as shown.

Tax	Status	Rate	Included In Price	Is Refundable
HST	Taxable	8	No	No

6 ➤ Click **OK** and return to the Home window.

Changing Settings for Item Number and Allocations

The Journal columns are not set the way we are used to. We are going to change some of the column fields.

1 ➤ Click the **RECEIVABLES** module, click on the **Sales invoices** icon. The Journal columns do not resemble what you have used in previous chapters.

2 ➤ With a Transaction **Invoice**, click on the 🖳 **Customize Journal** icon, in the left pane click **Columns** and change the items as shown next.

Sales Invoices

3 ➤ In the right pane, click on **Item Number** (the ☐ Account is grayed out), and **Divisions**, to insert a ✓ to NOT display both items.

Sales Orders

4 ➤ In the left pane, click **+** at **Sales Orders** and **Columns**. **Repeat step 3** to NOT display Item Number and Divisions.

Sales Quotes

5 ➤ In the left pane, click **+** at **Sales Quotes** and **Columns**. **Repeat step 3** to NOT display Item Number and Divisions.

Purchase Invoices

6 ➤ In the left pane near the top, click **+** at **Purchase Invoice** and **Columns**. **Repeat step 3** to NOT display Item Number and Divisions.

Purchase Orders

7 ➤ Click on the **Purchase Orders** and **Columns**. **Repeat step 3** to NOT display Item Number and Divisions.

Make Other Payment

8 ➤ Click on the **Make Other Payment** and **Columns**. **Repeat step 3** to NOT display Allocations.

9 ➤ Click **OK**. You do not need to change the other settings. The Invoice window columns will now resemble the ones you used previously. Note, you may have to repeat Exercise 2A-3 to Customize columns to widths that you want.

10 ➤ **Return** to the Home window.

Step 9a: Setting Up Subledgers–Vendors

Another part of the conversion process is to enter **vendors** and **vendor history** into the Vendors subledgers. The subledgers in Simply have the same purpose as those in a manual accounting system.

Detailed vendor balances in the Vendors subledger are compared in total to the balance of the ACCOUNTS PAYABLE account in the G/L.

Before setting up Vendors & Customers it is strongly recommended that you review Appendix Y, *To Cancel a History Invoice* at *www.simplyaccounting2010.nelson.com* under Student Resources, as this is a common mistake in Setting up invoices.

The following are the vendor details for Sarah's Kitchen Stores at Aug 31, 2016.

Exercise 4-12 – Setting Up Vendor Subledgers

Entering the Vendor Accounts

Create an account for each vendor as follows:

1 ➤ From the Home window, click **Setup**, **Setup Guide**, **Vendors**. You are in the Vendor Setup window.

2 ➤ Create the first vendor, with the following information:

Vendor	Office Stationery Plus
Contact	Owen Cliff
Telephone	905-675-6628
Street 1	987 Emerson Street
City	Hamilton
Province	Ontario
Postal Code	L8S 4W3

3 ➤ Before entering Balance Owing amounts, you will enter other Vendor information. Double-click the Vendor, **Office Stationery Plus**. This is using the same procedure as discussed in Chapter 3 – Exercise 3A-8 after step 16 information section, *Creating a New Vendor Account*.

4 ➤ Click the **Options** tab. Enter the information shown next.

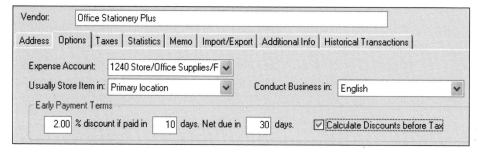

5 ➤ Click the **Taxes** tab. HST Exempt NO. Select Tax code **HS**.

6 ➤ Click the **Historical Transactions** tab.

7 ➤ Click the **Invoices** button. The Historical Invoices window is displayed.

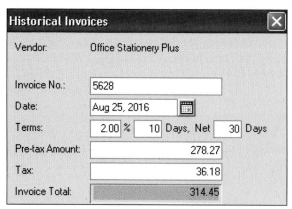

Fig. 4-39: Historical Invoices window.

8 ➤ Type the information from Fig. 4-39 into the fields in your window.

Pre-tax Amount	This field and the Tax field will not display if the vendor does not have Calculate Discounts before Tax field ✓. (See Exercise 4-12, step 4.) Only an amount field will display.

> Amount: [   ]

If there is no discount available, the program does not need a breakdown in the amount.

Tax	You would type the amount of the tax, HST where applicable. Note: the cost of the office goods purchased was 278.27. The 36.18 tax cost is HST.

*To cancel or correct a historical invoice, refer to Appendix **Y** at www.simplyaccounting2010.nelson.com under Student Resources.*

9 ➤ When your window resembles Fig. 4-39, click the **Record** button.

There are no other invoices to be entered for Office Stationery Plus.

10 ➤ **Close**   Click on the **Close** button when finished.

At the bottom of the window the vendor Balance Owing   314.45 now shows 314.45 for Office Stationery Plus. (See side note box.)

11 ➤ Click **X** to Exit.

12 ➤ Enter the other vendors information and outstanding balances (referred to as **History**).

Vendor	**Custom Cabinets Ltd.**	**Kitchen Gadgets Inc.**	**Your Name Landlord**
Contact	Toby Aharonhi	Sarah Ditlove	Carol Smith
Street 1	3890 Barton Street	200 Lakeshore Blvd	16 Main Street West
City	Hamilton	Hamilton	Hamilton
Province	Ontario	Ontario	Ontario
Postal Code	L8E 8Q2	L2X 4C3	L8S 4J1
Telephone	905-819-4751	905-623-3926	905-569-2863
Expense	5030	5030	5310
Terms	See Fig 4-41	See Fig 4-41	Net 3 days
Discounts	✓	✓	No
HST	Exempt No	Exempt No	Exempt No
Tax code	HS	HS	HS

Fig. 4-40: Vendor Names and Addresses.

Accounts Payable Outstanding Balances - August 31, 2016

Vendor	Inv. #	Date	Terms	Pre-Tax Amount	HS Tax Amount	Invoice Total
Custom Cabinets Ltd.	3620	Aug 16, 2016	2/10, net 30	7,810.00	1,015.30	8,825.30
Kitchen Gadgets Inc.	600	Aug 20, 2016	2/10, net 30	2,650.00	344.50	2,994.50
*Office Stationery Plus	5628	Aug 25, 2016	2/10, net 30	278.27	36.18	314.45

* entered in Exercise 4-12 $ 12,134.25

Fig. 4-41: Vendor Names and History.

History for vendors can be entered in detail by entering individual invoices and payments, or entered as one balance carried forward. The detail method provides an accurate aging of the payable balance.

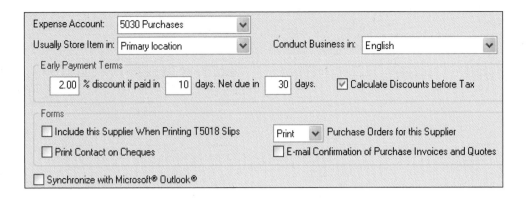

Expense Account: 5030 Purchases

Usually Store Item in: Primary location   Conduct Business in: English

Early Payment Terms

    2.00   % discount if paid in   10   days. Net due in   30   days.   ☑ Calculate Discounts before Tax

Forms

☐ Include this Supplier When Printing T5018 Slips   Print   Purchase Orders for this Supplier

☐ Print Contact on Cheques   ☐ E-mail Confirmation of Purchase Invoices and Quotes

☐ Synchronize with Microsoft® Outlook®

Remember to record the terms and ✓ the Calculate Discounts before Tax box for vendors that allow discounts to be taken on the purchase price of the goods before HST.

When you add the invoice details for an invoice that has no discount for paying early, the Pre-tax Amount box does not show. Record the full amount of the invoice owing.

Do NOT change any information for other fields. You may find information on what goes in the **Additional Info** tab in the Appendix Q, *Names Fields* at www.simplyaccounting2010.nelson.com under Student Resources.

---

13 ➤   When all vendors have been entered, you should see the following at the bottom. The amounts agree.

> Accounts Payable Balance: $12,134.25   equals   ⓘ   Total Balance Owing: $12,134.25

14 ➤   Close the Setup Guide and return to the Home window.

Depending on the configuration of your computer, the Home window Vendors Opening Balance amounts may not be updated. You will have to exit Simply and reopen the data base to update the amounts.

---

15 ➤   It would be a good idea to print the Vendor Aged Detail report and compare vendor totals. Using the Report Centre, display the **Vendor Aged Detail, Modify this report**, all vendors should be **selected**, click **Include Terms, OK** to display the aged vendor balances. ($12,134.25 to G/L ACCOUNTS PAYABLE account 2010. The amounts must be the same ($12,134.25**). This is done to prove that the starting PAYABLES module agrees with the COMPANY module (General Ledger).

Vendor Aged Detail As at Aug 31, 2016					
Source	Date	Terms	Transaction Type	Total	Current
Custom Cabinets Ltd.					
3620	Aug 16, 2016	2%/10, Net 30	Invoice	8,825.30	8,825.30
Total outstanding:				8,825.30	8,825.30
Kitchen Gadgets Inc.					
600	Aug 20, 2016	2%/10, Net 30	Invoice	2,994.50	2,994.50
Total outstanding:				2,994.50	2,994.50
Office Stationery Plus					
5628	Aug 25, 2016	2%/10, Net 30	Invoice	314.45	314.45
Total outstanding:				314.45	314.45
Total unpaid invoices:				12,134.25	12,134.25
Total prepayments/prepaid order:				-	-
Total outstanding:				12,134.25	12,134.25

Fig. 4-42: Vendor Aged Detail Aug 31, 2016.

16 ➤ **Exit** the Vendor Aged Detail window.

17 ➤ **Exit** the Report Centre window.

The history for the PAYABLES module is now complete.

18 ➤ **Back up** (save) your work before proceeding.

When the Vendors Ledger Does Not Agree with General Ledger

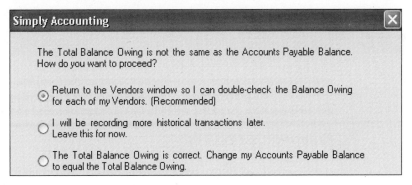

What would you do if the Vendor Aged Detail total does not agree with the General Ledger ACCOUNTS PAYABLE account 2010? Simply will not allow you to change from History to **Ready**. You would then take steps to find the error(s). Errors could be caused by:

a) one or more missing vendor information records.

b) one or more incorrect outstanding balances in the payable detail.

c) an error in the manual General Ledger (posting error).

Most companies would like to get the Simply system working as soon as possible. In the event that an error occurred, the business may enter an **UNKNOWN VENDOR** account for the difference between the Vendor Aged Detail total and the ACCOUNTS PAYABLE account.

If you see the above window, select the 2nd choice. **I will be recording more historical transactions later**. This will allow you to print the Aged Detail report and compare it to the manual records. You would then return to the Vendors area and add the missing amount(s) or correct an amount. See Appendix Y, *To Cancel a History Invoice* at www.simplyaccounting2010.nelson.com under Student Resources.

Difference	General Ledger Balance	Accounts Payable Detail	Difference To GL	Difference	Unknown Vendor Adjustment required
Short	$12,134.25	$11,924.25	$-210.00	Short	Positive Invoice
Over	$12,134.25	$12,449.25	$ 315.00	Over	Negative Invoice

The UNKNOWN VENDOR would be entered with an invoice number as:

a) **Unknown**, or
b) ? ? ? or
c) 9999999 or something similar to indicate an unknown invoice number.

You can get the Simply program working with the subledgers balanced; meanwhile, you will have time to find and correct the error. The error may be found when a vendor called for payment, a missing vendor card was located, a posting error was corrected, etc.

Step 9b: Setting Up Subledgers–Customers

Follow the same procedure that you used in Exercise 4-12 to create the Customer Ledger and enter Customer balances to add the dollar value to each customer history.

Exercise 4-13 – Setting Up Customer Subledgers

Entering Customers

1 ➤ From the Home window, click **Setup**, **Setup Guide**, **Customers.** You are in the Customer Setup window.

2 ➤ Create the following customers, with the following information.

Customer	Chaiken's Home Depot	Lee's Department Store
Contact	Marion Chaiken	Michael Lee
Street 1	268 Grandview Street	2075 Heron Road
City	Kitchener	Ottawa
Province	Ontario	Ontario
Postal Code	N2B 2B9	K1N 2A4
Telephone	519-745-1481	613-748-6358

3 ➤ Before entering Balance Owing amounts, you will enter other custom information. Double-click **Chaiken's Home Depot**. This is using the same procedure as discussed in Chapter 3 – Exercise 3A-8 after step 16 information section, Creating a New Vendor Account.

	Chaiken's Home Depot	Lee's Department Store
Options tab		
Revenue Account	4010	4010
Terms	2/10, net 30	2/10, net 30
Taxes tab		
HST	Tax Exempt, No	Tax Exempt, No
Tax code	HS	HS
Statistics tab		
Credit Limit	15,000.00	15,000.00

Customer	Inv. #	Date	Terms	Pre-tax Amount	HST Tax Amount	Invoice Total
Chaiken's Home Depot	598	Aug 23, 2016	2/10, n30	4,760.00	618.80	5,378.80
Lee's Department Store	613	Aug 28, 2016	2/10, n30	6,510.00	846.30	7,356.30

						$12,735.10

Fig. 4-43: Customer Outstanding Invoices.

Entering Customer Balances (History)

1 ➤ Click the **Historical Transactions** tab.

2 ➤ Click the **Invoices** button. The Historical Invoices window is displayed. Enter the invoice information in Fig. 4-43 for each customer. When complete, click **Record** and **Close** for each customer.

3 ➤ When you have entered both customers' historical transactions, **exit** the RECEIVABLES Ledger.

At the bottom of the Customer Setup window you will see:

Accounts Receivable Balance: $12,848.10   does not equal 🔵 Total Balance Owing: $12,735.10

You will notice that the total of the Customer Aged Detail report (Total Balance Owing) is $12,735.10 and **does not balance with** the $12,848.10 balance of the G/L ACCOUNTS RECEIVABLE Balance account 1200.

4 ➤ Click **Close** to exit to the Home window.

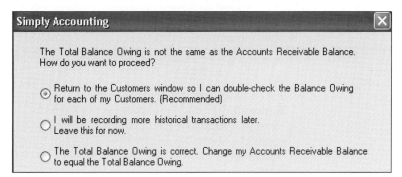

5 ➤ Click the 2nd choice as you will return to record another customer, and exit to the Home window.

6 ➤ From the top menu, click **Reports, Receivables, Customer Aged, Detail.** Both customers should be selected, **Include Terms, OK** to display the aged customer balances.

Customer Aged Detail As at Aug 31, 2016					
Source	Date	Terms	Transaction Type	Total	Current
Chaiken's Home Depot					
598	Aug 23, 2016	2%/10, Net 30	Invoice	5,378.80	5,378.80
Total outstanding:				5,378.80	5,378.80
Lee's Department Store					
613	Aug 28, 2016	2%/10, Net 30	Invoice	7,356.30	7,356.30
Total outstanding:				7,356.30	7,356.30
Total unpaid invoices:				12,735.10	12,735.10
Total deposits/prepaid order:				-	-
Total outstanding:				12,735.10	12,735.10

Fig. 4-44: Customer Aged Detail – not balanced.

Difference	General Ledger Balance	Accounts Receivable	Difference Detail	Difference To GL	Unknown Customer Adjustment required
Short	$12,848.10	$12,735.10	$-113.00	Short	Positive Invoice

As discussed in the vendor section, you may create an UNKNOWN CUSTOMER account to record the missing balance. This will allow the module to be turned to Ready and will give you time to locate the missing invoice.

A search of invoices issued has located all invoices except 615. Invoices 613, 614 and 616 were issued on Aug. 28, 2016; therefore, invoice 615 would have been issued on the same day. The Sales Journal on Aug. 28, 2016 has an entry for $100.00, plus 13% HST, for Kitchen Accessories for a total invoice of $113.00. However, the customer's name was not recorded, and the staff cannot remember to whom the sale was made.

The above invoice (615) was recorded correctly in the General Ledger.

You will enter the sales invoice information you have and try to locate the missing invoice.

You may not be able to locate information about the missing invoice(s) before turning the module to **Ready**. A suggested solution is to add an **Unknown Customer**, similar to step 8, with an unknown invoice number or other code, for the missing amount.

7 ➤ Add a customer ledger for **Unknown Customer,** with **no address information**, Ship to Address is the **same as mailing address**, leave **Revenue Account** field blank as you do not know what Revenue account this customer normally uses. Terms **2/10, net 30** given to all customers. Click the **Taxes** tab, HST **No**, Tax Code **HS**. Click the **Statistic** tab, Credit Limit **$113.00**.

8 ➤ Add historical invoice number **#615** with the following: Date **August 28, 2016**, Pre-tax Amount **$100.00**, Tax **13.00**, Invoice total **113.00**. If the invoice number is not known, use a code similar to **Unknown, ? ? ?,** or **999999,** etc., as discussed in Exercise 4-12 after step 18.

9 ➤ After entering the Unknown Customer, **exit** the Receivable Ledger. At the bottom of the Customer Setup window you will see:

Accounts Receivable Balance: $12,848.10   equals ⓘ Total Balance Owing: $12,848.10

The sub-ledger now agrees to the General ledger balance. Click **Close** and **Exit** to the Home window.

10 ➤ Display the **Customer Aged Detail** report as shown:

Customer Aged Detail As at Aug 31, 2016

Source	Date	Terms	Transaction Type	Total	Current	31 to 60
Chaiken's Home Depot						
598	Aug 23, 2016	2%/10, Net 30	Invoice	5,378.80	5,378.80	-
Total outstanding:				5,378.80	5,378.80	
Lee's Department Store						
613	Aug 28, 2016	2%/10, Net 30	Invoice	7,356.30	7,356.30	-
Total outstanding:				7,356.30	7,356.30	
Unknown Customer						
615	Aug 28, 2016	2%/10, Net 30	Invoice	113.00	113.00	-
Total outstanding:				113.00	113.00	
Total unpaid invoices:				12,848.10	12,848.10	-
Total deposits/prepaid order:				-	-	-
Total outstanding:				12,848.10	12,848.10	-

Fig. 4-45: Customer Aged Detail – after correction.

Compare the Customer Aged Detail $12,848.10 to the General Ledger again to prove that the starting CUSTOMERS module agrees with the General Ledger.

11 ➤ **Exit** to the Home window.

The history for the CUSTOMERS module is now complete.

Step 10: To Add Credit Card Information

To process credit card transactions, you must set up the information for the specific credit card company that your firm accepts.

Exercise 4-14 – To Add Credit Card Information

The following procedure is used to add credit card information:

1 ➤ At the bottom, Related Tasks, click **Settings,** click ➕ at **Company,** click **Credit Cards.**

Credit Cards Used

2 ➤ In the right pane, click **Used**. The blank Settings window for **Credit Cards Used** appears.

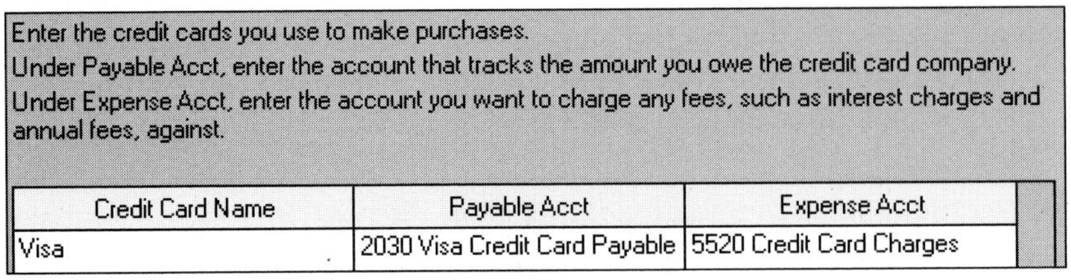

Credit Card Name	Payable Acct	Expense Acct
Visa	2030 Visa Credit Card Payable	5520 Credit Card Charges

Enter the credit cards you use to make purchases.
Under Payable Acct, enter the account that tracks the amount you owe the credit card company.
Under Expense Acct, enter the account you want to charge any fees, such as interest charges and annual fees, against.

Fig. 4-46: Credit Cards used window.

Sarah's Kitchen Stores uses a business credit card from the Visa Credit Card Company for their purchases.

3 ➤ Type the information as shown in Fig. 4-46.

Credit Card Name	**Visa**. Sarah will use this card to make purchases for the business. She may apply for other business credit cards later.
Payable Acct	**2030 Visa Credit Card Payable** is the account where the amounts owing to the credit card company will be charged.
Expense Acct	**5520 Credit Card Charges** is the account where the amounts that the credit card company charges the business for annual fees, etc., will be recorded. This is the same account to which the discount fee on customer credit card sales is charged. Sarah's Kitchen Stores has decided to use one account for all credit card fees and charges.

Credit Cards Accepted

4 ➤ In the left pane, click the **Credit Cards Accepted** item.

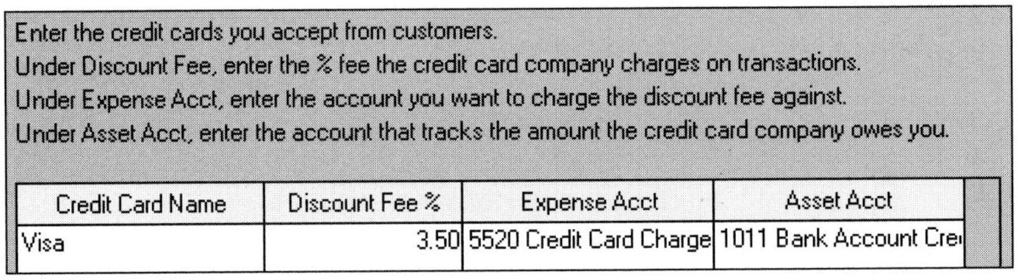

Enter the credit cards you accept from customers.
Under Discount Fee, enter the % fee the credit card company charges on transactions.
Under Expense Acct, enter the account you want to charge the discount fee against.
Under Asset Acct, enter the account that tracks the amount the credit card company owes you.

Credit Card Name	Discount Fee %	Expense Acct	Asset Acct
Visa	3.50	5520 Credit Card Charge	1011 Bank Account Cre

Fig. 4-47: Credit cards accepted window.

5 ➤ Type the information as shown in Fig. 4-47.

Credit Card Name	**Visa** (maximum 13-characters). Sarah has decided to accept only the Visa Credit Card for use by her customers. Other credit cards may be added later.
Discount Fee %	When you entered the Visa name above, a 0.00 appeared in this column. The rate would be the discount fee the credit card company charges the business for using the credit card. The Visa credit company charges a fee of **3.5%** on the sales value including taxes. (e.g., Sale 100.00, plus $13.00 HST = $113.00.) The discount fee would be $3.96 (3.5% of $113.00).

Expense Acct	**5520 Credit Card Charges** is the account where the discount fee will be charged as an expense.
Asset Acct	**1011 Bank Account Credit Card Receivable** is the asset account where the receivable (cash) amount from the credit card company will be charged.

6 ➤ Click **OK** to Exit.

VERY IMPORTANT: Back up your data before proceeding.

Step 11: Setting Modules to Ready

The final step in the setup process is to set the modules to **Ready** (change from History). The journals can be used for transaction entries from September 1, 2016 onwards. The modules that are being used for Sarah's Kitchen Stores are COMPANY, PAYABLES and RECEIVABLES.

Here's a last-minute checklist:

1. All sections in the Chart of Accounts must begin with an **H** and end with a **T**.

2. All **A** type accounts must be followed by an **S**.

3. All Accounts must be in logical order.

4. All Linked accounts needed should have been set up. You may change or modify the linked accounts at any time in the future, as the need arises.

5. Before the system can be made **Ready**, all subledger module balances must agree with the associated Linked account balances in the General Ledger. They now agree.

6. It is best to print a Trial Balance, Income Statement, Balance Sheet, Schedules of Accounts Payable and Accounts Receivable, and verify that the balances agree.

⚠️ Mistakes made in entering History **cannot** be changed once the module is set to **Ready**.

Back up your data and use the backup to correct History errors. Once the errors are corrected, another backup must be made before setting to Ready.

Remember, **BACK UP** before proceeding. Make *TWO* backup copies of your data. *THIS IS VERY IMPORTANT.* In Chapter 5, Sarah's Kitchen Stores is used to enter transactions. An extra backup, *before setting the modules to Ready,* could be vital. It should be kept in case you have to start Chapter 4 again, or fix errors when entering transactions.

If the above conditions are met, you can turn the modules to **Ready**.

Setting the System to READY

The following procedure will turn the COMPANY, RECEIVABLES and PAYABLES modules to **Ready**, and the quill pens (History icons), will disappear from the window.

Exercise 4-15 – To Set the System to READY

1 ➤ On the menu bar, click on **History**, and then **Finish Entering History**.

If the PAYABLES or RECEIVABLES do not balance with the General Ledger, you will receive an error message similar to the following:

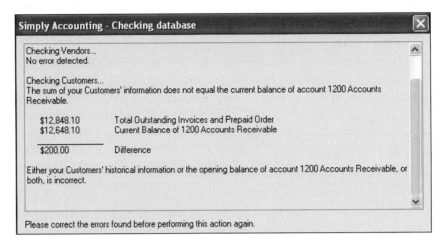

The Simply database verifies that all modules displayed are error-free. If errors exist, the program identifies the area where the error occurred (see above).

You will need to go back to the module that is not balanced and correct the error.

If you have not set up the Chart of Accounts in a logical order, an error message similar to the following is displayed, preventing you from changing to Ready and continuing. The error must be fixed before you can turn the Modules to Ready.

Checking Accounts...
Your accounts are not in logical order. The reason is: there is a missing Subgroup Total before account '2299 Total Current Liabilities'.

Until this issue is resolved, you cannot open some of your reports.

When the subledger balances agree with the G/L, you will see the following window and warning message to back up your data files:

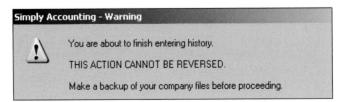

2 ➤ Click **Proceed**.

The screen will flicker and the quill pens will disappear. The RECEIVABLES, PAYABLES, BANKING and COMPANY modules, with all historical data, are now in READY mode and are **Ready** to use.

CONGRATULATIONS! The Journals in RECEIVABLES (Sales Quotes, Sales Orders, Sales Invoices and Receipts), PAYABLES (Purchase Orders, Purchase Invoices, and Payments), COMPANY (Chart of Accounts and General Journal) and BANKING (Reconcile Accounts) are ready to use. If you wish to use other modules, the setup and conversion process must be performed for the module before making the module **Ready**. The setup for other modules is covered in later chapters in this book.

3 ➤   **Exit** Simply.

Chapter 5 continues to use the Sarah's Kitchen Stores data file, and will provide a review of journalizing transactions in the COMPANY, PAYABLES and RECEIVABLES modules using simulated source documents.

Exercise 4-16 –Verify Information in SAI Data File

This procedure will allow you to verify/confirm the SAI data file information that you entered in the Sarah's Kitchen Stores data file, or can be used to verify other data files. This exercise does not take the place of an up-to-date log book.

1 ➤   **Open** Windows Explorer.

2 ➤   In the left pane, **locate** and **click** on the + beside the **C:\Simply Data 2010** folder.

3 ➤   In the left pane, click on the **Sarah's Kitchen Stores** folder containing the SAI file you want information about.

4 ➤   In the right pane, **click** on the [Sarah's Kitchen Stores.SAI] file, then **right-click**.

5 ➤   Select **Properties**. The Sarah's Kitchen Stores.SAI properties window appears.

6 ➤   Click on the **Simply Accounting** tab. Information about the SAI file will display.

This window will confirm the information you entered in this file, or any other Simply SAI file. This exercise does not take the place of an up-to-date log book.

7 ➤   **Exit** the window.

In future exercises, refer to **Slideshow 4** when creating a new G/L account, setting up a new vendor or a new customer.

Before Moving On...

Read the following questions and make sure you know the answers to them; otherwise, read the corresponding part in the chapter before moving on.

1. Explain the differences between the following dates: **Fiscal Start**, **Fiscal End**, **Earliest Transaction**, **Session**, **Latest Transaction** and **Historical Transactions**.

2. Before assigning account numbers, why is it important to know what accounts go with each account group number; e.g., 1000, 2000, 3000, 4000 or 5000?

3. What is the difference between **postable** and **non-postable** accounts? How do you designate a postable account?

4. Assume that mistakes have been made in entering the history balances and the system has been changed to **Ready**. What are two ways to correct this problem?

5. What does setting a module to **Ready** mean?

6. What is a **Linked** account?

7. Briefly explain each category of the account types **H A S G T** and **X**.

8. What is the purpose of the **X** account in the chart of accounts?

9. Would you enter the history balance of HST Paid on Purchases account as a positive or a negative number? Explain why.

10. Briefly explain what is meant by **Class Options** in Accounts.

Challenge Exercise 04 C4-1, Balloons Store

Conversion to Simply Accounting (G/L, A/R & A/P)

1 ➤ Use the **Wizard** to create a new company from scratch.

The trial balance provided shows only postable accounts. It is expected that you will use the techniques shown in Sarah's Kitchen Stores (Chapter 4) to:

- a) Add Headings (**H**), Postable accounts (**A** and **G**) with Subtotal (**S**) accounts and Total (**T**) accounts. You should have a minimum of 3 **S**-type accounts.
- b) Create **Linked accounts** for the COMPANY, PAYABLES and RECEIVABLES modules.
- c) Select **Class Options** required.
- d) Add **Vendor** and **Customer** invoice information.

Balloons Store is assumed to be a sole proprietorship business. It sells various kinds of party balloons.

This review assignment does not use all accounts that may be used by a typical business – it uses only the RECEIVABLES (Customers), PAYABLES (Vendors), and COMPANY modules. Balloons Store does not use the budget feature, credit cards, or shippers. When all data has been entered, turn the related modules to **Ready**.

A) The business using a calendar fiscal year has the following important dates:
Opened for business **Sep 12, 1987**
Year-end this year **Dec 31, 2016**
Year-end last year **Dec 31, 2015**
Manual books stopped **Apr 30, 2016**. This will be the conversion date the manual accounting records will be transferred to Simply.

B) The business is: Balloons Store, Your Name, 936 Alfred St., Sarnia, Ontario N7V 3K7.

> ***Remember, your name must appear on all reports.***

C) Business number is Z345.

D) Forms use the next number on:
Invoices (342)
Cheques (384)
All other forms start at **1**, except for:
Receipts (# blank)
Customer Deposits (# blank)
Direct Deposit Stubs (# blank)

E) Discounts are calculated **before tax** for both customer and vendor invoices, with Customer early payment terms **2/10 net 30**.

F) The computer financial statements should be set up with the following sections:
Current Assets Owner's Equity
Capital Assets Revenue
Current Liabilities Cost of Goods Sold
Long Term Liabilities Store Expenses

The **normal** account balances from the Apr 30, 2016 Balloons Store Trial Balance are listed below. Use appropriate **account classes** in setting up your accounts.

Account Names	Balance	Class	Other
Bank Account	$ 3,187	Bank	Cheque #384
Accounts Receivable	6,780	Accounts Receivable	
Supplies Store & Office	800		
Inventory	See below		
Store Furniture	34,400		
Accumulated Amortization	6,100		
Accounts Payable	9,718	Accounts Payable	
HST on Sales	2,463		
HST on Purchases	900		
Bank Loan Payable	24,600	Long Term Debt	8 year loan
Capital, your actual name	26,504		
Capital, Additional Investments	0		
Drawings, your actual name	6,500		
Sales Revenue	186,000		
Sales Returns	3,046		
Sales Discounts	312		
Beginning Inventory	See below		
Purchases	148,000		
Purchase Returns	2,000		
Purchase Discounts	2,086		
Ending Inventory	See below		
Rent Expense	16,221		
Advertising Expense	1,325		
Amortization Expense	0		
Inventory at Beginning of fiscal year	was $38,000		
Inventory at April 30, 2016	is $61,360		

G) Tax Classes, Codes and Rates:

HST rate is 13%, HST registration # R1234, and HST is refundable.

HS code is HST at 13%
HI code is HST at 8%

H) Customize the Journals as shown in Exercise 4-11, Setting up Tax Classes, Codes, Rates & Customization.

I) Set up Customers and Vendors:

Accounts Receivable Customers	**Accounts Payable Vendors**
Belair Hospital (balloons for rooms & patients)	"Your Last Name Here" Balloon Supply
Contact: Jordan Royes	Contact: Kylie Lunn
85 Colborne Road	289 Talford Street
Sarnia, Ontario, N7V 5B3	Sarnia, Ontario, N7T 6L4
Phone: (519) 826-7520, Fax –None	Phone: (519) 726-7520, Fax –None
Terms: 2/10, net 30. Credit Limit $10,000.	Terms: 2/10, net 30.
Revenue Account: Sales Revenue	Invoice #349 April 25, 2016, $8,500
Price List: Regular	HST $1,105. Total invoice: $9,605.
Invoice #340 April 26, 2016 $6,000;	Expense Account: Purchases
HST $780. Total invoice $6,780	Tax Code HS
Tax Code HS	

J) Set the related modules, accounts, vendors and customers to **Ready** mode.

2 ➤ Print the following reports.

> **As of Apr 30, 2016**
> a) Income Statement Jan 1- Apr 30
> b) Balance Sheet
> c) Customer Aged Detail report
> d) Vendor Aged Detail report

3 ➤ Record and **post** the next two transactions.

May 2   Purchase return (from original invoice # 349) of 10 cases of Red 40th Birthday balloons at $10.00 each plus HST, to "Your Last Name Here" Balloon Supply.

May 2   Sold to retail customer, Mirella Nostopolis, 3 party packages of children's balloons at $15.00 per package plus HST. Received her cheque #315 as payment in full.

4 ➤ Print the following reports.

> **As of May 1, 2016**
>
> a) Income Statement Jan 1- May 1
> b) Balance Sheet
> c) Customer Aged Detail report
> d) Vendor Aged Detail report
> e) All Journal Entries

Challenge Exercise 04 C4-2, Kojokaro

(Setup of a company file, using G/L, A/R & A/P)

1 ➤ Refer to Exercise 1-1, to unzip the **04 C4-2 Kojokaro.exe** file.

2 ➤ Open the **04 C4-2 Kojokaro** file with a date of Jan. 01.

This exercise is a review of the setup of a company file.

The account structure – Chart of Accounts, with many errors, was created by an employee of Kojokaro Sales Company. Account classes have not been shown in the information below. As a consultant hired to help with the setup of the company you will:

1 ➤ Identify the errors.

2 ➤ Add, Modify and Delete accounts necessary to fix the account structure.

3 ➤ Print the Balance Sheet.

4 ➤ Print the Income Statement.

5 ➤ Print the Chart of Accounts List.

Chart of Accounts

ASSETS

1000 Current Assets	**H**
1001 Cash in Bank	A
1030 Total Cash	S
1050 Accounts Receivable	A
1059 Accounts Receivable Net	S
1100 Store Supplies	A
1299 Total Current Liabilities	S
1400 Capital Assets	**H**
1410 Equipment	A

LIABILITIES

2000 Current Liabilities	**H**
2005 Accum Amortization/Deprec.	G
2100 Accounts Payable	G
2200 Drawings by Owner	G
2500 Long Term Liabilities	**H**
2530 Bank Loan -Mortgage	G

EQUITY

3010 Owner's Equity	A
3020 Inventory	A
3030 Capital	A
3600 Current Earnings	X

REVENUE

4010 Sales	**H**
4020 Sales -All	A
4040 Sales Discounts	A
4050 Sales Returns	G
4100 HST on Sales	G

EXPENSE

5000 Cost of Goods Sold	**H**
5020 Purchases	A
5030 Purchase Discounts	A
5040 Purchase Returns	A
5050 HST on Purchases/Service	A
5080 Ending Inventory	A
5090 Beginning Inventory	A
5099 Cost of Goods Sold	G
5300 Rent Expense	G
5310 Amortization/Deprec Expense	G
5325 Telephone Expense	A
5390 Other Expenses	S

Challenge Exercise 04 C4-3, Skates Stores

Conversion to Simply Accounting, using G/L, A/R & A/P

1 ➤ Use the **Wizard** to create a new company from scratch.

The trial balance provided shows only postable accounts in alphabetical order. It is expected that you will use the techniques shown in Sarah's Kitchen Stores (Chapter 4) to:

   a) Add Headings (**H**), Postable accounts (**A** and **G**) with Subtotal (**S**) accounts and Total (**T**) accounts. You should have a minimum of 3 **S**-type of accounts.
   b) Use a **Difference at Startup** account.
   c) Create **Linked accounts** for the COMPANY, PAYABLES and RECEIVABLES modules.
   d) Select **Class Options** required.
   e) Add **Vendor** and **Customer** invoice information.

Skates Stores is assumed to be a sole proprietorship business. It sells figure skates and hockey skates.

This review assignment does not use all accounts that may be used by a business, and uses only the COMPANY, PAYABLES (Vendors) and RECEIVABLES (Customers) modules. Skates Stores does not use the budget feature, credit cards, or shippers. When all data has been entered, turn the related modules to **Ready**.

   A) The business using a calendar fiscal year has the following important dates:
Opened for business	**February 15, 1986**
Year-end this year	**December 31, 2016**
Year-end last year	**December 31, 2015**
Manual books stopped	**May 31, 2016.** This will be the conversion date the manual accounting records will be transferred to Simply.

   B) The business is: Skates Stores, Your Name, 514 Semple Avenue, Your Town, Ontario, L0N 1B0.

   > ***Remember, your name must appear on all reports.***

   C) Business Registration # R1176.

   D) Forms: use the next number on:

   Invoices (#983)
   Cheques (#468)
   All other forms start at **1**, except:
   Receipts (# blank)
   Customer Deposits (# blank).

   E) Discounts are calculated **before tax** for both customer and vendor invoices, with Customer early payment terms **2/10 net 30**.

   F) The computer financial statements should be set up with the following sections:

Current Assets	Owner's Equity
Capital Assets	Revenue
Current Liabilities	Cost of Goods Sold
Long Term Liabilities	Store Expenses

The <u>normal</u> account balances from the May 31, 2016, Skates Stores. Trial Balance in alphabetical order is next:

Account Name	Balance	Class	Other
Accounts Payable	$ 1,356.00	Accounts Payable	
Accounts Receivable	1,243.00	Accounts Receivable	
Accumulated Amortization	4,100.00		
Amortization Expense All	0.00		
Beginning Inventory Jan 1	3,900.00		
Capital – Additional Investments	0.00		
Capital –Your last name	9,240.00		
Cash in Bank	4224.00	Bank	Cheque #468
Drawings –Your last name	1,000.00		
Ending Inventory	6,100.00		
HST on Sales	252.00		
HST Paid on Purchases	136.00		
Inventory	6,100.00		
Notes Payable (Long Term)	21,400.00		
Purchases	15,730.00		
Purchase Discounts	125.00		
Purchase Returns	345.00		
Rent Expense	3,200.00		
Sales Discounts	300.00		
Sales Returns	350.00		
Sales Revenue	14,165.00		
Store Equipment	23,700.00		
Store Supplies	200.00		
Telephone Expense	800.00		

G) Tax Classes, Codes and Rates:

    HST rate is 13%, HST registration # R1234, and HST is refundable.

    HS code is 13%.

    HI code is 8%

H) Customize the Journals as shown in Exercise 4-11, Setting up Tax Classes, Codes, Rates & Customization.

l) Set up Customers and Vendors:

Accounts Receivable customers:
Elvis Skates Corp., Contact Elvis Schafer
2 Huron Street
Woodstock, Ontario, N4S 1A5
Phone 519-546-8588 - Fax: none
Terms 2/10, net 30
Invoice #980, date May 24, 2016
Invoice amount $1,243.00 (including $143.00 HST)
Revenue Account: Sales Revenue
Tax: HS

Credit Limit: $5,000.00

Accounts Payable vendors:
Skates Supply Ltd., Contact Greg Johnson
43 McKay Avenue
Windsor, Ontario, N9B 1A4
Phone: 519-675-8940
Terms 2% 10, net 30
Fax: 416-675-8930
Invoice # 6512, date May 10, 2016
Invoice amount $791.00 (including $91.00 HST)
Expense Account: Purchases
Tax: HS

Manufacture Supply Inc., Contact Jessie Grant
645 Bancroft Drive
Sudbury, Ontario, P3B 8T4
Phone: 705-672-4860 - Fax: 705-672-4860
Terms 2% 10, net 30
Invoice # 1431, date May 28, 2016
Invoice amount $565.00 (including $65.00 HST)
Expense Account: Purchases
Tax: HS

2 ➤ Turn the system to **Ready** and **Record** the inventory adjustment entry for May 31, 2016. Ending inventory at close of business is $3,000.00.

3 ➤ After the ending inventory has been recorded, **print** the following reports:

a) Income Statement, year-to-date
b) Balance Sheet
c) Vendor Detail report
d) Customer Detail report
e) Journal Entries-General

Back up your file regularly.

Challenge Exercise 04 C4-4, R. Park Uniforms

(Conversion to Simply Accounting, using the G/L)

1 ➤ Refer to Exercise 1-1 to unzip the **04 C4-4 Uniforms.exe** file.

2 ➤ Open the Simply file **04 C4-4 Uniforms**. This file contains only the account 3600 Current Earnings account. See Fig. 4-11 as a reference.

Mr. Roland Park has asked for your assistance in setting up the General Ledger in Simply. The manual paper records were dropped on the floor and mixed up and are not in the proper order, but he knows that the Trial Balance which he cannot find now was balanced.

The bookkeeper had to leave this morning to attend to an important family matter in another province and will not be back for a week. The individual Accounts Receivable customer and Payable vendor pages are in her car. She will need your help with the PAYABLES and RECEIVABLES modules when she returns.

3 ➤ Set up the General Ledger accounts with balances using appropriate H A S G T account classes.

Other information:

The business opened	June 1, 2001
Year-end this year	December 31, 2018
Year-end last year	December 31, 2017
Manual books stopped	July 31, 2018

Business Name is R. Park Uniforms, any address (file created with Ontario)
Business number is R56-B37
HST rate is 13%, registration #R1234 and HST is refundable
HS   code is 13%
HI   code is 8%
HO   code is 5%
Next Cheque # and all Forms start at 1
Discounts are all 2/10, net 30

R. Park Uniforms: List of accounts (not in order) at July 31, 2018

HST Charged on Sales	7,124
Bank	27,868
Inventory Asset	39,900
Beginning Inventory	16,500
HST Paid on Purchases/Services	1,846
Ending Inventory	39,900
Salaries Expense	78,600
Prepaid Insurance	750
Accounts Payable	7,910
Advertising Expense	9,000
Capital R. Park	11,000
Mortgage Payable (Due March 2020)	31,020
Rent Expense	19,500
Purchases	117,580
Sales/Revenue	226,960
Accounts Receivable	9,040
Drawings R. Park	0
Sales Discounts	5,000
Purchase Returns	1,670

4 ➤ Print the following:
   a)   Trial Balance as at July 31
   b)   Income Statement, year-to-date
   c)   Balance Sheet as at July 31

Relevant Appendices

 The following appendices are available at www.simplyaccounting2010.nelson.com under Student Resources.

Appendix 2010 E	**Budgets — General Ledger**
Appendix 2010 F	**Printing in Batches**
Appendix 2010 H	**New Business Guide**
Appendix 2010 I	**Checklists for Task Completion**
Appendix 2010 M	**Post-Dated Cheques**
Appendix 2010 Q	**Names Fields**
Appendix 2010 U	**Add Notes/Footer to Statements**
Appendix 2010 X	**Removing an Account from a Wrong Section**
Appendix 2010 Y	**To Cancel a History Invoice**
Appendix 2010 AA	**Setting Up a New Company File using a Template**
Appendix 2010 AD	**Time and Billing Journals**

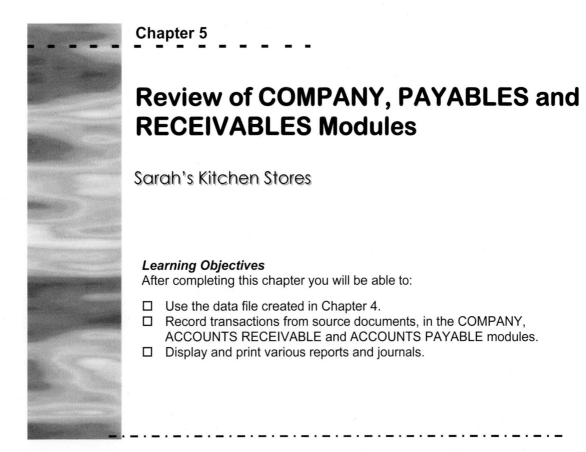

Chapter 5

Review of COMPANY, PAYABLES and RECEIVABLES Modules

Sarah's Kitchen Stores

Learning Objectives

After completing this chapter you will be able to:

☐ Use the data file created in Chapter 4.
☐ Record transactions from source documents, in the COMPANY, ACCOUNTS RECEIVABLE and ACCOUNTS PAYABLE modules.
☐ Display and print various reports and journals.

This chapter contains transactions that will allow you to review the concepts and procedures you have learned so far. You will be presented with source documents, and will need to determine what type of transaction each of them represents, and which module to use to process them. After processing the transactions, you will be required to print financial statements and reports.

The setup of the COMPANY, PAYABLES and RECEIVABLES modules for Sarah's Kitchen Stores was covered in Chapter 4. The modules have been set to **Ready**; therefore, you can start entering transactions in the various modules at any time.

Sarah's Kitchen Stores Profile

Before starting work in this chapter, display the Sarah's Kitchen Stores Balance Sheet and Income Statement and be sure that they are the same as those shown in Fig. 4-37b in Chapter 4. If you have any differences, check with your instructor.

1 ➤ The following source document transactions should be recorded using appropriate modules with dates in September 2016. If you are not sure which module to use, look back to Chapters 1, 2A, 2B, 3A and 3B, or ask your instructor for assistance. Begin recording the transactions assuming you work only 1 day a week, starting on Friday, September 3, 2016. Advance your Session Date appropriately.

Note: **SD** refers to Source Document.

Some important points to note are as follows:

- Make sure that you enter appropriate descriptions, and invoice credit or debit note numbers with proper codes where required.

- You may have to create new vendors, customers and G/L accounts.

- There is no HST on discounts.

- Discount on Office Supplies should be charged to the Office Supplies account.

- Late payment amounts on Utilities should be charged to the Utilities account.

- Remember that the HST remittance is calculated from the difference between the HST CHARGED ON SALES account and the balance of HST PAID ON PURCHASES account in previous months.

2 ➤ When you have finished, print the following reports:

- Trial Balance as of	Sep 30
- Income Statement for	Sep 01 to 30
- Vendor Detail report as of	Sep 30
- Customer Detail report as of	Sep 30
- All Journal Entries	Sep 01 to 30
- General Ledger from	Sep 01 to 30
- Cash Projections as of	Sep 30

Compare your reports to those given in the Solutions Manual provided to your instructor. If you have any differences, try to find out which transaction(s) caused the difference. To correct any errors, you must enter adjusting (or correcting) entries. You cannot change the existing entries once they have been posted. Refer to Chapters 1, 2A, 2B, 3A and 3B, or 13 for correcting errors.

Transactions

Transactions are recorded using the original date of the document to ensure that our records match the records of our suppliers and customers for discount periods, etc. (E.g., a 2%/10, net 30 day purchase invoice dated September 23, received on September 24, and approved on September 25, would be recorded as a purchase using the September 23 date, as this is the date the discount starts.)

SD-1

Quote

Sarah's
Kitchen Stores   339 Hudson Court, Hamilton ON L9C 6B3

To: Chaiken's Home Depot   Ship To:
    268 Grandview Street   (Same)
    Kitchener ON N2B 2B9

Quote NO.	DATE
1	Sep 01, 2016

Qty.	Order	Back Order	Description	Base Price	Disc. %	Price	Tax	Amount
	1		Set Kitchen Cabinets Model L45	$3,675.00		$3,675.00	HS	3,675.00
	1		Sink Model D256	300.00		300.00	HS	300.00
	1		Group Specialty Drawers & Knives	325.00		325.00	HS	325.00

Subtotal	4,300.00
HST #R4675 2567 HST 13%	559.00

Shipping Date: Sep 07, 2016
Terms: 2%/10, Net 30 days

TOTAL DUE
$4,859.00

SD-2

RECEIVED   Sep 02 2016

FOR DEPOSIT ONLY

Chaiken's Home Depot
268 Grandview Street
Kitchener, ON N2B 2B9

CHEQUE NO.   **791**

DATE 0 1 0 9 2 0 1 6
       D D M M Y Y Y Y

PAY   Five Thousand Two Hundred Eighty Three and 60/100 $**5,283.60
To The
Order Of   Sarah's Kitchen Stores

Bank of Nova Scotia   **Chaiken's Home Depot**
936 Grandview Street
Kitchener, ON N2B 2D3   *Marion Chaiken*

⑈791⑈ ⑆0289⑆006⑆ 116⑆93351⑈2

- -
DETACH BEFORE CASHING

Chaiken's Home Depot   CHEQUE NO.   **791**

Date	Description	Amount
Sep 01, 2016	#598	$ 5,283.60

SD-3

Sarah's
Kitchen Stores

339 Hudson Court, Hamilton ON L9C 6B3

CHEQUE NO.   **642**

DATE   0 1 0 9 2 0 1 6
D D M M Y Y Y Y

PAY   Two Thousand Three Hundred Seventy Three and 00/100 $**2,373.00

To   Your Name Landlord
The   16 Main Street West
Order   Hamilton ON L8S 4K1

Toronto Dominion Bank   **Sarah's Kitchen Stores**
2 Palace Rd.
Hamilton, Ontario L3X 1T3   **S. Kafa**

⑆642⑈   ⑆2614⑈007⑈   192⑈991 2⑈

- -
Please Detach Before Cashing

Sarah's Kitchen Stores   CHEQUE NO.   **642**
  Your Name Landlord   Sep. 01, 2016
                                              $2,373.00

Note: Rent $2,100, plus 13% HST payment for month based on lease.

SD-4

Order

Sarah's
Kitchen Stores   339 Hudson Court, Hamilton ON L9C 6B3

To: Chaiken's Home Depot   Ship To:
    268 Grandview Street   (Same)
    Kitchener ON N2B 2B9

Order NO.	DATE
1	Sep 02, 2016

Qty.	Order	Back Order	Description	Base Price	Disc. %	Price	Tax	Amount
	1		Set Kitchen Cabinets Model L45	$3,675.00		$3,675.00	HS	3,675.00
	1		Sink Model D256	300.00		300.00	HS	300.00
	1		Group Specialty Drawers & Knives	325.00		325.00	HS	325.00

Subtotal	4,300.00
HST #R4675 2567 HST 13%	559.00

TOTAL DUE
$4,859.00

Shipping Date: Sep 07, 2016
Terms: 2%/10, Net 30 days

SD-5

**Sarah's
Kitchen Stores**

339 Hudson Court, Hamilton ON L9C 6B3

CHEQUE NO.   **643**

DATE 0 2 0 9 2 0 1 6
        D D M M Y Y Y Y

PAY   Three Hundred eight and 88/100 $**308.88

To   Office Stationery Plus
The   987 Emerson Street
Order   Hamilton ON L8S 4W3

Toronto Dominion Bank   Sarah's Kitchen Stores
2 Palace Rd.
Hamilton, Ontario L3X 1T3   *S. Kafa*

⑈643⑈ ⑊2614⑊007⑈ 192⑊991 2⑈

- -

Please Detach Before Cashing

Sarah's Kitchen Stores   Discount   Cheque No.   **643**
  Office Stationery Plus   Inv. 5628   5.57   Sep. 02, 2016
                                                                $308.88

SD-6

Jack Daly
614 Manley Street
Hamilton, ON L9K 3A5

CHEQUE NO.   **501**

DATE 0 6 0 9 2 0 1 6
        D D M M Y Y Y Y

PAY One Hundred Eleven and 00/100 $**111.00

To The   Sarah's Kitchen Stores
Order   339 Hudson Court
Of   Hamilton, ON L9C 6B3

Central Bank
601 Main St.   J. Daly
Hamilton, ON L9Z 1M2

⑈050 1⑈ ⑊1133050 1⑈   91   890⑈

RECEIVED *Sep 06, 2016*   FOR DEPOSIT ONLY

Note: This is the cheque from the missing customer. Change the name and customer information to Mr. Daly and increase credit limit to $200.00.

SD-7

LEE'S Department Stores	CHEQUE NO. **4680**
2075 Heron Road	
Ottawa, ON K1N 2A4	**D A T E** 0 6 0 9 2 0 1 6
	D D M M Y Y Y Y

To the
Order Of _____ Sarah's Kitchen Stores _____ $**7,226.10

PAY Seven Thousand two hundred twenty six -------------------------------------10/100 DOLLARS

Bank of Montreal   LEE'S Department Stores
618 Main St.
Erinvale, ON N0Z 1Z0   *M. Lee*
_____

⑆4680⑈   ⑈0003⑆012⑈   18023 2⑈ 5

- -
DETACH BEFORE CASHING

Date	Description	Amount	Discount	CHEQUE NO. **4680**
Sep 06, 2016	Payment re: 613	$7,226.10	130.20	LEE'S Department Stores

SD-8

Sarah's
Kitchen Stores   339 Hudson Court, Hamilton ON L9C 6B3

INVOICE

To: Chaiken's Home Depot   Ship To:
    268 Grandview Street   (Same)
    Kitchener ON N2B 2B9

Invoice NO.	DATE
922	Sep 07, 2016

Qty.	Order	Back Order	Description	Base Price	Disc. %	Price	Tax	Amount
1			Set Kitchen Cabinets Model L45	$3,675.00		$3,675.00	HS	3,675.00
1			Sink Model D256	300.00		300.00	HS	300.00
1			Group Specialty Drawers & Knives	325.00		325.00	HS	325.00

	Subtotal	4300.00
HST #R4675 2567	HST 13%	559.00

Reference: Sales Order 1
Shipped: Sep 07, 2016
Terms: 2%/10, Net 30 days

TOTAL DUE
$4,859.00

Order

Sarah's Kitchen Stores   339 Hudson Court, Hamilton ON L9C 6B3

To: Connoisseur Gadgets Ltd.
896 Shaw Park Road
Belfountain ON L0N 1B3

Ship To:
Sarah's Kitchen Stores
339 Hudson Court
Hamilton ON L9C 6B3

Order NO.	DATE
1	Sep 07, 2016

Qty.	Order	Back Order	Description	Base Price	Disc. %	Price	Tax	Amount
	10		Specialty Knives	$36.75		$36.75	HS	367.50
	8		Specialty Cutting Gadgets	9.95		9.95	HS	79.60
	9		Food Processor Blades	12.00		12.00	HS	108.00

Subtotal		555.10
HST 13%		72.17

TOTAL DUE

$627.27

Shipping Date: Sep 10, 2016
Terms: 2%/10, Net 30 days

- CREDIT MEMO -

Sarah's Kitchen Stores   339 Hudson Court, Hamilton ON L9C 6B3

To: Chaiken's Home Depot
268 Grandview Street
Kitchener ON N2B 2B9

Ship To:
(Same)

Invoice NO.	DATE
922Rt	Sep 08, 2016

Qty.	Order	Back Order	Description	Base Price	Disc. %	Price	Tax	Amount
-1			Returned: Sink Model D256 Small crack in fittings	$300.00		$300.00	HS	-300.00

HST #R4675 2567

Subtotal		-300.00
HST 13%		-39.00

Total Credit

$ -339.00

SD-11

Connoisseur Gadgets Ltd.
896 Shaw Park Road,
Belfountain ON L0N 1B3

HST# 118 112 113

Invoice # 15838

TO:
Sarah's Kitchen Stores
339 Hudson Court
Hamilton ON L9C 6B3

DATE	CUSTOMER #	TERMS	P.O. #
Sep 08, 2016	*4040*	*2/10 n30*	*1*

QUANTITY	UNIT	BACKORDERED	DESCRIPTION	UNIT PRICE	TOTAL
10	*sets*		*Specialty Knives*	*36.75*	*367.50*
7	*sets*	*1*	*Specialty Cutting Gadgets*	*9.95*	*69.65*
8	*sets*	*1*	*Food Processor Blades*	*12.00*	*96.00*
				Subtotal	*533.15*
				HST	*69.31*
				TOTAL	*$ 602.46*

SD-12

Sarah's Kitchen Stores
339 Hudson Court, Hamilton ON L9C 6B3

CHEQUE NO.   **644**

DATE 0 8 0 9 2 0 1 6
          D D M M Y Y Y Y

PAY   One Hundred Thirteen and 00/100 $**113.00

To   Auto-Rite Mechanics
The   6589 Rexford Drive
Order   Hamilton ON L8W 7P3

Toronto Dominion Bank
2 Palace Rd.
Hamilton, Ontario L3X 1T3

Sarah's Kitchen Stores

S. Kafa

⑆644⑈ ⑈261400 7⑇ 192⑈991 2⑈

- -
Please Detach Before Cashing

Sarah's Kitchen Stores   Cheque No.   **644**
 Auto-Rite Mechanics   Sep. 08, 2016
 Re: Invoice 3396 ($100.00 +HST $13.00 $113.00
      maintenance husband's personal car)

SD-13

Connoisseur Gadgets Ltd.

▸ **CREDIT MEMO** ◂

896 Shaw Park Road,
Belfountain, ON L0N 1B3

HST# 118 112 113

TO:
Sarah's Kitchen Stores
339 Hudson Court
Hamilton ON L9C 6B3

▸ **DEBIT MEMO** ◂

DATE	CUSTOMER #	TERMS	INVOICE #
Sept. 10, 2016	*4040*	*2/8, n 28*	*15838Rt*

QUANTITY	UNIT	BACKORDERED	DESCRIPTION	UNIT PRICE	TOTAL
-3	*sets*		*Returned Food Processor Blades*	*12.00*	*-36.00*
			- Original Invoice 15838		
				Subtotal	*-36.00*
				HST	*-4.68*
				TOTAL	*$- 40.68*

SD-14

INVOICE

Sarah's Kitchen Stores

339 Hudson Court, Hamilton ON L9C 6B3

To: Kurpreet Gilbert
Visa Credit Card

Ship To:
Pickup

Invoice NO.	DATE
923	Sep 11, 2016

Qty.	Order	Back Order	Description	Base Price	Disc. %	Price	Tax	Amount
8			Kitchen Gadgets	$8.95		$8.95	HS	71.60

Subtotal	71.60
HST #R4675 2567 HST 13%	9.31

TOTAL DUE
$80.91

Shipped: Sep 11, 2016

SD-15

Metro Hydro

55223 Electric Drive, Hamilton ON L6Y 3B3

Sarah's Kitchen Stores		Phone	(905) 448-6320
339 Hudson Court		Date:	Sept 13, 2016
Hamilton ON L9C 6B3			

Service to Sept. 8	$212.39		
HST. R142887665	27.61		
Current charges including tax.	**$240.00**	DUE BY SEPT. 20	
If paid after DUE DATE	**$250.00**		

APPROVAL	RECEIVED Sep. 14, 2016
Date Sep 14, 2016	
Acct. # Utilities	
Approved *SW*	

Note: *Rec*ord $240.00 amount. It is anticipated that we can pay this invoice by the due date.

SD-16

Sarah's
Kitchen Stores

339 Hudson Court, Hamilton ON L9C 6B3

CHEQUE NO.   **645**

DATE   1 5 0 9 2 0 1 6
        D D M M Y Y Y Y

PAY   Two Thousand One Hundred Seven and 50/100 $**2,107.50

To   Receiver General
The   875 Heron Road
Order   Ottawa ON K1A 1A3

Toronto Dominion Bank   **Sarah's Kitchen Stores**
2 Palace Rd.
Hamilton, Ontario L3X 1T3   *S. Kafa*

⑆645⑈   ⑆2614⑉007⑆   192⑈991 2⑈

- -
Please Detach Before Cashing

Sarah's Kitchen Stores   CHEQUE NO.   645
  Receiver General   Sep 15, 2016
  Re: HST at end of Aug 31, 2016 $2,107.50

SD-17

Sarah's Kitchen Stores
339 Hudson Court, Hamilton ON L9C 6B3

INVOICE

To: Mr. Lennie Bercovitch
Visa Credit Card

Ship To:
612 Harmony Avenue
Hamilton ON L8H 1P6

Invoice NO.	DATE
924	Sep 15, 2016

Qty.	Order	Back Order	Description	Base Price	Disc. %	Price	Tax	Amount
1			Set Kitchen cupboards (includes installation)	$5,300.00	10	$4,770.00	HS	4,770.00

Subtotal	4,770.00
HST #R4675 2567　HST 13%	620.10

Shipped: Sep 11, 2016
* 10% Senior Discount

TOTAL DUE
$5,390.10

SD-18

Sarah's Kitchen Stores
339 Hudson Court, Hamilton ON L9C 6B3

CHEQUE NO.　**646**

DATE　1 6 0 9 2 0 1 6
　　　　D D M M Y Y Y Y

PAY　Five Hundred Fifty One and 84/100　　　$**551.84

To The Order　Connoisseur Gadgets Ltd.
896 Shaw Park Road
Belfountain ON L0N 1B3

Toronto Dominion Bank
2 Palace Rd.
Hamilton, Ontario L3X 1T3

Sarah's Kitchen Stores

S. Kafa

⑈646⑈　⑆2614⑈007⑉　1920991⑈2⑈

- - - - - - - - - - - - - - - - Please Detach Before Cashing - - - - - - - - - - - - - - - -

Sarah's Kitchen Stores
Connoisseur Gadgets Ltd.
Re: Invoice 15838, 15838Rt

CHEQUE NO.　**646**
Sep. 16, 2016
$551.84

SD-19

**Sarah's
Kitchen Stores**

339 Hudson Court, Hamilton ON L9C 6B3

CHEQUE NO.   **647**

DATE   3 0 0 9 2 0 1 6
          D D M M Y Y Y Y

PAY   Two Hundred Fifty and 00/100 $**250.00

**To
The
Order**
Metro Hydro
55223 Electric Dr.
Hamilton ON L6Y 3B3

**Toronto Dominion Bank
2 Palace Rd.
Hamilton, Ontario L3X 1T3**

Sarah's Kitchen Stores

S. Kafa

⑆647⑆ ⑈2614⑈007⑉ 192⑈991 2⑊

- -
Please Detach Before Cashing

Sarah's Kitchen Stores
Metro Hydro
Re: Sep. 13 bill. Includes late payment $10 (Utility Expense)

CHEQUE NO.   **647**
Sep. 30, 2016
$250.00

SD-20

Note: Students should make a
new account:
#5390 Tools Expense
Type: G
Class Option: Expense

Smith & Sons Tool Company
SCO – 06-6168
159 Main Street, North York ON M6W 4X6

Date: Sep. 30, 2016   Inv. # 515807
Time: 11:10 am   By: Al
Type: Visa

281-8275 Various tools $83.00 B

-------------------------SUBTOTAL ----------------------   83.00
HST: 13.00%   10.79

---------------------------TOTAL -----------------------   93.79

============AMOUNT(S) TENDERED================
VISA   93.79

===================SOLD TO ===================
Sarah's Kitchen Stores
339 Hudson Court,
Hamilton ON L9C 6B3
VISA Account: Z320-011-007
Exp.Date: 02/20

S. Kafa
Customer's Signature

Chapter 6

Challenge
COMPANY, RECEIVABLES, PAYABLES
Setup and Transactions

Shirts & Ties

Learning Objectives
After completing this chapter you will be able to:

☐ Create a new data file using knowledge gained from Chapter 4.
☐ Record transactions from source documents, in the COMPANY, RECEIVABLES, and PAYABLES modules.
☐ Display and print various reports and journals.

This chapter provides a challenge for you to set up the COMPANY, RECEIVABLES and PAYABLES modules for a company, and process transactions using source documents in the appropriate modules.

Study the information for the company and set up the various modules. Use your last name followed by Shirts & Ties as the company name (e.g., Smith Shirts & Ties) with the following address: 8 Shirt Drive, Ottawa, ON K2Z 1Z1. Supply all other missing details.

Analyze and process the source documents that follow.

> You can also complete this Challenge exercise using the Perpetual Inventory method, after you complete Chapter 8.
>
> See Challenge Exercise 08 C8-6 Shirts & Ties–PI.

(Your Last Name) Shirts & Ties: Company Profile

(Your Last Name) Shirts & Ties (business number R133922445) sells special shirts and ties to other businesses. The company has recently experienced rapid growth both in sales dollars and in sales volume, forcing management to look into another more efficient accounting system. The company books, up to this point, had been kept manually by your friend, but the increased size of the company has forced the business to computerize the accounting records. You are to convert this manual system to Simply Accounting, and help your friend with the first month of computerized operation (August 2016).

The company follows a **calendar fiscal year** and would like to convert after business closed on July 31, 2016.

The July 31, 2016 Trial Balance and details of Accounts Receivable and Accounts Payable are shown on the next two pages.

Some points to remember:

- Suggested company data file name is Shirts.

- The Trial Balance provided shows only postable accounts. You will have to create headings, subtotals and total accounts so that the appropriate financial statements can be printed.

- The Discount Fee percentage for credit cards accepted is 3.5%.

- Add Tax codes HS at 13% and HI at 8%.

- Remember to make a backup before setting the modules to Ready.

- Remember to enter appropriate invoice numbers, cheque numbers, descriptions, etc., for the transactions (audit trail).

- When you allocate account numbers for your system, always leave a gap of at least 5 to 10 numbers to allow for future accounts to be inserted. Here is an example of why this is so important:

  Assume your number sequencing is similar to:

      5110 Purchases
      5120 Purchase Returns
      5130 Ending Inventory

  You discover after turning the system to **Ready** mode that you missed adding the "Purchase Discounts" account into your chart of accounts.

  You will be able to easily insert Purchase Discounts as account number 5125 or any number between 5121 and 5129.

  If you had numbered the above three accounts as:
      5110 Purchases
      5111 Purchase Returns
      5112 Ending Inventory

  You would have a lot of work to do to fix all four of the accounts.

(Your Last Name) Shirts & Ties
Trial Balance Jul 31, 2016

	Debits	Credits
Bank Account Chequing	21,430.00	-
Accounts Receivable	15,350.32	-
Credit Card Receivables	0.00	-
Inventory	21,265.00	-
Prepaid Expenses	1,420.00	-
Warehouse Equipment	63,650.00	-
Accum Amortiz Warehouse Equip	-	21,300.00
Office Equipment	25,800.00	-
Accum Amortiz Office Equip	-	10,350.00
Accounts Payable	-	6,751.75
Universal Credit Card Payable	-	0.00
HST Charged on Sales	-	3,100.00
HST Paid On Purchases	950.00	-
Bank Loan Payable (Long Term)	-	75,000.00
Capital Your Last Name	-	13,847.57
Drawings Your Last Name	7,000.00	-
Sales	-	269,385.00
Sales Returns	2,650.00	-
Sales Discounts	2,800.00	-
Beginning Inventory	38,200.00	-
Purchases	88,800.00	-
Purchase Returns	-	3,000.00
Purchase Discounts	-	1,628.00
Ending Inventory	-	21,265.00
Wages Expense	98,030.00	-
Warehouse/Office Supplies Expense	1,790.00	-
Other Office Expenses	1,850.00	-
Travel & Entertainment Expense	2,630.00	-
Utilities Expense	2,800.00	-
Telephone Expense	2,400.00	-
Legal Expenses	1,600.00	-
Amortization Expense-All	2,900.00	-
Rent Expense	14,000.00	-
Credit Card Charges	7,512.00	-
Insurance Expense	800.00	-
	----------------	----------------
	425,627.32	425,627.32
	==========	==========

Accounts Receivable Details   [Credit limit - all customers $15,000.00]
Jul 31, 2016

	Tax Code	Invoice Number	Invoice Date	Amount	Taxes	Inv. Amt	Terms
Flight Airways Inc. 2983 Somerset Street W Ottawa ON K2P 3W2 (613) 889-8855 Contact: John Stammers	HS	5686	Jul 30, 2016	4,184.35	543.97	$4,728.32	Net 30
McBurger Chain 903 Wheeler Street Ottawa ON K2J 5J3 (613) 554-2236 Contact: Jim Muir	HS	5681	Jul 26, 2016	2,400.00	312.00	$ 2,712.00	2/10, net 30
Radisser Hotels Inc. 3865 Pickford Drive Ottawa ON K2J 5Z6 (613) 554-8833 Contact: Sandra Wilson	HS	5683	Jul 30, 2016	7,000.00	910.00	$ 7,910.00	2/10, net 30
						$15,350.32	

Accounts Payable Details
Jul 31, 2016

	Tax Code	Invoice Number	Invoice Date	Amount	Taxes	Inv. Amt	Terms
Arrow Clothing Centre 2830 Appollo Way Ottawa ON K4A 6N8 (613) 938-4220 Contact: Legoria Simmons	HS	2531	Jul 24, 2016	3,975.00	516.75	$ 4,491.75	2/10, net 30
Polo Accessories 36 Canter Blvd Ottawa ON K2G 4L7 (613) 338-4322 Contact: Kiran Kenth	HS	6528	Jul 27, 2016	2,000.00	260.00	$ 2,260.00	2/10, net 30
						$ 6,751.75	

Transactions

Transactions are recorded using the original date of the document to ensure that our records match the records of our suppliers and customers for discount periods, etc. (e.g., a 2%/10, net 30 day purchase invoice dated August 23, received on August 24, and approved on August 25, would be recorded as a purchase using the August 23 date, as this is the date the discount starts.)

1 ➤ The following transactions took place in August 2016. Enter them in the appropriate journals.

SD-1

Shirts & Ties
8 Shirt Drive
Ottawa ON K2Z 1Z1

CHEQUE NO. **5001**

DATE 0 1 0 8 2 0 1 6
D D M M Y Y Y Y

PAY One Thousand Eight Hundred Fifty three   and 20/100 $**1,853.20

To The Order Of   McTavish Building Management
80 Scott Street
Ottawa ON K4Z 1K9

Shirts & Ties

Bank of Central Ontario
601 Duke St.
Ottawa, ON K0Z 1Z2

Per _____ *YST* _____
Authorized Signature

⑆00500 ⑈" ⑆ ⑈11330501⑈ 91⑈1055⑉

Shirts & Ties Inc.   *Please Detach Before Cashing*   CHEQUE NO.   **5001**

Aug 1, 2016   Re: Lease ($1,640.00 plus HST) $1,853.20

SD-2

Shirts & Ties
8 Shirt Drive
Ottawa ON K2Z 1Z1

CHEQUE NO. **5002**

DATE 0 2 0 8 2 0 1 6
D D M M Y Y Y Y

PAY Four Thousand Four Hundred twelve ----------------25/100 $**4,412.25

To The Order Of   Arrow Clothing Centre
2830 Appollo Way
Ottawa ON K4A 6N8

Shirts & Ties

Bank of Central Ontario
601 Duke St.
Ottawa, ON K0Z 1Z2

Per _____ *YST* _____
Authorized Signature

⑆00500 2⑈" ⑆ ⑈11330501⑈ 91⑈1055⑉

Shirts & Ties Inc.   *Please Detach Before Cashing*   CHEQUE NO.   **5002**

Aug 2, 2016   Paid #2531   Discount $79.50 $4,412.25

SD-3

Shirts & Ties
8 Shirt Drive
Ottawa ON K2Z 1Z1
Phone: (613) 927-3838

INVOICE

Sold:	Flight Airways Inc.	Ship To:
To	2983 Somerset St. West	(Same)
	Ottawa ON K2P 3W2	

Invoice NO.	DATE
5694	Aug 04, 2016

Qty.	Order	Back Order	Description	Base Price	Disc. %	Price	Tax	Amount
250			Shirts style FA-6	$21.00		$21.00	HS	$5,250.00

						Subtotal		5,250.00
				R133922445		HST 13%		682.50

TOTAL DUE
$5,932.50

Shipping Date: Aug 04, 2016
Terms: Net 30 days

SD-4

Ottawa Hydro Company

55223 Electric Drive, Ottawa ON K6Y 3I3

Shirts & Ties	Phone:	(613) 445-8875
8 Shirt Drive	Date:	Aug 04, 2016
Ottawa ON K2Z 1Z1		

Service to July 29 $403.54
H.S.T. R142887665   52.46

Current charges including tax **$456.00**

If paid after August 19 pay **$466.00**

> *Note...*
> Record 456.00 amount owing. If
> payment is late, the additional cost is
> charged to Other Office Expenses.

APPROVAL
Date Aug 5, 2016
Acct. # Utilities
Approved   *GK*

RECEIVED **Aug 05, 2016**

SD-5

McBurger Chain
903 Wheeler Street
Ottawa ON K2J 5J3

CHEQUE NO. **665**

DATE 0 5 0 8 2 0 1 6
D D M M Y Y Y Y

To the order of

Shirts & Ties
8 Shirt Drive
Ottawa ON K2Z 1Z1

Pay: Two Thousand Six Hundred Sixty Four and 00/100 $**2,664.00

Canadian City Bank
125 Mavis Dr., Ottawa ON K3Y 2M9

_____ JH Smith

⑈665⑈ ⑈2500 250080⑈ ⑈89662⑈

McBurger Chain			665
DATE Aug. 05, 2016	INV.NO. #5681	DISCOUNT 48.00	AMOUNT PAID $2,664.00

RECEIVED Aug 06, 2016

For Deposit Only

SD-6

Springman & Associates
6990 Winston Churchill Road
Caledon ON L0P 1P6
519-927-8885
GST Number: R222444666
Anne Springman

**PURCHASE ORDER
2180**

Date: Aug 9, 2016
Ship Date: Aug 11, 2016

To: Shirts & Ties
8 Shirt Drive
Ottawa ON K2Z 1Z1

Ship To:
(Same)

Ordered	Description	Unit Price	Unit	Tax	Total
38	Shirts Mod-36	$20.00	Each	HS	$ 760.00
38	Ties VA-Mac	$32.00	Each	HS	1,216.00
				Subtotal	$ 1,976.00
				HST	256.88
	Terms: 2/10, net 30			**TOTAL**	$ 2,232.88

SD-7

Radisser **H**otels **I**nc.
3865 Pickford Drive
Ottawa ON K2J 5Z6

CHEQUE NO.   **93288**

DATE   0 9 0 8 2 0 1 6
D D M M Y Y Y Y

PAY	Seven Thousand Seven Hundred Seventy and 00/100	$**7,770.00

To The Shirts & Ties
Order 8 Shirt Drive
Of Ottawa ON. K2Z 1Z1

Canadiania Bank
19 Moore Avenue
Nepean ON K4C 2A1

B J Radisser

⑆93288⑆   ⑆0426⑆004⑆   112⑈181 8⑈

DETACH BEFORE CASHING

Radisser Hotels Inc.   **93288**

DATE	DESCRIPTION	AMOUNT
Aug 09,2016	RE: Payment of Invoice #5683, less $140.00 discount	$ 7,770.00

RECEIVED   Aug 09, 2016
For Deposit Only

SD-8

Shirts & Ties
8 Shirt Drive
Ottawa ON K2Z 1Z1
Phone: (613) 927-3838

INVOICE

Sold: Springman & Associates   Ship To:
To   6990 Winston Churchill Road   (Same)
        Caledon ON L0P 1P6

Invoice NO.	DATE
5695	Aug 13, 2016

Qty.	Order	Back Order	Description	Base Price	Disc. %	Price	Tax	Amount
38			Shirts Mod-36	$20.00		$20.00	HS	$ 760.00
38			Ties, VA-Mac	32.00		32.00	HS	1,216.00
					Subtotal			1,976.00
			R133922445		HST 13%			256.88

PO 2180 Attn: Ann Springman
Shipping Date: Aug 13, 2016
Terms: 2%10, Net 30 days

TOTAL DUE
$2,232.88

SD-9a

Arrow Clothing Centre　　　　　　Invoice 2689

2830 Appollo Way
Ottawa ON K4A 6N8
HST# 53842

Aug 15, 2016

To:　Shirts and Ties
　　　8 Shirt Drive
　　　Ottawa ON K2Z 1Z1　　　　Terms: 2/10, net 30

30 Shirts Model 42	24.25 each	$ 727.50
	HST	94.58
	Total	$ 822.08

Received a $30.00 Canadian mail-in rebate form on this purchase. See SD-9b.

SD-9b

REBATE CHECKLIST	CUSTOMER $30 MAIL-IN REBATE
Purchase $200 or more to receive a $30.00 mail-in rebate.	PLEASE PRINT CLEARLY IN CAPITAL LETTERS

Purchase $200 or more to receive a $30.00 mail-in rebate.

To qualify for this rebate, you must submit:

❑ This completed rebate form.

❑ Copy of the dated invoice, or transaction record for qualifying purchase.

CUSTOMER $30 MAIL-IN REBATE

PLEASE PRINT CLEARLY IN CAPITAL LETTERS

SHIRTS MODEL 42
Product description

SHIRTS AND TIES
Name

8 Shirt Drive
Street Address (required)

OTTAWA	ON	K2Z 1Z1
City	**Province**	**Postal Code**

613-927-3838	(blank)
Phone Number	**E-mail address**

Mail to:　Rebate Centre
　　　　　　 81 Booth Street
　　　　　　 Ottawa ON K2R 5P2

This offer expires: October 31, 2016

Assume that this form was completed and mailed today. Create a customer "Rebate Centre." Use invoice 5696 to record this receivable.

SD-10

Shirts & Ties

8 Shirt Drive
Ottawa ON K2Z 1Z1
Phone: (613) 927-3838

INVOICE
Credit Memo

Sold: Springman & Associates   Ship To:
To   6990 Winston Churchill Road   (Same)
        Caledon ON L0P 1P6

Invoice NO.	DATE
5695Rt	Aug 15 2016

Qty.	Order	Back Order	Description	Base Price	Disc. %	Price	Tax	Amount
-2			Shirts Mod-36	$20.00		$20.00	HS	$-40.00

R133922445 Subtotal	-40.00
HST 13%	-5.20

PO 2180 Attn: Ann Springman
Shipping Date: Aug 15, 2016
Terms: 2%8, Net 28 days

TOTAL DUE
$-45.20

SD-11

Shirts & Ties

8 Shirt Drive
Ottawa ON K2Z 1Z1

CHEQUE NO.   **5003**

DATE   1 5 0 8 2 0 1 6
         D D M M Y Y Y Y

PAY   Two Thousand One Hundred Fifty and 00/100 $**2,150.00

To The   Receiver General
Order   875 Heron Road
Of   Ottawa ON K1A 1A3

                              Shirts & Ties

Bank of Central Ontario
601 Duke St.
Ottawa, ON K0Z 1Z2

Per
Authorized Signature

⑆005003⑈ ⑆113305 01⑈ 91⑈1055⑆

- -

Shirts & Ties Inc.   *Please Detach Before Cashing*   **CHEQUE NO.   5003**

Aug 15, 2016   Re: HST to July 31 $2,150.00

SD-12

MEMO

Shirts & Ties

August 19, 2016

To: Your Name

From: Robert Amber, Manager

Issue cheque today to pay the August 4, 2016 Ottawa Hydro (utilities) bill. This must be paid today to save $10.00.

Robert

SD-13

Shirts & Ties

8 Shirt Drive
Ottawa ON K2Z 1Z1
Phone: (613) 927-3838

INVOICE

Sold:	Your Name
To	Staff – Credit Card Sale

Ship To: (Same)

Invoice NO.	DATE
5697	Aug 19 2016

Qty.	Order	Back Order	Description	Base Price	Disc. %	Price	Tax	Amount
2			Shirts Mod-36	$20.00	30	$14.00	HS	$28.00

R133922445

Subtotal	28.00
HST 13%	3.64

Staff discount 30%
Shipping Date: Aug 19, 2016
Terms: Today

TOTAL DUE
$31.64

SD-14

Springman & Associates
6990 Winston Churchill Rd.
Caledon, ON L0P 1P6

CHEQUE NO.   556

DATE 2 3 0 8 2 0 1 6
D D M M Y Y Y Y

To the order of

Shirts & Ties
8 Shirt Drive
Ottawa ON K2Z 1Z1

Pay: Two Thousand One Hundred Forty-eight and 96/100- - - - - - - - - - - - - - - -$**2,148.96

Canadian City Bank
125 Mavis Dr., Ottawa, ON K3Y 2M9

S Springman

⑈00556⑈   ⑈2500 2080⑈ 8966 2⑈

Springman & Associates   CHEQUE NO. 556

DATE	INV.NO.		AMOUNT
Aug 23, 2016	#5695, 5695Rt	Paid order less return, discount	$2,148.96

RECEIVED   August 24, 2016

For Deposit Only

SD-15

Shirts & Ties

8 Shirt Drive
Ottawa ON K2Z 1Z1

CHEQUE NO.   **5005**

DATE 3 1 0 8 2 0 1 6
D D M M Y Y Y Y

PAY   One Thousand Four Hundred Seventy-four and 20/100 $**1,474.20

To The   Meadows Insurance Brokers Inc.
Order   197 Larange Avenue, Suite 125   Shirts & Ties
Of   Ottawa ON K8Z 4R9

Bank of Central Ontario   Per _____ *YST* _____
601 Duke St.
Ottawa, ON K0Z 1Z2   Authorized Signature

⑈005005⑈   ⑈11330501⑈ 91⑈1055⑈

Shirts & Ties Inc.   *Please Detach Before Cashing*   CHEQUE NO.   5005

Aug 31, 2016   Re: Insurance Renewal Aug. 1, 2016 through Jul. 31, 2017
                      $1,365.00 plus HST $1,474.20

SD-16

Shirts & Ties

M E M O

Aug 31, 2016

To: Your Name
From: Robert Amber, Manager

Please enter the following in the Simply system:

- Andrea Mosely, the new bank accounting clerk, completed the bank reconciliation to August 23 and advised that there are 2 items (Bank Charges $100.00 and Bank Interest Expense $500.00 on our loan) that have not been recorded. Please create 2 new accounts to record these 2 charges.

- The current ending inventory as counted by the stock department is $39,800.00. Record the proper inventory entries to adjust the new inventory value for the Asset Inventory account and the ending inventory in the Cost of Goods Sold section of the Income Statement.

Robert

2 ➤ At the end of the month, **print** the following:

- Income Statement   Jan 01 to Aug 31
- Balance Sheet at   Aug 31
- Vendor Aged Detail report at   Aug 31
- Customer Aged Detail report at   Aug 31
- Journal Entries–All for   Aug 01 - Aug 31
- Journal Entries General   Aug 01 - Aug 31

Chapter 7

EMPLOYEES & PAYROLL
Module Setup and Processing

Creative Wallpaper

Learning Objectives

After completing this chapter you will be able to:

☐ Set up a company's Payroll defaults and linking accounts.
☐ Create and modify employee accounts with specific payroll information.
☐ Record opening employee balances before turning the module to ready.
☐ Turn the module to ready.
☐ Record payroll transactions, using cheque run or individual cheques.
☐ Reverse a payroll cheque issued in error.
☐ Record Payroll advances and reimbursements.
☐ Record Payroll remittance for source deductions.
☐ Record Payroll vacation pay.
☐ Display and Print appropriate Payroll reports and journals.

This chapter allows you to set up the Employees ledger in the EMPLOYEES & PAYROLL module for **Creative Wallpaper**, and record some payroll transactions for the month (January 2014).

Important: This chapter was written using the Simply Accounting Premium 2010, Release A software. If you use a different version you may receive different payroll solutions.

The **Student Edition** of the software included with this textbook is the same software with restrictions. See Appendix A, located at the back of this textbook.

Businesses must purchase a Payroll ID code to activate the Automatic payroll calculations for taxes. The student edition does not require a Payroll activation code.

The payroll taxes are effective from January 1, 2009. If you are using a different Simply version (see information symbol note above) and, therefore, a different edition of the tax tables, which covers a different time period, the instructions still apply, but there may be a slight difference between your net pay amounts and those in the solution.

The following topics are covered:

- EMPLOYEES & PAYROLL Module 365
    Difference between Manual Accounting and Simply Payroll 366
- Creative Wallpaper: Company Profile.. 367
    Exercise 7-1 – Making the EMPLOYEES & PAYROLL Module Visible 369
    Exercise 7-2 – Recording Reversing Entry 371
  Step 1: Setting EMPLOYEES & PAYROLL Module Defaults 371
    Exercise 7-3 – To Set EMPLOYEES & PAYROLL Module Defaults 371
  Step 2: Setting Up Linked Accounts 377
    Exercise 7-4 – Linking Accounts with PAYROLL 377
    Exercise 7-5 – Linking PAYROLL Remittance Accounts 379

   Payroll Conversion...380
  Step 3: Entering Employee Payroll Information 381
   Exercise 7-6 – To Enter Employee PAYROLL Information 381
  Step 4: Setting the PAYROLL Module to Ready..390
   Exercise 7-7 – Setting PAYROLL to Ready 390
   Exercise 7-8 – Creating a New Employee Ledger 392
   Exercise 7-9 – To Issue Paycheques (Payroll Cheque Run) 394
   Exercise 7-10 – Issuing a Single Paycheque 398
   Exercise 7-11 – Reviewing PAYROLL Entries 403
   Exercise 7-12 – To Enter Payroll for Salaried Employees 405
   Exercise 7-13 – Recording Withholdings Payment 407
   Exercise 7-14 – More Payroll Transactions...408
   Exercise 7-15 – Processing Vacation Pay...410
   Exercise 7-16a – Making PAYROLL Corrections-Reverse cheque 412
   Exercise 7-16b – Making PAYROLL Corrections- Issue new cheque 414
   Exercise 7-17 – Payroll for Pay Period Ending Jan 31, 2014......................414
   Exercise 7-18 – Remittances for Payroll Deductions 415
   Exercise 7-19 – Recording PAYROLL Accruals..417
 ▪ Processing T4 Slips (or Relevé 1)..417
   Exercise 7-20 – Printing Month-End Employee-Related Reports 418
    To Print the PAYROLL Journal..418
    To Print an Income Statement for Jan 1 to Jan 31, 2014.....418
    To Print the Balance Sheet as at Jan 31, 2014....................419
    To Display a Cheque Log for Jan 1 to Jan 31, 2014...........419
    To Print the Employee Detail Report................................419
    To Print the Employee YTD (Year-To-Date) Report............420
  Payroll Entry with EHT (Employer Health Tax)..420
  Converting During the Year 420
  Garnishee and Reimbursement...421

 ▪ Before Moving On. 422
 ▪ Relevant Appendices 422

 ▪ Challenge Exercise 07 C7-1, Carpets 4Home 423

Instructions in this chapter assume that you have some knowledge of the basic principles of payroll accounting. If you are unsure of some of the accounting entries for payroll or government regulations, you should try to research these areas before starting the chapter. Refer to your accounting textbook for more information.

Accrual for wages owed for a short period of time, at the beginning of the month and at month-end, will be discussed in this chapter.

Slideshow 7A – Setting up the EMPLOYEES & PAYROLL Module explains in detail the important steps in setting the module to **ready**. Run this slideshow before proceeding.

EMPLOYEES & PAYROLL Module

The EMPLOYEES & PAYROLL module is used to record money earned by employees in a company during a calendar year. The EMPLOYEES Ledger is used to record employees' personal information and payroll information such as hourly rates of pay, additional deductions, etc. The **Paycheques** and **Payroll Cheque Run** journals calculate the gross pay, subtract government deductions (CPP, EI, Income Tax) and other deductions; e.g., safety shoes, insurance, dental plans and other benefits, charitable donations, etc., to arrive at Net Pay.

The Simply program contains tax tables and deduction formulas for all earnings amounts. Simply Accounting updates these tables and formulas on a regular basis, based on information received from Canada Revenue Agency (CRA). There is a fee for these updates.

The COMPANY, RECEIVABLES and PAYABLES modules have been set up and are **Ready** to use.

To set the EMPLOYEES & PAYROLL module to **Ready**, the following needs to be completed:

1. Make payroll-related adjustments.
2. Set the PAYROLL module default settings.
3. Set the PAYROLL module Linked accounts.
4. Create an employee record for each employee in the EMPLOYEES Ledger. Each record will contain the employee's name, address and other basic personal information, pay rates, deductions, etc.

Simply EMPLOYEES & PAYROLL module follows similar procedures to setting the default linked accounts in Chapter 4, and creating customer and vendor records in the RECEIVABLES and PAYABLES modules.

After the employee information is entered in the Employees ledger, the total of the individual balances must balance with the General Ledger PAYROLL related accounts.

Simply Accounting can print T4s (summary of each employee's earnings and deductions), an employee payroll summary, and Detail reports whenever required.

Creative Wallpaper data files will be used to record payroll transactions for the month of January 2014. The instructions in this chapter are based on Simply Accounting Premium Release 2010 version A for Windows issued in December 2009.

Your instructor will advise you which of the two Wallpaper data files to use in Exercise 7-1.

If you use the 07 Wallpaper file:

Data file **07 Wallpaper** follows the text exercises in the following sequence:

1. recording the reversing accrual entry,
2. setting defaults,
3. linking the appropriate accounts to the General Ledger,
4. entering each employee's data,
5. turning the EMPLOYEES & PAYROLL module to Ready, and
6. recording paycheques and payments – to the end of the chapter.

If you use the 07 Wallpaper2 file:

Data file **07 Wallpaper2** has the EMPLOYEES & PAYROLL module set to **Ready** (Steps 1 through 5 above have been completed for you). If you use it, start at

Exercise 7-8 (Creating a New Employee Ledger). Assume you have been hired to be the new payroll clerk and the EMPLOYEES & PAYROLL module was set up by your supervisor, Mrs. Singh.

If you use 07 Wallpaper2, you may want to review the steps that were completed, to have the module ready to use by reading through the steps shown in Exercises 7-1 to 7-7.

Difference between Manual Accounting and Simply Payroll

The following illustrates the difference in processing payroll in a manual system and Simply. The entries assume an employee's basic Wage is $1,000.00 ($12.50 per hour x 80 hours) plus 4% Vacation Pay ($40.00) per week.

Manual Accounting:

1.	**Payroll journal entry from payroll register as printed on employee pay-stub.**		$
	Wages Expense	$1,040.00	
	Bank Account Chequing		750.48
	Vacation Payable		40.00
	EI Payable		17.30
	CPP Payable		42.84
	Income Tax Payable		105.38
	Union Dues Payable		20.00
	Pension Plan Payable		40.00
	Medical Plan Payable		24.00
	Record payroll cheque information		
2.	**Payroll: deduction expense entry (expense for company)**		
	EI Expense	24.22	
	CPP Expense	42.84	
	EI Payable		24.22
	CPP Payable		42.84
	Record payroll benefit costs		
3.	**Payroll: other expenses (Expense for company)**		
	WSIB Expense	4.10	
	WSIB Payable		4.10
	Record other benefit costs		

Fig. 7-1a: Simply Payroll.

Simply Payroll:

Simply generates the following combined journal entry (parts 1, 2, and 3).

Simply - payroll entry: combines parts 1, 2, 3		
Wages Expense	1,040.00	
EI Expense	24.22	
CPP Expense	42.84	
WSIB Expense	4.10	
Bank Account Chequing		750.48
Vacation Payable		40.00
EI Payable		41.52
CPP Payable		85.68
Income Tax Payable		105.38
Union dues Payable		20.00
Pension Plan Payable		40.00
Medical Plan Payable		24.00
WSIB Payable		4.10

Fig. 7-1b: Simply Payroll.

Creative Wallpaper: Company Profile

Creative Wallpaper sells wallpapers, from many manufacturers, and related materials (tools, cutters, glue, cleaning solvents and other accessories). Information about the company's payroll is shown below.

- Hourly employees are paid bi-weekly (26 times a year).

- Commission employees are paid bi-weekly (26 times a year).

- Salaried employees are paid twice a month (bi-monthly), 24 times a year.

- Overtime is paid at the rate of time and one-half. (Regular pay plus ½ regular pay.)

- Vacation pay (4%) is retained for hourly and commission employees until the employee takes holidays. Vacation pay is not calculated or retained for salaried employees.

- The Employment Insurance (EI) rate (federal regulations) for the company is 1.4 times that which the employees have deducted from their paycheques.

- WCB or Workers' Safety and Insurance Board (WSIB Ontario) rate for the company is 0.41% (dot 41%).

- The Employer Health Tax (EHT-Ontario) expense is based on payroll costs. Effective January 1, 1999, employers with payrolls of less than $400,000 are exempt from this tax. The payroll example that follows assumes the payroll costs for Creative Wallpaper will be less than $400,000 and, therefore, the payroll entries will not indicate this expense. See the "Information Only" section at the end of the chapter for an example of a payroll entry that contains the EHT expense and EHT payable.

- Each payday, union dues of **$20.00** (before tax) are deducted from the wages of each of the hourly and commission employees.

- A company policy is that, in extenuating circumstances, employees may receive an advance of wages/salary up to $600.00. The advance is repayable by regular payroll installments. *Hourly* workers repay **$30.00** and *Salaried* employees repay **$45.00** each pay date. Mrs. Singh, store supervisor, approves advances.

- Full-time employees contribute **4%** of their wages or salary, not including vacation pay, to a pension plan. Contributions are sent to the pension plan quarterly.

Study the Trial Balance of Creative Wallpaper shown next.

Creative Wallpaper, Student's Name
Trial Balance As At Jan 01, 2014

		Debits	Credits
1010	Bank Account Chequing	16,800.00	-
1200	Accounts Receivable	15,142.00	-
1241	Advances Receivable	90.00	-
1260	Inventory of Goods	75,325.00	-
1280	Store/Office Supplies/Prepaid	600.00	-
1520	Equipment & Shelving	67,800.00	-
1540	Office Furniture & Fixtures	15,628.00	-
1620	Accumulated Amortization Equipment	-	21,200.00
1640	Accumulated Amort: Office Furn/Fixt	-	3,420.00
2200	Accounts Payable	-	16,610.00
2210	Accrued Payroll Payable	-	512.00
2300	Vacation Payable	-	900.00
2310	EI Payable	-	512.00
2320	CPP Payable	-	497.00
2330	Income Tax Payable	-	2,345.00
2390	United Way Donations Payable	-	260.00
2420	Union Dues Payable	-	220.00
2430	Pension Plan Payable	-	480.00
2440	Medical Plan Payable	-	200.00
2450	Safety Shoes Payable	94.00	-
2460	WSIB Payable	-	450.00
2650	HST Charged On Sales	-	1,432.00
2670	HST Paid On Purchases	1,050.00	-
3100	Capital R. Storozhko	-	143,491.00
3580	Drawings R. Storozhko	-	0.00
4010	Sales	-	0.00
4210	Sales Returns	-	0.00
4220	Sales Discounts	-	0.00
5020	CGS Beginning Inventory	0.00	-
5030	Purchases	0.00	-
5040	Purchase Returns	0.00	-
5050	Purchase Discounts	0.00	-
5090	CGS Ending Inventory	0.00	-
5120	Advertising Expense	0.00	-
5140	Bank Charges and Interest Expense	0.00	-
5160	Insurance Expense	0.00	-
5180	Office Supplies Expense	0.00	-
5200	Telephone Expense	0.00	-
5220	Utilities Expense	0.00	-
5240	Bad Debts Expense	0.00	-
5300	Wages Expense	0.00	-
5302	Salaries Expense	0.00	-
5304	Commissions Expense	0.00	-
5308	Wages-Overtime Expense	0.00	-
5310	EI Expense	0.00	-
5320	CPP Expense	0.00	-
5330	WSIB Expense	0.00	-
5395	Reimbursement Payroll Suspense	0.00	-
		192,529.00	192,529.00

$94.00 Debit balance is from the safety shoes payment, by the company, to the Safety Shoe Company. This balance will decrease as deductions are made from the employee's pay.

Fig. 7-2: Creative Wallpaper, Opening Trial Balance.

Exercise 7-1 – Making the EMPLOYEES & PAYROLL Module Visible

1 ➤ Refer to Exercise 1-1, to open the appropriate Wallpaper data folder as shown below.

If you are using **07 Wallpaper**, open the data file and **continue with step 2 in this exercise**.

If you are using **07 Wallpaper2**, open the data file and **continue with Exercise 7-8**.

2 ➤ Advance the date to **Jan 2, 2014** (the business was closed for New Year's Day). The year 2014 beginning data year file is used for the exercises in this chapter. It will demonstrate the use of two payroll accruals, **January 1** (reverse prior year December 2013 accrual) and the setup of a **January 31 2014** month-end accrual.

3 ➤ The EMPLOYEES & PAYROLL module is not visible and, therefore, not available for use. To make the EMPLOYEES & PAYROLL module available, click **Setup**, **User Preferences**, in the left panel click **View**, in the right panel, **Pages** section, at EMPLOYEES & PAYROLL, click the box. Two ✓ appear (one in the Icon Windows section). Click **OK** and the EMPLOYEES & PAYROLL module in History mode is displayed for use.

4 ➤ Study the Trial Balance in Fig. 7-2. You will notice that account numbers 2210 to 2460 are payable accounts, which are directly affected by Payroll and Payroll Accrual Adjustment transactions.

The normal pay date at the end of December 2013, based on Friday paydays, would have been Friday, December 27. To match revenue with expenses, you would have recorded an accrual for wages owed to employees who work on any of the 4 days December 28, 29, 30 and/or 31. Notice the grayed out dates on the calendar below.

As of **December 31, 2013**, there were accrued salaries/wages of $512.00 owing to hourly and commission employees. This December 31 accrual will need to be reversed at January 2, 2014. This topic will be discussed in more detail in Chapter 9, **Month-End/Year-End Processing**, and Chapter 10, **Year-End Closing**.

The hourly and commission employees will be paid on Friday, January 10, 2014. (See calendar below.)

At the end of January 2014, the normal pay date for hourly and commission employees would be Friday, January 24. An accrual would be recorded for the wages owed for the period Saturday, January 25 to Friday, January 31 (see Exercise 7-19). Employees would be paid on Friday, February 7.

December 2013								**January 2014**					
S	M	T	W	T	F	S		S	M	T	W	T	F	S
1	2	3	4	5	6	7					1	2	3	4
8	9	10	11	12	13	14		5	6	7	8	9	10	11
15	16	17	18	19	20	21		12	13	14	15	16	17	18
22	23	24	25	26	27	28		19	20	21	22	23	24	25
29	30	31						26	27	28	29	30	31	

The days that Doreen David and Jordan Currie worked were recorded in the month of December 2013 as shown below, based on a memo from Mrs. Singh, as an accrued wages and commission expense. (See Trial Balance, Fig. 7-2, account #2210 Accrued Payroll Payable.)

Study the memo below:

MEMO

From: Gurjeet Singh   Date: <u>December 31, 2013</u>
To: Accounting

Please record a payroll accrual for the following employees.

Doreen: 3 days (Dec 28, 30, 31) (8 hours each) at $14.00 per hour $336.00
Jordan: Commission for 2 days (Dec. 28, 30), estimated   <u>$176.00</u>

                           Total accrued wages owed   <u>$512.00</u>

Please remember to reverse this accrual in January 2014, before you record the cheques being issued on January 10, 2014.

The entry that was recorded on December 31st, 2013 for the accrued wages is shown below:

Dec. 31, 2013

Dr 5300 Wages Expense   **336.00**
Dr 5304 Commission Expense   **176.00**
Cr   2210 Accrued Payroll Payable   **512.00**

Accrued wages @ Dec. 31, 2013 per calculation

Accruals do not include EI, CPP and Income Tax Payable amounts because they are recorded when they are actually deducted from each employee on each pay date.

Doreen and Jordan will not get paid for the period December 28 to 31 until January 10, 2014, which is the end of a bi-weekly pay period.

The accounting records on January 2, 2014 should reverse the payroll accrual.

The General Ledger data, accounts and balances have been entered as of January 1, 2014. Payroll liability accounts remain active because the amounts are payable to the federal government, and other agencies, for payroll deductions collected up to December 31, 2013. Employee deduction history information for 2013 is used in the year 2013 T4 slips, and is not entered in the 2014 data file information. Year 2014 employee deduction history will be zero (0.00).

After the EMPLOYEES & PAYROLL system is turned to **Ready**, you will see how your payroll entries affect the General Ledger accounts and financial statements.

Making Payroll-Related Adjusting Entry

As discussed earlier, a payroll accrual adjusting entry was recorded at December 31, 2013 for wages owed to employees who worked on any of the 4 days at the end of December. On January 2, 2014, a reversing entry will be recorded and its purpose is twofold.

a) To ensure expenses are matched to revenues correctly in each of 2013 and 2014, and

b) To keep payroll processing straightforward and simple by removing the need to adjust the paycheques for the amount of the December accrual.

When the actual paycheques for the individuals who had accrued wages are paid, their paycheque amounts for December would be properly accounted for.

Exercise 7-2 – Recording Reversing Entry

---

1 ➤ **Record** and **Post** a January 2 entry to reverse the December 31, 2013 General Journal accrual entry based on the memo. Use the Recurring entry **"Reverse prior month wages accrual"** to **Post** a January 2 entry to reverse the December 31, 2013 General Journal accrual. Change the information as needed. The entry should be similar to the following:

General Journal Entry Jan 02, 2014 (J1)

Account Number	Account Description	Debits	Credits
2210	Accrued Payroll Payable	512.00	-
5300	Wages Expense	-	336.00
5304	Commissions Expense	-	176.00
Additional Date:	Additional Field:		
		512.00	512.00

2 ➤ **Update** the Recurring entry.

3 ➤ **Exit** the General Journal window.

Step 1: Setting EMPLOYEES & PAYROLL Module Defaults

You will now set the EMPLOYEES & PAYROLL module defaults that give information about the way the employees are paid.

Exercise 7-3 – To Set EMPLOYEES & PAYROLL Module Defaults

Names — Payroll

1 ➤ From the Home window, click **Setup**, click **Settings,** in the left pane, click ⊞ at **Payroll**, click ⊞ at **Names,** click **Incomes and Deductions** to display the fields.

Simply allows you to change the names of the default fields:

Income fields,   Income codes 1 through 20 are descriptions for
1 to 20   the type of payroll paid to employees by a company in
(Linked accounts) addition to regular wages. Income codes 4 through 20 are
    not used by Creative Wallpaper.

2 ➤ Income 3   Change Income Name field to **Reimburse,** Tab. This field would be used to pay an employee for money they spent on behalf of the business.

Deduction   Simply provides up to 20 linked accounts that can
fields, 1 to 20   be used for deductions because some companies have many deductions from employees' earnings.

3 ➤ Deduction 1-4   Change Deduction Name fields to the Names listed below.

In this exercise we are not removing the additional unused names for Income or Deductions. If you want to remove the Income or Deduction names from the Names column you would click on the name (e.g., Income 20 or, Deduction 11), press Delete and Tab. The wording will no longer display in journal windows. You may receive a warning confirmation message.

The default names for 1 through 4 are typical of the deductions that exist in many companies.

Income	Name		Deduction	Name	
Advance	Advance	▲	Deduction 1	Pension	▲
Benefits	Benefits		Deduction 2	Union Dues	
Benef. (Que)	Benef. (Que)		Deduction 3	Medical	
Vac. Earned	Vac. Earned		Deduction 4	Safety Shoes	
Vac. Paid	Vac. Paid		Deduction 5	Deduction 5	
Regular	Regular		Deduction 6	Deduction 6	
Overtime 1	Overtime 1		Deduction 7	Deduction 7	
Overtime 2	Overtime 2		Deduction 8	Deduction 8	
Income 1	Salary		Deduction 9	Deduction 9	
Income 2	Commission		Deduction 10	Deduction 10	
Income 3	Reimburse		Deduction 11	Deduction 11	

4 ➤ Prov. Tax   In the left pane, click **Additional Payroll**. Remove **Tax (Que),** Tab. This field would be used to name a provincial payroll tax not collected by the federal government. Certain provinces have such a tax. Ontario does not. Leave the box blank.

5 ➤ Worker's Comp Click ▼ and select **WSIB** (Workplace Safety and Insurance Board) as the appropriate code for Ontario. Tab. Other provinces have different codes.

Prov. Tax:	
Worker's Comp.:	WSIB ▼

6 ➤ When your Names Income & Deductions window and Additional Payroll windows resemble the above, click **OK** to accept changes. (See side note box.)

Printers

⚠ You may not be allowed to change settings in your network system. Check with your instructor. If not, skip this section – read for information.

The next step is to define printer settings.

1 ➤ From the Home window, click **Setup, Reports & Forms,** in the left pane click **Cheques** and in the right pane click on `1010 Bank Account Chequing` to display the Reports & Forms Options window.

2 ➤ This window allows setting changes for both the Payment Cheque and Payroll Cheque. The Next cheque number should be as shown.

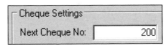

Cheque Settings
Next Cheque No: 200

The printer, form type, font and margin spacing are displayed in the Printer Forms Settings fields. No changes are necessary; however, check with your instructor to make sure that the settings are appropriate.

3 ➤ Click on the + at **Government Forms**.

Vendors	Used to print T5018 forms for subcontractors payroll information.
Federal Payroll	Used to print Record of Employment, T4 Slips and T4 Summary forms.
Quebec Payroll	Used to print Relevé 1 slips.

No changes are necessary. You can identify various printers (if available) for various reports.

In order to conserve paper, you will not be required to print payroll or payment cheques or T4/Relevé 1 slips in this chapter.

4 ➤ Click **OK**, to return to the Home window.

Payroll Settings

1 ➤ From the Home window, click **Setup, Settings**, click on the + at **Payroll** and click on **Incomes** to display the settings window. The option changes are shown as follows:

2 ➤ At Income **Regular**, in the column Type, triple-click the **Hourly Rate** and you will see two choices. DO NOT CHANGE.

Hourly Rate	The rate the employee earns per hour for regular work.
Differential Rate	Extra rate the employee earns per hour for working shifts, higher job classifications, etc.

3 ➤ Click **Cancel**, and at Income **Salary**, in the column Type, triple-click **Income** and you will see six choices. DO NOT CHANGE.

Income	Used to pay employees for regular work.
Benefit	Used for taxable employee benefits such as car allowance; paying employees for using their own vehicle (car, van, truck) for the business, or life insurance, etc., where the company pays the cost on the employee's behalf. Creative Wallpaper does not pay for these types of items.
Reimbursement	Used when an employee is being repaid for money they paid out for the company (e.g., traveling expenses, etc.). Using the PAYROLL module method will allow you to charge only one account for the reimbursement. In most situations, there are two accounts being charged, the Expense or Purchase account and an HST Paid account. Many companies use the PAYABLES module (Make Other Payment option) to reimburse the employee. See Appendix T, *Reimbursement (Payroll)* at www.simplyaccounting2010.nelson.com under Student Resources.

Hourly Rate   Information is the same as in Step 2.

Piece Rate   Employees can be paid based on the number of items (pieces) they can produce during the time they work. If the Piece Rate was chosen, then the Unit of Measure column would change to item.

Differential Rate Information is the same as in Step 2.

4 ➤ Click **Cancel** to leave the Salary line choice as **Income.**

Income	Type	Unit of Measure	Calc. Tax	Calc.	Calc. EI	Calc. Ins. Hours	Calc. CPP/QPP	Calc. EHT	Calc. QHSF	Calc. Vac.	Calc QPI
Advance	System	Period									
Benefits	System	Period	✓				✓	✓			
Benef. (Que)	System	Period		✓			✓		✓	✓	
Vac. Earned	System	Period									
Vac. Paid	System	Period	✓	✓	✓		✓	✓	✓		✓
Regular	Hourly Rate	Hour	✓	✓	✓	✓	✓	✓	✓	✓	✓
Overtime 1	Hourly Rate	Hour	✓	✓	✓	✓	✓	✓	✓	✓	✓
Overtime 2	Hourly Rate	Hour	✓	✓	✓	✓	✓	✓	✓	✓	✓
Salary	Income	Period	✓	✓	✓	✓	✓	✓	✓	✓	✓
Commission	Income	Period	✓	✓	✓	✓	✓	✓	✓	✓	✓
Reimburse	Reimbursem	Period									

Fig. 7-3: Payroll Incomes window after changes.

You will not be able to change any settings in the top blue section (System Type items).

The column is ✓ checked if you calculate the Income type before the column deductions. The column is   unchecked if you calculate the Income type after the column deductions. Therefore, the column is left checked ✓ as you may need the column calculations at a later time.

At the **Commission** line, leave the choice as **Income.**

| Calc. | This column is for Quebec. Leave the ✓ in the column even though Creative Wallpaper currently does not have any employees in Quebec. |

| Calc. EHT | Leave the ✓ in the column even though Creative Wallpaper is currently exempt from the (EHT) Employer Health Tax in Ontario. |

5 ➤ Reimburse At Reimburse, triple-click the **Income**, select **Reimbursement**. It will remove the ✓ marks from the Reimburse line. Reimbursement is not subject to any taxes, deductions or Vacation Pay.

6 ➤ Click the **bottom slider** to move to the right, as part of the right column is hidden. For all other line items use the following instructions.

| Calc. QHSF | Leave the ✓ in the Quebec Health Services Fund column even though Creative Wallpaper currently does not have employees in Quebec. |

| Calc. Vac. | There is no vacation pay on reimbursements. Leave the column unchecked. |

| Calc. QPIP | Leave the ✓ in the column Quebec Parental Insurance Plan. Creative Wallpaper currently does not have any employees in Quebec. |

Track Quebec DO NOT CHANGE. Creative Wallpaper currently has no
Tips Quebec employees.

Payroll Deductions

1 ➤ Click the **Deductions** item in the left pane.

The column is ✓ checked if you calculate the deduction after calculating Tax.
The column is   unchecked if you calculate the deduction before calculating Tax.

Deduction	Deduct By	Deduct After Tax	Deduct After	Deduct After EI	Deduct After CPP/QPP	Deduct After EHT	Deduct After QHSF	Deduct After Vacation	Deduct After QPIP
Pension	Percent of Gr		✓	✓	✓	✓	✓	✓	✓
Union Dues	Amount		✓	✓	✓	✓	✓	✓	✓
Medical	Amount	✓	✓	✓	✓	✓	✓	✓	✓
Safety Shoes	Amount	✓	✓	✓	✓	✓	✓	✓	✓

Fig. 7-4: Payroll Deductions window after changes.

Deduct After Tax	Means that the Income Tax calculations are based on the amount of income an employee earns each pay period, less deductions allowed for Income Tax purposes.

2 ➤

Deduct After Tax	**Pension:** Triple-click on the **Amount** in the **Deduct by** column and select **Percent of Gross,** `Tab`. Pension can be a set amount per week (e.g., $65.00 per pay period) or a percentage of the employee's gross pay.

Leave the column beside **Pension** and **Union Dues** blank (no checkmark) because these deductions are calculated before calculating Income Tax. Income tax is calculated on the Earned Income after these amounts are deducted.

Leave the ✓ in the columns beside **Medical and Safety Shoes.** Medical benefit cost and Safety Shoes are not allowable deductions for Income Tax purposes and are calculated and deducted after calculating Income Tax.

Deduct After	This column is for Quebec. Leave the ✓ in the column even though Creative Wallpaper currently does not have any employees in Quebec.

Deduct After EI	The deduction is calculated after the Employment Insurance amount is calculated.

Deduct After CPP/QPP	The deduction is calculated after the Canada Pension Plan/Quebec Pension Plan deduction amount is calculated.

Deduct After EHT	**Employee Health Tax.** Leave ✓ in column. Creative Wallpaper is currently exempt from this tax as the Payroll will not exceed $400,000 this year.

| Deduct After QHSF | Leave the ✓ in the Quebec Health Services Fund column even though Creative Wallpaper currently does not have employees in Quebec. |

| Deduct After Vacation | The deduction is calculated after the Vacation Pay amount is calculated. |

| Deduct After QPIP | Leave the ✓ in the column Quebec Parental Insurance Plan. Creative Wallpaper currently does not have any employees in Quebec. |

Payroll Taxes

1 ➤ In the left pane, click the **Taxes** item. Change the fields as shown.

EI Factor for new employees:	1.4
WSIB Rate for new employees:	0.41
EHT Factor:	0.0
QHSF Factor:	0.0

EI Factor — Current federal government law requires Creative Wallpaper, the employer, to contribute to EI based on an employee's EI payroll deduction times the factor **1.4**.

2 ➤ WSIB Rate — Workplace Safety and Insurance Board. Type **0.41** (zero dot .41). Premiums are paid by Creative Wallpaper based on a percentage of employees' gross earnings. Various industries pay various rates.

EHT Factor — Employee Health Tax. Do NOT Change. Creative Wallpaper is exempt from this tax as the Payroll will not exceed $400,000 this year.

QHSF Factor — Do NOT Change. Creative Wallpaper currently has no Quebec employees.

Payroll Entitlements

1 ➤ Click the **Entitlements** item in the left pane.

The number of hours in the work day: 8.00

Default Entitlements:

Name	Track Using % Hours Worked	Maximum Days	Clear Days at Year-end
Days 1	0.00	0.00	No
Days 2	0.00	0.00	No
Days 3	0.00	0.00	No
Days 4	0.00	0.00	No
Days 5	0.00	0.00	No

Note: You can change the entitlements for individual employees in their records.

Fig. 7-5: Payroll Ledger – Entitlements tab.

Some firms allow employees to accumulate sick days or leaves of absence based on the number of hours/days they have worked. The more hours worked the more accumulated sick days or leaves of absence employees can have off with pay. Creative Wallpaper does not accumulate entitlement days. There is no exercise in the text for entitlements. DO NOT CHANGE.

Payroll Remittance

Payroll Remittance is being skipped at this time. You will return to Payroll Remittance in Exercise 7-5, after the linked accounts are selected.

This feature allows the software to calculate the amount of the remittance to the Receiver General for the previous month.

Job Categories

1 ➤ Click the **Job Category** item in the left pane.

To add or change a job category, fill in the information below.
(Note: The Job Category of <None> cannot be renamed or removed.)

Job Category	Employees in Category submit time slips	Employees in Category are Salespersons	Status
<None>	√	√	Active

Job Categories would be used with the *Time & Billing Journals* (see Appendix AD, *Time & Billing Journals* at www.simplyaccounting2010.nelson.com under Student Resources) or when you want to classify employees working in various types of jobs. Wallpaper does not use this feature.

2 ➤ Click **OK** to save any changes in the Settings window and return to the Home window. You will return to the Settings window to set up the linked accounts in the next step.

Step 2: Setting Up Linked Accounts

The next step in the setup process is to select the **linked** accounts for the PAYROLL module. These accounts are the G/L accounts for which the entries will be automatically updated when entering data in the PAYROLL module. To link accounts, follow the procedure in the next exercise.

Exercise 7-4 – Linking Accounts with PAYROLL

1 ➤ From the Home window, click **Setup, Settings,** in the left pane, click the ⊞ at **Payroll**. Then in the left pane, click the ⊞ at **Linked Accounts**, in the left pane click **Incomes** to display the Payroll Linked Accounts window.

2 ➤ **Set up** the Payroll Linked Accounts as shown in Figures 7-6, 7-7, 7-8 and 7-9.

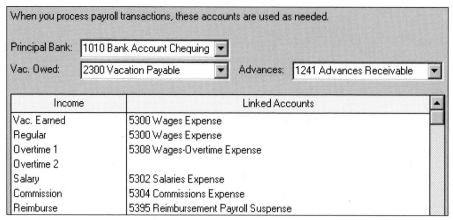

Fig. 7-6: Payroll Linked Accounts — Incomes window.

Payroll cheques will be credited from the bank account defined at the top of the window, and employee advances (if any) will be applied against the ADVANCES RECEIVABLE account.

Deduction	Linked Accounts
Pension	2430 Pension Plan Payable
Union Dues	2420 Union Dues Payable
Medical	2440 Medical Plan Payable
Safety Shoes	2450 Safety Shoes Payable

Fig. 7-7: Payroll Linked Accounts — Deductions window.

If your company does not deduct for any of the items, the field should be left blank.

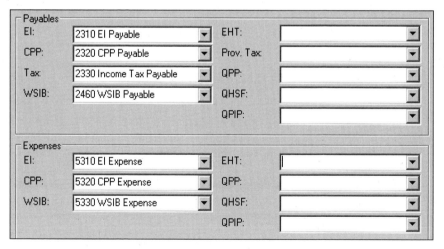

Fig. 7-8: Payroll Linked Accounts — Taxes window.

The **Payables** section contains the Balance Sheet accounts that employee deductions are posted to, which in turn, must be remitted on the employee's behalf to the federal government (EI, CPP, Tax), union, WCB (WSIB in Ontario), etc.

The **Expense** section contains the Income Statement expense accounts to which the company-related payroll expenses are charged.

Notice that there are no Linked accounts for the Quebec Payables and Quebec Expenses as the company currently has no Quebec employees.

Payroll User-Defined Expenses

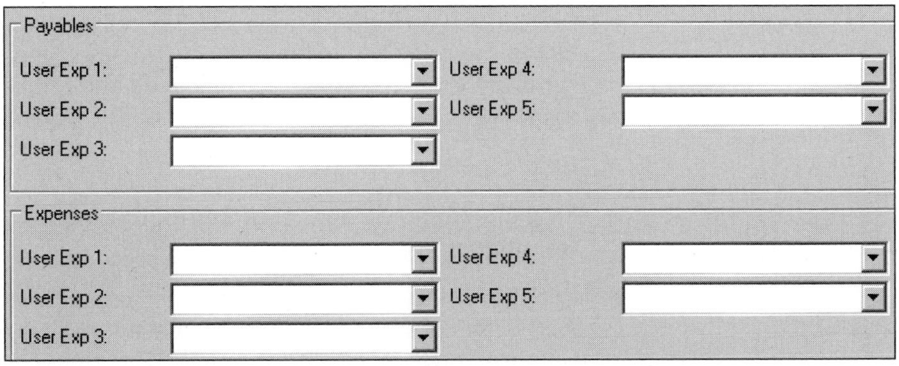

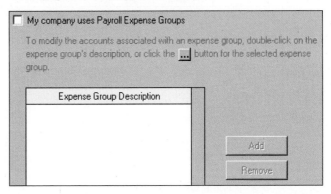

Fig. 7-9: Payroll Linked Accounts — User-Defined Expenses window.

The User-Defined Expenses and Payable accounts would be used when the company pays for various benefits (insurance, dental benefits, etc.). Creative Wallpaper does not pay for these types of items.

Fig. 7-10: Payroll Linked Accounts — Expense Groups window.

The Payroll Expense Groups would be used when you want to report the same employees payroll expenses at different locations, job categories, different administration departments, etc. There is no exercise for this feature.

3 ➤ Click **OK** when complete to exit to the Home window.

The next step in the setup process is to select the **Payroll Remittance Linked accounts** for the PAYROLL module. These accounts are the G/L accounts for which the entries will be automatically updated when entering data in the PAYROLL module. To link remittance accounts, follow the procedure in the next exercise.

Exercise 7-5 – Linking PAYROLL Remittance Accounts

The Receiver General-Payroll Taxes needs to be identified as the Vendor to be used for Payroll Remittances.

1 ➤ Click the **PAYABLES** module, click the **Vendors** icon.

2 ➤ Double-click **Receiver General–Payroll Taxes**.

3 ➤ In the lower-left corner click **Payroll Authority**. A ✓ appears.

4 ➤ Click **Save & Close**.

5 ➤ Repeat steps 2, 3 and 4 for **Accredited Pension Agency, London Medical Group, Union Local #569** and **Workplace Safety and Insurance Board**. Do NOT set up Safety Shoes as a Payroll Authority as Safety Shoes are paid by the company and reimbursed by the employee. The other Payroll Liability items are collected from the employees and remitted to the appropriate authority.

6 ➤ **Exit** to the Home window.

7 ➤ From the Home window, click **Setup, Settings**, click ⊞ at **Payroll, Remittance**.

8 ➤ Click in the **Payroll Authority** column, press **Enter** or triple-click the **Payroll Authority** column. Select and complete the window as shown next. The Balance Forward Date is actually the December 31 balances brought forward from the previous year.

Care must be taken if you are going to have payroll cheques issued on the Balance Forward Date. The amounts recorded are the amounts in the converted Trial Balance before any payroll entries.

Select the payroll authority to which you will remit taxes, deductions or expenses. After selecting the payroll authority enter in the end date of the last remittance period paid into the Bal. Forward Date column, and any amount still owing as of that date into the Bal. Forward column.

Payroll Liability	Payroll Authority	Balance Forward Date	Balance Forward
EI	Receiver General - Payroll Taxes	Jan 01, 2014	512.00
CPP	Receiver General - Payroll Taxes	Jan 01, 2014	497.00
Tax	Receiver General - Payroll Taxes	Jan 01, 2014	2,345.00
WSIB	Workplace Safety & Insurance Boa	Jan 01, 2014	450.00
Pension	Accredited Pension Agency	Jan 01, 2014	480.00
Union Dues	Union Local #569	Jan 01, 2014	220.00
Medical	London Medical Group	Jan 01, 2014	200.00
Safety Shoes			

You will use this feature and amounts in Exercise 7-18, when you are remitting Payroll amounts to the Receiver General. (See side note box.)

9 ➤ Click **OK** when complete.

The PAYROLL module defaults are complete.

This would be a good time to do a backup.

Payroll Conversion

Conversion in this chapter means changing from a manual payroll system to a system using the Simply Accounting program. It can also mean converting from another computerized software to Simply. All personnel records at a given time, usually after month-end, will be added to the PAYROLL module.

The Payroll Department must balance all payroll earnings, deductions, and liability accounts in the manual General Ledger system with the Simply Accounting personnel data information. When all the records have been entered and balanced, the PAYROLL module can be turned to **Ready** and payroll transactions can be entered.

1 ➤ Click the **EMPLOYEES & PAYROLL** module, click the **Paycheques** icon before turning the PAYROLL module to **Ready**. You will then receive this warning message.

Simply Accounting - Warning

⚠ Until you finish entering payroll history details, you must calculate and enter all taxes manually. Automatic calculation could generate inaccurate numbers if entering history has not been completed.

2 ➤ Click **OK**.

3 ➤ The icons (8th from left) *Calculate taxes automatically* and (9th from left) *Enter taxes manually* are grayed out and cannot be activated. **(No employee information has been entered; therefore, these options are not available at this time.)**

4 ➤ Click the ⊠ button to cancel the Payroll Journal and return to the Home window.

Step 3: Entering Employee Payroll Information

Employee names, personal information, payroll balance and amounts deducted from employees during the current year will be entered next.

Creative Wallpaper is converting at January 1, the beginning of a calendar year, and all employee balances of CPP, EI, Income Tax, Taxable Benefits, etc., except for vacation pay owed, would be 0 (nil). This will allow for payroll transaction information to be accumulated and used in preparing T4 slips at the end of 2014.

An example of the employee payroll information that would be entered if the conversion took place at June 30 is shown at the end of the chapter.

Before the EMPLOYEES module can be used, employee personal information must be set up, and payroll account dollar value information added by using the **History** option.

Exercise 7-6 – To Enter Employee PAYROLL Information

Creating Individual Employee Ledgers

You can also type **David, Doreen** and Simply will print the last name (DAVID) in capitals on the T4s as long as there is a comma between the names.

1 ➤ From the Home window, **click Setup, Setup Guide, Employees** and enter the following information.

      Employee   DAVID, Doreen

Enter Employee surname first (last name in CAPITAL letters); i.e., **DAVID,** then a comma, then the first name **Doreen**. (See side note box.)

Last name first in CAPITAL letters (required by Canada Revenue Agency [CRA]). The program prints the Last Name (Surname) in CAPITAL letters on the T4 slip.

* If you have difficulty entering date information, enter date information in step 3.

Birth date*	Apr 26, 1957
Tax Table	Ontario
Pay periods per year	26
SIN	456812635
Hire Date*	Mar 14, 1998
Street 1	17 Huron Street
City	London
Province	Ontario
Postal	N5Y 1Z5

2 ➤ Double-click on the **Employee Name** to display the Employees window. This window is similar to the Vendors and Customers windows.

3 ➤ Enter the Phone 1 information shown in Fig. 7-11, Personal Information.

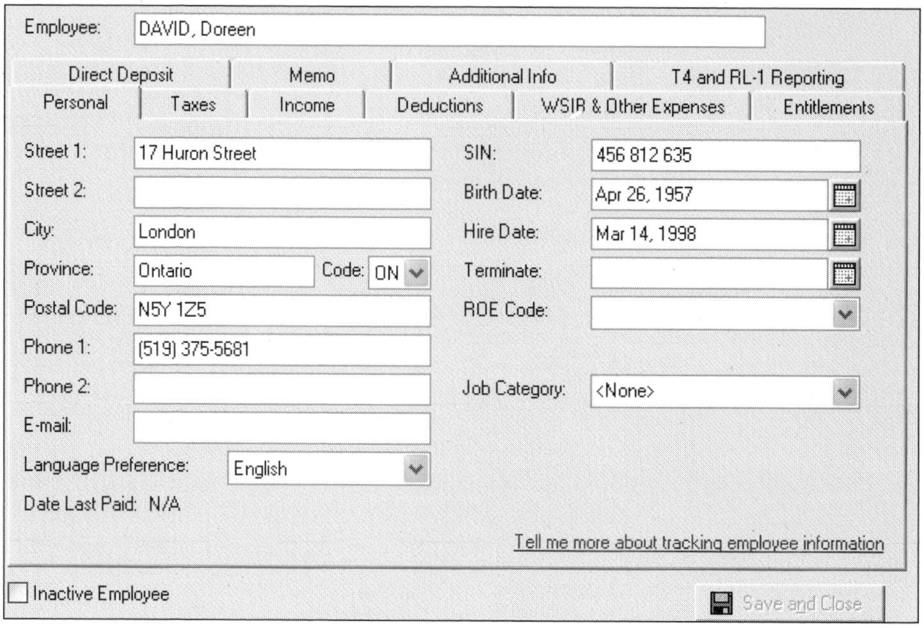

Fig. 7-11: Payroll Ledger window — Personal tab completed.

SIN	An Invalid Entry warning box will appear if you type an invalid SIN number, when you click Close or Save and Close.
Birth Date	This field is used by Simply to deduct CPP if the employee is 18 years or older. It is faster if you type the date (e.g., 042657, 04/26/1957 or apr26 57). Using the calendar feature, you could click on the calendar, click on January, a drop-down menu appears. Select the appropriate month. Click on 2014, a ⊞ appears. Click the up or down button to move to the appropriate year, and select the appropriate day. Using the calendar feature to go back years takes a little more time.
Terminate	Leave blank. This date field would be used when the employee leaves the company.
ROE Code	DO NOT CHANGE. If you click the ▼ a list of Record of Employment termination codes appears.
Job Category	Leave blank. This field would be used to identify job categories identified by management. Employees could be sorted for various reports. Creative Wallpaper does not use this feature.
Date Last Paid	The area to the right (gray area) will automatically show date information after each pay is issued.
Inactive Employee	☐ Inactive Employee The box would be checked (✓) if you have an employee who has temporarily left the firm (because of layoff, leave of absence, vacation, etc.) or has left the firm and is not expected to return.

4 ➤ When your window resembles Fig. 7-11, click the **Taxes** tab.

Taxes

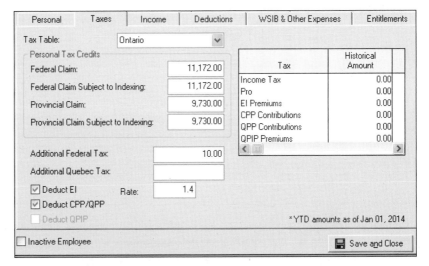

Fig. 7-12: Payroll Ledger — Taxes completed.

5 ➤ Complete the fields as indicated in Fig. 7-12.

Tax table   Click the ▼ arrow to see the other choices. Do NOT Change. (Doreen works and is taxed in Ontario.)

Personal Tax Credits

Federal Claim   **11,172.00** (amount from TD-1 form). This is the amount of income for the year that a person does not need to pay Federal Income Tax on. This allows the program to determine the income tax to be deducted from each employee.

Federal Claim Subject to Indexing   This is the amount of the Federal Claim that will be increased over time by the government. This amount may be different from the Federal claim. This will not be discussed in this text.

Provincial Claim   **9,730.00** The amount from TD1ON (Ontario). This is the amount of income for the year that a person does not need to pay Provincial Income Tax on. Ontario has its own tax rates for the provincial Income tax calculation.

Provincial Claim Subject to Indexing   This is the amount of the Provincial Claim that will be increased over time by the government. This amount may be different from the Provincial claim. This will not be discussed in this text.

 All employees, other than Doreen David, will have the same Federal and Provincial Personal Tax Credits Claim amounts.

Additional Fed Tax   This field will allow the firm to deduct extra income tax based on requests from employees. Doreen David has an extra **$10.00** for income tax deducted each pay period.

Deduct EI	✓ indicates that Doreen is eligible for Employment Insurance benefits.
Rate	Current federal government law requires Creative Wallpaper, the employer, to contribute to EI based on an employee's EI payroll deduction times the factor **1.4**.
Deduct CPP/QPP	The ✓ would be removed if the employee was receiving a disability pension and works on a full or part-time basis. It also applies to employees who are receiving Canada Pension. The individual cannot contribute to the Canada Pension plan while they are collecting benefits.
***YTD amounts as of Jan 01, 2014**	This will be discussed at the end of step 6 ➤.

6 ➤ When your window resembles Fig. 7-12, click the **Income** tab.

Income

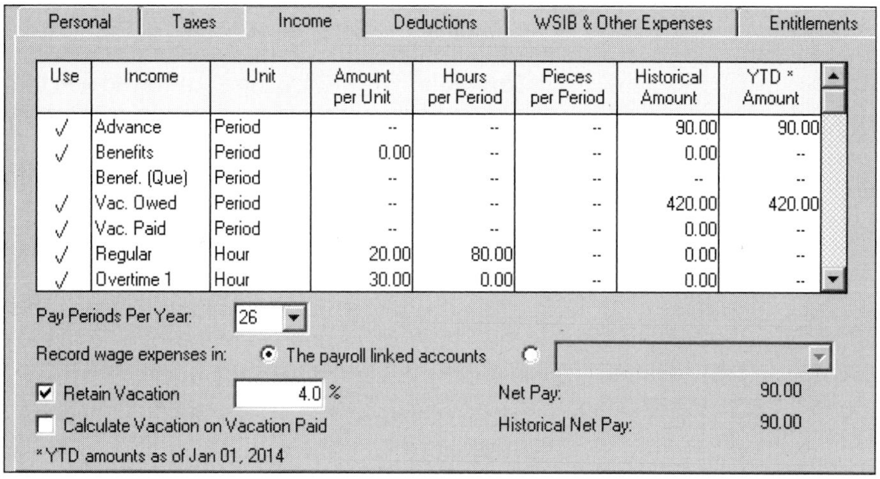

Fig. 7-13: Income tab completed.

ℹ️ All Historical and YTD amounts – Taxes, Income and Deductions will be 0.00, except for Advance 90.00 and Vacation Pay Owed 420.00, which are recorded at step 7. (The conversion of payroll information for Creative Wallpaper takes place at the beginning of the calendar year.)

7 ➤ Complete the fields as indicated in Fig. 7-13. (See side note box.)

Use	A ✓ would be in the field when the Income line is used.
Historical Amount **Advance**	**90.00** The amount that remains to be repaid by an employee for a payroll advance given. When you enter 90.00 in the field, the YTD * amount changes and cannot be amended unless the Historical amount is changed.
Benefits	DO NOT CHANGE. $ value benefits; e.g., additional life insurance, etc., are given to employees in addition to wages. There are no such benefits for Creative Wallpaper employees.
Benef. (Que)	This field would be for taxable benefits for Quebec employees. The company has no employees in Quebec.
Historical Amount **Vac. Owed**	**420.00** The accumulated amount of Vacation Pay owed to the employee for vacation from previous calendar year 2013. The YTD * amount changes and cannot be amended unless the Historical amount is changed.

ⓘ

| Hours Per Period for
employees is used for
Employment Insurance
eligibility and the Record
of Employment form.

Vac. Paid

DO NOT CHANGE. This would be the amount the employee has received in vacation pay this current calendar year.

**Regular
Amount Per Unit**

20.00 This field records the hourly wage rate that is paid to the employee in the current calendar year. This number will show up as a default when you enter the PAYROLL module to pay the employee.

**Regular
Hours Per Period**

80.00 This field records the normal weekly hours the employee works in the current calendar year. This number will show up as a default when you enter the PAYROLL module to pay the employee. (See side note box.)

**Overtime 1
Amount per Unit**

30.00 This field records the hourly wage rate that is paid to the employee for each hour of overtime.

Overtime 2

Overtime 2 fields are not used by Creative Wallpaper.

Salary per period

This field is lower down in the window. Use the down slider to see additional Income fields. Leave this field blank. Doreen is an hourly employee and does not receive a salary.

Commission

This field is lower down in the window. Shows the income earned for commission in the current calendar year.

Reimburse

This field is lower down in the window. Shows the amount of reimbursement the employee has received in the current calendar year.

Income 4-20

Leave this field blank. Creative Wallpaper does not use other Income categories.

**Pay Periods
Per Year**

26 Doreen is paid bi-weekly.

**Record wage
expenses in**

DO NOT CHANGE the default. The button to the right of the Payroll linked accounts would be clicked if the wages for an employee were to be charged to an account that was not identified on the Linked accounts — Income tab window (see Fig. 7-6). All employees use the Payroll Linked account button.

**Retain
Vacation**

The box would be (✓) to accumulate vacation pay. Doreen's vacation pay is 4% of her gross pay, and it accumulates week by week until she takes a vacation. Vacation paid to an employee will be shown in Exercise 7-15.

% field

Type **4.0, Tab**.

If you uncheck the **Retain** field, the vacation pay will be added to each paycheque. The employee would receive no vacation pay when going on vacation. The employee would have received it on a continual basis. DO NOT UNCHECK.

**Calculate Vacation
on Vacation paid**

DO NOT CHANGE the default as Ontario does not calculate vacation pay on vacation pay amounts paid to employees.

Net Pay	This field, calculated automatically by Simply, is the gross pay minus deductions. The 90.00 displayed is the outstanding payroll advance. You cannot change this field.
Historical Net Pay	This field, calculated automatically by Simply, is the gross pay minus deductions. The 90.00 displayed is the outstanding payroll advance. You cannot change this field.
*YTD amounts as of Jan 01, 2014	This * refers to the column YTD * Amount. The date will advance as the session changes. (e.g., `*YTD amounts as of Jan 10, 2014`).

8 ➤ When your window resembles Fig. 7-13, click the **Deductions** tab.

Deductions

Personal	Taxes	Income	Deductions	WSIB & Other Expenses	Entitlements

Use	Deduction	Amount per Pay Period	Percentage per Pay Period	Historical Amount	YTD Amount
✓	Pension	--	4.0000	0.00	--
✓	Union Dues	20.00	--	0.00	--
✓	Medical	24.00	--	0.00	--
✓	Safety Shoes	16.00	--	0.00	--

Fig. 7-14: Payroll Ledger – Deductions tab.

9 ➤ Complete the fields as indicated in Fig. 7-14.

Amounts entered in this window will be used by Simply to calculate net pay for each pay date. If necessary, the amounts may be edited on the paycheque at the time the pay is entered.

Pension	**4.0000** Full-time employees contribute 4% of gross salary, wages and/or commission to a registered pension plan.
Union Dues	**20.00** The amount taken from employees, bi-weekly pay for Union dues. It is a set amount that does not fluctuate based on income.
Medical	**24.00** The amount the employee pays, which is 100% of the cost for an extended medical and dental plan.
Safety Shoes	**16.00** Effective January 2, the amount Doreen will have deducted from each bi-weekly pay, to pay back $94.00 for new safety shoes. The shoes have been ordered.
Deductions 5-20	DO NOT CHANGE. Creative Wallpaper does not use these fields. These fields could be used for other deductions the employee and the firm agree upon; e.g., United Way, other charitable donations, etc.
Historical Amount	There are no Historical amounts to be recorded.

10 ➤ When your window resembles Fig. 7-14, click **WSIB & Other Expenses** tab.

WSIB & User-Defined Expenses

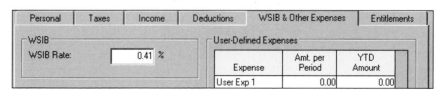

Personal	Taxes	Income	Deductions	WSIB & Other Expenses	Entitlements

WSIB

WSIB Rate: 0.41 %

User-Defined Expenses

Expense	Amt. per Period	YTD Amount
User Exp 1	0.00	0.00

> When a new employee is created, the WSIB current default rate is entered by Simply. When the WSIB rate changes, you must change the rate in every employee's ledger to the new rate.

WSIB Rate   As shown before, the rate is 0.41 (see side note box).

User-Defined   As shown previously, these fields are not used by
Expenses   Creative Wallpaper.

Entitlements

11 ➤   Click **Entitlements** tab.

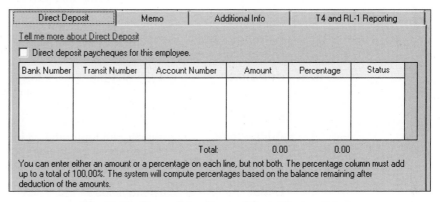

This window is similar to Fig. 7-5, but it now contains Historical Days & Net Days Accrued (Net days Accrued column partially hidden). No changes required.

Direct Deposit

12 ➤   Click **Direct Deposit** tab.

Bank Number	Transit Number	Account Number	Amount	Percentage	Status

Total: 0.00   0.00

You can enter either an amount or a percentage on each line, but not both. The percentage column must add up to a total of 100.00%. The system will compute percentages based on the balance remaining after deduction of the amounts.

Fig. 7-15: Payroll Ledger – Direct Deposit tab.

To use this feature, you must arrange with your bank to allow direct deposits of employees' net pay to one or more employee bank accounts.

Creative Wallpaper gives each employee a cheque for their pay and does not use this feature.

Memo

13 ➤   Click the **Memo** tab.

You may enter any personal information you may want to record about the employee, such as name and number to call in case of an emergency. See step 14 for additional fields. The memo notes can also display in the Daily Business Manager. DO NOT CHANGE.

Additional Information

14 ➤   Click the **Additional Info** tab. These fields can be used to keep personal information about the employee, similar to what was discussed at step 13. Some of the fields could be used to record wage increase dates, performance review date, etc. Refer to Appendix Q, *Names Fields* at www.simplyaccounting2010.nelson.com under Student Resources.

15 ➤ **Field 1:** Type **Payroll Advance $30.00** and click (✓) the Display Info box on the right. When the employee is chosen for a payroll transaction an information window will appear. Click the **T4 & RL-1 Reporting** tab.

T4 & RL-1 Reporting

Direct Deposit	Memo	Additional Info	T4 and RL-1 Reporting
	Current Year: 2014		Historical Amounts
El Ins. Earnings:		0.00	0.00
Pensionable Earnings:		0.00	0.00
QPIP Ins. Earnings:		0.00	0.00
RPP/DPSP Reg. No:		589896	
Pension Adjustment:		0.00	
T4 Emp. Code:			

E-file Information
Current Year: 2014

T4 E-file Submission ID:
T4 Date of Transmission:
RL-1 E-file Slip No.:
RL-1 Date of Transmission:

El Ins. Earnings (Historical)	This field would record El Insurable Earnings when employee records are being converted during the year.
Pensionable Earnings (Historical)	This field reports the Pensionable earnings that are recorded under the CPP plan for the current year.

16 ➤

RPP/DPSP Reg. No.	Type **589896**. This is the Registered Pension Plan number registered with the federal government.
Pension Adjustment	This field would contain a value for a Pension adjustment that reduces the RRSP deduction limit of persons who are in a company-sponsored registered pension plan. This topic is not discussed in this text.
E-file Information	These fields would contain information if the company sent T4 and/or Quebec RL-1E forms over the Internet to the government. DO NOT CHANGE.

17 ➤ Click the Save and Close button to save the Payroll Ledger information for Doreen David.

18 ➤ Use the same method as above to **enter employee payroll information for the other active employees**, MCINTYRE, Sharon, SINGH, Gurjeet, and CURRIE, Jordan as shown in Fig. 7-16 that follows.

When you finish making changes to the individual employee's historical data, and the balances in the Employee Ledger balance with the General Ledger, you may receive this message:

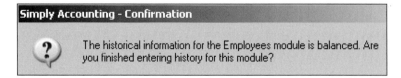

Simply Accounting - Confirmation

? The historical information for the Employees module is balanced. Are you finished entering history for this module?

19 ➤ If you see this box, click **No** and X to exit to the Employees window.

20 ➤ When you are finished entering all the employees, the Gross YTD and Deductions YTD should all be 0.00 because you have not paid the employees in the current calendar year. The Net YTD displays $90 for Doreen as this is the outstanding Payroll Advance she received (see Exercise 7-6, Fig. 7-13).

21 ➤ When finished, **Exit** to the Home window.

Employee	SINGH, Gurjeet	MCINTYRE, Sharon	CURRIE, Jordan **
Birth Date	Apr 02, 1952	May 20, 1966	Dec 11, 1953
Tax Table	Ontario	Ontario	Ontario
Pay Periods per year	24	24	26
SIN (No spaces)	445678907	623148392	719983256
Hire Date	Aug 18, 1997	Aug 06, 1990	Feb 12, 1989
Street 1	6342 Fanshawe Park Rd W	753 Regent Street	2132 Maitland Street
City	London	London	London
Province	Ontario	Ontario	Ontario
Postal	N6G 2T6	N5Y 7P6	N5Y 6B7
Personal Tab			
Phone 1	519 555-1212	519 826-2566	519 355-1269
Taxes Tab			
Tax Table	Ontario	Ontario	Ontario
Personal Tax Credits *	10,700.00	10,180.00	10,310.00
Additional Fed Tax	0.00	0.00	0.00
Deduct EI Rate	✓ 1.4	✓ 1.4	✓ 1.4
Deduct CPP/QPP	✓	✓	✓
Income Tab			
Historical Advance	0.00	0.00	0.00
Benefits	0.00	0.00	0.00
Vacation Owed	0.00	0.00	480.00
Regular Amount per unit **			0.00
Hours per period			0.00
Overtime 1 (per hour)			0.00
Salary	2,500.00, Hours 80	2,000.00, Hours 80	
Commission			0.00 Hours 0.00
Pay periods	24	24	26
Retain Vacation	No	No	✓ 4.0
Deductions Tab			
Pension	4.0	4.0	4.0
Union Dues			20.00
Medical	24.00	24.00	24.00
Safety Shoes	0.00	0.00	0.00
WSIB			
WSIB Rate	0.41	0.41	0.41
T-4 Reporting			
RPP/DPSP Reg. No.	589896	589896	589896

Fig. 7-16: Creative Wallpaper Employees PAYROLL Information.

* **Federal/Provincial**: All employees, other than DAVID, Doreen will have the same Federal and Provincial Personal Tax Credits claims amounts.

** **Note**: CURRIE, Jordan is a commission salesperson and does not receive an hourly wage.

Reviewing Related Payroll – G/L Balances

The history values entered for all employees must be equal to certain accounts in the General Ledger.

1 ➤   Display or print the Trial Balance as at January 2, 2014. This should agree with Fig. 7-2 except for the reversing entry for Wages Expense and Commissions Expense which now have a credit balance, and Accrued Payroll Payable is 0.00.

Review the balances for the following payable accounts:

> **2300 Vacation Payable**
> **2310 EI Payable**
> **2320 CPP Payable**
> **2330 Income Tax Payable**
> **2420 Union Dues Payable**

These accounts represent the employee deductions during December 2013 and the company portion of the same costs, where applicable (required by law), during the month of December 2013.

The asset 1241 ADVANCES RECEIVABLE is $90.00 which is equal to Doreen David's outstanding balance, which will reduce until repaid. A company policy is to lend individual employees up to $600.00 for emergencies. The amount must be repaid with $30.00 or $45.00 installments each payday.

2 ➤   Display the Balance Sheet at January 2, 2014 to verify the asset and payable amounts.

Step 4: Setting the PAYROLL Module to Ready

The last step is to set the module to **Ready**. It is important to back up your data files before setting a module to Ready. Once the modules are made **Ready**, you cannot go back to make changes to historical information.

Are you ready to make PAYROLL Ready?

Exercise 7-7 – Setting PAYROLL to Ready

1 ➤   Back up your data files now. Update your logbook, too.

2 ➤   From the menu bar, click **History, Enter Historical Information ▶ and click ✓ **Payroll**.

A warning message will be displayed if the balances of the Employees Ledger do not match the G/L linked accounts Vacation Payable and Advances Receivable. No warning message is displayed for the other linked accounts should any balances be different. You must review the balances carefully yourself.

This is an example of a warning message (see side note box):

Simply Accounting - Checking database

Checking Employees...
Your Employees' vacation pay owed does not equal the current balance of account 2300 Vacation Payable.

$420.00	Total Vacation Owed to Employees
$900.00	Current Balance of 2300 Vacation Payable
-$480.00	Difference

Either your Employees' historical information or the opening balance of account 2300 Vacation Payable, or both, is incorrect.

If the linked accounts balances are correct, you will receive a standard message to back up data files before proceeding.

  Backup

Remember to **Backup** before clicking Proceed to turn the PAYROLL module to **Ready**.

3 ➤ Click **Proceed**.

The PAYROLL module is ready to use for January 2014 and future transactions. Payroll Journal icons may now be selected.

 Start here if your instructor suggests that you use the data file **Wallpaper2**.

Slideshow 7B – Processing PAYROLL Transactions will help you better understand the tasks relating to PAYROLL transactions. Run it now.

Entering EMPLOYEE Transactions

The rule in setting the Session Date in the PAYROLL module is different from other modules. The PAYROLL module will record the session date as the processing date regardless of the Period Ending date you record. Simply uses the Session Date to determine which tax table to use.

The tax tables change according to government regulations (Simply provides software updates). As mentioned above, you may enter a Period ending date that is different from the Session Date, but the session date is posted. The limitation is the fiscal year. It is possible to back-date cheques in the PAYROLL module to previous months and also to a previous year if a system setting is changed. However, the Session Date is still considered the date of posting.

For the PAYROLL module, therefore, advance the Session Date for each work session.

The Creative Wallpaper store and office were closed for New Year celebrations and did not reopen until Wednesday, January 2.

Entering a New Employee

> **Jan 02, 2014 You will now enter your own personal information as a new employee who will work part-time for the first 3 months.**

Exercise 7-8 – Creating a New Employee Ledger

1 ➤ Enter a new employee account (see Exercise 7-6 for reference), using your name. In order to keep the window displays of existing employees and cheque numbers in proper sequence, **type your name with an A- before your actual last name** (e.g., A-BROWN, Wakina). Enter the rest of the profile as follows:

Personal	
Employee Name	A-Your LAST NAME, First Name
Birth Date	Jul 08, 1976
Tax Table	Ontario
Pay Periods	26
SIN	712336106
Hire Date	Jan 02, 2014
Street 1	690 Barker Street
City	London
Province	Ontario
Postal code	N5Y 8P3
Phone 1	519 841-5045

Taxes	
Tax Table	Ontario
Personal Tax Credits (Fed/Prov)	10,382.00
Deduct EI, Rate	✓ 1.4
Deduct CPP/QPP	✓

Income		
Regular Per Hour	14.00	40 hours
Overtime Per Hour	0.00	0
Retain Vacation	✓ 4.0	

Deductions		
Pension*	0.00	*only full-time staff belong to
Union	20.00	the Pension Plan and have
Medical*	0.00	medical benefits.

WSIB & Other	
WSIB Rate	0.41

Fig. 7-17: Your Name Information.

2 ➤ **Exit** from the Payroll Ledger and return to the Home window.

Payroll for Pay Period Ending Jan 10, 2014

1 ➤ Advance the Session date to **Jan 10, 2014**.

The payroll data may be entered in two different ways:

a) You may use the **Paycheques** icon to pay one employee at a time.

b) You may use the **Payroll Cheque Run** icon to pay multiple employees at the same time.

In the next Exercise 7-9 you will use the **Payroll Cheque Run,** method **b)**, to pay employees.

In Exercise 7-10, you will use method **a)** to pay one employee at a time.

To Issue Paycheques

At payroll preparation time, you would receive information from the manager or supervisor on memos or time cards similar to the following:

EMPLOYEE TIME SHEET   200

Date: Jan. 10, 2014

Employee Name: A-Your LAST NAME, First Name   Employee # __5__

Regular Hours	Overtime Hours	Commission Hours	Commission Amount	Deductions	Other Information
26	None	None		Pension No Union Dues $20.00	

Hint: Net Pay $326.35

Approved by: *G. S.*

EMPLOYEE TIME SHEET   201

Date: Jan. 10, 2014

Employee Name: Doreen David   Employee # __2__

Regular Hours	Overtime Hours	Commission Hours	Commission Amount	Deductions	Other Information
80	2	None		Pension $ 66.40 Union Dues 20.00 Medical 24.00 Safety Shoes 16.00	Advance Repaid $30.00

Hint: Net Pay $1,150.90

Approved by: *G. S.*

Jordan Currie's Employee Time sheet is not available at this time. A cheque will be issued later.

Exercise 7-9 – To Issue Paycheques (Payroll Cheque Run)

To reduce paper usage, you do not need to print paycheques for any exercise in this chapter. An example of what will print on the preprinted cheques appears in Fig. 7-19.

1 ➤ To issue bi-weekly paycheques to Doreen David and yourself, click the **Payroll Cheque Run** icon. A Payroll Run Journal window, similar to the following, will appear.

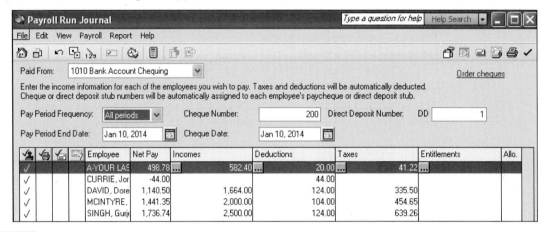

The Expand button shown in the first line of boxes will be seen as you move down the column.

Fig. 7-18: Payroll Cheque Run Journal, before changes. (See side note box.)

The Additional Info box advising you of the advance to be repaid by Doreen can be seen behind the top left of the Journal window.

⚠️ Your A-LAST NAME, First name will show as the first employee in the Employee column.

2 ➤ Move your mouse pointer and position it above [icons]. Look at the Payroll Run Journal status bar as you move your mouse.

🛈 A PAYROLL Direct Deposit Business Service is included with the Premium software that will deposit the net pay directly to the employee's bank account. There would be a setup and additional bank charges for using this module. This text does not have an exercise for using this special feature.

	Allows you to choose which employee is to be paid this pay date.
	Allows you to choose which employee cheque will be printed in this cheque run.
	Allows you to choose which employee payroll information will be e-mailed on this cheque run. Creative Wallpaper does not use this feature.
	Allows you to identify which employee will be paid by Direct Deposit. Creative Wallpaper does not use this feature. (See side note box.)

3 ➤ **Pay Period Frequency**
The ✓ is shown for all employees to be paid on this payroll date (not all employees are being paid on this pay date). Click the ▼ and select **26**, Tab to move to Cheque number. MCINTYRE and SINGH are not ✓, as they are paid twice a month. DO NOT CHANGE the ✓ for Jordan Currie. This will be explained later.

If there were an error printing the cheques, you could use this icon 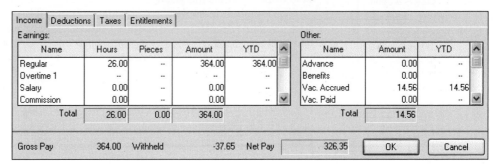 to renumber the cheques, and a message box would inform you that the summary report and cheques will need to be reprinted.

4 ➤ Cheque number Payroll and vendor cheques to be issued will start with this number. [Tab] to accept 200. (See side note box.)

5 ➤ Direct Deposit Number Press [Tab] to accept the default **1**. This field will not change as Creative Wallpaper does not use the Direct Deposit feature of Simply.

6 ➤ Pay Period End Date This is the pay for the week ended January 10, 2014, [Tab], [Tab].

7 ➤ Cheque Date This is the date that will be printed on the cheque and the date the payroll entry will get posted to the General Ledger. Simply will allow you to issue post-dated cheques. The manager, Gurjeet Singh, does not want to issue post-dated cheques. [Tab], [Tab] to accept Jan 10, 2014.

The Payroll Cheque Run feature assumes that default employee hours recorded in the Income tab window (Fig. 7-18) are correct. If an employee has worked overtime or has reduced hours then the hourly Income fields need to be updated.

You are going to change the hours for A-Your LAST NAME, First name from 40 Reg (regular) hours to 26 as follows:

8 ➤ Incomes Click the **Expand** button ▦ in the Income column and the Payroll Detail window appears.

9 ➤ Hours Change 40.00 to **26.00**, [Tab]. The Amount field will change to **364.00** and the Net Pay will change to **326.35**. The Payroll Detail Income tab window displays as shown next. Click **OK**, to return to the Payroll Run Journal window.

Income	Deductions	Taxes	Entitlements						

Earnings:

Name	Hours	Pieces	Amount	YTD		Other: Name	Amount	YTD	
Regular	26.00	--	364.00	364.00		Advance	0.00	--	
Overtime 1	--	--	--	--		Benefits	0.00	--	
Salary	0.00	--	0.00	--		Vac. Accrued	14.56	14.56	
Commission	0.00	--	0.00	--		Vac. Paid	0.00	--	
Total	26.00	0.00	364.00			Total	14.56		

Gross Pay	364.00	Withheld	-37.65	Net Pay	326.35	OK	Cancel

10 ➤ Notice the Additional Info box for Doreen David concerning the 30.00 repayment for her Advance. Click on the **Incomes column** line for **DAVID**. Click the ▦ to open the Detail window.

11 ➤ Advance Type **-30.00** (negative) to reduce the loan, [Tab].

Amount

Name	Amount	YTD	
Advance	-30.00	60.00	

Notice that 60.00 YTD, is the amount remaining to be paid on the Advance.

12 ➤ Overtime 1 Change the hours to **2**, [Tab]. The Net Pay changes to 1,150.90, click **OK**.

13 ➤ Click **Report**. Three different reports are listed.

14 ➤ Click **Print Payroll Cheque Run Summary**, the following message box appears.

> **Simply Accounting - Confirmation**
>
> ? The payroll formulas being used are valid only for session dates Jan 01, 2009 to Dec 31, 2009. Are you sure you want to continue with this transaction?

This message advises you that the tax tables used in this module to create paycheques are valid for dates between Jan 1, 2009 to Dec 31, 2009.

> If you do not use the same software, version 2010 version A, then the tax tables for the period (e.g., Jan 1, 2009 to Dec 31, 2009), may calculate different amounts from the solutions provided with this text for Canada Pension (CPP), Employment Insurance (EI) and Income Tax.

Payroll journal entries are part of one entry (e.g., J2) for display purposes. Each entry will be posted separately.

CURRIE, Jordan will not display in the Payroll Cheque Summary report as the amount is a debit (negative pay) to the BANK account and cannot be posted.

15 ➤ Although we are using a 2014 data file, click **Yes** to accept the formulas. The dates in the previous confirmation window should be the same.

A new warning message appears:

> **Simply Accounting - Confirmation**
>
> ? Negative cheques will not be posted. Do you want to continue printing the direct deposit stub summary?

This message informs you that an employee (Jordan) has a negative net pay (deductions but no income recorded) and cannot be posted in the Payroll Cheque Run. As discussed earlier, you will issue a paycheque to Jordan later in Exercise 7-10. (See side note box.)

16 ➤ Click **NO** to continue. The Summary report would print a copy of the cheque stubs (pay stubs) that the employees will receive. You and/or a supervisor would review the payroll amounts to verify that they are reasonable and approve the payment. You will verify this to the display. Hint: Boxes in the Employee's Time Sheet will advise you of the net pay amounts that are considered correct for the 2010 version A of the Payroll formulas.

17 ➤ Click **Report, Display Payroll Run Journal Entry**; the journal entry for 3 employees will display.

18 ➤ **Exit** from the Payroll Run Journal Entry window.

If a paycheque was printed, the printout on plain paper would be similar to Fig. 7-19. If the cheque was damaged while printing, or there is a serious error on the cheque (e.g., wrong amount), changes could be made and the cheque printed again with a new number (see Exercise 7-10). The payroll records and General Ledger are not updated until the entry is posted.

19 ➤ **Post** the payroll entry. You will see the same payroll date warning message throughout this chapter. Click **Yes** to continue.

You will see the negative pay warning message mentioning CURRIE, Jordan's name.

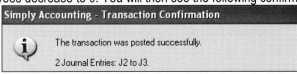

Simply Accounting - Confirmation

CURRIE, Jordan has a negative net pay amount and cannot be processed through the Payroll Cheque Run Journal. Employees with negative net pay amounts need to be processed through the Payroll Journal. Do you want to continue with this payroll run, omitting this employee?

20 ➤ Click **Yes** to process the pay omitting Jordan in this transaction.

When you click **Yes**, a message box will appear briefly with a message, "Selected employee payroll transactions are being processed" and you will see the number of employees decrease to 0. You will then see the following confirmation window.

Simply Accounting - Transaction Confirmation

The transaction was posted successfully.

2 Journal Entries: J2 to J3.

Click OK. You will be returned to the Payroll Run Journal window.

You could also click the Close other Simply windows icon to close the Additional Info box or boxes.

21 ➤ **Exit** the Payroll Run Journal.

22 ➤ **Additional Info Note** Click the **Close** button to close this window. You have made the deduction for the payroll advance. (See side note box.)

Creative Wallpaper, Student's Name
3106 Ambleside Drive
London, Ontario N3G 1V9

CHEQUE NO.	201
DATE	1 0 0 1 2 0 1 4
	D D M M Y Y Y Y

One Thousand One Hundred Fifty and 90/100 $1,150.90

DAVID, Doreen
17 Huron Street
London, Ontario N5Y 1Z5

Creative Wallpaper, Student's Name

DAVID, Doreen	Jan 10, 2014	201
For Pay Period	Jan 10, 2014	

	Period	YTD		Period	YTD		Period	YTD
Regular	1,600.00	1,600.00	CPP	75.51	75.51	Gross	1,660.00	1,600.00
Overtime	60.00	60.00	EI	28.72	28.72	Withheld	-479.10	-479.10
			Tax	248.47	248.47	Advance Paid	-30.00	-30.00
Gross Pay	1,660.00	1,660.00	Pension	66.40	66.40			
			Union Dues	20.00	20.00	Net Pay	1,150.90	1,150.90
Vacation Earned	66.40	486.40	Medical	24.00	24.00	EI Insurable Hours	82.00	
Vacation Owed		486.40	Safety Shoes	16.00	16.00	Days 1		
						Days 2		
			Withheld	479.10	479.10	Days 3		
						Days 4		
						Days 5		
						Regular: 80.00 @ $20.00/Hr		
						Overtime 1: 2.00 @ $30.00/Hr		

Fig. 7-19: Paycheque information printed on Easy Align cheques.

Jordan Currie arrives late and submits an Employee Time Sheet shown in Exercise 7-10. Jordan informed you that she was late due to her car not starting. The service station repair will cost $849.00 and she has asked for a $600.00 payroll advance to help pay for her car repairs. Mrs. Singh approved the advance based on Mrs. Currie's employment history.

Study the following payroll information for recording individual paycheques.

The PAYROLL Journal

When you need to issue a single paycheque, you can use the Paycheques icon as shown in the next exercise.

Exercise 7-10 – Issuing a Single Paycheque

1 ➤   Click the ▼ at the **Paycheques** icon, select **Create Paycheque**. The Payroll Journal window is displayed.

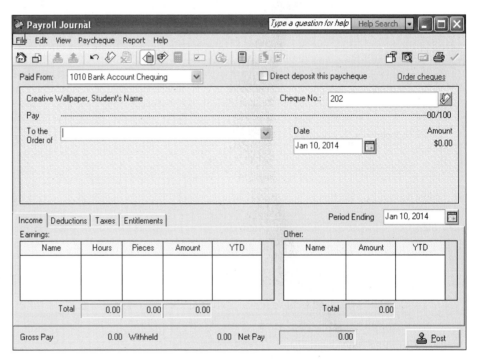

Fig. 7-20: Payroll Journal window.

The journal is intended to look like a payroll cheque with advice. You fill in the appropriate fields to complete the advice.

The Paycheque item on the paycheque menu bar is similar to other menus with drop-down lists. Many items are not available until after cheques have been processed.

Study the following icons on the toolbar:

Adjust Cheque: A previously posted payroll cheque (using the same pay period) can be recalled and corrected with the Adjust Cheque icon. If you are not adjusting the most recent paycheque for employees who have reached the maximum deduction for EI, CPP or WSIB, then errors in government deductions in the reversal amounts can occur. You can also adjust a cheque from the Home page, Paycheques icon, Adjust Paycheque. (See image in side box.)

This is also not a good choice if the tax tables have been updated and you are adjusting a paycheque that used a previous tax table, or adjusting a payroll entry from an earlier period (which used the current tax table), then the taxable income amounts may not be correct. You may see the following warning message.

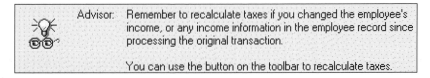

> Advisor: Remember to recalculate taxes if you changed the employee's income, or any income information in the employee record since processing the original transaction.
>
> You can use the button on the toolbar to recalculate taxes.

To reverse a paycheque in these circumstances, see Making PAYROLL Corrections (Exercise 7-16a and 7-16b).

Make sure the cheque date falls into the range of dates for the pay period that the cheque covers. This ensures that taxes are calculated properly for the revised cheque.

 You have seen this icon in previous chapters; it is used to reverse a paycheque before issuing a correct paycheque. See Making PAYROLL Corrections (Exercise 7-16a and 7-16b).

 Calculate Taxes Automatically: The program will calculate EI, CPP and Income tax automatically, based on defaults previously entered.

 Enter Taxes Manually: You will enter the EI, CPP and Income tax manually. This is used when reversing (canceling) a cheque.

 Recalculate Taxes: When used, Simply will recalculate the taxes if amounts entered have been changed.

EMPLOYEE TIME SHEET   202

Date: Jan. 10, 2014

Employee Name: Jordan Currie   Employee #   1

Regular Hours	Overtime Hours	Commission Hours	Commission Amount	Deductions		Other Information
None	None	77	$1,385.00	Pension	$ 55.40	Salary Advance $600.00
				Union Dues	20.00	
				Medical	24.00	

Hint: Net Pay $1,620.11

Approved by: *G. S.*

---

2 ➤ **To the order of**   Select **CURRIE, Jordan** and [Tab]. The employee name and address are displayed and will be printed on the payroll cheque. [Tab].

Cheque   202 is the correct next cheque number.

Date   Jan 10, 2014.

Regular and **Overtime 1** do not have a field available (--) for entering data. When Jordan was set up earlier, you indicated that she did not have an hourly rate for regular or overtime pay.

Some fields are not available because they are not defaults (e.g., Pieces).

3 ➤ Period Ending

Click the **calendar** icon. You are able to change the period ending date if the date displayed is not correct. [Tab] **twice** to accept Jan 10, 2014. This is Jordan Currie's pay for the week ended Jan 10, 2014. This is the date that the entry will get posted to the General Ledger.

(See side note box.)

Salary

These fields are for salaried employees only. Jordan is paid on a commission basis, therefore, there is nothing to record.

4 ➤ Commission Hours

This field is for the number of commission hours worked. Type **77**, [Tab].

5 ➤ Commission Amount

This field is the dollar amount of commissions earned by Jordan. Type **1385.00**, [Tab] to Advance. The Gross Pay and Net Pay amounts at the bottom of the window change.

 If you cannot see the Gross Pay at the bottom of the window, drag the Payroll Journal title bar up a bit. The bar should now be seen, or you can maximize this window.

Most firms would issue a separate cheque for an advance or reimbursement. This ensures that the payroll records are separate from other types of disbursements to employees.

6 ➤ Advance

Type **600.00**, [Tab]. The amount of any payroll advance issued or repaid would be recorded here. (See side note box.) To reduce a payroll advance you would enter a negative amount. The Net Pay field changes again to include the advance amount.

7 ➤ Benefits

[Tab] This field is for taxable employee benefits such as car allowance, life insurance, etc., for which the company pays the cost on the employee's behalf. Creative Wallpaper does not pay for this type of item.

If any amounts are entered, the program adds this amount to the gross pay before calculating the taxes.

8 ➤ Vac. Accrued

The amount of vacation pay earned this pay period. $1,385.00 commission x 4% = $55.40. This field is calculated from the default information entered previously.

If the amount is incorrect, it can be changed. [Tab].

Vac. Accrued YTD

This field will show the accumulated vacation pay (535.40) retained by the company for the employee.

9 ➤ Vac. Paid

Leave blank. This field is used to give some or all of the vacation pay retained by the company to the employee. This means that Jordan will not be paid the vacation pay earned. The $55.40 will be added to account: **2300 VACATION PAYABLE**.

10 ➤ Reimburse

Jordan has no reimbursement expenses to be repaid. [Tab].

Your Income tab should look like the following:

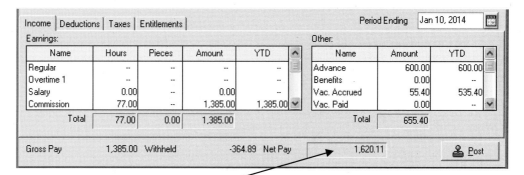

Fig. 7-21: Pay Window Income tab.

The Net Pay amount includes the Advance of 600.00.

11 ➤ Tab Tab . The window changes to the Deductions tab.

Deductions

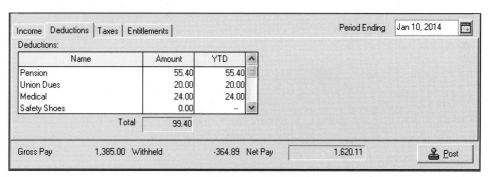

Fig. 7-22: Pay Window Deductions tab.

This window will display the default amounts that were entered when you set up the employee. The **Pension** field cannot be changed because this field is calculated by Simply. **Safety Shoes** does not have an amount because Jordan does not owe any money for safety shoes.

> If the amounts for **Union Dues** and **Medical** do not correspond to the text, check to see if you had entered the deductions incorrectly when setting up the employee ledger.

12 ➤ Press Tab Tab to accept the default amounts and to move to the Taxes window.

Taxes

You cannot change these fields because Simply calculates these amounts. The program will add the employee's EI, CPP, and Tax amounts, together with the business benefit cost of EI and CPP, to the liability (Payable) accounts.

The business will remit these amounts (employee's deductions and business expense) at regular intervals to Canada Revenue Agency (Receiver General). This is explained in Exercise 7-13.

The Taxes tab window should resemble Fig. 7-23.

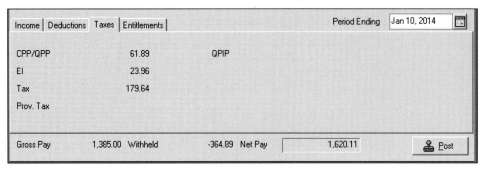

Fig. 7-23: Taxes tab.

13 ➤ Display the journal entry by clicking **Report** from the top menu, then **Display Payroll Journal Entry**.

The entry should be similar to the display in Fig. 7-24. If you upgraded from Simply 2010 Version A, your amounts may be different.

Creative Wallpaper, Student's Name
Payroll Journal Entry Jan 10, 2014 (J4)

Account Number	Account Description	Debits	Credits
1241	Advances Receivable	600.00	-
5300	Wages Expense	55.40	-
5304	Commissions Expense	1,385.00	-
5310	EI Expense	33.54	-
5320	CPP Expense	61.89	-
5330	WSIB Expense	5.68	-
1010	Bank Account Chequing	-	1,620.11
2300	Vacation Payable	-	55.40
2310	EI Payable	-	57.50
2320	CPP Payable	-	123.78
2330	Income Tax Payable	-	179.64
2420	Union Dues Payable	-	20.00
2430	Pension Plan Payable	-	55.40
2440	Medical Plan Payable	-	24.00
2460	WSIB Payable	-	5.68
Additional Date:	Additional Field:		
		2,141.51	2,141.51

Fig. 7-24: Payroll Journal Entry window.

The vacation pay portion of the commission earned by Jordan is charged to the Wages Expense #5300. The default link is to this account. Management has decided not to separate the vacation pay between regular pay and commission pay.

14 ➤ **Exit** from the Payroll Journal Entry window.

15 ➤ Click the **Post** button to post this payroll transaction.

16 ➤ You will see the date warning message. Click **Yes** to proceed, and **Exit** from the Payroll journal.

17 ➤ Click the **Employees** icon, double-click on **CURRIE Jordan** and click on the **Additional Info** tab. In Field 1, type **Payroll Advance $30.00** and click **Display this** ☑ . Click Save and Close .

18 ➤ Click 🔷 Simply Accoun... on the Windows bottom taskbar to display the Home page. Click the ⊠ Close all other windows icon to close the Employees window.

To Review PAYROLL Entries After Posting

Exercise 7-11 – Reviewing PAYROLL Entries

Review the entry for Doreen David as follows:

1 ➤ From the Home window, click the **Employees** icon to display the Employees window.

2 ➤ Click **Reports**, **Employee** and the Employee Report – Modify Report, window is displayed. Click the **Detail** Button. Change the information as shown in Fig. 7-25a and b.

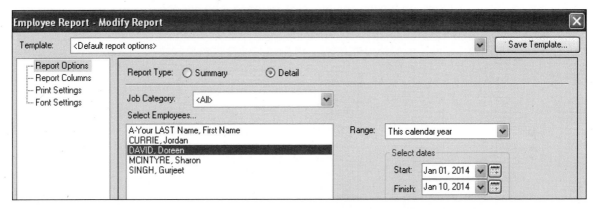

Fig. 7-25a: Employee Report Options window.

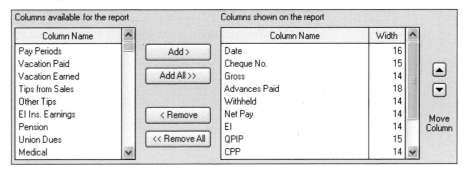

Fig. 7-25b: Employee Report Options window lower portion.

DO NOT CHANGE the start and finish dates, as they are appropriate for this exercise.

If you click Summary, the **Select dates** options are hidden.

3 ➤ By clicking the lower box (Fig 7-25b) payroll columns with no posted amounts will not display. Click **OK**. The report will display. If you repeated this step, but did not click the lower box, three columns QPIP, QPP and Prov Tax would display with 0.00 amounts.

4 ➤ **Exit** from the report. The next step will allow you to customize the columns.

5 ➤ Repeat step 2, but this time in the left pane click **Report Columns.**

6 ➤ Click the ⊙ Custom report column settings button and you will see the columns on the right side of the window that are currently shown in the report.

You have two choices.

Method a)   Click <<Remove All to move all the items to the left column. Then you can pick and choose the ones you want to see on the report by clicking an item and choosing Add> .

Method b)   In the right pane, click the items you do not want to see on the report and click on <Remove .

There are over 50 items available to choose from and we want to create a small report. The author has chosen Method a).

7 ➤   Click <<**Remove All** to move all items to the left.

8 ➤   In the left column, click on each, and choose **Add>** .
       Other columns could have been chosen.

Columns shown on the report	
Column Name	**Width**
Date	16
Cheque No.	15
Pay Periods	4
Gross	14
Withheld	14
Net Pay	14
Advances Paid	18

9 ➤   Click **OK** to display the report.

If you had customized by moving any of the other columns, the report would display, but you would need to use the slider button to see the other columns and, depending on the columns chosen, it may print on two pages. You would have to remove some columns if you wanted this report to print on one page or make the font size smaller, but then it will be more difficult to read.

A portion of the report is shown next. (See side note box.)

The P 26 refers to a bi-weekly pay period.

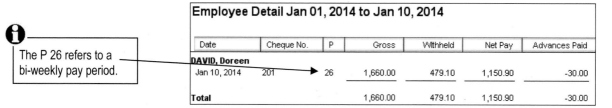

		Employee Detail Jan 01, 2014 to Jan 10, 2014					
Date	Cheque No.	P	Gross	Withheld	Net Pay	Advances Paid
DAVID, Doreen						
Jan 10, 2014	201	26	1,660.00	479.10	1,150.90	-30.00
Total			1,660.00	479.10	1,150.90	-30.00

10 ➤   Click X to return to the Employees window.

11 ➤   You can also see the YTD (Year-to-Date) payroll amounts. Double-click on **DAVID, Doreen**.

12 ➤   Click the **Income** tab. In the YTD * amount column, the amounts displayed are the amounts as of Jan 10, 2014. The YTD * column amounts will increase with the posted payroll amounts and the bottom date will increase based on the Payroll date. The Advance 60.00 is the amount remaining to be repaid.

13 ➤   **Exit** to the Employees window.

You can also display and/or print the Employee Summary.

14 ➤ Click **Reports, Employee**, select **Summary**, **DAVID, Doreen** should be selected. Make sure a ✓ is in the Show only Incomes, deductions and taxes box. This will display fields that are in use at this time.

15 ➤ Click **OK**.

ℹ️

Net Pay refers to the normal net pay considering Advances issued. Net Pay $1,150.90 plus Advance issued $90.00

If payroll cheques are not printed by Simply (money deposited by the Direct Deposit feature or other cheques issued), the print cheque feature is still available. The advice portion of the cheque can be given to employees for their records.

Employee Summary for 2014

DAVID, Doreen　　　　　　　　SIN _____ 456 812 635　　Birthdate _____ Apr 26, 1957

Tax Table ....Ontario	Regular 1,600.00	EI 28.72
Federal Claim 11,172.00/yr	Overtime 60.00	CPP 75.51
Provincial Claim 9,730.00/yr	Salary 0.00	Tax 248.47
Pay Periods 26/yr	Commission 0.00	Pension 66.40
WSIB Rate 0.41%	Benefits 0.00	Union Dues 20.00
Insurable ....Yes	Vacation Paid 0.00	Medical 24.00
Pensionable ....Yes		Safety Shoes 16.00
EI Factor 1.40	Gross Pay 1,660.00	
Vacation 4.00%	Less Benefits 0.00	
Retained ....Yes	Advances Paid 60.00	
Vacation on Vacation Paid ....No	Reimburse 0.00	Withheld 479.10
Regular 20.00/Hour		Net Pay 1,240.90
Overtime 30.00/Hour	Gross Paid 1,720.00	
Salary 0.00/Period		
Commission 0.00/Period	Vacation Owed 486.40	
Reimburse 0.00/Period	EI Ins. Earnings 1,660.00	
Benefits 0.00/Period	Pens. Earnings 1,660.00	
Additional Federal Tax 10.00/Period	Pension Adjust... .... 0.00	
	RPP/DPSP Reg.... 589896	
Days 1 .... 0.00	Days 2 .... 0.00	Days 3 .... 0.00
Days 4 .... 0.00	Days 5 .... 0.00	

Fig. 7-26: Employee Summary window. (See side note box.)

16 ➤ Click **X** and return to the Home window.

Payroll for Pay Period Ending Jan 15, 2014

Exercise 7-12 – To Enter Payroll for Salaried Employees

1 ➤ Advance the Session date to **Jan 15, 2014**.

2 ➤ Process the salaried employees' pay from the following time sheets using the **Payroll Cheque Run** option.

3 ➤ **Pay Period Frequency**　　**Change to 24**. Two ✓ appear on the left of the window.

4 ➤ Close the Additional Info notes for Doreen and Jordan as they are not needed at this time.

EMPLOYEE TIME SHEET   203

Date: Jan. 15, 2014

Employee Name: Sharon McIntyre   Employee # 3

Salary	Deductions		Other Information	
$ 2,000.00	Medical	$24.00	Pension	$80.00

Hint: Net Pay $1,441.35

Approved by: *G. S.*

EMPLOYEE TIME SHEET   204

Date: Jan. 15, 2014

Employee Name: Gurjeet Singh   Employee # 4

Salary	Deductions		Other Information	
$ 2,500.00	Medical	$24.00	Pension	$100.00

Hint: Net Pay $1,736.74

Approved by: *G. S.*

---

5 ➤   Display the **Payroll Run Journal entry**.

You will notice that salaried employees' pay is charged to #5302 SALARIES EXPENSE. Some businesses charge hourly employees' and salaried employees' earnings to the same account and do not split the expenses between accounts.

6 ➤   **Exit** the entry window and **Post** when correct.

7 ➤   **Exit** to the Home window.

Paying Receiver General Pay Withholdings

You are required to send the payroll deductions (CPP, EI and Income Tax) to the Receiver General on a regular basis. These are referred to as **source deductions**.

Depending on the procedures established in your company, your manager may or may not remind you to do this task. If it is your responsibility to make the payments, be sure to know the schedule for payments. The month's source deductions are usually due on the 15th day of the next month (e.g., January's deductions are due to be paid by February 15).

When you use this exercise (Pay Remittance feature) to issue the Receiver General Payroll Remittance cheque, please note that you cannot use the Reverse or Adjust a Cheque icons feature as shown in previous chapters. Verify the entry before Posting.

To make a correction, you would use the PAYABLES module, Make Other Payment option and create a negative cheque to correct the error.

Exercise 7-13 – Recording Withholdings Payment

Study the next memo:

M E M O   **205**

From: Gurjeet Singh   Date: Jan. 15, 2014
To: Accounting

To pay the Receiver General – Payroll Taxes, the EI, CPP and Income Tax amounts owing at December 31, 2013.

Hint: Review the Jan 01, 2014 Trial Balance for appropriate amounts.

Hint: Cheque amount = $3,354.00

This exercise is similar to the procedure to pay the Receiver General for HST OWING (Exercises 3B-30 and 3B-31), except we are paying the Payroll deductions owing at the end of the previous month. This Exercise will be using the new Simply feature Pay Remittance selection in Payments as shown next.

Creative Wallpaper has the following payroll payable accounts that need to be remitted to the Receiver General:

2310	EI Payable
2320	CPP Payable
2330	Income Tax Payable

Check the previous month's Trial Balance (on January 1, 2014, you would view the December 31, 2013 Trial Balance amounts). You could also check the Balance Sheet for the same date. The amounts to be paid are the amounts collected from the employees, plus the company's portion of the deductions where applicable by law. These amounts are recorded in the appropriate PAYABLE accounts.

1 ➤ From the Home page, click on the **Pay Remittance** icon, select **Receiver General-Payroll Taxes,** change the date to

End of Remitting Period	Jan 01, 2014	📅

and in the Amount Owing column, the amounts change to the Jan 01 Trial Balance amounts. In future months you would select the last day of the previous month.

Payroll Liability	Amount Owing	Adjustment	Payment Amount
CPP	497.00		497.00
EI	512.00		512.00
Tax	2,345.00		2,345.00
		Total	3,354.00

Reference No. | Ded Dec 2013

2 ➤ **Payment Amount**   Click in the **Payment Amount** column for each **EI, CPP** and **Tax**. ⌨Tab at 2,345.00 to update the total to 3,354.00.

3 ➤ **Reference No.**   An appropriate reference would be **Ded Dec 2013**, or Dec Pay Ded, or something similar to identify what is being paid.

Remember to view the entry before posting. You can not set this up as a recurring entry as the Store and Recall icons are grayed out.

4 ➤ Click **Post** and return to the Home window.

Exercise 7-14 – More Payroll Transactions

Payroll for January 24, 2014

1 ➤ Advance the date to **January 24, 2014**.

2 ➤ **Record** the bi-weekly payroll, using the **Payroll Cheque Run**, for the following employees based on the following time sheets:

EMPLOYEE TIME SHEET   206

Date: Jan. 24, 2014

Employee Name: A-Your LAST NAME, First Name   Employee #   5

Regular Hours	Overtime Hours	Commission Hours	Commission Amount	Deductions		Other Information
40	None			Pension	No	
				Union Dues	$20.00	

Hint: Net Pay $498.78

Approved by: *G. S.*

```
┌─────────────────────────────────────────────────────────────────────┐
│               EMPLOYEE TIME SHEET              207                    │
│                                                                       │
│   Date:___Jan. 24, 2014___                                            │
│                                                                       │
│   Employee Name:_____Jordan Currie_____   Employee # ___1___    │
│                                                                       │
│   Regular   Overtime  Commission  Commission              Other       │
│   Hours     Hours     Hours       Amount      Deductions   Information │
│                                                                       │
│   None      None      79          $1,560.00   Pension  $ 62.40  Advance Repaid  $30.00 │
│                                               Union Dues  20.00       │
│                                               Medical     24.00       │
│                                                                       │
│                    Hint: Net Pay $1,106.04                            │
│   Approved by: G. S.                                                  │
└─────────────────────────────────────────────────────────────────────┘
```

```
┌─────────────────────────────────────────────────────────────────────┐
│               EMPLOYEE TIME SHEET              208                    │
│   Date:___Jan. 24, 2014___                                            │
│                                                                       │
│   Employee Name:__Doreen David_____   Employee # __2____           │
│                                                                       │
│   Regular Overtime Commission  Commission                 Other       │
│   Hours   Hours    Hours       Amount       Deductions     Information │
│                                                                       │
│   80      4        None                     Pension  $ 68.80  Advance Repaid  $30.00 │
│                                             Union Dues  20.00         │
│                                             Medical     24.00         │
│                                             Safety Shoes 16.00        │
│                                                                       │
│                   Hint: Net Pay $ 1,187.94                            │
│                                                                       │
│   Approved by: G S.                                                   │
└─────────────────────────────────────────────────────────────────────┘
```

3 ➤ **Post** when correct and **Exit** to the Home window. Remember to close the Additional Info boxes.

Processing Vacation Pay

In the late afternoon of January 24, Jordan Currie receives a phone call about her parents suddenly taking ill, and she has requested one week off to help them. She wishes to collect her vacation pay, which has been retained by the company. A memo approving the request is received from Gurjeet Singh as shown next. To issue a cheque for vacation pay, follow the procedure in the next exercise.

MEMO   **209**

═══

From: Gurjeet Singh   Date:___January 24, 2014___
To: Accounting

Please issue vacation pay owing to Jordan Currie. Please adjust the time
period to allow for appropriate Income Tax to be deducted. Do not take any
advance repayments on vacation pay. Pension is $23.91.

Hint: Net Pay $463.17

Exercise 7-15 – Processing Vacation Pay

Jordan is paid commission bi-weekly. Jordan will receive her vacation pay for one
week, and when she comes back she will receive a pay for one week. She will,
therefore, receive two paycheques in a two-week period (vacation pay and regular
commission).

By taking all vacation pay for a one-week period (during a bi-weekly pay period),
Simply will not take off enough Federal Income Tax or CPP from the total pay. To
avoid this problem, the number of pay periods in the year can be increased from 26
(bi-weekly) to 52 (weekly) temporarily. Once the vacation paycheque and her one
week pay for commission, when she returns, have been posted, the pay periods
must be switched back to 26 per year.

The next pay period will be February 7. You will need to remember to issue a
separate commission paycheque for Jordan with the 52 week setting. After her
February 7 pay is paid, you will change the setting back to 26 and you can resume
paying Jordan in the Payroll Cheque Run window.

1 ➤ From the Home window, click the **Employees** icon.

2 ➤ Double-click the icon for **CURRIE Jordan** to display the Payroll Ledger
window for Jordan.

3 ➤ Click the **Income** tab and change the Pay Periods Per Year from 26 to **52**
(press ⬚Tab to accept the change). Click ⬚**Save & Close**.

4 ➤ **Exit** to the Home window.

5 ➤ Click the **Paycheques** icon.

6 ➤ Select **CURRIE, Jordan,** ⬚Tab.

7 ➤ Jordan is not receiving commission, therefore, do not enter any amount.

8 ➤ The vacation pay accumulated and retained by the company $597.80 for
Jordan can be found in the YTD column.

| Vac. Accrued | 0.00 | 597.80 |

You want to pay this amount to Jordan. In the Vac. Paid Amount column, type **597.80**, `Tab`.

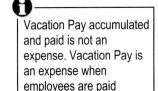

9 ➤ You will see | Vac. Paid | 597.80 | 597.80 |. The Vac. Accrued Amount changes to 0.00 and the Vac YTD Amount changes to - -.

10 ➤ Click the **Deductions** tab.

11 ➤ **Union Medical:** Press the *Delete* key to remove Union and Medical amounts in this window. These deductions are paid on weekly commissions which included vacation pay owed and, therefore, should not be deducted again.

12 ➤ View the Payroll entry. (See side note box.)

> Vacation Pay accumulated and paid is not an expense. Vacation Pay is an expense when employees are paid regular wages/salaries and commissions.
>
> EI, CPP, and WSIB expenses are calculated on actual amounts paid to employees. They are not calculated on vacation pay accumulated each pay period.

Creative Wallpaper, Student's Name
Payroll Journal Entry Jan 24, 2014 (J11)

Account Number	Account Description	Debits	Credits
2300	Vacation Payable	597.80	-
5310	EI Expense	14.48	-
5320	CPP Expense	26.26	-
5330	WSIB Expense	2.45	-
1010	Bank Account Chequing	-	463.17
2310	EI Payable	-	24.82
2320	CPP Payable	-	52.52
2330	Income Tax Payable	-	74.12
2430	Pension Plan Payable	-	23.91
2460	WSIB Payable	-	2.45
Additional Date:	Additional Field:		
		640.99	640.99

Fig. 7-27: Payroll Entry.

13 ➤ **Exit** the entry window and **post** when correct.

14 ➤ **Exit** from the Payroll Journal and return to the Home window.

Making Payroll Corrections

After the cheques were issued, Doreen brought to Mrs. Singh's attention that she had taken Tuesday off last week as an unpaid leave of absence and, therefore, should not have been paid for the day.

There are two ways to correct this problem.

At the Paycheques icon, click the ▼, select Adjust Paycheque and follow steps 1 through 6 and make changes required, including the cheque number. However, this will only work if the paycheque being corrected is from a recent paycheque date (e.g., Jan 24) and not a prior pay period (e.g., Jan 10).

When adjusting/correcting paycheques from prior pay periods (before the most recent pay period), please note the following:

- Income taxes have to be re-calculated AND
- extra precaution must be taken to ensure the revised cheque correctly includes all deductions AND
- double check to ensure Gross Pay and YTD figures are correct.
- THEREFORE, it is strongly recommended that every effort be made to make corrections for a pay period BEFORE processing the next pay period's entries.

Exercise 7-16a – Making PAYROLL Corrections- Reverse cheque

Step 1: Reverse Original Entry

1 ➤ At the Paycheques icon, click the ▼ , select **Adjust Paycheque,** you will see the following:

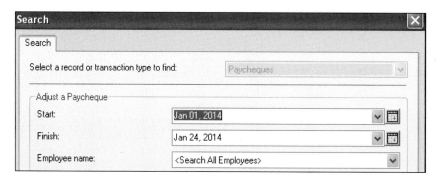

2 ➤ Do NOT change the settings. Click **OK** to see the next window.

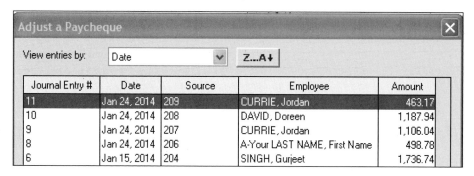

3 ➤ Only a partial window is shown here. Click the appropriate Journal Entry # line (**10**), and click **Select**.

4 ➤ Close the **Additional Info Note** window.

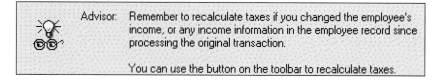

5 ➤ Click to **close** this window. You are in the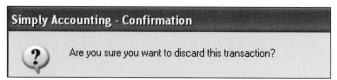

6 ➤ Click ✐ **Adjust paycheque** icon. You will see.

> **Simply Accounting - Confirmation**
>
> ? Are you sure you want to discard this transaction?

7 ➤ Click **No.** You are in the Adjusting Journal window. If you click Yes, you will be taken back to the image above step 2.

8 ➤ Click 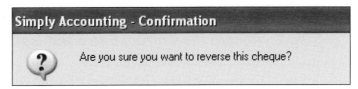 **Reverse paycheque** icon.

> **Simply Accounting - Confirmation**
>
> ❓ Are you sure you want to reverse this cheque?

9 ➤ When you are sure that this is the correct cheque you want to reverse, click **Yes**. You will see the confirmation window.

> **Simply Accounting - Transaction Confirmation**
>
> ⓘ This transaction was reversed successfully.

10 ➤ Click **OK**. You are returned to a blank Payroll Journal window. The original journal entry #10 for DAVID, Doreen has been reversed (cancelled) by Journal entry #12.

11 ➤ Click X to return to the Home window.

12 ➤ Click **Report Centre**, click **Financials**, click **All Journal Entries**, click **Modify this report**, click on **Journal Number,** change the Start and Finish fields to **12**. Click **Corrections**, and click **OK**.

All Journal Entries J12 to J12

		Account Number	Account Description	Debits	Credits
Jan 24, 2014	J12	ADJ208, Reversing J10. Correction is J12.			
		1010	Bank Account Chequing	1,187.94	-
		1241	Advances Receivable	30.00	-
		2300	Vacation Payable	68.80	-
		2310	EI Payable	71.42	-
		2320	CPP Payable	156.96	-
		2330	Income Tax Payable	265.02	-
		2420	Union Dues Payable	20.00	-
		2430	Pension Plan Payable	68.80	-
		2440	Medical Plan Payable	24.00	-
		2450	Safety Shoes Payable	16.00	-
		2460	WSIB Payable	7.05	-
		5300	Wages Expense	-	1,668.80
		5308	Wages-Overtime Expense	-	120.00
		5310	EI Expense	-	41.66
		5320	CPP Expense	-	78.48
		5330	WSIB Expense	-	7.05
				1,915.99	1,915.99

Fig. 7-28: Payroll Reversing Journal Entry for J10.

The entry will display with the following wording error.
`ADJ208, Reversing J10. Correction is J12.` J12 is actually the reversing entry and not the correction entry. The correcting entry will be shown in the next exercise.

13 ➤ Click X twice to return to the Home window.

Exercise 7-16b – Making PAYROLL Corrections- Issue new cheque

Step 2: Record the Correct Entry and Issue a New Cheque

EMPLOYEE TIME SHEET   210

Date:___Jan. 24, 2014___

Employee Name:___Doreen David___   Employee # ___2___

Regular Hours	Overtime Hours	Commission Hours	Commission Amount	Deductions		Other Information
76	None	None	None	Pension	$ 60.80	1 day leave of absence
				Union Dues	20.00	Advance Repaid $30.00
				Medical	24.00	
				Safety Shoes	16.00	

Hint: Net Pay $1,058.95

Approved by:* G. S. (revised)*

---

14 ➤   Click on the **Paycheques** icon.

15 ➤   **To the**   Select **DAVID, Doreen,** [Tab].
        Order of

16 ➤   Change the Regular hours from 80 to **76** for the correct hours. (Doreen David took an unpaid leave of absence, therefore, 80 hours – 8 plus 4 = 76 regular hours with no overtime.) The correct net pay should be **$1,058.95**.

(See side note box.)

17 ➤   **Post** when correct.

18 ➤   Click [X] to return to the Home window, and click **Close** to close the Additional Info Notes.

> Most companies pay overtime only if an employee has worked more than the normal regular hours based on the company's regular hours. Some businesses have 70 regular hours and others have 80 hours per bi-weekly pay.

Exercise 7-17 – Payroll for Pay Period Ending Jan 31, 2014

---

1 ➤   Advance the Session date to **Jan 31, 2014**.

Issue cheques to salaried employees Sharon McIntyre and Gurjeet Singh, based on time sheets 211 and 212.

For salaried employees use:

2 ➤   **Pay Period Frequency 24**

3 ➤   **Cheque Number   211**

4 ➤   **Pay Period End Date   Jan 31, 2014**

5 ➤   **Cheque Date   Jan 31, 2014**

6 ➤ **Record** and **post** the following salaried employee time sheets.

EMPLOYEE TIME SHEET   **211**

Date: Jan. 31, 2014

Employee Name: Sharon McIntyre   Employee #   3

Salary	Deductions		Other Information	
$ 2,000.00	Medical	$24.00	Pension	$ 80.00

Hint: Net Pay $1,441.35

Approved by :   *G. S.*

EMPLOYEE TIME SHEET   **212**

Date: Jan. 31, 2014

Employee Name: Gurjeet Singh   Employee #   4

Salary	Deductions		Other Information	
$ 2,500.00	Medical	$24.00	Pension	$ 100.00

Hint: Net Pay $1,736.74

Approved by :   *G. S.*

Jordan Currie has advised Mrs. Singh that she will be returning on Monday, February 3. There is no setting to change for her until after she gets paid on the 7th.

7 ➤ Click ☒ to return to the Home window, and click **Close** to close the Additional Info Notes.

Additional Transaction

During the month, the Payroll department must remit money collected from employees or on behalf of employees to appropriate vendors. Examples of these would be union dues payable to the local union branch, pension plan payable amount to the pension fund trustee, WSIB payment to the provincial association. There can be many others.

Exercise 7-18 – Remittances for Payroll Deductions

---

1 ➤ Use a procedure similar to the payment for the Receiver General to make these payments.

M E M O   **213**

From: Gurjeet Singh   Date:___Jan. 31, 2014___
To: Accounting

Please remit the funds at January 1, in account 2460 WSIB Payable, to
the WSIB office. Reference our file #2589-B-X304.

> Hint: *Review the Jan 01, 2014 Trial Balance for appropriate* **amounts**.

> Hint: *Cheque amount = $450.00*

M E M O   **214**

From: Gurjeet Singh   Date:___Jan. 31, 2014___
To: Accounting

Please remit the funds at January 1, in account 2420 Union Dues Payable,
to the Local Union office. Reference our file #569-2013-12.

> Hint: *Review the Jan 01, 2014 Trial Balance for appropriate amounts.*

> Hint: *Cheque amount = $220.00*

---

2 ➤ Return to the Home window.

Recording Payroll Accrued Wages

Study the calendar for the last week of January 2014 and the first week of February
2014. You pay employees every second Friday; therefore, the next pay date for
hourly paid employees is Friday, February ⃞7.

January 2014							February 2014						
S	**M**	**T**	**W**	**T**	**F**	**S**	**S**	**M**	**T**	**W**	**T**	**F**	**S**
19	20	21	22	23	24	25							1
26	27	28	29	30	31		2	3	4	5	6	⃞7	8

To record January expenses properly according to GAAP, a payroll expense accrual
for the period Saturday, January 25 to Friday, January 31 must be recorded. Payroll
accruals are recorded in the General Journal.

Mrs. Singh has checked the time cards for the employees and as per her memo,
calculated the following:

```
DAVID, Doreen      5 days at 8 hours per day at $20.00 per hour  800.00
STUDENT'S Name  5 days at 8 hours per day at $14.00 per hour   560.00
                              Total Accrual          $1,360.00
```

Exercise 7-19 – Recording PAYROLL Accruals

---

1 ➤ Click the **COMPANY** module, click the **General Journal** icon.

2 ➤ Click the **Recall Recurring** icon.

3 ➤ Select **Setup Wages accrual for month end**.

4 ➤ Enter the accrual as shown in Fig. 7-29. Your General Journal window should resemble the following:

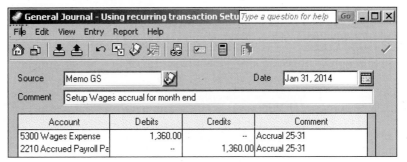

Fig 7-29: Payroll Accrual.

5 ➤ **Post** when correct and **Exit** to the Home window.

Processing T4 Slips (or Relevé 1)

T4s and Relevé 1 slips must be completed at the end of a calendar year after the payroll for the entire year has been processed. They are completed on special forms created by using a Simply Reports & Forms setting of Plain-paper laser & Inkjet form, or creating them on similar forms provided by Canada Revenue Agency or Quebec government. To save paper, do not print T4s or Relevé 1 slips. Study a sample T4 in Fig. 7-30.

Your instructor will have the printouts of all the T4 employees to date. It is possible to print regular T4s on plain paper, but the Report and Forms setting would need to change. There is no exercise for this procedure. Your instructor will have the setting for printing. Printing T4s uses a lot of paper.

At year-end, you will need to back up your data and keep a copy in a locked cabinet to ensure that you always have a backup in case the original payroll data is lost or corrupt. If the data were to become lost or corrupt, the firm would need someone to manually create T4s for all employees. Once you advance the Session date to a new calendar year, Simply resets all the T4 or Relevé 1 information to zero to start the new calendar year.

Before you proceed, back up your data. It is very important that you are able to print T4s again in case of errors. Without a separate backup, T4s could not be printed again.

Also, once you advance the Session date to a new calendar year, the T4 data is placed in the previous year.

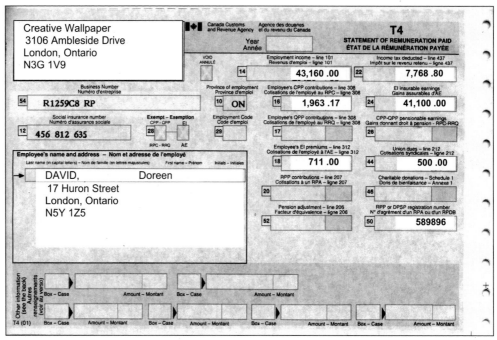

Fig. 7-30: A sample T4 form.

There is no exercise for this procedure. (See side note box.)

Printing Month-End Employee-Related Reports

All of the transactions for the Creative Wallpaper PAYROLL module for January have been completed. As part of the normal month-end procedures for any company, you should print reports for the month's transactions.

The Payroll Journal report lists only payroll transactions. The payroll transactions are also contained in the All Journal Entries report.

Exercise 7-20 – Print Month-End Employee-Related Reports

To Print the PAYROLL Journal

Entries #1 and #18 are General Journal entries and are listed in the All Journal Entries report. Entry #7, #16 and #17 (cheques #205, #213 & #214) are not payroll transactions and are listed in the All Journal Entries and or Payments reports.

1 ➤ Click **Report Centre**, click **Employees & Payroll**, click **Payroll Journal Entries**, click **Modify this report**, click **Show Corrections**. (See side note box.) Dates should be: Start date **Jan 01, 2014**, Finish date **Jan 31, 2014**, click **OK**.

(See side note box.)

To Print an Income Statement for Jan 1 to Jan 31, 2014

Refer to instructions shown in previous chapters.

Review the balances in the accounts shown. The Wages Expense is the total of the regular pay and vacation pay the employees earned. Salary, commission and overtime pay are recorded separately.

The other expenses (EI, CPP and WSIB) are benefit costs of hiring employees and are normally referred to as payroll or benefit expenses.

Companies will normally group these expenses together and calculate a percentage of the benefits, and compare them to the Wages Expense. Creative Wallpaper's cost of benefits is 7.8%.

To Print the Balance Sheet as at Jan 31, 2014

To print the Balance Sheet, refer to instructions as shown in previous chapters.

Review the balances for the payroll related G/L accounts:

- ADVANCES RECEIVABLE is owed to the company by employee(s).

- VACATION PAYABLE is owed to the employees for accrued vacation.

- EI PAYABLE, CPP PAYABLE and INCOME TAX PAYABLE are owed to the federal government (Receiver General) and are normally paid monthly.

- United Way Donations Payable records the amounts collected from employees during a recent campaign and is not deducted from paycheques. This money will be sent to the United Way in February.

- UNION DUES PAYABLE are owed to the union to which the employees belong.

- WSIB (WCB) PAYABLE is owed to the provincial Workplace Safety and Insurance Board and is normally paid monthly.

To Display a Cheque Log for Jan 1 to Jan 31, 2014

i — You do not need to print the following reports at this time. Use the information for future reference. These reports are normally used by management to verify information regarding employees.

1 ➤ **Display** a Cheque Log for cheques issued from January 1, 2014 to January 31, 2014. Refer to Exercise 3B-36. You **DO NOT NEED** to print this report at this time. The report (partial) shown next, indicates that cheque #208 was reversed. Notice that J12, the canceling cheque entry, is not shown.

(See side note box.)

208	Payroll	DAVID, Doreen	1,187.94	Jan 24, 2014	0	Reversed	J10	Jan 24, 2014
209	Payroll	CURRIE, Jordan	463.17	Jan 24, 2014	0	Yes	J11	Jan 24, 2014
210	Payroll	DAVID, Doreen	1,058.95	Jan 24, 2014	0	Yes	J13	Jan 24, 2014

To Print the Employee Detail Report

The Employee Detail Report is a list of the employees' payroll information for the current year. The information is listed by pay period, and can be displayed and/or printed for one date or a range of dates.

You **DO NOT NEED** to print this report at this time. You would print this report, however, if you need to verify employee payroll details. If you were to print this report, you would do the following from the Home window:

- Click Reports, Payroll, Employee.
- Click Detail, set the range of dates, Start Jan 01, 2014 to Finish Jan 31, 2014.
- Select DAVID, Doreen or Select All to include all employees.
- Check the Show only incomes, deductions and taxes that are currently in use, or that have a YTD amount item.
- Click OK. You may need to scroll down or click the full window icon to see the balance of the report.

The program will keep these default boxes for all employees until you change them.

To Print the Employee YTD (Year-To-Date) Report

The Employee YTD Report is a list of the employees' YTD payroll information for the current year. The information is listed in summary for the Year-to-Current Session date.

You **DO *NOT* NEED** to print this report for this exercise.

Click Reports, Payroll, Employee.

Click Summary.

Select a specific employee, or Select All to include all employees, OK.

You may need to maximize the window, or scroll down to see other employees.

Compare your printouts to those in the Creative Wallpaper section of the instructor's Solutions Manual. Remember, the payroll entries and amounts may be slightly different if you are using a version of Simply that is different from Version Premium 2010 A.

The following section is **FOR INFORMATION ONLY**. Use it for future reference.

Payroll Entry with EHT (Employer Health Tax)

Payroll Journal Entry Jan 31, 2014 (J19)

Account Number	Account Description	Debits	Credits
5300	Wages Expense	1,040.00	-
5310	EI Expense	24.22	-
5320	CPP Expense	42.84	-
5330	WSIB Expense	4.10	-
5360	EHT Expense	9.80	-
1010	Bank Account Chequing	-	725.89
2300	Vacation Payable	-	40.00
2310	EI Payable	-	41.52
2320	CPP Payable	-	85.68
2330	Income Tax Payable	-	113.97
2395	EHT Payable	-	9.80
2420	Union Dues Payable	-	20.00
2430	Pension Plan Payable	-	40.00
2440	Medical Plan Payable	-	24.00
2450	Safety Shoes Payable	-	16.00
2460	WSIB Payable	-	4.10
Additional Date:	Additional Field:		
		1,120.96	1,120.96

Converting During the Year

Do not enter the next example. If payroll conversion takes place during a calendar year (e.g., June 30), Historical employee deductions for EI, CPP, Income tax and other payroll deductions would be entered as of June 30. The payroll information for the conversion (January 1 to June 30) and payroll information entered for the months of July - December are accumulated by the program, and will be used in preparing T4 slips for the complete year. See Fig. 7-31.

Employee data, converted at June 30

__Personal__
Employee name and information

__Historical Income__

Regular Wages:	12,800.00
Overtime Wages 1:	395.00
Taxable Benefits:	250.00
Vac Pay Paid:	177.80
Vac Pay Owed:	350.00
EI Earnings:	12,760.00
Net Pay:	9,165.22

__Historical Deductions__

Pension:	527.80
Union:	260.00
Medical:	312.00

__Historical Taxes__

Income Tax:	2,399.54
EI Premiums:	396.89
CPP Premiums:	311.35

Fig. 7-31: Conversion information during the year.

Garnishee and Reimbursement

Information on *Payroll Garnishment* (Appendix P) and *Reimbursement (Payroll)* (Appendix T) can be found at www.simplyaccounting2010.nelson.com under Student Resources.

This is the **end of the INFORMATION SECTION**.

Before Moving On...

Read the following questions and make sure you know the answers to them; otherwise, read the corresponding part in the chapter before moving on:

1. Briefly describe how the Simply PAYROLL module works:

    - its purpose.

    - the records or forms it can automatically produce.

    - built-in tables and formulas.

2. After entering the employee payroll for January 2014, the total of year-to-date employees' gross pay plus vacation pay owed must equal the balance of which G/L accounts?

3. Why is the session date particularly important to consider when processing in the Simply PAYROLL module? If you set a particular session date, what restrictions are set by Simply?

4. Why is it particularly important to back up your data before printing Tax slips for employees and/or the CRA at December 31?

5. What is the procedure for correcting an error in posting a paycheque in the PAYROLL module?

Relevant Appendices

 The following appendices are available at www.simplyaccounting2010.nelson.com under Student Resources.

Appendix 2010 P	**Payroll Garnishment**
Appendix 2010 Q	**Names Fields**
Appendix 2010 T	**Reimbursement (Payroll)**
Appendix 2010 AD	**TIME and BILLING Journals**

Challenge Exercise 07 C7-1, Carpets 4Home

(PAYROLL and PAYABLES modules)

This exercise is a review of the PAYROLL and PAYABLES modules.

1 ➤ Refer to Exercise 1-1 to unzip the **07 C7-1 Carpets.exe** file.

2 ➤ Open the **07 C7-1 Carpets** file.

Payroll information:

- All employees are paid bi-weekly.

- Overtime is paid at time and a half (regular pay plus 1/2 regular pay).

- Vacation pay (4%) is retained from hourly and commission employees until the employee takes a vacation. Vacation pay is not calculated or retained for salaried employees.

- The EI rate is 1.4% times the employee deductions.

- It is assumed that the employer is exempt from the Employee Health Tax (EHT).

- Union dues are deducted from hourly and commission employees' paycheques.

- The company does not have a pension plan.

- The company allows employees to receive a payroll advance up to $700.00 for extenuating circumstances. The advance is repayable by all employees at $20.00 per pay. Hardeep Singh has a $500.00 advance owing at January 1.

- Commission employee Vibeke Ipanaque is on a medical leave of absence and is expected back to work by the middle of January.

3 ➤ **Record** and **Post** the following transactions for 2014:

Jan 2   Change employee "YOUR ACTUAL LAST, First Name" to your own name before processing payroll transactions.

Jan 2   Memo 1-YM received from Owner, to reverse the Accrued Payroll Payable entry created in the previous year. See the January 1 Trial Balance. (There was no accrual for commission employees.)

Jan 3   Pay by Payroll Cheque Run, pay period effective today:
        Hardeep Singh   80 hours, she is repaying her advance by $20.00 per pay
        Herve Lions   80 hours and 1 hour overtime
        Your Actual Last, First Name   for salary

Jan 3   Hardeep Singh (normally paid bi-weekly) will go on a one week vacation starting this evening. She will return on January 13. As discussed in the chapter, change the pay periods to 52 and then issue a vacation paycheque $650.00 of the amount accrued. Use the Paycheques icon to pay the Vacation Pay. Union dues and/or advance repayments are not deducted on vacation pay.

Jan 3   Manager called Herve Lions, before he left for lunch, to advise him his cheque was incorrect. He had been 2 hours late for work on January 2 (he slept in) and the cheque should have been for 79 hours at his regular wage rate. Received and reversed original cheque. Issued a corrected cheque.

Jan 13   Employee Vibeke Ipanaque and Hardeep Singh both returned to work today. They will each be working just one week in this pay period (ending Jan. 17). Make sure their employee setup reflects this (Income tab) to ensure taxes will be deducted properly.

Jan 13   Canada Revenue Agency (CRA) payroll auditor arrived today to do an audit on the previous year payroll records.

Jan 14   The payroll auditor verified that the previous year files and records were in order. The manager approved issuing the next cheque to the Receiver General, for December 31, amount owing for PAYROLL amounts (Trial Balance amounts at January 1).

Jan 17   Pay by **Payroll Cheque Run**, pay period effective today.

Singh, Hardeep	for 40 hours. She is repaying her advance by $20.00 per pay.
Ipanaque, Vibeke	for $912.00 commission for 40 hours.
Lions, Herve	for 80 hours and 1 hour overtime.
Your Actual Last, First Name	for salary.

After the payroll cheque run is completed, return Vibeke and Hardeep to 26 pay periods per year.

Jan 21   The owner has given you a memo to update the accounting records by recording a payroll accrual for $976.00 salary and $350.00 commission, for the period ending today. The owner needs the reports, listed below, for a meeting with the bank for a loan to buy specialty carpets.

4 ➤ Print the following reports for the manager:
   a)   Balance Sheet.
   b)   Income Statement (All amounts will be zero, except for payroll).
   c)   Journal Entries Payroll, with corrections, for the month to the current date.
   d)   Journal Entries-All, with corrections, for the same period.
   e)   Journal Entries General for the same period.
   f)   Cheque log for January 1 to January 21.

Chapter 8

INVENTORY & SERVICES Module Setup and Transactions Review: G/L, A/P, A/R

Printers Company

Learning Objectives

After completing this chapter you will be able to:

- [ ] Create and modify inventory and service item information.
- [ ] Set up the module defaults and Linking accounts.
- [ ] Turn the module to Ready.
- [ ] Record transactions (Sales and Purchases) using perpetual inventory items.
- [ ] Display and print appropriate inventory reports and journals.

This chapter reviews the setup procedures for the Simply INVENTORY & SERVICES module and provides practice in processing inventory transactions using the **Printers Company** files. The COMPANY, PAYABLES and RECEIVABLES modules are also used. Refer, also, to Fig. 8-1a and Fig. 8-1b, **Comparison of Periodic** and **Perpetual Inventory methods**.

This chapter assumes that you have some knowledge of perpetual inventory accounting. If you are unsure of the procedures, you should research the topic before starting this chapter.

The contents of this chapter are as follows:

- INVENTORY & SERVICES Module Overview.. 426
- Printers Company: Company Profile.. 427
- Comparison of Periodic and Perpetual Inventory Methods 428
- Conversion 431

      Exercise 8-1 – Starting the INVENTORY & SERVICES Module 432
      Exercise 8-2 – Setting INVENTORY & SERVICES Module Defaults 433
      Exercise 8-3 – To Set Up INVENTORY& SERVICES Linked Accounts..... 434
      Exercise 8-4 – Creating Inventory & Service Item Ledgers 435
      Exercise 8-5 – To Display Inventory Details 441
      Exercise 8-6 – Setting the INVENTORY & SERVICES Module to READY 443
      Exercise 8-7 – Journalizing Inventory-Related Sales 444
      Exercise 8-8 – Determining What Items to Order 448
      Exercise 8-9 – To Record a New Inventory Item 448
      Exercise 8-10 – Display the Pending Purchases Report 450
      Exercise 8-11 – Journalizing Inventory Purchases 452
      Exercise 8-12 – Journalizing a Cash on Delivery (COD) Sale................... 455
      Exercise 8-13 – Journalizing an Inventory Sales Return 458
      Exercise 8-14 – Journalizing an Inventory Purchase Return 460
      Exercise 8-15 – Recording an Inventory Payment with Cash Discount...... 462
      Exercise 8-16 – To Create Ledger Accounts & Service Items................... 463
      Exercise 8-17 – To Journalize an Invoice for Warranty Repairs................ 465

Exercise 8-18 – To Change the Selling Price 466
Exercise 8-19 – To Correct Invoice Price after Posting 467
Exercise 8-20 – Recording the INVENTORY Adjustments 469
Exercise 8-21 – Using the Build from Bill of Materials Journal 472
                  Information for the Build from Item Assembly Journal 475
Exercise 8-22 – To View INVENTORY Reports 476
                  Other Reports 476

- Before Moving On... 477
- Relevant Appendix.. 477

Challenge Exercise 08 C8-1, Stain Company (Your Name)....................... 478
Challenge Exercise 08 C8-2, Charlie's Hair Styling.................................... 480
Challenge Exercise 08 C8-3, Vet Services 481
Challenge Exercise 08 C8-4, Luggage–PI.. 483
Challenge Exercise 08 C8-5, Toys–PI.. 485
Challenge Exercise 08 C8-6, Shirts–PI... 487
Challenge Exercise 08 C8-7, Bears.. 489

INVENTORY & SERVICES Module Overview

The INVENTORY & SERVICES module is used to keep track of the quantity and cost of a company's inventory items (i.e., goods for sale) and services (e.g., veterinary services, repairs to equipment, office visits, etc.). This chapter illustrates the use of the **Perpetual Inventory Ledger**, where detailed records of purchases and sales of each item of inventory are kept. The quantity and cost are increased by each purchase and decreased by each sale.

Companies that use the INVENTORY & SERVICES module charge the cost of inventory **purchased for resale** (e.g., printers, ink, cables, etc.) to a **G/L asset inventory** account (e.g., INVENTORY INKJET PRINTERS) rather than the PURCHASES account.

When goods are sold:

a) The asset Inventory account (in the Balance sheet) is reduced ↓ by the cost of the goods.

b) The Cost of Goods Sold account in the Income Statement is increased ↑ by the cost of the goods.

The Simply INVENTORY & SERVICES module keeps track of inventory at **Average Cost** or **First In, First Out** (**FIFO**) methods. The average cost method takes the total cost of the individual goods divided by the number of items in stock.

Example: Inventory item: **Laser Black Cartridge** = $1,056.00. Divide by 16, (the number of items in stock) = average cost of $66.00. If you buy 10 more cartridges for $645.00 = $1,701.00 total cost for 26 total cartridges. The new average cost = 65.42 (1,701.00/26). Refer to your accounting textbook for further explanation. This is also illustrated in Exercise 8-11.

Simply will allow you to change from the Average Cost method to the FIFO method, but you cannot change back. Simply does not allow the use of the Last In, First Out (LIFO) costing method.

When goods are purchased, the transactions are recorded in the PAYABLES module, and the INVENTORY & SERVICES module records (cost and quantity) are increased ⬆.

When goods are sold the transactions are recorded in the RECEIVABLES module, and the INVENTORY & SERVICES module records (cost and quantity) are decreased ⬇.

Simply allows you to have regular and preferred pricing for customers. Preferred pricing, which is a reduction in the selling price, would be given to customers who buy a large amount (quantity) of merchandise and/or services. See Exercise 8-4 and 8-7.

Before the INVENTORY & SERVICES module can be used, the COMPANY, PAYABLES and RECEIVABLE modules must be set to **Ready**. Inventory items must be added to the INVENTORY module, and the quantities and cost of the goods must be entered as of the conversion date.

Run **Slideshow 8A – Setting Up the INVENTORY Module** now. It explains the various steps required to set the INVENTORY & SERVICES module to **ready**.

Printers Company: Company Profile

Printers Company is in the business of buying and selling computer printers, black ink cartridges and printer cables. The company carries only 2 types of printers, related ink cartridges, and printer cables. The company is planning to sell colour cartridges at a later date. Printers Company sells to other companies that sell directly to the public, and does not normally sell retail.

The management of Printers Company has hired you to set up the INVENTORY & SERVICES module and use it to process transactions.

INVENTORY Policies and Procedures

Sales invoices and purchase payment cheques are prepared manually and are entered in the computer on a weekly basis. In the workplace, the same documents can be printed using the Simply program on special preprinted form paper.

CASH DISCOUNTS are allowed to all customers based on the selling price of the items sold before taxes.

The company does not use the Additional Information fields.

Comparison of Periodic and Perpetual Inventory Methods

In the following examples HST, GST and/or PST is NOT included in the transactions. This will highlight the differences between the two methods.

Transactions	Periodic Inventory	Ref			Perpetual Inventory	Ref		
Buy Merchandise for resale	Dr. Purchases	A	400		Dr. Inventory (Asset)	L	400	
	Cr. Accounts Payable	B		400	Cr. Accounts Payable	M		400
Return part of goods	Dr. Accounts Payable	C	100		Dr. Accounts Payable	N	100	
	Cr. Purchase Returns	D		100	Cr. Inventory (Asset)	O		100

At this point, we have $300 of goods (at cost) available for sale in both methods. Periodic (Net Purchases) Perpetual (Inventory [Asset])

Transactions	Periodic Inventory	Ref			Perpetual Inventory	Ref		
We sell goods for $320 costing $200	Dr. Accounts Receivable	E	320		Dr. Accounts Receivable	P	320	
	Cr. Sales	F		320	Cr. Sales	Q		320
					Dr. Cost of Goods Sold	R	200	
					Cr. Inventory (Asset)	S		200

General Ledger Accounts (Periodic)

Accounts Receivable	Ref	Debit	Credit	Balance
	E	320		320 Dr

Accounts Payable	Ref	Debit	Credit	Balance
	B		400	400 Cr
	C	100		300 Cr

Sales	Ref	Debit	Credit	Balance
	F		320	320 Cr

Purchases	Ref	Debit	Credit	Balance
	A	400		400 Dr

Purchase Returns	Ref	Debit	Credit	Balance
	D		100	100 Cr

General Ledger Accounts (Perpetual)

Accounts Receivable	Ref	Debit	Credit	Balance
	P	320		320 Dr

Inventory (Asset)	Ref	Debit	Credit	Balance
Purchase of goods	L	400		400 Dr
Return of goods	O		100	300 Dr
Goods sold	S		200	100 Dr

Accounts Payable	Ref	Debit	Credit	Balance
	M		400	400 Cr
	N	100		300 Cr

Sales	Ref	Debit	Credit	Balance
	Q		320	320 Cr

Cost of Goods Sold	Ref	Debit	Credit	Balance
	R	200		200 Dr

Fig. 8-1a: Comparison of Periodic and Perpetual Inventory Methods.

Perpetual Inventory Method

Trial Balance

Accounts Receivable	320	
Inventory (Asset)	100	
Accounts Payable		300
Sales		320
Cost of Goods Sold	200	
	620	620

Income Statement

Sales	320
Cost of Goods Sold	200
Gross Margin	120

Balance Sheet

Accounts Receivable	320
Inventory (not sold)	100
Assets	420
Accounts Payable	300
Net Income	120
Liabilities & Owner Equity	420

Periodic Inventory Method

Trial Balance

Accounts Receivable	320	
Accounts Payable		300
Sales		320
Purchases	400	
Purchase Returns		100
	720	720

Income Statement

Sales		320
Beginning Inventory		0
Purchases	400	
Purchases Returns	100	
Net Purchases	300	
Goods Available for Sale	300	
Less: Ending Inventory (count)	-100	
Cost of Goods Sold		200
Gross Margin		120

Balance Sheet

Accounts Receivable	320
Inventory (not sold)	100
Assets	420
Accounts Payable	300
Net Income	120
Liabilities & Owner Equity	420

Fig. 8-1b: Comparison of Periodic and Perpetual Inventory Methods.

Printers Company, Student's Name
Trial Balance As At Jan 01, 2014

		Debits	*Credits*
1020	Bank Account	8,131.00	-
1200	Accounts Receivable	15,068.55	-
1250	Inventory InkJet Printers	7,950.00	-
1260	Inventory Laser Printers	5,800.00	-
1270	Inventory Ink Cartridges InkJet	800.00	-
1280	Inventory Ink Cartridges Laser	1,056.00	-
1290	Inventory Printer Cables	350.00	-
1330	Prepaid Store Supplies	800.00	-
1510	Equipment	53,146.00	-
1515	Accum Amort. Equipment	-	26,000.00
1520	Office, Warehouse Furniture	28,560.00	-
1525	Accum. Amort. Office/Warehouse	-	13,490.00
2200	Accounts Payable	-	15,992.73
2650	HST Charged on Sales	-	400.25
2670	HST Paid on Purchases	210.56	-
2710	Bank Loan Payable	-	0.00
3100	Capital Gavin Mosely	-	65,989.13
3230	Drawings Gavin Mosely	-	0.00
4100	Sales InkJets	-	0.00
4110	Sales Lasers	-	0.00
4120	Sales Cables	-	0.00
4150	Sales Discount	-	0.00
4200	Sales Returns & Allowances	-	0.00
5010	Cost Of Goods Sold- InkJets	0.00	-
5020	Cost Of Goods Sold- Lasers	0.00	-
5030	Cost Of Goods Sold- Cables	0.00	-
5040	Purchase Discounts	0.00	-
5050	Inventory Adjustments	0.00	-
5310	Wages Expense	0.00	-
5400	Rent Expense	0.00	-
5410	Advertising Expense	0.00	-
5420	Bank Charges & Interest	0.00	-
5430	Insurance Expense	0.00	-
5440	Office/Store Supplies Expense	0.00	-
5450	Telephone Expense	0.00	-
5460	Utility Expense	0.00	-
5470	Bad Debts Expense	0.00	-
		---------------	---------------
		121,872.11	121,872.11

Fig. 8-2: Printers Company Trial Balance as at Jan 01, 2014.

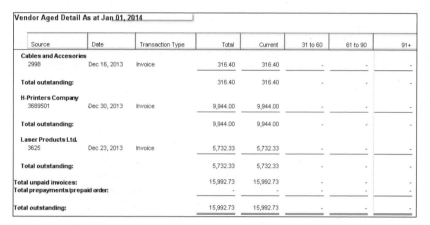

Fig. 8-3: Printers Company Customer Aged Detail report.

Vendor Aged Detail As at Jan 01, 2014							
Source	Date	Transaction Type	Total	Current	31 to 60	61 to 90	91+
Cables and Accesories							
2998	Dec 16, 2013	Invoice	316.40	316.40	-	-	-
Total outstanding:			316.40	316.40	-	-	-
H-Printers Company							
3689501	Dec 30, 2013	Invoice	9,944.00	9,944.00	-	-	-
Total outstanding:			9,944.00	9,944.00	-	-	-
Laser Products Ltd.							
3625	Dec 23, 2013	Invoice	5,732.33	5,732.33	-	-	-
Total outstanding:			5,732.33	5,732.33	-	-	-
Total unpaid invoices:			15,992.73	15,992.73	-	-	-
Total prepayments/prepaid order:			-	-	-	-	-
Total outstanding:			15,992.73	15,992.73	-	-	-

Fig. 8-4: Printers Company Vendor Aged Detail report.

Conversion

As in other modules, when a conversion is made from a manual to a computerized system or from one computerized system to another, the General Ledger, RECEIVABLES, PAYABLES and INVENTORY balances in the new system should match the old system.

There are two files at www.simplyaccounting2010.nelson.com under Student Resources that refers to **Printers Company**: **08 Printers** and **08 Printers2** which can be used to record INVENTORY & SERVICES transactions for this chapter. Your instructor will advise you which of the two **Printers** data files you are to use.

If you use the 08 Printers data file:

You need to use the data file **08 Printers** to do all the chapter exercises, which cover the following topics:

1. setting defaults
2. linking the appropriate accounts to the General Ledger
3. creating individual inventory item ledgers
4. setting the INVENTORY & SERVICES module to Ready
5. recording perpetual inventory transactions

If you use 08 Printers2 data file:

In data file **08 Printers2,** the INVENTORY & SERVICES module was set up by your supervisor and has been set to **Ready.** It is, therefore, ready for processing transactions. You have been hired to be the new accounting clerk. If you wish to review the steps that your supervisor completed to have the module ready to use, read the instructions for Exercises 8-1 to 8-6.

Exercise 8-1 – Starting the INVENTORY & SERVICES Module

---

1 ➤ Refer to Exercise 1-1, to unzip the appropriate **08 Printers,** or **08 Printers2** file.

2 ➤ Start **Simply** and open the appropriate **08 Printers** or **08 Printers2** data file.

If you are using 08 Printers2, proceed to Exercise 8-7: Journalizing Inventory-Related Sales.

If you are using the **08 Printers** file, proceed to step 3.

3 ➤ Accept the Session date of **Jan 01, 2014**. The Printers Company Home window is displayed.

4 ➤ To view and update the INVENTORY & SERVICES module, from the top menu click **Setup, User Preferences,** click **View,** in the Pages area, click the **Inventory & Services** box, and both the Pages and Icon Window boxes now have a ✓.

5 ➤ Click **OK**. The INVENTORY & SERVICES module is displayed on the left side of the Home window.

6 ➤ Click the **INVENTORY & SERVICES** module. The appropriate icons are now displayed and the module is available to update.

The Inventory and Services icons are described below.

The Inventory & Services Journals

Inventory & Services — This journal is used to add, modify, view or remove an Inventory & Service item. Only items with no item count and no dollar value information can be removed.

Build from Bill of Materials — This journal can be used on a regular basis for the transfer of several items into one finished item. When an item icon is highlighted, the journal automatically inserts **item code**, **description**, **unit of measure** and **cost**. See Exercise 8-21.

Build from Item Assembly — This journal is used on a random basis for the transfer of several items into one finished item. When an item icon is highlighted, the journal automatically inserts **item code**, **description**, **unit of measure** and **cost**. See Information only section at the end of Exercise 8-21.

Adjust Inventory — This journal is used for recording adjustments to item quantity or cost. When an item icon is highlighted, the Adjustments journal automatically inserts **item code**, **description**, **unit of measure** and **cost**.

Transfer Inventory — You use this icon to transfer inventory from one location (warehouse or store) to another location. This feature is not shown in the text.

> Failure to remove the ✓ from the 5 column items as indicated, will not allow you to record the perpetual inventory purchases and sales properly.

7 ➤ Remember that Printers Company uses the **Perpetual** inventory method.

To allow individual inventory items to be used in Purchase and Sales invoices, quotes and orders, click the **PAYABLES** module on the left, click the

Purchase Invoices icon. Click the **Customize Journal** icon. In the left pane, the Purchase Invoices selection should be shown with a ⊟. If a ⊞ is displayed at **Purchase Invoices**, click the ⊞ then click **Columns**. You need to remove the ✓ in the **Item** field. Repeat the ⊞ procedure for the following column items: **Purchase Orders** (Purchase Quotes are not used by Printers) and **Sales Invoices, Sales Orders, Sales Quotes**. (See side note box.)

8 ➤ Click **OK**. The item column is now available for use.

9 ➤ **Exit** to the Home window.

10 ➤ **Display** the Chart of Accounts. Click **Report Centre, Accounts, Chart of Accounts**, click **Modify this report**, the Current Year (2014) is in blue, click **OK**. Notice that inventory accounts #1250 to 1290 are **Inventory** class, and accounts #5010 to 5050 are **Cost of Goods Sold** class. For the INVENTORY module to work, you must have the Inventory and Cost of Goods Sold class accounts identified. Click X to close the report. Return to the Home window.

Step 1: Setting the INVENTORY & SERVICES Module Defaults

Exercise 8-2 – Setting INVENTORY & SERVICES Module Defaults

---

1 ➤ From the top menu click **Setup, Settings**, click the ⊞ at **Inventory & Services**, click **Options**.

Inventory Costing Method

> Inventory Costing Method:
> ⦿ Average Cost   ○ First In, First Out (FIFO)

As discussed at the beginning of this chapter (Overview), Simply Premium can record inventory using the methods shown. This chapter will use the Average Cost method. DO NOT CHANGE the default **Average Cost**.

Profit Evaluation Method

> Profit Evaluation Method:
> ○ Markup   ⦿ Margin

The default shows the method used by Simply to calculate the Gross Profit percentage. **Markup** or **Margin** is the difference between the inventory items, selling price and average cost. **Gross profit** is displayed using 1 of 2 methods:

Markup % = (Selling Price - Cost)/Cost

Margin % = (Selling Price - Cost)/Selling Price

DO NOT CHANGE the default **Margin**.

Sort Inventory & Services by

Sort Inventory & Services by:

○ Number   ● Description

Inventory items in this ledger can be sorted by **Number**, or by **item description**. **Description** should be selected.

Allow inventory levels to go below zero

☐ Allow inventory levels to go below zero

DO NOT CHANGE. Printers Company does not allow inventory levels to go below zero.

2 ➤ In the left pane, click **Price List** to display the default price list names. This will be explained in Exercise 8-4. DO NOT CHANGE.

3 ➤ In the left pane, click **Locations**. The user can identify various locations where inventory is stored (warehouse, in another city, etc.). There is no exercise for this feature. DO NOT CHANGE.

4 ➤ In the left pane, click **Categories** to display the heading and note as shown next. If the business had thousands of similar items in stock with various inventory codes, the user could identify the items as part of a category (e.g., printers or print cartridges) and the report would display the category items. There is no exercise for this feature. DO NOT CHANGE.

☐ My company uses Categories for inventory and service items

Use categories to group related inventory and service items together. To add a new category, enter a category name on a new line.

Leave this window open for the next exercise.

Step 2: Setting the INVENTORY & SERVICES Linked Accounts

The next step in the setup process is to define the **linked** accounts in order to update the INVENTORY module when relevant journal information (Journal transaction) is entered in the PAYABLES and RECEIVABLES modules.

Sales invoices for inventory items are recorded in the RECEIVABLES module.

Purchase invoices for inventory items are recorded in the PAYABLES module.

Purchase and Sales invoices include inventory descriptions, quantities bought or sold, and prices.

___

Exercise 8-3 – *To Set Up INVENTORY & SERVICES Linked Accounts*
___

The INVENTORY & SERVICES Linked accounts are set up as follows:

1 ➤ In the left pane click **Linked Accounts**.

When you process inventory adjustments or assemble items with Item Assembly, these accounts are used as needed.

Item Assembly Costs: _____ ▼

Adjustment Write-off: _____ ▼

Item Assembly Costs   DO NOT CHANGE. (Leave the field blank.) This would be used when a business takes a number of parts and makes them (assembles them) into a product for sale (e.g., a number of different computer parts are made into a saleable computer system). Printers Company does not assemble new printers, therefore, they do not use this feature.

Adjustment Write-Off   There are various ways for a firm to keep track of **inventory differences.**

Some companies use an account INVENTORY ADJUSTMENTS when the computer inventory records need to be updated to the actual goods on hand due to theft, damage, shrinkage, overage, etc.

Some firms may also use an account DAMAGED GOODS when goods for sale are damaged and cannot be sold. Printers Company does not use a Damaged Goods account.

These accounts would be in the Cost of Goods section of the Income Statement.

There are many other accounts that could be used to record differences. Each firm would use account names that would best represent what has happened to the inventory.

> **ℹ**
> Many companies do not keep a separate account for adjustments/changes to inventory. Adjustments, therefore, would be posted to a **Cost of Goods Sold** (Cost of Sales) account.

2 ➤   Adjustment Write-Off   Type **5050**, ⌨**Tab** for **Inventory Adjustments.** If adjustments have to be made to inventory costs, they will be posted to this G/L expense account.

Adjustment Write-off: | 5050 Inventory Adjustments |

3 ➤   Click the **OK** button to save changes and **Exit** to the Home window. (See side note box.)

The Linked accounts for INVENTORY & SERVICES are now set up. The Linked accounts for the other modules have been set up for you earlier.

Step 3: Creating Inventory Item Ledgers

In order to keep track of increases and decreases for each INVENTORY item, you need to create individual Inventory or Service item ledgers. You cannot use the Setup Guide to enter inventory items. The procedure is very similar to creating individual customer and vendor ledgers.

Exercise 8-4 – *Creating Inventory & Service Item Ledgers*

1 ➤   From the Home window, click the **INVENTORY & SERVICES** module, click the **Inventory & Services** icon.

The Inventory & Services window is similar to previous windows used to create the Customers, Vendors and Employees lists. The difference is in the **Journal** option on the menu bar.

Journal	Reports	Help
Bill of Materials & Item Assembly Journal		
Inventory Adjustments Journal		

The toolbar has icons for the same journals.

2 ➤ From the **Inventory & Services** window, click the **Create** icon to display the **Inventory Ledger** window. The Quantities tab displays.

Inventory Information

Study this chart. The first inventory item (first line in Fig. 8-5) will be set up through the completion of steps 3 to 12. Step 13 will return you to this figure to set up the rest of the inventory items. (Do not include an asterisk when setting up InkJet Printer 5 in 1.)

		Quantities Tab		Pricing Tab			Linked Tab			History Tab	
Inventory Name	Inventory Item #	Show Quantities in	Minimum Level	Regular	Preferred	Web Price	Asset	Revenue	C.O.G.S	Opening Quantity	Opening Value
InkJet Black Cartridge	IBC-01	Each	26	38.50	37.50	0.00	1270	4100	5010	40	800.00
InkJet Printer 5 in 1*	IP-001	Each	30	245.00	235.00	0.00	1250	4100	5010	53	7,950.00
Laser Black Cartridge	LBC-01	Each	10	99.00	98.00	0.00	1280	4110	5020	16	1,056.00
Laser Printer 20P	LP001	Each	12	400.00	385.00	0.00	1260	4110	5020	20	5,800.00
Printer Cable USB	C-01	Each	20	15.00	14.50	0.00	1290	4120	5030	50	350.00
											15,956.00

* Printer, copier, scanner, fax, PC fax.

Fig. 8-5: Summary of Fig. 8-8 and 9a and 9b Inventory items and values.

3 ➤ Enter the information shown on the first line of Fig. 8-5 through to step 13.

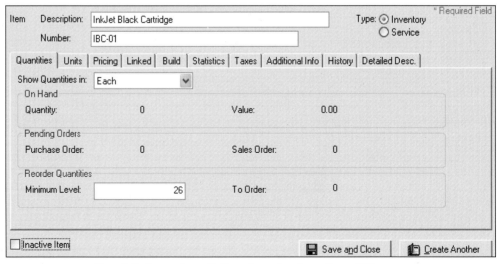

Fig. 8-6: Inventory & Services Ledger Quantities.

Item Description	Description of the item.
Item Number	Management has decided to use a combination of numbers and letters for the internal company numbering system. Simply will allow a combination of 14 numbers and/or letters for item number. The letter codes **I** and **L** identify the item as an InkJet or Laser. The other numbers are a numerical sequence increasing for future items that may be sold. The codes *IBC* and *LBC* refer to: InkJet **B**lack **C**artridge and Laser **B**lack **C**artridge. The red * will disappear when information is entered in a required field.
Type	DO NOT CHANGE the Inventory default. Printers Company sells items of inventory. Service items will be shown later in this chapter.

Quantities

Show Quantities In	This is a unit of measure of how goods are sold. Some companies may sell items in boxes, packages, etc.
On Hand	These fields are shaded because the information has not been entered in the other tab fields.
Pending Orders	These fields are shaded because the information has not been entered in the other tab fields.
Reorder Quantities	Minimum level is the lowest number of items that should be on hand before ordering new items. Simply will provide a warning message, when the inventory item falls below the reorder point. (See Exercise 8-7.) View the Inventory & Service Quantity report. The **To Order** column will indicate the quantity that is below the reorder point. See Exercise 8-8.

4 ➤   Click the **Units** tab.

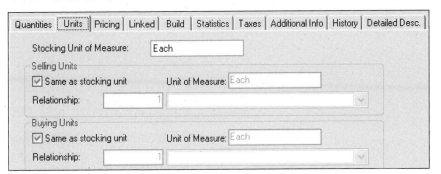

Stocking Unit of Measure	DO NOT CHANGE. As noted on the previous window, this field can indicate **each**, **boxes**, etc.
Selling Units	DO NOT CHANGE. If the selling unit is different from the stocking unit you would remove the ✓ and change the appropriate fields (e.g., you stock units by the box, and sell individual items).
Buying Units	DO NOT CHANGE. If the buying unit is different from the stocking unit, you would remove the ✓ and change the appropriate fields (e.g., you stock units by items and buy by the box).

Pricing

5 ➤ Click the **Pricing** tab and enter the information shown next:

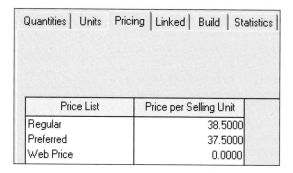

> ⓘ As you input the first amount, the same price amount is recorded for all Selling units.

> ⓘ Simply 2010 allows up to 1,000 different price lists.

(See side note boxes.)

Regular Price   This is the normal selling price of the item.

Preferred Price   This is the price at which you will sell this item to your customers who buy a large quantity of goods from your firm. The manager has decided to give only one customer this preferred status. This will be shown in a later exercise.

Web Price   Change to 0, then ⌷Tab⌷. The amount changes to 0.0000. (See side note box at step 12 for information about Simply removing all 0.0000 amounts in the Price per Selling Unit.) Printers Company does not have a Web-based Store.

Linked

6 ➤ Click the **Linked** tab, and **enter** the information shown next:

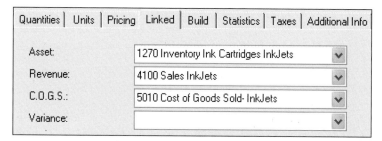

Asset   **1270 Inventory Ink Cartridges Inkjets**. This field contains the G/L Balance Sheet linked account that will increase when you buy items, and will decrease when you sell items.

Revenue   **4100 Sales InkJets**. This field contains the G/L Income Statement linked account that will increase when you sell items and will decrease when items previously sold are returned.

C.O.G.S. **5010 Cost of Goods Sold - InkJets**. This field contains the G/L Income Statement linked account that will increase by the cost of the items sold and will decrease when items previously sold are returned.

Variance Leave blank. This field would be used when you allow negative inventory levels. Printers Company does not allow negative inventory. This topic is not discussed in this text.

Build

7 ➤ Click the **Build** tab.

Build DO NOT CHANGE. Management has decided to use this feature when they create packages for sale (printers, ink and cables). You will see how this works in Exercise 8-21 as you cannot create a build without inventory items.

| Quantities | Units | Pricing | Linked | Build | Statistics | Taxes | Additional Info | History | Detailed Desc. |

Build ☐ 0 of this item from the following components (all quantities are in stocking units):

Item	Unit	Description	Quantity	

Statistics

8 ➤ Click the **Statistics** tab.

Year To Date DO NOT CHANGE. When the module is turned to Ready, information about previous sales will be available for statistical analysis.

Date of Last Sale DO NOT CHANGE. When the module is turned to Ready, this field will show the last sales transaction date.

Last Year DO NOT CHANGE. Printers Company has decided not to research previous sale information and will track statistical information from the conversion date of the INVENTORY module.

Taxes

9 ➤ Click the **Taxes** tab. DO NOT CHANGE.

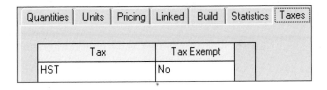

| Quantities | Units | Pricing | Linked | Build | Statistics | Taxes |

Tax	Tax Exempt	
HST	No	

Additional Info

10 ➤ Click the **Additional Info** tab. DO NOT CHANGE. These fields, together with the Detailed Desc. fields, can describe the item. The fields could display the companies we are able to buy the inventory item from. See Appendix Q, *Names Fields* at www.simplyaccounting2010.nelson.com under STUDENT RESOURCES.

History

11 ➤ Click the **History** tab and **enter** the appropriate information from summary Fig. 8-5.

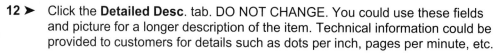

| Quantities | Units | Pricing | Linked | Build | Statistics | Taxes | Additional Info | History | Detailed Desc. |

Stocking Units On Hand

Opening Quantity: 40   Opening Value: 800.00

> ℹ️ Opening value divided by Opening Quantity = Average cost.

On Hand
Opening Quantity — The number of items you currently have in stock. (See Fig. 8-5, also Fig. 8-7, 8-8 and 8-9a and 8-9b.)

On Hand
Opening Value — The total cost value of the items in stock. (See Fig. 8-5, also Fig. 8-7, 8-9a and 8-9b.) (See side note box.)

Detailed Desc.

> ℹ️ After you finish recording the inventory item, click Create Another or Save and Close. Simply will remove the 0.0000 amounts from any Selling Unit.
>
> Return to the Pricing tab (step 5) to see the 0.0000 removed in the Web Price field.

12 ➤ Click the **Detailed Desc**. tab. DO NOT CHANGE. You could use these fields and picture for a longer description of the item. Technical information could be provided to customers for details such as dots per inch, pages per minute, etc.

13 ➤ Click | **Create Another** | to save this item. Return to Fig. 8-5 to input the rest of the inventory items using previous steps 2 to 12. (See side note box.)

Add Additional Inventory Items

14 ➤ When you have finished entering the last item with the dollar quantities and values, the software may (or may not) advise you, with a message box shown next, that the total dollar value of the inventory asset accounts is equal to the totals of the individual inventory items you have just entered.

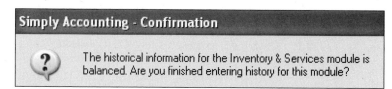

Simply Accounting - Confirmation

? The historical information for the Inventory & Services module is balanced. Are you finished entering history for this module?

15 ➤ If you see the Confirmation message box shown, click **No**. If you click Yes Simply will turn the INVENTORY module to **Ready**, and you do not want to do that at this point.

The best thing to do at this time is to display and print out the reports in Exercise 8-5 to verify what you have entered so far. If the information printed matches the information in Figures 8-7, 8-8 and 8-9b, then you can proceed. You should make a backup after Exercise 8-5 before proceeding.

16 ➤ Click on the **Display by** icon 🔲. This display does not provide the user with any Quantity or Value information.

17 ➤ Click **Display by name** icon 🔲. Your inventory window should resemble Fig. 8-7 with five inventory items and Quantity and Total Value Information.

Balances are as of the latest transaction date	Quantity	Total Value
InkJet Black Cartridge IBC-01	40	800.00
InkJet Printer 5 in 1 IP-001	53	7,950.00
Laser Black Cartridge LBC-01	16	1,056.00
Laser Printer 20P LP001	20	5,800.00
Printer Cable USB C-01	50	350.00

Fig. 8-7: Inventory window.

To Display Inventory Details

Exercise 8-5 – To Display Inventory Details

To review the information entered, use the following steps:

1 ➤ Click the **Select a Report** icon 📇. Click the ▼ to display a list of available reports, select **Quantity**, **Select**, the Asset accounts should be highlighted in blue, or click Select All if they are not in blue, **OK**.

The window display (Fig. 8-8) shows the items on order and items to order that are below minimum stock. (See Exercise 8-8 for an example or information in the To Order column.) Note: The displayed and printed report will not indicate any date. **Exit** this window.

Inventory Quantity

Description △	Item No.	Unit	Quantity	Minimum	On Purc...	On Sale...	To Order
InkJet Black Cartridge	IBC-01	Each	40	26	0	0	-
InkJet Printer 5 in 1	IP-001	Each	53	30	0	0	-
Laser Black Cartridge	LBC-01	Each	16	10	0	0	-
Laser Printer 20P	LP001	Each	20	12	0	0	-
Printer Cable USB	C-01	Each	50	20	0	0	-

Fig. 8-8: Printers Company Inventory Quantity.

2 ➤ Click the **Select a Report** icon. Click the ▼ to display a list of available reports. Select **Summary**, **Select**. All inventory items should be highlighted in blue, or otherwise click Select All.

At the bottom left of the window you have two choices of displaying/printing the report.

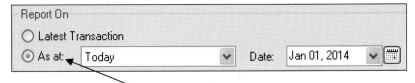

The default selection is As at.

3 ➤ Latest Transaction   The report can be displayed only after the latest transaction. Click **Latest Transaction** button. The As at date line is grayed out. Click **OK**.

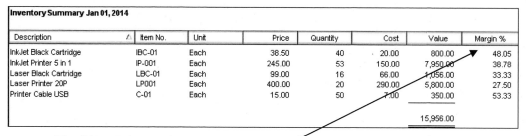

Inventory Summary Jan 01, 2014							
Description	Item No.	Unit	Price	Quantity	Cost	Value	Margin %
InkJet Black Cartridge	IBC-01	Each	38.50	40	20.00	800.00	48.05
InkJet Printer 5 in 1	IP-001	Each	245.00	53	150.00	7,950.00	38.78
Laser Black Cartridge	LBC-01	Each	99.00	16	66.00	1,056.00	33.33
Laser Printer 20P	LP001	Each	400.00	20	290.00	5,800.00	27.50
Printer Cable USB	C-01	Each	15.00	50	7.00	350.00	53.33
						15,956.00	

Fig. 8-9a: Printers Company Inventory Summary with Margin (%).

This report displays the Margin % of profit earned on the sale of individual items (average inventory cost).

4 ➤ Click **Modify, Report Options**. Click **As at**. The selection is available.

5 ➤

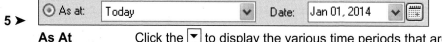

    ◉ As at: Today   ▾   Date: Jan 01, 2014   ▾ 🗓

As At   Click the ▾ to display the various time periods that are available during a fiscal year. Do Not change the date. Click **OK**. This report does not display the Margin %.

Inventory Summary As at Jan 01, 2014					
Description	Item No.	Unit	Quantity	Cost	Value
InkJet Black Cartridge	IBC-01	Each	40	20.00	800.00
InkJet Printer 5 in 1	IP-001	Each	53	150.00	7,950.00
Laser Black Cartridge	LBC-01	Each	16	66.00	1,056.00
Laser Printer 20P	LP001	Each	20	290.00	5,800.00
Printer Cable USB	C-01	Each	50	7.00	350.00
					15,956.00

Fig. 8-9b: Printers Company Inventory Summary (without Margin %).

Look at these two reports to notice that some of the information is the same and some is different. The displays are the result of the input you just completed. The Summary As At date report cannot display the Selling price and or Margin % as the selling price of items could have changed during the period and, therefore, the Margin % cannot be calculated.

The authors believe the Summary report with Margin % is more important to management as it identifies which inventory items are making less of a profit for the business. Users must be aware that the % may be low due to a temporary reduction in the sales price.

6 ➤ Exit the **Summary** report, and click the **Select a Report** icon. Click **Select** to accept the **Display Inventory and Services list**, the window changes, click **OK**. Compare the displayed information to the Summary chart, Fig. 8-5, to verify your input. Note: Ignore the Uncategorized column.

7 ➤ **Exit** this window and return to the Home window.

Make a backup before proceeding. Name your backup similar to: **Printers_B4_Ready**.

The conversion process is now complete.

Step 4: Setting the INVENTORY & SERVICES Module to READY

The INVENTORY & SERVICES module is ready to change from History to **Ready** mode. The COMPANY, PAYABLES and RECEIVABLES modules have been set to **Ready** for you. Only the INVENTORY & SERVICES module needs to be set to **Ready** at this point.

1 ➤ Double check that the total cost of the inventory on hand, as entered in the Inventory Ledger, is equal to the balance of the Inventory accounts 1250 to 1290 in the G/L. If the balances are not equal, return to the **Inventory & Services Ledger**, and correct where necessary.

Before making the module Ready, it is important to back up your data files. Once the modules are made Ready, you cannot go back to make changes.

2 ➤ If you did not back up your files before, do it now.

Back up your files before proceeding and record details in your logbook.

Exercise 8-6 – Setting the INVENTORY & SERVICES Module to READY

Set the INVENTORY & SERVICES module to **Ready** as follows:

1 ➤ From the Home window, click **History, Enter Historical Information** ▶, **Inventory & Services**.

A warning message is displayed if the inventory account balances do not balance with the General Ledger inventory accounts.

The normal warning message box shown next is seen when inventory details are balanced to the G/L. Make sure you have a backup.

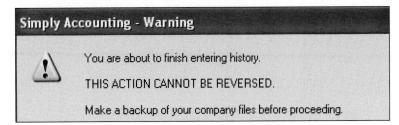

Simply Accounting - Warning

⚠ You are about to finish entering history.

THIS ACTION CANNOT BE REVERSED.

Make a backup of your company files before proceeding.

2 ➤ Click **Proceed** to continue. The Quill pen is removed, because history information has been entered and is complete.

Slideshow **8B – Journalizing Inventory-Related Transactions** demonstrates how the INVENTORY & SERVICES module works and the accounting principles relate to the various inventory-related tasks. Run it now.

Step 5: Journalizing Inventory-Related Sales

Start here from Exercise 8-1 if your instructor suggested that you use the data file **Printers2**.

Exercise 8-7 – Journalizing Inventory-Related Sales

---

1 ➤   Advance the Session date to **Jan 06, 2014**.

2 ➤   Click the **RECEIVABLES** module, and click the **Sales Invoice**s icon. Notice the Sales Invoice window does *not* indicate a preferred status field. **Exit** to the Home window.

Preferred Pricing

Study this transaction:

> **Jan 06, 2014**   **The manager has finalized plans to extend preferred pricing only to customer More Computers Ltd. effective today, as they normally buy a large quantity of merchandise from the firm.**

To have More Computers Ltd. receive preferred pricing, complete the next 3 steps.

1 ➤   Click the **Customers** icon, and double-click **More Computers Ltd**.

2 ➤   Click the **Options** Tab, at Price List, click the ▼, select **Preferred**, Tab .

3 ➤   Click Save & Close and X to return to the Home window.

Inventory-Related Sale on Credit

Study this transaction:

> **Jan 06, 2014**   **The following inventory items are sold with HST to More Computers Ltd. (a preferred customer) on invoice #11592 dated today with terms 2/10, net 30 days.**
>
> | | | |
> |---|---|---|
> | 15 InkJet Printer 5 in 1 at | $ | 235.00 ea. plus HST |
> | 15 InkJet Black Cartridge at | $ | 37.50 ea. plus HST |
> | 15 Printer Cable USB at | $ | 14.50 ea. plus HST |
> | Invoice total = | $ | 4,864.66 |

This transaction is a normal inventory-related sale on credit and is entered in the RECEIVABLES module as follows:

1 ➤   From the Home window, click the **Sales Invoices** icon.

The procedures to record the credit sale are similar to Exercise 2A-13, in RECEIVABLES (Chapter 2A), except that inventory item numbers and descriptions are entered.

(See side note box.)

Enter the invoice as indicated below:

ℹ️

In many situations, the branch office orders the goods, and the invoices are sent to Head Office for payment, or vice versa.

---

2 ➤   **Customer**   Select **More Computers Ltd**. Tab .

Shipping Address   DO NOT CHANGE. (See side note box.)

	Invoice No.	Do not change. This is the next invoice to be issued.
	Order/Quote No.	Printers Company does not use sales orders or quotes at this time. Leave blank.
3 ➤	**Item Number**	Press [Enter] (or double-click in the first line of the Item column) to display a list of inventory items. Before Selecting, notice that the display shows the quantity of each item in stock. Select **InkJet Printer 5 in 1**. Automatically the Item number, Unit, Item Description, Base Price, Price, Tax code, and G/L account for Sales InkJets are displayed in the first row of the invoice. This information is retrieved from the Inventory ledger as you enter the item.

> ℹ️ There is no indication in the Sales Invoice window that preferred pricing is being used for this customer. The reference, as noted, is in the customer ledger window.

(See side note box.)

4 ➤	**Quantity**	Type **15** (items sold), [Tab] to **Base Price**.
5 ➤	**Base Price**	[Tab] to accept the price of **235.00**. This price can be changed by typing the new price if the actual selling price is different from the regular or preferred price.
6 ➤	**Discount %**	[Tab] to move to Price. This client has previously been given a preferred selling price.
7 ➤	**Price**	[Tab] to accept the amount of **235.00**.
8 ➤	**Amount**	[Tab] to accept the amount of **3,525.00**. The Amount field is automatically calculated as **quantity** times **price**.
9 ➤	**Tax**	HS, [Tab]. The goods are being purchased
10 ➤	**Account**	[Tab] to accept the G/L account number **4100 Sales InkJets**. This field can be changed as needed (e.g., returns).

The cursor moves to the second row of the invoice.

Using the mouse, resize the columns to approximate Fig. 8-10.

> ℹ️ Printers Company Ltd. does not charge for delivery. If the customer is charged for delivery, a linked account in the RECEIVABLES module for Freight Revenue needs to be added. Then you would enter an amount in the **Freight** field.

11 ➤	**Enter** the other sales items on the next 2 rows by using the above procedure. The G/L sales account is different for the cable items.	
	Terms	DO NOT CHANGE.

(See side note box.)

The Sales Invoice should display like Fig. 8-10.

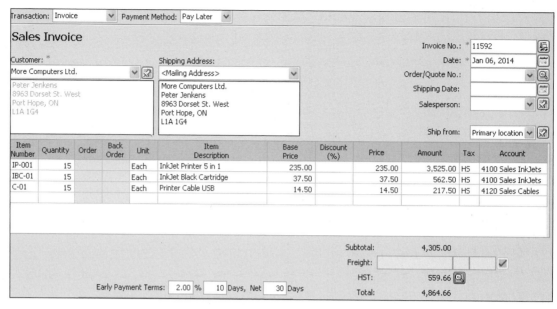

Fig. 8-10: Sales Invoice window.

12 ➤ Display the **Sales Journal Entry**. The entry should be as follows:

Sales Journal Entry Jan 06, 2014 (J1)

Account Number	Account Description	Debits	Credits
1200	Accounts Receivable	4,864.66	-
5010	Cost Of Goods Sold- InkJets	2,550.00	-
5030	Cost Of Goods Sold- Cables	105.00	-
1250	Inventory InkJet Printers	-	2,250.00
1270	Inventory Ink Cartridges InkJet	-	300.00
1290	Inventory Printer Cables	-	105.00
2650	HST Charged on Sales	-	559.66
4100	Sales InkJets	-	4,087.50
4120	Sales Cables	-	217.50
Additional Date:	Additional Field:		
		7,519.66	7,519.66

Fig. 8-11: Sales Journal Entry.

13 ➤ **Exit** from the entry window.

Simply combines two journal entries into one entry when an inventory sale is recorded.

1. **The Sales entry:**

	DR	CR
Accounts Receivable	4,864.66	
HST Charged on Sales		559.66
Sales InkJets		4,087.50
Sales Cables		217.50

2. **The Cost of Goods Sold entry:**

Cost of Goods Sold- InkJets	2,550.00	
Cost of Goods Sold- Cables	105.00	
Inventory InkJet Printers		2,250.00
Inventory Ink Cartridges InkJet		300.00
Inventory Printer Cables		105.00

The credits to the **Sales** accounts (Section 1) are based on the **selling price** of the items.

```
┌─────────────────────────────────────────────────────────────────────────────────┐
│                                                                                   │
│  Printers Company , Student's Name                                    11592       │
│  1075 Aberdeen Avenue                                                             │
│  Vaughan, Ontario L4L 8V7                                          Jan 06, 2014   │
│                                                                                   │
│                                                                        1          │
│                                                                                   │
│        More Computers Ltd.              More Computers Ltd.                        │
│        Peter Jenkens                    Peter Jenkens                             │
│        8963 Dorset St. West             8963 Dorset St. West                      │
│        Port Hope, Ontario L1A 1G4       Port Hope, Ontario L1A 1G4               │
│                                                                                   │
│   IP-001      15  Each    InkJet Printer 5 in1      HS    235.00    3,525.00      │
│   IBC-01      15  Each    InkJet Black Cartridge    HS     37.50      562.50      │
│   C-01        15  Each    Printer Cable USB         HS     14.50      217.50      │
│                                                                                   │
│                           Sub-total:                                 4,305.00     │
│                           HS- HST added at 13%                                    │
│                           HST                                          559.66     │
│                                                                                   │
│                                                                                   │
│                           Terms: 2%/10, Net 30. Due Feb 05, 2014                 │
│                                                                                   │
│                                                                                   │
│  Printers Company , Student's Name HST: #Rx25693                                 │
│                                                                                   │
│  Thank you for your order.                                           4,864.66     │
│                                                                                   │
└─────────────────────────────────────────────────────────────────────────────────┘
```

Fig. 8-12: Invoice details printed on plain paper.

The debits to the **Cost of Goods Sold** accounts and the credits to **Inventory** accounts (Section 2) are based on the **average cost** of the items in inventory.

14 ➤   **Post** when correct.

A message window should appear advising you that an item quantity has fallen below the minimum level (reorder point).

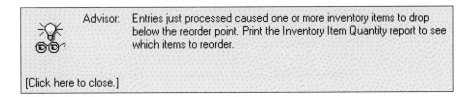

Advisor: Entries just processed caused one or more inventory items to drop below the reorder point. Print the Inventory Item Quantity report to see which items to reorder.

[Click here to close.]

15 ➤   **Click** anywhere in the box.

16 ➤   **Exit** from the Sales Journal window.

Back up your files regularly and update your logbook.

Refer to Fig. 8-12 to see the invoice details that will print on preprinted forms.

Determining Inventory Items to Order

You should check the number of items in stock on a regular basis to determine if there are stock items that need reordering. In Exercise 8-7, step 14, a message window advised you that one or more items have dropped below the reorder point. You may view and/or print a report that will show you all the items that need reordering.

Exercise 8-8 – Determining What Items to Order

In this exercise, you will view the Inventory Quantity report that will show you what items need reordering.

1 ➤ Follow the procedures in Exercise 8-5 to display an Inventory **Quantity** report for all Inventory items. Alternatively, from the Home window, click **Reports** and then click **Inventory & Services**, **Quantity.** On the right, ensure your screen shows **Inventory by Asset** and **Stocking units** selected and all inventory items are highlighted in blue. Click **OK.**

Description	Number	Unit	Quantity	Minimum	On Pur Order	On Sal Order	To Order
InkJet Black Cartridge	IBC-01	Each	25	26	0	0	1

The 1 listed in the **To Order** column means that the InkJet Black Cartridge is one below the minimum quantity, therefore, an order to purchase should be placed.

2 ➤ **Exit** to the Home window.

Recording a New Item

There are two ways to add a new item to the INVENTORY listing:

a) Click the Inventory & Services icon and create the new item as you learned earlier.

b) Add the new inventory item as you record the Purchase Order.

Using method b, follow the steps in Exercise 8-9 to record a Purchase Order and to add a new inventory item.

Exercise 8-9 – To Record a New Inventory Item

Jan 06 2014   **After many requests for colour InkJet cartridges from customers, the manager ordered from InkJet Cartridges Ltd., the following on Purchase Order #65:**

50 InkJet Colour Cartridges at $27.00 each plus HST.
60 InkJet Black   Cartridges at $20.00 each plus HST.

Terms are 2/10, n30, with a shipping date of Jan 09, 2014. Total Purchase Order is $2,881.50.

To record the Purchase Order, follow these steps:

1 ➤ Click the **PAYABLES** module, click the **Purchase Orders** icon.

Transaction   Leave selection as Purchase Order.

2 ➤ Vendor   Select **InkJet Cartridges Ltd.**, `Tab`.

Order No.   The next PO is 65.

3 ➤ Date   **Jan 06, 2014,** `Tab` `Tab`.

4 ➤ Shipping Date   **Jan 09, 2014,** `Tab`.

5 ➤ Item Number   Press `Enter` and the Select Inventory/Service window appears with the first line as:

<Add new inventory/service>

6 ➤ Click **Select**.

Enter the inventory item and details as shown next:

The **On Hand Quantity**, **Pending Purchase Order**, **Sales Order** and **Value** fields are not available as this is a new item. These fields are updated when a purchase or a sale is completed.

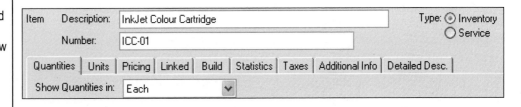

(See side note box.)

7 ➤ Minimum Level: 10, `Tab`. Click the **Pricing** tab.

Pricing

8 ➤ Enter the pricing as follows.

Price List	Price per Selling Unit
Regular	44.0000
Preferred	43.0000
Web Price	0.0000

9 ➤ Click the **Linked** tab, and set the linked accounts (**1270**, **4100** and **5010**) which are the same as the InkJet Black Cartridges.

Taxes

10 ➤ Click the **Taxes** tab. DO NOT CHANGE. We do not know which of our customers can buy inventory items HST-Exempt.

11 ➤ Click **Save & Close**.

After item #ICC-01 has been added to the inventory list, enter the Purchase Order as shown next:

12 ➤ **Item** `Tab` to accept ICC-01, InkJet Colour Cartridge.

13 ➤ **Order** Type **50**, `Tab`.

14 ➤ **Back Order** `Tab` to accept 50. `Tab` to Price.

15 ➤ **Price** Type **27.00**, `Tab`. (See side note box.)

16 ➤ **Tax** `Tab` to accept **HS**.

17 ➤ **HST** `Tab` to accept 175.50. `Tab`.

18 ➤ **Amount** `Tab` to accept **$1,350** in the Amount column.

Account The account number should be 1270 (the linked account for InkJet Cartridges) and the total Purchase Order amount is 1,525.50.

19 ➤ **Enter** the order for 60 InkJet Black Cartridges using the same procedure.

Terms **2/10, n/30**.

> The price field in the Purchase Order is blank because this is the first time a cost is being entered for this item.
>
> When the invoice is received and posted, the average cost shown for this item will be $27.00. It will change after each purchase, if the cost price changes.

The Purchase Order should be as shown in Fig. 8-13.

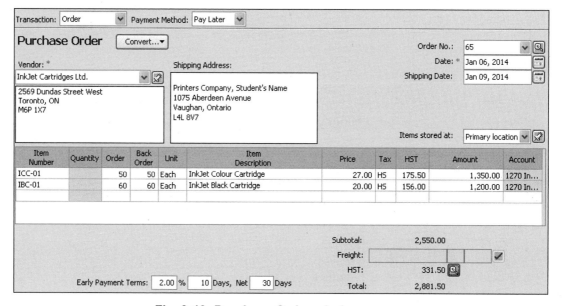

Fig. 8-13: Purchase Order window.

20 ➤ **Record** when correct. **Exit** to the Home window.

Exercise 8-10 – Display the Pending Purchases Report

Study the next transaction and record as follows:

Display the Pending Purchases Report

1 ➤ From the main menu, click **Reports, Payables, Pending Purchase Orders, By Vendor, Summary,** if all items are not highlighted in blue, click **Select All,** change the date to **Jan 09, 2014, OK.** The report as shown next will display outstanding Purchase Orders. If you want to see the details of the Purchase Order, drill down by double-clicking on any item on the line. (See side note box.)

ⓘ If you selected Vendor Detail you would be able to view details about Item, Description, Unit, Back Ordered Quantities.

Pending Purchase Orders Summary by Vendor As at Jan 09, 2014

Purchase Order Number	Purchase Order Date	Ship Date	Amount Original Order
Ink Jet Cartridges Ltd.			
65	Jan 06, 2014	Jan 09, 2014	2,881.50
			2,881.50
			2,881.50

2 ➤ **Exit** to the Home window.

Other Transactions

1 ➤ Advance the Session date to **Jan 07, 2014.**

2 ➤ **Record** and **Post** this transaction.

This transaction is a normal cash receipt from a customer. Use the Receipts journal with a deposit date of Jan 07, 2014 to record this transaction.

Jan 07, 2014 Received cheque #998 in the amount of $3,330.00 from Do-It Yourself Inc. in payment of Invoice 11575.

The Discount Available column indicates 0.00. A discount of $60.00 for paying within 10 days will be allowed (Discount Taken column), due to the volume of mail delivery during the holiday season.

The envelope was dated and postmarked December 31.

Your window should appear as follows:

Invoice Date	Invoice or Deposit	Original Amount	Amount Owing	Discount Available	Discount Taken	Amount Received
Dec 23, 2013	11575	3,390.00	3,390.00	0.00	60.00	3,330.00

3 ➤ **Record** and **Post** this transaction.

Jan 07, 2014 Sold to Davis Computers, for immediate shipment today, the following items at regular price plus HST:
7 Laser Printers 20P
7 Laser Black Cartridges
7 Printer Cable USB

Terms 2/10, n30. Invoice 11593, total $4,065.74.

A low inventory warning message should appear.

4 ➤ Click anywhere in the box to **close** the window. **Return** to the Home window.

5 ➤ Display the **Inventory Quantity** report. You may have to expand the column to see the heading wording.

The report indicates that:

On Pur Order   Under this column, opposite the black and colour InkJet cartridges are the quantities on order for these items.

To Order   1 item below the minimum quantity for the Laser Black Cartridge. This item should be ordered.

1 Item above the minimum quantity for the Laser Printer 20P.

6 ➤ **Exit** to the Home window.

7 ➤ **Record** the following Purchase Order:

Jan 07, 2014 The manager asked you to issue Purchase Order #66 to Laser Products Ltd. for the following items plus HST.

25 Laser Printer 20P   at $290.00 each
25 Laser Black Cartridges   at $66.00 each

Terms 2/10, net 30 and ship by Jan 09, 2014.

Total Purchase Order $10,057.00.

---

8 ➤ **Exit** to the Home window.

9 ➤ Advance the Session date to **Jan 09, 2014**.

Journalizing Inventory Purchases

Notice that items purchased under the **Perpetual** method do not go to the PURCHASES account, but rather go to the INVENTORY account on the Balance Sheet. When the items are sold, the cost of the inventory is taken out of the INVENTORY account and charged to COST OF SALES.

Exercise 8-11 – Journalizing Inventory Purchases

Study the next transaction and record as follows:

INKJET CARTRIDGES LTD.

2569 Dundas Street West
Toronto, Ontario, M6P 1X7

INVOICE # 25831

Date: Jan. 9, 2014
Your P.O. 65
Terms: 2/10, n 30

-We sell Quality Products -

SOLD TO:
Printers Company, Student's Name
1075 Aberdeen Avenue
Vaughan, ON
L4L 8V7

HST # 332 445 667

QTY	B/O	DESCRIPTION	HST		UNIT PRICE	AMOUNT
50		InkJet Colour Cartridges	HS		27.00	1,350.00
50	10	InkJet Black Cartridges	HS		19.50	975.00
					Sub Total	2,325.00
					HST	302.25
			Total Invoice Amount			$2,627.25

Received the above invoice with a note from the vendor's manager that effective Jan 07, 2014 a price decrease to $19.50 each was given on the InkJet Black Cartridges. The note also stated that 10 InkJet Black Cartridges are backordered and should be shipped by Jan 14, 2014.

This transaction is a purchase of inventory items from a Purchase Order.

1 ➤   From the Home window, click the **Purchase Invoices** icon.

Transaction   **Invoice**.

Payment Method **Pay later**.

2 ➤ **Order No.**   Click the **Finder** icon [🔍] and the Select Order or Quote appears. Select **PO 65**. Automatically, details from Purchase Order 65 are retrieved and displayed in the invoice.

3 ➤ **Invoice**   Type **25831**, [Tab].

4 ➤ **Quantity**   For colour cartridges, type **50**, [Tab].

5 ➤ **Back Order**   [Tab] to accept a blank field.

   Price   The 27.00 unit price displayed is the cost of the individual inventory items on the PURCHASE ORDER.

   [Tab] to Quantity on the next line.

The cursor does not allow entry to the **Acct** field because this account is the default linked account. To change the account number, you would have to reassign the specific linked account.

6 ➤ **Quantity**   For black cartridges, type **50,** [Tab].

7 ➤ **Back Order**   Notice that 10 cartridges are backordered. [Tab].

8 ➤ **Price**   Type **19.50**. This is the new price of the cartridges. As a result of this price change, the average cost of the InkJet Black Cartridge will decrease to $19.6667 each. This will be explained later. [Tab] to accept.

9 ➤ Display the Purchases Journal Entry.

Purchases Journal Entry Jan 09, 2014 (J4)

Account Number	Account Description	Debits	Credits
1270	Inventory Ink Cartridges InkJet	2,325.00	-
2670	HST Paid on Purchases	302.25	-
2200	Accounts Payable	-	2,627.25
Additional Date:	Additional Field:		
		2,627.25	2,627.25

10 ➤ **Exit** from the Journal Entry. **Post** when correct and **Exit** to the Home window.

11 ➤ Display the **INVENTORY Summary** report, with **Latest Transaction** selected.

Inventory Summary Jan 09, 2014

Description	Item No.	Unit	Price	Quantity	Cost	Value	Margin %
InkJet Black Cartridge	IBC-01	Each	38.50	75	19.6667	1,475.00	48.92
InkJet Colour Cartridge	ICC-01	Each	44.00	50	27.00	1,350.00	38.64
InkJet Printer 5 in 1	IP-001	Each	245.00	38	150.00	5,700.00	38.78
Laser Black Cartridge	LBC-01	Each	99.00	9	66.00	594.00	33.33
Laser Printer 20P	LP001	Each	400.00	13	290.00	3,770.00	27.50
Printer Cable USB	C-01	Each	15.00	28	7.00	196.00	53.33
						13,085.00	

Note that the InkJet Black Cartridge average cost per unit has changed due to the reduction in the purchase price of the last order. Simply calculates the cost of inventory on hand using the **Average Cost** method.

25 items on hand   @ $20.00 each = $ 500.00
50 items purchased   @ $19.50 each = $ 975.00
75 items total cost   = $1,475.00

The average cost of each InkJet Black Cartridge is:

$1,475.00 / 75 items = $19.6667 (See side note box.)

The gross margin has increased from an average of 48.05% to 48.92%. The manager has decided not to decrease the selling price of the InkJet cartridges at this time.

> **ℹ**
> Simply calculates AVERAGE COST to 4 decimal places.

12 ➤ **Exit** the Summary window.

Another Transaction

1 ➤ **Record** the following transaction. Select the purchase order number, then enter the invoice number and verify the date, click the **Fill Backordered Quantities** 🔲 icon and the **Quantity** column will fill with the items ordered.

The Fill Backordered Quantities icon can be useful when you have ordered many items on a Purchase Order and the complete order has been filled. You would still have to verify all received items with the invoice total.

Jan 09, 2014 Received Invoice #3661 dated today from Laser Products Ltd. for the goods ordered on Purchase Order #66, and 5 extra printers ordered yesterday by the manager without changing the Purchase Order. Terms 2/10, net 30.

30 Laser Printers 20P	**$ 8,700.00**
25 Laser Black Cartridges	**1,650.00**
HST	**1,345.50**
Total	**$ 11,695.50**

Notice that the Backorder column amounts are removed because the purchase order request has been received in full.

2 ➤ Change the Laser Printer 20P quantity to **30,** [Tab] .

3 ➤ **Post** when correct. A message box will appear advising you that the Purchase Order has been filled, because there are no items on backorder.

4 ➤ Click **OK** and **Exit** to the Home window.

5 ➤ Advance the Session date to **Jan 15, 2014**.

To Journalize a Cash on Delivery (COD) Sale

Normally a COD (Cash on Delivery) sale is processed as a **cash** sale. However, if you are giving the customer a sales discount, you would process the transaction a bit differently from a normal cash sale.

In this particular case, you are not sure if this customer will purchase again in the future. Therefore, the customer's information will be added to the customer list, but will be given a 0.00 (nil) credit limit.

Exercise 8-12 – Journalizing a Cash on Delivery (COD) Sale

This customer has applied for credit, and the credit application is being processed. In the meantime, you will give the customer a sales discount of 2%, which you usually provide for regular customers for early payment.

1 ➤ Study the following transaction:

Jan 13, 2014   Sold the following goods to a new customer, McPherson's Computers Co., terms COD, on our invoice #11594 dated today. Sale is made with 13% HST.

A 2% discount for paying for the goods at time of sale is given to McPherson's Computers Co. Cheque #1362 in the amount of $1,681.65 (not certified) was received when Mrs. van Ingen picked up the equipment.

Create a customer ledger with the following information:

McPherson's Computers Co.
310 Kendalwood Road
Whitby, Ontario, L1N 2G3
905 430-2830

Contact: **Mrs. Diane van Ingen**
Revenue Account: **Select 4100 Sales InkJets**.
Terms: **Leave blank**.
Taxes **HS**
Credit Limit: **0.00**
Memo: **Credit check requested Jan 13, 2014 by our manager**.

To-Do Date: **Jan 24, 2014**

2 InkJet Black Cartridges	$ 38.50	each
2 InkJet Colour Cartridges	44.00	each
2 InkJet Printer 5 in 1	245.00	each
2 Laser Printers 20P	400.00	each
4 Printer Cables USB	15.00	each

Total (including HST) before discount **$1,711.95**

---

2 ➤   From the Home window, click the **Receivables Module**, click the **Sales Invoices** icon to display the Sales Journal window.

     Transaction   **Invoice**

3 ➤   **Payment method** Select **Cheque**, [Tab] [Tab] to Cheque.

4 ➤   **Cheque No.**   Type **1362**, [Tab] to Sold to.

5 ➤   **Customer**   Type **McPherson's Computers Co.**, [Tab], select **Full Add**. Enter the appropriate information (see the above information box). Select Save and Close. [Tab].

6 ➤   **Date**   Select **Jan 13, 2014**. [Tab].

7 ➤   **Details**   Enter the rest of the invoice with inventory items from the information box. You may have to drag the bottom of the window down to see the 5 items in the window. You could also maximize the window.

8 ➤   **Message**   Change to: **Thank you for your order. COD paid by cheque** (this will show on the invoice that this is a cash sale and the invoice has been paid), [Tab] twice to Early Payment Discount.

9 ➤ Early Payment Type **2.00**, [Tab]. The box to the right of % will display:
      Discount ☐   30.30, which is the discount for paying early.

The Total invoice and Cheque Amount should be as follows:

Cheque Amount:	1,681.65

($1,711.95 less $30.30 discount equals cheque amount).

[Tab] to Post.

10 ➤ Display the journal entry (see side note box). It should be as follows:

<table>
<tr><td colspan="4">Sales Journal Entry Jan 13, 2014 (J6)</td></tr>
<tr><th>Account Number</th><th>Account Description</th><th>Debits</th><th>Credits</th></tr>
<tr><td>1020</td><td>Bank Account</td><td>1,681.65</td><td>-</td></tr>
<tr><td>4150</td><td>Sales Discount</td><td>30.30</td><td>-</td></tr>
<tr><td>5010</td><td>Cost Of Goods Sold- InkJets</td><td>393.33</td><td>-</td></tr>
<tr><td>5020</td><td>Cost Of Goods Sold- Lasers</td><td>580.00</td><td>-</td></tr>
<tr><td>5030</td><td>Cost Of Goods Sold- Cables</td><td>28.00</td><td>-</td></tr>
<tr><td>1250</td><td>Inventory InkJet Printers</td><td>-</td><td>300.00</td></tr>
<tr><td>1260</td><td>Inventory Laser Printers</td><td>-</td><td>580.00</td></tr>
<tr><td>1270</td><td>Inventory Ink Cartridges InkJet</td><td>-</td><td>93.33</td></tr>
<tr><td>1290</td><td>Inventory Printer Cables</td><td>-</td><td>28.00</td></tr>
<tr><td>2650</td><td>HST Charged on Sales</td><td>-</td><td>196.95</td></tr>
<tr><td>4100</td><td>Sales InkJets</td><td>-</td><td>655.00</td></tr>
<tr><td>4110</td><td>Sales Lasers</td><td>-</td><td>800.00</td></tr>
<tr><td>4120</td><td>Sales Cables</td><td>-</td><td>60.00</td></tr>
<tr><td>Additional Date:</td><td>Additional Field:</td><td></td><td></td></tr>
<tr><td></td><td></td><td>2,713.28</td><td>2,713.28</td></tr>
</table>

> ℹ️ BANK ACCOUNT is debited and not ACCOUNTS RECEIVABLES since this is a cash sale. The entry shows the **sales discount** amount.

11 ➤ Exit the entry window, **Post** when correct and **Exit** to the Home window.

Another Transaction

1 ➤ Record and **post** this transaction.

> **Jan 13, 2014** Purchase from new vendor, Rotex Printing Ltd., 212 Caster Avenue, Vaughan, Ont. L4L 7U9, Phone 905-675-6629, Invoice #4012 for $200.00 plus HST for 1 box of new sales invoices for the store. Terms N20 days, Invoice total $226.00.

The default expense account for these sales invoices is **1330 Prepaid Store Supplies**. This is a purchase of supplies for store use and is not a purchase of inventory for resale, therefore, when recording the invoice you:

a) Do not use the Item column in the Purchases Invoice window.
b) Do not add this to the inventory listing of goods for sale.

Item Number	Quantity	Order	Back Order	Unit	Item Description	Price	Tax	HST	Amount	Account
	1			box	Sales Invoices	200.00	HS	26.00	200.00	1330 P...

2 ➤ Exit to the Home window.

Journalizing an Inventory Sales Return

Goods returned must be entered in the RECEIVABLES module as a **negative** sale. A Sales Return in a business using the perpetual method of accounting for inventory, records the return of goods to the INVENTORY module at the cost value. They do not use a Sales Return account.

Exercise 8-13 – *Journalizing an Inventory Sales Return*

Study this transaction:

> **Jan 14, 2014** **Received cheque #720 in the amount of $5,068.05 from Computers and More, re invoice #11568 with a letter from Larry Richards, Operations Manager, asking why they have not received a credit memo in the amount of $452.00 for the return of 1 Laser printer 20P on Jan 3, 2014. You have checked and found that the printer was received on Jan 3, but the paperwork did not get to Accounting.**

You will issue **Credit Memo 11568Rt CM61**, referenced back to the original invoice for the returned item, and adjust your Accounts Receivable and Inventory accounts accordingly.

This transaction with Computers & More must be recorded in two steps:

    a.   Enter the goods returned.
    b.   Record the cash receipt.

Step 1: Record the Sales Return

1 ➤   Click the **RECEIVABLES** module, click the **Sales Invoices** icon from the Home window.

2 ➤   **Enter the return** as shown in Fig. 8-14.

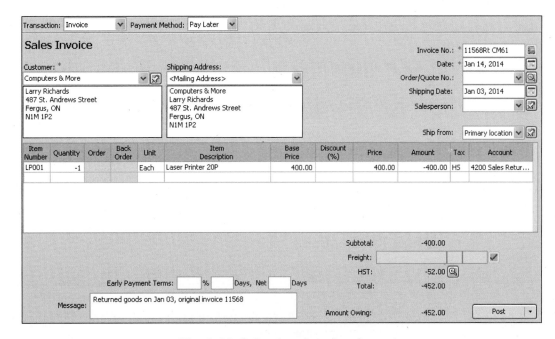

Fig. 8-14: Sales Invoice showing return.

Transaction	Invoice (**Sales** and **Sales Returns** use the same window).
Ship Date	This date records the actual date the goods were returned.
Date	This records the date the return was recorded in the accounting records. In this situation, there is no effect on a discount and the Comment Field also records the actual date received.
Quantity	**-1**. The minus sign will result in items being added to the inventory quantity and reduce the ACCOUNTS RECEIVABLE subledger for Computers and More.
Price	You may have to retype the price amount if the customer received a special or different price. The original 11568 sales invoice price was **400.00.**
Acct	**4200 Sales Returns and Allowances**. The entry results in a **debit** to Sales Returns and Allowances, and a **credit** to Accounts Receivable (see side note box).
Comment	Add appropriate information (see Fig. 8-14).
Terms	We are receiving payment for the invoice less the return and the terms would have no effect on the payment. Leave the Terms field blank.

Printers Company Ltd. does not use separate accounts for the different types of returns and records them in account 4200 Sales Returns & Allowances.

Some companies may not use a Sales Returns account and would record sales returns as **negative** sales.

3 ➤ **Display** the Sales Journal entry. It should display as follows:

Sales Journal Entry Jan 14, 2014 (J8)

Account Number	Account Description	Debits	Credits
1260	Inventory Laser Printers	290.00	-
2650	HST Charged on Sales	52.00	-
4200	Sales Returns & Allowances	400.00	-
1200	Accounts Receivable	-	452.00
5020	Cost Of Goods Sold- Lasers	-	290.00
Additional Date:	Additional Field:		
		742.00	742.00

The Inventory asset account and Sales Returns account are debited, and the Cost of Goods Sold account is credited using the **average** cost of the inventory.

4 ➤   **Exit** the entry window. **Post** when correct, and **Exit** to the Home window.

Step 2: Record the Cash Receipt from Computers and More

5 ➤   **Record** cheque **#720** for **$5,068.05** from Computers and More on Jan. 14.

Remember to apply the receipt against Invoice 11568 and the Return 11568Rt CM61, resulting in a net receipt of $5,068.05.

6 ➤   **Post** when correct, and **Exit** from the Receipts Journal.

More Transactions

1 ➤   **Record** and **post** the following transactions:

Jan 14, 2014 Issue a $316.40 cheque to pay Cables and Accessories for invoice 2998.

Jan 14, 2014 Received cheque #1012 from More Computers Ltd. in the amount of $4,778.56 for invoice #11592.

Jan 15, 2014 Received cheque #712 in the amount of 10,224.24 from Davis Computers in payment of invoices #11571 and #11593.

2 ➤   Return to the **Home** window.

3 ➤   Advance the Session date to **January 18, 2014**.

Journalizing an Inventory Purchase Return

Returned goods must be removed from the INVENTORY ledger by entering a **negative** purchase.

Exercise 8-14 – Journalizing an Inventory Purchase Return

Study the next transaction:

> **Jan 18, 2014** **You received a memo from your Sales Manager that one Laser Printer 20P in inventory is damaged. It is from the shipment from Laser Products Ltd. on invoice 3661.**
>
> **You contacted Laser Products Ltd., who agreed you could return the printer for credit. They faxed a credit memo to you (#C103) dated today for $327.70 including HST. The printer was returned.**

You will process the return of the printer in this exercise. In the next exercise, you will pay the invoice with a cash discount.

1 ➤ Click the **PAYABLES** module, click the **Purchase Invoices** icon from the Home window.

      Transaction   **Invoice.**

      Payment Method Pay later.

2 ➤ **Purchased From**   Select **Laser Products Ltd.**, ⌜Tab⌟.

3 ➤ **Invoice**   **3661Rt C103,** ⌜Tab⌟.

      Date   **Jan 18, 2014.**

4 ➤ **Item Number**   Select **LP001 Laser Printer 20P.**

5 ➤ **Quantity**   **-1**. A minus will result in items being reduced from INVENTORY and will reduce the Accounts Payable subledger for Laser Products Ltd., ⌜Tab⌟.

      Price   **290.00** is the original purchase price for these printers and is the amount of the credit memo issued by Laser Products Ltd. If the price was different, you would change it here. ⌜Tab⌟.

      Tax   HS, the original code used when the printer was purchased.

      Account   The cursor does not stop at Account as the account shown is the linked account for inventory. Using the **Perpetual Inventory method** for purchases, costs of goods bought and sold are charged to Asset Inventory accounts. Goods returned are charged to the INVENTORY account and not to a Purchase Returns account. In this exercise the cost of the returned printer is charged to the asset 1260 INVENTORY LASER PRINTERS account.

6 ➤ **Terms**   Refer to original invoice. Date of invoice Jan 09, 2014 with terms of 2/10, net 30. The return is subject to the same terms as the original invoice. The terms should be:

                        2% 2 days, Net 22 days.

7 ➤ **Display** the Purchases Journal Entry. The entry should be as follows:

Purchases Journal Entry Jan 18, 2014 (J13)			
Account Number	Account Description	Debits	Credits
2200	Accounts Payable	327.70	-
1260	Inventory Laser Printers	-	290.00
2670	HST Paid on Purchases	-	37.70
Additional Date:	Additional Field:		
		327.70	327.70

8 ➤ **Post** when correct, and return to the **Home** window.

Recording a Payment with Cash Discount

When goods are purchased using the perpetual INVENTORY module, the INVENTORY asset account increases.

In the transaction that follows, you will pay the invoice related to the purchase return you posted in the last exercise, and take a cash discount. To allocate the cash discount to INVENTORY you have to break down the discount based on the purchase price of each item. However, on invoices with many items, this technique is not practical.

The discount is not charged to the INVENTORY asset account, but is charged to the PURCHASES DISCOUNT account in the COST OF GOODS SOLD section.

Exercise 8-15 – Recording an Inventory Payment with Cash Discount

Study the following transaction:

Jan 18, 2014   **Paid Laser Products Ltd. for invoices #3625, 3661 and 3661Rt C103, with the next cheque, in the amount of $16,898.93 taking advantage of a 2% cash discount on Invoice 3661 less the return on invoice 3661Rt C103.**

Record the transaction as follows:

1 ➤ From the Home window, click **Payments**.

2 ➤ **Pay To**   Select **Laser Products Ltd.,** [Tab].

   Date   **Jan 18, 2014**.

3 ➤ **Invoice/Pre-pmt**   Click 3625. [Tab] [Tab] [Tab] to accept Payment Amount of **$5,732.33** for invoice #3625.

4 ➤ **Disc. Taken**   The cursor should be in the **Disc. Taken** column for Invoice 3661. [Tab] [Tab] to accept **$207.00** Discount Taken and Payment Amount **$11,488.50**.

5 ➤ **Disc. Taken**   The cursor should be in the Disc. Taken column for invoice 3661Rt C103. [Tab] **two** times to accept **-5.80** Discount Taken and Payment Amount **$-321.90**.

   The Total payment will be **$16,898.93**.

	Merchandise	HST	Total
3661	$ 10,350.00	$ 1,345.50	$11,695.50
3661Rt C103	$ -290.00	$ - 37.70	$ -327.70
Net Purchase	$ 10,060.00	$ 1,307.80	$11,367.80

2% discount based on **$10,060.00** (net purchase) equals **$201.20**.

Discount Taken shown in window	$ 207.00
less	$ -5.80
equals	$ 201.20

Due Date	Invoice or Prepayment	Original Amount	Amount Owing	Discount Available	Discount Taken	Payment Amount
Jan 22, 2014	3625	5,732.33	5,732.33	0.00		5,732.33
Feb 08, 2014	3661	11,695.50	11,695.50	207.00	207.00	11,488.50
	3661Rt C103	-327.70	-327.70	-5.80	-5.80	-321.90
					Total	16,898.93

Fig. 8-15: Payment with discount.

Payments Journal Entry Jan 18, 2014 (J14)

Account Number	Account Description	Debits	Credits
2200	Accounts Payable	17,100.13	-
1020	Bank Account	-	16,898.93
5040	Purchase Discounts	-	201.20
Additional Date:	Additional Field:		
		17,100.13	17,100.13

6 ➤ **Post** when correct and return to the Home window.

7 ➤ Advance the Session date to **January 22, 2014**.

New Services Provided

A number of customers and individuals who live in the area have asked your firm to repair printers that are out of warranty. The manager agreed to provide this service, with a 30 day warranty for repairs, and by memo, asked you to create new General Ledger accounts and Service items.

In this exercise you will create new General Ledger accounts for repair revenue and Inventory & Service items for repairs of InkJet and Laser Printers.

Exercise 8-16 – To Create Ledger Accounts & Service Items

To create new Ledger Accounts

1 ➤ From the Home page, click the **COMPANY** module.

2 ➤ Click the **Chart of Accounts** icon. Click **Create** icon.

3 ➤ **Account**   Type **4310**, [Tab] type **Repairs InkJet Printers**, [Tab].

4 ➤ **Type**   Select **Group** Account, if it is not already selected.

5 ➤ **Allow Division Allocations**   Remove the ✓.

Class Options Tab

6 ➤ Click the **Class Options** Tab and select **Revenue** [Tab].

7 ➤ Click **Create Another**.

8 ➤ Repeat steps 3 to 6 to create account **4320 Repairs Laser Printers**, with the same settings. Click **Save & Close**.

9 ➤ **Exit** to the Home window.

To Create New Service Items

1 ➤ From the Home window, click the **INVENTORY & SERVICES** module. Click the **Inventory & Services** icon.

2 ➤ Click the **Create** icon.

3 ➤ **Description**   Type **Repair InkJet Out of Warranty**.

4 ➤ **Number**   OWI-01 (**O**ut of **W**arranty **I**nkJets).

5 ➤ **Type**   Click the **Service** option button.

Unit Tab

6 ➤ **Unit of Measure**   Change to **Unit**.

Pricing Tab

7 ➤ Click the **Pricing** tab, and record as follows. (The unit price will be for each 20 minutes of service.)

Price List	Price per Selling Unit
Regular	20.0000
Preferred	19.0000
Web Price	0.0000

Linked Tab

With Service Items there are 2 linked accounts, whereas, with Inventory Items there are 4 linked accounts.

8 ➤ Click the **Linked** tab. (See side note box.)

9 ➤ **Revenue**   Select **4310 Repairs InkJet Printers**.

    Expense   DO NOT CHANGE. There is no associated expense account with this service. Leave this field blank. The manager assumes that if parts are required, they would be ordered specifically for each service call.

10 ➤ Click **Create Another**.

11 ➤ Repeat steps 3 to 8 to create service item **Repair Laser Out of Warranty**, with code **OWL-01**, same pricing and link account **4320**. Click **Save & Close** .

12 ➤ **Exit** to the Home window.

Exercise 8-17 – To Journalize an Invoice for Warranty Repairs

---

The Manager has decided that each warranty repair will be set up with the name of the customer with a name code that begins with W- and the customer name. (W- to represent the warranty work.) The customer file will contain the customer's address with a memo note stating the warranty dates.

> **Jan 22, 2014** **Mrs. Judy Marsh, on the recommendation of Computers and More, brought in her older model Laser Printer (out of warranty), that was not printing properly even with a new cartridge. One of your technicians worked on the printer for approximately 40 minutes and it is now in working order. Bill Mrs. Marsh for 2 units of service, plus HST. Invoice total $45.20. Mrs. Marsh paid with her cheque #653.**

1 ➤ From the Home window, click the **RECEIVABLES** module. Click the **Sales Invoice** icon.

2 ➤ **Payment Method** Change to **Cheque,** Tab twice.

3 ➤ **Cheque** Type **653**. Tab .

4 ➤ **Customer** Create a customer account (Full Add) for Mrs. Marsh, with a name code of **W-Marsh Judy**, address, **635 Sonoma Blvd, Vaughan, Ontario, L4H 6P8**, Phone **905 897-8632**, Options tab, Link **4320**, remove the terms, Taxes tab, select **HS**, Statistics tab- Credit limit field type **0.00**, Memo tab type **Laser Warranty repair Jan 22 to expire Feb 21 (30 days)**, Save and Close .

5 ➤ **Item Number** Double-click and select **Repair Laser Out of Warranty (OWL-01)**.

6 ➤ **Quantity** Type **2** (2 units of 20 minutes). Tab .

Tax This service is a retail sale and requires HST to be charged.

7 ➤ **Message** Change to: **Warranty for 30 days**.

The journal entry should be as follows:

```
Sales Journal Entry Jan 22, 2014 (J15)

 Account Number   Account Description        Debits    Credits
 1020             Bank Account               45.20        -
 2650               HST Charged on Sales        -        5.20
 4320               Repairs Laser Printers      -       40.00
 Additional Date:  Additional Field:
                                            _____   _____
                                             45.20     45.20
```

8 ➤ **Post** when correct, and **Exit** to the Home window.

Changing Selling Prices

You may increase or decrease the selling price of goods when the purchase price changes. Some companies change the selling price only when the lower-cost goods are sold.

In the next exercise, you will **reduce** the selling price of an INVENTORY item. The same procedure would be used to **increase** a selling price.

Exercise 8-18 – To Change the Selling Price

1 ➤ Advance the Session date to **Jan 28, 2014**.

Jan 27, 2014 **The Manager noted that other wholesalers in your area have reduced the price of the 5 in 1 Inkjet Printers by $15.00. He advised you, by memo, to reduce the selling price of IP-001 to $230.00 for regular customers and to $220.00 for preferred customers on all future sales.**

---

2 ➤ Click the **INVENTORY & SERVICES** module. Click the **Inventory & Services** icon.

3 ➤ Double-click **InkJet Printer 5 in 1 IP-001**.

4 ➤ Click the **Pricing** tab, and **change the prices** as noted previously.

5 ➤ Click Save and Close and return to the Home window.

More Transactions

1 ➤ **Record** and **Post** the following transactions:

Jan 27, 2014 Do-It-Yourself Inc. requested a Sales price quote (#1) on the following goods (retail sale), plus HST. Requested shipping date is Jan 28, 2014 and terms are 2% 10 days, net 30 days.

2 InkJet Printer 5 in 1 at	$ 230.00 each
2 InkJet Black Cartridges at	38.50 each
2 InkJet Colour Cartridges at	44.00 each
2 Printer Cable USB at	15.00 each
Total quote including taxes	$740.15

> Jan 28, 2014 The manager of Do-it-Yourself Inc. called and agreed to the price quote of Jan 27, 2014. Record the sale from Sales Quote #1.

The journal entry should look like this:

Sales Journal Entry Jan 28, 2014 (J16)			
Account Number	Account Description	Debits	Credits
1200	Accounts Receivable	740.15	-
5010	Cost Of Goods Sold- InkJets	393.33	-
5030	Cost Of Goods Sold- Cables	14.00	-
1250	Inventory InkJet Printers	-	300.00
1270	Inventory Ink Cartridges InkJet	-	93.33
1290	Inventory Printer Cables	-	14.00
2650	HST Charged on Sales	-	85.15
4100	Sales InkJets	-	625.00
4120	Sales Cables	-	30.00
Additional Date:	Additional Field:		
		1,147.48	1,147.48

2 ➤ **Post** when correct, and return to the Home window.

3 ➤ Advance the Session date to **Jan 29, 2014**.

Correcting Wrong Price after Posting

To make a correction for an invoice containing an incorrect price or quantity, there are three ways to make the correction:

a) Use the Adjust Invoice icon (refer to Exercise 2B-23b or Chapter 13, Correcting Transaction Errors After Posting), and issue a corrected invoice by correcting the price of the printer. All items on the original invoice would be shown.

b) Correct the item(s) (assuming one or two items) in a new invoice. This method makes it easier for the customer to see that the price change has taken place. The customer would receive two invoices (original and correction).

c) Reverse (Cancel) the original invoice Exercise 2A-18, then issue a correct invoice. If the invoice contains many items, this method takes too long and is a waste of an employee's time. The customer would receive two invoices (original and correction).

Method **b** will be shown as follows:

Exercise 8-19 – To Correct Invoice Price After Posting

> Jan 29, 2014 Do-It-Yourself Inc. advised you, by fax, that the items shipped on the 28th were received in good condition, but the 2 InkJet printers were priced at $230.00 each, which was $5.00 higher than what your manager quoted. You checked with Mrs. Davis and she confirmed her verbal agreement with Do-it-Yourself Inc. Mrs. Davis forgot to inform you of the change to $225.00 and, therefore, requested that you change the selling price for this invoice.

You will be preparing a net negative invoice:

1 ➤ Click the **Sales Invoices** icon from the Home window.

     Transaction   **Invoice.**

     Payment Method **Pay later.**

2 ➤ **Customer**   Select **Do-It Yourself Inc.,** Tab .

3 ➤ **Invoice**   **11596Co** (Co for correction), Tab .

     Date   **Jan 29, 2014.**

To Remove the Incorrect Item

4 ➤ **Item Number**   **InkJet Printer 5 in 1**.

5 ➤ **Quantity**   **-2,** Tab . The minus sign will result in items being added back to the inventory quantity, and the customer's account will be reduced by the amount of the negative sale.

Item Number	Quantity	Order	Back Order	Unit	Item Description	Base Price	Discount (%)	Price	Amount	Tax	Account
IP-001	-2			Each	InkJet Printer 5 in 1	230.00		230.00	-460.00	HS	4100 Sales InkJets

6 ➤ Tab across the invoice fields.

     Base Price   Accept $230.00 (the original price).

     Amount   -460.00 (this is a negative amount since it is a reduction in the amount owed by the customer).

     Tax   Accept HS.

     Account   To accept 4100 Sales. (This is a price adjustment not a sales return.)

To Insert the Item with the Correct Sales Amount

7 ➤ **Item Number**   **InkJet Printer 5 in 1,** Tab .

8 ➤ **Quantity**   **2,** Tab to Base Price.

IP-001	2			Each	InkJet Printer 5 in 1	225.00		225.00	450.00	HS	4100 Sales InkJets

9 ➤ **Base Price**   **225.00**. This is the correct selling price as agreed upon.

     Amount   Accept **450.00**.

10 ➤ **Terms**   **2.00**%, **9** Days, Net **29** days.

11 ➤ **Message**   Type **To correct invoice #11596 re error in price.** Tab . The net invoice total should be $-11.30.

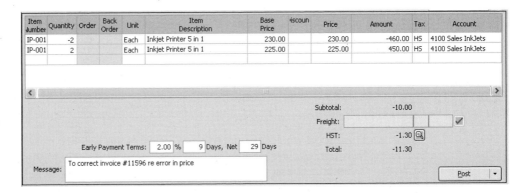

Item Number	Quantity	Order	Back Order	Unit	Item Description	Base Price	Discoun	Price	Amount	Tax	Account
IP-001	-2			Each	Inkjet Printer 5 in 1	230.00		230.00	-460.00	HS	4100 Sales InkJets
IP-001	2			Each	Inkjet Printer 5 in 1	225.00		225.00	450.00	HS	4100 Sales InkJets

Subtotal: -10.00
Freight: ☑
HST: -1.30
Total: -11.30

Early Payment Terms: 2.00 % 9 Days, Net 29 Days

Message: To correct invoice #11596 re error in price

Post

The journal entry should be as follows:

Sales Journal Entry Jan 29, 2014 (J17)

Account Number	Account Description	Debits	Credits
2650	HST Charged on Sales	1.30	-
4100	Sales InkJets	10.00	-
1200	Accounts Receivable	-	11.30
Additional Date:	Additional Field:		
		11.30	11.30

12 ➤ **Post** when correct, and **Exit** to the Home window.

13 ➤ Advance the Session date to **Jan 30, 2014**.

Making Inventory Adjustments

Simply allows the user to use the Adjustments journal for two types of adjustments:

a. Adjustment to cost only.
b. Adjustment to quantity only.

For an adjustment to cost only (e.g., if you wish to increase or decrease the cost of an item without adjusting the quantity on hand), then leave the **Qty.** field blank and enter the adjustment amount into the **Amount** field.

For an adjustment to quantity only (e.g., if you wish to increase or decrease quantity without adjusting the total cost of the item) enter the quantity change into the **Qty.** field but leave the **Amount** field blank.

Exercise 8-20 – Recording the INVENTORY Adjustments

Study the following scenario:

> **Jan 30, 2014** **The accountant suggested that an inventory count be completed by staff to verify goods available for sale.**

1 ➤ **Print** the Inventory Quantity report (refer to Exercise 8-5).

The inventory report should be as follows:

Inventory Quantity

Description	Item No.	Unit	Quantity	Minimum	On Pu...	On Sal...	To Order
InkJet Black Cartridge	IBC-01	Each	71	26	10	0	-
InkJet Colour Cartridge	ICC-01	Each	46	10	0	0	-
InkJet Printer 5 in 1	IP-001	Each	34	30	0	0	-
Laser Black Cartridge	LBC-01	Each	34	10	0	0	-
Laser Printer 20P	LP001	Each	41	12	0	0	-
Printer Cable USB	C-01	Each	22	20	0	0	-

This report would be printed and a copy of the first two columns, **Description** and **Number**, showing items the firm sells, would be given to the clerks counting the inventory. The actual counted report would be compared to the computer report above, and any variances or discrepancies adjusted.

It is not normal to give the counting staff the complete report, including the **Quantity** column, because it may cause them to count inaccurately.

The following counted inventory report was returned from the supervisor: The shortage of both types of InkJet cartridges was noted and a recount was completed. The missing inkjet cartridges were not located and an extra printer cable was found.

INVENTORY REPORT

Printers Company , Your Name

Date ___Jan 30, 2014___

Signed: ___*JCD*___

Description	Number	Unit
InkJet Black Cartridge	IBC-01	69 each
InkJet Colour Cartridge	ICC-01	45 each
InkJet Printer 5 in 1	IP-001	33 each
Laser Black Cartridge	LBC-01	34 each
Laser Printer 20P	LP001	41 each
Printer Cable-USB	C-01	23 each

Note: One 5 in 1 printer damaged and removed from inventory. The Repair Department reports that it is damaged beyond repair. Not saleable.

The IP-001 printer actually fell from the display shelf when the bracket holding the shelf broke. See note on count at the bottom of the inventory report.

As a result of the above report, the manager has ordered new, stronger display shelf brackets and a lockable display cabinet to hold the InkJet cartridges for safekeeping.

The missing ink cartridges and the broken printer must be written off to various accounts. Some companies may write off damaged goods that cannot be sold to a DAMAGED GOODS account in the expense section of the Income Statement. Other companies may record the above changes to the **Adjustments** account in the Cost of Goods Sold section of the Income Statement.

The management of Printers Company has decided to record this type of change to the **Adjustment** account. If the dollar value became a larger amount, then management may decide to use two or three accounts to record INVENTORY changes.

2 ➤ From the Home window, click the **INVENTORY & SERVICES** module, click the **Adjust Inventory** Journal icon.

This journal is used to record only adjustments to inventory quantity and value due to loss, damage, etc.

Many of the drop-down menus and icons have been discussed previously. The Adjustment menu item will allow the entry to be Stored, Recalled, Allocated and/or Posted.

3 ➤ **Record** the Adjustment as shown below.

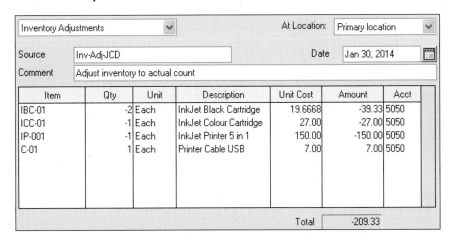

| Inventory Adjustments | | | | At Location: | Primary location | |

Source	Inv-Adj-JCD				Date	Jan 30, 2014
Comment	Adjust inventory to actual count					

Item	Qty	Unit	Description	Unit Cost	Amount	Acct
IBC-01	-2	Each	InkJet Black Cartridge	19.6668	-39.33	5050
ICC-01	-1	Each	InkJet Colour Cartridge	27.00	-27.00	5050
IP-001	-1	Each	InkJet Printer 5 in 1	150.00	-150.00	5050
C-01	1	Each	Printer Cable USB	7.00	7.00	5050
					Total	-209.33

Fig. 8-16: Inventory Adjustments Journal window.

Source	**Inv-Adj-JCD** (For Inventory Adjustment, memo with approval received from manager (initials JCD).
Qty	**-2**, Negative amounts indicate that items are to be removed from inventory because they are missing (probably theft). Positive amounts indicate that items are to be added to inventory when more items are counted as being in stock compared to the Simply Quantity listing.
Unit Cost	The average unit cost of this item is **19.6668**. This field cannot be changed at this point.
Amount	Quantity times unit cost.
Acct	The G/L account for INVENTORY ADJUSTMENTS was set up as the **Integration** account.

4 ➤ Display the Adjustments Journal entry (select **Report** and then **Display Inventory Adjustments Journal Entry**). The entry should be as follows:

Inventory Adjustments Journal Entry Jan 30, 2014 (J18)

Account Number	Account Description	Debits	Credits
1290	Inventory Printer Cables	7.00	-
5050	Inventory Adjustments	209.33	-
1250	Inventory Inkjet Printers	-	150.00
1270	Inventory Ink Cartridges Inkjets	-	66.33
Additional Date:	Additional Field:		
		216.33	216.33

5 ➤ The inventory quantity and inventory value will be reduced and/or increased by this adjustment. **Exit** from the entry window.

6 ➤ Post when correct and **Exit** to the Home window.

(See side note box.)

To correct or cancel an
Inventory adjustment,
refer to Chapter 13.

Correcting Inventory Errors

Errors that originate from entries posted in the Sales or Purchases journal should be corrected using **the same** journal. As with other modules, the best way is to reverse the original entry for both **quantity** and **cost** and then enter a new entry.

The Adjustments journal is used to correct inventory errors (damaged goods, theft or obsolescence) as shown in Exercise 8-20. Errors in the average cost and/or quantity may also be made using the Adjustments journal.

Build from Bill of Materials and/or Build from Item Assembly Journal

Sometimes a company may decide to group inventory items as a package for special promotions or transfer inventory (and costs) from one item to another item; for example, when individual parts are used to make (assemble) a smoke detector.

A new inventory number must be set up that will combine all the inventory items into the new item.

The **Build from Bill of Materials Journal** is used when you are building packages of items that you normally build or assemble (on a regular basis) and then sell.

The **Build from Item Assembly Journal** can be used to build the same packages or special order packages that do not occur on a regular basis.

Exercise 8-21 – Using the Build from Bill of Materials Journal

1 ➤ Advance the Session date to **Jan 31, 2014**.

Jan 31, 2014	**A number of customers have requested buying a package consisting of a printer, ink cartridges and printer cable for a special price. The manager has decided that the firm will sell an InkJet package deal on a regular basis. The manager has moved 5 InkJet printers, 5 black cartridges, 5 colour cartridges and 5 printer cables to the front of the store for this special deal.**

Printers Company will use the Build from Bill of Materials Journal feature to have the software create and record the special package deal.

2 ➤ Create a new General Ledger account #**1292 Inventory InkJet Package Deal**. Select **Subgroup Account**, Class Options **Inventory**.

3 ➤ Create a new inventory item with the following information:

Item Description	**InkJet Package Deal**
Item number	**IJP-01**
Type	Select **Inventory**

Quantities tab

Minimum Level **2** (if we sell 3 units, we will need to make more packages).

Pricing tab

Pricing **Regular price $294.00** (Normal selling price of all components is $327.50.) The Package Sales price will be a 10% reduction ($32.75 plus 75 cents).

The Preferred Pricing will be $284.00 and the Web Store Pricing will be 0.00.

Linked tab

Linked Accounts **1292, 4100** and **5010**.

Build tab

Enter the following information:

Quantities	Units	Pricing	Linked	Build	Statistics	Taxes	Additional Info	Detailed Desc.

Build ☐ 1 of this item from the following components (all quantities are in stocking units):

Item	Unit	Description	Quantity
IP-001	Each	InkJet Printer 5 in 1	1
IBC-01	Each	InkJet Black Cartridge	1
ICC-01	Each	InkJet Colour Cartridge	1
C-01	Each	Printer Cable USB	1

Additional Costs: 0.00 Record additional costs in: ☐ ▼

You will be using one of each component to build one promotion package (see step 5).

Additional Costs This field would be used for any additional costs such as labour or freight expenses. Printers Company does not have additional costs associated with building these packages.

Record additional costs in To use this field, you would need to create an Income Statement account such as Wages Expense Transfer, which must be specified when defining the Linked accounts for the INVENTORY module. There is no exercise for this feature.

4 ➤ Click **Save and Close** and **Exit** to Home window.

5 ➤ Click the **Build from Bill of Materials** icon. Input the information shown in Fig. 8-17.

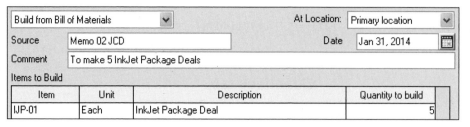

Build from Bill of Materials		At Location: Primary location	
Source	Memo 02 JCD	Date	Jan 31, 2014
Comment	To make 5 InkJet Package Deals		

Items to Build

Item	Unit	Description	Quantity to build
IJP-01	Each	InkJet Package Deal	5

Fig. 8-17: Build from Bill of Materials Journal.

6 ➤ View the entry. The cost of the components has been moved from the individual inventory accounts to the new #1292 account.

Bill of Materials & Item Assembly Journal Entry Jan 31, 2014 (J19)

Account Number	Account Description	Debits	Credits
1292	Inventory InkJet Package Deal	1,018.33	-
1250	Inventory InkJet Printers	-	750.00
1270	Inventory Ink Cartridges InkJets	-	233.33
1290	Inventory Printer Cables	-	35.00
Additional Date:	Additional Field:		
		1,018.33	1,018.33

	Individual Cost	5 units Total cost
5 in 1 Printer	$150.00	750.00
Black cartridge	19.6669	98.33 (rounded)
Colour cartridge	27.00	135.00
USB cable	7.00	35.00
Total for one unit	203.67 (rounded)	1,018.33

7 ➤ **Exit** the Journal entry, **Post**. Simply will create the 5 package deals.

The following warning message appears:

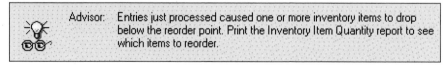

Advisor: Entries just processed caused one or more inventory items to drop below the reorder point. Print the Inventory Item Quantity report to see which items to reorder.

This message informs the user that even though the inventory has not been sold, that some of the individual items are below the reorder point. If the package deals sell, new inventory will need to be ordered. Click anywhere in the gray box to close the warning message.

The Build from Bill of Materials and Build from Item Assembly Journal entry can be reversed (negative amount) to cancel the promotion and return the unsold items to normal inventory status.

8 ➤ **Close** the Advisor and **Exit** to the Home window.

9 ➤ On the Home page, Inventory section, you will see

▼ InkJet Package Deal IJP-01	5	$1,018.33

(See side note boxes.)

ℹ️ If you make a package deal such as this, it may cause one or more of the individual parts quantities to fall below the reorder point. The manager and staff will have to review the Inventory Quantity report to monitor the inventory.

ℹ️ To correct or cancel an Inventory Assembly Journal entry, refer to Chapter 13.

Information only

If you were to use the Build from Item Assembly Journal to make the packages, the window would look similar to the following. If the top window does not show all the items, click the bottom right of the window, and drag (move) to the right until all items show. The completed Assembly Journal is shown in Fig. 8-18.

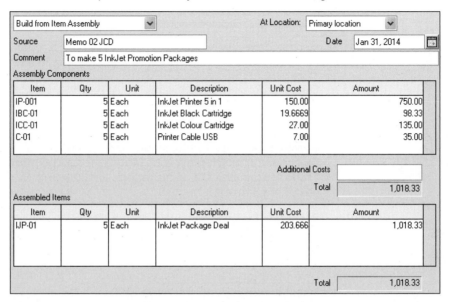

Fig. 8-18: Build from Item Assembly Journal.

Assembly Components

This section contains the components that will make up the new product or item.

Unit Cost   (This is the average cost of each item being moved.)

Amount   (This is the total cost of individual items being moved.)

Additional Costs

Discussed in Exercise 8-21.

Assembled Items

This section contains the item(s) that have been made up to sell as one unit.

Unit Cost	This is the average cost of the items being made (total cost of all parts used/divided by the number of items, $1,018.33/5 = **$203.666**). (See side note box.)
Amount	$1,018.33 (this is the total cost of the items being made). **Note**: You may have to adjust the Unit Cost to make the amount agree with the Assembly Components Amount due to rounding of fractions of a cent.

> If you TAB past the Unit Cost field and enter the total cost (1,018.33) in the Amount field, Simply will calculate the Unit cost for you.

The Build from Item Assembly Journal can be reversed to cancel the promotion and return the unsold items to normal inventory status.

End of Information section

Inventory Reports

There are a number of inventory reports available. Study each one so you will know what to print when the need arises.

Exercise 8-22 – To View INVENTORY Reports

In this exercise, from the Home window you will print 3 reports (steps 1 and 2). In steps 3 through 5 you will view others, without printing to save paper.

1a ➤ Quantity Report Print this report. At Reports, click ▼ , select **Inventory Quantity**, click **Display**. This report (similar to Fig. 8-8) lists details of items outstanding on Purchase or Sales Orders.

1b ➤ Summary Report Print this report. At Reports, click ▼ , select **Inventory Summary**, click **Display**, click **Modify**, **Report Options**, select **Latest Transaction,** click **OK**. This report (similar to Fig. 8-9a) lists details of cost, total cost margin %, etc.

2 ➤ Statistics Report Print this report. At Reports, click ▼ , select **Inventory and Services Statistics,** click **Display**. This report will help management see which items have not sold during the period, or have not been sold recently.

3 ➤ Inventory and Services List Display - DO NOT PRINT. At Reports, click ▼ , select **Inventory and Services List,** click **Display**. This will display a list of all inventory items on hand, with the Average Cost value. Ignore the Category column. Study the report, then exit.

4 ➤ Sales Report Display - DO NOT PRINT. At Reports, click ▼ , select **Inventory and Services Sales Summary (or Detail),** click **Display**. This will display a Y-T-D report (summary or detail) of dollar revenue, and cost of goods sold including dollar profits and margin %.

5 ➤ Transaction Report Display - DO NOT PRINT. At Reports, click ▼ , select **Inventory and Services Transaction Summary (or Detail),** click **Display**. Click **Modify**, **Report Options**. You can print the report with or without Bill of Materials and/or Adjustments & Transfers. This will display a Y-T-D report of Quantity In (Purchase) and Quantity Out (Sales) with dollar amounts for each listing.

Other Reports

6 ➤ Print the following reports:

    a) Customer Aged Detail report as at Jan 31, 2014.
    b) Vendor Aged Detail report as at Jan 31, 2014.
    c) Journal Entries-All for the month of January 2014.
    d) Income Statement for the month of January 2014.
    e) Balance Sheet as of Jan 31, 2014.
    f) Cheque Log.

7 ➤ Compare your printouts to the Printers Company solutions with your instructor.

Before Moving On...

Read the following questions and make sure you know the answers to them; otherwise, read the corresponding part in the chapter before moving on.

1. Explain the difference between the **Margin** and **Markup** methods of calculating gross profit.

2. Which journal is used to process:

   Sales returns of inventory items?

   Purchase of inventory items?

3. State at least one benefit of using the **Minimum** field in the INVENTORY ledger window.

4. When are adjustments made on inventory items? What types of adjustments can be made?

5. What inventory valuation methods are used by Simply Accounting?

6. What is the difference between the Bill of Materials Journal and the Item Assembly Journal?

7. How do you make corrections for posting errors related to inventory purchases and sales?

8. What is preferred pricing?

Review **Slideshows 8A** and **8B** before doing the challenge exercise(s) assigned to you.

Relevant Appendix

The following appendix is available at www.simplyaccounting2010.nelson.com, under Student Resources.

Appendix 2010 -Q   **Names Fields**

Challenge Exercise 08 C8-1, Stain Company (Your Name)

COMPANY, RECEIVABLES, PAYABLES, INVENTORY & SERVICES

1 ➤   Refer to Exercise 1-1 to unzip the **08 C8-1 Stain.exe** file.

2 ➤   Open the **08 C8-1 Stain** file and enter transactions for January.

You are the new accounting clerk for the **Stain Company Your Name** (Your name is the student's name).

Company Accounting Policies:

- Terms of 2/10, net 30 are applied to credit sales and purchases unless other information is provided.
- All cash discounts are calculated on price before tax.
- Sales invoices and cheques are assumed to be in numerical order.
- HST at 13% is used for Sales and Purchases.
- HST at 13% is used for Retail Sales and Purchases of goods for own use.
- Tax codes HS and HI can be used in this challenge case.
- This company does not use Purchase Orders.
- Ignore Shipped by field.
- Address information is not important.

Note: Accounts Receivable Subsidiary customer balances are nil.
Accounts Payable   Subsidiary vendor   balances are nil.

3 ➤ Record and **Post** the transactions in the appropriate module.

Jan 2   Based on special requests from customers, we received a new stain, as indicated below, on invoice 9873 from new vendor Kevin Paint Supply (address not important) terms 2/10, net 30. Tax code HS, Expense Account - you decide.

Item Description	Stain – Indoor-Better
Item Number	ST-I-BQ
Received	20 items at $11.10 each plus HST.
Selling price	$21.00 each
Minimum is	5 items, as this is the first time we will carry this type of stain.

Jan 3   New Retail customer, Mrs. Pottery, purchased 4 Stain - ST-I-GD at 10.60 each, plus HST paid by Universal Credit Card.

Jan 3   Sold the following goods to Paint Plus with HST. The sale is with normal terms of 2/10, net 30:

Quantity	Item	Unit	Description	Selling Price Plus HST
20	ST-O-BE	each	Stain - Outdoor-Better	$ 12.50
30	ST-O-E	each	Stain - Outdoor-Excellent	$ reduced to $12.90

Note: Ignore "inventory low" message if seen.

Jan 4   Purchased from Canada Paint Ltd. 50 Stain - Indoor-GD at $5.30 each, plus HST. Invoice #5512 with terms 2/10, net 30.

Jan 4   Purchased store supplies from Office Supplies Company on Invoice #825, terms 2/10, net 30, with the following information:

   10 rolls of special wrapping material at $15.00 each, plus HST.

Jan 5   Retail sale to Bayview Terrace of the following items. Terms 2/10, net 30.

Quantity	Item	Unit	Description	Selling Price
20	ST-I-E	each	Stain - Indoor E	$11.00 plus HST
5	BR-Ex	each	Brushes-Excellent	$ 7.00 plus HST

Jan 7   Received from Painters Supplies, per their invoice 4912, twenty (20) each of Stain - Indoor GD at $5.30 each, plus HST, terms 2/10, net 30.

Jan 9   The manager noticed that three (3) of the Stain - Indoor GD purchased on invoice #4912 have a small leak in the container and must be returned for replacement. All the other containers are OK. Returned the three containers, for full credit, to Painters Supplies.

Jan 10 During the night, a display cabinet shelf broke and 5 Stain - Outdoor Better paint cans were damaged and spilled over the floor. The manager issued a memo to write off these items.

Jan 11 Paid insurance agent, Marshall Insurance, $240.00 plus HST, for a one-year fire damage policy #5689B effective January 1. Charge the January cost of insurance to expense.

Jan 11 The owner, A-Your Name (First and Surname) withdrew $1,205.00 for a monthly draw. *Note*: Use A- before your name.

Jan 12 Received cheque #362 from Paint Plus for amount owing.

Jan 14 Prepayment of $250.00 issued to Canada Paint Ltd.for a future order of paint. A Purchase Order was not issued.

Jan 14 Paid Office Supplies Company for Invoice #825.

Jan 16 Paid Receiver General for HST owing at Jan 1.

Jan 18 A purchase order received from retail customer, Bayview Terrace, for 10 Stain-Indoor E at $11.00 each plus HST, to be delivered on January 21. Issued Sales Order #125, terms 2/10, n30.

4 ➤   Print the following reports:

   a)   Income statement from the beginning of the year to session date.
   b)   Accounts Receivable Customer Aged Detail for all customers.
   c)   Accounts Payable Vendor Aged Detail for all vendors.
   d)   Journal Entries All entries.
   e)   Inventory Synopsis for all items of inventory.
   f)   Pending Sales Order report dated January 21.

Challenge Exercise 08 C8-2, Charlie's Hair Styling

COMPANY, ACCOUNTS RECEIVABLE, ACCOUNTS PAYABLE, INVENTORY & SERVICES

Charlie's Hair Styling cuts ladies' and men's hair and sells hair products. *Note*: All haircuts and products are subject to 13% HST. Ignore the Shipped by field.

1 ➤ Refer to Exercise 1-1 to unzip the **08 C8-2 Hair.exe** file.

2 ➤ Open the **08 C8-2 Hair** file.

3 ➤ **Record** and **Post** the following transactions for March:

Mar 1   Change the customer name "Your First and Last Name" to your own name before recording transactions.

Mar 1   Issued next cheque to pay $600.00 rent plus HST at 13% to Mega Mall Ltd.

Mar 2   Ms. Rodrigues paid by Universal Credit Card for 1 lady's haircut at $30.00 plus taxes, and 1 bottle of regular shampoo (SG01) at $12.00 plus HST.

Mar 3   Mr. Miguel Santos paid by cheque #569 for a man's haircut at $20.00 and a child's haircut at $10.00 plus HST.

Mar 3   Cash sale of 2 bottles shampoo (SB01) $13.00 each and 2 bottles conditioner (CB01) $14.50 each, plus HST, to Mrs. Kiran Kenth.

Mar 5   Your First and Last Name ordered a new style hair dryer on sales order #16 at $40.00 plus HST, terms leave blank. Item will be delivered March 13. Create the new item with the following information.

         Description   New Style Hair Dryer #23
         Number   HD-23
         Selling Price $40.00
         Link   Sales Other
         Minimum Quantity   0

Mar 5   Issued Purchase Order #19 to Hair Products International for 3 new style hair dryer #23 at $28.00 each, plus HST. Delivery date, Mar 7. This is a new item described on March 5. Terms 2/10, net 30.

Mar 6   Mrs. Chen purchased 2 bottles of mousse (MB01) at $18.00 each, plus HST. Cheque #126 received in full payment.

Mar 7   Issued cheque to new vendor Flooring Specialty (address not important) for 2 gallons (6 months supply) of Heavy Duty Floor Cleaner at $125.00 per gallon, plus HST. Invoice #9682. Charge to Store Supplies.

Mar 7   Two new hair dryers were delivered by Hair Products International on invoice #6589 at price agreed on Purchase Order #19. The remaining dryer is backordered and will be available in 6 days.

Mar 8   The manager called Your First and Last Name to tell them that the hair dryer arrived. Received their cheque #257 to pay for the hair dryer on invoice #236. (Sales Order # 16.)

Mar 10 Mrs. Del Rosario had a haircut $30.00, and purchased 1 each of shampoo (SB01) $13.00, conditioner (CB20) $16.00 and mousse (MB01) $18.00, plus HST. She paid with her Universal Credit Card.

Mar 10 Mrs. Del Rosario returned the mousse because she decided she did not want the product at this time. Process a credit card adjustment to accept the return.

4 ➤ **Print** the following reports:
     a)   Income Statement for January 1 to March 10
     b)   Balance Sheet to March 10
     c)   Journal Entries All to March 10
     d)   Outstanding Purchase Orders

Challenge Exercise 08 C8-3, Vet Services

COMPANY, ACCOUNTS RECEIVABLE, ACCOUNTS PAYABLE, INVENTORY & SERVICES

This exercise provides practice in recording transactions for a business that combines service revenue and sales of goods (to keep track of the quantity and cost of a company's inventory items). The data file for **Vet Services** has been set up to use the COMPANY, PAYABLES, RECEIVABLES, and INVENTORY & SERVICES modules.

1 ➤ Refer to Exercise 1-1 to unzip the **08 C8-3 Vet.exe** file.

2 ➤ Open the **08 C8-3 Vet** file.

Company Accounting Policies:

- Vet Services provides services for dogs and cats and is owned by Dr. Katherine DiGenova.
- Each client is charged for an office visit (**0-1 Office Visit**).
- Fiscal year is January 1 to December 31.
- The staff use the memo tab record to include the name of the pet, breed name, sex, and other relevant information.
- Full payments from clients for goods and services are required after the veterinarian has seen the pet.
- A 10% discount will be given to seniors for Office visits and lab tests. Seniors will pay regular prices for medication. The only senior client at this time is Mr. Jason Alexander.
- The office does not sell pet food and keeps only a small amount of medication on hand.
- Cheques are issued when necessary for purchases of goods and services. Vendor purchase and/or service invoices are normally with terms of 2/10, n30 days, unless other information is provided.
- HST at 13% is used for all services. Tax code HS is set up as a default because most services and medications are sold with HST.
- The office does not use Purchase Orders.
- Ignore Shipped by field.
- Address information is not important.
- Universal Credit Card is accepted for services and medication. Occasionally she has a client who does not have a credit card and cannot pay cash.
- One client, Mrs. Wakenna Zia, has an outstanding account.

Inventory Summary Jan 01, 2017							
Item No. △	Description	Unit	Price	Quantity	Cost	Value	Margin %
Meds-1	Medicine Antibiotic	Each	20.00	40	10.00	400.00	50.00
Meds-2	Medicine-pain	Each	12.00	100	6.00	600.00	50.00
Meds-3	Flea Treatment plan	Each	47.00	15	20.00	300.00	57.45
Meds-4	Rabies Needle	Each	15.00	0	0.00	0.00	100.00
						1,300.00	

Vet Services Inventory Summary.

3 ➤ Advance the date on a daily basis after **January 3,** and **record** the following transactions. The Daily Business Manager has been set up to advise Katherine of clients who need to be contacted to bring their pets in for various reasons. The receptionist would call the client to arrange a suitable appointment.

Jan 3   Mrs. Helen Tyson brought her 10-year-old cat, Smoky, who was not feeling well, for an examination. The veterinarian examined the cat and prescribed one antibiotic medication which was supplied by the vet. If the cat is not feeling better within 4 days, the cat is to be brought back to see the vet. Mrs. Tyson paid the $62.09 invoice by Universal Credit Card.

Jan 4   Mrs. Eileen Rosen brought in her dog, Kuhlau, for a consultation about fleas. She asked the veterinarian to clip the dog's nails as she was having trouble keeping the dog still while trying to do it herself. Katherine decided that since she has been asked to do this procedure many times, she will now start charging for this service. Katherine provided a regular check-up and prescribed a flea program for the dog. The total invoice amount is $101.64, paid by Universal Credit Card.

           Create a new Service item, Description: Nail Clipping Dog with Item Number: S-5, Unit of Measure should be: Each, Pricing Regular Price 8.00, Preferred Price 7.20, Web Price 0.00, Linked tab, 4330 Veterinary fees – Other, Expense: There is no associated expense account with this service, Taxes tab. Tax HS.

Jan 4   Received from Medical Supplies Inc. 25 Rabies Needles at $7.00 each, plus HST. A purchase order was not issued. Invoice #3280 for $197.75. Terms 2/10, net 30.

Jan 5   A new client, Your Actual First and Last Name, Contact: **Dalmatian Male: Salem, 3 Ann Street, Guelph, Ontario, N1H 2Z4**; Ship-to-Address tab: Same as mailing address; Options tab: Revenue Account **4310, no terms**; Taxes tab: **HS**; Statistics tab: Credit Limit **0.00**; Memo tab: **Dalmatian Male: Salem, born Oct 3, 2009. Jan 05, 2012 special blood tests ordered. Patient to return on Monday, Jan 9, 2012 at 4:00 PM**; To-Do-Date: **Jan 07, 2012**. The vet ordered special blood tests (the clinic charges a $10.00 laboratory test fee plus HST) and the results will be back from the lab on Friday. Your Actual First and Last Name has been scheduled for a return visit as noted on the Memo tab. Prepare an office visit and lab fee invoice. Total fee $50.79 paid by cash.

Jan 7   Issue a cheque to pay Medical Supplies Inc., invoice # 265.

Jan 7   Mrs. Carol Wright brought in her cat, Lucky, for her rabies needle. Bill her for the office visit (annual check-up) and the regular price for 1 rabies needle. Total invoice $56.44 paid by Universal Credit Card. After posting the transaction, change the To-Do date to Jan 07, 2018 in Mrs. Wright's memo file.

Jan 7   The Ontario Lab Testing results for Your Actual First and Last Name pet arrived, Invoice #7763 in amount of $6.78 (lab test $6.00 and HST $.78). Record this invoice, terms n10. (*Note*: Charge 5345 Laboratory fees. Do not use lab item.)

Jan 9   Your Actual First and Last Name brought in Salem and the vet informs her that the lab tests show Salem has an infection that requires antibiotic medication.

           Issue an invoice $62.09, for an office visit and one antibiotic medication paid by personal cheque #442. The vet informs Your Actual First and Last Name that a follow-up visit (at no charge) is required within 2 weeks to see if the medication has cleared the problem. Add a notation to Your Actual First and Last Name memo file: vet needs to see Salem on Jan 23, for a special office visit (check-up) at no charge.

Jan 11   Cheque #634 in the amount of $58.25 received from Mrs. Zia. Mrs. Zia also sent a letter of appreciation for allowing her a few days to make the payment.

Jan 11   Mr. Nathan brought his cat Akia in for an office visit and check-up as Akia is continually scratching. The vet prescribed the flea medication plan. Invoice of $92.60 paid by personal cheque #813. Change the To-Do Date to Jan 11, 2018.

Jan 11   Mr. Alexander brought Samtu in as she was in a fight with a porcupine. The vet removed 5 quills and prescribed one antibiotic and one pain medication. Mr. Alexander receives a 10% seniors discount on office visits, paid with a Universal Credit Card. Invoice total $71.71. Mr. Alexander's follow-up visit scheduled for Jan 18, 2017.

   4 ➤   Print the following reports:

                 - Journal Entries - All for January 1 to January 11
                 - Income Statement - for January 1 to January 11

Challenge Exercise 08 C8-4, Luggage–PI

Recording Chapter 2A transactions using the Perpetual Inventory method

It is assumed that you will attempt this exercise only after you have completed Chapter 2A and Chapter 8.

This exercise is a repeat of the transactions from Chapter 2A, however, you will be using the 08 C8-4 Luggage-PI (Perpetual Inventory) data file.

1 ➤ Unzip and open the **08 C8-4 Luggage-PI** file.

The following Trial Balance accounts are different in the date file 08 C8-4 Luggage-PI, due to the transfer of the data file to the Perpetual Inventory method.

Chapter 2A, Figure 2A-2			*Challenge Exercise 08 C8-4* **Luggage PI**	
Cost of Goods Sold – Periodic			Cost of Goods Sold – Perpetual	
5010　Beginning Inventory	21,000.00		5010　Cost of Goods Sold　24,320.00*	
5040　Purchases	28,000.00			
5050　Purchase Returns		1,000.00		
5080　Purchase Discounts		335.00	5080　Purchase Discounts	335.00
5090　Ending Inventory		23,680.00		

* The Perpetual Inventory Method amount of 24,320.00 combines the Periodic amounts in gray.

2 ➤ Record and **Post** the following transactions using the Perpetual Inventory method. Change the session date as required.

Mar 1　Luggage 4U has requested a quote for the following items that are to be picked up by their van on March 3. Their purchasing manager was very specific that the goods must be received by March 3 or the order will not be accepted. Their delivery van driver will pick up the quote before 2:30 p.m. today. Your manager has asked you to complete the Sales Quote, as the items requested are in stock and have been put aside for this customer:

　　　　5 Laptop Back Paks at $70.00 each
　　　　9 Suitcase w/w regular size at $56.00 each
　　　　8 Suitcase w/w (with wheels) large size at $62.00 each

　　　Add HST at 13% to all purchases. Luggage 4U purchases are with terms 2/10, net 30.

Mar 2　The Purchasing Manager of Luggage 4U confirmed, by fax, to your Sales Manager the approval of Quote #103. Change the sales quote into a sales order.

Mar 3　All goods ordered by Luggage 4U on Sales Order #103 are ready to be shipped. Record the sale.

Mar 3　Havarah Leather Goods returned 2 Laptop Back Paks, as they had ordered too many. The Back Paks were originally purchased on invoice #2253 at 70.00, plus HST. We sent Havarah Leather Goods our credit memo #124 dated today in the amount of $158.20, and referenced it to invoice #2253Rt.

Mar 3　　Received cheque #438 for $1,221.00 from Royes Luggage Inc. in full payment of invoice #2256.

Mar 3　　Received cheque #159, in the amount of $2,000.00, from Sandler Travel Stores as a partial payment on their outstanding invoice #2197 from January 26.

Mar 4　　A clerk from Havarah Leather Goods is being sent to pick up 2 Laptop Back Paks. Record and Post the sale (invoice #2311) in the regular way at $70.00 each, plus HST. Terms 2/10, n30. Invoice total $158.20.

Mar 4　　As the Havarah Leather Goods clerk is preparing to leave the store, he receives a cell-phone message that he is to change the order to 3 extra large Laptop Back Paks. Your store does not carry this particular item and your supplier does not stock this item. The clerk confirms with his boss that the order for 2 Laptop Back Paks is to be cancelled. They will go elsewhere.

Mar 5　　You have made a sale to a new customer. The details are: A-Your Name Luggage Rack; Contact: Your Name; 256 Trillium Way, Oakville, Ontario, L6J 2H8; telephone 905-699-8000, extension 2563; fax number 905-699-8010; Revenue Account 4100, terms 2/10 n30, credit limit $3,000.00

6 Carry on bags – small	@ $21.00 each, plus HST
3 Suitcase w/w large	@ $62.00 each, plus HST
4 Power adapters	@ $10.50 each, plus HST

The goods are to be picked up by their own delivery truck and delivered to Jackie Welland at the 939 Fennel Avenue West, Hamilton, Ontario, store, L9N 3T1.
Note: You will be recording the Hamilton Store information in the Ship-to Address tab.

Mar 6　　Sold to Zehr Luggage with Terms 2/10, net 30, Invoice 2313, $953.72.

　　　　　　　10 Suitcases w/w Large size　@ $62.00 each plus HST
　　　　　　　4 Suitcases w/w Regular size @ $56.00 each plus HST
　　　　　　　　plus HST on all items.

Mar 6　　You made a sale to another new customer, Hanlan's Luggage Store, 2318 Avondale Drive, Oakville, Ontario, L6H 5A1; telephone 905-399-5000, Revenue Account 4100, Terms No %, 0 days, Net amount 0 days, HST.AT 13%. Credit limit $3,000.00, and they paid by business cheque #739. Record this as a sale and then record the receipt separately.

The goods shipped on this first order are:

　　　　　　　6 Carry on bags – small @ $21.00 each, $126.00 plus HST

Mar 7　　Zehr Luggage returned 3 Suitcases w/w Large as the zippers do not work properly. The suitcases will need to be returned to the manufacturer. Record the Sales Return. You do not need to record a return to the manufacturer.

Issued Credit Memo #125, with reference to original sales invoice. Terms amended to 9 days, net 29 days.
　　　　　　　–3 Suitcases w/w Large @ $62.00, plus HST (net return –$210.18)

3 ➤　　**Print** the following:

　　a)　Journal Entries All, with corrections　Mar 1 to Mar 7
　　b)　Income Statement for period　　　　Jan 1 to Mar 7
　　c)　Balance Sheet at　　　　　　　　　Mar 7
　　d)　Customer Aged Detail report at　　　Mar 7

Challenge Exercise 08 C8-5, Toys–PI

This exercise is a review of the PAYABLE and the INVENTORY & SERVICES Modules

It is assumed that you will attempt this exercise only after you have completed Chapter 3A and/or 3B and Chapter 8.

This exercise is a repeat of selected transactions from Chapter 3A and 3B, however, you will be using the Perpetual Inventory method on data file 08 C8-5 Toys–PI (perpetual inventory).

1 ➤   Unzip and open the **08 C8-5 Toys-PI**.

The following Trial Balance accounts are different in the data file 08 C8-4 Toys-PI, due to the transfer of the data file to the Perpetual Inventory method.

Chapter 3, Figure 3A-1			_Challenge Exercise 08 C8-5 Toys - PI_	
Cost of Goods Sold – Periodic			Cost of Goods Sold – Perpetual	
5010 Beginning Inventory	5,421.49		5010 Cost of Goods Sold	16,623.00*
5040 Purchases	18,408.80			
5050 Purchase Returns		300.00		
5080 Purchase Discounts		289.80	5080 Purchase Discounts	289.80
5090 Ending Inventory		6,907.29		

* The Perpetual Inventory Method amount of 16,623.00 combines the Periodic amounts in gray.

2 ➤   Record and **Post** the following selected transactions from Chapter 3A and 3B, using the Perpetual inventory method. Change the session date as required.

Apr 1   Jerry Tyson issued purchase order # 82 to Markham Toy Manufacturing for 35 Trucks small for $14.32 each, plus HST. The trucks will be delivered on Apr 5. Credit terms are 2/10, net 30. The next PO is # 82.

Apr 1   Jerry Tyson reviewed purchase order #82 to Markham Toy Manufacturing and decided to increase the order to 40 Trucks small for $14.32 each, plus HST. The other information did not change.

Apr 5   Mr. Tyson issued PO # 83 to a new vendor A-Your Name Toy Parts, contact Your Name, 956 West Credit Avenue, Mississauga, Ontario, L6X 3K9. Phone number 905-820-3865 extension 2056, Fax 905-820-3865. Ordered 100 Truck wheels (to be sold as parts) at 99 cents plus HST, per wheel, terms 2/10, net 30, calculate discounts before tax. Total Purchase Order is $111.87 and the wheels are to be shipped on Apr 15, by Vendor Truck.

Apr 6   Purchased from Thomson Toy Makers 10 Trucks large at $30.00 each plus HST, terms 2/10, net 30. Total Purchase is $339.00. Invoice # 996.

Apr 6   Mr. Tyson ordered and received 1 box of 1,000 cheques, form style, number # 10188 from NAS Business Forms. The special printing of cheques, on invoice # 4556 dated today, is in the amount of $300.00, plus 13% HST. Terms are 2/10, net 30. A purchase order number was not issued for this purchase. Note: Charge 1330 Prepaid Office Supplies because the cheques have not been used. The cost will be charged to an expense (adjustment) as they get used.

Apr 7   Mr. Tyson called you on his cell phone, and he will pick up a cheque payable to Willowdale Mall Ltd. for $2,100.00 plus 13% HST cheque for the monthly mall rent at 93 Betty Ann Drive. Issued cheque # 2511.

Apr 7   The items ordered from Markham Toy Manufacturing on purchase order # 82 arrived today in good condition with Invoice #1693 dated Apr 6. Record the transaction with a purchase date of Apr 6 because the 2% discount period starts on the 6th. Mr. Tyson was aware the trucks would arrive late.

Apr 7   Returned 13 Trucks small, received this morning from Markham Toy Manufacturing due to paint peeling from the driver's side of truck. The cost of each returned item is $14.32 plus HST. Markham Toy Manufacturing faxed us their credit memo # CM265 today in the amount of $-210.36.

Apr 7   Per special arrangements, Mr. Tyson sent back 30 trailer trucks at $10.00 each plus HST to Lanting Speciality Toys that were originally purchased on invoice # 6198 dated Feb 22. Total return including HST is -339.00 (negative). There are no terms on this return.

Apr 16   Mrs. Tyson purchased a second new briefcase (wide) for $135.00, plus HST, for a total price of $152.55 from Santos Luggage, 65 Semple Avenue, Toronto, Ontario M9L 1V5. She is going to Vancouver for a toy conference and her old briefcase does not look good and needs some repairs. Mrs. Tyson used her business credit card to pay for the purchase. Received invoice # 2401. Charge this purchase to Office/Store Supplies Expense.

Apr 16   Received invoice # 646 dated today, in the amount of $384.93 for 15 Cars medium at $22.71 each plus HST, from Thompson Toy Makers. A PO was not issued. Terms 2/10, net 30.

Apr 16   The complete Purchase Order # 83 of truck wheels from A-Your Name Toy Parts arrived in good condition with invoice # 65839 for $111.87 dated today.

Apr 20   A local service club has ordered 16 Orderly Vanline trucks. The trucks need to be received on Apr 29, as 10 of the trucks will be used as prizes in a children's contest, sponsored by the service club. Issue a Purchase Order (# 84) to Thompson Toy Makers for these trucks at $25.66 each plus HST, Total $463.93. Terms 2/10, Net 30. Thompson requires a $200.00 prepayment, as this is a special order of trucks. Inventory code Ord-Vanline, selling price $34.64, minimum quantity is 0.

Apr 29   Received 14 of the trucks ordered on PO # 84, from Thompson Toy Makers. The other 2 trucks will be delivered on May 4. Invoice # 1007 dated Apr 28 was received. Total invoice $405.94.

Apr 30   Paterson's Wood Working, 698 Beech Avenue, Suite 6, Toronto, Ontario, M4E 9A3, delivered and installed 2 new Store Equipment (display) cabinets. They were ordered by Mrs. Tyson to display new and current toys. A PO was not issued. The cabinets cost $900.00 each, plus HST. Received $2,034.00 invoice # 2696 dated today, with terms net 10 days.

3 ➤ Print the following reports:

     a. Income Statement for period Jan 1 to Apr 30.
     b. Balance Sheet at Apr 30.
     c. The Journal Entries - All of the transactions entered to date.
     d. The Vendor Aged Detail report, as at an appropriate date Apr 30.
     e. Pending Purchase Orders as at April 29.

Challenge Exercise 08 C8-6 Shirts–PI

Using the Chapter 6, Challenge Shirts & Ties Periodic Inventory solution, before entries, to change a Periodic Inventory system to a Perpetual Inventory system for Shirts & Ties.

It is assumed that you will attempt this challenge exercise to set up the COMPANY, RECEIVABLES, PAYABLES and the INVENTORY & SERVICES modules for this company, only after you have completed Chapters 6 and 8.

1 ➤ **Locate** and **open** your Challenge Exercise Shirts & Ties solution ready file before entries. If you did not complete Chapter 6, see step 3.

2 ➤ i) Change the company name to: **Your last name and initials,** followed by **Shirts-PI** (e.g., Malakowski-B Shirts-PI).

A revised Trial Balance (for Perpetual Inventory) is provided.

Chapter 6			*Challenge Exercise 08 C8-6 Shirts-PI*	
Cost of Goods Sold – Periodic			Cost of Goods Sold - Perpetual	
Beginning Inventory	38,200.00		Cost of Goods Sold	102,735.00*
Purchases	88,800.00			
Purchase Returns		3,000.00		
Purchase Discounts		1,628.00	Purchase Discounts	1,628.00
Ending Inventory		21,265.00		
			Inventory Adjustment	0.00

* The Perpetual Inventory amount of 102,735.00 combines the Periodic amounts in gray.

   ii) Remove Vendor-Options tab, linking Expense Account xxxx Purchases, from Apple Clothing Centre and Polo Accessories. Leave the field blank, to work with Perpetual Inventory.
   iii) Customize the columns to include the 'Item Number' for quotes, orders, and invoices for both Sales and Purchases.
   iv) Add the accounts required to amend the Cost of Goods Sold section. Use Group accounts.
   v) Create a General Journal entry to close the accounts in gray and move the balance to the new Cost of Goods Sold account shown above.
   vi) Return to the General Ledger Accounts window. Locate the accounts you closed in step v and click ☑ Omit from Financial Statements if Balance is Zero . Change the name of each account to include the words: Do Not Use-(e.g., Do Not Use-Beginning Inventory).
   vii) Make the INVENTORY & SERVICES module available, insert the inventory items as shown (Fig. 08 C8-6-2) and complete the linking for **Asset**, **Revenue** and **C.O.G.S**. accounts.
   viii) Go to **Setup, Settings, Inventory & Services, Linked Accounts** and select **Inventory Adjustment**.
   ix) Record source documents SD-1 through SD-10 inclusive from Chapter 6.
        Note: For SD-9b Receivable, do not use 'Item Number' column and use the Inventory Adjustment account.
   x) a) Print an Income Statement Jan 01 to Aug 16
       b) Balance Sheet Aug 16
       c) Vendor Aged Detail report at Aug 16
       d) Customer Aged Detail report at Aug 16
       e) Inventory Summary report at Aug 16

3 ➤ i) If you DID NOT complete Chapter 6, set up the company data file using a file name of **Your last name** and **initials**, followed by **Shirts PI**, (e.g., Malakowski-B Shirts-PI).
   ii) Complete the 'Ready file' before entries as per Chapter 6.
   iii) Complete step 2 above.

Your Last Name & initials Shirts-PI
Trial Balance As At Jul 31, 2016

	Debits	Credits
Bank Account Chequing	21,430.00	-
Accounts Receivable	15,350.32	-
Credit Card Receivables	0.00	-
Inventory	21,265.00	-
Prepaid Expenses	1,420.00	-
Warehouse Equipment	63,650.00	-
Accum Amortiz Warehouse Equip	-	21,300.00
Office Equipment	25,800.00	-
Accum Amortiz Office Equip	-	10,350.00
Accounts Payable	-	6,751.75
Universal Credit Card Payable	-	0.00
HST Charged on Sales	-	3,100.00
HST Paid On Purchases	950.00	-
Bank Loan Payable (Long Term)	-	75,000.00
Capital Your Last Name	-	13,847.57
Drawings Your Last Name	7,000.00	-
Sales	-	269,385.00
Sales Returns	2,650.00	-
Sales Discounts	2,800.00	-
Beginning Inventory	38,200.00	-
Purchases	88,800.00	-
Purchase Returns	-	3,000.00
Purchase Discounts	-	1,628.00
Ending Inventory	-	21,265.00
Wages Expense	98,030.00	-
Warehouse/Office Supplies Expense	1,790.00	-
Other Office Expenses	1,850.00	-
Travel & Entertainment Expense	2,630.00	-
Utilities Expense	2,800.00	-
Telephone Expense	2,400.00	-
Legal Expenses	1,600.00	-
Amortization Expense-All	2,900.00	-
Rent Expense	14,000.00	-
Credit Card Charges	7,512.00	-
Insurance Expense	800.00	-
	---------------	-----------------
	425,627.32	425,627.32
	==========	==========

Fig. 08 C8-6-1: Perpetual Inventory information Trial Balance.

Inventory Information

Inventory Name		Inventory Item #	Quantities Tab		Pricing Tab			Linked Tab			History Tab	
			Show Quantities in	Minimum Level	Regular	Preferred	Web Price	Asset	Revenue	C.O.G.S	Opening Quantity	Opening Value
Shirts	FA4	FA4	Each	30	19.00	17.10	0.00				300	2,850.00
Shirts	FA6	FA6	Each	30	21.00	18.90	0.00				419	4,399.50
Shirts	Mod-34	Mod-34	Each	30	19.00	17.10	0.00				275	2,612.50
Shirts	Mod-36	Mod -36	Each	30	20.00	18.00	0.00				325	3,250.00
Shirts	Mod-42	Mod-42	Each	30	36.00	32.40	0.00				166	2,988.00
Ties	VA-Mac	VA-Mac	Each	40	32.00	28.80	0.00				206	3,296.00
Ties	KB-21	KB-21	Each	40	21.00	18.90	0.00				178	1,869.00
										Total		21,265.00

Fig. 08 C8-6-2: Summary of Inventory items and values.

Challenge Exercise 08 C8-7, Bears

Perpetual Inventory Average Cost and First In First Out (FIFO)

This Challenge Exercise will allow you to record transactions in both Perpetual Inventory methods: Average Cost and First In First Out (FIFO) and compare results for both Cost of Goods Sold and Balance Sheet Inventory.

The Bears Company is a new company started by Jessica Jordan that will sell stuffed Teddy Bears to toy stores. She is not sure which Perpetual Inventory method to use and will record the first few entries in both data files for comparison. She plans to sell only 1 type of teddy bear for the first few weeks.

A college student has created 2 data files for this company that will open for business on Jan 2.

Note: Both data files **08 C8-7 Bears –PI -1 (Avg)** and **08 C8-7 Bears – PI -2 (FIFO)** are identical. You will change data file PI-2 to use the FIFO method.

1 ➤ Unzip and open the **08 C8-7 Bears –PI -1 (Avg)** data file.

2 ➤ Click **Setup, Settings, +** at **Inventory & Services, Options**. The Inventory Costing method: Average Cost should be selected. Click **Cancel** to return to the Home page.

Note: To assist in learning the difference between the 2 methods, **taxes** are *ignored* in the following transactions.

After each transaction, record the appropriate amount in the tables at Exercise 7D.

Exercise 7A – Record Transactions using the Average Cost Method

---

3 ➤ Record the following transactions, using the Average Cost method.

   a) After the input of each transaction, fill in the appropriate table in Exercise 7D.
   b) After the completion of all transactions, complete Exercise 7E.

Jan 2   Received from David Morris Company, 60 Bears at $10.00 each on Invoice #67888, dated today, terms 2% 10 days, net 30 days. They will sell for $20.00 each.

Jan 3   40 bears are sold to Ditlove Toys Inc. for $20.00 each on invoice 1, terms 2% 10 days, net 30 days. Before posting the entry display the Journal entry.

Jan 4   Received from David Morris Company, 50 bears at $12.00 each on invoice #67897, terms 2/10, net 30. The selling price is not changed as another warehouse store in the area sells similar bears for the same price.

Jan 5   Sold 30 bears to Jen Milton Toys for $20.00 each, on the next invoice.

Jan 6   Received from David Morris Company, 20 more bears at $12.50 each on Invoice #68002, with terms of 2/10, net 30. The selling price is not changed as another warehouse store in the area sells similar bears for the same price.

Jan 7   Sold 35 bears to Ditlove Toys Inc. for $20.00 each, on the next invoice, terms 2% 10 days, net 30 days.

Exercise 7B – Change Inventory Costing Method to the First In First Out (FIFO)Method

1 ➤ Unzip and open the **08 C8-7 Bears –PI -2 (FIFO)** data file.

2 ➤ Click **Setup, Settings, click ⊞ at Inventory & Services,** click **Options**. The Average Cost Inventory Costing Method is selected. Select **First In, First Out** (**FIFO**). Click **OK**.

The following warning message appears.

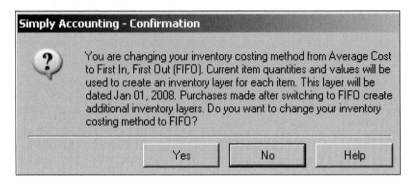

3 ➤ Click **Yes** to change to FIFO, and return to the Home page.

Exercise 7C – Record Transactions Using the First In First Out (FIFO) Method

1 ➤ Record the same transactions from Exercise 7A and record the information in the tables.

Exercise 7D – Record information in the following tables

Cost of Purchases (Average Cost)

Date	Items Purchased	$ Cost
Jan 02	60	
Jan 04	50	
Jan 06	20	
Total	130	$

Cost of Purchases (FIFO)

Date	Items Purchased	$ Cost
Jan 02	60	
Jan 04	50	
Jan 06	20	
Total	130	

Cost of Goods Sold (Average Cost)

Date	Items Sold	$ CGS
Jan 03	40	
Jan 05	30	
Jan 07	35	
Total	105	

Cost of Goods Sold (FIFO)

Date	Items Sold	$CGS
Jan 03	40	
Jan 05	30	
Jan 07	35	
Total	105	

Exercise 7E – For both methods, print the following; and record information in the following tables

---

1 ➤ From the ACCOUNTS PAYABLE module window, what is the total cost of the bears purchased from David Morris Company?

$_____

2 ➤ For both methods, print the Income Statement and Balance Sheet and record information below:

a) **Income Statement**   (Compare Cost of Goods Sold amounts)

Cost of Goods Sold – (Average Cost)	Cost of Goods Sold – (First In First Out)
$	$

b) **Balance Sheet**   (Compare Inventory amounts)

Inventory Average Cost	Inventory First In First Out
$	$

3 ➤ Print the Inventory & Service, Summary report at Jan 07, and record information (Compare

Inventory Summary - Average Cost
Jan 07 ____items at $_____= $_____

4 ➤ Print the Inventory & Services, FIFO Costing Report at Jan 07, and record information (Compare

Jan 04 _____ items at $_____ $

Jan 06_____ items at $_____ $_____
                        Total $_____0

                                    Average Cost (FIFO) $_____

5 ➤ Comparison of both methods:

Average Cost	FIFO
Cost of Goods Sold: $	Cost of Goods Sold: $
Balance Sheet Inventory _____	Balance Sheet Inventory _____
Total inventory values $_____	Total inventory values $_____

Chapter 9

Month-End/Year-End Processing

Kafa Sweaters

Learning Objectives
After completing this chapter you will be able to:

☐ Record various month-end adjusting entries in the General Journal.
☐ Add new General Ledger accounts as required.
☐ Display and print various reports and journals.

This chapter reviews recording adjusting entries at month-end or year-end and starting a new fiscal year. Reversing entries are discussed and shown.

The instructions assume that you are familiar with manual accounting, processing month-end and year-end adjustments, and closing a year for a company. Procedures vary from company to company, depending upon the Simply modules used and the nature of the business; e.g., merchandise versus service.

The chapter contains the following:

- Kafa Sweaters: Company Profile 494
    - Reviewing Existing Accounting Data 494
    - Trial Balance for Kafa Sweaters 494
- Entering Month-End (Period-End) Adjustments 494
    - Exercise 9-1 – Entering Period-End Adjustments 496
        - Bank Reconciliation...496
        - Prepaid Expense Adjustment: Office Supplies.......................................497
        - Prepaid Expense Adjustment: Prepaid Insurance..................................498
        - Accrued Expenses 499
        - Accrued Interest 501
        - Accrued Wages Payable 502
        - Amortization Adjustment 503
        - Periodic Inventory: Month-End Adjustment...504

- Backing Up the Data Files...505
- Printing Month-End and Year-End Reports...505
- Summary 506
- Before Moving On 506

Kafa Sweaters: Company Profile

Kafa Sweaters has been in business for 5 years and sells a selection of sweaters to both retail and wholesale customers. All transactions for the year have been entered into the accounting records, except for the year-end adjusting entries. Mr. Kafa has hired you to assist in recording the December month-end adjustments and closing the books (shown in Chapter 10) for the year.

The COMPANY module is used to record the normal month-end and year-end adjustments. Some of these adjustments will be reversed in the new year.

Kafa Sweaters does not use **recurring entries** or the **Track Additional Transaction Details** feature.

Reviewing Existing Accounting Data

1 ➤ Refer to Exercise 1-1, to **unzip** the **09 Kafa.exe** file.

*(Do NOT use the **10 Kafa2** data file.)*

2 ➤ Start Simply and open the **09 Kafa** data file.

3 ➤ Accept the Session Date of December 31, 2014 (the fiscal year-end of the firm).

Trial Balance for Kafa Sweaters

> Most companies will have printed a Trial Balance and a General Journal before adjustments are made. The accountant or manager would review the accounts and $ values to see if the $ values need changing.

4 ➤ **Display** and compare the Trial Balance at December 31, 2014 to Fig. 9-1. All previous entries have been cleared. Only the adjusting entries will display when reviewing your work in this chapter.

(See side note box.)

Entering Month-End (Period-End) Adjustments

Adjustments are made after all the regular monthly transactions have been entered. Most of the adjustments shown in this chapter are typical monthly entries. Some entries (Accrued Revenue and Expense) are reversed in the next month.

All of the adjustments shown in this chapter should be entered in the COMPANY module using the Dec 31, 2014 date.

Usually one of the accounting clerks would be responsible for recording all adjustments at month-end. The manager has decided you are the individual to record all accrued entries at December 2014.

Kafa Sweaters, Student's Name
Trial Balance As At Dec 31, 2014

Account	Name	Debits	Credits
1100	Bank Account	9,725.00	-
1200	Accounts Receivable	13,860.00	-
1260	Inventory of Goods	60,320.00	-
1300	Prepaid Insurance	1,200.00	-
1420	Equipment	88,129.00	-
1440	Furniture	31,020.00	-
1520	Accum Amortiz–Equipment	-	35,252.00
1540	Accum Amortiz–Furniture	-	12,408.00
2200	Accounts Payable	-	13,545.00
2231	Accrued Liabilities	-	0.00
2310	EI Payable	-	589.00
2320	CPP Payable	-	523.00
2330	Income Tax Payable	-	3,233.00
2350	HST on Sales	-	3,561.00
2360	HST Paid on Purchases	1,841.00	-
2710	Bank Loan Payable	-	21,000.00
3120	Capital Nathan Kafa	-	86,635.00
3140	Drawings Nathan Kafa	10,000.00	-
4010	Sales-All	-	327,600.00
4210	Sales Returns	3,980.00	-
4220	Sales Discounts	5,725.00	-
5020	Beginning Inventory	48,680.00	-
5030	Purchases	140,370.00	-
5040	Purchase Returns	-	5,260.00
5050	Purchase Discounts	-	1,942.00
5090	Ending Inventory	-	60,320.00
5110	Rent Expense	24,000.00	-
5120	Wages Expense	86,300.00	-
5122	EI Expense	3,452.00	-
5124	CPP Expense	3,193.00	-
5260	Office Supplies Expense	2,540.00	-
5330	Telephone Expense	3,720.00	-
5340	Advertising Expense	15,137.00	-
5350	Amortization Expense-All	0.00	-
5360	Bad Debts Expense	2,438.00	-
5410	Water/Hydro Expense	4,568.00	-
5510	Bank Charges Expense	1,380.00	-
5530	Bank Interest on Loan	1,540.00	-
5540	Insurance Expense	2,100.00	-
5550	Automobile Expense	2,810.00	-
5560	Automobile Lease	3,840.00	-
		---------------	---------------
		571,868.00	571,868.00
		==========	==========

Fig. 9-1: Trial Balance for Kafa Sweaters.

It is important to understand what month-end and year-end adjustments you need to do and why you need to do them; the GAAPs related to the various tasks; and how the adjustments affect your financial statements. Keep these in mind when you run **Slideshow 9 – MONTH & YEAR-END PROCESSING**.

Exercise 9-1 – Entering Period-End Adjustments

Bank Reconciliation

At month-end, differences between the company's bank statement and accounting records must be reconciled. Bank charges and deductions from your company's bank account must be recorded in your company's accounting system. You have not yet learned how to do bank reconciliation in Simply, but it will be covered in detail in Chapter 12.

All bank adjustments are processed in the COMPANY module, General Journal.

The bank statement for December for Kafa Sweaters would not be received until some time in the middle of January. During each month, the manager of Kafa Sweaters would receive debit and/or credit memos from the bank to alert the company to any changes made to the bank account. Examples of these entries are: NSF cheques, regular service charges, etc. This also makes the company aware of entries that occur regularly, such as lease payments, normal bank charges, etc.

Kafa Sweaters' bank normally charges bank service fees at the end of the month. The bank has not sent the normal Debit memo for bank service fees.

> If the company has access to the bank account using the internet, then the manager can locate the actual bank charges. If the actual amount is being used, then the Chapter 10 reversal for bank charges does not need to be reversed.

Mr. Kafa sent you a note to prepare an entry to the bank account for estimated bank service charges of $33.00.

This adjusting entry will be reversed on the first day of the next period.

1 ➤ From the Home window, **COMPANY** module, click the **General Journal** icon.

2 ➤ **Source:**   **Dec-Adj-1** (code December adjustment #1).

3 ➤ **Date:**   **Dec 31, 2014**

4 ➤ **Comment:**   **Estimated Bank Service Fees per N. Kafa.**

> This entry is recorded on a monthly basis. If desired, you could set it up as a Recurring Transaction entry. Remember that the Recurring Entry feature is optional. It is designed to help save you time in making repetitive entries and to minimize chances of making errors.

The entry should be recorded as follows:

5510	Bank Charges Expense	33.00	
1100	Bank Account		33.00

5 ➤ **Comment**   **Estimated Service Fees (for both lines).** (See side note box.)

6 ➤ **Post** after verifying accuracy.

Prepaid Expense Adjustment: Office Supplies

Most companies charge office supplies purchased to an asset account, similar to Prepaid Office Supplies On Hand. At month-end, the asset is adjusted for the amount of supplies consumed (used) during the period. The consumed supplies are normally charged to an expense account similar to Supplies Expense.

Study the following memo:

Kafa Sweaters

Memorandum

Date: December 31, 2014

To: Jordan Royes, Accounting Department

From: Nathan Kafa, General Manager

Our auditor has suggested that we record office supplies as an asset (which we have normally entered as an expense). The office staff have determined, by counting and calculating the cost price, that we have $370.00 worth of office supplies on hand.

*Please open a new asset account, **Prepaid Office Supplies On Hand**.*

Prepare an entry to reduce the expense account and increase the new asset.

Fig. 9-2: Memo on Prepaid Office Supplies.

1 ➤ Add a new G/L account **#1270 Prepaid Office Supplies on Hand**, select **Group Account** type, click **Class Options** tab, and select **Current Asset**.

2 ➤ **Record** and **Post** the following journal entry **Dec-Adj-2**:

Comment line   **Setup new asset- Office Supplies on Hand**

1270	Prepaid Office Supplies on Hand	370.00	
5260	Office Supplies Expense		370.00

Comment column for: 1270 - **Office Supplies on Hand**
                     5260 - **Office Supplies Not Used**

Use appropriate Comments for remaining adjustments.

Prepaid Expense Adjustment: Prepaid Insurance

The two Prepaid Expense adjustments (Prepaid Insurance and Prepaid Office Supplies On Hand), are examples of proper matching of revenues earned with expenses incurred. This results in a more accurate financial statement for Kafa Sweaters. If the adjustments were not made, the profits of the company would be higher than the true profits for 2015 and lower for 2014.

Kafa Sweaters

Memorandum

Date: December 31, 2014

To: Jordan Royes, Accounting Department

From: Nathan Kafa, General Manager

Re: Insurance policy FT2786-09

The FT (Fire/Theft) Insurance Policy purchased on November 15 expires in 4-1/2 months.

Prepare an entry to record the insurance used from November 15 to December 31.

Fig. 9-3: Memo on Prepaid Insurance Expense.

You need to reduce the ledger account **1300 Prepaid Insurance** to show that only 4-1/2 months of insurance remain in effect, after the year-end.

$1,200.00/6 months = $200.00 per month.

1-1/2 months used up = $300.00. This will leave $900.00 in the PREPAID INSURANCE account for the following year. (See side note box.)

Proper matching results from recording the prepaid insurance premiums as an expense as the policy expires.

1 ➤ **Record** and **Post** the following journal entry **Dec-Adj-3**:

5540	Insurance Expense	300.00	
1300	Prepaid Insurance		300.00

This expense adjustment occurs each month and could be set up as a recurring entry for $300.00.

Accrued Expenses

GAAP **Matching Principle** requires that all expenses incurred to earn revenues must be reported in the same time period as the corresponding revenues. The revenues are to be "matched" with the expenses spent to earn them. These expenses are what are referred to as **accrued expenses**. Proper matching of the revenues and expenses results in an accurate accounting of net income or loss.

In this section you will match the expenses recorded in December with the corresponding revenues earned by Kafa Sweaters in the same month.

Study the following memo:

Kafa Sweaters

Memorandum

Date:	*December 31, 2014*
To:	*Jordan Royes, Accounting Department*
From:	*Gus Hollin, Accounting Supervisor*

In reviewing the trial balance, we noticed the following expense bills have not been received or entered. Would you please process an accrual entry.

	Amount Subject To Tax	HST Amount
Telephone	*$260.00*	*33.80*
Electricity	*340.00*	*44.20*
Automobile Gas	*90.00*	*11.70*
Totals	*$690.00*	*89.70*

Fig. 9-4: Memo on Accrued Expense.

5330	Telephone Expense	260.00	
5410	Water/Hydro Expense	340.00	
5550	Automobile Expense	90.00	
2360	HST Paid On Purchases	89.70	
2231	Accrued Liabilities		779.70

1 ➤   **Record** and **Post** the following journal entry **Dec-Adj-4**:

Remember to view the transaction before posting.

Entries similar to this will occur each month; however, it should **not** be set up as a recurring entry, as the expense accounts may be very different each month.

When you click the **Post** icon you will see a confirmation window.

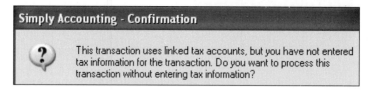

In Chapter 1 the General Journal was used to record entries without HST.

In Chapter 2A and 2B, when you recorded entries in the Purchases Journal, you identified the purchase amount before HST was added. Simply then allocated taxes based on the tax codes and rates that were previously set up.

In the General Journal when you record an entry affecting the taxes accounts (HST), the program requires the pre-tax amounts.

2 ➤ Click **No** to process the transaction entering the tax information. If you click Yes (entering without tax information), you would have to manually adjust the Simply HST report when submitting the report to the Receiver General.

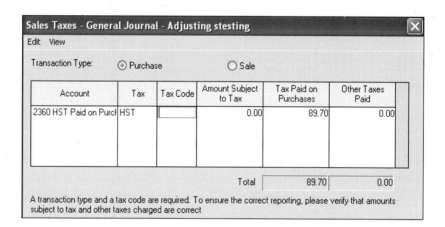

> You entered an HS tax code for HST at 13% $690.00 appears in the Amount Subject to Tax column.
>
> Simply divides the HST amount entered in the HST Paid on Purchases account #2360 ($89.70) by .13 (the HST rate) to determine the amount subject to HST tax ($690.00).

3 ➤ **Tax Code**   Type **HS** or select HS, ⎡Tab⎤. (See side note box.)

4 ➤ **Other Taxes Paid**   See side note box. ⎡Tab⎤.

> The $0.00 (Other Taxes Paid) column would be used where PST is applicable. Ontario no longer collects PST after June 30, 2010.

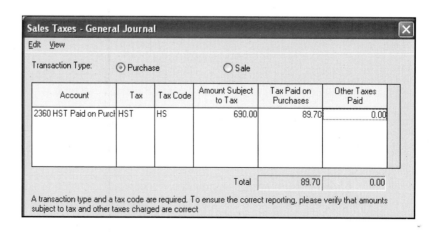

5 ➤ Click **OK**.

(See side note box.)

6 ➤ You need to click the **Post** icon again to post the entry.

Accrued Interest

This entry is very similar to the previous entry for ACCRUED EXPENSES.

Kafa Sweaters

Memorandum

Date: *December 31, 2014*

To: *Jordan Royes, Accounting Department*

From: *Nathan Kafa, General Manager*

The loan interest for December is due on January 1, 2015. Would you please accrue, to account #2231 Accrued Liabilities, the loan interest as of December 31, 2014.

The loan balance is $21,000.00; the loan interest rate is 8% per year. The monthly interest cost is $140.00.

Fig. 9-5: Memo on Accrued Interest.

$21,000.00 x 8% /12 months = $140.00 per month.

(See side note box.)

1 ➤ **Record** and **Post** the following journal entry **Dec-Adj-5**:

5530	Bank Interest on Loan Expense	140.00	
2231	Accrued Liabilities		140.00

This entry will occur each month as the interest expense accrues on the loan, and could be set up as a recurring monthly entry.

Remember to view the transaction before posting.

(See side note box.)

Accrued Wages Payable

This scenario occurs at the end of some months during the year depending on when employees are paid. This adjustment could be set up, therefore, as a monthly recurring entry.

 Kafa Sweaters

Memorandum

Date: *December 31, 2014*

To: *Jordan Royes, Accounting Department*

From: *Nathan Kafa, General Manager*

The payroll department has advised me that we need to accrue $1,809.00 in wages for December 31. Employees were last paid up to and including December 25, 2014.

Ignore employee benefits for this period. The benefit accrual is not material in amount.

Open a new account for WAGES PAYABLE.

Fig. 9-6: Memo on Accrued Wages Payable.

1 ➤ Before this transaction can be recorded, add a new G/L account **#2220 Wages Payable**. Select **Group Account** and **Other Payable** on the Class Options tab.

2 ➤ **Record** and **Post** the following journal entry **Dec-Adj-6**:

5120	Wages Expense	1,809.00	
2220	Wages Payable		1,809.00

Amortization Adjustment

Amortization represents the reduction of the value of a **capital asset** such as machinery, equipment, building, etc. The cost minus the expected salvage value is divided by the estimated life of the asset. This amount would be the amortization cost per year.

Kafa Sweaters

Memorandum

Date:	December 31, 2014
To:	Jordan Royes, Accounting Department
From:	Nathan Kafa, General Manager

We have determined, based on the amortization schedules, that we need to record yearly amortization in the amounts of:

Equipment	$ 8,813.00
Furniture	$ 3,102.00

Please make a note to record Amortization next year on a monthly basis.

Fig. 9-7: Memo on Amortization.

1 ➤ **Record** and **Post** the following journal entry **Dec-Adj-7:**

5350	Amortization Expense – All	11,915.00	
1520	Accum Amortiz – Equipment		8,813.00
1540	Accum Amortiz – Furniture		3,102.00

Remember to view the journal entry before posting.

This entry will occur each month as the capital assets are used up and could be set up as a monthly recurring entry.

Periodic Inventory: Month-End Adjustment

Refer to Chapter 3B, Tyson's Toys Exercise 3B-34, for inventory adjustments.

 **Kafa Sweaters**

Memorandum

Date: *December 31, 2014*

To: *Jordan Royes, Accounting Department*

From: *Nathan Kafa, General Manager*

The physical inventory has been counted and valued at $55,850.00, our cost.

Fig. 9-8: Memo on Inventory.

1 ➤   Our auditor has suggested that we adjust inventory in two steps:

Step 1 – Dec-Adj-8:   Remove November ending inventory.

5090	Ending Inventory	60,320.00	
1260	Inventory of Goods		60,320.00

Step 2 - Dec-Adj-9: Set up the December ending inventory.

1260	Inventory of Goods	55,850.00	
5090	Ending Inventory		55,850.00

These entries will occur each month as the inventory changes, and could be set up as a recurring monthly entry.

Alternative Adjustment...

The inventory could also be adjusted in one step, by adjusting for the difference in the two amounts. $60,320.00
                                        −$55,850.00

                                      = $ 4,470.00

You have to be careful how you enter the difference. In this case we need to reduce the inventory. The entry could be:

5090 Ending Inventory	4,470.00	
1260 Inventory of Goods		4,470.00

With the two-step method you used in the last exercise for Dec-Adj-8 and Dec-Adj-9, it is easier to check that you have removed the old inventory dollar value correctly.

All of the month-end/year-end adjustments and accruals have now been made.

Backing Up the Data Files

After all adjustments have been made, make a backup copy of the data files for Kafa Sweaters. This is very important for a number of reasons:

- Once the Session Date is advanced to a new fiscal year, no more entries should be entered in the year ended December 31, 2014, except for the fiscal year-end adjusting entries from the accountant.

- The company's accountants will review the accounting data and may make adjustments including Audit adjustments after the fiscal year is completed. The backup copy can then be used to make the adjustments and print revised final financial statements that agree with the audited statement.

- Data loss may occur (very rarely, but it could happen) during the Simply year-end closing procedures.

Back up your data now and record details in your logbook.

Printing Month-End and Year-End Reports

Month-End/Year-End reports are made available for review by management, accountants, and in some cases shareholders, banks and other parties that have a major financial interest in the company.

It is also good practice to keep a hard copy of the month's/year's activity, just in case computer data is lost. Back up at regular intervals.

1 ➤ **Print** the following reports for Kafa Sweaters at year-end and retain for future use. There would be other reports printed if other modules were used.

a) Trial Balance as at Dec 31.
b) Balance Sheet as at Dec 31.
c) Income Statement for the year from January 1 to Dec 31.
d) Journal Entries - All for Dec 31.
e) General Ledger Listing (all G/L account activity in detail) for Dec 31.

2 ➤ Compare your results with those in the instructor's Solutions Manual.

If you find differences, you should make adjusting entries to correct the problems. See your instructor if you need help.

Summary

The adjustments and accruals entered for Kafa Sweaters' month-end/year-end processing are typical month-end and year-end entries.

Entries could be stored and recalled at future month-ends as a time-saving feature.

Financial statements and reports are printed at period-end.

The Year-End close is performed by advancing the Session Date into the new fiscal year. See Chapter 10.

Before Moving On...

Read the following questions and make sure you know the answers to them; otherwise, read the corresponding part in the chapter before moving on.

1. Explain the concept of matching revenues with expenses in a specific accounting period.

2. What kind of adjustment is required to Prepaid Expenses at the end of an accounting period?

3. What are accrued expenses? Give at least two examples.

4. What is accrued interest? Why is it necessary to make an adjustment to this account at the end of the accounting period?

5. Name two major reasons why backing up data files is necessary before doing the year-end closing in Simply.

6. What is the benefit of using recurring entries?

Chapter 10

Year-End Closing

Kafa2 Sweaters

Learning Objectives

After completing this chapter you will be able to:

☐ Close the previous year's financial records (year-end).
☐ Record appropriate reversing entries.
☐ Update Inventory accounts at the start of the fiscal year.
☐ Display and print various reports and journals.

This chapter continues with Kafa Sweaters data, from Chapter 9, after all adjusting entries have been entered. The balances in each account are the final balances before year-end closing entries. You will be using the **Kafa2** company files for **Kafa2 Sweaters**. The files are at www.simplyaccounting2010.nelson.com under Student Resources.

- To Close the Books (Fiscal Year-End) 508
    - Exercise 10-1 – Closing the Fiscal Year...510
    - Exercise 10-2 – To View the New Year's Statements 512
    - Exercise 10-3 – To Close the Owner's Drawing Account.......................512
    - Exercise 10-4 – To Reverse Prior-Year Accrued Entries 513
        - Bank Service Charge 513
        - Office Supplies 514
        - Prepaid Insurance...514
        - Accrued Expenses 514
        - Accrued Interest..515
        - Accrued Wages Payable..515
        - Amortization 515
    - Exercise 10-5 – Updating INVENTORY Accounts.................................516

- Summary...516
- Before Moving On 517
- Inventory Entry at the *End of the First Month* of the Fiscal Year......................518

- Challenge Exercise 10 C10-1 (Chapters 9-10), Rama Magazines....................519
- Challenge Exercise 10 C10-2 (Chapters 9-10), City Gravel.............................520

How do you close the fiscal year at year-end? What do you need to do at the end of the year, after year-end adjustments are posted? How do they affect the financial statements? These are the questions that **Slideshow 10 – YEAR-END CLOSING** will answer. Run it now.

To Close the Books (Fiscal Year-End)

The final step for Kafa Sweaters' year-end processing is to close off the fiscal year.

In a manual system:

To close the books at year-end, you would do the following:

For a sole proprietorship:
a) Prepare and post a Journal entry to transfer the Revenue and Expense accounts to the CAPITAL account.
b) Close the DRAWINGS account to the CAPITAL account.

For a corporation:
a) Prepare and post a Journal entry to transfer the Revenue and Expense accounts to the RETAINED EARNINGS account.
b) Close the DIVIDENDS DECLARED account to the RETAINED EARNINGS account.

In the Simply system:

a) Make backups of your data before proceeding and put the backups in a safe place. Start the new fiscal year with new backup storage devices.

b) In Simply you would advance the Session Date to the first day of the new fiscal year.

c) Simply automatically records and posts the closing entry (after giving you a warning) which effectively closes the Revenue and Expense accounts and then transfers the net profit or loss to the default Capital or Retained Earnings account. Note: Simply does not make or prepare a closing journal entry.

d) In addition, Simply clears journal entries and resets journal numbers to 1. PROJECT/Division detail is accumulated as one balance forward amount (removing the detail, therefore, you need printouts and backups before period-end processing).

Kafa2 Sweaters: Company Profile

The Fiscal Start date becomes the first day of the new fiscal year (for Kafa2 Sweaters, it is January 1, 2015), and the Fiscal End date is the last day of the new fiscal year (December 31, 2015).

Study the following Trial Balance of **Kafa2 Sweaters** as at Dec 31, 2014. This will be the basis of the closing entries.

Make sure you have a backup before proceeding!

Kafa2 Sweaters, Student's Name
Trial Balance As At Dec 31, 2014

Account		Debits	Credits
1100	Bank Account	9,692.00	-
1200	Accounts Receivable	13,860.00	-
1260	Inventory of Goods	55,850.00	-
1270	Prepaid Office Supplies on Hand	370.00	-
1300	Prepaid Insurance	900.00	-
1420	Equipment	88,129.00	-
1440	Furniture	31,020.00	-
1520	Accum Amortiz–Equipment	-	44,065.00
1540	Accum Amortiz–Furniture	-	15,510.00
2200	Accounts Payable	-	13,545.00
2220	Wages Payable	-	1,809.00
2231	Accrued Liabilities	-	919.70
2310	EI Payable	-	589.00
2320	CPP Payable	-	523.00
2330	Income Tax Payable	-	3,233.00
2350	HST on Sales	-	3,561.00
2360	HST Paid On Purchases	1,930.70	-
2710	Bank Loan Payable	-	21,000.00
3120	Capital Nathan Kafa	-	86,635.00
3140	Drawings Nathan Kafa	10,000.00	-
4010	Sales-All	-	327,600.00
4210	Sales Returns	3,980.00	-
4220	Sales Discounts	5,725.00	-
5020	Beginning Inventory	48,680.00	-
5030	Purchases	140,370.00	-
5040	Purchases Returns	-	5,260.00
5050	Purchase Discounts	-	1,942.00
5090	Ending Inventory	-	55,850.00
5110	Rent Expense	24,000.00	-
5120	Wages Expense	88,109.00	-
5122	EI Expense	3,452.00	-
5124	CPP Expense	3,193.00	-
5260	Office Supplies Expense	2,170.00	-
5330	Telephone Expense	3980.00	-
5340	Advertising Expense	15,137.00	-
5350	Amortization Expense-All	11,915.00	-
5360	Bad Debts Expense	2,438.00	-
5410	Water/Hydro Expense	4,908.00	-
5510	Bank Charges Expense	1,413.00	-
5530	Bank Interest on Loan	1,680.00	-
5540	Insurance Expense	2,400.00	-
5550	Automobile Expense	2,900.00	-
5560	Automobile Lease	3,840.00	-
		582,041.70	582,041.70

Fig. 10-1: Kafa2 Trial Balance as of December 31, 2014.

Exercise 10-1 – Closing the Fiscal Year

---

1 ➤ Unzip the **10 Kafa2.exe** file from www.simplyaccountingnelson.2010.com under Student Resources.

2 ➤ Start Simply and select **10 Kafa2** as the company file.

3 ➤ Accept Session Date of **Dec 31, 2014, OK**.

4 ➤ Display and Print the Balance Sheet at December 31, 2014 and note the dollar values of the Equity accounts. File for Audit Trail.

Owner's Equity	
Capital Nathan Kafa	86,635.00
Drawings Nathan Kafa	-10,000.00
Current Earnings	20,362.00
Total Owner's Equity	96,997.00

5 ➤ Display and **Print** the Income Statement **for the fiscal year** to view the Revenue, Expenses and Net Income. File for Audit Trail.

In this exercise you are not required to back up; however, in a real-life business year-end situation, you should create backups every step of the year-end closing process in case you need to restore your data.

6 ➤ Return to the Home window.

7 ➤ **Session Date**   Click the **Calendar**. Click the ▼ and select **Jan 01, 2015**, click **OK**. (See side note box.)

The following message window appears:

Simply Accounting - New Fiscal and Calendar Year

⚠️ You have entered both a new calendar and a new fiscal year. If you proceed, the program will move the current year's data into last year, close all revenue and expense account balances into the Retained Earnings linked account, and set the new fiscal year's dates. Print all employee reports and make a backup before proceeding.

If you have chosen to keep financial history for a certain number of years, you can still see financial reports for those years.

Do you want the program to back up your data before beginning the new fiscal and calendar year?

◉ Yes   ○ No

You are using a 2014 data file. In a real business setting, the file can also contain 2013 prior year data.

Study the whole message before proceeding. It is assumed that you are now in the year 2015. This is a warning that four things will happen:

1a. The year 2013 data (currently in Simply) will be **deleted**.

1b. The 2014 year's data is **moved** into the previous year's storage area.

2. The previous year's data (2014) revenue and expense account balances will be **closed** (changed to zero) and the balance will be transferred to the **Retained Earnings** linked account. The Retained Earnings linked account can be one of the following:

   a. Capital Account (Sole Proprietorship)
   b. Retained Earnings (Corporation)
   c. Net Profit Holding account (Partnership) for later allocation to the partners.

3. The new fiscal year's (2015) dates will be set.

4. All journal entry records will be cleared, and Journal entry numbers for 2015 are reset to 1. All employee data for 2015 will start at 0.

8 ➤ Click the **No** button regarding backing up your data. In this exercise there is no need to back up. When ready, click **OK**.

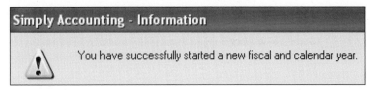

9 ➤ Click **OK**.

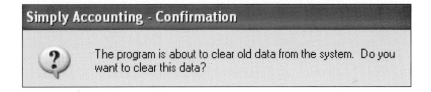

10 ➤ This message refers to item 1a in step 7 above. Any previous data in the storage area (e.g., 2013) will be deleted from the system.

The current 2014 year data will move to the storage area and the 2015 year data fields will be created and will remain in the system. Click **Yes**.

The screen will flicker and you will see the following message window:

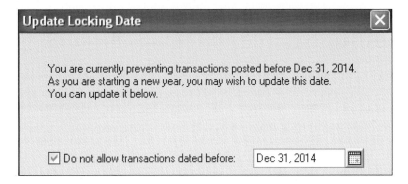

This window would allow you to post transactions to a previous year data file. You have removed the 2013 data and will not be posting any information to 2013. You should update this field to Jan 01, 2015. This will prevent posting entries to the previous 2014 year. This field could be changed later in the Setup, System Settings, Setting window.

11 ➤   In the Update Locking Date box, change the date to **Jan 01, 2015**, and click **OK**.

You return to the Home window. Continue with the next exercise.

Starting a New Fiscal Year

As you start a new fiscal year, you need to:

1. View the 2015 Statements to make sure the Income Statement accounts have zero balances.

2. Record entries in the General Journal to:
    a) Close the Owner's Drawing Account.
    b) Reverse the prior year-end accrued entries.
    c) For a Periodic Inventory system, update the Inventory accounts.

Exercise 10-2 – To View the New Year's Statements

You should be at the Kafa2 Home window.

1 ➤   To verify that the year-end procedure was done correctly, repeat the steps to view the Current Year Income Statement.

You will see that the dates are now **Jan 01, 2015** (1st day of **new fiscal year**) and all Revenue and Expense accounts are zero (0).

2 ➤   View the Balance Sheet and you will see that the balance of the CAPITAL account has increased by the amount of the net income (Current Earning) from 2014.

Owner's Equity	
Capital Nathan Kafa	106,976.20
Drawings Nathan Kafa	-10,000.00
Current Earnings	0.00
Total Owner's Equity	96,976.20
TOTAL EQUITY	96,976.20

The data file is now ready to record transactions in 2015. The first entry should be to transfer the balance of Drawing for a sole proprietorship, or Dividends Declared for a corporation, to the appropriate equity account.

Exercise 10-3 – To Close the Owner's Drawing Account

Mr. Kafa, by memo, has asked you to prepare a General Journal entry to close the Drawings Nathan Kafa account with the following information:

1 ➤   From the Home window, click the **General Journal** icon.

2 ➤   **Source:**   Memo N. Kafa, [Tab].

         Date: Jan 01, 2015.

3 ➤   **Comment:**   **Close the Owner's Drawing account.**

4 ➤ Record and **Post** the following journal entry:

3120	Capital Nathan Kafa	10,000.00	
3140	Drawings Nathan Kafa		10,000.00

In a corporation to close the DIVIDENDS DECLARED account, the entry would be similar to:

3120	Retained Earnings	xx,xxx.00	
3140	Dividends Declared		xx,xxx.00

Exercise 10-4 – To Reverse Prior-Year Accrued Entries

The next step is to reverse any accrued revenues and expenses recorded in the previous year (2014). You will not be able to use the Reverse entry icon for previous fiscal year entries.

Accrued expenses and accrued revenues that were recorded in the previous year (for matching purposes) must be reversed in the current year. The reversing entry amounts are opposite to the original entry(ies) made in December 2014.

Accruals are amounts that have been estimated or based on source documents that have not yet been received from suppliers, or invoices that have not yet been issued by our firm in time to process at year-end. When the vendor documents arrive or Kafa2 issues the corresponding invoices, they will be processed as usual in the RECEIVABLES or PAYABLES module.

If reversing entries are not made for accrued items, the amounts will have been recorded twice, once in the previous year (2014) and again in the current year (2015). The accrued payable account will also not be correct.

The accountant would need to review the entries that were made at year-end to determine which entries need to be reversed.

The adjusting entries that need to be made at year-end, and why they need to be reversed or not reversed, are shown next.

Bank Service Charge

The estimated bank service charge needs reversing, because the correct service charge will be recorded when the December bank reconciliation is completed in January. (See side box.)

1 ➤ Open the **General Journal**.

As discussed in Chapter 9, Exercise 9-1, it is possible to record an actual bank charge if the business has access to the Internet. If you recorded an actual bank charge, then you do not need to reverse the entry.

To reverse the accrual, the following is the suggested wording for each field:

2 ➤ Source   **Yr-End-Reversal**.

  Date   **Jan 01, 2015**.

3 ➤ Comment   **Reverse Estimated December bank fees**. (A better comment line would include the original December Journal entry number to cross-reference for audit trail purposes.)

4 ➤ Comment column   Record the information shown below. The comment column includes information about the entry number Adj-1 (from 2014) to cross-reference the entry (2015 year) for audit trail purposes.

Account	Debits	Credits	Comment
1100 Bank Account	33.00	--	Reverse 2014 Yr-End Adj-1
5510 Bank Charges Expe	--	33.00	Reverse 2014 Yr-End Adj-1

Source: Yr-End-Reversal Date: Jan 01, 2015
Comment: Reverse Estimated December bank fees

5 ➤ **Post** when correct to reverse the original accrual made December 31.

Office Supplies

Does not need a reversal; the correct cost of supplies used in December was recorded in December.

Prepaid Insurance

Does not need a reversal; the correct cost of insurance used in December was recorded in December.

Accrued Expenses

The accruals for the Telephone, Electricity and Automobile expenses in 2014 were estimated and, therefore, need to be reversed. The actual December invoices will be recorded as an expense in January.

1 ➤ Click the **General Journal** and reverse the entry as shown below.

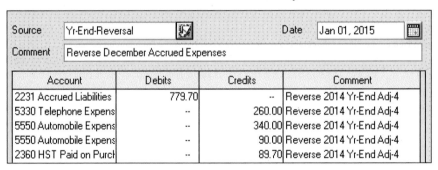

Source: Yr-End-Reversal Date: Jan 01, 2015
Comment: Reverse December Accrued Expenses

Account	Debits	Credits	Comment
2231 Accrued Liabilities	779.70	--	Reverse 2014 Yr-End Adj-4
5330 Telephone Expens	--	260.00	Reverse 2014 Yr-End Adj-4
5550 Automobile Expens	--	340.00	Reverse 2014 Yr-End Adj-4
5550 Automobile Expens	--	90.00	Reverse 2014 Yr-End Adj-4
2360 HST Paid on Purch	--	89.70	Reverse 2014 Yr-End Adj-4

Notice that the amounts are opposite to the original entry made on December 31, 2014.

2 ➤ **Post** when correct and you will see the Tax Linked confirmation window.

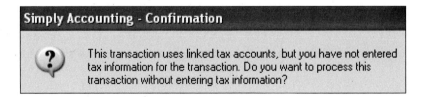

Simply Accounting - Confirmation

This transaction uses linked tax accounts, but you have not entered tax information for the transaction. Do you want to process this transaction without entering tax information?

3 ➤ Click **No** to continue.

4 ➤ **Enter** the information as shown below (with negatives). This is opposite to what was recorded in Chapter 9.

Transaction Type:	⊙ Purchase		○ Sale		
Account	Tax	Tax Code	Amount Subject to Tax	Tax Paid on Purchases	Other Taxes Paid
2360 HST Paid on Purch	HST	HS	-690.00	-89.70	0.00

5 ➤ If you do not see the **OK** button at the bottom of the Sales Taxes - General Journal, click **View, Restore**, then **OK**, to continue. A blue ✓ appears in the Sales Tax button to indicate sales taxes were recorded.

6 ➤ **Post** to record the entry.

Accrued Interest

Does not need a reversal; the correct cost of interest was recorded as an expense in December.

Accrued Wages Payable

This needs to be reversed; otherwise, the full amount of the actual payroll cheques will be recorded in January as an expense. The January debit expense for the payroll will be reduced by the January reversal credit entry. When reversed, the payroll expense for the first pay period in the current year would be January 1 to January 6.

1 ➤ **Record** and **Post** the following journal entry:

Source	Yr-End-Reversal			Date	Jan 01, 2015	
Comment	Reverse December accrued Wages Expense					

Account	Debits	Credits	Comment
2220 Wages Payable	1,809.00	--	Reverse 2014 Yr-End Adj-6
5120 Wages Expense	--	1,809.00	Reverse 2014 Yr-End Adj-6

Amortization

Does not need a reversal; the correct cost of amortization expense used in the year 2014 was recorded in December.

Updating Inventory Accounts

Kafa Sweaters uses the **Periodic Inventory** method to record purchases of merchandise for resale. If a business is using the **Perpetual Inventory** method to record purchases for resale, the following entries are not required because the inventory account is used to record all purchases and is changed when goods are sold. See Chapter 8 for purchase and sales entries using the Perpetual Inventory method.

When you displayed the new Income Statement, you should have noticed that all Revenue and Expense accounts were closed, including the two Cost of Goods Sold inventory accounts.

(See side note box.)

The **Jan. 1, 2015** Trial Balance, therefore, contains the following values:

		DR	CR
ASSET	1260 Inventory of Goods	$55,850.00	
*COGS	5020 Beginning Inventory	0.00	
*COGS	5090 Ending Inventory	0.00	

*COGS = Cost of Goods Sold

On the first day of the new fiscal year; i.e., January 1 in this example, the Beginning Inventory (last year's Ending Inventory) is $55,850.00. Since the Opening or Beginning Inventory value in the Income Statement accounts is currently $0, we need to record an entry to set up the beginning inventory value for the year.

Exercise 10-5 – Updating INVENTORY Accounts

---

1 ➤ **Record** and **Post** a **Jan 01, 2015** entry, similar to the following, in the General Journal to update the inventory records.

Source	Inventory Adj-1		Date	Jan 01, 2015	
Comment	Set up Opening Inventory Jan 01, 2015				

Account	Debits	Credits	Comment
5020 Beginning Inventory	55,850.00	--	Set up Jan 01 Beg Inventory
1260 Inventory of Goods	--	55,850.00	Set up Jan 01 Beg Inventory

The **January 1 trial balance** would now contain the following values:

			DR	CR
ASSET	1260 Inventory of Goods		0.00	
COGS	5020 Beginning Inventory		55,850.00	
COGS	5090 Ending Inventory		0.00	

> **ℹ**
> It is assumed that financial statements would not be printed until the end of the first month and no additional entries are required. When statements before the end of the month are needed, additional entries would be required to update accounts 1260 and 5090 to correct values.

(See side note box.)

Printing Reports

2 ➤ **Print** Journal Entries-All for **Jan 01, 2015** and review the entries made. Check with the instructor's Solutions Manual.

3 ➤ **Print** Income Statement at **Jan 01, 2015**.

4 ➤ **Print** a Balance Sheet at **Jan 01, 2015**.

5 ➤ **Print** a Trial Balance at **Jan 01, 2015**.

The Kafa2 Sweaters company file is now set up for you to record transactions for January 2015.

Summary

The year-end close is performed by advancing the Session date into the new fiscal year. Reports are displayed to see the result of closing of Income Statement accounts to the Capital for a Sole Proprietorship or Retained Earnings for a Corporation.

Using the January 1, 2015 date:

- Drawings accounts or Dividends Declared are closed.
- Reversing entries are made to avoid recording of revenues and expenses to the next accounting period.
- The Income Statement amounts for Beginning Inventory are set up.

Before Moving On...

Read the following questions and make sure you know the answers to them; otherwise, read the corresponding part in this chapter before moving on.

1. Why is it necessary to enter reversing entries for accruals after closing the year?

2. Why is it necessary to record opening inventory in the Income Statement at the beginning of the year for a company using the periodic method for inventory?

3. What steps are involved in closing the current year in a manual system? How is this done in Simply?

4. What are two reasons why you would back up the data files before doing the year-end closing in Simply?

Inventory Entry at the *End of the First Month* of the Fiscal Year

Assume that the physical count of INVENTORY at January 31, 2015 amounted to **$98,000.00**.

The inventory balances would need to be updated. The same procedure we followed in Chapter 3, Tyson's Toys, or Inventory Month-End for Kafa Sweaters would be followed.

Since the values in accounts 1260 and 5090 are already $0, there is no need to remove "old" values. All that is needed is an entry to update these accounts to the current ending inventory value.

Comment line could be similar to: **Set up January ending Inventory**.

The entry would be:

			DR	CR
ASSET	1260	Inventory of Goods	$98,000.00	
COGS	5090	Ending Inventory		$98,000.00

The resulting **Jan. 31** trial balance would contain the following values:

		DR	CR
1260	Inventory	$98,000.00	
5020	Beginning Inventory	55,850.00	
5090	Ending Inventory		$98,000.00

For each successive month to the end of the year, you will process inventory adjusting entries as shown in Chapters 3B and 9.

Review **Slideshows 9** and **10** and make sure you understand the GAAPs related to month- and year-end adjustments. Also focus on the effects of the adjustments on both the Balance Sheet and the Income Statement.

Challenge Exercise 10 C10-1 (Chapters 9-10), Rama Magazines

Month-End Procedures Review

This exercise is a review of month-end procedures.

1 ➤ Refer to Exercise 1-1 to unzip the **10 C10-1 Magazines.exe** file.

2 ➤ Open the **10 C10-1 Magazines** file.

3 ➤ Record January 31, month-end adjustments for Rama Magazines, a company that provides various magazines, candy and small toys to businesses. Rama Magazines is using the COMPANY, PAYABLES and RECEIVABLES modules and does not use the Account Reconciliation journal.

Rama Magazines has the following adjustments for the January month-end:

a) Bank service charges for the month are estimated to be $43.50.

b) The Prepaid insurance account balance represents 4 months insurance that has not been used as of January 1. Adjust the account accordingly.

c) A part-time employee (use YOUR ACTUAL NAME as the part-time employee's name in the comment line) did not submit his time sheet and was not paid $158.00, the regular wages for the pay period ending January 28. (Magazine Sales charges all salaries and wages to Salaries Staff Account #5290.) Accrue the wages for the period (ignore CPP and EI).

d) The value of the Store Supplies on hand was counted, and is $358.00.

e) Amortization of Store Equipment is $1,500.00 for the year ($125.00 per month).

f) The long-term bank loan arranged on December 31, 2011 with the Canadian Bank is for a 5-year period at an interest rate at 9% (per annum). Monthly payments of $1,000.00 are due at the end of each month. The January 31, automatic bank payment of $1,000.00 (including interest of $333.30) has not been made or recorded.

g) A new vendor, Snowgone Services, a snow removal operator, submitted invoice #5631 dated today for $140.00 plus HST, net 30 days (Rent Expense), for your cost of snow removal services at the mall during January.

h) The previous ending inventory adjustment of $61,320.00 was made on January 15, for a manager's meeting. The inventory was counted today, after the close of business, and the INVENTORY amount is $59,738.00.

4 ➤ Print **Journal Entries-All** for the entries above.

5 ➤ Print a **Trial Balance** as at January 31.

6 ➤ **Back up** your data before moving on.

Your instructor may require you to:

i) advance the date to February 1.

j) reverse the appropriate accruals on February 1.

7 ➤ If required, print **Journal Entries-All** for the **February reversing entries** above.

Challenge Exercise 10 C10-2 (Chapters 9-10), City Gravel

Month-End Procedures Review

This exercise is a review of month-end procedures and year-end procedures.

1 ➤   Refer to Exercise 1-1 to unzip the **10 C10-2 Gravel.exe** file.

2 ➤   Open the **10 C10-2 Gravel** file.

3 ➤   Record the following December 31, month-end adjustments for City Gravel, a company that provides various types of gravel to construction companies. City Gravel uses the COMPANY, PAYABLES and RECEIVABLES modules and does not use the Account Reconciliation journal.

     a.   Bank service charges for the month are estimated to be $37.90.

     b.   The Prepaid insurance account balance represents 3 months insurance that has not been used as of December 1. Adjust the account accordingly.

     c.   The value of the Office Supplies on hand was counted, and is $266.00.

     d.   Amortization of Equipment is estimated at $8,760.00 for the year and has been recorded for 11 months.

     e.   Amortization of Office Furniture is estimated at $3,120.00 for the year and has been recorded for 11 months.

     f.   The manager forgot to create an invoice for 40 cubic yards of gravel at $80.00 per cubic yard plus HST, to a new customer, Your Name Builders, a mall builder. Your actual first and last name must appear as a customer, credit limit $8,000.00. Address is not important. Create an invoice for this customer dated December 31, with credit terms 2/10 net 30 days.

     g.   The long-term bank loan arranged on December 31, 2011 with the Bank of Montreal is for a 5-year period at an interest rate at 8% (per annum). Monthly payments of $325.00 are due at the end of each month. The December 31, automatic bank payment of $325.00, which has not been recorded in our records, includes interest of $80.00.

     h.   Keith Barrett is a part-time employee. The manager made an error in Mr. Barrett's time sheet and Mr. Barrett was underpaid by $58.00 for the period ending December 31. City Gravel charges all salaries and wages to Pit Crew Wages Expense #5310. The $58.00 will be paid with the next paycheque. Accrue the wages for the December period (ignore CPP and EI).

     i.   The previous ending inventory adjustment of $101,500.00 was made on November 30.

     j.   The inventory was counted today (December 31) after the close of business, and the INVENTORY amount is $89,325.00.

4 ➤   Print **Journal Entries-All** for the entries above.

5 ➤   Print a **Trial Balance** as at December 31.

6 ➤   **Back up** your data before moving on.

Your instructor may require you to:

     k)   Advance the date to January 2, (business closed for New Years).
     l)   Reverse the appropriate accruals on January 2, and set up the required inventory value.

7 ➤   If required, print Journal Entries-All for the January reversing entries above.

Chapter 11

DIVISION* Module
Setup and Transactions

HotTubs Company Ltd.

Learning Objectives

After completing this chapter you will be able to:

☐ Set up a company's Division Title name.
☐ Set up a company's Individual Division names.
☐ Record regular transactions and allocate revenues and costs to individual Divisions.
☐ Record regular transactions and Adjust Inventory and Cost of Sales with allocations to individual Divisions.
☐ Display and print appropriate Division reports and journals.

*The name of the DIVISION module can also be called Projects, Job Sites, Crops, Properties, etc., depending on the type of business you operate.

This chapter reviews the setup of the Simply DIVISION module, and then provides practice on transaction processing using **HotTubs Company** to record related transactions for a month using the COMPANY, RECEIVABLES, PAYABLES, EMPLOYEES & PAYROLL and DIVISION modules.

The contents of this chapter are as follows:

- The DIVISION Module 522
- HotTubs Company: Profile.. 522
- Financial Reports and Other Information................................... 523
- Setting Up the DIVISION Module 525
  Step 1: To Display the DIVISION Module..................................... 525
    Exercise 11-1 – Setting Up a Division 525
  Step 2: To Set Up Division Settings 525
    Exercise 11-2 – Setting Up Division Settings 525
  Step 3: To Set Up a Division Name/Balance Forward.................... 527
  Step 4: To Enter Other Divisions 528
- Processing Transactions in the DIVISION Module 528
    Exercise 11-3 – Processing Transactions 529
    Exercise 11-4 – To Allocate a Purchase to a Division(s)............. 531
    Exercise 11-5 – To Allocate Cash Sales to a Division(s) 534
    Exercise 11-6 – To Allocate Payroll to a Division(s).................. 536
    Exercise 11-7 – To Allocate Credit Sales to a Division(s) 539
    Exercise 11-8 – To Allocate Sales Returns to a Division(s)........ 540
- Correcting DIVISION Errors 541
    Exercise 11-9 – To Record Payroll Accrual to a Division(s)........ 542
    Exercise 11-10 – To Adjust INVENTORY and Cost of Sales 544
    Exercise 11-11 – To Print DIVISION -Related Reports 546
- Before Moving On 548

The DIVISION Module

Division (or Projects, Job Sites, Crops, Properties, etc.) refers to a group of accounts where costs and revenues are allocated and accumulated for particular business activities. A Division is a job or activity; (e.g., building a house, assembling a computer, etc.) or a cost centre (division or department of a company, etc.).

The DIVISION module is used to record revenue and expenses including employees' wages from the PAYROLL module, and allocate them to one or more divisions. For example, you may allocate RENT, ADVERTISING, SUPPLIES, etc. to various divisions. Similarly, if a company has several salespeople and they are paid according to sales volume, the company needs to keep track of sales (and expenses) for each salesperson's territory. Each territory may be specified as a separate division or other appropriate name.

Run **Slideshow 11A – Setting Up the DIVISION Module** to get a good understanding of how the DIVISION module works before you do the practice exercises in setting the module to **ready**.

HotTubs Company: Profile

HotTubs Company has been in business for 5 years. The business sells 4 models of hot tubs, accessories, chemicals, and arranges for the installation and service of the hot tubs. The fiscal year will end on December 31, 2014.

The manager has decided to use the Simply Accounting DIVISION module to track revenues and expenses for the following divisions:

- hot tubs – all models
- all chemicals

A recent college graduate has just completed the conversion of the manual accounting records to Simply Accounting at June 30, 2014. The COMPANY, RECEIVABLES, PAYABLES and EMPLOYEES & PAYROLL modules have been set up and set to **Ready**. You will display the DIVISION module and set up the individual divisions. The manager has decided not to use the **Perpetual** inventory system (INVENTORY module) at this time, and the **Track Additional Transaction Details** is not being used.

The manager, Mrs. Shortt, would like to allocate Revenue and Expenses to the various models of hot tubs and chemicals being sold to determine the profitability of each type of hot tub in addition to the chemical sales. Each staff member was asked, as of July 2, to keep a record of the time they spend on selling each model, including talking to customers, writing up sales orders, and making sure the hot tubs are delivered and installed correctly.

Division Group Name

Mrs. Shortt has decided to use the Division group title name of **Tubs/Chemic** into which you will enter the names of six individual Divisions that will be tracked. Division revenues and expenses are tracked only from the day the DIVISION module names are set up and used.

Invoices and cheques will be prepared manually and recorded in Simply, and will not be printed by the computer program.

Financial Reports and Other Information

The following financial information is available:

Employee Details: Two employees, **Hillary Buchanan**, and **Vivian Shortt** have been set up in the PAYROLL module.

Hillary Buchanan	Wages per hour: $20.00
Vivian Shortt	Wages per hour: $25.00

The company uses a 26 pay-period system. **WSIB, EHT** and **Vacation Pay** are not shown in this chapter to make it easier to illustrate the salary allocation.

The Employment Insurance (EI) rate is: **1.4**

Accounts Payable Details

The following vendors have been set up in the company PAYABLES module. Purchase orders were issued manually to these companies and are not set up in Simply.

Acrylic Moldings Inc.	Terms: 2/10, net 30
Eco Fittings Canada Ltd.	Terms: 2/10, net 30
George Kouretsoes & Associates*	Terms: Due on Receipt
Markham Lumber	Terms: 2/10, net 30

*George Kouretsoes & Associates prepare, deliver, and install all hot tubs.

Outstanding Vendor Invoices:

Acrylic Moldings Inc.
Invoice #7530 dated: Jul 25, 2014, Amount $2,260.00, Terms 2/10, net 30.

Other Vendor:

Receiver General for Canada – used for payroll remittances.

Accounts Receivable Details

The company has received orders from the following customers:

Carol's Bed & Breakfast	Terms: 2/10, net 30
Mrs. Faygie Noble	Terms: net 3 days

Outstanding Sales Invoices:

Carol's Bed & Breakfast
Invoice #640 dated Jul 30, 2014, amount $5,650.00, Terms 2/10, net 30.

The majority of the transactions in this chapter will affect accounts that have been shaded in Fig. 11-1.

HotTubs Company Ltd., Student's Name Trial Balance As At Jul 31, 2014	*Debits*	*Credits*
1020 Bank Account	21,000.00	-
1200 Accounts Receivable	5,650.00	-
1310 Inventory-Bases	2,200.00	-
1320 Inventory-Fittings	870.00	-
1330 Inventory-Wood Skirts	1,050.00	-
1350 Inventory-Chemicals	8,500.00	-
1370 Display Hot tub-models	12,770.00	-
1380 Prepaid Store Supplies, etc.	250.00	-
1510 Display Fixtures/Cabinets	22,800.00	-
1515 Accum. Amort. Display Fixtures/Cabi	-	6,600.00
1520 Office, Warehouse Furniture	24,200.00	-
1525 Accum. Amort. Office/Ware Equipment	-	6,672.00
2200 Accounts Payable	-	2,260.00
2205 Payroll Accrual	-	0.00
2220 EI Payable	-	181.66
2225 CPP Payable	-	163.55
2230 Income Tax Payable	-	873.98
2650 HST Charged on Sales	-	3,084.00
2670 HST Paid On Purchases/Services	2,010.00	-
3100 Common Stock	-	1,000.00
3201 Retained Earnings	-	49,245.81
3230 Dividends Declared	2,000.00	-
4100 Sales-Hot tubs	-	216,800.00
4110 Sales-Hot tubs Allowances	400.00	-
4200 Sales-Chemicals	-	8,620.00
4210 Sales Returns-Chemicals	100.00	-
4310 Sales - Discount	1,200.00	-
5010 Cost Of Sales-Bases	48,870.00	-
5020 Cost Of Sales-Fittings	13,032.00	-
5030 Cost Of Sales-Wood Skirts	18,462.00	-
5040 Cost Of Sales-Outside Labour	28,236.00	-
5060 Cost Of Sales-Chemicals	4,310.00	-
5070 Purchase Discounts	-	1,412.00
5310 Wages Expense	28,000.00	-
5320 EI Expense	1,124.00	-
5330 CPP Expense	840.00	-
5410 Advertising Expense	22,090.00	-
5420 Bank Charges & Interest	620.00	-
5430 Insurance Expense	11,400.00	-
5450 Credit Card Expense	3,535.00	-
5540 Office/Warehouse Supplies Expense	2,850.00	-
5550 Telephone Expense	1,109.00	-
5560 Utility Expense	825.00	-
5570 Truck Expenses-gas, repairs	1,810.00	-
5580 Truck Lease Expense	2,700.00	-
5590 Legal Expense	2,100.00	-
5600 Amortization Expense – All	0.00	-
	296,913.00	296,913.00

Fig. 11-1: HotTubs Trial Balance.

Starting Simply Accounting

1 ➤ Refer to Exercise 1-1, to unzip the **11 HotTubs** file.

2 ➤ Open the **11 HotTubs** data file.

3 ➤ Advance the Session Date to **Aug 01 2014**. The HotTubs home window is displayed. Remember to **add your name** to the Company Name.

Setting up the DIVISION Module

The following exercises will show you how to use the DIVISION module. To get the DIVISION module to work, you need to go through the following steps:

- Display the DIVISION module
- Set up the DIVISION module settings
- Set up the Division Title Name default
- Set up the Division Names
- Enter the Balance Forward

You will then be ready to process transactions allocating expenses/revenues and/or payroll to the specific Divisions.

Step 1: To Display the DIVISION module

Exercise 11-1 – Setting Up a DIVISION

1 ➤ From the top menu, click **Setup, User Preferences, View**, at **Pages** click the **DIVISION** box (2 ✓appear), **OK**.

The DIVISIONS module now displays and is available to modify.

Step 2: To Set Up DIVISION Settings

The following steps refer to setting up the default DIVISION module settings.

Exercise 11-2 – Setting Up DIVISION Settings

1 ➤ From the top menu click **Setup**, **Settings**, in the left pane click the **+** at Division. Click **Names**.

The Project Title determines the title of the icon and the Division window.

Project Title: | Tubs/Chemic |

2 ➤ **Project Title:** Change to ⌊_____⌋.

Do not change the Title field names.

3 ➤ In the left pane, click on **Budget**.

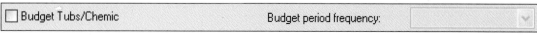

☐ Budget Tubs/Chemic   Budget period frequency: ⌄

Fig. 11-2a: Budget Settings window.

Budget: DO NOT CHANGE. Management has decided to defer (hold off) the budget process until they have a new financial plan in place.

Allocation

4 ➤ In the left pane, click on **Allocation**, and select the options shown in Fig. 11-2b.

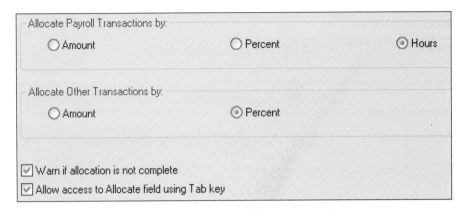

Fig. 11-2b: Allocation Settings window.

Allocate refers to the way that expenses and revenues are divided (split) among divisions. The allocation could be a set amount, an amount based on a percentage, or by employee hours.

Allocate Payroll Transactions by	The default setting for distributions is by Percent rather than by Hours. HotTubs' management has decided to distribute payroll by **hours** spent on each model and chemical sales. Employee hours are averaged to the nearest one-quarter (.25) of an hour.
Allocate Other Transactions by	DO NOT CHANGE.
Warn if allocation is not complete	The box should be ✓ so that if an amount is not fully distributed, a warning message will appear.
Allow access to Allocate field using the Tab key	The box should be ✓ to allow you to tab to the Allocate field, instead of using the mouse.

5 ➤ Click **OK** to accept the changes. You will see the following window.

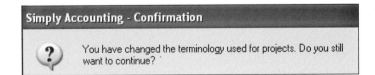

6 ➤ The term 'Projects' is a default term and cannot be changed in this window. Click **Yes** to continue and return to the Home window.

The module column now displays the new name Tubs/Chemic.

Step 3: To Set Up a Division Name/Balance Forward

Division Names are the names of the individual divisions within the **Division Title**.

Tubs/Chemic

1 ➤ From the Home window, click the **Tubs/Chemic** icon to display the Tubs/Chemic window; click the **Create** icon and enter the information as shown in Fig. 11-3.

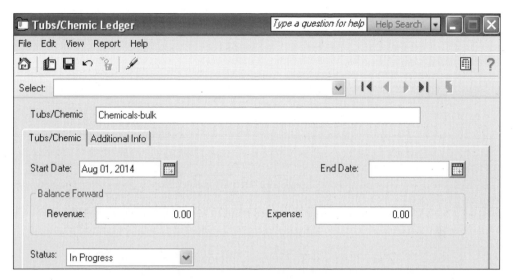

Fig. 11-3: Tubs/Chemic Ledger.

Tubs/Chemic	This field will contain the name of the particular division, project, job, or department for which you want revenues and expenses tracked.
Start Date	This field will contain the date the Division is expected to start.
End Date	This field will contain the date the Division is expected to end.
Balance Forward	These fields (Revenue and Expense) record Division values that are being converted (moved) to Simply.

You could enter Division revenue and expense totals brought forward from the previous year or previous accounting system. However, in the case of HotTubs Company Ltd., the staff does not have any records of their time before this date, and sales and expenses were not allocated to the various models or chemicals. You will, therefore, start recording division information in Simply as of Aug 01, 2014.

Status	There are 4 choices, select **In Progress**.

Pending:	Division may start in the near future.
In Progress:	Division currently in use.
Cancelled:	Division cancelled, not started.
Completed:	Division finished.

Step 4: To Enter Other Divisions

1 ➤ Click │ **Create Another** │ button to add the other division names.

2 ➤ Repeat the procedure, adding the five remaining division names (see Fig. 11-4), all with a Start Date of **Aug 01, 2014** and Status: In Progress.

	Start date	End date	Status
Chemicals-bulk	Aug 01, 2014	--	In Progress
Chemicals-individual	Aug 01, 2014	--	In Progress
HT 1.0 HP 72" x 72"	Aug 01, 2014	--	In Progress
HT 4.0 HP 84" x 84"	Aug 01, 2014	--	In Progress
HT 4.4 HP 84" Gazebo	Aug 01, 2014	--	In Progress
HT 4.6 HP 84" Enclosed	Aug 01, 2014	--	In Progress

Fig. 11-4: Division names.

3 ➤ Click │Save and Close│ to Exit to the Tubs/Chemic window.

The display window is using the **Display by Name** icon.

The codes in the names mean the following:

HT	Hot tub
1.0 HP	Power of the motor
72" x 72"	Size of hot tub

4 ➤ **Exit** to the Home window.

The ledgers in the RECEIVABLES, PAYABLES, EMPLOYEES & PAYROLL and COMPANY modules were previously set to **Ready**.

The DIVISION module is automatically set to **Ready**.

Slideshow 11B – Processing Transactions in the DIVISION Module helps you do the various allocations in the DIVISION module. Run it now.

Processing Transactions in the DIVISION Module

You are now able to process transactions in the DIVISION module.

HotTubs Company Ltd. does not use **perpetual** inventory records; however, they use individual general ledger accounts (#1310 -1350) to record purchases of goods to be made into complete hot tubs and chemical purchases. The inventory accounts are adjusted periodically to update the cost of sales accounts (#5010-5060) for goods sold.

There are two ways to record Sales Quotes and Sales Orders using Simply.

1. Click the RECEIVABLES module, click on Sales Quotes or Sales Orders and continue.

2. Click the TUBS/CHEMIC module, click Sales Invoices, at Transaction, click ▼ select the appropriate journal and continue.

Exercise 11-3 – Processing Transactions

1 ➤ **Record** the following transaction using either method.

Aug 01, 2014 Mrs. Vivian Shortt sent you a memo to issue Sales Order #423 ($36,232.78) to a new customer, Radisser Hotels Inc., contact Alvina Cassiani, 3890 Glen Erin Street, Mississauga, Ontario, L6X 3B9, phone number 905 841-3363, Revenue Account 4100, Standard Discount 5%, due to the value of order. Terms 2/10, net 30, Tax Code HS, Credit Limit $40,000. The tubs are to be installed and working by Monday, August 18. The Sold by field cannot be used in this order, as both Mrs. Shortt and Mrs. Buchanan worked together on this order.

Order	Description	Price
1	HT 1.0 HP 72" x 72"	$4,630.00 each, less 5% discount plus HST
4	HT 4.0 HP 84" x 84"	$5,580.00 each, less 5% discount plus HST
1	HT 4.4 HP 84" Gazebo	$6,802.00 each, less 5% discount plus HST

You cannot allocate a sales or purchase order. You will allocate the sales invoice as shown in Exercise 11-4.

The *Salesperson* field will not be used on individual sales invoices, or sales orders.

There are two ways to record Purchase Quotes and Purchase Orders using Simply.

1. Click the PAYABLES module, click on Purchase Quotes or Purchase Orders and continue.

2. Click the TUBS/CHEMIC module, click Purchase Invoices, at Transaction, click ▼ select the appropriate journal and continue.

1 ➤ **Record** the following transactions using either method.

Aug 01, 2014 Issued Purchase Order #28 to Acrylic Mouldings Inc. to buy:

Order	Description	Price
10	Acrylic base #10	$1,000.00 each plus HST
16	Acrylic base #12	$1,200.00 each plus HST
14	Acrylic base #15	$1,500.00 each plus HST

Terms 2/10, net 30. Total PO amount including HST was $56,726.00. Shipping date was noted as Aug 27, 2014. They will be able to ship 12 various mouldings on Aug 05, 2014 as these are currently in stock, and the rest will be available on Aug 27, 2014.

The Moldings will be put into (charged to) Asset #1310 INVENTORY-BASES. As the hot tubs are completed and sold (fittings and parts installed), the bases will be allocated to the various Divisions. This entry does not use revenue or expense accounts, and would not be recorded as a Tubs/Chemic entry.

Aug 01, 2014   Issued Purchase Order #29 to Eco Fittings Canada Ltd. to buy sets of brass and plastic fittings.

Order	Description	Price
10 sets	Fittings package #3	$350.00 each plus HST
16 sets	Fittings package #5	$320.00 each plus HST
16 sets	Fittings package #11	$400.00 each plus HST

Terms 2/10, net 30. Total PO amount including HST was $16,972.60. Shipping date Aug 05, 2014.

The fittings will be put into (charged to) Asset #1320 INVENTORY-FITTINGS. As the hot tubs are completed and sold, the fittings will be allocated to the various hot tub Divisions. This entry does not use revenue or expense accounts and would not be recorded as a Tubs/Chemic entry.

Aug 01, 2014   Issued Purchase Order #30 to Markham Lumber to buy 4 skids of various wood products, to make 20 sets of wood skirts for the various hot tubs being produced. (Note: some hot tubs are enclosed in ceramic tile and do not require wood skirts.) Each skid costs $1,200.00 plus HST. Total PO amount including HST is $5,424.00.Terms 2/10, net 30. Shipping date Aug 05, 2014.

The wood products will be put into (charged to) Asset #1330 INVENTORY-WOOD SKIRTS. As the hot tubs are completed and sold, the wood will be allocated to the various hot tub Divisions. This entry does not use revenue or expense accounts, and would not be recorded as a Tubs/Chemic Division entry.

Aug 01, 2014   Issue cheque today, to arrive by due date August 04, to pay Acrylic Moldings Inc. for Invoice #7530.

---

1 ➤ Advance Session date to **Aug 05, 2014**.

2 ➤ **Record** and **post** the following transactions:

Aug 05, 2014   Received the complete order from PO #29, in good condition, from Eco Fittings Canada Ltd. on Invoice #36781, dated today, $16,972.60.

This entry does not use revenue or expense accounts, and would not be recorded as a Tubs/Chemic entry.

> **Aug 05, 2014** Received partial order from PO #28 issued to Acrylic
> Mouldings Inc., Invoice #34218, total $16,611.00, terms are
> 2/10 net 30.
>
> | Quantity | Description | Price |
> |---|---|---|
> | 3 | Acrylic base #10 | $1,000.00, plus HST |
> | 6 | Acrylic base #12 | $1,200.00, plus HST |
> | 3 | Acrylic base #15 | $1,500.00, plus HST |

This entry does not use revenue or expense accounts, and would not be recorded
as a Tubs/Chemic entry.

> **Aug 05, 2010** Received invoice #6568 from Markham Lumber with a total
> of $5,424.00 for wood products ordered on PO #30.

This entry does not use revenue or expense accounts, and would not be recorded
as a Tubs/Chemic entry.

Allocating a Purchase to a Division(s)

HotTubs does not charge all expenses or revenues to Divisions. Only expenses and
revenues directly related to hot tubs or chemical sales are charged to Divisions.
However, some companies allocate all revenue and expense accounts to Divisions.
This procedure ensures that all expense and revenue items are accounted for,
resulting in much better cost control. When Division costs and revenues are totaled,
the totals match the corresponding revenue and expense accounts on the Income
Statement.

1 ➤ Advance the Session date to **Aug 08, 2014**.

Exercise 11-4 – To Allocate a Purchase to a Division(s)

To allocate a purchase to various Divisions means to divide the purchase price
among various Divisions.

> **Aug 08, 2014** Paid George Kouretsoes & Associates $800.00 plus HST,
> re their invoice #465 for installing some of the fittings in
> the tubs and preparing the wood skirts. Terms: Payment
> upon receipt. Per instructions, his invoice allocated 32
> hours as follows:
>
> | | |
> |---|---|
> | HT 1.0 HP 72" x 72" | 12.5% |
> | HT 4.0 HP 84" x 84" | 66.5% |
> | HT 4.4 HP 84" Gazebo | 21.0% |

To allocate this vendor invoice to the Tubs Divisions follow these instructions:

1 ➤ Click the **Payments** icon.

2 ➤ **Pay Purchase**   Click ▼ select **Make Other Payment**.
      Invoices

3 ➤ **To the**   Select **George Kouretsoes & Associates**, [Tab].
    Order of

   Acct.   The default account **5040 Cost of Sales-Outside Labour**
                        is shown. This account is used to record all work done by
                        non-employees; i.e., businesses or individuals hired to
                        work on the hot tubs but who are not employees. If you
                        want a different account, double-click the account shown
                        and select an account from the list.

4 ➤ **Description**   Type **Time spent on Hot Tubs**, [Tab].

5 ➤ **Amount**   Type **800.00**, [Tab].

6 ➤ **Tax**   [Tab] to accept code HS.

7 ➤ **HST**   [Tab] to accept **40.00**.

8 ➤ **Allo**   Click the **Allo** column to display the **Tubs/Chemic
                        Allocation - Payments Journal** window or click the
                        allocate icon ✓ on the toolbar.

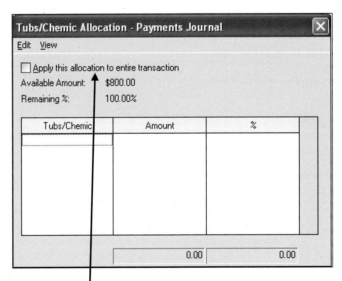

On the top left of window is the **$800.00** amount to be allocated.

☐ Apply this allocation to entire transaction   The box would be ✓ if there was more than 1
item on the sales or purchase invoice with the same % to be allocated. This will be
shown in Exercise 11-5.

9 ➤ **Tubs/Chemic**   Press [Enter] to display the chemical and hot tubs Divisions.

                        Select **HT 1.0 HP 72" x 72"**, the cursor jumps to the %
                        column with an amount of 100%.

10 ➤ **%**   Change the 100% to **12.5**. (This represents 12.5% of
                        George Kouretsoes & Associates' time spent on

                        preparing this model for sale.) Press [Tab]. The Amount
                        field changes to $100.00; the cursor moves to the next
                        line. Note at top that the Remaining % changes to
                        87.50%.

11 ➤ **Tubs/Chemic** Press **Enter**, then select **HT 4.0 HP 84" x 84"**. Change the % to **66.5,** [Tab].

12 ➤ **Tubs/Chemic** Press **Enter**, then select **HT 4.4 HP 84" Gazebo,** [Tab] to accept **21.00%**.

The Tubs/Chemic Allocation-Payments Journal window should appear as follows:

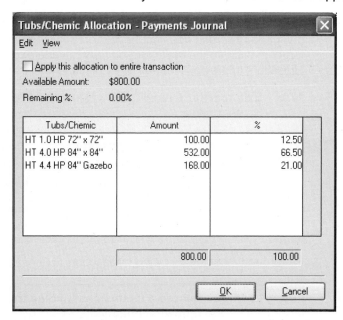

13 ➤ The Amount column Total should be **800.00** and the % column should be **100%**. The Remaining % to be allocated is 0.00%, therefore, the $800.00 amount has been allocated.

Mr. Kouretsoes did not do any work on Model 4.6 HP 84" Enclosed, therefore, there is no allocation.

14 ➤ Click **OK** to accept the distribution.

The window changes back to the Payments Journal, and you will notice the **Allo** column has a ✓ indicating that the allocation has taken place.

15 ➤ **Invoice/Ref.** Type **465** [Tab]. (Invoice 465.)

The bottom portion of the Payments Journal window should resemble the following:

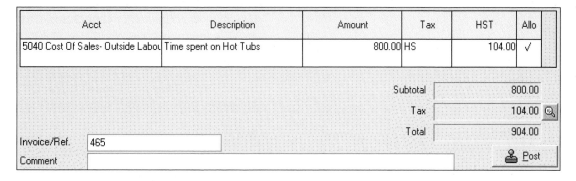

16 ➤ **Display** the Payments Journal Entry.

Payments Journal Entry Aug 08, 2014 (J5)

Account Number	Account Description	Tubs/Chemic	Debits	Credits	Tubs/Che...
2670	HST Paid On Purchases		104.00	-	
5040	Cost Of Sales- Outside Labour		800.00	-	
		- HT 1.0 HP 72" x 72"			100.00
		- HT 4.0 HP "84 x 84"			532.00
		- HT 4.4 HP 84" Gazebo			168.00
1020	Bank Account		-	904.00	
Additional Date:	Additional Field:				
			904.00	904.00	

If your entry screen does not have the Tubs/Chemic allocation on the right, you forgot to allocate the costs, or you may have to expand the window to see the allocation. In previous journal entry displays the Tubs/Chemic wording was Division.

17 ➤ **Exit** from the Journal Entry window and **Post** when correct, and **Exit** to the Home window.

Allocating Cash Sales to a Division(s)

1 ➤ Advance the Session date to **Aug 12, 2014**.

Exercise 11-5 – To Allocate Cash Sales to a Division(s)

Record and post the following transaction:

Aug 12, 2014	Record a cash sales invoice to cash customers for the following chemicals:

Ship	Unit	Description	Price	Amount	Tax
40	each	Chemicals-individual	12.75	510.00	HS
320	each	Chemicals-bulk	10.50	3,360.00	HS

Total Sales invoice amount is **$4,373.10**

1 ➤ Click the **Sales Invoices** icon.

Transaction   Invoice.

2 ➤ **Payment Method** Select **Cash**, [Tab].

3 ➤ **Customer** Type **Various Cash Customers**, [Tab], select **Full Add** to add the name to the file, click the **Options** tab, Revenue Account select **4200 Sales-Chemicals** and remove the early payment terms. The terms should all be blank. Click the **Taxes** tab. The Tax code should be **HP**. Click the **Statistics** tab. Leave the Credit Limit blank. Click **Save and Close**. [Tab]. On future cash sales, the default fields will display in the Invoice.

Invoice   #642

4 ➤ **Quantity** Type **40**, [Tab].

5 ➤ **Unit** Type **each**, [Tab].

6 ➤ **Description** Type **Chemicals-individual**, [Tab].

7 ➤	**Base Price**	Type **12.75**, `Tab` to Amount.
8 ➤	**Amount**	`Tab` to accept 510.00.
9 ➤	**Tax**	`Tab` to accept HS.
10 ➤	**Account**	`Tab` to accept 4200 Sales-Chemicals.
11 ➤	**Allo**	Press `Enter` to display the Sales Journal Allocation window.

> In step 12, you will click in the box to apply the allocation to the entire transaction, but the allocation should be separate, for each sales item. This error is to show you how this feature works. It will be corrected in step 20.

12 ➤　Click the ☑ Apply this allocation to entire transaction box.

Simply Accounting - Information

⚠ The current allocation will be applied to the entire transaction. Therefore, any allocation previously defined will be overwritten. To undo this action, un-check the checkbox.

13 ➤　Click **OK** to accept. The 100% allocation will be applied to both Sales items.

14 ➤	**Tub/Chemic**	Double-click and select **Chemicals-individual**.
15 ➤	**%**	`Tab` to accept 100.00.

16 ➤　Click **OK** to accept the allocation. A ✓ appears in the Allo column as a result of the selection made in step 12.

17 ➤　**Repeat** from step 4 to 10 to enter the Chemical-bulk sales to the invoice. A ✓ appears in the Allo column as a result of the selection.

The lower portion of the Sales window should appear as follows:

Quantity	Order	Back Order	Unit	Item Description	Base Price	Discount	Price	Amount	Tax	Account	s/Che
40			each	Chemicals-individual	12.75		12.75	510.00	HS	4200 Sales-...	Ch...
320			each	Chemicals-bulk	10.50		10.50	3,360.00	HS	4200 Sales-...	C...✓

18 ➤　**Display** the Sales Journal entry. You will see that both sales amounts have been allocated to the Chemicals-individual Division, which is not correct.

4200	Sales-Chemicals	-	3,870.00
	- Chemicals-individual		3,870.00

> You will now enter the correct allocation Division.

19 ➤　**Exit** the entry. Click in the **Allo** column for the Chemicals-individual sales line.

20 ➤　Remove the ✓ at "apply this allocation to the entire transaction."

> **Simply Accounting - Information**
>
> The current allocation will apply only to the current entry. Any allocations previously defined for other entries will remain. To undo this change, check the checkbox.

Click **OK** to accept. Click **OK** to return to the Sales Invoice window.

21 ➤ Click the **Allo** column for the Chemicals-bulk sales line and **Allocate** 100% to Chemical-bulk sales.

22 ➤ Click **OK**, to return to the Sales Invoice window. You will notice that the lower portion has not changed.

23 ➤ **Display** the Sales Journal entry. The entry now allocates the sales to the two Divisions.

4200	Sales-Chemicals	-	3,870.00	
	- Chemicals-individual			510.00
	- Chemicals-bulk			3,360.00

 The ☑ Apply this allocation to entire transaction would be used only when all sales lines on an invoice apply to one division or project, etc. An example of this would be if sales invoices were prepared for each customer with individual sales items listed on the invoice that apply to one division.

24 ➤ **Exit** from the Journal window, **Post** when correct and **Exit** to the Home window.

25 ➤ Advance the Session date to **Aug 15, 2014**.

Allocating Payroll to a Division(s)

To allocate Payroll to various Divisions, you would process the allocation in the PAYROLL module. Allocation is based on hours spent by particular employees on specific Divisions.

Exercise 11-6 – To Allocate Payroll to a Division(s)

You may allocate 100% or any percentage of the payroll to a specific Division(s) (see step 12).

In this exercise you will be allocating payroll costs using the PAYROLL module.

Aug 15, 2014	**Issued the company payroll, Payroll Cheque Run, based on the allocations prepared by each of the employees. Vivian and Hillary worked 80 hours each from Monday, August 1st to Friday, August 15th.**
	Hours are estimated for Friday, August 15. Allocated hours will be shown in Fig. 11-5, Payroll Run Journal.

1 ➤ From the Home window click the **EMPLOYEES & PAYROLL** module, then the **Payroll Cheque Run**.

2 ➤ **Pay Period Frequency** Click ▼ and select **26**, [Tab].

3 ➤ **Cheque Number** [Tab] to accept 863.

4 ➤ **Direct Deposit** DO NOT CHANGE. HotTubs Company Ltd. does
 Number   DD not use this feature. [Tab] to move to Pay Period
 End Date.

5 ➤ **Pay Period End Date** [Tab] **twice** to accept Aug 15, 2014.

6 ➤ **Cheque Date** [Tab] **twice** to accept Aug 15, 2014.

In the column 🖳 to the left of both employees' names, make sure a ✓ appears in
the column.

7 ➤ **Incomes** column, click on the ▦ **payroll button** for Hillary Buchanan. Click
 OK to return to the Payroll Run Journal.

 Repeat for Vivian Shortt. You will see that they both have 80.00 in the
 Regular Hours column.

8 ➤ Click **Report, Display Payroll Run Journal Entry**. The total of the
 expense account numbers 5310, 5320 and 5330 is:

 Hillary $1,711.29
 Vivian $2,140.78

 Some or all of the total expense amounts can be expensed in the
 allocation. Vivian also works on administrative duties that will not be
 allocated to a Division. The bottom total is **$3,852.07**.

9 ➤ **Exit** from the Journal entry window.

10 ➤ Select the Line for **Buchanan, Hillary** and click on the **Allo** field or click
 the ✓ on the top right corner of the window beside the printer icon.

11 ➤ **Tubs/Chemic** Below the blue shaded area, **double-click**, or press [Enter].

12 ➤ Enter the Allocation (Regular hours column) shown in Fig. 11-5.

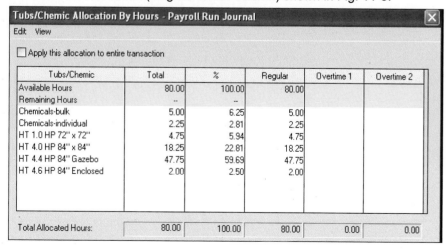

Fig. 11-5: Payroll Run Journal – Allocation for Hillary Buchanan.

13 ➤ Click **OK** when correct.

14 ➤ Click **Report, Display Payroll Run Journal Entry**.

The window portion for Hillary is shown below. Note that the entry shows the detail split of payroll expense $1,711.29 among the Tubs/Chemic Divisions.

Payroll Run Journal Entry Aug 15, 2014 (J7)					
Account Number	Account Description	Tubs/Chemic	Debits	Credits	Tubs/Che...
BUCHANAN, Hillary					
5310	Wages Expense		1,600.00	-	
		- Chemicals-bulk			100.00
		- Chemicals-individual			45.00
		- HT 1.0 HP 72" x 72"			95.00
		- HT 4.0 HP "84 x 84"			365.00
		- HT 4.4 HP 84" Gazebo			955.00
		- HT 4.6 HP 84" Enclosed			40.00
5320	EI Expense		38.75	-	
		- Chemicals-bulk			2.42
		- Chemicals-individual			1.09
		- HT 1.0 HP 72" x 72"			2.30
		- HT 4.0 HP "84 x 84"			8.84
		- HT 4.4 HP 84" Gazebo			23.13
		- HT 4.6 HP 84" Enclosed			0.97
5330	CPP Expense		72.54	-	
		- Chemicals-bulk			4.53
		- Chemicals-individual			2.04
		- HT 1.0 HP 72" x 72"			4.31
		- HT 4.0 HP "84 x 84"			16.55
		- HT 4.4 HP 84" Gazebo			43.30
		- HT 4.6 HP 84" Enclosed			1.81
1020	Bank Account		-	1,250.09	
2220	EI Payable		-	66.43	
2225	CPP Payable		-	145.08	
2230	Income Tax Payable		-	249.69	
Additional Date:	Additional Field:				
			1,711.29	1,711.29	

15 ➤ **Exit** from the window.

16 ➤ Continue with Vivian's allocation as follows; no overtime:

Chemicals-bulk	**8.00 hours**
Chemicals individual	**1.00 hours**
HT 1.0 HP 72″ x 72″	**4.75 hours**
HT 4.0 HP 84″ x 84″	**19.50 hours**
HT 4.4 HP 84″ Gazebo	<u>**38.75 hours**</u>
	72.00 hours

72 hours only are allocated to Divisions. The other 8 hours were spent on management duties and are not allocated.

17 ➤ Click **OK** to continue. A Confirmation window will appear.

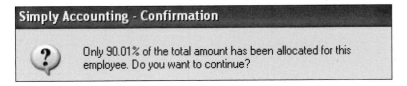

18 ➤ 72 hours divided by 80 hours equals 90.00%. Due to rounding of individual %, the allocation is 90.01% of the total. Click **Yes** to continue.

19 ➤ Display the **Payroll Run Journal Entry**. Note the bottom totals. Vivian's total expense is $2,140.78 and the total of the Debit and Credit columns is $3,852.07. Note also that there is no total for the allocated Tubs/Chemic column.

The net pay for Hillary is $1,250.09 and for Vivian is $1,494.98.

20 ➤ **Exit** from the Payroll Journal entry.

21 ➤ **Post** the **Payroll Cheque Run** entry when correct. A Confirmation window will appear.

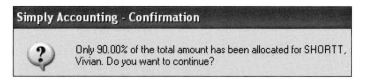

Simply Accounting - Confirmation

Only 90.00% of the total amount has been allocated for SHORTT, Vivian. Do you want to continue?

22 ➤ This confirmation % is slightly different to the step 17 confirmation % window. This is a programming error. Click **Yes** to Continue.

23 ➤ Click **Yes** to the warning message about the payroll dates needing to be between Jan 01, 2009 and Dec 31, 2009.

24 ➤ **Exit** to the Home window.

To Allocate Credit Sales to a Division(s)

Unlike allocating PAYROLL, you would allocate credit sales to a Division(s) based on percentage of the amount for each item. Simply will automatically calculate the specific amount based on the percentage you enter.

Exercise 11-7 – To Allocate Credit Sales to a Division(s)

In this exercise, you will be allocating credit sales invoices to specific Divisions, similar to what you did in Exercise 11-5 Cash Sales.

1 ➤ Advance the Session date to **Aug 18, 2014**.

Aug 18, 2014   Issue sales invoice #643 to Radisser Hotels for the hot tubs based on Sales Order #423.

---

2 ➤ As noted earlier, click the **Sales Invoices icon** in the **TUBS/CHEMIC** module.

Transaction:	**Invoice**
Paid by:	**Pay later**

3 ➤ **Order/Quote No.:**   Click the 🔍 and select **423**, ⌨Tab.

The window fills with the information from the Sales Order.

4 ➤ All items ordered have been installed and are working to the satisfaction of the Hotel Assistant Manager. Click the **Fill backordered quantities** icon.

Quantity: The fields fill with the quantities ordered. Invoice total is $36,232.78.

5 ➤ **Allo:**   Click in the **Allo** column. The Tubs/Chemic Allocation - Sales Journal window is displayed.

6 ➤ Allocate each line on the invoice 100% to the appropriate Division. Click **OK** to accept the distribution.

7 ➤ **Display** the Sales Journal Entry. It should be as follows:

Sales Journal Entry Aug 18, 2014 (J9)					
Account Number	Account Description	Tubs/Chemic	Debits	Credits	Tubs/Che...
1200	Accounts Receivable		36,232.78	-	
2650	HST Charged On Sales		-	4,168.38	
4100	Sales -Hot Tubs		-	32,064.40	
		- HT 1.0 HP 72" x 72"			4,398.50
		- HT 4.0 HP "84 x 84"			21,204.00
		- HT 4.4 HP 84" Gazebo			6,461.90
Additional Date:	Additional Field:				
			36,232.78	36,232.78	

8 ➤   **Exit** from the entry window, **Post** when correct and return to the **Home** window.

Allocating Sales Returns to a Division(s)

In Exercise 11-5 you recorded sales to various customers and allocated the sale amounts 100% to each Division. When sales are returned, the return should be allocated back to the same Division(s).

Exercise 11-8 – To Allocate Sales Returns to a Division(s)

---

1 ➤   Advance the Session date to **Aug 19, 2014**.

> **Aug 19, 2014   A cash customer, Mr. John Stammers, from the Chemicals-individual summary sales records on Aug 12, 2014, (our invoice #642) returned 2 bottles of chemicals at $12.75 each, plus HST, due to leaking containers. Vivian Shortt checked the remaining stock and found that 3 additional containers were leaking.**
>
> **The manufacturer's representative will be replacing the stock of this item.**
>
> **Total Invoice = $ -28.82**

Mr. Stammers is interested in purchasing an Ozonator accessory for his hot tub and wants to have this return credited to an account in his name. Mrs. Shortt is looking into ordering this new accessory.

Create an account for Mr. Stammers and issue a credit refund for the returned chemicals as shown in this exercise. **Do not forget to allocate the return to the Division**.

2 ➤   Click the **Sales Invoices** icon to:

- Set up a customer account.
- Issue a credit refund.

Transaction	**Invoice**.
Paid by	**Pay Later**.

3 ➤   **Customer**   Type **Mr. John Stammers**, ⌷Tab⌷, click ⌷**Full Add**⌷, record with any address information. Terms **net 10 days**, leave revenue account blank, Tax code **HS**, credit limit **$500.00** and click ⌷**Save and Close**⌷.

4 ➤   **Invoice**   Type **642Rt Cash**, ⌷Tab⌷. Click the **Quantity** column.

5 ➤   **Record** the return as shown in the next window portion:

Quantity	Order	Back Order	Unit	Item Description	Base Price	Discount	Price	Amount	Tax	Account	is/Chei
-2			each	Chemicals-individual	12.75		12.75	-25.50	HS	4210 Sales ...	✓

Subtotal:	-25.50
Freight:	✓
HST:	-3.32
Total:	-28.82

Early Payment Terms: ___% ___ Days, Net **10** Days

Message: Return accepted - leaking container

6 ➤   **Allo**:   Allocate the -25.50 return to the Division, **OK**.

7 ➤   **Display** the entry.

Sales Journal Entry Aug 19, 2014 (J10)

Account Number	Account Description	Tubs/Chemic	Debits	Credits	Tubs/Che...
2650	HST Charged On Sales		3.32	-	
4210	Sales Returns -Chemicals		25.50	-	
		- Chemicals-individual			-25.50
1200	Accounts Receivable		-	28.82	
Additional Date:	Additional Field:				
			28.82	28.82	

8 ➤   **Exit** the window, **Post** when correct and **Exit** to the Home window.

9 ➤   **Record** and **post** the following entry:

Aug 19, 2014	**Received George Kouretsoes & Associates' invoice #468 dated today for $4,300.00, plus HST for time spent on completing the fittings, delivery and installing the tubs at the Radisser Hotel. Total invoice $4,859.00. Terms: Payment upon receipt. Cheque issued. Allocation of his staff time of 172 hours is as follows:**
	HT 1.0 HP 72"x72" **12.5%**
	HT 4.0 HP 84"x84" **66.5%**
	HT 4.4 HP 84" Gazebo **21.0%**

10 ➤   Return to the **Home** window. Advance the Session date to **Aug 22, 2014**.

Correcting DIVISION Errors

It is common to make errors in allocations to Divisions. For example, the wrong Division could be selected, the wrong percentage may be used, or the Division allocation forgotten. As with other modules, to correct the error, you can reverse the entry and then enter a new transaction to record the correct entry, or you can make an adjusting entry to correct the item(s) that need correcting.

The reversal should be made in the originating module (TUBS/CHEMIC, RECEIVABLES, PAYABLES, or EMPLOYEES & PAYROLL). The reversal must be the exact original amount. As mentioned, the correction can be entered using the **Reverse** invoice icon or **Adjust** icon. The corrections are the same as those covered in previous chapters, except that the allocation must be reversed as well.

The Payroll Accrual

Although PAYROLL allocation can be allocated by hours, the PAYROLL accrual must be allocated by percent, because Simply will not allow Payroll accruals to be allocated by hours (see Fig 11-2b).

Exercise 11-9 – To Record Payroll Accrual to a Division(s)

Aug 22, 2014 **The owner has asked you to prepare a Division report as of the end of business today. The staff has prepared the information below to assist you in updating all Division records:**

Salary accrual report for five days is allocated as follows:

	Vivian Shortt Hours	Hillary Buchanan Hours	Total Hours	Total Percent
Chemicals-bulk	5.00	2.50	7.50	9.40%
Chemicals individual	3.75	4.25	8.00	10.00%
1.0 HP 72" x 72"	10.50	9.50	20.00	25.00%
4.0 HP 84" x 84"	16.75	21.75	38.50	48.10%
4.4 HP 84" Gazebo	2.00	1.25	3.25	4.00%
4.6 HP 84" Enclosed	2.00	0.75	2.75	3.50%
Totals	40.00	40.00	80.00	100.00%

	Hours	Rate	Amount
Vivian Shortt	40.00	$25.00	1,000.00
Hillary Buchanan	40.00	$20.00	800.00
			1,800.00

Fig. 11-6: Salary Accrual Report.

Follow the steps below to record the information.

1 ➤ Click the **COMPANY** module, click the **General Journal** icon.

2 ➤ Source   Type **Payroll Accrual**, ⌨Tab.

3 ➤ Comment   Type **Payroll Accrual August 16 – 22**, ⌨Tab.

4 ➤ Account   Select **5310 Wages Expense**.

5 ➤ Debits   Type **1,800.00** (40 hours at $25.00 per hour and 40 hours at $20.00 per hour). ⌨Tab.

6 ➤ Comment   Type **Payroll Accrual**, ⌨Tab.

7 ➤ Allo   Press enter or click the column at the **5310 Wages Expense** line.

8 ➤ Enter the percentages from the Salary Accrual report in Fig. 11-6 and click **OK** when complete. ⌨Tab to move to the Account column.

9 ➤ Account   Select **2205 Payroll Accrual**.

10 ➤ Credits   `Tab` to accept 1,800.00.

The payroll accrual allocation journal entry should resemble the following:

General Journal Entry Aug 22, 2014 (J12)					
Account Number	Account Description	Tubs/Chemic	Debits	Credits	Tubs/Che...
5310	Wages Expense		1,800.00	-	
	Payroll Accrual				
		- Chemicals-bulk			169.20
		- Chemicals-individual			180.00
		- HT 1.0 HP 72" x 72"			450.00
		- HT 4.0 HP 84" x 84"			865.80
		- HT 4.4 HP 84" Gazebo			72.00
		- HT 4.6 HP 84" Enclosed			63.00
2205	Payroll Accrual		-	1,800.00	
Additional Date:	Additional Field:				
			1,800.00	1,800.00	

The PAYROLL accrual, as a General Journal entry, would be allocated to Tubs/Chemic Divisions in the same manner as when the payroll cheques are issued. The payroll accrual does not normally record EI and CPP Expense, because they are expensed only when actually paid.

11 ➤ Post when correct and return to the Home window.

> The payroll accrual, including the allocation, would be reversed before the next actual paycheques are issued. This will allow the cheque entry for actual pay on August 29 to be allocated without being adjusted for accruals.

Another Transaction

1 ➤ Record and **post** the transaction that follows.

Aug 22, 2014	Made the following cash sales from Aug 13, 2014 to Aug 22, 2014.

Do not forget to allocate the sales to the corresponding divisions!

Quantity	Unit	Description	Price	Amount	Tax	Total
23	each	Chemicals-bulk	10.50	241.50	HST	
251	each	Chemicals-individual	12.75	3,200.25	HST	

Total cash sales   **$3,889.18**

Adjusting INVENTORY and Cost of Sales

As discussed in Chapter 3B, the dollar value of goods on hand inventory (e.g., bases, fittings, wood skirts and chemicals) at the end of a period should be adjusted (reduced) to show the actual cost of material used during the month. The corresponding adjustment (increase) is shown in the Cost of Goods Sold during the period.

Exercise 11-10 – To Adjust INVENTORY and Cost of Sales

The INVENTORY of all materials on hand was counted and verified to determine the actual cost of all products sold. Following are the costs of all items (Debit column) which would have been included in the cost of installing the fittings, wood skirts, delivering the tubs to the locations and all installation work, including electrical wiring and plumbing work.

Fittings and wood that were damaged during installation, and cannot be repaired, are recycled because they cannot be reused or sold.

1 ➤ **Journalize** a **General Journal entry** as shown in Fig. 11-7 and from the Cost and Allocation Schedule % amounts, shown in Fig. 11-8.

Source	Memo VS		Date	Aug 22, 2014	
Comment	Inventory cost per schedule				

Account	Debits	Credits	Comment	Allo
5010 Cost Of Sales-Base	7,300.00	--	Cost per Schedule	✓
5020 Cost Of Sales-Fittin	2,330.00	--	Cost per Schedule	✓
5030 Cost Of Sales-Woc	2,750.00	--	Cost per Schedule	✓
5060 Cost of Sales-Chen	2,107.00	--	Cost per Schedule	✓
1310 Inventory-Bases	--	7,300.00	Cost per Schedule	
1320 Inventory-Fittings	--	2,330.00	Cost per Schedule	
1330 Inventory-Wood Sk	--	2,750.00	Cost per Schedule	
1350 Inventory-Chemica	--	2,107.00	Cost per Schedule	
	--	--		
Total	14,487.00	14,487.00		

Fig. 11-7: General Journal – Inventory.

2 ➤ **Allocate** the following costs to the appropriate Cost of Sales expense account.

All amounts are rounded to nearest dollar in this schedule. When you enter the percentage in the Allocation schedule, the individual amounts will be out less than $1.00.

	Costs Used	HT 1.0	HT 4.0	HT 4.4	HT 4.6	Chemicals Bulk	Individual
Bases Allocation %	$7,300.00	$1,000.00 **13.7%**	$4,803.00 **65.8%**	$1,497.00 **20.5%**	-----	----	----
Fittings Allocation %	$2,330.00	$ 303.00 **13.0%**	$1,545.00 **66.3%**	$482.00 **20.7%**	-----	-----	-----
Wood Skirts Allocation %	$2,750.00	$ 349.00 **12.7%**	$1,801.00 **65.5%**	$600.00 **21.8%**	-----	-----	-----
Chemicals Allocation %	$2,107.00		-----	-----	-----	$1,780.00 **84.5%**	$327.00 **15.5%**

Fig.11-8: Cost and Allocation Schedule.

3 ➤ View the General Journal Entry and compare with Fig. 11-9:

General Journal Entry Aug 22, 2014 (J14)

Account Number	Account Description	Tubs/Chemic	Debits	Credits	Tubs/Che...
5010	Cost Of Sales-Bases Cost per Schedule		7,300.00	-	
		- HT 1.0 HP 72" x 72"			1,000.10
		- HT 4.0 HP 84" x 84"			4,803.40
		- HT 4.4 HP 84" Gazebo			1,496.50
5020	Cost Of Sales-Fittings Cost per Schedule		2,330.00	-	
		- HT 1.0 HP 72" x 72"			302.90
		- HT 4.0 HP 84" x 84"			1,544.79
		- HT 4.4 HP 84" Gazebo			482.31
5030	Cost Of Sales-Wood Skirts Cost per Schedule		2,750.00	-	
		- HT 1.0 HP 72" x 72"			349.25
		- HT 4.0 HP 84" x 84"			1,801.25
		- HT 4.4 HP 84" Gazebo			599.50
5060	Cost of Sales-Chemicals Cost per Schedule		2,107.00	-	
		- Chemicals-bulk			1,780.41
		- Chemicals-individual			326.59
1310	Inventory-Bases Cost per Schedule		-	7,300.00	
1320	Inventory-Fittings Cost per Schedule		-	2,330.00	
1330	Inventory-Wood Skirts Cost per Schedule		-	2,750.00	
1350	Inventory-Chemicals Cost per Schedule		-	2,107.00	
Additional Date:	Additional Field:				
			14,487.00	14,487.00	

Fig. 11-9: Inventory Journal entry.

This entry would be recorded on a monthly basis, therefore, it could be set up as a recurring transaction. There is no need to set a recurring entry in this Division, but you should be aware that it could be done.

4 ➤ Exit from the window and **post** when correct.

After the previous entry is posted, the values (at August 22) of the following accounts should be:

1310 Inventory-Bases	$ 9,600.00
1320 Inventory-Fittings	$13,560.00
1330 Inventory-Wood Skirts	$ 3,100.00
1350 Inventory-Chemicals	$ 6,393.00

Printing Month-End DIVISION Reports

There are no other transactions to be recorded for this exercise. Reports should be printed as part of the normal month-end procedures.

Exercise 11-11 – To Print DIVISION-Related Reports

1 ➤ From the Home window, click **Reports**, move to **Tubs/Chemic**, select **Income** to display the Tubs/Chemic Income Report Options window.

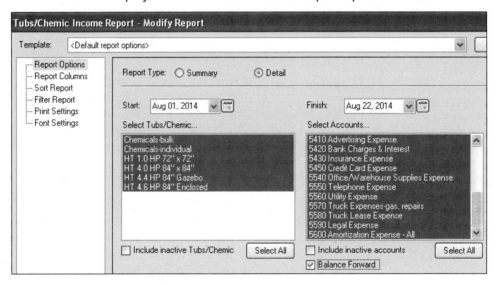

Fig. 11-10: Tubs/Chemic Income Report window.

The Tubs/Chemic Income Reports are based upon Revenue and Expense accounts only, and the divisions can be selected for display.

2 ➤ Select the options as shown in Fig 11-10. (**Detail**, **Start** and **Finish** dates.)

3 ➤ **Select Tubs/Chemic**   If the division names are not blue, click **Select All**. They turn blue.

4 ➤ **Select Accounts**   If the account names (Revenue and Expense accounts) are not blue, click **Select All**. They turn blue.

Note: The report may be printed for one or more revenue or expense accounts.

5 ➤ **Balance Forward**   Check ✓ the ☐, **OK**. This will produce a complete Income Statement for each HotTubs Division with the balance forward from previous periods. The balance forward amount is 0.00 since we have no previous period information.

6 ➤ Maximize the report to fill the screen.

Depending on the size of the font used, the report may be six or more pages long. Smaller fonts may allow one Division on each page. Notice the details for expenses shown in the report.

7 ➤ You may want to print only one or two Division reports. This will show you the detail available in the reports. **Repeat** the procedure above and choose any individual Division report(s) that you would like to see.

8 ➤ Click **File, Print** to print the Division reports you requested.

The **Summary** report, like a financial statement, will show the balance of each Revenue and Expense account only. If you need more detail, you can drill down to the line or lines on which you need more detail, or you could print the complete **Detail** report.

Journal Entries

1 ➤ Print **Journal Entries-All** transactions for the period **Aug 01, 2014** to **Aug 22, 2014**.

Don't forget to ✓ ☑ Tubs/Chemic Allocations in the Modify Report Options. If you forget, the **Division Distributions** detail will not print on the report.

This report in default mode will print over 6 pages. You could print the report over 3 pages, by resizing the column widths. You could also print the report in Landscape format, but you will have to remember to change it back to Portrait for the other reports, otherwise all reports will print in Landscape mode.

Income Statement

2 ➤ Print the Income Statement for the period **Aug 01, 2014** to **Aug 22, 2014**.

The Income Statement cannot be printed with Division detail.

Balance Sheet

3 ➤ **Print** the Balance Sheet for **Aug 22, 2014**.

4 ➤ **Compare** the Inventory accounts to the amounts suggested in Exercise 11-10.

5 ➤ **Compare** your printouts to those in the instructor's Solutions Manual.

Review **Slideshows 11A** and **11B** before proceeding.

Before Moving On...

Read the following questions and make sure you know the answers to them; otherwise, read the corresponding part in the chapter before moving on.

1. Explain briefly the use of the Simply DIVISION module.

2. Explain briefly how the RECEIVABLES, PAYABLES, and EMPLOYEES & PAYROLL modules may be used effectively with the DIVISION module in producing a detailed picture of a company's financial position.

3. What two options are available for allocation of the dollar value of Divisions?

4. Why would most companies that use the Simply DIVISION module allocate 100% of revenues and expenses to Divisions? (To assist with this answer, compare the total of the Division reports to the Income Statement.)

5. How should you correct an error in allocating amounts to Divisions?

Chapter 12

BANKING Module
Reconciliation & Deposits

Wedding Flowers Company

Learning Objectives

After completing this chapter you will be able to:

☐ Set up the BANKING module, Reconciliation & Deposits, Linked accounts.
☐ Prepare the Reconciliation & Deposits with Outstanding Bank Items.
☐ Turn the module to Ready.
☐ Reconcile the bank account by identifying cleared items and various other items such as outstanding deposit(s) or cheque errors, etc.
☐ Display and print appropriate reports and journals.

This chapter illustrates the Simply BANKING module feature using the **Reconciliation & Deposits Journal**.

The chapter assumes you have some knowledge of bank reconciliation and the types of items that require reconciling. If you are unsure of bank reconciliation theory and procedures, refer to your accounting textbook.

Topics in this chapter include:

- Accounting and Simply Accounting Terminology 550
- Banking Codes 550
- The Reconciliation & Deposits Journal 551
- The Wedding Flowers Company 551
  - Exercise 12-1 – Setting Up the Reconciliation & Deposits Journal 553
    - To Set Up Linked Accounts 553
    - Reconciling Bank Accounts in Simply 555
    - Steps to Complete a Bank Reconciliation in Simply 556
  - Exercise 12-2 – Using the Reconciliation & Deposits Journal 556
  - Exercise 12-3 – To Clear the Unresolved by Recording the NSF Cheque . 563
  - Exercise 12-4 – To Print Reconciliation & Deposits Reports 564
  - Other Reconciliation & Deposits Features 566

- Summary 566
  - Reconciliation Errors 566

- Before Moving On 568
- Relevant Appendix 568
- Challenge Exercise 12 C12-1, China 569

The Accounting and Simply Accounting Terminology has been deliberately placed at the beginning of this chapter in order to help you better understand account (bank) reconciliation concepts and principles. Read them carefully before you proceed with the exercises.

Accounting and Simply Accounting Terminology

Bank: A basic definition used in the context of this text is: A financial institution that holds amounts of money for personal or commercial use.

Bank Reconciliation: The process of determining and processing the differences in the company bank account(s) as shown in the company's records, and the balance as shown on the bank statement.

Canceled Cheque: A client's cheque which has been cashed by the bank and deducted from the customer's bank account.

Cash: In business terms this refers to actual cash, cheque or credit card payment.

NSF: **N**ot **S**ufficient **F**unds. The customer did not have enough money in the bank account to allow the bank to pay the cheque.

Outstanding cheque: Cheque issued by the company and recorded in the General Ledger, but has not been cashed by the bank by the statement date.

Outstanding deposits: Deposits recorded in the company General Ledger that have not been deposited (credited) by the bank into the customer's account by the statement date. This could be due to a deposit being taken to the bank late during the day and the bank recording the deposit on the next day, or a deposit processed in the books but not yet taken to the bank.

Reconciliation: See *Bank Reconciliation*.

Unresolved Balance: The difference between the bank statement and the General Ledger bank account. The difference may be from bank errors or errors in processing transactions in Simply.

Banking Codes

A (Adjustment) for transactions posted as adjustments to a bank account.

C (Cleared) items (matched deposits with depositor cheques) that are recorded in your General Ledger bank account and that have been processed by the bank (on the bank statement).

D (Deposit Error) is used for deposits that are recorded in your General Ledger bank account but which differ from the bank statement. The difference must be recorded with a journal entry and assigned the Deposit Error code. When both D codes are entered, they can be cleared with the C code. The original deposit coded as a D and the error correction coded as a D can be cleared together with a C (cleared) code.

N (NSF) Means **N**ot **S**ufficient **F**unds. Cheques returned by the bank to the depositor when there is not enough money in the customer's bank account.

P (Payment Error) is used for cheques that are recorded in your General Ledger bank account but which differ from the bank statement. The difference must be recorded with a journal entry and assigned the Payment Error code. When both P codes are entered, they can be cleared with the C code. The original cheque, coded as a P, and the error correction, coded as a P, can be cleared together with a C (Cleared) code.

R (Reversed) When a cheque is received by the bank as a deposit, it is entered as a credit on the depositor's bank statement. When the cheque is canceled (usually because of NSF), the entry in the depositor's bank statement is reversed, so the entry is assigned the **R** (Reversed) code. The reversing entry is normally recorded in the company's Sales Journal. A reversing entry is required and is then assigned the **A** (Adjustment) code.

V (Void) is used to identify cheques that were canceled because they were issued incorrectly. A reversing entry is required and is then assigned the **A** (Adjustment) code.

Slideshow 12 – **BANKING-Reconciliation & Deposits** is designed to help you relate the RECONCILIATION & DEPOSITS module to manual bank reconciliation. Run it before you proceed.

BANKING Module

The Reconciliation & Deposits Journal

The **Reconciliation & Deposits** journal is where all BANK (cash) transactions are tracked by the Simply program for selected bank accounts. At month-end or period-end, when the bank reconciliation is performed, the Reconciliation & Deposits Journal is used to identify items (cheques or deposits, etc.) that are not shown on the bank statements. Items on the bank statement that have not been recorded in the company files must be journalized in the Accounts RECEIVABLE, PAYABLE, or General Journal as required.

Receive Payments

This icon is the same as the RECEIVABLES module journal used to record receipts from customers. Either journal can be used. This journal is not used in this chapter.

Make Deposit

This journal can be used to record deposits which consist of a number of customer receipts. This feature is not used in this text.

Transfer Funds

This journal is used to transfer funds between different business bank accounts. This feature is not used in this text. It could have been used in Chapter 2A or 2B to transfer funds between a regular bank account and a credit card bank account.

Pay Bills ▼

This icon is the same as the PAYABLE module journal used to record payments to Vendors. Either journal can be used. This journal is not used in this chapter.

Reconcile Accounts

This journal (**Reconciliation & Deposits**) is used to reconcile bank accounts. It will be used in Exercise 12-2.

The **Wedding Flowers Company** has been preparing reconciliations manually, and now intends to use the Reconciliation & Deposits journal in Simply. The last bank reconciliation was completed for the period ending April 30, 2014.

The Reconciliation & Deposits journal must be set up before it can be used. Wedding Flowers Company is currently using the COMPANY, RECEIVABLES, and PAYABLES modules, and all transactions have been recorded up to May 31, 2014.

The Wedding Flowers Company

The company records include cheque and deposit information from May 1, 2014 to May 31, 2014. You will now use the Reconciliation & Deposits journal to perform a reconciliation between the CASH IN BANK account 1060 and the May 31 bank statement.

It would be helpful for you to do a manual bank reconciliation before attempting to use the Simply BANKING module. This will enable you to understand what you are processing in the Reconciliation & Deposits journal.

You will use the following to complete a manual bank reconciliation: Fig. 12-1, Fig. 12-2 and Fig. 12-5.

General Ledger Report May 01, 2014 to May 31, 2014
Sorted by: Transaction Number

Date	Comment	Source #	JE#	Debits	Credits	Balance
1060	**Cash in Bank**					1,185.00 Dr
May 02, 20...	Etobicoke Newspaper	623	J1	-	113.00	1,072.00 Dr
May 05, 20...	Dorothy Wadkins	801	J2	222.00	-	1,294.00 Dr
May 05, 20...	Receiver General for Canada	624	J3	-	885.00	409.00 Dr
May 14, 20...	Rowena's Wedding Boutique	753	J4	1,260.00	-	1,669.00 Dr
May 16, 20...	Judy Johnson, Payroll	625	J5	-	400.00	1,269.00 Dr
May 16, 20...	Etobicoke Hydro	626	J6	-	113.00	1,156.00 Dr
May 16, 20...	Better Built Builders	627	J7	-	500.00	656.00 Dr
May 19, 20...	226, Sales -cheque Shierel	342	J8	226.00	-	882.00 Dr
May 31, 20...	227, Sale Cash- Larson	Cash	J9	79.10	-	961.10 Dr
				1,787.10	2,011.00	

Fig. 12-1: Cash in Bank Report.

Fig. 12-2 shows the manual reconciliation that was completed for the April 30 bank statement. The unrecorded service charge item on the reconciliation has been recorded in the General Ledger at April 30.

Wedding Flowers Company
Bank Reconciliation at April 30, 2014

Balance per Bank Statement April 30, 2014	$ 1,185.00
Add: Outstanding Deposits	None
Less: Outstanding Cheques	None
(All previous cheques have been cashed)	
Adjusted Bank Balance	$ 1,185.00

Balance per General Ledger April 30, 2014	$ 1,203.00
Add: Interest earned on account not recorded	None
Less: Service Charges* not previously recorded	-18.00 (negative)
Adjusted Bank Balance	$ 1,185.00

Fig. 12-2: Bank Reconciliation.

*The service charges were recorded in the General Ledger before the trial balance at April 30, 2014.

The first time the Reconciliation & Deposits journal is used, you must enter background information about the **linked accounts** you want to use. This is done only once for each bank account.

Background information includes:

1. The starting and ending dates of the month(s) you want to reconcile the bank (cash) account from the General Ledger.
2. The beginning and ending dates on the bank statement that you are going to reconcile.
3. Transactions that were posted to the bank account before you started to use the Reconciliation & Deposits journal.

Setting Up the Reconciliation & Deposits Journal

You will now set up the linked accounts for the Reconciliation & Deposits journal. Follow the steps in the exercise that follows:

Exercise 12-1 – Setting Up the Reconciliation & Deposits Journal

---

1 ➤ Unzip the **12 Weddings.exe** file from www.simplyaccounting2010.nelson.com under Student Resources.

2 ➤ Start Simply and open the **12 Weddings** data file.

3 ➤ Session Date will be **May 31, 2014**.

This will allow you to enter all bank reconciliation information into **History** for the period. Simply will gather cheque and deposit information previously entered and make it available for use in the Reconciliation & Deposits journal.

To Set Up Linked Accounts

1 ➤ From the Home window, click the **COMPANY** module, click the **Chart of Accounts** icon, to display the Accounts windows.

2 ➤ Double-click **1060 Cash in Bank** to display the General Ledger window.

3 ➤ Click the **Reconciliation & Deposits** tab.

Reconciliation & Deposits

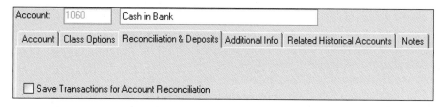

Fig. 12-3: General Ledger – Reconciliation & Deposits tab.

4 ➤ Click the **Save Transactions for Account Reconciliation** box. The **Set Up** button appears near the bottom on the right side. (See side note box.)

In the future, if you decide not to use the RECONCILIATION & DEPOSITS Journal to assist with the bank reconciliation, uncheck the **Save Transactions for Reconciliation** box. If you do not uncheck the box, the program will continue to accumulate bank data, using storage space unnecessarily.

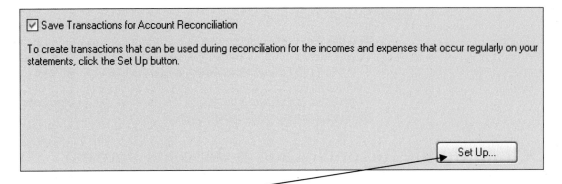

5 ➤ Click the **Set Up** button. The Account Reconciliation Linked Accounts window appears.

6 ➤ **Change** the fields to those shown in Fig. 12-4.

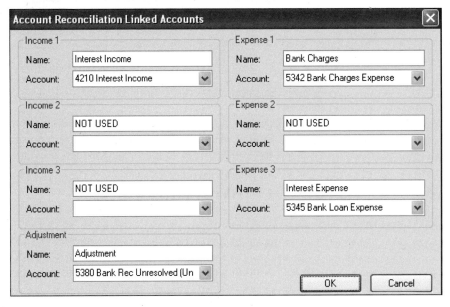

Fig. 12-4: Linked Accounts window.

Income 1 **Interest** **Income**	The accounts that appear when you click the ▾ would be in the 4000-4999 range (Revenue accounts). As a result of this selection, unrecorded Interest Income amounts identified on the Bank Statement can be posted automatically to this account number.
Adjustment **Unresolved**	The accounts that appear when you click the ▾ would be in the 4000 to 5999 range (Revenue and Expense accounts). As a result of this selection, unresolved amounts will be posted to this account. You will take steps to locate information that will allow this item to be resolved.
Expense 1 **Bank** **Charges**	The accounts that appear when you click the ▾ would be in the 5000-5999 range (Expense accounts). As a result of this selection, unrecorded bank charge amounts identified on the Bank Statement can be set to be posted automatically to this account number.

Expense 3	The accounts that appear when you click the ▼
Interest	would be in the 5000-5999 range (Expense accounts).
Expense	As a result of this selection, unrecorded bank loan interest, identified on the Bank Statement, can be posted automatically to this account.

7 ➤ Click **OK** to save the changes and return to the **General Ledger** window for account 1060.

The Reconciliation & Deposits journal default names and Linked accounts have now been set up.

A company can have several bank reconciliation accounts (i.e., U.S. dollar accounts, several local chequing accounts, etc.). However, you will be using only one bank account for bank reconciliation purposes in this chapter.

8 ➤ Click X twice to return to the **Home** window.

Reconciling Bank Accounts in Simply

Simply may now be used for bank reconciliation. The next reconciliation date is May 31, 2014. The May 31, 2014 bank statement is received and the reconciliation can be completed.

Commercial Bank of Canada
1234 Main Street Toronto, Ontario L5X 2Y9

Wedding Flowers Company
3896 Athol Street
Whitby, ON L1M 6U2

Account Number: 256-589-4   May 31, 2014

(OD = Overdrawn)

Date	Information	Cheques	Deposits	Balance
May 01	Balance Forward			1,185.00
May 04	Cheque 623	113.00		1,072.00
May 05	Deposit		222.00	1,294.00
May 14	Cheque 624	885.00		409.00
May 14	Deposit		1,260.00	1,669.00
May 16	Cheque 625	400.00		1,269.00
May 19	NSF item	1,260.00		9.00
May 20	Cheque 626	113.00		-104.00 OD
May 27	Deposit Interest		1.40	-102.60 OD
May 28	Service Charge	10.00		-112.60 OD
May 28	Loan Interest	100.00		-212.60 OD

Fig. 12-5: Bank Statement. (See side note box.)

ℹ **OD** means Overdrawn or Overdraft. May 28 service charge is for Overdraft protection.

Before attempting the Simply Reconciliation & Deposits for the first time, prepare a manual reconciliation first. This will help you understand what you are updating in the Reconciliation & Deposits journal.

Steps to Complete a Bank Reconciliation in Simply

There are five basic steps in completing a bank reconciliation in Simply:

1. Compare the deposits and withdrawals on the bank statement to the debits and credits (General Ledger bank account transactions) that are processed by Simply in *rows*. Enter the appropriate codes as shown below:

C	Cleared (the two sources match)	**R**	Reverse
D	Deposit error	**V**	Void
P	Payment error	**A**	Adjustment
N	Not Sufficient Funds	**O**	Outstanding (The item is in the General Ledger but NOT on the bank statement or vice versa.)

2. Using the designated Income and Expense Fields, enter the Interest Earned and Service Charges as shown on the bank statement.

3. After displaying the bank reconciliation, the "unresolved" amount(s) if any, need to be investigated.

4. Journal entries to clear any unresolved amounts should be made. Return to the Reconciliation & Deposits process to complete the codes for the resolved items.

5. Print the General Ledger bank account to confirm that the entries have been made and the ledger amounts have been updated.

Using the Reconciliation & Deposits Journal

Exercise 12-2– Using the Reconciliation & Deposits Journal

1 ➤ Click the **BANKING** module, click **Reconcile Accounts** icon. Fill in the fields in the Reconciliation & Deposits Journal as follows:

Account	Click the ▼ and select **1060 Cash in Bank**. The Statement Start, End and Reconciliation Dates are automatically filled in.
Statement Opening Balance	Type **1185.00,** ⌷Tab⌷. This is the May 01 Balance forward from the bank statement Fig 12-5.
Statement End Balance	Type **–212.60,** ⌷Tab⌷. This is the ending balance from the bank statement dated May 31. (See side note box.)
Comment	Type **Reconciliation at May 31, 2014.**

> 🛈 The **Statement End Balance** amount is the Bank Statement balance.

Read the important information on the Transactions tab.

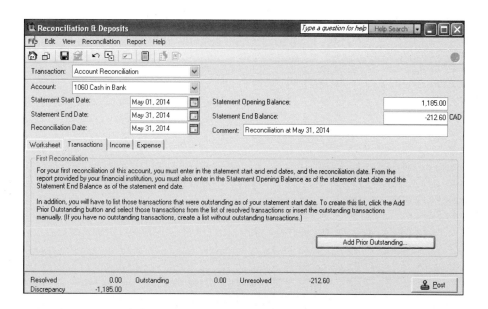

2 ➤ Click on the **Add Prior Outstanding** button.

A message box to save the changes to the Journal appears.

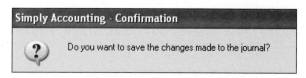

3 ➤ Click **Yes** to save the date and amount changes. The Add Outstanding Transactions window appears.

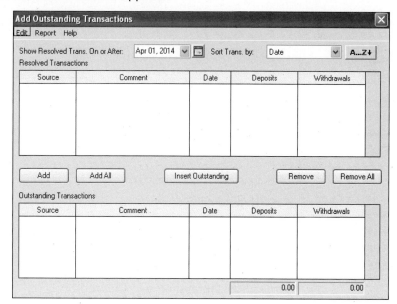

This window allows you to add in previous Resolved and Outstanding transactions.

4 ➤ The Bank Reconciliation Fig. 12-2, prepared on April 30, 2014, for Wedding Flowers Company had no outstanding transactions (cheques or deposits) and the bank service charge was recorded in the month of April.

Show Resolved   Click ▼ select **Apr 30, 2014**, click **OK**.
Trans. On or After

The Reconciliation & Deposits Journal appears showing the Outstanding items for May. You may have to drag the bottom-right corner to the right to see the window below.

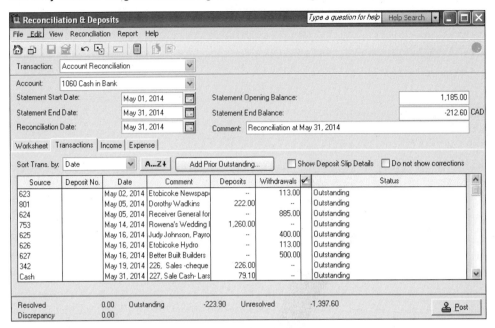

The unresolved balance should be **-1,397.60**. This represents the amount that has to be reconciled.

Show Deposit Slip Details   This feature is not used with Wedding Flowers Company. If a business identified individual cheques as being part of a single deposit then the details of the deposit made can be shown.

5 ➤   DO NOT POST. Click **Report, Display Account Reconciliation Journal Entry**.

Account Reconciliation Journal Entry May 31, 2014

	Account Number	Account Description	Debits	Credits
May 31, 2014	Account Rec., Reconciliation at May 31, 2014			
	1060	Cash in Bank	-	1,397.60
	5380	Bank Rec Unresolved (Unknown)	1,397.60	-
Additional Date:	Additional Field:			
			1,397.60	1,397.60

6 ➤   **Exit** from the entry.

The transactions that have cleared the bank, as indicated by the bank statement, must be identified in the journal by clicking under the ☑ column icon next to the Withdrawals column. A ✓ will identify the item as cleared, and the Status column changes from **Outstanding** to **Cleared**.

> If the item appears as the same dollar amount on the bank statement as it is recorded in the General Ledger, identify the item as **cleared**. If the dollar amount is not the same, accept the appropriate code (shown in the information section).

7 ➤ Mark the following transactions as **cleared** (both the General Ledger transaction and the bank item agree as to the amount):

Source	Date	Vendor	Debit	Credit
623	May 02, 2014	Etobicoke Newspaper		113.00
801	May 05, 2014	Dorothy Wadkins	222.00	
624	May 12, 2014	Receiver General for Canada		885.00
753	May 14, 2014	Rowena's Wedding Boutique	1,260.00	
625	May 16, 2014	Judy Johnson, Payroll		400.00
626	May 16, 2014	Etobicoke Hydro		113.00

The lower portion of the window should resemble the following:

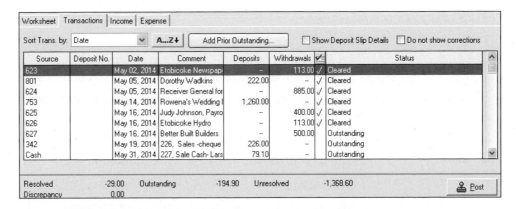

8 ➤ **View** the journal entry created by the above changes. The unresolved amount has changed to $1,368.60.

Account Reconciliation Journal Entry May 31, 2014					
		Account Number	Account Description	Debits	Credits
May 31, 2014		Account Rec., Reconciliation at May 31, 2014			
		1060	Cash in Bank	-	1,368.60
		5380	Bank Rec Unresolved (Unknown)	1,368.60	-
Additional Date:	Additional Field:				
				1,368.60	1,368.60

9 ➤ **Exit** the entry.

Income tab

10 ➤ Click the **Income** tab, and on the Interest Income line, update the information as follows:

Source No.   Type **Bank Statement**, [Tab].

Date   Change the date to **May 27, 2014** (the date the interest was deposited to the bank account). [Tab] to Amount.

Amount   Type **1.40**, [Tab]. The Unresolved amount changes to $1,370.00.

Name	Source No.	Date	Comment	Acct	Amount
Interest Income	Bank Stateme	May 27, 2014	Interest Income	4210 Interest	1.40
NOT USED		May 31, 2014	NOT USED		--
NOT USED		May 31, 2014	NOT USED		--

11 ➤ **View** the journal entry created by the previous changes.

Account Reconciliation Journal Entry May 31, 2014				
	Account Number	Account Description	Debits	Credits
May 27, 2014	Bank Statement, Interest Income			
	1060	Cash in Bank	1.40	-
	4210	Interest Income	-	1.40
May 31, 2014	Account Rec., Reconciliation at May 31, 2014			
	1060	Cash in Bank	-	1,370.00
	5380	Bank Rec Unresolved (Unknown)	1,370.00	-
Additional Date:	Additional Field:			
			1,371.40	1,371.40

12 ➤ **Exit** the entry.

Expense tab

13 ➤ Click the **Expense** tab.

14 ➤ On the Bank Charges line, change the information as follows:

Source No.	Type **Bank Statement**, `Tab`.
Date	Change the date to **May 28, 2014** (the date the charges were taken out of the account), `Tab`.
Comment	Change to **Service Charges**. `Tab` to Amount.
Amount	Type **10.00**, `Tab`.

On the Interest Expense line, change the information as follows.

Source No.	Type **Bank Interest**, `Tab`.
Date	Change the date to **May 28, 2014** (the date the charges were taken out of the account). `Tab`.
Comment	Change to **Loan Interest**. `Tab` to Amount.
Amount	Type **100.00**, `Tab`.

The lower portion of the window appears as follows and the Unresolved amount changes to $1,260.00.

Name	Source No.	Date	Comment	Acct	Amount
Bank Charges	Bank Stateme	May 28, 2014	Service Charges	5342 Bank C	10.00
NOT USED		May 31, 2014	NOT USED		--
Interest Expense	Bank Interest	May 28, 2014	Loan Interest	5345 Bank L	100.00

15 ➤ **View** the journal entry created by the additional activity.

Account Reconciliation Journal Entry May 31, 2014

		Account Number	Account Description	Debits	Credits
May 27, 2014		Bank Statement, Interest Income			
	1060		Cash in Bank	1.40	-
	4210		Interest Income	-	1.40
May 28, 2014		Bank Statement, Service Charges			
	1060		Cash in Bank	-	10.00
	5342		Bank Charges Expense	10.00	-
May 28, 2014		Bank Statement, Interest Expense			
	1060		Cash in Bank	-	100.00
	5345		Bank Loan Expense	100.00	-
May 31, 2014		Account Rec., Reconciliation at May 31, 2014			
	1060		Cash in Bank	-	1,260.00
	5380		Bank Rec Unresolved (Unknown)	1,260.00	-
Additional Date:	Additional Field:				
				1,371.40	1,371.40

Fig. 12-6: Reconciliation & Deposits Journal entry.

16 ➤ Exit the entry.

Simply has created entries for the linked items identified earlier and for the 1,260.00 unresolved balance, which is the same as the NSF item on May 18.

DO NOT POST YET.

In the manual bank reconciliation shown in Fig. 12-7, the items that have been reconciled so far are shaded. The only cheque that has not cleared the bank (cashed by the bank) is cheque #627 for $500.00. This cheque has the Outstanding status.

There is still an unresolved amount of **-1,260.00**, which is the NSF item from Rowena's Wedding Boutique. This will be adjusted in Exercise 12-3.

Wedding Flowers Company
Bank Reconciliation at May 31, 2014

Balance per Bank Statement				($ -212.60)	Overdrawn
Add: Outstanding Deposits	May 31	226.00			
	May 31	79.10		305.10	
	Subtotal			92.50	
Less: Outstanding cheque #627				500.00	
Adjusted Bank Balance				($ 407.50)	Overdrawn
Balance per General Ledger				$ 961.10	
Add: Deposit interest				1.40	
	Subtotal			962.50	
Less: Bank Charges		10.00			
Loan Interest		100.00			
NSF cheque -					
Rowena's Wedding Boutique		1,260.00		1,370.00	
Adjusted Bank Balance				($ 407.50)	Overdrawn

Fig. 12-7: Manual Bank Reconciliation.

17 ➤ Post when correct. All of the entries in Fig. 12-6 will be posted, including the one for the unresolved amount of $1,260.00.

A warning message advising the fourth entry in Fig. 12-6 will be posted.

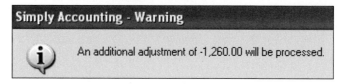

18 ➤ Click **OK** to accept.

The Select Adjustment Account window requires you to identify the account where the unresolved adjustment amount is to be posted.

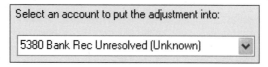

19 ➤ Click the ⯆. A selection of accounts that can be used for the adjustment are displayed. With the default 5380 account selection, click **OK**.

20 ➤ When posting, the Simply Advisor reports that the chequing account (1060 Cash in Bank) is overdrawn. **Click in the box** to proceed. Arrangements have been made to cover overdrafts up to $5,000.00.

After posting the entry, the Reconciliation & Deposits journal has been updated (the reconciled items have been deleted from the Reconciliation & Deposits data base).

21 ➤ Account   Click the ⯆ and select **1060 Cash in Bank**. The **Statement Start Date** has been updated to June 01, 2014. Outstanding cheque **#627** is shown as carried forward, as well as the two outstanding deposits. The window now reflects the balance forward for the next period (June). (July dates would be changed to June 30 when preparing the next reconciliation.)

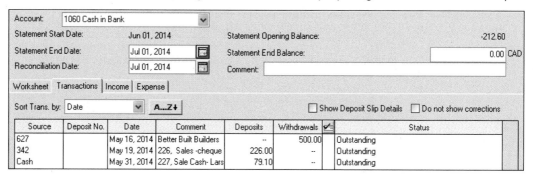

Fig. 12-8: Reconciliation & Deposits Journal.

22 ➤ DO NOT POST. If you Post, you will update the June Bank Reconciliation, which you do not want to do. **Exit** to the Home window.

23 ➤ Display the Income Statement and locate the Expense account **5380 Bank Rec Unresolved (Unknown)**. The balance is $1,260.00. We need to enter the NSF cheque information in the CUSTOMERS module, to charge the customer with the amount they owe the business. Their cheque to pay invoice #221 was not valid. If the customer is not charged for the NSF cheque, the amount will be an expense to the business and the account reconciliation will NOT be complete.

24 ➤ Exit to the Home window.

Exercise 12-3– To Clear the Unresolved by Recording the NSF Cheque

1 ➤ Using the Sales Orders & Quotes, **Sales Invoice Journal**, record NSF cheque #753 from Rowena's Wedding Boutique original invoice 221, following procedures learned in Chapter 2B. Terms fields should be blank. Use account **5380 Bank Rec Unresolved (Unknown)**. There are no bank charges. The May 19 entry (date the cheque became NSF in our account) to update Rowena's Receivable account will be:

Sales Journal Entry May 19, 2014 (J14)		Debits	Credits
Account Number	Account Description		
1200	Accounts Receivable	1,260.00	-
5380	Bank Rec Unresolved (Unknown)	-	1,260.00
Additional Date:	Additional Field:		
		1,260.00	1,260.00

The CREDIT entry will be to **5380 Bank Rec Unresolved (Unknown)**, not 1060 BANK.

2 ➤ **Exit** the entry, **Post** when correct, and **Exit** to the Home window. The Customers section (top right) displays the $1,260.00 balance for Rowena's account.

Some banks charge a fee to the company or individual depositing an NSF cheque. Some banks do not charge a fee for this type of transaction. If the bank charges a fee for this type of entry, the entry remains the same except that the bank fee should be added to the NSF cheque amount. The customer should pay this fee. Assuming the bank fee was $5.00, the entry to Rowena's account would be:

Dr 1200 Accounts Receivable   **1,265.00**
Cr   5380 Bank Rec. Unresolved (Unknown)   **1,265.00**

If the firm charges the customer a handling fee for NSF cheques, they would need to open a Revenue account (e.g., 4220 Handling Fee) for the fee received. If the bank charged a service fee of $5.00, and the business charged a handling fee of $15.00, the entry to Rowena's account would be:

Dr   1200 Accounts Receivable   **1,280.00**
Cr   5380 Bank Rec. Unresolved (Unknown)   **1,265.00**
Cr   4220 Handling fee   **15.00**

---

3 ➤ **Display** the Income Statement and locate account **5380 Bank Rec. Unresolved (Unknown)** account. After the NSF Adjustment, the account balance should be 0.00.

Printing Reconciliation & Deposits Reports

Exercise 12-4 – To Print Reconciliation & Deposits Reports

---

1 ➤ From the Home page, click **BANKING** module, click **Report Centre**, click **Banking, Reconciliation Transactions Detail**, click **Display.** The report for Account 1060 Cash in Bank is displayed. Note: A vertical line on the display will indicate it will display/print on 2 pages (see arrow).

Reconciliation Transactions Detail Report Jan 01, 2014 to Jul 01, 2014

Account: 1060 Cash in Bank

Date	JE#	Comment	Source	Deposits	Withdrawals	Deposit No.	CI	Status
May 02, 2014	J1	Etobicoke Newspaper	623	-	113.00		Y	Cleared
May 05, 2014	J2	Dorothy Wadkins	801	222.00	-		Y	Cleared
May 05, 2014	J3	Receiver General for Canada	624	-	885.00		Y	Cleared
May 14, 2014	J4	Rowena's Wedding Boutique	753	1,260.00	-		Y	Cleared
May 16, 2014	J5	Judy Johnson, Payroll	625	-	400.00		Y	Cleared
May 16, 2014	J6	Etobicoke Hydro	626	-	113.00		Y	Cleared
May 16, 2014	J7	Better Built Builders	627	-	500.00		N	Outstanding
May 19, 2014	J8	226, Sales -cheque Shierel	342	226.00	-		N	Outstanding
May 31, 2014	J9	227, Sale Cash- Larson	Cash	79.10	-		N	Outstanding
				1,787.10	2,011.00			

Fig. 12-9: Reconciliation Transactions Detail Report (with no banking codes). (See Fig. 12-11.)

2 ➤ To display/print the report on one page, click the ⟦Modify ▾⟧ icon, then **Report Options**. In the left pane, click **Report Columns**, in the right pane, click **Custom report columns settings.** In the Columns shown in the report pane, change four columns:

Journal Number, from 10 to **5**
Comment   from 35 to **30**
Source Number from 18 to **10**
Deposit Number, from 15 to **10**

3 ➤ Click **OK**, to display the report.

The report should resemble Fig. 12-9, and will display/print only on one page.

4 ➤ **Exit** to the Home window.

General Journal

> The entry for Rowena's NSF cheque does not show in the Reconciliation & Deposits journal entries, because it was prepared in the Sales, Invoice Journal as an entry for an NSF cheque.

1 ➤ From the Home page, click **Report Centre**, click **Banking** (if not selected) click **Account Reconciliation Journal Entries**. Click **Display**.

The report should resemble Fig. 12-6, except that each entry has a Journal Entry number.

(See side note box.)

2 ➤ **Print** the Report. **Exit** to Report Centre window.

3 ➤ Click **Financials,** click **All Journal Entries**, click **Display** to see Rowena's NSF adjustment entry (J14).

4 ➤ **Exit** to the Report Centre window.

General Ledger – 1060 BANK ACCOUNT

Display the report as follows:

1 ➤ At **Financials,** click **General Ledger**, click **Modify this report**,
  Start date **May 01, 2014**,
  Finish date **May 31, 2014**, select **Account 1060, Sort by Date**, **OK**.
  Notice that the **J13 May 31, 2014** entry is done automatically by Simply.
  The report should resemble Fig. 12-10.

General Ledger Report May 01, 2014 to May 31, 2014
Sorted by: Date

Date	Comment	Source #	JE#	Debits	Credits	Balance
1060	**Cash in Bank**					1,185.00 Dr
May 02, 20...	Etobicoke Newspaper	623	J1	-	113.00	1,072.00 Dr
May 05, 20...	Dorothy Wadkins	801	J2	222.00	-	1,294.00 Dr
May 05, 20...	Receiver General for Canada	624	J3	-	885.00	409.00 Dr
May 14, 20...	Rowena's Wedding Boutique	753	J4	1,260.00	-	1,669.00 Dr
May 16, 20...	Judy Johnson, Payroll	625	J5	-	400.00	1,269.00 Dr
May 16, 20...	Etobicoke Hydro	626	J6	-	113.00	1,156.00 Dr
May 16, 20...	Better Built Builders	627	J7	-	500.00	656.00 Dr
May 19, 20...	226, Sales -cheque Shierel	342	J8	226.00	-	882.00 Dr
May 27, 20...	Interest Income	Bank Statement	J10	1.40	-	883.40 Dr
May 28, 20...	Service Charges	Bank Statement	J11	-	10.00	873.40 Dr
May 28, 20...	Interest Expense	Bank Interest	J12	-	100.00	773.40 Dr
May 31, 20...	227, Sale Cash- Larson	Cash	J9	79.10	-	852.50 Dr
May 31, 20...	Reconciliation at May 31, 2014	Account Rec.	J13	-	1,260.00	407.50 Cr
				1,788.50	3,381.00	

Fig. 12-10: General Ledger Report.

Notice that the ending Cash in Bank balance of 407.50 Cr is equal to the Manual Bank Reconciliation Adjusted Bank Balance of ($407.50) shown in Fig. 12-7.

2 ➤ Return to the Home window.

General Ledger – 5380 BANK REC UNRESOLVED (Unknown)

1 ➤ At **Financials,** click **General Ledger**, click **Modify this report**,
  Start date **May 01, 2014**,
  Finish date **May 31, 2014**, select **5380 (Bank Rec Unresolved (Unknown)**,
  Sort by Date, **OK**.

The report should resemble Fig. 12-11.

General Ledger Report May 01, 2014 to May 31, 2014
Sorted by: Date

Date	Comment	Source #	JE#	Debits	Credits	Balance
5380	**Bank Rec Unresolved (Unknown)**					- Dr
May 19, 20...	Rowena's Wedding Boutique	221NS ck753	J14	-	1,260.00	1,260.00 Cr
May 31, 20...	Reconciliation at May 31, 2014	Account Rec.	J13	1,260.00	-	- Dr
				1,260.00	1,260.00	

Fig. 12-11: General Ledger report on account 5380 Bank Rec Unresolved.

2 ➤ Return to the **Home** window.

Other Reconciliation & Deposits Features

There are some other features of the Reconciliation & Deposits journal that are not covered in this chapter. They are as follows:

a) A deposit slip containing numerous receipts can be entered into the Transactions display of the journal. If each receipt is identified with the deposit slip number, then the status of all the receipts can be changed to "Cleared" in one step by clicking the ☑ button at the top of the check mark column.

b) The ☑ button in the Transactions display can be used to change the status of **all** items to "Cleared."

c) The "Clear Account Rec. Data" option under the Maintenance menu is used to clear selective data from the reconciliation for space reasons. Transactions that cannot be cleared are Outstanding items.

Summary

The BANKING module, Reconciliation & Deposits journal, can be activated, then set up for a company with information from the most recent manual bank reconciliation. The Reconciliation & Deposits Journal will maintain a running record of all transactions affecting the bank accounts specified.

The Simply program will allow you to:

- identify normal recurring items; e.g., bank interest.
- identify all bank statement items as cleared or error items.
- record entries to update client files for NSF cheques, etc., which will update the Reconciliation & Deposits journal.

This next section is **FOR INFORMATION ONLY**. Do NOT follow the instructions – use them for future reference.

Reconciliation Errors

This should be done only after the previous work in the chapter has been completed.

1 ➤ Click the **Reconcile Accounts** icon.

2 ➤ Account   Select the **1060 Cash in Bank** account.

3 ➤ ☑ column   For source cheque #627 click in the column to change the blank to a ✓ and the status will change to "cleared."

4 ➤ Triple-click in the **Status column** and the Select Transaction Status window appears as shown below. A list of alternatives for the status of the transaction is displayed.

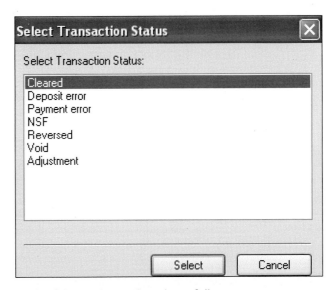

An explanation for each of the status options is as follows:

Cleared   The default status for a normal transaction that has cleared the bank and matches the amount recorded in the General Ledger.

Deposit Error   To identify a deposit on the bank statement that is different from the General Ledger amount due to a recording error. The error difference must be recorded with a journal entry and assigned the Deposit Error (D) status also. The original deposit coded as a D and the error correction coded as a D can be cleared together with a C (cleared) code.

Payment Error   To identify a payment on the bank statement that is different from the General Ledger amount due to a recording error. The error difference must be recorded with a journal entry, and assigned the Payment Error (P) status code. The original payment coded as a P and the error correction coded as a P can be cleared together with a C (cleared) code.

NSF   To identify customer deposit cheques that were returned by the bank to you because there was not enough money in the customer's bank account to cover the cheque. An adjusting entry (to record the NSF cheque and the bank charges) must be made in the Sales Journal. If the Sales Journal is not ready for use, then the NSF cheque and bank charges would be recorded in the General Journal.

                       The adjustment must then be assigned the **A (Adjustment)** status (explained later).

Reversed   To identify cheques that the firm has canceled by recording a reversing entry to the bank. The reversing entry is normally made in the Sales or Purchases Journal. A reversing entry is required and is then assigned the A (Adjustment) code.

Void   For a cheque that has not been used or has been canceled. A reversing entry is required for a canceled cheque and is then assigned the A (Adjustment) code.

Adjustment   For transactions posted as adjustments in other journals as described above.

5 ➤ Select the **Adjustment** as an example. You are returned to the Reconciliation window. Notice that the Status has now changed to ✓ Adjustment.

The above procedure is to show you how you can change the status to fit the situation.

6 ➤ Click the **X** to cancel the above procedure.

7 ➤ At the message box, click **NO** to cancel the changes.

This is the end of the INFORMATION ONLY section for Chapter 12.

Reviewing **Slideshow 12** will help you make sense of the reconciliation procedure in Simply.

Before Moving On...

1. What are the steps required to activate and set up a Reconciliation & Deposits Journal?

2. Explain the term "Unresolved Balance."

3. If a deposit does not match figures/entries on the bank statement, what possible causes could there be for the difference?

4. If a cheque does not match entries on the bank statement, what possible causes could there be for the difference?

Relevant Appendix

The following appendix is available at www.simplyaccounting2010.nelson.com under Student Resources.

Appendix 2010 AI   **Transfer Funds – Transfer money between bank accounts**

Challenge Exercise 12 C12-1, China

COMPANY, ACCOUNTS RECEIVABLE, ACCOUNTS PAYABLE, and Reconciliation & Deposits)

This challenge exercise is using the Challenge Exercise 03 C3B-2 solution file from Chapter 3B.

1 ➤ Open the **China solution** file. Change the company name to **China Co Bank Rec**, **Your Name**.

2 ➤ Add a new GL account **#5380 Bank Rec Unresolved,** with a Class type of **Expense**.

3 ➤ From the **General Ledger #1010 Bank Account,** click on **Reconciliation & Deposits** tab and follow the steps outlined in the chapter to set up the linked accounts. For: **Adjustment** Bank Rec Unresolved and **Expense 1** Bank Charges and Interest.

Note: The company does not have any Bank Income earned on investments, nor do they have any Bank Loan Payable amounts.

Note: The bank reconciliation was completed last month (Feb) and there were no outstanding cheques. Bank service charges were recorded in Feb.

As noted in the Challenge Exercise in Chapter 3, the bank manager, on March 19, asked the owner to provide financial statements. The bank provided the following interim bank statement.

Commercial Bank of Canada
2098 Victoria Street West, Alliston ON L9R 6P2

China Company
1012 Victoria Street East
Alliston ON L9R 3Z4

Account Number: 158-2591-3   Mar 19, 2018

(OD = Overdrawn)

Date	Information	Cheques	Deposits	Balance
Mar 01	Balance Forward			3,120.00
Mar 09	Cheque 625	800.00		2,320.00
Mar 10	Cheque 624	700.00		1,620.00
Mar 14	Cheque 626	721.50		898.50
Mar 17	Cheque 627	111.00		787.50
Mar 17	Deposit		116.55	904.05
Mar 19	NSF item Plates & More	116.55		787.50
Mar 19	Service Charge	9.10		778.40

ℹ **OD** means Overdrawn or Overdraft. Mar 19 service charge is for regular bank charges.

4 ➤ From the **BANKING** module, click on **Reconciliation Accounts** and complete the bank reconciliation noting the following dates: Statement Start Date: **Mar 1, 2018**, Statement End Date: **Mar 19, 2018** and Reconciliation Date: **Mar 19, 2018**.

5 ➤ **Reconcile** the bank account in Simply and make the appropriate journal entries to update the Financial Statements. *Note*: Refer to the original deposit entry to see if there was a discount on the receipt.

6 ➤ **Prepare** the following revised reports:
   a) Year-to-date Income Statement
   b) Customer Aged Detail Report as at Mar 19
   c) All Journal Entries (for all activity)

Chapter 13

Correcting Transaction Errors After Posting

Learning Objectives

After completing this chapter, you will be able to:

☐ Reverse and adjust posted entries or other information (quotes or orders).

The contents are as follows:

COMPANY Module
    Exercise 13-1 – Print General Journal Entries 573
    Exercise 13-2 – Correcting General Journal Entries 574

RECEIVABLES Module
    Exercise 13-3 – Correcting a Sales Order or Quote 576
    Exercise 13-4 – Correcting a Sales Invoice 578
    Exercise 13-5 – Correcting Sales Receipt Entry 579

PAYABLES Module
    Exercise 13-6 – Canceling or Correcting Purchase Orders or Quotes 581
    Exercise 13-7 – Correcting Purchase Journal Entries for Merchandise 582
    Exercise 13-8 – Correcting Purchase Journal Entry for Non-Merchandise. 584
    Exercise 13-9 – Correcting Vendor Payments 585
    Exercise 13-10 – Correcting Payments (Make Other Payment) 587

EMPLOYEES & PAYROLL Module
    Correcting Payroll Cheque Items 588

INVENTORY & SERVICES Module
    Exercise 13-11 – Correcting Inventory Adjustments 589
    Exercise 13-12 – Correcting Build from Inventory Assembly 590

No one is perfect, and we all make mistakes from time to time. This chapter will help you correct errors in invoices, quotes, orders and/or journal entries after you have posted your transactions.

You can avoid having to do these corrective steps if you view each entry before posting. See Exercise 1-7 if you wish to review the procedure.

Errors in wrong vendor, customer, employee, wrong number of items shipped, wrong description of item being sold, wrong general ledger account number, etc., may all be corrected. Remember, that it is **very** important to document any corrections you make. Write a memo explaining the original error, including the posting entry number (e.g., J125), how the entry was corrected, including the new posting entry number (e.g., J147). This memo notation is part of what is called an **Audit trail**. This trail is how someone else can trace or track what has happened in accounting records.

Always use codes to identify corrections made to entries. See Exercise 2A-14 for a sample listing of error codes. Companies may use many other codes to identify corrections. The secret of effective use of these codes is **consistency**.

There are three ways to correct entries:

a) You may use the 🖼 Lookup icon to locate the entry that needs correcting. The window changes and the header will be similar to: Sales Journal – Invoice.

   Lookup. You would then click on 🖼 Adjust icon and the header changes to: Sales Journal -Adjusting Invoice No. 2310. You make the necessary changes and post when correct.

   Using this method the original and reversing entries **Do NOT** show in the Customer or Vendor aged detail listings. Only the corrected invoice will show in the report.

   When you display journal entries (with corrections) that have been corrected and posted, you will see the reversing entry with a source field similar to: ADJ2310, Reversing J3, Correction is J5. The correcting entry will have a source field based on the changes that you have made.

b) If you want to see the original, reversal and correcting entries in the Customer or Vendor aged detail reports, you will need to record and post:

   i.   A reversing entry with a code similar to 2310Rv (2310 Reversed). In the reversing entry, accounts that were originally debited are credited, and accounts that were credited originally are now debited.

   ii. The correct entry, new invoice 2314 (assumed new invoice number), will display the way it should have been recorded.

   The Aged Detail report will show the original 2310, the 2310Rv and 2314.

c) If you want to reverse an entry (cancel) because the entry was in error and there is no correction (new entry not needed), you may use the 🖼 Reverse icon.

The Adjustment icon method (a) and Reverse an entry icon will be shown in this chapter. You will see:

   1. information about the original entry.
   2. a screen display of the original entry.
   3. a screen display of the original posted journal entry.
   4. correcting screen display.
   5. correcting screen display of the revised entry.

Remember to **view** the reversing entry before posting. This will allow you to verify that the reversing entry you are making is correct; otherwise, you will complicate the problem even further.

1 ➤   Refer to Exercise 1-1 to unzip the **13 Corrections.exe** file at www.simplyaccounting2010.nelson.com under Student Resources.

2 ➤   Open the **13 Corrections** file and accept the date of **Jan 04, 2016**.

The **Corrections Prizes Company** sells various games and prizes for home and office party loot bags.

The Corrections Prizes Company was closed for the holiday period and re-opened on January 4, 2016. Unfortunately the bookkeeper was tired from partying during the New Year's weekend and made many mistakes. He was going to correct the errors, but was called out of town for a personal family situation. You were called in, for the afternoon, to print the entries that he made and correct them.

You will be shown how to correct each type of error using the Adjustment icon and/ or Reversing icon.

Exercise 13-1 – Print General Journal Entries

The first thing you need to do is to print the General Journal entries to identify the entries that need to be corrected.

1 ➤   **Print** Journal Entries - All for January 4, 2016.

Correcting General Journal Entries

Jan 04, 2016	The bank faxed the debit memo for printing new cheques. Information on the fax was New cheques $43.00, HST $5.59, total debit to the account $48.59.

The General Journal entry recorded in error was:

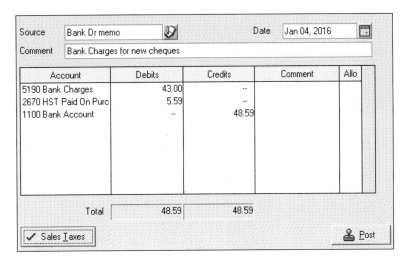

New cheques are normally charged to a Prepaid Office Supplies account and expensed as they are used. In this situation the cost of printing the cheques is not a large amount (immaterial amount) and is charged to Office Supplies Expense account. Cheques are normally not charged to Bank Charges.

In Chapter 1 (Photos Company), there were no taxes (HST) recorded when using the General Journal. The following correction entry will show you how Sales taxes are recorded in the General Journal.

Exercise 13-2 – Correcting General Journal Entries

---

1 ➤   To correct this entry, click the **COMPANY** module, click the **General Journal** icon.

2 ➤   Click the 🔖 **Adjust a previously posted entry** icon.

3 ➤   At the Search window, do not change dates, click **OK**.

4 ➤   At the Select Entry to Adjust window, select **Journal # 1**, with a description of Bank charges for new cheques. Notice that only General Journal entries recorded show in this display.

5 ➤   Change the **accounts, amounts and comments** to reflect the journal shown next. The bank withdrew the money on January 4.

Source	Bank Dr memo			Date	Jan 04, 2016	
Comment	Bank Charges for new cheques					

Account	Debits	Credits	Comment	Allo
5220 Office Supplies Exp	43.00	--	new cheques	
2670 HST Paid On Purc	5.59	--		
1100 Bank Account	--	48.59		

6 ➤   **View** the entry before posting.

General Journal Entry Jan 04, 2016 (J10)

Account Number	Account Description	Debits	Credits
5220	Office Supplies Expense	43.00	-
	new cheques		
2670	HST Paid On Purchases	5.59	-
1100	Bank Account	-	48.59
Additional Date:	Additional Field:		
		48.59	48.59

As discussed in Exercise 1-12, all adjusting entry numbers will be increased due to the automatic reversing entry, therefore, after posting, J9 would be the reversing entry and J10 would be the correction.

Jan 04, 2016	J9	ADJBank Dr memo, Reversing J1. Correction is J10.

7 ➤   Click the **Sales Tax** button (with the blue✓). See the information field after step 9.

8 ➤   The Sales Taxes- General Journal – Adjusting Bank Dr Memo window displays.

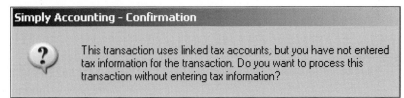

Edit   View

Transaction Type: ⊙ Purchase   ○ Sale

Account	Tax	Tax Code	Amount Subject to Tax	Tax Paid on Purchases	Other Taxes Paid
2670 HST Paid On Purc	HST	HS	43.00	5.59	0.00
			Total	5.59	0.00

A transaction type and a tax code are required. To ensure the correct reporting, please verify that amounts subject to tax and other taxes charged are correct

The window records amounts affecting linked tax accounts. In order for the HST Tax report to be correct, the cost of the cheques and taxes must be recorded properly.

If the original entry did not use the sales taxes button and, therefore, the linked tax accounts did not get recorded properly, you would see the following window.

Simply Accounting – Confirmation

This transaction uses linked tax accounts, but you have not entered tax information for the transaction. Do you want to process this transaction without entering tax information?

You should click No, to record taxes properly. The tax information window appears and should be filled in as noted in step 9.

HS Tax Code would be the appropriate code for this transaction.

The **Amount Subject to Tax** and **Other Taxes Paid** column amounts appear as shown.

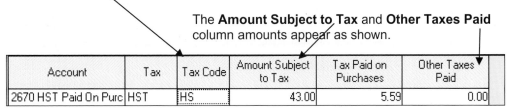

Account	Tax	Tax Code	Amount Subject to Tax	Tax Paid on Purchases	Other Taxes Paid
2670 HST Paid On Purc	HST	HS	43.00	5.59	0.00

Simply divides the HST amount (Tax Paid on Purchases) $5.59 by .13 (the HST rate) to determine the amount subject to HST tax ($43.00).

9 ➤ Click **OK** to continue. The Sales Tax button has the blue ✓ to indicate that Sales Tax (purchase taxes) information will be updated for the report.

10 ➤ **Post** when correct.

11 ➤ Return to the Home window.

Correcting or Canceling Sales Orders or Quotes

Exercise 13-3 – Correcting a Sales Order or Quote

> The bookkeeper recorded a Sales Quote for 10 Prizes Adults-metal (P20).
> This should have been a quote for 15 prizes.

Sales Quote recorded in error

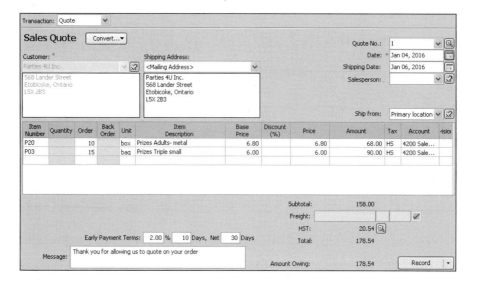

To Change a Sales Order or Quote

1 ➤ Click the **RECEIVABLES module,** click the **Sales Quotes** icon.

2 ➤ **Quote No.**   Click the ▼, select **1** and `Tab`. The original Quote is displayed.

3 ➤ Click on 🔲 **Adjust quote** icon and change the order for P20 Prizes Adults-
metal to **15** `Tab`.

4 ➤ The new total is $216.96. **Record** when correct, click **OK**, then return to the
Home window.

To Cancel (Remove) a Sales Order or Quote

1 ➤ Click the **Sales Quotes** icon.

2 ➤ **Quote No**.   Click the ▼, select **1,** `Tab`. The revised quote is displayed.

3 ➤ Click on 🔲 **Remove quote** icon.

4 ➤ You will be asked: Are you sure you want to remove this Quote? Click **No**
to leave the Sales Quote with 15 units of each item ordered, and Return to
the Home window.

Correcting Sales Journal Entry for Merchandise

There are two scenarios shown below, illustrating different ways to adjust or reverse a Sales journal entry for goods for resale.

Scenario: Invoice with errors has *not* been sent to the customer.

Method One

To correct

Use the Simply **Adjust Invoice** feature that will allow you to change the item(s) that are in error, and post. This will reverse the original customer's invoice and prepare a correct invoice.

Method Two

Use the **Reverse** icon feature to cancel the original entry if there are many errors. This will allow you to create a new invoice with the correct amounts.

As discussed earlier, methods one and two do not provide an audit trail for the customer, because the original and reversing entries will not show in the customer's ledger record. Only the new corrected invoice will appear in the Journals All report.

Method Three

Scenario: Invoice with errors has *been* sent to the customer.

If the invoice has been sent to the customer, method one and two are not appropriate because the original and reversing entries will not show in the customer's ledger record. Only the new corrected invoice will appear. This discrepancy between your company records and those of the customer could present a problem later.

There are two ways to resolve the problem:

a) **Assuming there are a few items on the invoice**.

    (1) Reverse the original invoice entry to cancel the original invoice (Method 2).

    (2) Record a correct invoice with appropriate comments to reference the original invoice.

b) **Assuming there are many items on the invoice**.

    Record an invoice reversing only the item with the error. This in effect is canceling the sale of those items with the error. On the next line, record the **correct** item with the correct information. This is similar to Exercise 8-19.

An example of b) is shown in Exercise 13-4.

Exercise 13-4 – Correcting a Sales Invoice

> The original sales entry (invoice #11504) was recorded to the Rideau Social Club. Their manager called stating that the price given by our manager for the Prizes Adults-metal should be $6.70. Your manager confirmed the price. You will create an invoice adjustment for the Prizes Adults-metal item.

Original Sales Journal

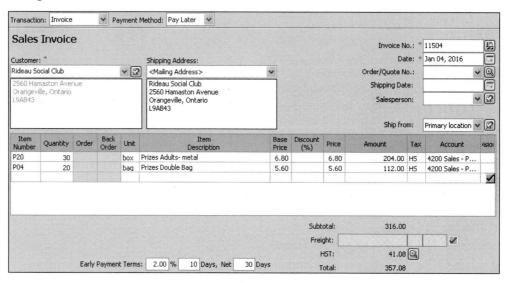

Original Sales Journal entry

Sales Journal Entry Jan 04, 2016 (J6)

Account Number	Account Description	Debits	Credits
1200	Accounts Receivable	357.08	-
5080	Cost Of Sales - Prizes	159.08	-
1280	Inventory -Prizes	-	159.08
2650	HST Charged On Sales	-	41.08
4200	Sales - Prizes	-	316.00
Additional Date:	Additional Field:		
		516.16	516.16

1 ➤ Click the **Sales Invoices** icon.

2 ➤ Create a **Partial Revised** Sales invoice #11504 as shown next. Invoice number code **PtCo** refers to **Part correction**. Comments section can also contain relevant information.

Revised Sales Invoice

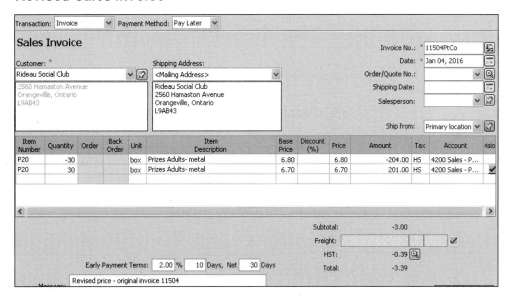

Revised Sales Invoice Journal entry

Sales Journal Entry Jan 04, 2016 (J11)

Account Number	Account Description	Debits	Credits
2650	HST Charged On Sales	0.39	-
4200	Sales - Prizes	3.00	-
1200	Accounts Receivable	-	3.39
Additional Date:	Additional Field:		
		3.39	3.39

3 ➤ Post when correct. Return to the Home window.

Correcting Sales Receipt Entry

Exercise 13-5 – Correcting Sales Receipt Entry

The original receipt of $399.60 was recorded as shown below.

The clerk forgot to record the $7.20 discount.

Before correcting this Receipt, note that the Customers area displays an outstanding balance of $7.20. Simply has converted the $7.20 Discount Available in the Original Receipt window (below), to an Outstanding Receivable balance of $7.20.

Original Receipt window

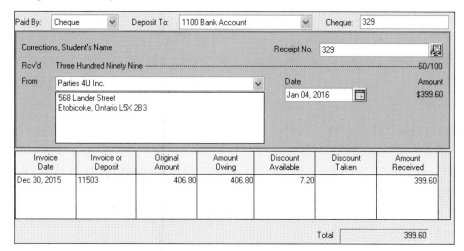

Original Receipt entry

Receipts Journal Entry Jan 04, 2016 (J8)

Account Number	Account Description	Debits	Credits
1100	Bank Account	399.60	-
1200	Accounts Receivable	-	399.60
Additional Date:	Additional Field:		
		399.60	399.60

To Reverse the Original entry:

1 ➤ Click the **Receipts** icon.

2 ➤ Click the 📇 **Lookup** icon.

3 ➤ At the Search window, do not change dates, click **OK**.

4 ➤ At the Select a Receipt window, select **Journal #8**, with customer Parties 4U Inc.

5 ➤ Click on the **Reverse Receipt** 📄 icon. You will see the following window.

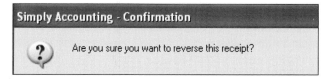

6 ➤ You want to reverse this receipt. Click **Yes.** You are returned to a blank Receipts Journal. The original receipt has been reversed as shown next.

Jan 04, 2016	J12	ADJ329, Parties 4U Inc.: Reversing J8. Correction is J12.		
		1200	Accounts Receivable	399.60	-
		1100	Bank Account	-	399.60

You will notice that the debit entry is to Accounts Receivable.

7 ➤ **Rec'd From** Select **Parties 4U Inc**. in the Receipts window; you will now record the proper cheque amount with a cheque number of **329Co** as shown next.

Correct Receipts window

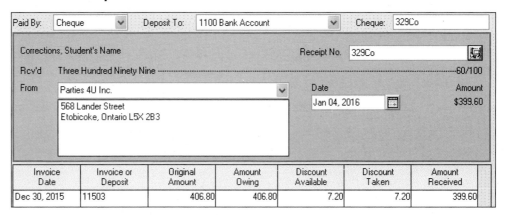

Correct Receipts entry

Receipts Journal Entry Jan 04, 2016 (J13)

Account Number	Account Description	Debits	Credits
1100	Bank Account	399.60	-
4290	Sales Discounts, all items	7.20	-
1200	Accounts Receivable	-	406.80
Additional Date:	Additional Field:		
		406.80	406.80

8 ➤ Post when correct. Return to the Home window.

Canceling or Correcting Purchase Orders or Quotes

Exercise 13-6 – Canceling or Correcting Purchase Orders or Quotes

A Purchase order issued for 55 boxes of Games Wooden Medium size 1 was recorded as 50 boxes in error as shown next.

You will be adjusting the quantity ordered in this exercise.

Original Purchase Order window

To Change a Purchase Order or Quote

1 ➤   Click the **PAYABLES** module, click **Purchase Orders** icon.

2 ➤   **Order No.**   Click ▾, select **1** `Tab`. The original Purchase order is displayed.

3 ➤   Click on 🖻 **Adjust purchase order** icon and change the order quantity to **55**. `Tab`.

Item Number	Quantity	Order	Back Order	Unit	Item Description	Price	Tax	HST	Amount	Account	ⁱsioⁱ
G-W-1		55	55	box	Games Wooden Medium size 1	5.2813	HS	37.76	290.47	1260 Invent...	

4 ➤   The new total is $328.23. **Record** when correct.

5 ➤   Return to the Home window.

To Cancel (Remove) a Purchase Order or Quote

1 ➤   Click the **Purchase Orders** icon.

2 ➤   **Order No.**   Click ▾, select **1**, `Tab`. The original Purchase order is displayed.

3 ➤   Click on 🗑 **Remove purchase order** icon.

4 ➤   You will be asked: Are you sure you want to remove this order? Click **No** to leave Purchase Order 1 with 55 items ordered.

5 ➤   Return to the Home window.

Correcting Purchase Journal Entries for Goods for Resale (Merchandise)

Exercise 13-7 – Correcting Purchase Journal Entries for Merchandise

This exercise, using the Adjusting icon method, will demonstrate how to adjust purchase invoices, assuming that the quantity amount should have been 35.

If you wanted the vendor record to show the original incorrect entry, the reversal and the correction entry, you will need 2 entries to correct the original:

1. Record a negative invoice (negative quantity) to reverse the original invoice.
2. Record the correct entry.

(See side note box.)

The Purchase Journal Invoice entry for merchandise for resale that was recorded in error is shown next.

Original Purchase Invoice entry

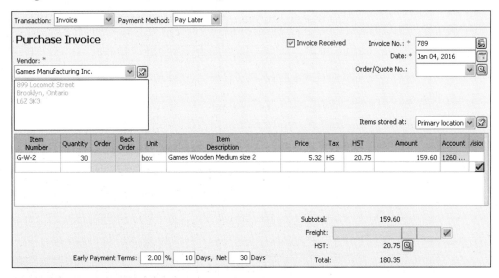

Purchase Journal entry

Purchases Journal Entry Jan 04, 2016 (J2)

Account Number	Account Description	Debits	Credits
1260	Inventory -Games	159.60	-
2670	HST Paid On Purchases	20.75	-
2200	Accounts Payable	-	180.35
Additional Date:	Additional Field:		
		180.35	180.35

1 ➤ Click on **Purchase Invoices** icon.

2 ➤ Click on 🖳 **Lookup an invoice** icon.

3 ➤ At the Search window, do not change dates, click **OK**. Outstanding invoices are listed. Select **Games Manufacturing Inc.** entry dated **Jan 04, 2014** (invoice **789**) in the amount of $180.35.

4 ➤ Click on the **Adjust invoice** icon and change the Quantity amount to **35**, [Tab]. The invoice total changes to 210.41.

Purchase Journal Adjusted

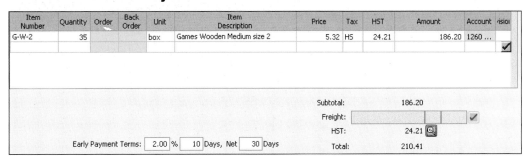

Purchase Journal Adjusted entry

Purchases Journal Entry Jan 04, 2016 (J15)

Account Number	Account Description	Debits	Credits
1260	Inventory -Games	186.20	-
2670	HST Paid On Purchases	24.21	-
2200	Accounts Payable	-	210.41
Additional Date:	Additional Field:		
		210.41	210.41

5 ➤   **Post** when correct. Return to the Home window.

To cancel the Invoice (Information only)

To cancel the invoice completely, click on 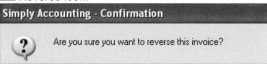 Lookup icon, and select the invoice to be reversed.

Click on 🗐 Reverse icon.

Simply Accounting - Confirmation

❓   Are you sure you want to reverse this invoice?

Click Yes, if this is the correct invoice to cancel. Do not reverse the above entry.

The entry is reversed (Cancelled).

End of Information section.

Correcting Purchase Journal Entries for Non-Merchandise

Exercise 13-8 – Correcting Purchase Journal Entry for Non-Merchandise

> **This exercise assumes the wrong price of 300.00 was recorded. The price should have been 200.00.**

Purchase Journal (non-merchandise) entry that was recorded in error.

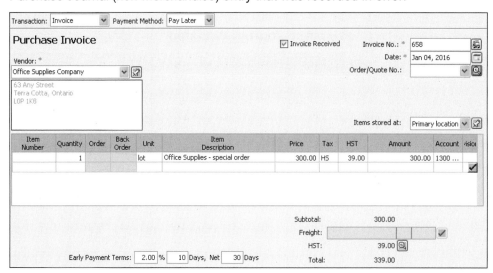

Purchases Journal Entry Jan 04, 2016 (J3)

Account Number	Account Description	Debits	Credits
1300	Office Supplies On Hand	300.00	-
2670	HST Paid On Purchases	39.00	-
2200	Accounts Payable	-	339.00
Additional Date:	Additional Field:		
		339.00	339.00

1 ➤ Click the **Purchase Invoices** icon.

2 ➤ Click the [icon] **Lookup** icon.

3 ➤ At the Search window, do not change dates, click **OK**. Outstanding invoices are listed.

4 ➤ Select **Office Supplies Company** entry **#3,** dated **Jan 04, 2014** (invoice **658**) in the amount of $339.00.

5 ➤ Click on the **Adjust invoice** icon and change the Price amount to **200.00,** `Tab`. The invoice total changes to 226.00.

Purchase Journal Adjusting Invoice

Item Number	Quantity	Order	Back Order	Unit	Item Description	Price	Tax	HST	Amount	Account	vision
	1			lot	Office Supplies - special order	200.00	HS	26.00	200.00	1300 ...	✓

Subtotal: 200.00
Freight: ✓
Early Payment Terms: 2.00 % 10 Days, Net 30 Days   HST: 26.00
Total: 226.00

Purchase Journal entry

Purchases Journal Entry Jan 04, 2016 (J17)

Account Number	Account Description	Debits	Credits
1300	Office Supplies On Hand	200.00	-
2670	HST Paid On Purchases	26.00	-
2200	Accounts Payable	-	226.00
Additional Date:	Additional Field:		
		226.00	226.00

6 ➤ **Post** when correct. Return to the Home window.

Correcting Vendor Payments

Exercise 13-9 – Correcting Vendor Payments

The clerk issued a cheque to Games Manufacturing to pay invoice #731, but he entered $621.00 in the Payment field. He did not accept the discount amount of $11.00 that Simply was showing.

You will cancel (Reverse) the original payment (with the error) and record a correct payment.

Original Payment

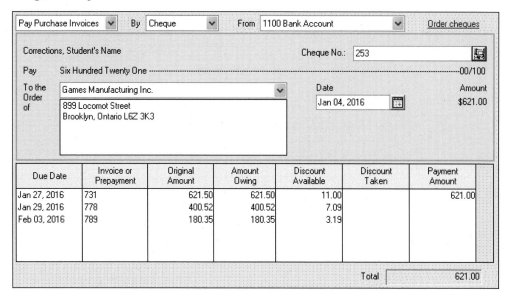

Original Payment entry

Payments Journal Entry Jan 04, 2016 (J5)

Account Number	Account Description	Debits	Credits
2200	Accounts Payable	621.00	-
1100	Bank Account	-	621.00
Additional Date:	Additional Field:		
		621.00	621.00

1 ➤ Click the **Payments** icon.

2 ➤ Click the ![lookup] **Lookup** icon.

3 ➤ At the Search window, do not change dates, click **OK**, journal entry payment #5 is listed.

4 ➤ Select **Games Manufacturing Inc.**, entry **#5,** dated **Jan 04, 2014** in the amount of $621.00.

5 ➤ Click on **Reverse payment** ![icon] icon. You will see the following:

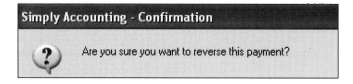

6 ➤ You want to reverse this payment. Click **Yes.** Return to a blank Payments journal window.

Record the Correct Payment

7 ➤ **Record** a correct payment to Games Manufacturing Inc. Issue replacement **cheque #254** as shown next.

Due Date	Invoice or Prepayment	Original Amount	Amount Owing	Discount Available	Discount Taken	Payment Amount
Jan 27, 2016	731	621.50	621.50	11.00	11.00	610.50
Jan 29, 2016	778	400.52	400.52	7.09		
Feb 03, 2016	789	210.41	210.41	3.72		
					Total	610.50

Correct Payment entry

Payments Journal Entry Jan 04, 2016 (J19)

Account Number	Account Description	Debits	Credits
2200	Accounts Payable	621.50	-
1100	Bank Account	-	610.50
5090	Purchase Discounts	-	11.00
Additional Date:	Additional Field:		
		621.50	621.50

8 ➤ **Post** when correct. Return to the Home window.

Correcting Payments (Make Other Payment)

Exercise 13-10 – Correcting Payments (Make Other Payment)

In this exercise, the HST on Sales and HST on Purchases amounts on a payment entry were not recorded correctly. Fortunately, the cheque has not been mailed. Reverse original cheque 252, and issue a new cheque for the correct amounts.

Original Payment

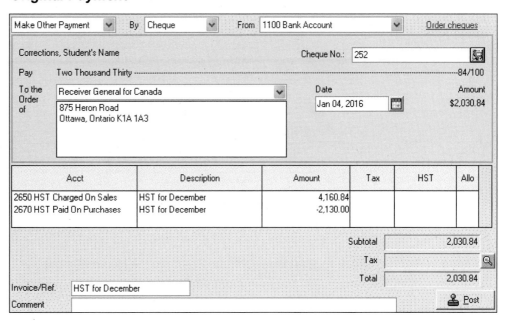

Payment Journal entry

Payments Journal Entry Jan 04, 2016 (J4)

Account Number	Account Description	Debits	Credits
2650	HST Charged On Sales	4,160.84	-
1100	Bank Account	-	2,030.84
2670	HST Paid On Purchases	-	2,130.00
Additional Date:	Additional Field:		
		4,160.84	4,160.84

1 ➤   Click the **Payments** icon.

2 ➤   **Pay Purchase**   Select **Make Other Payment**.
        Invoices

3 ➤   Click the 📇 **Lookup** icon.

4 ➤   At the Search window, do not change dates, click **OK**. Payments are listed.

5 ➤   Select **entry #4 dated Jan 04, 2016** (cheque 252) in the amount of $2,030.84.

6 ➤   Click on 📄 **Reverse payment** icon. You will see the Reverse confirmation window.

7 ➤   You want to reverse this payment. Click **Yes.** Return to a blank Payments journal window.

Record the Correct Payment

8 ➤   **Record** a correct Receiver General payment, cheque number **255**, as shown next.

Payment Correction

Acct	Description	Amount	Tax	HST	Allo
2650 HST Charged On Sales	HST for December	4,152.84			
2670 HST Paid On Purchases	HST for December	-2,113.22			

Subtotal	2,039.62
Tax	🔍
Total	2,039.62

Invoice/Ref.   HST for December

Payment Correction entry

Payments Journal Entry Jan 04, 2016 (J21)

Account Number	Account Description	Debits	Credits
2650	HST Charged On Sales	4,152.84	-
1100	Bank Account	-	2,039.62
2670	HST Paid On Purchases	-	2,113.22
Additional Date:	Additional Field:		
		4,152.84	4,152.84

9 ➤   **Post** when correct. Return to the Home window.

Correcting Payroll Cheque Items

You can **NOT** use the Payroll Cheque Run journal to correct payroll cheques. You must use the Paycheques journal to cancel (reverse) a cheque. See Exercise 7-16a and 16b.

Correcting Inventory Adjustments Journal Entries

There is no Adjust icon in the Inventory Adjustments Journal.

There are two ways to adjust INVENTORY adjustment errors:

1. Reverse the original entry, then record the correct entry.
2. Reverse and correct the entry in one step (shown below).

Exercise 13-11 – Correcting Inventory Adjustments

This adjustment assumes method 2 will be used to correct the error in one step.

The manager's memo stated that the Prizes Double bag should be reduced by 15 units. In error, the Prizes Single was reduced by 5 units.

Incorrect Inventory Adjustment

Incorrect Inventory Adjustment journal entry

Inventory Adjustments Journal Entry Jan 04, 2016 (J7)

Account Number	Account Description	Debits	Credits
5120	Inventory Adjustments	12.54	-
1280	Inventory -Prizes	-	12.54
Additional Date:	Additional Field:		
		12.54	12.54

You need to record a correction entry as shown next:

1 ➤ Click the **INVENTORY & SERVICES** module, click the **Adjust Inventory** icon.

2 ➤ Enter the **correct** entry shown as follows:

Correcting entry

Inventory Adjustments Journal Entry Jan 04, 2016 (J22)

Account Number	Account Description	Debits	Credits
1280	Inventory -Prizes	-	29.54
5120	Inventory Adjustments	29.54	-
Additional Date:	Additional Field:		
		29.54	29.54

3 ➤ **Post** when correct. Return to the Home window.

Correcting Build from Inventory Assembly Journal Entries

Exercise 13-12 – Correcting Build from Inventory Assembly

The manager sent a memo to set up 10 Games Loot Bag #1 as a promotional sales item using the Bill of Materials Journal.

This adjustment assumes the bookkeeper used the Build from Item Assembly Journal. This procedure may also be used to set up or cancel inventory items that do not occur on a regular basis.

The clerk set up the loot bag in error as shown next. There is no Adjust icon, and you cannot display a posted Item Assembly Journal.

Original Item Assembly Journal

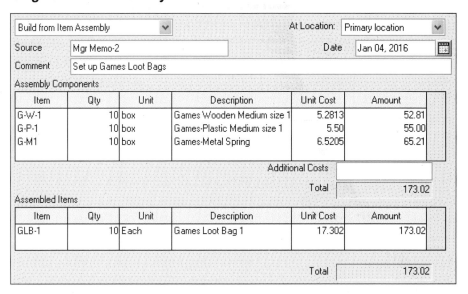

Original Item Assembly entry

Bill of Materials & Item Assembly Journal Entry Jan 04, 2016 (J8)

Account Number	Account Description	Debits	Credits

There is no data to report.

It appears that journal entry #8 with no amounts is created when the original entry is posted, but entry #8 is not created.

Simply Accounting - Information

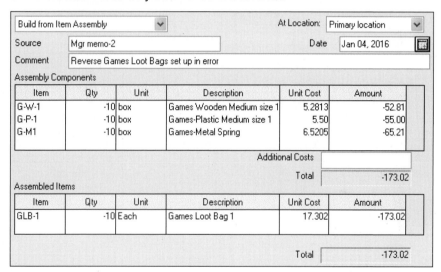

> Inventory quantities will be updated but no journal entry will be created for this build because the net change to each affected account is zero.

It is a transfer within the INVENTORY module. The Games Loot Bags use the same General Ledger linked accounts as the individual games items and there is no Journal entry created.

To Reverse an Item Assembly

1 ➤ Click the **Build from Item Assembly** icon. Leave the choice as **Build from Item Assembly**.

2 ➤ To **reverse** the setup of the Games Loot Bag, type the following information into the Item Assembly Journal as shown next.

Build from Item Assembly				At Location: Primary location		
Source	Mgr memo-2			Date	Jan 04, 2016	
Comment	Reverse Games Loot Bags set up in error					

Assembly Components

Item	Qty	Unit	Description	Unit Cost	Amount
G-W-1	-10	box	Games Wooden Medium size 1	5.2813	-52.81
G-P-1	-10	box	Games-Plastic Medium size 1	5.50	-55.00
G-M1	-10	box	Games-Metal Spring	6.5205	-65.21

	Additional Costs	
	Total	-173.02

Assembled Items

Item	Qty	Unit	Description	Unit Cost	Amount
GLB-1	-10	Each	Games Loot Bag 1	17.302	-173.02

	Total	-173.02

If you display the Journal, you will see:

Bill of Materials & Item Assembly Journal Entry Jan 04, 2016 (J23)

Account Number	Account Description	Debits	Credits
There is no data to report.			

3 ➤ **Post** the entry when correct.

Simply Accounting - Information

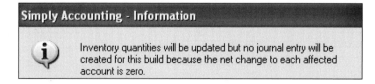

> Inventory quantities will be updated but no journal entry will be created for this build because the net change to each affected account is zero.

4 ➤ Click **OK** to continue. Click **OK** again. You will see an Inventory Low report.

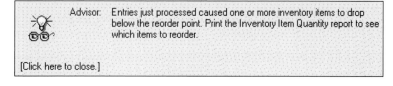

> Advisor: Entries just processed caused one or more inventory items to drop below the reorder point. Print the Inventory Item Quantity report to see which items to reorder.

[Click here to close.]

5 ➤ Ignore this report for this exercise. Click in the **box** to continue. **Return** to the Home window.

To set up the proper 10 Games Loot Bag #1 as a promotional sales item using the Bill of Materials Journal, complete the following steps. Refer to Exercise 8-21.

To set up the Build from Bill of Materials Loot Bag Build Information

1 ➤ Click the **Inventory & Services** icon (in Tasks area).

2 ➤ Locate and double-click **Games Loot Bag 1 GLB-1** icon.

3 ➤ Click on the **Build** tab.

4 ➤ Type the information as shown.

5 ➤ Click the Save and Close button. **Exit** to return to the Home window.

To Create the Loot Bag Using the Build from Bill of Materials Journal

1 ➤ Click the **Build from Bill of Materials** icon.

2 ➤ Type the information shown next.

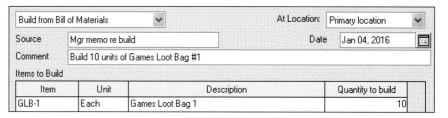

If you display the Journal, you will see:

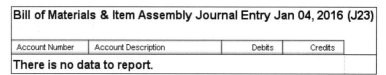

3 ➤ **Post** the entry when correct.

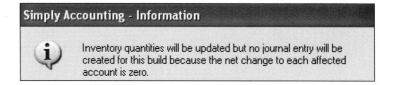

4 ➤ Click **OK** to continue. **Exit** to the Home window.

5 ➤ To confirm that the 10 units have been built, display the **Inventory Summary** or **Inventory Quantity report** to see the 10 units created.

6 ➤ **Print** Journal entries All (with corrections) for January 04, 2016.

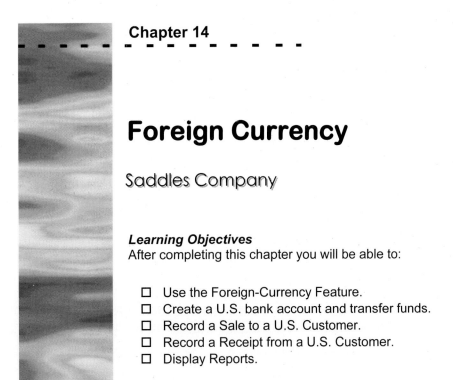

Chapter 14

Foreign Currency

Saddles Company

Learning Objectives

After completing this chapter you will be able to:

☐ Use the Foreign-Currency Feature.
☐ Create a U.S. bank account and transfer funds.
☐ Record a Sale to a U.S. Customer.
☐ Record a Receipt from a U.S. Customer.
☐ Display Reports.

The contents of this chapter are as follows:

* Foreign-Currency Overview 594

    Exercise 14-1 – Turn on Foreign-Currency Feature 594
    Exercise 14-2 – Create U.S. Dollar Bank Account..................................... 596
    Exercise 14-3 – Set Up Linked Accounts.. 598
    Exercise 14-4 – To Create U.S. Customer 598
    Exercise 14-5 – Transferring Money to the U.S. Account.......................... 600
    Exercise 14-6 – Recording a Sale to a U.S. Customer.............................. 601
    Exercise 14-7 – Record a Receipt from a U.S. Customer 602
    Exercise 14-8 – Reports... 603

* Challenge Exercise 14 C14-1, Saddles 607

Slideshow 14 – FOREIGN CURRENCY will demonstrate how easy, yet powerful, this Simply feature is. Run it now.

Foreign Currency Overview

There have been many requests from customers for saddles to be shipped to the United States. The business will be able to receive U.S. dollars for sales receipts and pay in U.S. dollars for a number of different saddle cleaners that can be purchased in the United States.

The Saddles Company business manager has decided to transfer Canadian funds, in order to open a new U.S. bank account, due to future receipts and payments being received and paid in U.S. funds.

1 ➤   Refer to Exercise 1-1, to **unzip** the **14 Saddles exe** file, from the www.simplyaccounting2010.nelson.com under Student Resources.

2 ➤   Start Simply Accounting and open the **14 Saddles** file.

3 ➤   Accept the session date of **Feb 01, 2017**.

Exercise 14-1 – Turn on Foreign-Currency Feature

Simply needs to know that you want the system to work with U.S. dollars (currency). The Premium version can work with as many different currencies as you need.

1 ➤   Click **Setup, Settings,** in the left pane, click ⊞ at **Company,** click **Currency**. This window shows that the currency to be used is Canadian (Simply calls this the Home Currency).

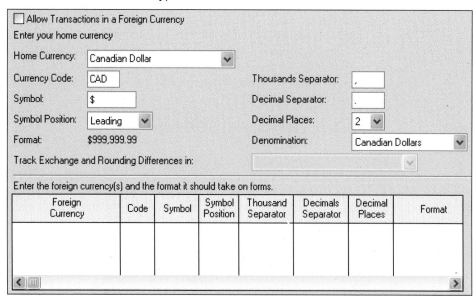

Home Currency	DO NOT CHANGE. If you click the ▼ you can see the selection of currencies available and the Home Currency could change. You want to leave it as Canadian.

Currency Code	DO NOT CHANGE from CAD.
Symbol	DO NOT CHANGE. Different currencies in the world use different symbols to represent their money.
Symbol Position	DO NOT CHANGE. Most currencies have the symbol at the beginning of the amount, similar to what we do in Canada. Some currencies have the symbol at the end of the amount.
Format	This is a display of the currency amounts (codes) above.
Thousands Separator	DO NOT CHANGE. Some currencies use a space, instead of a , (comma) as we do in Canada. If you change any of the settings, then the Format displayed below changes. Remember to change the settings back to a comma.
Decimal Separator	DO NOT CHANGE. Some currencies use a comma instead of a dot similar to what we do in Canada.
Decimal Places	DO NOT CHANGE. Some currencies only use 1 decimal place.
Denomination	DO NOT CHANGE. If you click the ▼ you can see a selection of currency wording available.

2 ➤ At the top, click on ☐ Allow Transactions in a Foreign Currency . A ✓ appears and the "Track Exchange and Rounding Differences in" field is now available (not grayed out).

3 ➤ **Track Exchange and Rounding Differences in** Click the ▼, select **5400 US Exchange Gains/ Losses**, Tab . Saddles has decided to record exchange differences in this account. This account could also have been set up in the Revenue section of the chart of accounts.

4 ➤ **Foreign Currency** Double-click and select **United States Dollars**. The USD currency code and other fields to the right are filled in. When you choose the currency, the Currency Code and Symbols change.

The Currency Information Currency tab window should appear as follows:

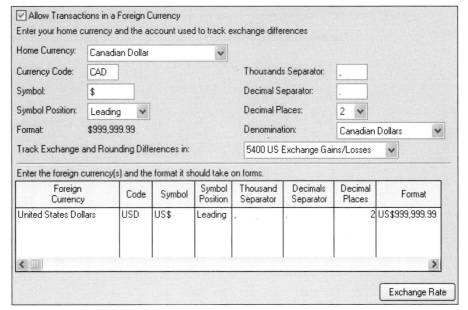

☑ Allow Transactions in a Foreign Currency
Enter your home currency and the account used to track exchange differences

Home Currency: Canadian Dollar

Currency Code:	CAD		Thousands Separator:	,
Symbol:	$		Decimal Separator:	.
Symbol Position:	Leading		Decimal Places:	2
Format:	$999,999.99		Denomination:	Canadian Dollars

Track Exchange and Rounding Differences in: 5400 US Exchange Gains/Losses

Enter the foreign currency(s) and the format it should take on forms.

Foreign Currency	Code	Symbol	Symbol Position	Thousand Separator	Decimals Separator	Decimal Places	Format
United States Dollars	USD	US$	Leading	,	.	2	US$999,999.99

Exchange Rate

5 ➤ Click the **Exchange Rate** button.

Display a reminder if the exchange rate is:	DO NOT CHANGE. You do not need to be notified if the rate is old. If you click the ▼ you will see other choices.
Currency Exchange Web Site	Leave blank. DO NOT CHANGE. You could enter an Internet URL (Uniform Resource Locater) web site where daily exchange rates are updated.

Exchange Rate Table

6 ➤ **Date**   Type **Feb 01, 2017**, ⬚Tab⬚.

7 ➤ **Exchange Rate** Type **1.0531**, ⬚Tab⬚. This is the U.S. dollar exchange rate to Canadian for this date. Simply adds the extra three zeros.

In business there are two rates for each of purchasing and selling U.S. dollars, one rate for under $1,000 and one rate for over $1,000. For this exercise we will only use 1 rate per day, because most businesses would use only one rate for the daily activity.

Your Exchange Rate tab should look like the following:

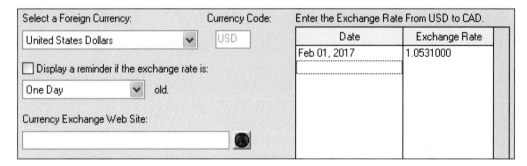

8 ➤ Click **OK** when correct. You are returned to the Setting window. Click **OK** to return to the Home window.

Exercise 14-2 – Create U.S. Dollar Bank Account

---

1 ➤ Click the **COMPANY** module, click the **Chart of Accounts** icon.

2 ➤ Click on the **Create** icon.

3 ➤ **Account**   Type **1080**, ⬚Tab⬚, **U.S. Chequing Account**, ⬚Tab⬚.

4 ➤ **Type**   Select **Subgroup Account**.

5 ➤ Click the **Class Options** tab. Click the ▼ and select **Bank**.

6 ➤ **Currency**   Click the ▼ and select **USD**. The account will record transactions in U.S. dollars. ⬚Tab⬚ to Next Deposit No.

7 ➤ **Next Deposit No.**   Remove 1 and leave blank, ⬚Tab⬚.

Do NOT click on [Change the Next Cheque Number]. If you click this selection, you will see the following:

Simply Accounting

Changes have been made to this account but they have not been saved. Save your changes if you want to change the next cheque number for this account.

Click **OK** to return to the General Ledger window.

---

8 ➤ Click [Save and Close] to create the account.

You will notice that the U.S. Chequing account is under the Canadian bank account. You should also notice that a new column Foreign Balance now shows the U.S. Chequing account with a U.S. $0.00 balance.

Balances are as of the latest transaction date	Type	CAD Balance	Foreign Balance
ASSETS			
📗 **1000 CURRENT ASSETS**	H		
📗 1060 Cash In Bank	A	3,120.00	
📗 1080 U.S. Chequing Account	A	0.00	US$0.00

You should also notice that both #1200 Accounts Receivable and #2200 Accounts Payable, show Canadian Dollars and Foreign Balances in United States Dollars (US$.00).

📘 1200 Accounts Receivable	G		
Canadian Dollar		2,712.00	
United States Dollars		0.00	US$0.00
Total		2,712.00	

📘 2200 Accounts Payable	G		
Canadian Dollar		5,989.00	
United States Dollars		0.00	US$0.00
Total		5,989.00	

There are two ways to enter the next cheque number for this account.

Method a) Follow the steps starting at step 9.

Method b) From the Home window, click **Setup**, **Reports & Forms**, in the left pane click the [+] at Cheques, click **1080 U.S. Chequing Account**. You will be taken to the Reports & Forms Options window. In the right pane, follow step 11 to enter the cheque number.

9 ➤ Using method a) Double-click **1080 U.S. Chequing Account,** click **Class Options** tab.

10 ➤ Click [Change the Next Cheque Number]. You will be taken to the Report & Form Options window as noted in 8b.

11 ➤ Next Cheque No. At the bottom type **101** [Tab]. Special cheques with the wording 'Pay in U.S. funds' should be purchased.

Click **OK**. You are returned to the General Ledger Accounts window.

DO NOT CHANGE the other fields for this exercise.

Notice at the bottom the new information.

Current Balance in CAD	0.00
Current Balance in USD	0.00

12 ➤ Click ☒ to return to the Accounts window. Return to the Home window.

Exercise 14-3 – Set Up Linked Accounts

---

1 ➤ From the Home window, click on **Setup**, **Settings**, in the left pane, click the ⊞ at Payables, click **Linked Accounts**. The right pane shows the Linked Accounts.

Select default bank accounts for currencies

Currency	Bank account to use
Canadian Dollar	1060 Cash In Bank
United States Dollars	

Accounts Payable:	2200 Accounts Payable
Freight Expense:	
Early Payment Purchase Discount:	5120 Purchase Discounts
Prepayments and Prepaid Orders:	2200 Accounts Payable

2 ➤ **Bank account**   Double-click on the **United States Dollars** line and select
to use   **1080 U.S. Chequing Account**.

Select default bank accounts for currencies

Currency	Bank account to use
Canadian Dollar	1060 Cash In Bank
United States Dollars	1080 U.S. Chequing Account

3 ➤ In the left pane, click the ⊞ at **Receivable,** click **Linked Accounts** and repeat step 2.

4 ➤ Click **OK** to return to the Home window.

Exercise 14-4 – To Create U.S. Customer

---

1 ➤ Click the **RECEIVABLES**, click the **Customers** icon, and click the **Create** icon.

2 ➤ **Customer**   Type **Saddle Barn Inc.**, and type the Address tab information as shown next:

Customer:	Saddle Barn Inc.

| Address | Ship-to Address | Options | Taxes | Statistics | M |

Contact:	Lydia Sullivan
Street 1:	2900 Steiger Avenue
Street 2:	
City:	Bronx
Province:	New York
Postal Code:	10932
Country:	US

Ship-to-Address tab

3 ➤ **Ship-to address** leave the selection as  ☑ Default ship-to address.

Options tab

4 ➤ Change the items indicated.

Revenue Account	**4010 Sales Saddles**
Currency	**USD**

Early Payment Terms
___ % discount if paid within ___ days. Net amount due within 20 days.

The bottom-right display now shows:

Balance Owing in CAD	0.00
Balance Owing in USD	0.00

The balance in the account will display both Canadian and U.S. dollars.

Taxes tab

5 ➤ **Tax Exempt**   Click to make Tax Exempt HST column **Yes**.
When goods are shipped to the U.S., there are no taxes.

Tax code   Select **No Tax** as the Tax Code.

Statistics tab

6 ➤ **Credit Limit**   Type CAD **6,000.00**   USD **5,600.00**.

7 ➤ Click Save and Close to create the account.

Customers window   The Balances for this customer are showing in U.S. dollars.

 Saddle Barn Inc.   US$0.00   US$0.00

8 ➤ Return to the Home window.

Exercise 14-5 – Transferring Money to the U.S. Account

An alternative method is to use the BANKING module, Transfer Funds feature. However, you will not be able *to* display the entry before posting.

See Appendix CD-AJ, *Transfer Funds* at www.simplyaccounting2 010.nelson.com under Student Resources.

1 ➤   Advance the date to **Feb 02, 2017**.

2 ➤   Click the **COMPANY** module, click the **General** Journal icon. (See side note box.)

3 ➤   **Source**   **Bank Transfer,** [Tab] to Comment.

4 ➤   **Comment**   **Transfer Canadian funds to open U.S. account.**

5 ➤   **Currency**   Click the ⏷ and select **USD**.

6 ➤   **Exchange Rate** The rate (1.0531) entered in Exercise 14-1, step 7 is displayed as 1.0531000.

7 ➤   Enter the information shown in the next figure.

The amount entered is in U.S. dollars (currency).
If you do not select USD, account 1080 will not display in the Account field.

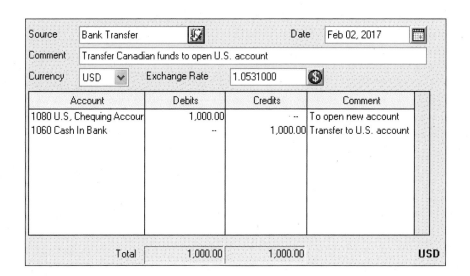

8 ➤   Display the General Journal entry. It should resemble the following:

Account Number	Account Description	Foreign A...	Debits	Credits
General Journal Entry Feb 02, 2017 (J1)				
1080	U.S, Chequing Account	US$1,000.00	1,053.10	-
	To open new account			
1060	Cash In Bank	US$1,000.00	-	1,053.10
	Transfer to U.S. account			
1 United States Dollars equals 1.0531000 Canadian Dollar				
Additional Date:	Additional Field:			
			1,053.10	1,053.10

Notice: It required $1,053.10 Canadian dollars to buy $1,000.00 U.S. dollars.

9 ➤   **Exit** the General Journal Entry and **Post** when correct.

10 ➤ **Exit** to the Home window.

Exercise 14-6 –Recording a Sale to a U.S. Customer

---

1 ➤ Advance the date to **Feb 03, 2017**.

Feb 03, 2017   **Shipped 2 model #501 saddles at $1,100.00 U.S. each to Saddle Barn Inc. (U.S. customer). Terms Net 20 Days.**

---

2 ➤ Click **RECEIVABLES** icon, click on the **Sales Invoices** icon.

3 ➤ **Sold To**   Select **Saddle Barn Inc**. Note that the Exchange Rate field now displays. `Tab`.

4 ➤ **Exchange Rate** Change the rate to **1.0526**, `Tab`.

Note: The actual rates may be very different when you do these entries. This is an example of how to record entries.

5 ➤ **Quantity**   Type **2**, `Tab`.

6 ➤ **Unit**   Type **each**, `Tab`.

7 ➤ **Description**   Type **Model #501 saddles**, `Tab`.

8 ➤ **Base Price**   Type **1,100** (the amount will be in U.S. funds) `Tab` to Account.

   Disc %   There is no discount at this time.

   Tax   As noted previously, when goods are shipped to the U.S., there are no taxes (HST).

9 ➤ **Account**   Leave as 4010 Sales Saddles. Some companies may want to have different sales accounts for Foreign Currencies. Saddles Company is using only one Sales account.

The Sales Invoice window should resemble the following:

The Total box | Total in USD | 2,200.00 |.

10 ➤ Display the Sales Journal Entry. It should resemble the following:

Account Number	Account Description	Foreign A...	Debits	Credits
1200	Accounts Receivable	US$2,200.00	2,315.72	-
4010	Sales Saddles	US$2,200.00	-	2,315.72

Sales Journal Entry Feb 03, 2017 (J2)

1 United States Dollars equals 1.0526000 Canadian Dollar
Additional Date: Additional Field:

| | | | 2,315.72 | 2,315.72 |

11 ➤ **Exit** the Sales Journal Entry and **Post** when correct.

12 ➤ **Exit** to the Home window.

Exercise 14-7 – Record a Receipt from a U.S. Customer

---

1 ➤ Advance the date to **Feb 23, 2017**.

> **Feb 23, 2017** **Received cheque # 867 in the U.S. amount of $1,200.00 from Saddle Barn Inc. as partial payment on our invoice 270.**

2 ➤ Click the **Receipts** icon.

3 ➤ **From**   Click the ▼ and select **Saddle Barn Inc**. The 'Deposit to' field changes to the 1080 U.S. Chequing Account. This is automatically set because you linked the U.S. dollar account in Exercise 14-3. Note that the Exchange Rate field displays. [Tab].

4 ➤ **Cheque**   Type **867**.

5 ➤ **Receipt No.**   Type **867**, [Tab] to Amount Received.

6 ➤ **Amount Received**   Type **1,200.00**. [Tab].

7 ➤ **Exchange Rate**   Type **1.0302** (the rate changes daily), [Tab].

8 ➤ Click on the **Exchange** icon [icon]. Previously used exchange rates are listed and may be used by selecting the rate required.

Exchange Rate

Enter a new exchange rate or select an existing one

Date	Exchange Rate
Feb 01, 2017	1.0531000
Feb 02, 2017	1.0531000
Feb 03, 2017	1.0526000

9 ➤ Click **Cancel**.

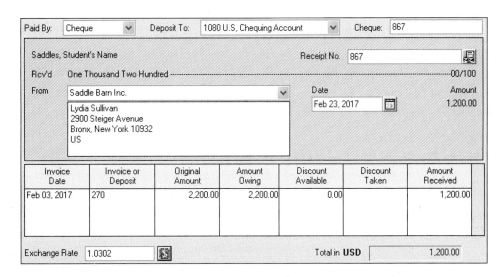

10 ➤ Display Receipts Journal Entry. It should resemble the following:

Account Number	Account Description	Foreign A...	Debits	Credits
Receipts Journal Entry Feb 23, 2017 (J3)				
1080	U.S, Chequing Account	US$1,200.00	1,236.24	-
5400	US Exchange Gains/Losses		26.88	-
1200	Accounts Receivable	US$1,200.00	-	1,263.12
1 United States Dollars equals 1.0302000 Canadian Dollar				
Additional Date:	Additional Field:			
			1,263.12	1,263.12

11 ➤ **Exit** the Receipts Journal Entry and **Post** when correct.

12 ➤ **Exit** to the Home window.

Similar procedures would be followed to record Vendor Purchases and Payments.

In Challenge Exercise 14-1 you will create a U.S. vendor and record a U.S. $ purchase and a U.S. $ payment.

Exercise 14-8 – Reports

View the Customer Aged Detail report as follows.

1 ➤ Click **Reports, Receivables, Customer Aged, Detail** should be selected, click **Show Foreign Amounts**, select **Saddle Barn Inc.**, remove the ✓ at Include Terms, **OK**. The report displays the amounts in U.S. dollars.

Source	Date	Transaction Type	Currency Code	Total	Current
Customer Aged Detail As at Feb 23, 2017					
Saddle Barn Inc. (amounts in United States Dollars)					
270	Feb 03, 2017	Invoice	USD	2,200.00	2,200.00
867	Feb 23, 2017	Payment	USD	-1,200.00	-1,200.00
Total outstanding:				1,000.00	1,000.00
Total unpaid invoices:					
Canadian Dollar				-	-
United States Dollars				1,000.00	1,000.00
Total deposits/prepaid order:					
Canadian Dollar				-	-
United States Dollars				-	-

2 ➤   **Exit** to the Home window.

If you did not click Show Foreign Amounts, the report would display the amounts in Canadian funds as follows:

Customer Aged Detail As at Feb 23, 2017				
Source	Date	Transaction Type	Total	Current
Saddle Barn Inc.				
270	Feb 03, 2017	Invoice	2,315.72	2,315.72
867	Feb 23, 2017	Payment	-1,263.12	-1,263.12
Total outstanding:			1,052.60	1,052.60
Total unpaid invoices:			1,052.60	1,052.60
Total deposits/prepaid order:			-	-
Total outstanding:			1,052.60	1,052.60

3 ➤   **Exit** to the Home window.

4 ➤   Click **Reports, Receivables, Customer Aged**, select **Report Type** as **Summary**, click **Show Foreign Amounts**, **Select All**, **OK**. The report displays the amounts in Canadian and U.S. dollars.

Customer Aged Summary As at Feb 23, 2017			
Name	Cur Co	Total	Current
Lonesome Ranch		1,695.00	1,695.00
Saddle Barn Inc. (amounts in Uni...	USD	1,000.00	1,000.00
Western Tack & Saddle Shop		1,017.00	1,017.00
Total outstanding in:			
Canadian Dollar		2,712.00	2,712.00
United States Dollars		1,000.00	1,000.00

5 ➤   **Exit** to the Home window.

Other Reports

1 ➤   Click **Reports, Financials, Realized Exchange Gain/Loss**, Start Date **Feb 01**, Finish Date **Feb 23**, **OK**.

This report will show the gain or loss difference between the Sale transaction exchange rate and the Receipt exchange rate.

Realized Exchange Gain/Loss Feb 01, 2017 to Feb 23, 2017								
Date	Name	Invoice/Source No.	Payment No.	Journal No.	Foreign Amt.	Original Rate	Payment...	Gain/Loss
1200 Accounts Receivable								
Feb 23, 2017	Saddle Barn Inc.	270	867	J3	US$1,200.00	1.0526000	1.0302000	-26.88
Total Realized Exchange Gain/Loss								-26.88

2 ➤   **Exit** to the Home window.

3 ➤   Click **Reports, Financials, Unrealized Exchange Gain/Loss**, **OK**.

The Exchange Rate: would be changed when the Financial Statements are being prepared and all U.S. accounts need to be recalculated based on the Exchange Rate on that date.

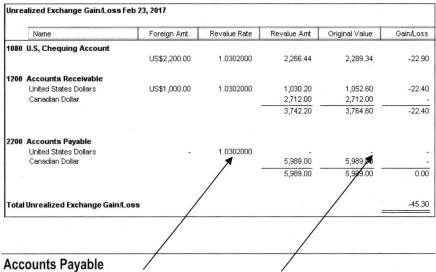

4 ➤   There are no changes required. Click **OK**.

Name	Foreign Amt.	Revalue Rate	Revalue Amt	Original Value	Gain/Loss
1080 U.S, Chequing Account					
	US$2,200.00	1.0302000	2,266.44	2,289.34	-22.90
1200 Accounts Receivable					
United States Dollars	US$1,000.00	1.0302000	1,030.20	1,052.60	-22.40
Canadian Dollar			2,712.00	2,712.00	-
			3,742.20	3,764.60	-22.40
2200 Accounts Payable					
United States Dollars	-	1.0302000	-	-	-
Canadian Dollar			5,989.00	5,989.00	-
			5,989.00	5,989.00	0.00
Total Unrealized Exchange Gain/Loss					-45.30

Unrealized Exchange Gain/Loss Feb 23, 2017

Accounts Payable
Revalue Rate: The rate displays, but there is no dollar amount, because we have not recorded any U.S. Purchases or Payments.

5 ➤   **Exit** to the Home window.

To Print a Balance Sheet

6 ➤   Click **Reports, Financials, Balance Sheet**.

7 ➤   Click the **Yes** button to revalue the accounts. A drop-down Exchange Rate window appears.

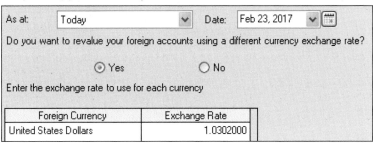

8 ➤ For this exercise, leave the choice as **Yes**, but do not change the Exchange rate at 1.0302000 (today's rate). All outstanding U.S. dollar values will be revalued at this rate. Click **OK**. The Statement displays the Canadian equivalent for the U.S. accounts (Accounts Receivable and Payable).

Accounts Receivable	3,742.20

(**Yes** choice)

	Balance Sheet with Yes choice	Balance Sheet with No choice
Lonesome Ranch	1,695.00	1,695.00
Saddle Barn	1,030.20 CDN	1,030.20 CDN*
Western Tack & Saddle Shop	$1,017.00	1,017.00
Sub-Total	3,742.20	3,742.20
Add: Unrealized Gain On U.S.		22.40 **
Accounts Receivable	3,742.20	3,764.60

* This is the Canadian equivalent of what the $1,000.00 U.S. was worth on the date the sale was made. Exchange rate was 1.0302.

** applies to Saddle Barn

If you had selected No, the exchange rate would default to the original U.S. Exchange rate for each transaction (which would include any Unrealized Gains or Losses on the U.S. dollar values). The original Exchange rate for the sale (Exercise 14-6) was 1.0526000. Click **OK**. The Statement displays the Canadian equivalent for the U.S. accounts (Accounts Receivable and Payable).

Accounts Receivable	3,764.60

Accounts Payable	5,989.00

Specialty Saddles Ltd.	2,260.00
Western Clothing Manufacturing	3,729.00
Accounts Payable*	5,989.00

*No U.S. dollar accounts

Information only

If you were to use a different Exchange Rate during a session date (assuming you are recording all transactions on the same invoice/receipt date), you will receive a confirmation message similar to the one below.

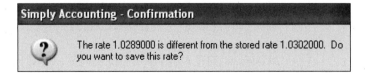

You would click "Yes" to save this rate instead of the previous rate used.

Challenge Exercise 14 C14-1, Saddles

Foreign-Currency Review

In this exercise you will be using the Chapter 14 data file solution to create a U.S. vendor, a U.S purchase and a U.S. payment.

1 ➤ Record and **Post** the following transactions.

Feb 23 Based on a customer's request, the manager has made arrangements to purchase a special design model saddle #623 from the Hersay Stables, 258 RR#6, Millerton, New York, 12683, ignore phone number, Expense Account 5100, Currency USD. Due to the special nature of the saddle, terms are payment on receipt of goods. Taxes for this vendor will be No taxes. The saddle will cost $1,300.00 U.S. (ignore Duty and HST taxes, etc., on this purchase to allow you to see the transaction without duty and taxes). The saddle will be delivered by courier on Feb 25. Issued Purchase Order #15, exchange rate has not changed.

Feb 25 The saddle from Hersay Stables arrives in good condition. Invoice #1389 for $1,300.00 U.S., accompanies the shipment.

Feb 25 Issue U.S. cheque #101 to Hersay Stables for invoice #1389.

2 ➤ Print the following:

a) Journal Entries All, with Foreign Amounts for all entries.
b) Income Statement for Feb 1 to Feb 25.
c) Balance Sheet at Feb 25, without changing the currency exchange rate. Leave choice as No.

Chapter 15

Taxes (HST, GST and PST)

Brittany Company

Learning Objectives

After completing this chapter you will be able to:

- ☐ Identify the difference between HST, GST and PST.
- ☐ Determine who pays the taxes.
- ☐ Specify how they are reported to the separate governments.

The contents of this chapter are as follows:

- Information on HST or GST Goods and Services Tax 610
- Method of Recording HST or GST 611
- HST, What Account Do You Charge? 613
- (PST) Provincial Sales Tax, (RST) Retail Sales Tax 614
- GST Sales Tax 615
- PST, What Account Do You Charge? 615

Information on HST or GST Goods and Services Tax

The Goods and Services tax (GST), presently at 5%, or blended (Harmonized- HST) with some provincial taxes at different rates (e.g., Ontario at 13%,) is levied by the federal government of Canada, Canada Customs and Revenue Agency, on most goods and services in Canada.

In Ontario, New Brunswick, Newfoundland & Labrador, and Nova Scotia, the GST and PST are blended together, harmonized, at a rate of 13%. British Columbia is harmonized at 12%. The harmonized tax operates the same as the GST, with the HST Paid on Purchases deducted from the HST Charged on Sales.

The HST rate of 13% is used in this text and reflected in the solutions. When on the job be sure to use the appropriate HST or GST and PST rates.

Refer to Fig. 15-10, at the end of this chapter, for a chart of the tax rates levied by various governments.

Some goods and services are not taxed as follows:

1. **Tax exempt** (i.e., GST is not calculated on these goods. GST is, therefore, not collected or paid).

2. **GST non-taxable** (i.e., there is no tax rate on these services or goods; therefore, GST is not collected or paid).

3. **GST taxable at a zero rate** (i.e., the current GST rate on these goods or services is zero (0) percent; therefore, GST is not collected or paid).

Tax codes used in this text are:

HS	Harmonized at 13%
HI	Harmonized at 8%
No Tax	Used on some items (paying HST or GST to the Receiver General, drawings or withdrawals to the owner, etc.).

(PST) Provincial Sales Tax

Provinces (except Alberta) levy a provincial sales tax (PST), which is included in the HST, and may include or exclude the GST in the price on which the PST is calculated. The companies in this text exclude the GST in calculating the PST.

PST also may be called Retail Sales Tax (RST).

HST or GST Charged on Sales

HST or GST is charged on goods or services regardless of whether they are sold to a retail customer (consumer) or to another company (merchandiser, wholesaler or service company). The **HST Charged on Sales** or **GST Charged on Sales** is entered as a liability.

HST or GST Paid on Purchases

When a company buys goods for resale or for its own use, HST or GST is paid on the purchase price, regardless of whether or not the purchased item is intended for resale. The **HST Paid on Purchases or GST Paid on Purchases** is entered as a contra-liability.

Method of Recording HST or GST

A business may use the **Regular** method of recording HST or GST, in which the HST or GST is recorded on each sale and purchase. At the end of the reporting period the business will either send the difference (more HST or GST collected than paid) or claim a refund (more paid than collected) to the Receiver General of Canada. Depending on the size of the business, it will report on a monthly or quarterly basis.

A business may use the **Quick** method, which calculates the HST or GST to be paid based on a rate of 1 to 5 percent of net sales. This method may be used by some grocery and convenience stores.

The companies in this text use the Regular method of recording the GST.

To avoid double taxation, a business is allowed to deduct the **HST or GST Paid on Purchases** from the **HST or GST Charged on Sales**. The usual business practice is to locate the **HST or GST Paid on Purchases** account in the liability section of the Balance Sheet, with the **HST or GST Charged on Sales**. Some companies use one account only, HST or GST Payable, to record both the HST or GST collected and paid.

Registration

A business with annual sales of more than $30,000 in a single calendar quarter or in four consecutive calendar quarters, which exceed the small supplier limit, **must** register to collect the HST or GST. Registering will allow a business to recover any HST or GST paid on its purchases. Registration is optional for a business in which sales are less than $30,000.

Accounting Examples Using the Regular Method of Recording HST

In this chapter the cents .00 are not shown, and it is assumed the province is Ontario, with an HST rate of 13%.

If Brittany Company buys merchandise **for resale** from Dustin Company the entry on each company's books is shown in Fig. 15-1.

Brittany Company			Dustin Company		
buys goods			**sells** goods		
Dr Purchases	200		Dr Cash or Accounts Receivable 226		
Dr HST Paid on purchases	26		Cr Sales		200
Cr Cash or Accounts Payable		226	Cr HST Charged on Sales		26

Fig. 15-1

If Brittany Company **sells** merchandise, including HST, to Chad Company, another merchandising company, the entries on each company's books are shown in Fig. 15-2.

```
Brittany Company                      | Chad Company
  sells goods                         |   buys goods
Dr Cash or Accounts Receivable  565   | Dr  Purchases                    500
Cr    Sales                     500   | Dr  HST paid on Purchase          65
Cr    HST Charged on Sales       65   | Cr    Cash or Accounts Payable         565
```

Fig. 15-2

- Most firms add the HST to the selling price of the goods or services on the invoice.

- The $500 price, plus 13% HST, equals invoice amount of $565.

HST or GST Paid to the Federal Government

The clerk will determine the amounts in the two HST or GST accounts, at the report date, and calculate the difference as being a payment to be made or a refund requested. See Exercise 3B-30.

For Brittany Company, at reporting time (month or quarter), the value of **HST Paid on Purchases** ($26) is subtracted from **HST Charged on Sales** ($65), and the difference ($39) is paid to the government, Receiver General, by the appropriate date.

Assuming different dollar values:

If the **HST Paid on Purchases** ($420) is subtracted from HST Charged on Sales ($390), the difference ($30) is reported to the government, and a refund is claimed.

HST Examples for Showing Remittances

The Receiver General is set up as a vendor in the PAYABLES module. To record the payment of HST, Brittany Company must reduce the amount in both HST accounts, and the difference will be paid by cheque using the Make Other Payment option to the Receiver General for Canada. See Fig. 15-3.

```
DR HST Charged on Sales       65
CR    HST Paid on purchases           26
CR    Cash                            39
```

Fig. 15-3

HST, What Account Do You Charge?

A common question that comes up when you buy goods or services is, to which account is the HST (Harmonized Sales Tax) posted?

You pay the HST; therefore, it should go into the HST Payable account, or should it?

To answer that, look at the following Ontario example:

Business Supplies
85 Shaw Avenue   **INVOICE**
Toronto, ON M2W 3A6   **4557**
Phone 416-333-2255 ❖ Fax 416-333-2211

SOLD TO:

Taras Rai   P.O. _____
21 Nina Drive   Date: _April 5, 2016_
Rexdale, ON M9N 1Z2   Shipped By: _Our Truck_

#	*ITEM*	*QTY.*	DESCRIPTION	AMOUNT
	various		Various Office Supplies	$ 100.00
			HST	13.00
			TOTAL	$ 113.00

	Personal	**Business**
Office supplies bought above	$100.00	$100.00
HST Paid (included in invoice)	13.00	13.00
Total paid	$113.00	$113.00
Rebate from Provincial Government	nil	nil
Rebate from Federal Government	nil	13.00 (Federal)
The true cost	$113.00	$100.00

You cannot get any other rebates from governments, therefore:

- the personal true cost of the office supplies becomes $113.00
- the business true cost of the office supplies becomes $100.00

If the true cost of supplies for business is $100.00, then the cost of the supplies and HST should be charged as follows.

The business entry would be:

Office Supplies On Hand (Asset)	$100.00	
HST Paid on Purc/Serv	13.00	
Cash or Bank or Accounts Payable		$113.00

(PST) Provincial Sales Tax, (RST) Retail Sales Tax

Provinces (except Alberta) levy a Provincial Sales Tax (PST). It may also be called Retail Sales Tax (RST), and may include or exclude the GST in the price on which the PST is calculated. As noted previously, some provinces blend (harmonize) their PST with the GST (the tax is called HST). The following discussion is for provinces that collect the PST from retailers.

The Provincial Sales Tax, normally referred to as PST or RST, is collected by the selling company on goods or services sold within the province. The company that sells the product or service is required by the provincial government to collect the tax at the time of sale, and forward the amount collected to the provincial taxation office in the following month.

If Brittany Company **purchases** merchandise for resale from other vendors, the merchandise purchased is exempt from provincial tax (PST). This means that Brittany Company does not pay PST on items purchased that are going to be resold to customers. A purchasing firm (e.g., Brittany) would apply for a PST exemption certificate, and the certificate number would have to be given to a seller to advise them that the goods were purchased PST-Exempt.

If Brittany Company **sells** merchandise to a final consumer (Retail sale) the entry to record the sale is shown as in Fig. 15-4. It is assumed that the PST is calculated only on the selling price and not on the selling price plus GST.

Retail Sale with PST @ 8% and GST at 5%

Brittany Company		Mrs. Marion Chaiken	
sells goods		**buys** goods for her personal use.	
Dr Cash or Accounts Receivable 452		Does not keep accounting records	
Cr Sales	400	and, therefore, does not record entries	
Cr GST Charged on Sales	20		
Cr PST Charged on Sales	32		

Fig. 15-4

If Brittany Company **sells** <u>different</u> merchandise to another merchandising company, the PST-exemption entry to record the sale is shown as in Fig. 15-5.

Merchandiser/Wholesaler

Brittany Company		Delta Company		
sells goods		**buys** goods		
Dr Cash or Accounts Receivable 525		Dr Purchases	500	
Cr Sales	500	Dr GST Paid on Purchases	25	
Cr GST Charged on Sales	25	Cr Cash or Accounts Payable		525

Fig. 15-5

PST Paid to the Provincial Government

Brittany Company will determine the amounts in the PST account at the report date. As shown in Fig. 15-4, Brittany Company owes the provincial government $32.

To record the payment, Brittany Company would set up a Vendor, the Minister of Finance of the province, and would issue a cheque in Payments using Make Other Payment option and record the following entry. See Fig. 15-6.

```
Dr PST Charged on Sales     32
Cr    Cash                         32
```

Fig. 15-6

GST Sales Tax

Assume that Brittany Company is in Prince Edward Island with a Provincial Sales tax of 10%. The entry to record the sale is as shown in Fig. 15-7.

```
Brittany Company                    | Ditlove Company
 sells goods                        |  buys goods
Dr Cash or Accounts Receivable 420  | Dr Purchases               400
Cr    Sales                    400  | Dr GST Paid on Purchases   20
Cr    GST Charged on Sales      20  | Cr    Accounts Payable          420
```

Fig. 15-7

When goods for resale are **purchased**, entries similar to the following are recorded:

```
Brittany Company                    | Darwin Company
  buys goods                        |   sells goods
Dr Purchases               300      | Dr Cash or Accounts Receivable  315
Dr GST Paid on Purchases    15      | Cr    Sales                     300
Cr   Cash or Accounts Payable  315  | Cr    GST Charged on Sales        15
```

Fig. 15-8

At the end of the recording period for Brittany Company, the net GST is remitted to the Receiver General with a procedure similar to HST as shown in Fig. 15-9.

Note: The provincial portion of the GST is not paid separately.

```
Dr GST Charged on Sales      20
Cr   GST Paid on Purchases      15
Cr   Cash                        5
```

Fig. 15-9

PST, What Account Do You Charge?

A common question that comes up when you buy goods or services is to which account is the PST (Provincial Sales Tax) posted?

You pay the PST; therefore, it should go into the PST Payable account, or should it?

To answer that, look at the following Manitoba example:

Business Supplies
856 Tranner Avenue   **INVOICE**
Brandon, MB, M2W 3A6   **3658**
Phone 204-783-4689 ❖ Fax 204-783-8528

SOLD TO:

Geraldine Anrason   P.O. _____
2561 Louise Avenue   Date: _April 5, 2016_
Brandon, MB   R7A 6C3   Shipped By: _Our Truck_

#	ITEM	QTY.	DESCRIPTION	AMOUNT
	various		Various Office Supplies	$ 100.00
			GST	5.00
			PST	7.00
			TOTAL	$ 112.00

	Personal	**Business**
Office supplies bought above	$100.00	$100.00
PST Paid (included in invoice)	7.00	7.00
GST Paid (included in invoice)	5.00	5.00
Total paid	$112.00	$112.00
Rebate from Provincial Government	nil	nil
Rebate from Federal Government	nil	5.00(Federal)
The true cost	$112.00	$107.00

You cannot get any other PST rebates from governments, therefore:

- the personal true cost of the office supplies becomes $112.00
- the business true cost of the office supplies becomes $107.00

If the true cost of supplies for business is $107.00, then the cost of the supplies and GST should be charged as follows.

The business entry would be:

Office Supplies On Hand (Asset)	$107.00	
GST Paid on Purc/Serv	5.00	
Cash or Bank		$112.00

HST, GST and PST rates by Province & Territory (at July 1, 2010)

	HST	GST	PST	Total
Prince Edward Island	-	5.0	10.0	15.0
British Columbia	12.0	-	-	12.00
New Brunswick	13.0	-	-	13.0
Newfoundland & Labrador	13.0	-	-	13.0
Nova Scotia	13.0	-	-	13.0
Ontario	13.0	-	-	13.0
Quebec	-	5.0	7.5	12.5
Manitoba	-	5.0	7.0	12.0
Saskatchewan	-	5.0	5.0	10.0
Alberta	-	5.0	-	5.0
North West Territories	-	5.0	-	5.0
Yukon	-	5.0	-	5.0

Fig. 15-10

Simply Accounting by Sage Premium 2010 Student Version Installation Instructions

Installing Simply Accounting

When you install Simply Accounting, you need to know how many computers must have access to your company data and how your company's computers are set up.

Do you store your company data on a file server?

If your company data is, or will be, stored on a Windows file server, perform a **server-only** installation of Simply Accounting on your server. This option installs the MySQL Connector and the Simply Accounting Connection Manager service that manages all connections to your company data. It **does not** install the Simply Accounting program. To learn more, see Standard Network setup below.

Note that if you store your data on a Windows Server (2003, 2008, or Small Business Server 2003), you need to perform additional setup tasks so that other users can access your Simply Accounting data.

Additional setup tasks for Windows

Using Linux?

You can also store your data on a number of supported Linux servers. To learn more about supported Linux distributions, and to download the Simply Accounting Connection Manager for Linux, visit www.simplyaccounting.com/install.

Standalone Computer

User PC

This is the most common installation choice for small businesses. If you only need to use Simply Accounting on one computer,

You or your system administrator need to:

Perform a Full Installation of Simply Accounting on your computer.

Full Install
company
data

Fig. A-1: A portion of the Installation Guide. Credits Sage Software, Inc.

Free to you available as a software download from Simply, is the **Simply Accounting by Sage Premium 2010, Student Version**, which we will refer to as the Student Version.

These instructions assume that you have a previous version of Simply installed on your computer. You need to uninstall the previous version of Simply. If you do not have Simply installed, move to Exercise 1c.

Make sure your computer meets the following system requirements for optimal performance.

The System Requirements are:

- Processor operating at 1 GHz or higher (2.0 GHz recommended).
- 512 MB RAM (1 GB recommended)
- 820 MB hard disk space [additional 100 MB of hard disk space needed for installation]
- Internet Explorer 5.5 SP2
- Microsoft® Windows® 2000, XP, Vista or 7.
- 256 colour or higher SVGA monitor optimized for 1024 x 768; supports 800 X 600 with small fonts
- ACT! By Sage integrations requires ACT! 2009 or ACT! 2010
- CD-ROM Drive
- Forms that can be sent via e-mail require MAPI compliant e-mail client, Internet connection, e-mail service and word processor
- Word and Excel integration requires Microsoft Word and Microsoft Excel 2003 or 2007
- Multi-user (Premium and higher) optimized for Windows 2000, XP, Vista and 7 peer-to-peer networks for Windows 2000 and XP file server networks. Dedicated server recommended: Windows Server 2003 R2, Windows Small Business Server 2003 R2 and 2008, Windows Server 2008, Red Hat Enterprise, Linux 5.0 or SUSE Linux Enterprise Server 10 by Novell.

If you do not have Word, Excel or Outlook as noted, you can still use Simply.

Restrictions and other information

The student edition of the 2010 Premium software has the following restrictions:

1. Can be used for a maximum of 14 months after installation. The software will expire after 14 months.

2. Can NOT open data created in previous versions.

3. You will NOT be able to convert data from this version into future student versions.

4. Technical support may be available from instructors, or for a fee from the Simply technical support number.

- Exercise A-1 Remove Prior Simply Programs from Your Computer 620
- Exercise A-2 Run the Simply Version Utility from the Website 621
- Exercise A-3 Download the Simply Premium Software from the Simply Server 622
- Exercise A-4 Student Registration and Activation 628

Exercise A-1: Remove Prior Simply Programs from Your Computer

IMPORTANT: If you have previously installed *any* version of Simply Accounting on your computer, uninstall that version, then run the Student Version Utility (Exercise 1b) before you install the Student Version of Simply Accounting. If you do not run the Utility, you will have problems using the software.

1 ➤ Click **Start, Settings, Control Panel**, double-click on **Add or Remove Programs**, scroll down to the Simply program (e.g., Simply Accounting by Sage 2009**)**, click on it, click **Remove**.

After a brief time, you will then see a window similar to the following:

2 ➤ To continue click **OK**.

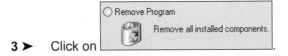

3 ➤ Click on [   ].

4 ➤ Click **Next**. You will see:

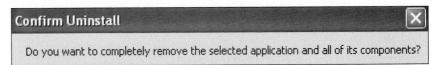

5 ➤ Click **OK**.

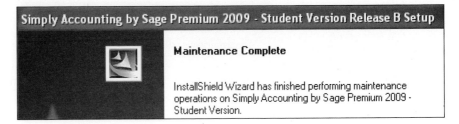

6 ➤ Click **Finish**.

7 ➤ Click **X** to return to the Home page.

Exercise A-2: Run the Simply Utility from the Website

1 ➤ Open **Internet Explorer,** or your browser.

2 ➤ In the address field, type the following:

http://www.simplyaccounting.com/downloads/student/, press **Enter**.

3 ➤ Click on the **Student Version Utility** link on the top right of the window.

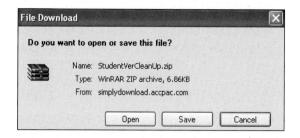

4 ➤   Click on Open. You will see the following.

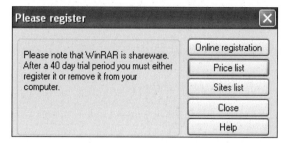

5 ➤   You will be using this software once. Click Close.

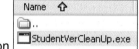

6 ➤   Double-click on .

7 ➤   You should see the following message that the Simply cleanup was successful.

8 ➤   Click OK to close the window and click X to return to the Home window.

Exercise A-3: Download the Simply Premium Software from the Simply Server

---

The author suggests that you save the download file to your hard drive before installing the software.

1 ➤   Using Windows Explorer, **create a folder** on the C drive named: **Simply Download 2010**.

2 ➤   Open **Internet Explorer**.

3 ➤   In the Address field, type the following:
http://www.simplyaccounting.com/downloads/student/, press **Enter**.

4 ➤   **Locate and write down** the Simply 2010 product serial number.

5 ➤   **Download**
Student Version Click on **Simply Accounting 2010**.

6 ➤   Click on the **2010 download** link to download the software.

7 ➤   On the left side under the Simply box, click on the Download button.

8 ➤ Under the Download via the Sage Download Manager, click on **Download Now**.

9 ➤ Click **Install**.

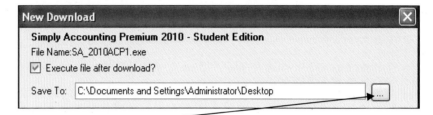

10 ➤ Click the **Browse** button, and locate the Simply Download 2010 folder created in step 1.

11 ➤ The window should be:

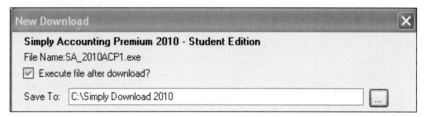

12 ➤ Click **OK**.

13 ➤ Click **Next**.

Fig. A-2: Choose Installation Language.

14 ➤ With a selection of English, click **OK**.

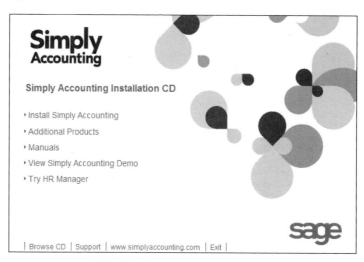

Fig A-3: Install window.

You can view a brief (8 minute) Simply Accounting Demo about the software program.

You can download a trial version of the HR (Human Resource) Manager. There is no exercise for this feature. Note: The HR Manager requires a retail version of Simply and the HR Manager sells for $149.99 for use on 1 computer and 1 user. There is no exercise for the HR Manager in this text.

15 ➤   Click on **Install Simply Accounting**

16 ➤   With a selection of English, click **OK**.

17 ➤   With a selection of **Yes**, click **Next**.

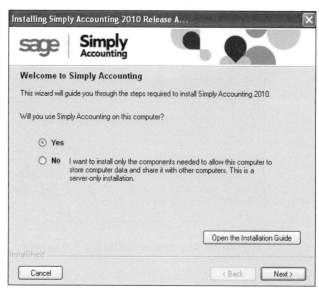

⊙ I have a serial number:

[   ] - [   ]

Fig A-4: Serial number.

18 ➤   Type **242P2U2 1000001**. Click **Next**.

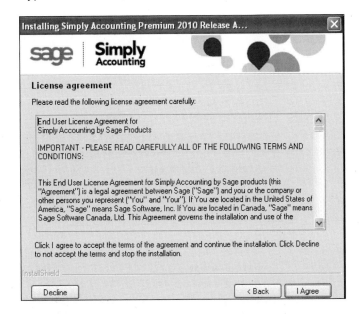

19 ➤   Click **I Agree**.

You will see one of the next two windows regarding the Firewall.

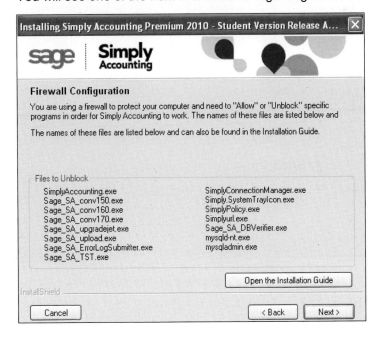

20a ➤   Click **Next** or

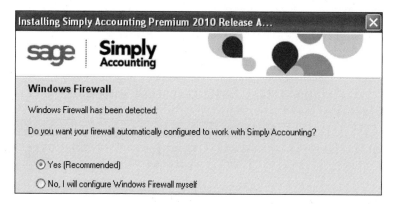

20b ➤   With a selection of **Yes**, click **Next**.

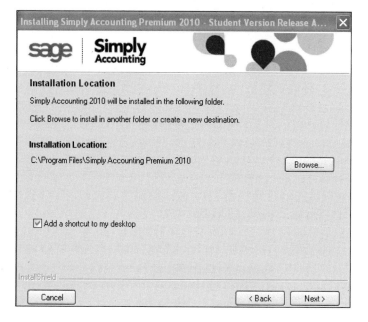

21 ➤   Click **Browse** and **add Student Version** to the file name. Click **OK**.

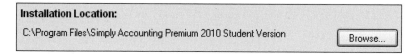

22 ➤   Click **Next**.

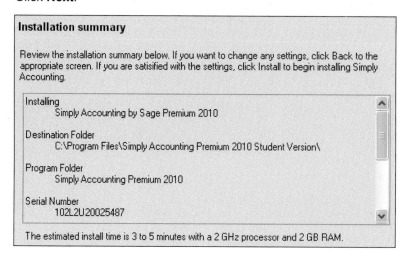

23 ➤   Click **Install**.

Note: Depending on the speed of your computer, the speed of your Internet provider and the number of students downloading, the download may take more than the time indicated. Be patient.

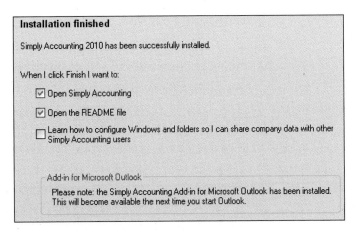

24 ➤   With the selection as shown, click **Finish**.

The ReadMe file lists no changes.

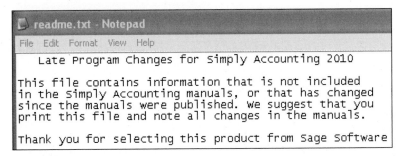

25 ➤   Click **X** to close the window.

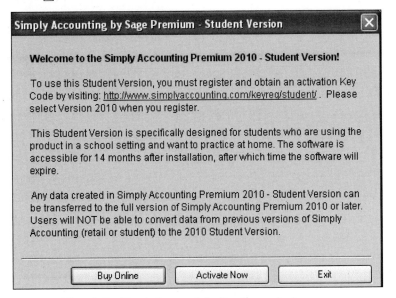

Fig. A-5: Register and Activation window.

Exercise A-4: Student Registration and Activation

1 ➤ Click on the **website** link, and you are taken to the Simply Accounting by Sage, Student Version Registration window.

If you do not have Internet access from your own computer, write the website link address on a piece of paper, or type it in a word processing document. You can use the school Internet access by typing the website into the Internet Address window and link to the Simply website.

2 ➤ Click on **Version 2010 (Premium)**.

3 ➤ Complete the **Company Name** (your student name) and **Email Address** fields. Do **NOT** type a company name, as the registration will be rejected. You must use your own name. You may also fill the information in the lower section.

4 ➤ Click **Submit** (lower down in the window). You should receive an immediate response (Serial Number and Key Codes) as shown below as well as an e-mail response.

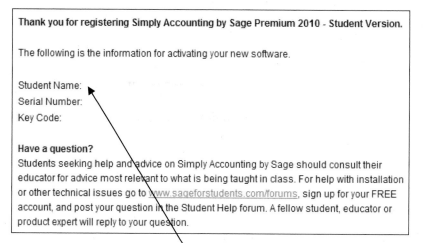

Thank you for registering Simply Accounting by Sage Premium 2010 - Student Version.

The following is the information for activating your new software.

Student Name:
Serial Number:
Key Code:

Have a question?
Students seeking help and advice on Simply Accounting by Sage should consult their educator for advice most relevant to what is being taught in class. For help with installation or other technical issues go to www.sageforstudents.com/forums, sign up for your FREE account, and post your question in the Student Help forum. A fellow student, educator or product expert will reply to your question.

5 ➤ The author has removed the Student Name, Serial Number and Key Code from the above image. **Exit** from your Internet browser.

6 ➤ **Open** your e-mail program and you should have received the activation codes. **Print** the document. It will be easier to enter the codes if you can read them. Put the document in a safe place in case you need to reinstall the software.

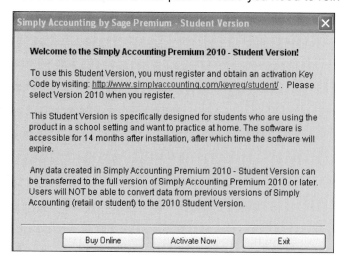

Simply Accounting by Sage Premium - Student Version

Welcome to the Simply Accounting Premium 2010 - Student Version!

To use this Student Version, you must register and obtain an activation Key Code by visiting: http://www.simplyaccounting.com/keyreq/student/ . Please select Version 2010 when you register.

This Student Version is specifically designed for students who are using the product in a school setting and want to practice at home. The software is accessible for 14 months after installation, after which time the software will expire.

Any data created in Simply Accounting Premium 2010 - Student Version can be transferred to the full version of Simply Accounting Premium 2010 or later. Users will NOT be able to convert data from previous versions of Simply Accounting (retail or student) to the 2010 Student Version.

Buy Online   Activate Now   Exit

7 ➤ Click the **Activate Now** button.

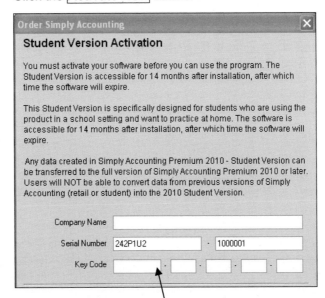

8 ➤ Company Name Enter **your name** in the field exactly as it is spelled in the documents received.

9 ➤ Key Code   Enter the **Key Code** as indicated in the document. All letters must be entered in CAPITAL letters. Click **OK** when complete.

If you receive an error message, carefully double check the code again.

10 ➤ Click **OK**.

11 ➤ You will see the Simply Premium window similar to Fig. 1-1a in Chapter 1. Click **Exit** to return to the Installation window. It is assumed that you have not completed Chapter 1, Exercise 1-1: Unzipping the Master Data Files from the website at www.simplyaccounting2010.nelson.com under Student Resources.

12 ➤ Click **Exit** to close the Installation window.

Complete text Exercise 1-1 to unzip the Master Data Files and continue with the text exercises.

If you didn't get a chance to enter the Activation code at step 7, you can Activate later. When you open Simply Accounting to start the program, you will be prompted to enter the Activation code then.

Glossary

Account: A form in which transactions are recorded individually. Each account has a name (e.g., Cash, Accounts Receivable, etc.) and is identified with a number (e.g., 1010 to represent Cash, 1200 to represent Accounts Receivable, etc.) An account will have a left side (Debit) and a right side (Credit). Accounts are contained in a ledger.

Account Class: An identification for specific groups of accounts. The class identifies each group's main purpose or function; Cash, Bank, Payable, Debt, Expenses, etc. (refer to Exercise 4-5, step 14 and Fig. 4-33). This is different from Account Types or Account Numbers.

Account Numbers: A range of numbers established by Simply for each particular type of account (Asset, Liability, Equity, Revenue and Expense). This system is used by Simply in determining the normal balance of each account, and where the account is located in the Balance Sheet or Income Statement.

Account Type: An identification code, or category, for each account; e.g., Asset, Liability, Equity, etc. Each code has a specific function and placement on financial statements.

Accrual: Recording the revenues and expenses for goods received and/or services completed but not paid for in a particular accounting period; e.g., salaries/wages owed to employees at the end of a period. The entries are normally reversed in the next period (see Exercise 10-4, To Reverse Prior Year Accrued Entries). The Accrual Method is the generally accepted accounting treatment in Canada, as it more accurately reflects revenues and expenses in a specific period. The alternative is to record revenue or expense when paid (Cash Method). The Cash Method, however, is not acceptable for income tax purposes in Canada.

Accrued Expenses: Expenses incurred in the period but no invoice or bill has been received (e.g., electricity or water bills attributable to the month ending). The amount is estimated and recorded for the month ending.

Accrued Revenue: Revenue earned in the period, but no sales invoice has been issued (e.g., a partial shipment made but an invoice was not issued). The amount is estimated and recorded for the month-end.

Accrued Salaries/Wages: If the pay period spans two months (i.e., the pay period starts in one month and the pay date falls in the following month), the pay amounts that relate to the previous month are referred to as **accrued salaries/wages**. For example, if the work week goes from December 29 to January 4, the wages for December 29 to 31 must be accrued.

Adjustment: Journal entries recorded in order to bring the balance of an account up to date; e.g., to transfer the Prepaid Insurance amount used or consumed during a period, from the Asset account to the Insurance Expense account.

Advance: An amount of money "borrowed" by an employee against future wages/salaries. This advance may be issued on a separate company cheque or it can be added to a regular paycheque. If the employee agrees to repay the advance with regular payments, the firm will reduce the regular net pay by the agreed-upon repayment. Advances are issued and repaid without any deductions for CPP, EI or Income Tax.

Advance to a new year: This is a Simply Accounting term that means advancing the Session Date to a new fiscal year. This results in the transfer of the balances of all Revenues and Expenses to Capital account (for a sole proprietorship) or Retained Earnings (for a Corporation). The closing entry is recorded automatically by the Simply program when you perform year-end processing.

Advice: A detachable form on a cheque that provides the business receiving the cheque with details of the payment.

Aging: A process of sorting Accounts Receivable transactions in predefined categories: 30, 60, or 90 days based on the current session date; e.g., an invoice dated 26 days before the session date would appear in the "30 day" column in the Accounts Receivable Customer Aged report.

Allocate: To divide (split) revenues and/or expenses to various divisions (projects, jobs, etc.). By reviewing Division costs, the management can see the revenue, expense and the profitability of each division.

Amortization: Represents the process of allocating the cost of the capital asset to expense over the useful life of the asset. The cost minus expected salvage value is divided by the estimated life of the asset. This amount would be the amortization cost per year.

Approval Stamp: A stamp on the back of the vendor invoice on which an authorized person in the purchasing department indicates the G/L account number(s) to which the invoice must be charged. It is approved usually by showing the person's name or initials, and dated.

Backordered: Goods or merchandise ordered by a customer, but currently not in stock. The sales order will be filled at a later date when stock is available.

Backup: A copy of your data on another medium such as a USB storage device, CD-ROM or DVD drive using a computer operating system such as Windows or specialized software (e.g., CD-Creator). If the original storage device is lost or damaged, you can restore the data from the backup copy.

Balance Sheet: A financial report that shows a business's assets (what they own), liabilities (what they owe) and equity (owners' or shareholders' investment) at a certain date.

Bank: A basic definition used in the context of this text is: A financial institution that holds amounts of money for personal or commercial use.

Banking Codes:

A (Adjustment) for transactions posted as adjustments to a bank account.

C (Cleared) items (matched deposits with depositor cheques) that are recorded in your General Ledger bank account and that have been processed by the bank (on the bank statement).

D (Deposit Error) is used for deposits that are recorded in your General Ledger bank account but which differ from the bank statement. The difference must be recorded with a journal entry and assigned the Deposit Error code. When both D codes are entered, they can be cleared with the C code. The original deposit coded as a D and the error correction coded as a D can be cleared together with a C (cleared) code.

N (NSF) Means **N**ot **S**ufficient **F**unds. Cheques returned by the bank to the depositor when there is not enough money in the customer's bank account.

P (Payment Error) is used for cheques that are recorded in your General Ledger bank account but which differ from the bank statement. The difference must be recorded with a journal entry and assigned the Payment Error code. When both P codes are entered, they can be cleared with the C code. The original cheque, coded as a P, and the error correction, coded as a P, can be cleared together with a C (Cleared) code.

R (Reversed) When a cheque is received by the bank as a deposit, it is entered as a credit on the depositor's bank statement. When the cheque is canceled (usually because of NSF), the entry in the depositor's bank statement is reversed, so the entry is assigned the **R** (Reversed) code. The reversing entry is normally recorded in the company's Sales Journal. A reversing entry is required and is then assigned the **A** (Adjustment) code.

V (Void) is used to identify cheques that were canceled because they were issued incorrectly. A reversing entry is required and is then assigned the **A** (Adjustment) code.

Bank Reconciliation: The process of determining and processing the differences in the company bank account(s) as shown in the company's records, and the balance as shown on the bank statement.

Benefit: Refers to items such as dental plans, life insurance, drug plans, etc., for which the firm pays the cost of the items, either in full, or partly shares the cost with its employees.

Cash: In business terms this refers to actual cash, cheque or credit card payment.

Cash Sale: Sale for which cash, cheque, credit card is received. In many businesses these sales are recorded in a cash register and are summarized daily.

Clear: To remove (delete) paid vendor invoices from the data records.

Close the books: See *Advance to a new year*.

Close the year: See *Advance to a new year*.

Codes: Abbreviations of words to indicate action taken. The code Rv indicates a reversal; the code Rt indicates a return item. (See Exercise 2A-14.)

Commission: Amount of money earned by an individual working in sales, based on a percentage of Net Sales made by the individual. The firm would keep records of sales by each staff member, and may pay the commission on a weekly, bi-weekly, semi-monthly or any other agreed-upon time schedule.

Company Data: Transaction entries and general ledger files referring to one particular company, which are stored in one directory/folder separate from data belonging to other companies.

Conversion: The change from one accounting system to another, usually from manual accounting to a computerized system, or from one computerized accounting software to another.

Conversion Date: See *Earliest Transaction Date*.

Correction: An entry to correct errors in posting. These entries are made on a regular basis and are not necessarily part of the month-end/year-end procedures.

Cost Centre: Refers to a group of accounts where expenses and revenues are allocated and accumulated. This can also mean a division/department in a company.

Credit Memo (Seller): A memo similar to an invoice sent to customers to advise them that the amount owed to your company has been reduced as a result of a return of goods or price reductions.

Credit Memo (Vendor): A memorandum sent by a vendor to the purchaser to indicate that the purchaser's account has been **reduced**, usually because of a return of the purchased goods. It is a **credit** memo because the vendor is crediting **their** customer's ACCOUNTS RECEIVABLE account; therefore, the purchaser would **debit** ACCOUNTS PAYABLE in their books.

Customer Aged Report: A report of all amounts to be received from each customer in the CUSTOMERS subledger aged according to specified aging period; e.g., **Current, 30 days overdue, 60 days overdue,** etc. The report may be listed in **Summary** (total owed by each customer) or **Detail** (individual outstanding invoices per customer not paid in full).

Debit Memo: A memo similar to an invoice sent to customers to advise them that the amount owed to your company has increased, usually as a result of errors in the original invoice, price changes that were overlooked in the original invoice, or extra charges for NSF cheques.

Deductions: Amounts of money deducted from an employee's earnings for items such as CPP, EI, Income Tax, charities, employee benefits, etc.

Default: A preset value; e.g., the default date format is month, day, year, unless the user changes it.

Deposit: 1) A sum of money paid in advance by customers for a guarantee that goods will be reserved for them. 2) Required of a new customer who has not yet established a good credit rating. 3) From a regular customer who has had trouble making payments on previous orders. May also be referred to as **Prepayment**.

Deposit: See *Prepayment*.

Depreciation: See *Amortization*.

Distribute: See *Allocate*.

Division: A project, job, activity or enterprise, e.g., building a house (or houses); or a cost centre, e.g., a department or a branch of the company. It refers to a group of accounts where revenues and costs are allocated and accumulated.

Drive Letter: **C:** in a standalone hard drive computer system or D or any letter after C: for a USB or other storage device, CD-ROM or DVD drive. The letter indicates that you are at the root directory of the current drive, or any letter after C in a network system, indicating that you are at the root directory of your current drive.

Earliest Transaction Date: This is the date when the manual books are converted to the computer system, or converted from one computerized system to another; e.g., May 31 month-end conversion. This is the conversion date as defined by Simply Accounting.

Expense: Purchase of goods not for resale or services used in running a business.

Export: A feature that allows you to transfer reports produced in Simply into a format that can be used by other software programs; e.g., Lotus 1-2-3, Excel, most word processing, etc.

Finish Date: The end of the fiscal year.

Folders: A separate location, in Windows, where you can keep various reports or data files. May also be called directories or subdirectories.

GAAP: **G**enerally **A**ccepted **A**ccounting **P**rinciples are guidelines used by ethical practitioners in the Accounting field.

Garnishee: To deduct money from an employee's paycheque, due to a legal Court Order. See Appendix P, *Payroll Garnishment* at www.simplyaccounting2010.nelson.com under Student Resources.

Gross Margin Income Statement: Is an Income Statement that breaks down the Expenses into two categories; **Cost of Goods Sold** and **Expenses**. The Gross Margin Income Statement can also be called the **Gross Profit Income Statement**.

Gross Pay: The amount of money earned by employees before deductions.

GST: **G**oods and **S**ervices **T**ax. See Chapter 15 *Taxes*.

GST Remittance: GST paid on purchases is deducted from GST collected from sales. If GST collected from sales is larger, the difference must be paid (remitted) to the government. If the reverse is true, a GST refund will be requested. The GST remittance may be made monthly, quarterly, or annually depending on volume of business.

History: Account balances and other pertinent information in a module. Historical information needs to be entered before the module can be set to **Ready**.

HST: Harmonized **G**oods and **S**ervices **T**ax. In the PAYABLES module, HST paid to vendors is posted to the account HST Paid On Purchases. It is based on 13% of the goods purchased amount. In the RECEIVABLES module, HST received from customers is posted to the account HST Charged on Sales. It is based on 13% of the goods sold amount.

HST Remittance: HST paid on purchases is deducted from HST collected from sales. If HST collected from sales is larger, the difference must be paid (remitted) to the government. If the reverse is true, an HST refund will be requested. The HST remittance may be made monthly, quarterly, or annually depending on volume of business. See Chapter 15 Taxes.

Icon: A symbol, normally a graphic image that represents a menu item within Windows.

Import: To bring data into a file from another file or program; e.g., importing data from an Excel worksheet into Simply.

Income Statement: A financial report that shows revenues (earnings) less expenses (costs) resulting in net profit/loss for a period.

Integrated Accounting Software: A type of accounting software in which the subledgers are linked to the General Ledger. When entries are posted in the subledgers, the General Ledger is updated.

Integration: See *Linking*.

Inventory Adjustment: The decrease or increase of inventory in the INVENTORY & SERVICES module, due to a difference in the actual physical count of inventory and the computer records (see Exercise 8-20).

Inventory Assembly Costs: The costs of the parts used when a business takes a number of parts and makes them into a product for sale (e.g., a number of different computer parts are made into a saleable computer system).

Invoice: A bill sent or given to a customer for goods or services sold.

Job: See *Division*.

Job Cost: See *Division*.

Journal Entry: The process of recording an accounting transaction, which may consist of one or more debit entries (DR) and one or more credit (CR) entries. Total Debits must equal total Credits.

Linking: A feature of Simply that allows you to enter a transaction in one module and automatically update other modules.

Logbook: A dated record of activities, which will contain information on the material covered (the last page of text read or work completed), and the storage file name used for backup.

Manual Cheque: A cheque written by hand and not printed by Simply. A numbering system different from computer-generated cheques may be used for manual cheques.

Markup Method: A method used in Simply for calculating gross profit by the following formula:
(Selling Price–Cost)/Cost. [($100–$60)/$60 = 66.67%]

Matching Principle: This accounting principle requires that if revenues earned in an accounting period are recorded, then expenses incurred to earn those revenues must also be recorded in that period.

Merchandise: Goods that were purchased or manufactured by a company for the purpose of resale.

Minimum: A field in the INVENTORY ledger window that allows you to enter the lowest number of items that must be in stock. At any time, you can display a report of stock items that need to be reordered. The **Inventory Quantity** report shows the amount below minimum quantity in the **To Order** column.

Module: Referring to a part of a software program designed for a specific function. A module may be separate from the other parts of the program (as in a modularized accounting software), or it may be linked with other modules (as in integrated accounting packages such as Simply Accounting).

Month-End Processing: Entering adjustments and accruals, to match Revenue with Expenses during the period.

Net Pay: The amount of money earned by employees after deductions is taken off. Also called **take-home pay**.

Network: Two or more computers connected directly or through a server, and able to share data files and peripheral equipment; e.g., printers or scanners.

NSF: **N**ot-**S**ufficient **F**unds: A bank advice that a cheque received from a customer and deposited in your bank account was returned because the customer did not have enough money in their bank account to cover the cheque. You would ask the customer to issue a new cheque.

O/L (Outside Labour): The cost, to the company, of hiring individuals or companies outside the company (non-employees) to produce work/goods for sale, or provide consulting services, etc.

Obsolescence: When an inventory item has become outdated by new technology or upgrade, it is described as being **obsolete**. Normally, the realizable value (the amount the item could be sold for) drops (in many cases below original cost), and an adjustment should be made to reflect this loss in value. There are common accounting practices that should be followed in these cases.

Outstanding Cheque: Cheque issued by the company and recorded in the General Ledger, but has not been cashed by the bank by the statement date.

Outstanding Deposits: Deposits recorded in the company General Ledger that have not been deposited (credited) by the bank into the customer's account by the statement date. This could be due to a deposit being taken to the bank late during the day and the bank recording the deposit on the next day, or a deposit processed in the books but not yet taken to the bank.

Path: Also referred to as pathname; includes the drive and the folder/directory name directing the system to specific files. For example, if you have a set of company files on drive C in a folder called PHOTOS, the path or pathname would be **C:\01 PHOTOS\PHOTOS**. When indicating a path, one must be careful of the spelling, spacing between names, filename extensions and backslashes.

Pay Period: A specified time interval for which employees are paid, usually every week, every two weeks (bi-weekly), middle and end of the month (bi-monthly), or every month.

Payroll: The record of wages/salaries earned by each employee less deductions, which is completed on a regular basis.

Periodic Inventory Method: When goods for resale are purchased, they are recorded in the Purchases Account in the Cost of Goods Sold section of the Income Statement. The Cost Of Goods Sold section (Ending Inventory account) is adjusted at various times (periodically) during the year, usually at month-end and year-end.

Perpetual Inventory Method: When goods for resale are purchased, they are recorded in an Asset account (INVENTORY). When goods are sold, the INVENTORY account is reduced, and the Cost Of Goods Sold account is increased by the cost of the goods.

Physical Count: The actual counting of inventory in the store, warehouse, etc.

Physical Inventory: For a company that uses the periodic method of inventory control, the INVENTORY accounts are usually adjusted at the end of an accounting period (monthly, quarterly, semi-annually, yearly) by making a physical count of inventory on hand. The actual inventory on hand at this time is usually called the **physical inventory**. This amount is set up as INVENTORY ON HAND on the Balance Sheet, and COST OF GOODS SOLD Ending Inventory account is correspondingly reduced.

Post: To transfer the information recorded in a journal transaction to the appropriate subledger and/or general ledger, thus updating the company data.

Preferred Pricing: A reduction in the normal selling price of goods or services given to customers who buy a large amount (quantity) of merchandise and/or services.

Prepaid Expenses: These are expenses paid ahead of time; e.g., leases, insurance, subscriptions, etc. and are recorded as assets. The amounts in these accounts are reduced by an amount that corresponds to the portion used or consumed in the period. This amount is then entered as an expense. (Also see *Adjustment* above.)

Prepayment: An advance payment made to a vendor against a future invoice to show a commitment to purchase. In the RECEIVABLES module Simply refers to advance payments from a customer as a **deposit**. Also see *Deposit*.

PST: **P**rovincial **S**ales **T**ax. In provinces that do not have HST, companies selling to the public have to collect PST, except from companies involved in wholesale distribution and which have an exemption licence.

Purchase: Includes transactions involving purchase of merchandise for resale, or the purchase of goods used to produce goods for resale.

Purchase Order (PO): A business form issued by a company, usually the Purchasing Department, to place an order for goods or services with a vendor or supplier. A purchase order, usually abbreviated PO, is a formal request for goods or services to be shipped at a specified date, price and quantity.

Purchase Quote: A business form issued by the vendor (supplier) to advise the customer that it can and will supply the products and/or services listed at the prices quoted by the date specified.

Purchase Return: A company may return goods to a vendor, that were originally purchased for a number of reasons; damaged goods, wrong items, late shipment, or over shipment. Purchase returns reduce Purchases and are recorded as a negative purchase invoice. This account refers only to goods purchased for resale. Returned items that are not for resale are recorded as a reduction to the original account charged when purchased. (e.g., Office Supplies).

Range of Dates: A time period, generally between two dates, in which data may be entered. The transaction date must be on or between the two dates.

Ready: The last step in the conversion process is to set the module to **Ready** for recording transactions. Before setting up a module from History to Ready mode, the total of individual subledger balances must agree with the corresponding General Ledger control accounts.

Reconciliation: See *Bank Reconciliation*.

Reimbursement: An amount of money repaid to an employee for money the employee paid on behalf of the business; e.g., traveling expenses, purchase of goods needed in a hurry, long-distance business calls from home phone, petty cash, etc.

Release: Payment of vacation pay accumulated from prior periods. Vacation pay is set up as a payable each pay period. When vacation pay is released (just before the employee goes on vacation or when the employee leaves the company), the payable is reduced by the amount released to the employee. At this point, Simply calculates deductions as though the released amount is gross pay. The employee receives a cheque for the vacation pay.

Relevé 1: Form provided to employers by the Quebec government for employers to indicate payroll information for each employee. See *T4 slip*.

Reversing Entries: Accrued revenues and expenses (usually adjustments) that pertain to a particular accounting period are reversed at the start of the next accounting period. This results in a zero balance (nil) in the original General Ledger account in the new period or fiscal year when the revenue or expense is finally recorded.

Salary: A fixed amount paid to an employee every pay period, expressed usually in total annual amount; e.g., $30,000 per annum (also see *Wages*).

Sales Order: A form issued to a customer to confirm that the goods or services listed on the Sales Quote are acceptable and will be shipped as indicated on the Sales Order form.

Sales Quote: A form requested by a customer advising them of selling price(s) for goods (merchandise) or services.

Sales Return: Goods returned from a previous sale for a number of reasons; e.g., wrong goods delivered, damaged goods received, etc.. In Simply, it is entered in the RECEIVABLES module as a **negative** sale. The goods are added back into Inventory, and Cost Of Goods Sold is adjusted accordingly.

Services: A sale not involving goods, but the seller provides assistance (auto or computer repair, etc.) or advice to the buyer.

Session Date: In Simply, it is the actual working date when you are using the computer. In this text, the simulated date is advanced on a regular basis for classroom use.

Standalone: A computer system that is working on its own and not connected to a network.

Start Date: The beginning of the current calendar year, or fiscal year, or the date when the business started this year.

Supplier: *See Vendor.*

T4 slip: Form provided to employers by Canada Revenue Agency. The employer completes the form with a summary of each employee's earnings and deductions for the previous calendar year, and submits the four copies as follows: 1) for Canada Revenue Agency, 2) for the employee's use in completing their personal tax return, 3) copy for employee, and 4) copy for the employer.

TD-1: Form supplied by Canada Revenue Agency to employers, to be completed by employees, which calculates the basic income exemption each employee is entitled to claim.

Template: A data file supplied with the software that contains a set of linked and non-linked General Ledger accounts with section and group headings. Each of the templates has accounts that are similar in nature to specific businesses.

Terms (of Sale): The time allowed to pay an invoice; e.g., **net 30 days** to pay the full amount within 30 days. Terms of **2%/10, net 30** means that a 2% discount will be given if paid within 10 days; if not, the full amount is due within 30 days.

Unearned Revenue: Money received from customers (clients) before the work (service) or goods are delivered to the client, usually a deposit received in advance; e.g., prepaid subscriptions to a magazine company.

Unresolved Balance: The difference between the bank statement and the General Ledger bank account. The difference may be from bank errors or errors in processing transactions in Simply.

Vendor: A business from which another firm buys goods or services. May also be called Supplier.

Vendor Aged Report: A report of all amounts owing to each vendor in the VENDORS subledger aged according to specified aging period; e.g., **Current**, **30 days overdue**, **60 days overdue,** etc. The report may be listed in **Summary** (total owed to each vendor) or **Detail** (individual outstanding invoices per vendor not paid in full).

Wages: Amount paid to an employee each pay period based on an hourly rate. This will also include overtime and any shift premiums (see *Salary*).

WCB: See *Workers Safety Insurance Board*.

Wizard: A smart step-by-step help feature that takes you through the necessary procedure in completing a process (e.g., setting up a new company).

Workers Safety Insurance Board (**WSIB**). As of January 1, 1998, in Ontario the name was changed from Workers Compensation Board (**WCB**). Simply refers to this as WCB.

Write-off: Journal entry to reduce an outstanding balance from a customer's account, when the amount is no longer collectable for any reason; e.g., the customer is bankrupt or refuses to pay the amount. ***Note:*** A part or the full amount of the outstanding amount may be written off.

Index

A

Account(s)
    add an account · 292
    add new account · 29, 34
    compound entry · 34
    contra · 309
    correcting number · 30
    delete · 299
    entering balances (history) · 306
    entering vendor · 314
    field · 29, 34
    linking · 302
    modify · 300
    numbering structure · 261
    remove from section · 298
    write-off · 146
Accountant's Copy · 18
Accountant's Tasks · 18
Accrual
    wages/salary · 369
Accrual Basis
    method of accounting · 4
Accrued Interest · 501
Accrued wages payable · 502
Additional Information feature · 46
Adjust previously posted entry · 41
Adjust Inventory Journal · 432
Adjusting Inventory · 244
Adjusting Journal Entry · 40
Adjustments
    Accrued Expense · 499
    Accrued Interest · 501
    Accrued wages payable · 502
    Amortization · 503
    bank reconciliation · 496
    correct entry · 26
    month-end · 494
    Periodic Inventory, Month-End · 504
    Prepaid Expense · 497, 498
Adobe Reader · 256
Advance the Session Date · 33
Audit trail · 129, 165

B

B/O (Back Order) · 93
Back Order) · 93
Back Up
    Year-end · 505
Backup · 56, 57
    procedures · 57
    restoring a data file · 67
Balance Sheet
    display · 25
    display and print · 178
Bank
    Account Options · 295
    charges · 227
    codes · 550, 556
    Service Charge · 513
Bank Reconciliation · 550
    Items journalizing · 227
    Period-End Adjustments · 496
Banking Module · 549

Beginning Inventory · 243
Benefits (Que) · 384
Bi-monthly Payroll · 367
Budget Feature · 62, 282
Build from Bill of Materials Journal · 432, 472
Build from Item Assembly Journal · 432, 472
Business Number · 276
Business Performance icon
    Daily Business Manager · 97

C

C.O.G.S. · *See* Cost of Goods Sold
Calendar button · 12
Cash Basis
    accounting · 277
    method of accounting · 4
Cash Discount · 105, 427
    recording a payment · 462
Cash Flow Projection Report · 218
Cash Sale
    One-time Customer · 142
    with Discount · 151
Chart of Accounts · 18, 291
    adding an account · 292
    delete an account · 299
    modify an account · 300
    structure · 271
Checklists · 273
Cheque Log
    view or print · 248
Cheques
    change number · 301
    Post-Dated · 169
    Simply easy align · 398
Close
    Year-End · 508
COD (Cash on Delivery) · 455
Codes for Invoices · 103
Commission Income · 385
Company
    changing information · 22
    set up · 259
Compound entry · 34
Conduct Business in
    another language · 122
Contra asset account · 309
Conversion · 261
    date · 291
    process · 290
Copy EXE (exe) files · 8
Correcting
    Inventory errors · 472
    posted invoice · 135
    transaction errors after posting · 572
    wrong account number · 30
    wrong price after posting · 467
Correcting entries
    Display option · 42
Cost of Goods Sold · 241
Cost of Sales
    inventory adjusting · 544

CRA (Canada Revenue Agency) · 365
Credit · 306
Credit Card
    accepted · 322
    company set up · 321
    purchase · 218
    Sale · 144
Credit Limit · 123
Credit Memo for return · 202
Currency change · 279
Current Earnings · 264
Customer
    account write-off · 146
    add a new record · 117
    history · 313
    One-time · 117
    statements · 164
    subledger records set up · 318
    unknown account · 320
Customer Aged Report · 77, 111
    Summary and Detail · 77
Customers Ledger · 116
Customize
    icon · 82
    Purchase Orders Journal · 180
    Sales Journal Columns · 81, 83

D

Daily Business Manager · 18
Damaged Goods · 435, 470
Data Management · 18
Date
    conversion · 291
    earliest transaction · 291
    range of dates · 12
    session · 11, 176
DBM (Daily Business Manager) · 95
    to Display · 97
    to Hide · 97
Debit · 306
Deductions tab
    Pension, Union, Medical · 386
Defaults
    changing settings · 276
    setting · 271, 273
Deposit · 139
Detail option · 177
Direct Deposit · 387
Discount · 105, 136
    merchandise · 208
    non-merchandise · 220
    on Cash Sale · 151
    Senior's · 151
Dividends Declared account · 512
Division Module
    allocate credit sales · 539
    allocating a purchase to · 531
    allocating cash sales · 534
    allocating payroll · 536
    correcting errors · 541
    print month-end reports · 546
    record payroll accrual · 542
    Sales Return · 540
    set up Project Title Name · 525

transactions · 528
Drill Down (Trace Back) · 47

E

Earliest Transaction Date · 291
Early Payment Discount · 457
EHT (Employer Health Tax) · 367
EI (Employment Insurance) · 367
E-mail
 format · 281
 receipt · 109
Employee Module
 entering employee information · 381
 Federal Claim · 383
 Provincial Claim · 383
Employee Related Reports
 Printing · 418
Employees & Payroll Module
 setting defaults · 371
Enter Additional Information feature · 39
Entitlements · 387
Entitlements tab · 376
Equity section · 297
Exchange Rate · 596
Expense account · 178
Expense section · 298

F

Federal Claim · 383
FIFO (First In, First Out) · 426
Files
 copying exe · 8
Fill Backordered Quantities · 454
Fiscal Year · 12
 closing · 510
 start new year · 512
Foreign Currency · 279
Foreign Currency feature · 594
Form Designer · 19
Forms
 setting up · 280
Full Add · 119

G

Garnishment · 421
General Journal · 18
 Comment field · 28
 correcting entries · 574
 display and print · 48
 double entry recording · 26
 transactions · 27
General Ledger · 18
 display and print report · 52
 entering Account Balances, history · 306
GIFI code · 293
Government Forms · 373
Graphs · 168
 view, print · 168
Gross Margin Income Statement · 166

Gross Profit
 percentage · 433
GST
 rates Province & Territory · 256
GST (Goods and Services Tax) · 610

H

H A S G T
 account codes · 262
 structure · 291
HI code · 88
History symbol · 18, 75
History tab
 Inventory · 440
HS code · 87
HST · 84
 rates Province & Territory · 256
HST (Harmonized Sales Tax) · 610
 account to charge · 613
 HST Paid on Purchases · 234
 journalize remittance · 234
 method of recording · 611
 registration · 611
 report · 233
HST Report · 166

I

Import/Export tab · 124
Income Statement
 Comparative · 247
 display · 23
 display and print · 178
Institution
 banking · 295
Inventory
 adjusting · 244, 544
 Adjustments · 435
 Beginning · 243
 correcting errors · 472
 End of First Month of Fiscal Year · 518
 journalize Sales Return · 458
 journalizing Sales Return · 458
 making Inventory Adjustments · 469
 ordering items · 448
 Periodic and Perpetual comparison · 428
 Periodic method · 175
 Purchase Return · 460
 recording a new item · 448
 reports · 476
 set up inventory items in ledger · 436
 sort by · 434
 Summary report · 442, 454
Inventory & Services
 average cost · 426
 FIFO · 426
 Item Ledger · 435
 Journal · 432
 Linked Accounts, setting up · 434
 Module · 425

setting to READY · 443
Inventory Adjustments Journal
 correct entries · 589
Inventory Assembly Journal
 correct entries · 590
Inventory tabs
 Build tab · 439
 History tab · 440
 Linked tab · 438
 Pricing tab · 438
 Quantities tab · 437
 Statistics tab · 439
 Taxes tab · 439
 Units tab · 437
Invoice
 adding a salesperson's name · 87
 cancel after posting · 114
 codes · 103
 Lookup feature · 134
 without HST · 238
Invoice Lookup feature · 135
Item Assembly Costs · 435
Item Assembly Journal · 475

J

Journal columns
 customize · 83
Journal Columns
 customizing · 81
Journal entry
 Additional Date · 32
 Additional Field · 32
 adjusting · 40
 compound entry · 33
 displaying · 32
Journalize
 deposit (prepayment) · 139
 invoice to a deposit · 157
 partial receipt · 111
 partial write-off · 148
 purchase · 199
 receipts paid by credit card · 159
 vendor payment · 205
 write-off · 146
Journals
 Adjust Inventory · 432
 Build from Bill of Materials · 432, 472
 Build from Item Assembly · 432, 472
 General Journal · 18
 Inventory & Services · 432
 Payments · 179
 Purchase · 179
 Purchase Orders · 180
 Receipts · 79, 105
 Reconciliation & Deposits · 549
 Sales · 80

L

Language
 change · 279
 change to another · 122
Learning Centre · 19

Lease Payment
  recording · 233
Ledgers
  Customers · 116
  General Ledger · 18
  Inventory & Service Item · 435
Liability section · 297
Linking Modules/Accounts · 302
Logbook
  or Diary · 60

M

Margin
  or markup · 433
Master Data Files
  to unzip · 6
Memo tab · 123
Menu Bar
  Home window · 17
Merchandise Discount · 208
Mini-Guide
  Receivables and Payables · 173,
    257
  Receivables or Payables: · 91
Modify icon · 43
Modules · 17
  Banking · 549
  Company · 1
  Division · 521
  Employees & Payroll · 363, 365
  Inventory & Services · 425
    setting defaults · 433
  linking or Integration · 303
  Payables · 174, 216
  Receivables · 74, 132
  setting to Ready · 323
  Time and Billing · 377
Month-End
  entering adjustments · 494
  Processing · 493
  Reports · 211, 247

N

Names Fields · 124, 283, 287
Network Procedures · 10
New Business Guide · 259
Notes feature
  Daily Business Manager · 96
Notes/Footers
  adding · 24
Not-Postable accounts · 262
NSF (Not Sufficient Funds) cheque ·
  154, 550

O

One-time Customer · 117, 142
One-time Vendor
  purchase and payment · 224
Overtime wages · 367
Owner Investment · 39, 161
Owner's Drawings · 228, 512

P

Partner's/Proprietor's Drawing · 228
Payables
  module · 174, 216
  Options · 284
Paycheques
  Journal · 365
  to issue · 393
Payments
  correct (make other payment) ·
    587
  Journal · 205
  method of payment · 100
  toolbar · 205
  with Cash Discount · 462
  with discount · 208
  Non-Merchandise Discount · 220
Payments Journal · 174
Payroll
  Cheque Run · 394
  Conversion · 380
  corrections · 411
  deductions · 375
  Entitlements · 376
  Garnishment · 421
  recording accrued wages · 416
  Reimbursement · 421
  remittance · 377
  reversing entry · 371
  taxes · 376
  toolbar icons · 398
Payroll Cheque Run Journal · 365
Payroll Conversion
  during the year · 420
Payroll Journal · 398
Payroll Ledger
  Deductions tab · 386
Payroll Module
  entering new employee · 392
  Remittance linked accounts · 379
  Session Date · 391
  set up Linked Accounts · 377
  setting to Ready · 390
Pending Purchase Orders Report ·
  204
Pending Purchases Report · 451
Pension · 375
Pensionable earnings · 388
Period-End
  Reports · 247
Periodic Inventory · 81, 175
Perpetual Inventory · 81, 243
  Ledger · 426
Post · 26
Postable accounts · 263
Post-Dated Cheques · 169
Preferred pricing · 444
Prepaid Asset account · 178
Prepayment · 139
  to Vendor · 231
Price
  correct wrong price · 467
  remove incorrect item · 468

Printer
  define setting · 288
  define setting for payroll · 372
Printing
  Balance Sheet · 53
  Cash Flow Projection Report ·
    218
  cheque log · 248
  Comparative Income Statement ·
    247
  Cost of Goods Sold report · 241
  Customer Aged Report · 77
  customer statement · 164
  General Journal · 48
  in Batches · 281
  Income Statement · 53
  Month-End and Year-End Reports
    · 505
  Month-End Division reports · 546
  Month-End Employee Reports ·
    418
  Packing Slips: · 101
  Payroll Balance Sheet · 419
  Pending Purchase Orders Report
    · 204
  Pending Sales Orders Report · 97
  Period-End Reports · 129, 165,
    211
  Period-End/Month-End Reports ·
    247
  Receipts Journal · 168
  Reconciliation & Deposits Report
    · 564
  Sales Journal · 168
  statements · 164
  Trial Balance · 241
  Vendor Aged Report · 177
Project Module
  Credit Sale to project · 539
Projects · 18
Provincial Claim · 383
PST
  rates Province & Territory · 256
PST (Provincial Sales Tax) · 610,
  614
  account to charge · 615
Purchase
  by Credit Card · 218
  Goods Not for Resale · 193
  Invoice · 179
  of Services · 194
  Order · 179
  pending orders · 204
  Quote · 178
  returns · 202
  with no PO · 189
Purchase Journal · 174
Purchase Orders Journal · 180
Purchase Orders or Quotes
  correct or cancel · 581

Q

Quantity discount · 152
Quick Add · 119

Quick Search
  Help · 21

R

Receipt(s) · 79, 107
  correct an error · 113
  Journal · 105
  Journal transactions · 79
Receipt(s) Lookup icon · 113
Receivables module · 74, 132
  types of transactions · 74
Receiver General · 234
  withholdings · 406
Reconciliation & Deposits
  errors · 566
  features · 566
  Journal · 549
  Journal setting up · 553
  Linked Accounts · 554
  Reconcile Bank Accounts · 555
Record a Receipt
  from U.S. customer · 602
Record button · 91, 95
Recurring Entries · 38
  to remove · 44
  Transaction · 45
Registered Pension Plan · 386
Reimbursement · 373
Relevé 1
  processing · 417
Report Centre · 19
Reports
  Income Statement · 241
  printing month-end · 546
  to customize · 289
  Trial Balance · 241
Restoring a Data File
  From a Backup Data File · 67
Retained Earnings · 304
Returns · 202
Revenue section · 298
Reverse entry · 41
ROE (Record of Employment) Code
  · 382
RPP (Registered Pension Plan) ·
  388
RST (Retail Sales Tax) · 614

S

Sales
  credit card · 144
  Invoice · 79
  Order · 79
  Quote · 79
Sales Invoice
  correct · 578
  customize style · 83
  from Sales Order · 98
  type of customer · 119
Sales Journal · 80
  correct (merchandise for sale) ·
  577
  Payment Method · 80

Sales Order
  converting from a Sales Quote ·
  92
  correct or cancel · 576
  Pending Report · 97
Sales Quote
  recording in Sales Journal · 84
  revise form · 90
Sales Returns · 102, 458
  Returns and Allowances · 459
Sample Company
  to open · 10
Save Template button · 24
Save, Save As · 55
Search
  Help · 16, 17
Select an existing company · 176,
  216
Selling price
  change price · 466
  margin · 433
Senior's Discount · 151
Service Items
  create new · 464
Session Date · 11, 12, 176
  advance · 33
Setting up a company · 259
  using a Template · 264
  using a Template · 261
  using Scratch method · 264
Setup Wizard · 265
Ship-to Address · 121
Shortcuts · 22
  Customize · 53
Show Notes button · 24
Simply
  company conversion · 261
  Help feature · 20
Sort Report · 49
Source field · 28
Statements
  add notes/footer · 293
Statistics tab · 123
Summary option · 177

T

T4
  processing · 417
T4 & RL-1 Reporting · 388
Taxes
  HST, GST, PST · 609
  ID · 123
  list of tax codes · 87
  rate chart by Province & Territory
  · 617
  set up classes, codes, rates · 311
  Tax Summary icon · 127
  taxes tab · 122
TD-1 · 383
Terms, for payment · 122
Time and Billing · 272
Toolbar
  icons, top menu · 17

Payments · 205
Trace Back (Drill Down) · 47
Track Shipments icon · 126
Tracking Number: · 88
Trade discount · 152
Transactions
  correcting errors after posting ·
  572
Transferring money · 600
Trial Balance · 217
  display · 311

U

U.S. Account
  transferring money · 600
U.S. Customer · 598
  record receipt · 602
Unit Cost · 475
Unknown vendor · 317
Unresolved Balance · 550, 637
Unzip files · 6
User Preferences · 271

V

Vacation Pay · 409
  earned · 400
  rate · 367
Vendor
  Aged Detail report · 237
  correct/cancel Payments · 585
  enter new vendor · 185
  entering accounts · 314
  history · 313
  invoice guidelines and procedures
  · 178
  one-time · 224
  subledger setup · 313
  unknown · 317
Vendor Ledger
  Accounts Payable subledger ·
  174
Vendors Subledger · 185

W

Wages/Salary, Accrued · 369
Warranty Repairs
  to journalize · 465
WCB, See WSIB. · 367
Withdrawals
  Partner/Proprietor · 228
Wizard
  Setup · 265
WSIB (Worker's Safety and
  Insurance Board) · 367

Y

Year-End
  Close the Books · 508
  Closing · 507
  Processing · 493
  update inventory accounts · 515

Work Logbook for Simply Accounting Premium 2010   See Exercise 1-24, *Maintaining a Logbook.*

Date	Backup #	Data Information (Where you get to each class)	Name of File in Storage Location
Sept 08	1	Finished Ex. 1-13, page 1-44	01_Photos_Sep_08_2009a